RENEGOTIATING BOUNDARIES

VERHANDELINGEN
VAN HET KONINKLIJK INSTITUUT
VOOR TAAL-, LAND- EN VOLKENKUNDE

238

RENEGOTIATING BOUNDARIES

Local politics in post-Soeharto Indonesia

Edited by

HENK SCHULTE NORDHOLT and GERRY van KLINKEN

KITLV Press
Leiden
2007

Published by:
KITLV Press
Koninklijk Instituut voor Taal-, Land- en Volkenkunde
(Royal Netherlands Institute of Southeast Asian and Caribbean Studies)
P.O. Box 9515
2300 RA Leiden
The Netherlands
website: www.kitlv.nl
e-mail: kitlvpress@kitlv.nl

KITLV is an institute of the Royal Netherlands Academy of Arts and Sciences (KNAW)

Cover: Creja ontwerpen, Leiderdorp

The design is based on the painting 'Topeng' (Mask) by the Bandung artist, Ropih Amantubillah, and the reproduction here appears with his permission (photo courtesy of Dewi Watson).

ISBN 90 6718 283 4

Printed in the Netherlands

Contents

List of maps

Preface

For decades almost the only social scientists who visited Indonesia's provinces were anthropologists. Anybody with a special interest in politics or economics spent most of their time in Jakarta, where the action was. The usual pressures facing foreign researchers contributed to this weakness – shrinking budgets and the waning of area studies in the West, a slow research visa process in Indonesia. As a result, academic expertise on the regions beyond Java became fragmented and patchy. Yet as field visits grew shorter, conclusions about the nature of 'Indonesia' became more sweeping in their generality. Our view of the world's fourth largest country threatened to become simplistic, lacking that essential graininess and heterogeneity.

Just then, in 1998, Indonesia was plunged into a crisis that could not be understood with simplistic tools. Massive demonstrations, amidst an economic crisis triggered by a plunging exchange rate, forced President Soeharto to resign. After 32 years of enforced stability, the New Order was at an end. Things began to happen in the provinces that no one was prepared for. Democratization was one of them. Everyone wanted it, but there was no doubt that the movement was not equally strong all over the country. The demands were stronger in Java – especially Jakarta – than outside it. The 1999 elections, the freest since 1955, showed strong regional differences. Decentralization was another new development. The push for that was almost the inverse of the democratization drive – stronger outside Java than within. Powers were transferred from Jakarta to the local level, precisely the level to which scholars had paid little attention during the centralizing New Order. The decentralization process set off dynamics for which we hardly had a vocabulary. Ethnic and religious identities emerged that had lain buried under the blanket of the New Order's modernizing, secular ideology. Unfamiliar forms of political competition came to light. Mostly these remained civil, but in a few cases they became violent. New modes of economic exchange came into view. And all this took place in an atmosphere of political and economic crisis.

Today, almost a decade after those tumultuous events of 1998, some of the changes hurriedly introduced back then have turned out to be ephemeral.

The New Order political party Golkar was back in power in 2004. So was a former general in the presidential palace. Decentralization, too, was being wound back to some extent. Security had improved. But even if the six years between 1998 and 2004 described in this book turn out to be a momentary irruption – and we are convinced they are far more than that – then they still imply profound changes in the way we need to think about the state and society in Indonesia. Our total surprise at the volume of demands for new districts to be carved out of old, and at the emergence of local identity politics – to name just two developments – suggests there was a gap in our understanding. We had made progress at describing Indonesia under conditions of stability, but we had no idea what to expect when stability broke down. To speak about 'chaos', as many did at the time, was no substitute for understanding. Indonesia had far more structure than that word suggests.

This book is the result of a two-year research project, based at the Koninklijk Instituut voor Taal-, Land- en Volkenkunde (KITLV, Royal Netherlands Institute of Southeast Asian and Caribbean Studies), and entitled 'Renegotiating boundaries; Local politics in post-Soeharto Indonesia'. It brought together a remarkably international group of 24 scholars – mainly from Indonesia and the Netherlands but also from the United States, Australia, Germany, Canada and Portugal. The KITLV hosted a work-in-progress workshop in July 2004, attended by a number of authors, and invited seven of the authors to spend between a month and six months at the institute for research.[1] Both editors did their work at the KITLV. The Indonesian Institute of Sciences (LIPI) co-hosted the final conference in Jakarta in December 2004, at which the authors discussed each others' work. The entire project was generously funded by the Royal Netherlands Academy of Arts and Sciences (KNAW). To the directors and staff at the KITLV, LIPI, and KNAW, we wish to extend our sincere appreciation for their unstinting support. We hope the results, concretely in this book but also in terms of strengthening academic exchanges, will justify the confidence they placed in us.

Just four days after the Jakarta conference ended, one of our authors lost his life in the tsunami that swept the coasts of Aceh. M. Isa Sulaiman had been an enthusiastic participant in the project throughout its duration. He will be greatly missed. An obituary included in this volume describes his work. We dedicate this book to his memory.

1 They were Lorraine Aragon, Erwiza Erman, Syarif Hidayat, Isa Sulaiman, Arianto Sangaji, Andi Faisal Bakti and Carole Faucher.

Map 1. The Indonesian archipelago

HENK SCHULTE NORDHOLT and GERRY VAN KLINKEN

Introduction

Renegotiating boundaries

After the monetary and political crisis of 1997 and 1998, which was followed by a period labelled 'Reformasi', many observers said Indonesia had entered a transitional phase from authoritarian rule towards a new democratic system of government in which civil society played a more prominent role.[1] The transition was, moreover, accompanied by a process of decentralization, bringing regional autonomy and democracy while making government more transparent.

Others contested this optimistic perception and sketched a negative transition from 'order to disorder'. After decades of authoritarian centralist governance, attempts to introduce political and economic change seemed doomed, in the face of bureaucratic sabotage, corrupt power politics, short-term opportunism, and the absence of a widely shared vision of the future. In the light of outbursts of ethnic and religious violence in various regions of the archipelago, regional resistance movements, the inability to restructure both the army and the economy and to curb collusion, nepotism and corruption, pessimists were inclined to classify Indonesia in the category of 'failing' or 'messy' states. In short, they predicted further disintegration, which could eventually lead to the breaking up of the nation-state.

Recently the process of decentralization in Indonesia was equated with a process of democratization and the rise of civil society.[2] These are, however, three very different processes. A shift from centralized to a decentralized government is not synonymous with a shift from authoritarian to democratic rule nor does it automatically imply a shift from a strong state towards a strong civil society. The weakening of the central state does not automatically result in more local democracy. On the contrary, decentralization can under certain conditions be accompanied by new forms of authoritarian rule.

Although the term 'transition' can also be used to indicate the transfer

1 Parts of this introduction draw on Schulte Nordholt 2003.
2 Antlöv 2003; Aspinall and Fealy 2003; Shaikhu Usman 2002.

from one authoritarian system to another, it does not capture the complexity of the historical processes that are creating contemporary Indonesia, nor does it offer the opportunity to trace 'changing continuities' in Indonesian politics. Given that a 'new Indonesia' still seems out of reach and that the present period is marked by a certain amount of stagnation, it seems, for the time being, wiser to use the more neutral term 'post-Soeharto Indonesia'.

This book is the latest in a growing series of studies providing 'snapshots' of Indonesia after the resignation of President Soeharto. Some of these have focused mainly on the democratization.[3] Others dealt more with the dynamics of decentralization.[4] The present volume belongs to this second category. Like its predecessors it takes up questions that range from the political, such as democratization versus 'elite capture' of local state institutions, to the cultural, especially ethnic identities that emerge along with regional autonomy.[5] However, coming in behind the front-runners has permitted us to be a little more ambitious. Firstly because almost all the contributors have conducted in-depth field studies for their chapter. A new research agenda that takes local dynamics seriously is beginning to bear fruit. And secondly, the longer view has allowed us to realize that what we are observing is not exclusively the result of the decentralization agenda. Often these are patterns of politics that may be new to observers from outside the region, but have been practised for decades in the provinces. Decentralization comes into this world not as a *deus ex machina* but as a rearrangement of existing force fields. This view from below gains credibility by the biographical interest of some contributions in this book.

This book aims to explore new approaches to local politics in post-Soeharto Indonesia. In order to understand the dynamics of these politics we propose to investigate the nature and role of regional elites, particularly in the fields of bureaucratic, economic and identity politics. First, we will focus on the role of regional bureaucratic elites in the huge increase in the number of administrative districts, from 300 in 1999 to 440 in 2004. This process is aptly called *pemekaran*, or 'blossoming'. As we will demonstrate, this 'administrative involution' was driven by the interests of particular bureaucratic and political elites who often mobilized ethnic sentiments to achieve their goals. In the second place, we will concentrate on the economic policies of certain bureaucratic and political interest groups. Here we will introduce the concept of the 'shadow state',

3 Aspinall 2000; Arief Budiman et al. 1999; Emmerson 1999; Kingsbury and Arief Budiman 2001; Liddle 2001; Manning and Diermen 2000.

4 Aspinall and Fealy 2003; Erb et al. 2005; Kingsbury and Aveling 2003; Sakai 2002.

5 A separate but related literature has focused on the violence that surrounded the end of the New Order in some places: Anderson 2001; Bertrand 2004; Colombijn and Lindblad 2002; Van Klinken forthcoming-a; Törnquist 2000; and Wessel and Wimhöfer 2001.

which is used in Indian and African settings in order to indicate the vital connections between formal and informal arrangements that characterize the regional economy. Related to these themes are questions regarding an economy of violence and the relative weakness of civil society. Finally, we focus on aspects of regional identity politics as they are manifested in terms of ethnicity, religion, and/or region. We take a particular interest in the role played by provincial urban middle class intellectuals. Taken together, the reorganization of power relationships at the regional level implies a fundamental renegotiation of boundaries in terms of bureaucratic competences, political power, economic arrangements and the (re-)definition of group identities. Throughout this book we aim to identify the major actors in these fields in order to understand the nature of (old and new) regional elites and the role they play.

Before we introduce these themes in more detail, we will briefly review the dominant approaches to Indonesian politics during the New Order and discuss some of the implications of the recent focus on regional dynamics. The sudden demise of the strong New Order state in 1998 came as a surprise to many professional Indonesia watchers. What seemed to be a solid and invincible regime turned out to be a fragile state, in which regional, religious, and ethnic identity politics became more dominant.[6] The collapse of Soeharto's regime in 1998 invites us to abandon the concept of the strong centralized state in favour of a model that offers room for a more fragmented polity. It is in this respect not only necessary to find new concepts to describe the present situation in Indonesia, but it is also imperative to rethink established views on the New Order.

The appearance of order

When after 1966 the New Order gradually took shape, the focus of academic research shifted away from the tensions between processes of nation-building and primordial attachments – which emphasized the importance of local attachments expressed in terms of kinship, religious community, language or customs (Geertz 1963) – and concentrated to a large extent on the nature of the state.[7] In an influential essay, Harry Benda had characterized the late

6 But see the last chapter of Michael Vatikiotis' book, titled 'The fragile state' (Vatikiotis 1993:206-19).

7 Geertz (1963) borrowed Edward Shils' notion of 'primordial sentiments' and argued that they formed an obstacle to the civil politics of the new nation-states. It required an 'integrative revolution' to adjust old societies to the needs of the new states. Today we would label these primordial attachments 'ethnic' (see for example Liddle 1970), but we would no longer apply the evolutionary transition from traditional/local/primordial attitudes to the modernization process of nation-building.

colonial state as a *beamtenstaat* (Benda 1966). Framed in a Weberian model this state was seen as an apolitical administrative polity that was staffed by Dutch and 'native' officials – but with the Dutch firmly in control – for whom sound and centralized administration mattered most. It was a state that emphasized modern, efficient developmental governance.

Due to the rise of the strong New Order state, large groups in society were soon excluded from the political domain, which was restricted to competing factions within a small political elite. Harold Crouch (1979) argued that the New Order should be seen as a patrimonial cum military regime in which patron-client ties kept the state together. He also perceived a gradual process towards rational policy-making. There was considerable consensus among scholars about the patrimonial nature of the state.

Modifying the (neo-)patrimonial approach, Dwight King (1982) launched the concept of a bureaucratic authoritarian regime that is characterized by a high degree of corporatism. Instead of individual patron-client ties, various groups within the state as well as in society were collectively tied to the leaders of the state. Apart from the disciplining effects of the incorporation of these groups, there was, according to King, also a modest possibility for upward interest representation.

The New Order was, of course, not a static phenomenon, but evolved gradually into a relatively hegemonic regime (Mackie and MacIntyre 1994). Apart from the broad consensus about the (neo-)patrimonial cum corporatist nature of the New Order, scholars also agreed on the strength of the state and its autonomy vis-à-vis society.

Ruth McVey and Benedict Anderson introduced in this respect a comparative historical perspective. McVey (1982) took Benda's idea of the *beamtenstaat* as her point of departure when she compared the late colonial state with the New Order. Although the colonial state was basically run by civil servants and the New Order by the military, the similarities were compelling because both regimes were ultimately based on force, political demobilization, and a technocratic approach towards the modernization of society.

The continuity from the late colonial state to the New Order regime was further elaborated in a paradigmatic article by Benedict Anderson (1983). Referring to the book *Old societies and new states* edited by Geertz in 1963, Anderson gave his article the reversed title 'Old state, new society' because he located the origins of the New Order in the late colonial state. It was no longer society, but the state that had the most solid foundations.

By emphasizing the autonomy of the state qua state, Anderson took issue with Marxist interpretations of the state as a tool of international capital and the ruling bourgeoisie. Both McVey and Anderson reinforced a tendency among Indonesia watchers to conceptualize the state as disconnected from society. And since the state was growing stronger and did achieve economic growth, studies of Indonesia were primarily focused on the New Order regime and its centre, Jakarta.

Criticizing the scholars who studied Indonesian politics from a strict Weberian perspective, Richard Robison initiated an alternative political economy approach in the 1980s. Indonesia was now situated within a broader context of international flows of capital, but the strength and relative autonomy of the state could not be ignored. Due to the absence of a strong indigenous bourgeoisie, Robison (1986) located the origins of the new capitalism within the bureaucracy, which was financed by oil income and international aid, while a small and dependent class of capitalists operated outside the state. The concept of authoritarian-bureaucratic capitalism was born in which the state figured prominently.

Meanwhile, however, economic growth had facilitated capitalist bureaucrats to become more independent of the state, and it accelerated the formation of a domestic capitalist class primarily of Chinese-Indonesian descent. Paradoxically the fall of oil prices in the 1980s undermined the monopolistic position of the state and necessitated a diversification of the economy, which opened possibilities for new groups to enter the market (Robison 1988). Whereas Jeffrey Winters (1988) had questioned the actual size of the new capitalist class, Andrew MacIntyre (1991) argued that fundamental changes were indeed taking place in the Indonesian economy. Elaborating both the corporatist nature of the regime suggested by King, and the political economy approach, MacIntyre demonstrated that from the late 1980s onwards a substantial group of indigenous entrepreneurs had been established that operated outside the state on a relatively autonomous basis.

Acknowledging its economic success, most authors now labelled the New Order an authoritarian interventionist developmental state. As long as Soeharto managed to maintain a balance between various competing groups, favouring the spendthrift 'high tech' people in affluent times, and pushing the cautious technocrats centre stage in times of crisis, the Indonesian economy and its regime performed well in terms of growth, crisis management and stability. A good illustration of the widespread confidence in the Indonesian economy and the quality of the regime is Hal Hill's book from 1996. After a thorough analysis of developments since the 1960s, he was optimistic about the capacity of the government to handle the conditioning factors that shape the future (Hill 1996).

Blinded by its economic success, many observers tended to conceptualize the New Order in terms of a rather well-integrated set of institutions that operated apart from society and facilitated the gradual growth of a relatively free market economy. More than ever Jakarta was the place to be for anyone interested in the impressive success story of Soeharto's regime. Under his paternal rule an expanding and affluent middle class inhabited the new suburbs, shopping malls and traffic jams of the capital, where they consumed new air-conditioned life-styles and where during the mid-1990s 70% of all the money in the Indonesian economy circulated.

A backstage perspective

Just as Indonesia's international respectability grew during the 1980s, cracks began to appear in the decent image of the New Order. In East Timor (1975-1999), Tanjung Priok (1984) and Lampung (1989) the regime showed its ruthless face, while the so-called Petrus murders (1983) and brutal military actions in Papua and Aceh showed how the regime manifested itself as a boss among other criminals.

As long as the Cold War was not over, the international community noticed these violent practices but tolerated them. After the fall of the Berlin Wall however, Soeharto faced serious problems in defending the legitimacy of his aging regime. Video footage of the Santa Cruz massacre in East Timor in November 1991 was broadcast all over the world, while in 1996 the headquarters of the relatively small opposition party PDI was attacked by a government-sponsored mob. The 1990s witnessed an increase in political violence and criminality as protest movements faced repression and militias were engaged in intimidating campaigns and political gang wars. At the same time the presidential family was increasingly portrayed as being at the centre of unprecedented corruption, damaging Jakarta's image as a booming metropolis of modern business. It seemed that the future of the nation-state was no longer threatened by 'primordialism from below', but by 'criminality from above'.

With the wisdom of hindsight one may wonder how strong the New Order actually was in institutional terms. Adrian Vickers (2001) has argued that the New Order was a regime that mainly kept itself busy keeping up appearances. While the bureaucracy produced the appearance of rational administration, it consisted of inefficient clusters of largely incompetent institutions with overlapping responsibilities, overstaffed with underpaid employees. The state produced an appearance of order, expressed primarily in elaborate ceremonies. The New Order even tried to keep up the appearance of democracy by staging elections every five years. As John Pemberton (1986) showed, it was not the results that mattered but the campaigning that preceded the elections, which could easily turn into violence and disorder. If the government was able to maintain order during that period it had demonstrated its legitimacy.

The regime also tried to keep up the appearance of orderly capitalism operating in a free market. But rent or crony capitalism and patrimonial hierarchies reinforced each other in such a way that nobody could escape the structure of corruption controlled from the centre. Estimates indicate that over a period of 30 years of New Order rule 30% of the 30 billion US dollars of foreign aid disappeared into private pockets. Apart from routine corruption – paying for access, protection, loyalty, and licenses – the system also allowed for large scale plunder of natural resources.

When the Asian monetary crisis hit Jakarta in August 1997 the regime collapsed within nine months. John Sidel (1998) has shown how the financial and political crisis of 1997-1998 can be conceptualized as a *macet total*, or a total traffic jam of the patrimonial networks leading to the centre of the regime. Various groups, from old aristocracies, Christians, and socialists, to modernist Muslims, who had initially supported the New Order, had been gradually marginalized and lost their access to the sources of wealth at the centre. A similar thing happened to high ranking military officers who had enjoyed the spoils of power at the centre while on active duty but fell by the wayside upon retirement, and Chinese entrepreneurs who lost their privileged position through miscalculation. Many people thus removed from the network felt betrayed, while others were dissatisfied with the 'traffic jam', which increased dramatically because of the monetary crisis. When the money flow from the centre stagnated, large groups of people lost their loyalty to the president. The collapse of the patrimonial regime soon followed.

Towards the end of the New Order and especially during its demise, it became clear that a sharp analytical distinction between state and society was no longer valid, and it probably never had been. The security state had blurred the boundaries between (legitimate) state violence and (illegal) criminality, and between formal institutions and semi-informal criminal gangs. Problems were ultimately not solved by the rule of law or bureaucratic procedures but by violent means.

Rethinking analytical categories

It seems that the image of the bureaucratic interventionist developmental state, heir of the colonial *beamtenstaat*, has now changed into that of a messy, criminal crony state. Does this imply that we need a fundamental shift of paradigm in order to understand why the New Order state so suddenly 'failed'? Do we perhaps need new ways of looking at 'the state' in order to incorporate various arrangements that link formal institutions with informal networks, which help to undermine artificial distinctions between 'state', 'society' and 'market'?

Particularly relevant here is the continuity of patrimonial patterns during the colonial and post-colonial period. The New Order regime distributed large amounts of so-called INPRES (*Instruksi Presiden)* funds, in such a way as to suggest that the president himself had personally paid for specific projects. Meanwhile a substantial amount of state income was generated by informal means, underlining once more the patrimonial character of the system. The armed forces rely only for 30% on state revenues and depend for the remaining 70% on their own sources of income. The army has therefore been characterized not as a hierarchically integrated organization, but instead as an archipelago of semi-independent 'warlords'. In terms of violence there are also continuities from the colonial into the post-colonial period (Schulte Nordholt 2002), and protection against intimidation and violence involves the payment of informal taxes. Old notions of invulnerability are in this respect still relevant, but they do not in the first place refer to efforts by potential victims to protect themselves against violence and corruption, but to perpetrators who are allowed to act above and beyond the law.

A comparable system of informal taxation and 'bottom up' distribution of income characterized and still characterizes the Indonesian bureaucracy as well. Underpaid bureaucrats supplement their salaries with informal sources of income by selling licenses and levying personalized forms of taxation. The sheer lack of independent state institutions reinforces the reproduction of these patrimonial hierarchies.

The New Order was also part of a wider set of capitalist structures, which should be taken into account in order to understand how capital, production, labour and markets were controlled. The patron-client nature of patrimonial networks helped to obscure and deny issues of class. But New Order Indonesia did of course produce rather clear-cut class divisions.

In many respects post-Soeharto Indonesia shows continuities with the previous period, albeit the central leadership of the old regime has been weakened, making way for a considerable degree of 'factionalization' and decentralization of power. It is therefore misleading to see the New Order too much as an integrated set of institutions operating primarily apart from society, and having its origins in the late colonial *beamtenstaat*. Artificial distinctions between 'state' and 'society', 'state' and 'market', and 'formal' and 'informal' relationships need to be critically reviewed.

It is even too simplistic to conclude that the state in Indonesia has weakened since 1998. This is perhaps true if we look in a restricted and purely institutional way at the central state. But if we look at power structures throughout the country, which include both formal institutions and informal networks, a very different picture emerges. Here a comparison can be made with provincial Thailand, where the formal domains of politics and economics are interwoven with illegal economic activities and criminality, in which bureaucrats, politicians, military, police, businessmen and criminals maintain intimate relationships, while distinctions between their respective professions are often blurred (McVey 2000; Phongpaichit et al. 1998).

Apart from historical continuities, changes in global political and economic arrangements had an impact on Indonesia as well. Since the 1980s a world-wide neo-liberal revolution has gained ground. Neo-liberalism attacked the belief in the regulating role of the state in the field of social and economic policies. The Western welfare state was downsized while the fall of the Berlin Wall signalled the failure of the socialist model. The end of the Cold War also marked the end of many authoritarian regimes in the Third World. Neo-liberalism needed open markets and advocated less state in exchange for more democracy. It was argued that a small and non-political administration would increase good governance, while a strong civil society would reinforce a democratic system that guaranteed transparency and accountability. The only concession in this respect was motivated by the war on terror after '9/11', which necessitated the strengthening of the security sector of the state. Summarized in ideological terms, decentralization would thus result in less state and more democracy. Taken together this would result in open markets, economic growth and higher standards of living. This optimistic scenario was based on the belief that markets and governance could be separated from political interests and conflicts. However, Robison and Hadiz (2004) have pointed out the illusory character of this neo-liberalist view, and demonstrated the resilience of political and economic oligarchies in Indonesia. It is against the backdrop of this fractured structure of patrimonial relationships that recent developments in the regions should be understood.

Bringing the regions back in

Decentralization is not a new phenomenon in Indonesia. The first legislation dates back more than a century. In 1903 the urban European elites were allowed a limited measure of self-government. The law offered, however, next to nothing in terms of autonomy (Benda 1966:241). While the first colonial measures were primarily aimed at urban areas, the following decades saw a transfer of a range of administrative functions to provinces and large districts. The decentralization law of 1922 created new provinces, which had a fair degree of administrative autonomy. Apart from these new macro administrative units, in Java the so-called Ethical Policy of *ontvoogding*, or 'de-tutelization', resulted at the district level in the establishments of councils in which the local elites were represented. Most of these councils were conservative and functioned as bastions against nationalism (Sutherland 1979). Under colonial rule, decentralization had nothing to do with democratization and very little with the strengthening of civil society.

The reforms of the 1920s caused, nevertheless, a blurring of the lines of responsibility between European and indigenous administrators, which led to confusion and irritation. Eventually the communist uprisings of the mid-1920s in West Java and West Sumatra reinforced a conservative turn among the European rulers, and from 1931 onwards colonial rule was re-centralized.

By and large, the colonial system was characterized by indirect rule, in which the conservative European administrative elite controlled a subordinate body of indigenous administrators. Moreover, European law was restricted to the European elite (and to some extent the Chinese), whereas the indigenous population was ruled according to 'their own' customary, or *adat* law. Moreover, the appointment of descendants of old dynasties as representatives of colonial rule reinforced the conservative character of indirect rule in the Outer Islands. This system was primarily intended to isolate the small nationalist movement within urban sectors by keeping the countryside and the areas outside Java under control through colonized traditional rule.

During the Indonesian Revolution, the Dutch tried to revive pre-war plans for a federation of Indonesian states along provincial lines in order to isolate the Republican forces. The Dutch also stimulated the establishment of regional rule by local aristocracies, also in order to counteract revolutionary nationalists. This strategy failed. In 1950 Indonesia chose for a unitary nation-state, and the concept of federation became strictly taboo.

In reality, however, regional governments and military commands had a high degree of autonomy, since the centre lacked the means to exert strict control. Due to pressure from the regions and especially the political parties who wanted to dismantle the monopoly of the post-colonial bureaucracy, far-reaching reforms were formulated in Law no. 1/1957 regarding the decentralization of provincial and regional government (Legge 1961; Malley 1999). The law entitled provincial and district parliaments to appoint their own governor and district head, or *bupati*. For the first time power was transferred from appointed administrators to elected politicians and this measure invited the nation to participate in the state (Anderson 1983). An important side effect was an increase in the number of provinces from 12 in 1950 to 20 in 1958.[8] However, the fiscal side of the decentralization measures was highly centralist in character as a result of which many regions remained dependent on the centre.

Decentralization did not get a chance to take root, because of regional rebellions in Sumatra and Sulawesi against Jakarta, and the subsequent proclamation of martial law, increased military power and, in 1959, the rise of authoritarian rule aborted this brief experiment. Law no. 1/1957 was abolished by Presidential Decree no. 6/1959 (Magenda 1989:18).

At the end of the turbulent years between 1959-1974, during which the

8 Or more precisely: ten provinces plus two special regions in 1950; see Legge 1961:62-83.

central state regained its dominant position, Law no. 5/1974 formalized the supremacy of the centre over the regions. Although the law defined provinces and districts as 'autonomous' levels and elected councils were established in order to generate a bottom-up representation, regional government consisted in practice of the top-down execution of developmental interventions initiated by the state, accompanied by strict surveillance. Although provincial and district councils were entitled to nominate candidates for the position of governor and district head, they were actually appointed by the President and the Home Minister. These regional administrators were in fact agents of the centre. Law no. 5/1974 was accompanied by Law no. 5/1979 on village government, which made village administration uniform throughout Indonesia, and reinforced the grip of the centre on local politics.

The appearance of development and order, and strict obedience to protocol, were as important as the channelling of large sums of routine and development funds from the centre to the regions, which made the system work. Due to an abundance of central resources – originating from oil exports and aid imports, later supplemented by foreign investments – the regions depended heavily on the centre. The flows of money entering the regions resulted in the formation and reinforcement of state agencies, which penetrated deeply into local society (Schiller 1996). Parallel to a tight centralization, there was a de-concentration of authority, which implied that central Ministries, like Agriculture, Public Works, and Religion, had their own representatives in the regions executing central policies at the regional level.

An even more powerful parallel state structure was formed by the military presence running from the centre, through the province, district, and sub-district down to the village level. Moreover, the military had entered the civilian bureaucracy as well. At the high point in 1970, 20 out of the 26 provincial governors were recruited from the military, while in 1997 they still formed a majority: 14 out of 27 (Malley 1999; Jaya and Dick 2001).

Despite their dependency on the central government, regional governments were relatively powerful in terms of local administration because they also offered employment and channelled government funds. This facilitated the reproduction of patrimonial patterns of rule at the local level, while informal networks connected the interests of both local businessmen and bureaucrats.

The agony of decentralization: 1999 and after

As indicated above, neo-liberalism over the last several decades has been accompanied around the world by a huge wave of decentralization in Latin America, Africa, Eastern Europe and Asia. Powerful organizations like the

World Bank embraced the neo-liberal idea that decentralization would stimulate both the economy and democracy. When neo-liberalism met Reformasi in Indonesia at the turn of the present century, this resulted in an unprecedented measure of decentralization.

Decentralization can be interpreted in three different ways (Dormeier-Freire and Maurer 2002): 1. as the delegation of specific tasks while the centre retains its overall responsibility, which is comparable with the law of 1974; 2. deconcentration, which refers to a relocation of decision-making within a centralized state, which is reflected in the law of 1957; and 3. devolution, which concerns the actual transfer of power to lower levels of government, and this was implemented in 2001.[9]

Looking back at the period 1998-2004 one may conclude that the most important reform measures were taken by the Habibie presidency (May 1998-October 1999). Apart from press freedom, the freedom to establish political parties, free elections, and the granting of a referendum in East Timor, the Habibie government also pushed two important laws through parliament in great haste, which set in motion a process of administrative decentralization.

The laws were primarily designed by a small group of bureaucrats, without any feedback from the regions (Malley 2004; Turner et al. 2003). Known as the Team of Seven, the core individuals were American-trained academics-cum-bureaucrats who maintained close links with overseas agencies ideologically committed to decentralization. The same team had earlier designed the new electoral laws. However, amid the excitement of democratizing reforms, the decentralizing initiative attracted little metropolitan public debate. One month before the general elections in June 1999, the national parliament – whose members ironically still belonged to the New Order era – agreed without much debate to implement Laws no. 22 and 25, which provided the administrative and fiscal framework for a process that seemed to change the very foundation of the unitary nation-state.

One of the main reasons why the government wanted to accelerate this process was to accommodate the anti-Jakarta sentiments in many regions outside Java while the still-ruling Golkar party, which was on Java under political fire, tried to maintain its power bases in the outer islands by supporting regional autonomy. The sense of panic about their own future led policy-makers to take drastic action.

The proposed two-year period of transition and implementation was even shortened by six months, which meant that the biggest administrative reorganization in the history of the Indonesian state had to be completed by

[9] The most far-reaching form of decentralization is, of course, privatization (Frerks and Otto 1996).

1 January 2001.[10] A period of eighteen months was too short to get things done properly, and this was a major reason why the responsible deputy minister Ryaas Rashid resigned.[11] Moreover there were considerable differences between various ministries and levels of government about the desirability of the decentralization moves. Many within the Interior Ministry (and later in the presidential palace under Megawati) feared that, far from taming disintegrative dynamics, decentralization might unleash even more dangerous localist sentiments. Officials in the regions, meanwhile, often supported decentralization but for the wrong reasons – they wanted not less but more government.

In a sense the laws of 1999 revived the process of decentralization that was stopped in the late 1950s, but they went much further. Because the new autonomy was located at the level of districts and municipalities, the power of the provinces was dismantled, while a process of political fragmentation was stimulated. Seen from this perspective, decentralization was a divide-and-rule strategy from the centre, aimed at permitting administrative fragmentation while maintaining fiscal control at the centre.

Law no. 22 was written by the Home Ministry with the stated intention of achieving a substantial devolution of power in order to bring government closer to the people and to offer more transparency. Similar to Law no. 1/1957, governors, district administrators and mayors were no longer appointed by the centre but elected by regional parliaments. This brought regional political leaders back onto the stage.[12] The chapter by M. Isa Sulaiman in this collection explains the electoral rules at this time, and how they shaped local politics in one province.

At first sight the role of the central government seemed to resemble the so-called night watch state. The few remaining responsibilities included national defence and security, foreign policy, fiscal and monetary matters, macro-economic planning, natural resources, justice and religion. Regions have autonomy with regard to public works, education and culture, health care, agriculture, transport, industry, trade, investments, environmental issues, cooperations, labour, and land (Ray and Goodpaster 2003). But in order to assess the nature of this decentralization effort it is important to look at the fiscal arrangements as well. Whereas Law no. 22 facilitated devolution of power, Law no. 25, made by the Ministry of Finances, was centralist

10 At least in theory more than a thousand government regulations and presidential decrees and instructions had to be revoked (Amzulian Rifai 2002:33; see also Turner et al. 2003).

11 Actually the department he headed was only in operation as a relatively independent unit during a limited period, from April till August 2000 (World Bank 2003).

12 Part of the operation was a massive transfer of 2.1 million state employees – 50% of whom were schoolteachers – to the regions. Since it concerned primarily a financial operation it did not imply actual mass migrations (Rohdewohld 2003).

in character. This implied that the central government maintains its grip on the main sources of revenue of the regions, namely 80% of the income tax, value added tax, import duties and export taxes, and foreign aid, while it still controls a sizable number of government enterprises. What we actually witnessed in Indonesia was a decentralization of administrative power that was heavily subsidized by the central government.[13] No less important is the way competition for power was organized at the regional level. The new law on political parties (No. 2/1999, written by the same Team of Seven) did not permit the establishment of regional parties – in contrast with the 1950s when they were allowed. Parties remained centralized in the hands of Jakarta party bosses, allowing little room for manoeuvre at the local level. This led to considerable friction between local branches and central headquarters, and even to local efforts to subvert the party system by forming cross-party alliances based on ethnicity or district of origin.

By the time Megawati Sukarnoputri became president in July 2001, the earliest, breathless phase of reforms had passed. Problems with the decentralization process were now regularly aired in the media, including 'money politics' among district parliamentarians electing new district heads and municipal mayors, the allegedly excessive power of district parliaments to dismiss heads annually, and the corruption of the now much more autonomous heads. Clearly some of these concerns were fanned by interests within the central government that had long regarded decentralization as dangerous. In the dying days of Megawati's presidency two new laws were passed to deal with them. Technically, Law no. 32/2004 on Regional Government and Law no. 33/2004 on Fiscal Balance between the Central Government and Regional Governments did not merely amend the previous laws but replaced them altogether (Malley 2004). Once again, the two laws passed with almost no public debate. The fiscal law did not much alter the power balance between the centre and the regions. But the law on regional government did substantially cut back on the powers previously given to heads and parliaments. Local parliaments now cannot remove heads, while the central

13 The central government keeps 75% of all these revenues, and distributes 25% to the regions in the form of a general grant (DAU, Dana Alokasi Umum), 90% of which goes to the autonomous regions while the provinces receive 10%. In 2001 in total Rp 60.5 trillion, or US$ 6.1 billion flowed from Jakarta to the regions. The criteria for the distribution of funds among the variety of districts are complex, depending on the relative size of the population, the poverty rate, geographical conditions and price indices.
The contentious provinces Papua and Aceh received special autonomy (respectively Laws no. 18 and 21/2001), granting Aceh 80% of the oil and gas revenues, and Papua 80% of its mining revenues and 70% of the revenues from oil and gas. It is ironic that in the case of both Aceh and Papua autonomy was granted to the province instead of the districts. One might expect this could favour separatist sentiment in the rebellious provinces. However, both provincial administrations are still dominated by old Golkar elites and the army, who control the flows of money.

government can unilaterally suspend them for corruption or if they 'threaten security'. Also, heads (called mayors if they head towns) are now elected directly by the voters, in a process that mirrors the direct presidential election introduced in that same year. Thus in one stroke the district parliament was taken out of the most crucial parts of the power circuit – election and dismissal of the executive. Moreover the election of heads is supervised by regional electoral commissions following national government guidelines, rather than by the national electoral commission, raising fears of government interference. As a result the position of the regional administrators has on the one hand become more dependent on the central state, but on the other hand more powerful vis-à-vis the local parliaments since they can make use of their popular mandate.[14]

Nevertheless, the changes have so far not led to protests. The first direct district head elections passed smoothly in dozens of districts in June 2005. People voted for candidates they knew and trusted, rather than for party symbols as in the past. Democratically contested elections had become a routine affair in Indonesia, and participation rates were high.[15]

Professional optimism versus realistic pessimism

Differences of opinion concerning the effects of decentralization can be found among various groups, depending on the extent to which they are involved in the process. Professional optimism can be found among organizations with an institutional interest in decentralization. NGOs like SMERU, and donor organizations like Support for Decentralization Measures (SfDM), Ford Foundation, Asia Foundation and financial giants like the World Bank and the Asian Development Bank actively support decentralization and proclaim a firm ideological belief in its success. In the SMERU report, decentralization is basically seen as a big administrative operation in which possible weaknesses can be improved (Syaikhu Usman 2002). The World Bank sees it as a huge financial operation – with the ominous title 'Big Bang' – which can be successfully managed (Hofman and Kaiser 2002; World Bank 2003). And in a publication sponsored by the Asian Development Bank it is said that 'The great achievement of decentralization in Indonesia is that it took place, and on schedule' (Turner et al. 2003:136). Such a technocratic approach erases

14 Law no. 32/2004 seems to offer more possibilities for provinces to strengthen their position vis-à-vis districts and autonomous towns. Personal communication Gustaaf Reerink.

15 Since our research focused on the early days of decentralization, the effects of direct elections of mayors and district heads, which started in 2005, are not included in this volume, but will be discussed in future publications by some of the members of our research group.

questions referring to power struggles among competing interests groups (Hadiz 2003b).

Decentralization is supported by a coalition of financial institutions and organizations like the Asia Foundation and the Ford Foundation, which support it because it is supposed to strengthen democracy and civil society. Between the lines, however, one can find carefully phrased doubts and concerns about the outcome of the 'transition'.[16]

Critical publications by authors without direct institutional involvement give voice to a more pessimistic attitude.[17] A brief list of unresolved issues in this respect justifies an attitude of realistic pessimism.

World Bank experts have measured that 'on aggregate' the regions receive enough revenues to cover the costs of their own autonomous administrative apparatus. However this does not imply that they have adequate funding for education, health care and poverty alleviation. Wihana Kirana Jaya (2002:39) remarks, moreover, that whereas Law no. 25/1999 reduces the vertical imbalance between centre and regions, it is likely to increase horizontal imbalances among regions. The richest region has 50 times more income than the poorest one. Rich areas will try to develop their own trans-national networks, whereas poor regions will fall further behind and become increasingly isolated.[18]

A precise demarcation of responsibilities and claims between central government, province, and districts and municipalities does not yet exist. There seems to be a tendency for regions to issue their own regulations in fields not yet regulated by the central government, which may cause confusion and contention.

Especially the district level suffers a general lack of administrative expertise. Most career paths head towards Jakarta, leaving few bright young people behind (Fanany 2003). Moreover, regional bureaucrats used to a wait-and-see attitude now have to play a much active role over against the centre, something they were never trained for.

District parliaments (Dewan Perwakilan Rakyat Daerah, DPRD) are slow in initiating legislation and have a limited capacity to do so. Also lacking are mechanisms to resolve conflicts between DPRD and the executive adminis-

16 Although they professed their faith in the outcome of decentralization, Hofman and Kaiser (2002:7) state that more than one year into decentralization, much remained unclear on what exactly had been decentralized and which administrative functions had been decentralized (World Bank 2003).

17 Dormeier-Freire and Maurer 2002; Hadiz 2003a; Hadiz and Robison 2003; Kingsbury and Aveling 2003; Malley 2003.

18 World Bank 2003. This does not necessarily mean that Indonesia will fall apart into a Balkanized archipelago of small states. The example of the recently formed resource-rich province of Bangka-Belitung (the islands southeast of Sumatra) shows that loyalty towards Jakarta increased considerably when autonomy was granted (Sakai 2003a).

trators, while members of the DPRD do not show much eagerness to represent their constituencies. Ryaas Rashid (2003) remarks that DPRD are by and large controlled by national party bosses who protect in the first place the special interests of their own party. There are indications that members of local parliaments prioritize substantial increases in their own salaries and travel budgets at the cost of education and health care (Dormeier-Freire and Maurer 2002; Shaikhu Usman 2002).

Because most regions are subsidized by the centre, regional governments tend to become spending machines (Ray and Goodpaster 2003). In general, financial management and accountability is weak, while 'money politics' seem to prevail. There are widespread complaints that corruption has increased since regional autonomy was implemented. Elections of governors and district administrators by provincial and district parliaments were generally accompanied by massive transfers of money (at least until the introduction of Law no. 32/2004), while budgets for development and construction projects are characterized by mark ups of 50-100%, which are divided among alliances of administrators and businessmen.[19]

In order to acquire additional funds, regional administrations tend to burden their regions with extra taxes, while they pay little or no attention to environmental issues. Because of a lack of coordinating power at a supra-regional level, decentralization encourages interregional competition and conflict. One of the reasons that Bangka-Belitung wanted to become a separate province is that they did not want to share their mining revenues with the province and the other districts on the mainland. Conflicts between neighbouring districts along the north coast of Java about the demarcation of their fishing territories have been a regular occurrence. Elsewhere trade restrictions, which already existed under the New Order, are reinforced by new regulations (Ray and Goodpaster 2003).

Measures that favour locals and exclude minorities may increase ethnic conflict. Cultural identity politics reinforce economic and political competition between districts, also in regions that are ethnically homogeneous.

It is revealing that in the writings of the 'professional optimists' the role of the army and the police as important actors at the regional level is completely ignored. Both the World Bank (2003) and the Asia Foundation (2002) sketch in their reports an Indonesia without army, militias and organized crime.

For those familiar with the literature on decentralization in post-colonial states, the issues mentioned here do not come as a surprise. In a general review of the subject worldwide, Frerks and Otto (1996) concluded that the

19 The World Bank (World Bank 2003) refers to the surprisingly large number of newly elected district heads (*bupati*) who are not affiliated with majority parties in their region, and admits that substantial amounts of money from the centre seem to disappear once they reach the region.

overall results of decentralization were rather disappointing and far behind initial expectations. They refer in this respect also to reports by USAID and the World Bank from the 1990s, illustrating the structural amnesia of these institutions.[20]

Both the literature and the examples mentioned here illustrate that decentralization does not necessarily result in democratization, good governance and the strengthening of civil society at the regional level. Instead we often witness a decentralization of corruption, collusion and political violence that once belonged to the centralized regime of the New Order, and is now moulded into the existing patrimonial patterns at the regional level. We may expect that the continuity of these patterns will prevent the establishment of transparent rules, democratic procedures and control mechanisms. The district head plays a crucial role in this system. This official receives most of the funds from the centre and controls the channels through which money is distributed. If they manage to cooperate with the chairperson of the district parliament and leading businesspeople, and if they are able to accommodate the military commander, they can rule the district and maintain their patronage network without encountering much opposition. Various people call the new autonomous regions 'little kingdoms', but do we know where the kings come from? Except for a few scholars (Hadiz 2003a; Van Klinken 2002; Malley 2003) this question is by and large ignored in recent publications on decentralization.

Pemekaran and the dynamics of ethnicity

The most remarkable aspect of the decentralization process was quite unplanned. *Pemekaran* is the Indonesian word for the subdivision of existing districts and provinces to create new units. It does occur in other countries. In the United States it is called redistricting and concerns electoral politics.[21] It occurred often in some Eastern European countries after the end of the Soviet era, particularly Hungary and the former Czechoslovakia. Scholars described it there as a 'far-reaching and spontaneous fragmentation of the territorial administrative structure' (Illner 2000; Majcherkiewicz 2000). It aimed to undo Soviet era amalgamation and return to earlier, smaller units. Neither

20 A USAID report in 1995 on decentralization identified a lack of planning, the failure to mobilize enough local resources, competition between local officials, and poor natural resource management as major problems. The World Bank stated in 1992 that a weak administrative capacity at the local level would lead to waste and corruption, while resources are arguably open to capture by elite groups at the local level (Frerks and Otto 1996).

21 http://www.lib.purdue.edu/govdocs/redistricting.html.

in the United States nor in Eastern Europe has the process been particularly controversial. In Indonesia, by contrast, it has often been a highly contested development involving strong localist identity movements. Yet the new units often had only a flimsy connection with previous boundaries. Sometimes protagonists invoked colonial history, but that was beyond living memory.

We believe there are good grounds for regarding the Indonesian process as unique in the world for its extent and its politicization, and have therefore retained the Indonesian expression *pemekaran*, which literally means 'flowering'. Strictly speaking this is a misnomer, since the movement is not out and up but turned in upon itself in endlessly repeated subdivision. 'Administrative involution' is another appropriate term, reminiscent of Geertz's notion of agricultural involution when too many people need to live off the same piece of land. It reflects the same talent for improvisation in hard times.

The foreign-trained policy-makers who wrote the Indonesian decentralization legislation did not intend it to trigger a rush of *pemekaran* (Turner et al. 2003). The extensive literature on decentralization around the world is about transferring powers from one administrative level to another, not about redrawing administrative boundaries at the same time. Yet that is what happened in Indonesia. In the space of a few years the number of provinces increased from 27 to 33 while the number of districts (sometimes called regencies or *kabupaten*) increased by almost 50% to 440.

Pemekaran after 1998 was largely driven from below. Despite objections from Interior Ministry officials in Jakarta that *pemekaran* was often unnecessary and costly, time and again politicians in the regions managed to force them to authorize new provinces and districts anyway. Usually the regional politicians made their approach to Jakarta not directly through the bureaucracy but via the national parliament, which then passed legislation instructing the formation of new units. To add force to their argument that *pemekaran* would bring government 'closer to the people', they quietly handed out large amounts of money. Each new district promised a building contractors' bonanza, as they had to be equipped with an array of new offices. The military and police supported *pemekaran* because their parallel territorial command structures were usually upgraded to reflect the change soon afterwards.

The combination of two essentially different processes – administrative decentralization and popular democratization – produced much freer competition between local elites for control of the state. They often conducted their competition in ethnic terms. A district for each faction could be the answer to competing claims. *Pemekaran* is therefore a case study in the question 'why is provincial statecraft so ethnic in moments of formal state weakness?' The rush for *pemekaran* had a parallel in the late 1950s, when Jakarta's formal powers were also weakened by factional struggles at the centre and armed revolts in the provinces. The centre responded then by creating eight new provinces.

But it would be a mistake to see this as a victory for centrifugal forces. Behind the fervor of local identity movements lay not a desire to secede but rather to outdo rivals in loyalty to Jakarta, which was still the source of cash. Indeed Jakarta offered new provinces as perks to loyalists in the regions in order to outmanoeuvre the separatists (Van Klinken 2006).

The first section of the present volume concerns the politics of *pemekaran* after 1998. Two authors – Myrna Eindhoven on Mentawai Island (West Sumatra) and Lorraine Aragon on Poso (Central Sulawesi) – explore the ethnic turn in provincial statecraft that accompanied them. Mentawaian intellectuals found themselves in the city of Padang at a moment of opportunity provided by the administrative flux of decentralization. Lacking a political party infrastructure, an ethnic ideology of indigeneity became their best weapon in the struggle to carve out a bureaucratic niche for themselves. But the ideology had nothing to say to the predatory combination of timber interests and a rent-seeking officialdom that threatened to despoil their island. Despite their best intention, and illustrating the weak foundations of critical NGOs, they were eventually swallowed up by it themselves. In Poso, bureaucrats who had long been blandness personified turned suddenly into champions of religious and (later) ethnic ideologies when they had to compete for their positions in the newly democratizing order. Informal business interests pushed and pulled behind the scenes. Aragon's chapter illustrates how elections plus rent-seeking results in ethnic competition. Thus both studies raise painful questions about the unintended consequences that can arise when two of the modern world's most prized ideals become a reality – democracy and the rights of indigenous peoples. A third author in another section of this book (on civil society) also describes ethnicized regional politics but reaches a more positive conclusion. Taufiq Tanasaldy, writing about West Kalimantan, argues that ethnic politics can be civil. Ethnic 'power-sharing' at the district level, based on new census data, has effectively short-circuited ethnic violence. Indeed ethnicity has taken on emancipatory meanings for Dayak, who deployed it as an ideology to help reverse their hitherto marginalized political status.

This section of the book also includes two studies of, thus far, failed *pemekaran* movements – one by Jacqueline Vel on Sumba (East Nusa Tenggara) and another by Dik Roth on Luwu (South Sulawesi). In a few years time these movements may have been forgotten even by their protagonists. However, these studies are interesting not as chronicles of failure but because they show us exactly how the game was played. They take a close interest in networking. Networks of influence are key sites for researchers interested in less institutionalized, more personalized paradigms of state-society relations. They stretched from the remotest region all the way to Jakarta, often via the provincial capital. An ethic of family-like trust binds them together – whether derived from a common place of origin, descent, or religion. Thus

Roth and Vel are moving beyond provincial studies towards a new theoretical integration, in which networks of influence with a (sub-)provincial focus acquire a national scope.

The salience of ethnic and religious identities (in the Indian context often conflated as 'communal identity') is the most striking feature of provincial Indonesia since the end of the New Order. In the four chapters in this section ethnicity was an ideology in a political struggle, but it was at the same time more than an ideology. It evoked a real depth of feeling. A little history may help to explain this, as well as provide a broader context for the detailed observations by Vel, Aragon, Eindhoven and Roth.

The colonial period, as we have seen, contains the key to understanding the connection between regional elites and ethnicity in present day Indonesia. Mahmood Mamdani (2001b) has noted that African colonial systems were marked by contrasts between Western overlords and local ethnicity, and between Western legal systems and local forms of customary law. This resulted in forms of indirect governance whereby regional ethnic elites acquired power. There are striking similarities with the situation in Indonesia, where in many regions local aristocracies came to power during the colonial period. Customary law was an important mechanism to regulate local relations and to keep ordinary people trapped in an ethnically ordered system. In the late colonial period a strong though relatively limited central state allied itself with aristocratic elites in the regions in order to reinforce a cheap but stable form of indirect rule.

Dutch colonial thinking conceptualized its rule in the Netherlands Indies – especially in the islands outside Java – in dualistic terms. These ideas, which separated European interests from local society, were materialized in the fields of economy, education and law.[22] In terms of law the Dutch created a corpus of knowledge about local customs, which not only separated 'natives' from Europeans (and Arabs and Chinese) but also produced sharp divisions among indigenous groups themselves. There was among 'ethically' inspired Dutch administrators a genuine ideal to respect and protect local cultures against the ambitions of the penetrating colonial state to introduce uniform rule. This was, however, also part of a strategy of divide and rule intended to counter the spread of Islam, while it later served as a conservative 'medicine' against the virus of nationalism.

Throughout the archipelago ethnic groups and *adat* boundaries were defined in the sense that fluid communities with flexible boundaries were now demarcated in rigid terms and located within fixed territorial structures.[23] In many parts of the archipelago the Dutch administered these ethnic groups and *adat*

22 Burns 2004; Van Klinken 2003b; Lev 1985; Stoler 1995.
23 Kingston 1991; Kipp 1993; Laksono 2002; Schrauwers 2000; H. Schulte Nordholt 1994.

communities, through local aristocracies. And it was this colonial legacy that determined to a large extent post-colonial relationships. As a consequence of this colonial imprinting of ethnic identities, the first manifestations of nationalism in Indonesia (Jong Java and so on) had a strong ethnic flavour.[24]

Although ethnicity was a topic of scholarly discussion during the 1950s (Skinner and Bruner 1959), the dominant discourse was primarily focused on nation-building, the role of political parties and the so-called *aliran* (political pillars) on Java. As Ichlasul Amal (1992) has argued, this approach obscured to a large extent the importance of ethnic factors shaping Indonesian politics at the same time.

Neither Geertz (1963) nor Liddle (1970) paid much attention to the colonial moulds within which post-colonial discourses of ethnicity had been shaped. For them 'primordial' sentiments referred to something that was authentic and without much history. Nevertheless, Liddle did notice that at least until 1959 people in north Sumatra were at the same time organized along ethnic lines and deeply committed to the nation (Liddle 1970:208). Geertz (1963:270) even went one step further when he stated that 'it is the very process of the formation of a sovereign civil state that [...] stimulates sentiments of parochialism, communalism, racialism [...] because it introduced into society a valuable new prize over which to fight and a frightening new force with which to contend'. Today the idea that ethnic identities might in fact be 'products' of colonial state formation has become widely accepted (Yinger 1985).

Under the New Order, ethnicity, religion, race and class (summarized in the acronym SARA) were political no-go areas, which implied that public discourse about these topics was under close surveillance. However, there were still discourses about culture, *adat*, religion, and ethnicity, and these formed a complex repository for identity formation. Issues concerning religion and *adat* were monitored by state agencies, while the phenomenon of class was simply silenced. Culture was, moreover, both bureaucratized and folklorized (Acciaioli 1985; Kipp 1993). Officially ethnicity was taboo because of its explosive potential, but the national motto – Unity in Diversity – seemed to legitimize diversity. And it was precisely the interpretation of what diversity meant and who was in control of this meaning that was to become a bone of contestation. Rita Smith Kipp (1993) has analysed the ambiguous and contested nature of concepts like ethnicity, religion and culture in New Order Indonesia. She illustrates how since the colonial period the state has encouraged a process of dissociation by which she means that there is no longer an

24 Van Klinken 2003a; H. Schulte Nordholt 2000. David Henley argues in the final chapter of his book on Minahasa (Henley 1996) for a distinction between *adat* and more modern notions of ethnicity. *Adat* was emphasized in areas with indirect rule, whereas ethnicity played an important role in areas where the influence of Western institutions was more strongly felt.

overlap of religious and ethnic identities (like in the old Malay world where *masuk Melayu* was synonymous with the conversion to Islam). Contrary to the old idea that national integration and increased contact between different groups would erode ethnic identities, government policy, migration and intensified competition for scarce resources had led since the 1980s to an intensification of ethnic consciousness. The New Order believed that it could handle the variety of differences it had helped to create. For, ethnic diversity diminished religious unity, religion pluralized ethnic groups, and both ethnicity and religion denied class (Kipp 1993:261). However, the violent conflicts in the Moluccas, Central Sulawesi and West- and Central Kalimantan, which accompanied the demise of the Soeharto regime, demonstrate that a monster of Frankenstein had been created. Because the New Order had transformed Soekarno's popular nationalism with its mobilizing qualities into state-monitored ceremonialism, ethnic identification seemed to become more powerful. Like nationalism, discourses based on ethnicity imagine bonds of loyalty also in terms of kinship and emotions, which persuade people to risk their lives and cleanse their territories from evil enemies.

Thus by the late 1990s a language of ethnic and religious identity was taking shape that at one and the same time was blessed by the regime yet offered ample possibilities of refuge from and even resistance to that state. This idiom was, as Charles Tilly and his students put it (McAdam et al. 2001), part of a 'repertoire' of action, which could be deployed for a variety of purposes at the appropriate moment. The many cross-cutting possibilities offered by ethnic and religious identifications gave it a theatrical quality, and this did not escape the notice of some of the authors in the present volume. Jacqueline Vel in particular has paid attention to the theatre of ethnic protest in Sumba, which appears to arouse great emotion in the heat of battle but then dims again just as rapidly.

Shadow states and the black economy

Emotions and political theatre often hide a very different reality, in which hard economic interests are at work. This section takes us to one of the core concerns of this book. It explores the contrast between the main visualizations about the state and the economy of Indonesia in the western literature hitherto, and the reality that may be observed on the ground today. The chapters in this section present a wealth of grounded observations to challenge the orderly images of the state and the economy found in mainstream scholarship during the New Order. The criminalization of the state, the blurring of boundaries between state and society, and the informalization of the economy are here closely observed in different parts of the country. They occur not merely in the wild frontiers of upriver Central Kalimantan (as described by John McCarthy), or in the war zone of Aceh (Isa Sulaiman), but also in the quiet tin-mining islands of Bangka-Belitung (Erwiza Erman), and even in Banten, the new province just west of Jakarta (Syarif Hidayat). Two of these are examples of resource-based rent-seeking (timber and tin), while two others illustrate the simple 'transfer rent', in which money is moved out of the government into private pockets at the regional level.

Even when these authors do not adopt an explicit terminology to capture the confusing interpenetration of state, society, and economy that they observe, they offer fascinating material to anybody inclined to develop one. Certainly none see anything resembling the autonomous, bureaucratic or corporatist state that became accepted notions during the New Order. McCarthy does acknowledge the importance of the state regulations and institutions, but his contribution also illustrates how essential it is to avoid the reification of the state in inappropriate ways. This position reflects a literature arguing that endlessly qualifying the ideal Weberian state with predicates such as 'weak' or 'messy' has reached the limit of the absurd, since no actual state in the world comes anywhere near this ideal (Migdal 2001). A different perspective allows us to see that 'the state' does many things that are remote from what it is expected to do by policy-makers. Decentralization, moreover, made certain hidden aspects of the state more explicit as it revealed the extent to which local actors used the state for their own interests.

Isa Sulaiman undertakes a similar move when he analyses Acehnese politics, not in terms of institutional interests, but in those of the personal relationships among its leading actors. District of origin is the major binding factor. Here we see a continuity of neo-patrimonial models mentioned earlier.[25]

Erwiza Erman and Syarif Hidayat, by contrast, do deploy a concept of the state. But it is not the kind of empowered state familiar to all since Weber defined it as 'a human community that (successfully) claims the monopoly of the legitimate use of physical force within a given territory' (Gerth and Wright Mills 1946:77-128). It is the 'shadow state', a notion borrowed from the Indianist Barbara Harriss-White (2003:89), who in turn took it from the Africanist William Reno (1995). The key idea is that political authority can be drawn, not from the possession of undisputed force, but from the ability to control markets and material rewards, or, in other words, from hegemony in the 'black economy'. This implies a blurring of boundaries between state and informal economy. The shadow state expands across that border. Whereas the 'formal' state resembles the set of institutions Weber would have recog-

25 Indonesia provided much of the material upon which the neo-patrimonial model was first based (Eisenstadt 1973; Roth 1968).

nized, the 'shadow state' is larger than this formal state, and also has greater reality. Harriss-White (2003:89) defines it as:

> that part of the informal, 'real' economy that cannot operate without the particular form taken by the State. While it might be considered to be analytically separate from the definition of the State as a set of institutions of political and executive control centred upon government, with which we embarked, the 'shadow' State is part of the actually existing state [...] Hence the real State, including its shadow, is bigger than the formal State, and has a vested interest in the perpetuation of a stricken and porous formal State.

Syarif Hidayat detects a typical shadow state activity when he describes Banten's main businessman, whose livelihood comes from government contracts, going to great lengths to ensure he controls the new province's parliament, which in turn makes executive appointments. Erwiza Erman similarly describes the 'King of Tin' in Bangka-Belitung turning himself into a major competitor for the state-owned tin mining company PT Tambang Timah by colluding with the local district and police chiefs. In each case the crucial observation is that the system only yields a profit to all participants because some of them are there 'in their official capacity'. In Banten, parliament must appoint the district head who will agree to the monopolistic terms set by that contractor. In Bangka-Belitung, the district head needs to argue to his superiors in Jakarta that regional autonomy justifies special dispensations for local tin operators, and the police chief needs to cooperate with 'illegal' tin shipments.

These are not stories of individual moral lapses, nor do they simply reflect a continuity of New Order practices. The shadow state is a system of authority and exchange that is firmly embedded in local relationships and that has staying power. Nevertheless, more effort is needed to develop a conceptual model of the post-New Order state and its fragments which is as clear as the one we used during the New Order. It should account for the privatization of formal institutions and the institutionalization of private interests, but also for the ethnic turn of local politics in moments of formal state weakness discussed in the previous section, as well as the security failures discussed in the next.

Fear and the failure of security

Security is a topic that is almost entirely neglected in the expert literature on decentralization in Indonesia. This reflects its origins in the corridors of the multilateral agencies that have attempted to depoliticize decentralization and turn it into a technical exercise for bureaucrats (Hadiz 2003b). Yet both the decentralization process and the associated democratization have repeatedly led to violence. This is not a book about post-authoritarian communal violence in Indonesia (but see Van Klinken forthcoming-a), nor do we want to suggest that all post-New Order changes were inherently violent. In most places they unfolded peacefully. But when violence did occur it often involved the same actors. Lorraine Aragon's chapter on Poso makes this clear.

Violence is so destructive because it produces a psychology of insecurity that lingers long after the killing has stopped, and spreads to other places where violence never occurred. A threatening climate of fear poisons hopes and erodes the basic trust without which no democracy can flourish. The most fundamental political good that a state is expected to provide is security (Rotberg 2003). If democracy is a process of protected consultation, then the absence of protection spells its death. Democracy needs a functioning state. Suggestions that democracy is all about civil society pushing back the state (the 'counterweight' theory of civil society (Foley and Edwards 1996) are misleading because they ignore the indispensable role of the state in this area. When violence does break out, blame ought to lie in the first place with the state. Anto Sangaji correctly points out in his chapter on Poso that a minimally functional security capacity, subject to civilian control, is a legitimate state role.

The chapters in this section of the book complement the previous ones on the black economy and the shadow state. For both, the gap between conventional understandings of the Weberian state and the observed reality is so wide yet so systematic that we are driven to search for a more adequate concept. The security failures observed in Poso by Anto Sangaji, and in Lombok by John MacDougall, can be as little explained by speaking of individual moral lapses as could the rent-seeking behaviour of state officials in the previous section. Lack of professionalism, too, while real, often does not capture the dynamics of failure.

As in the previous section, these authors are often not yet in a position to formulate a more adequate concept. But we do have some hints, and they relate once more to the logic of the shadow state. The failure of the security forces in Poso could be traced to their preoccupation with both formal and informal business activities. Having built business relationships with key local players whose activities spanned the government, the economy and the district's religious and ethnic life, security officers may have been reluctant to imperil those friendships by taking repressive action (Mietzner 2003). Sometimes the interests of key players in the shadow state are better served not by withholding repressive capacity but by actually (mis-)applying it. Thus Sangaji and MacDougall both describe murky connections between the military and various private militias who in fact promote violence rather than reducing it.

How civil is civil society?

In the next section on civil society the somewhat breathless sense of crisis of the previous chapters is tempered. It also turns our attention to the question, 'under what conditions can democratization be successful at the regional level?'. Is, to put it more sharply, democratic decentralization possible in the presence of ethnic and religious claim-making? Standard literature on modernization would have the answer 'no' ready before you could finish this sentence. In this volume we do not take such a dogmatic position. Contrary to the pessimistic tone of other writing about the provinces, also in some parts of this book, three of the contributions in this section portray societies with salient religious and ethnic identities that are also reasonably democratic. They are the predominantly Christian North Sulawesi (described by David Henley, Maria Schouten and Alex Ulaen), majority Muslim Jepara, a town in Central Java (Jim Schillers), and the ethnically plural West Kalimantan (Taufiq Tanasaldy).

The argument of these chapters will not be uncontested but deserves to be heard. If democracies are those places where talking trumps fighting, then it will be noticed that West Kalimantan had two serious episodes of ethnic violence, in 1997 and 1999, while Jepara had its share of political violence before the 1999 election. Nevertheless, a democracy does not necessarily have to be free of political violence, as India can testify.

For Jepara and North Sulawesi, it helps to have a majority religion – NU-oriented Islam in one, Protestant Christianity in the other – while minority groups know their place. But, as David Henley and his colleagues argue, responsible leadership embedded in strong religious institutions plays a role as well. It also helps to be reasonably prosperous. Jepara and North Sulawesi's capital Menado are comfortable towns each with a small but self-confident middle class, while in North Sulawesi the extremes of wealth and deprivation found in other parts of Indonesia are largely absent. In neither, moreover, has the military been particularly meddlesome – even during the New Order they preferred to stay in the background. Both these places survived the end of the New Order without political collapse. It is therefore just as important, as Henley and his colleagues note correctly, to study 'the anatomy of peace' as to study its pathological collapse.

West Kalimantan is even more interesting. The province does not score highly on economic indicators. It is deeply divided into several ethnic groups, which became salient after the violent episodes of the late 1990s. And the military has left a deep imprint on it through decades of interference caused mainly by its proximity to Malaysia. Yet precisely the violent episodes of 1997 and 1999 put in motion a set of ethnic 'power-sharing' arrangements to prevent the recurrence of trouble. This is an important example of consociational democracy as a conflict-resolution approach (Lijphart 1977). This is, moreover, the first time West Kalimantan has been studied in terms of an anatomy of peace.

Finally the chapter by Andi Faisal Bakti on Wajo, South Sulawesi, shows that social change is slower than often thought. Established elites are eager to maintain privileges and adapt easily to new circumstances. It may seem that non-government organizations multiply to create the appearance of a civil society, but often they do not act accordingly. For that matter, this chapter is a salutary reminder of the truth of Partha Chatterjee's remark that civil society is itself a problematic saviour. Its middle class members are born and raised in the warm embrace of the state. They speak on behalf of the 'masses' but are secretly afraid of them (Chatterjee 1993:85-102).

Identities under construction

The last set of essays investigates discussions about regional identities which are constructed with bricks made of ethnicity, religion and custom, and mortar taken from a nation-wide middle class seminar culture. It is in this context important to note that decentralization and regional autonomy have excluded a fundamental discussion about the meaning of citizenship in contemporary Indonesia, which forms an important cornerstone of democracy. Facing rapid political and economic changes, regional intellectuals try to conceptualize who they are, how they are tied to their region and how they relate to Indonesia. These discussions are marked by ambivalence, complexity and contradiction, which pretty much reflects Indonesian societies today. A closer look at discourses on regional identities shows an interesting paradox, in the sense that regional authenticity is often emphasized in a very 'Indonesian' way. More in general we may conclude that throughout the archipelago differences are increasingly expressed in similar ways (see for example Van Klinken forthcoming-b). Two factors contribute to the Indonesian way these regional differences are expressed. In the first place discourses about regional authenticity are firmly rooted in a body of colonial texts which share a set of assumptions on the nature of these societies. These texts are moreover expressed in a bureaucratized New Order language which moulds them into a highly uniformed format. Therefore discussions about the essence and resilience of Balinese culture, or how the *nagari* is considered to be the basis of Minangkabau culture, as elaborated in the essays by Henk Schulte Nordholt and Franz and Keebet von Benda-Beckmann, reflect an 'Indonesian' way of identifying cultural keys, as much as they express concerns about regional identities. If we look at the main participants in these discourses we encounter urban middle class intellectuals who are born, educated and socialized in the New Order. Although they tend to emphasize their unique regional identity, this group of people seems to embody at the same time the core of a national Indonesian middle class culture. Henk Schulte Nordholt takes the discussion about 'Ajeg Bali' (the Resilience of Bali) as a point of departure in an effort to give an integrated analysis of recent political changes which are seen in a wider Indonesian context. Franz and Keebet von Benda-Beckmann analyse the discourse concerning the *nagari* as a key to Minangkabau community and identity. They emphasize the inward-looking nature of this debate but show also that apart from local actors, participants at the provincial, national and international level are involved.

Regional identities are also heavily contested, and this is elaborated in the essays by Carole Faucher on Riau and Jaap Timmer on Papua. In Riau aristocratic ideas compete with the threatening proximity of Singapore's modernity, while the younger generation opts for a more outspoken Indonesian identity. The picture which emerges from Faucher's essay is one of confusion. Despite the existence of large groups if immigrants, the Malay elite tries to impose a coherent image of Malayness, which is contradicted by practices of exclusion by Singapore and Malaysia, while the high school curriculum is still to a large extent determined by Jakarta. Timmer, meanwhile, criticizes the idea of a unified and homogeneous Papua resisting Jakarta oppression. Instead he emphasizes the ethnic and demographic fault lines along which regional elites compete with each other. Increasingly, Papuan elites have accommodated to Indonesian ways of doing politics and found their way to political circles in Jakarta. In Papua a process of '*pemekaran* from above' has increased tensions and conflicts between elites and their constituencies, as a result of which the hopes of reform expressed during the 'Papua Spring' of 2000 have faded.

Taken together the essays in this book aim to document the hopes and anxieties in Indonesian societies at the turn of the twenty-first century, especially in its neglected regions. The idea of the nation is damaged, the legitimacy of the state questioned, the nature and future of regional identities contested, and the boundaries between 'state', 'nation' and 'region' have become zones of conflict. Yet amid this flux of boundaries renegotiated, Indonesians are also demonstrating an admirable confidence that futures can be made anew, a surprising resilience in the face of uncertainty and (let us not forget) poverty, and (also too often overlooked) a remarkable civility amid the differences.

GERRY VAN KLINKEN

M. Isa Sulaiman (1951-2004)

Isa Sulaiman was one of Aceh's most important social scientists. Unlike other talented Acehnese, he did not move to Jakarta, nor did he go into politics or the bureaucracy. He stuck to his scholarship as if it was a calling. Three days after returning from the workshop that produced this book, on the morning of 26 December 2004, he was among the multitude of human beings swept away by the tsunami. His extensive archives also disappeared in the water.

Isa Sulaiman was born on 28 June 1951 in Manggeng, Labuhan Haji, a small town in South Aceh. It lay near Meulaboh that was to be destroyed by the tsunami; the area was hurt by fighting in the 1990s. In 1977 he graduated from the History Department of the Faculty of Education at the Syiah Kuala University, in the provincial capital Banda Aceh. His thesis, on religion in his home town after independence, marked the beginning of two abiding interests – things that happen in small places, and how religion gets on in modernizing times. The Australian historian Lance Castles was one of his mentors. Impressed, the university offered him a lectureship.

Academic work at a state university in an authoritarian system can be deadening. The 1980s were the height of the militaristic New Order. Some of Isa's early work was little more than anthropological list-making. In order somehow to shape a national culture, the government asked social scientists around the country to make exhaustive 'inventories' of traditional rituals such as weddings.[1] The ruling idea was that cultures are static things that need only be classified to be understood.

In 1979 he was invited to Makassar (then Ujung Pandang), in South Sulawesi. The innovative Pusat Latihan Penelitian Ilmu-Ilmu Sosial (PLPIIS, Centre for Social Sciences Research Training) was one of four sponsored by the Ford Foundation. Another stood in Banda Aceh. He wrote a fine field study on a Buginese ironworking village (Isa Sulaiman 1979). His supervisor, the Bugis specialist Christian Pelras, then arranged for him to write a doctoral dissertation in Paris. This was Isa's big break. Separated from wife and two

1 Isa Sulaiman 1978; Syamsuddin, Hasan Husin and Isa Sulaiman 1981; Hasan Husin, Isa Sulaiman Mahmud Main et al. 1982.

young sons, he learned French and wrote a 365-page dissertation in that language within the required three years (Isa Sulaiman 1985a). Denys Lombard was his supervisor. This solid study on the struggle for Aceh between aristocrats and religious leaders in the years of occupation and revolution 1942-1951 remains unpublished, though he wrote several articles based on it (Isa Sulaiman 1985b, 1985c).

The same thorough approach informed his next book-length work, which also did not circulate widely because it was self-published. It was a transcription with a long introduction of four epic poems (*hikayat*) about the Cumbok War, the decisive battle between the aristocracy and radical nationalists in Pidie in December 1945-January 1946 (Isa Sulaiman 1990b).

In 1997 his *Sejarah Aceh (*History of Aceh appeared with a major Jakarta publisher. It covered the tumultuous period 1942-1962 and thus incorporated and extended his dissertation work. This was his debut for a wider public. A foreword by the redoubtable T.H. Ibrahim Alfian placed him among only nine Acehnese with substantial work on Aceh's politics and history, though only Isa and Ibrahim Alfian were historians.[2] *Sejarah Aceh* is carefully crafted. He trawled archives in the Netherlands and Jakarta for it, persuaded key Acehnese actors to talk, and tracked down rare documents in private and public collections in Aceh. This bloody period covers the end of Dutch rule, the Japanese occupation, the independence struggle including the social revolution of early 1946, and the Darul Islam revolt of the 1950s.

Far more than a chronology, he also brought his own interpretation to this period. Till then the dominant Indonesian explanation of the Darul Islam revolt came from Nazaruddin Syamsuddin (Isa Sulaiman 1985, 1990), who portrayed it as persistent Acehnese primordialism obstructing national integration. Isa preferred to read the entire period as a struggle within Aceh itself, a fruitful struggle for an emerging modernity. He had been working on this theme for some time (Isa Sulaiman 1988a, 1988b). Like Nazaruddin he was a modern intellectual who only occasionally showed a touch of nostalgia for the 'harmony' of traditional village life (Isa Sulaiman 1990a). If we read between the lines we can perhaps even detect some regret at his own role, Snouck Hurgronje-like,[3] of lending his intellect to aid the destructive penetration by the modern bureaucratic state into this rural idyll (Isa Sulaiman 1988c; Isa Sulaiman, Hasan Husin et al. 1995). Yet more than Nazaruddin, Isa wrote about Aceh from within, and he refused to despair. The radicals who took

2 The others were Ali Hasjmy, Nazaruddin Syamsuddin, Hasan Saleh, Amran Zamzami, Sjamaun Gaharu and Fachry Ali, to which we must add Ibrahim Alfian himself.

3 Snouck Hurgronje was the late nineteenth century colonial anthropologist and official who advised the Dutch army in Aceh. Indonesian nationalists naturally regard him as a villain. However, Isa portrayed him more positively as a careful observer, who moreover trained Acehnese researchers (Isa Sulaiman 2004).

on the aristocrats in 1946, and who went on to challenge Jakarta in the 1950s, were self-made individuals arising from the common people. They educated themselves in private religious schools in the 1930s because the Dutch and the Acehnese aristocrats had conspired to block their rise. The fact that they themselves later adopted the same patrimonial leadership style as those they had opposed merely led to new revolts from their own ranks. Thus in Isa's view, the characteristic Acehnese heroism may have caused blood to run, but it was certainly not atavistic.[4]

Heroism was not something just to write about, but to do. When Reformasi came also to Aceh, Isa did not sit on the fence. He introduced his book on the Gerakan Aceh Merdeka (GAM, Free Aceh Movement) (Isa Sulaiman 2000) by saying he hoped it would add a historical dimension to a strident indictment of military human rights abuse written earlier by Al-Chaidar (1998). Once again it was well-documented, and it displayed a fearlessness and compassion that few could match. It refused to bow to ideology – whether nationalist Indonesian, Acehnese, or religious. Accuracy and balance were everything. It was written at a moment when both the Indonesian armed forces and GAM carried out assassinations against civilian activists and academics who displeased them.

The book led to an invitation to join the 'Acehnese civil society task force' in Banda Aceh, which hoped to create a democratic space amid the fighting. In November 2002 the international mediation group Henry Dunant Centre (HDC) invited him and others to Geneva to shore up negotiations between the Free Aceh Movement and the Indonesian government. It was his first meeting with Acehnese leaders in exile, and he was impressed with them.

Just when the tsunami claimed him, Isa seemed to be going from strength to strength. His chapter for the present book was not quite finished. It was another well-documented indictment of the political order (Isa Sulaiman and Van Klinken 2006). He knew the whole cast personally, but refused to let his need for acceptance overwhelm his judgment of them. In May 2004 he co-convened a conference at the Asia Research Institute in Singapore on the historical background of the Aceh problem. He had just done fieldwork in the remote Simeulue Island off Sumatra's west coast. He planned to write about the left, which disappeared from Aceh and from the history books in 1965 (he admired the socialist youth movement Pesindo). He wanted to write about Indonesian literature and social change in Aceh between 1927 and 1962. And he taught large classes in Banda Aceh.

During his four and a half months at the Koninklijk Instituut voor Taal-,

4 Although he was only one of the ghost-writers, the biography of Abdul Muluk, Aceh's best-known engineer who was also born in South Aceh, illustrates the same confidence that modernity and Aceh do go together (Isa Sulaiman 2001).

Land- en Volkenkunde (KITLV, Royal Netherlands Institute of Southeast Asian and Caribbean Studies) in Leiden in 2003, Isa was usually quiet in company. But when the ice was broken he could laugh, loudly. When he spoke about Aceh there was fire in his voice. That fire also lit up his scholarship. Aceh deserves no less.

Bibliography M. Isa Sulaiman

1977 'Beberapa aspek pengaruh pesantren Darussalam Labuhan Haji terhadap perkembangan keagamaan di Aceh Selatan, 1945-1975'. MA thesis, History Department, Faculty of Education, Universitas Syiah Kuala, Banda Aceh.

1978 *Adat dan upacara perkawinan di daerah adat istiadat Aneuk Jamèe*. Banda Aceh: Pusat Dokumentasi dan Informasi Aceh.

1979 *Dari Gecong hingga ke Rotary; Perkembangan usaha kerajinan pandai Besi Massepe kabupaten Sidrap*. Ujung Pandang: Hasanuddin University Press.

1985a *Les ulèebalang, les ulémas, et les ensignants de madrasah; La lutte pour le pouvoir local en Aceh de 1942 à 1951*. PhD thesis, Ecoles des Hautes Etudes en Sciences Sociales, Paris.

1985b 'Islam et propagande anti-Néerlandaise; Abdullah Arief et le Seumangat Atjeh 1945-1946', *Archipel* 30:207-17.

1985c 'Islam, etnisitas dan propaganda anti Belanda; Suatu tujuan terhadap semangat empat lima'. Paper, Seminar Sejarah Nasional 4, Yogyakarta, 16-19 December.

1988a 'Banda Aceh dalam siklus perdagangan internasional; Suatu tinjauan historis'. Paper, Seminar Hari Jadi Kota Banda Aceh, Banda Aceh, 26-29 March.

1988b 'Madrasah dan pembentukan elite modernis di Aceh'. Paper, Seminar Temu Budaya Nusantara, Banda Aceh, 28-29 August.

1988c 'Kebudayaan daerah sebagai sumber dalam menunjang kebudayaan nasional; Kasus kebudayaan Aceh'. Paper, Seminar Temu Budaya Nusantara, Banda Aceh, 28-29 August.

1990a 'Modernization and bureaucratization in developing the village; The Aceh experience'. Paper, Workshop on Centres and Peripheries, DEVI-CNRS, Paris, 17-18 October.

1990b *Hikayat Prang Cumbok; Fungsinya sebagai karya sastra dan sumber sejarah Aceh*. Banda Aceh: M. Isa Sulaiman.

1997 *Sejarah Aceh; Sebuah gugatan terhadap tradisi*. Jakarta: Pustaka Sinar Harapan.

2000 *Aceh merdeka; Ideologi, kepemimpinan, dan gerakan*. Jakarta: Pustaka Al-Kautsar.

2004 'C. Snouck Hurgronje dan pengembangan kebudayaan Aceh'. Paper, Seminar Kajian Kritis Pandangan Snouck Hurgronje tentang Aceh, Jakarta.

Joint publications

Syamsuddin, T., T.A. Hasan Husin, M. Isa Sulaiman et al.
1981 *Sistem kesatuan hidup setempat daerah propinsi Daerah Istimewa Aceh.* Banda Aceh: Proyek Inventarisasi dan Dokumentasi Kebudayaan Daerah Istimewa Aceh, Pusat Penelitian Sejarah dan Budaya, Departemen Pendidikan dan Kebudayaan.
T.A. Hasan Husin, M. Isa Sulaiman, Mahmud Main et al.
1982 *Upacara tradisional daerah propinsi Daerah Istimewa Aceh.* Banda Aceh: Proyek Inventarisasi dan Dokumentasi Kebudayaan Daerah, Direktorat Sejarah dan Nilai Tradisional, Direktorat Jenderal Kebudayaan, Departemen Pendidikan dan Kebudayaan.
M. Isa Sulaiman, Achmadi, T.A. Hasan Husin et al.
1995 *Kehidupan sosial budaya masyarakat terasing di Desa Alue Waki, kecamatan Darul Makmur, Kabupaten Aceh Barat.* Banda Aceh: Lembaga Penelitian, Universitas Syiah Kuala, Kantor Wilayah Departemen Sosial Propinsi Daerah Istimewa Aceh.
Abdul Muluk, edited by M. Isa Sulaiman and Sayid Abu Bakar
2001 *Anak desa diajarnya berkata, dibimbingnya berjalan.* Jakarta: Pustaka Sinar Harapan.
M. Isa Sulaiman and Gerry van Klinken (eds)
2006 'The rise and fall of governor Puteh', in: Gerry van Klinken en Henk Schulte Nordholt, *Renegotiating Boundaries; Local politics in post-Soeharto Indonesia,* pp. 225-52. Leiden: KITLV Press. [Verhandelingen 238.]

References

Al-Chaidar
1998 *Aceh bersimbah darah; Mengunghap penerapan status Daerah Operasi Militer (DOM) di Aceh 1989-1998.* Jakarta: Pustaka Al-Kautsar.
Syamsuddin, Nazaruddin
1985 *The republican revolt; A study of the Acehnese rebellion.* Singapore: Institute of Southeast Asian Studies.
1990 *Pemberontakan kaum republik; Kasus Darul Islam Aceh.* Jakarta: Grafiti.

Local society and the dynamics of ethnicity

LORRAINE V. ARAGON

Elite competition in Central Sulawesi

Maps and dreams

The post-1999 reorganization of Indonesia's regional boundaries, literally termed 'blossoming' (*pemekaran*), is being done in the name of good governance, democratization, and regional autonomy.[1] The use of this botanical term suggests a natural and organic unfolding of new parts, as the nation matures like a healthy plant. Yet the creation and financing of political units in Indonesia is anything but biologically natural. At least in some provinces, decentralization has less to do with good governance than revised incentives for seeking political rents from natural resources, which encourage the re-drawing of administrative maps.[2] This essay explores how rent seeking at the district level and social discrimination interacted with competitive elections and decentralization in Central Sulawesi. In the Poso District, elite competition turned to religious and then to ethnic identity politics when district executives encountered both the enrichment possibilities of decentralizing governance and the risks of newly competitive, more democratic, elections.

Several new districts have been formed in Central Sulawesi since 1999, and lobbying efforts now aim to create a new East Sulawesi Province.[3] There are many pedestrian issues for negotiation, such as which towns will become new capitals, which leaders from which groups will become district heads, and which people will receive new civil service jobs. Yet, the region's decentralization has been coterminous with post-Soeharto collective violence.

1 I wish to thank the Wenner-Gren Foundation for Anthropological Research, a Research and Writing Grant from the John D. and Catherine T. MacArthur Foundation, and the Koninklijk Instituut voor Taal-, Land- en Volkenkunde (KITLV) Modern Indonesia program for research support and collegiality. For helpful comments on an earlier draft, I am grateful to Arianto Sangaji and Jacqueline Vel.

2 As used by economists, 'rent-seeking' describes how fees are garnered by state agents when governments stand in a monopoly position as contractual owners of public resources (Törnquist 1990; R. Williams 1999).

3 We can contrast Central Sulawesi with provinces like Bali, where a long history of districts based on prior kingdoms with little internal ethnic diversity seems to have made the idea of *pemekaran* uninteresting.

Ethnic constellations mobilized for religiously polarized violence largely overlap with groups increasingly separated by most new district plans. Thus, the 1999 regional autonomy laws constructed under President Habibie revamped local politics and accentuated religious and ethnic competition through administrative fragmentation and the intensified extraction of natural resources made accessible by new roads.

Central Sulawesi's crony capitalism, violence between Muslim and Christian factions, and the push to redraw political boundaries are related. But their synergy is generated through multiple lines of local agency in conjunction with periodic state agent support, rather than top-down state control.[4] Although continuous with practices from the Soeharto era, corruption in Poso has in fact 'blossomed' under competitive elections, regional violence, and the potential for controlling local resources through *pemekaran*.[5] These events stem from the ways transition economies in newly organized districts put public property 'up for grabs' to the marketplace, while elections evoke targeted patronage to insure the continued profits of public office.

Many observers became disillusioned as promises of Indonesia's pro-democracy movement fizzled in the wake of faltering national leadership, economic crisis, regional violence, and bureaucratic corruption. In 2002 I spoke with a seasoned program director for an international NGO in Jakarta. Although more optimistic than many, he commented that the equal opportunity dream of Indonesia's Reformasi movement was now mainly a reality of 'equal opportunity buying'. Power over public resources and legal processes merely had shifted from the Soeharto regime into the hands of other wealthy people who could buy a piece of the decentralizing political economy system.

In some regions, though, the same sums of money could not always buy the same slice. In Central Sulawesi's capital of Palu, job seekers quoted different sums required for access to entry-level jobs. There was a low amount asked from those with relatives or ethnic cohorts already working in local government and a much higher amount requested from people with no strings to pull. In September 2003, non-insiders were asked to guarantee 20 million rupiah (almost US$ 2,000) at civil service testing time when applying for a junior post. A 50% down payment was made to the department head (*kepala dinas*) before selections were announced. If lobbying for a paying client

4 This 'decentralized articulation' argument and background on the first years of the Poso conflict can be found in Aragon 2001. For ensuing events, see Human Rights Watch 2002; ICG 2004; George Junus Aditjondro 2003, 2004a; Aragon 2005; S. Sinansari Ecip, Darwis Waru, and Alip Yog Kunandar 2002; or Tahmidy Lasahido 2003.

5 To avoid misunderstanding, my thesis does not therefore recommend a return to centralized military control and rigged elections as seen under Soeharto, but rather for legal checks, community institutions, and press monitoring that better safeguard public funds and resources. See Jenkins and Goetz 1999.

was overruled at the district secretary's office, the payment was not refunded. The loser only received assurances of lobbying the following year.

This was not equal opportunity buying, I concluded. It was un-equal opportunity buying. The bureaucracy was corrupt in both social and financial aspects.[6] This matches many political patronage patterns worldwide, as well as Indonesia's local markets, where stores offering fixed prices are recent phenomena, which strangely displace personal negotiations over social difference and the local value of goods. Michele Ford (2003) describes a Batak man in Riau forced to pay higher prices for kerosene because of his non-Muslim, non-Malay identity. In that case, the Batak was considered an outsider to the majority population. Perhaps Muslim Malay migrants have similar problems near Lake Toba. Yet even people who consider themselves 'indigenous' encounter such problems in many Indonesian regions. The politics of discrimination is something that local politicians, both native sons and migrants, understand well and manipulate to organize patronage alliances, now linked to voting.

Given the history of shifting populations and privileges in Poso, corruption at the district level came to operate according to ethno-religious alliances as well as material incentives. This claim challenges economic approaches to corruption that assume the income-maximizing behaviour of individuals in all cases. Rather, the Central Sulawesi case entails non-market or parochial corruption based on personal ties (Scott 1972:88-9). Such corruption often involves material risk because it is 'socially conditioned and sustained by complex and enduring social networks', rather than following an omniscient and maximizing economic model with short-term goals (R. Williams 1999:508). For example, if a bureaucrat helps a member of his ethnic community to gain a job, he may or may not receive a direct economic benefit from that action. To give an example relevant for Poso, a bureaucrat may misuse his position to facilitate a militia killing for either material or non-material motives. These include monetary gain, revenge – if his family was harmed – or ideological reasons if he thinks in ethnic or religious conspiracy terms. This approach to corruption probes a wider cultural view of the 'private gain' aspect of the 'misuse of public office'.

One native Central Sulawesi family who had sacrificed heavily for their children's college degrees found that good performance on civil service exams could not outweigh the deficiencies of their minority status and

6 Corruption is defined briefly as 'the misuse of public office for private gain' (Robertson-Snape 1999:589). This Weberian type of definition has been critiqued for assuming too clean a line between public and private spheres, or too monolithic a public assessment of 'misuse of office'. Yet, a legal-focused definition serves here better than economic ones, which introduce positivist 'rational choice' biases I wish to avoid. See also R. Williams 1999 and Scott 1972.

shallow pockets. The educated children were unable to find government or private jobs in their fields. The one who graduated with a promising specialized agriculture degree eventually migrated to another island to assume unskilled work through the family's church organization. Some income was better than nothing, the family decided. The older child, with a law degree, stayed home to help her mother with housework. When I asked this bright young woman in 2003 whether there were any possibilities for her to use her university training and bring home a salary for her family, her answer was simple. If one of the newly proposed districts were authorized, a requisite set of civil servants would be needed. She was waiting for her chance to apply. Her dreams depended upon new maps.

The example of 'unequal opportunity buying' warrants expanded theories of 'non-market corruption', and illustrates how urban ethnic groups on the losing end of 'unequal buying' still hope for the benefits of a 'trickle-down' effect when bureaucratic jobs are created for new districts. They thus often support plans to split up districts conceived to benefit particular religious or ethnic groups. Both the elite plans and broader popular support are based in competitive rather than cooperative views of citizenship. The resulting 'transaction costs' (Bakker and Schulte Nordholt 1996) are rarely figured into analyses of decentralization or corruption at the policy level.

Partition of existing districts to create new, smaller ones requires lobbying in Jakarta, regional support, and sufficient local resources to make a new bureaucracy potentially self-supporting. Sponsors of *pemekaran* are motivated to control future capital from Jakarta, bureaucratic positions, and natural resource profits. Jakarta and regional politicians will share much of that income, along with business and military associates who protect them. What Jakarta or provincial officials seek in return for backing new districts and their would-be leaders are kickbacks (often termed 'tribute', *upeti*; or 'allotment', 'bribe', *jatah*), business cooperation, and political constituencies who can be counted on in the next election. Competitive elections and uncensored requests for greater public control over policies are the kernels of democracy nestled within patrimonial administrations now managed by the regions' so-called 'little kings' (*raja kecil*). These newly empowered district heads (*bupati*), shift more of the authoritarian structure anchored in cronyism from Jakarta to the districts (H. Schulte Nordholt 2003; Hadiz 2003a). This 'elite capture' process is perhaps less a matter of what Michael Mann (2005) terms 'the dark side of democracy' than Indonesia's lingering 'dark side of autocracy'.[7]

My discussion below targets four main issues. First, I discuss the rise and transformations of some ethno-religious groups seeking to control the Poso

7 I thank Gerry van Klinken for suggesting this comparison. This is also akin to what Charles Tilly (2003:43) calls the 'zone of fragmented tyranny'.

District.[8] Ethnic identities, consolidated through Dutch influences and publicly fossilized during the New Order, moved in flux with political opportunities linked to the global market, regional bureaucracy, and informal economy. These ethno-religious constellations also developed historically in conjunction with colonial and post-colonial visions of 'indigenous' versus 'migrant' statuses. The situation in Poso thus emerged differently from what Rita Smith Kipp (1993) described for the Karo region of North Sumatra, where religious and ethnic identities became increasingly dissociated during the New Order.

Second, I describe how the Soeharto family's precedent of *korupsi, kolusi, dan nepotisme* (KKN, corruption, collusion, and nepotism) was realized in Poso. Whereas most literature on crony capitalism in Southeast Asia focuses on macro-economic structures and national elites,[9] the focus here is on district heads, their business links, and popular reactions to their activities. The Poso District illustrates how government institutions and illegal practices can construct each other to benefit incumbents who become inspired to maintain power at any social price. The Poso regimes echo the way Soeharto's illicit practices were sheltered under the kinship metaphor of 'Daddy-ism' (Bapakism), where a good father provides well for his family (Saya Shiraishi 1997). The most successful Poso political leaders of the late New Order were Sulawesi Muslims who claimed both 'native' ethnic and Muhammadiyah credentials as patronage shields for their profiteering activities.

Third, I document how Poso's violence became a catalyst for regime change at the district level from an ethnic Tojo network to a Bungku network. The two district heads' ethnic origins, Tojo and Bungku, can be traced back to pre-colonial entrepôt polities (Atkinson 1989; Velthoen 1997), setting an historic precedent for the emergence of 'little kingdoms' under decentralization. Historically, the political economy of such 'statelets' is characterized as inherently unstable, being based on competitive 'trading and raiding'. Indeed, the initial solidarity of the winning Bungku administration gives way to resentments about 'Bungkuism' from other Muslim ethnic groups. The district's corruption eventually moves beyond the routine siphoning of funds designated for government services into the less accepted misuse of humanitarian funds intended for Poso conflict survivors. Post-violence military deployments provide additional business opportunities for incumbents.

Fourth, I examine how successful district heads pursue *pemekaran* to counteract transfers of power at the end of their terms. Ethno-religious and

8 The term 'ethno-religious' indicates where ethnic and religious identities usually overlap and are not readily disentangled with respect to most local perceptions or inter-actional behaviour. Examples, which will be elaborated below, include Protestant Pamona and Muslim Bungku.

9 I. Brown 1997; Robertson-Snape 1999; N. Schulte Nordholt 1996; White 2004; Winters 1996; Yoshihara 1988.

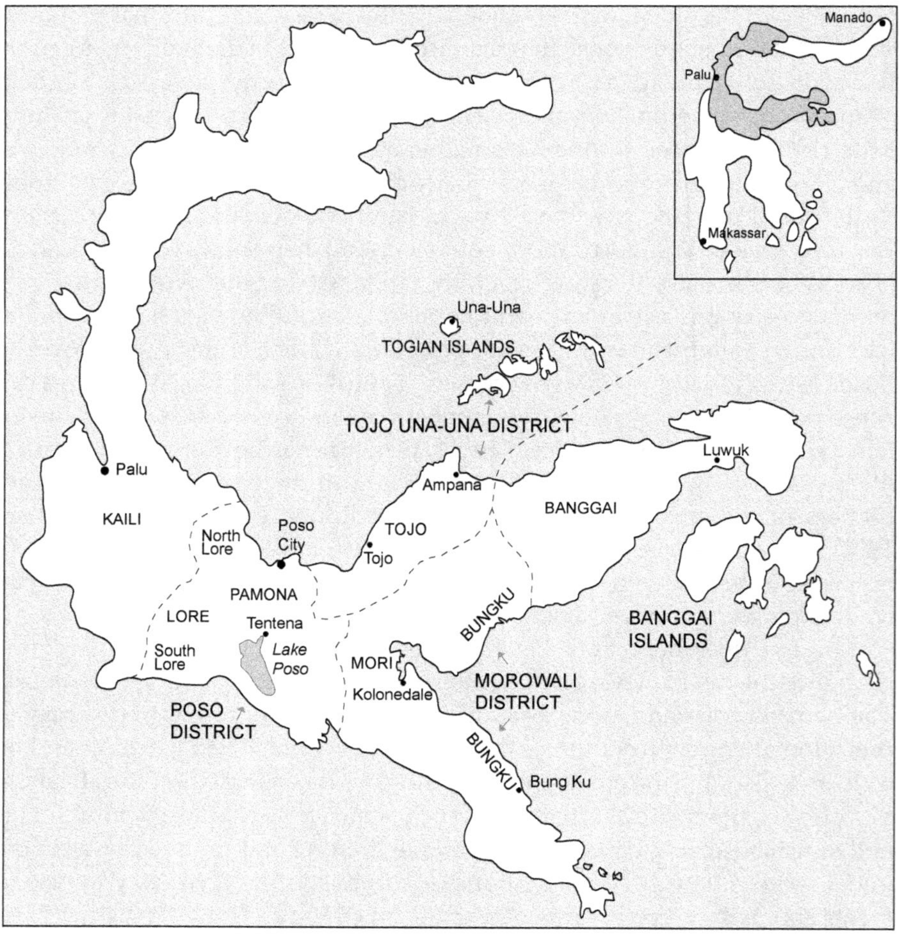

Map 2. Central Sulawesi (1)

political debates surround the newly formed Morowali and Tojo Una-Una districts, as well as proposals for an East Sulawesi Province. It is through the realization of these 'models for' new districts and provinces that ambitious groups and leaders hope to prosper through natural resource extraction businesses. By contrast, Protestant minorities propose new districts in their homeland areas with little chance of authorization.

With increased migration during the Soeharto regime, Central Sulawesi's population gradually became less rural and more linked to 'de-territorialized' religious and ethnic networks based in major population areas. When Jakarta placed an outsider Christian governor and district head in charge from the mid-1970s to the mid-1980s, coastal urban Muslims saw themselves as repressed 'native sons' (*putra daerah*). By the late 1990s, however, national politics had shifted in their favour. Politicians with Golkar and ICMI backing built family-based patronage constituencies along nationally supported lines of Muslim identity politics.[10] Because national migration incentives led to a demographic Muslim majority in Poso, Muslim politicians strategically sought votes in 1998 by appealing to religious competition. Subsequent violence re-territorialized and separated different ethno-religious groups within the Poso District, as Protestants fled to the highlands centred in the mission town of Tentena while Muslims fled to the coasts, centred in Poso City. Seeing opportunity in the regional autonomy laws, Muslim politicians then lobbied for new districts to govern when their terms expired, offering to bring government jobs and development business to their ethnic constituencies. Thus far, newly created districts such as Morowali (centred on ethnic Bungku) and Tojo Una-Una (centred on ethnic Tojo), and plans for an East Sulawesi province have led to demonstrations and wrangling rather than eased regional tensions.[11]

Emerging ethnic and religious constellations in Poso

Layers of individuals' multiple social identities – including sex, community, ethnicity, religion, or class – become more firmly envisioned when governmentally sanctioned or privileged by local economies. Indonesia's decentralization process introduced newly selective opportunities for some ethnic groups although their ascendance and 1998 mobilization is better under-

10 ICMI stands for Ikatan Cendekiawan Muslim se-Indonesia, or Indonesian Association of Muslim Intellectuals. See Hefner 1993. Golkar was the professional organization to which all civil servants automatically belonged, but it functioned as a privileged corporatist political party under Soeharto's rule.

11 Violent conflict also occurred in September 2003, October 2004, and April 2005 during a process of *pemekaran* in the new province of West Sulawesi when some Muslims contested the inclusion of their villages within Protestant majority districts; see ICG 2005.

stood in the light of a longer history. At the turn of the twentieth century, most Central Sulawesi inhabitants followed local cosmological traditions and there was little demand for purity from the few migrants professing foreign religions. Most native groups' identities were based on known kinship ties and related claims to ancestral land (Aragon 2000). It was only the arrival of migrants, world religions, and state population controls that cultivated formal 'ethnic' categories, which colonial officers based partly on religious conversions. The results of these state and religious pressures were naturalized as the ethnic categories listed in government reports, and the religions listed on Indonesian identity cards.

Dutch colonial categories of indigenous 'native' and foreign 'settler' also became grafted onto religious and ethnic identities in post-colonial Indonesia, much as Belgian ones became grafted onto racial identities in central Africa.[12] Although the Dutch colonial regime created and favoured native Protestants in eastern Indonesia, both domestic migration and Muslims' political power increased during the late Soeharto regime. Competing views about the relative legitimacy of migrants and natives often split along Muslim-Christian lines, increasingly supported through distant religious networks. As competition over land and business increased in Poso, the interpretive framing of economic problems shifted from local frustration to broader religious agendas. The native versus migrant overlap with Christian versus Muslim populations was accentuated before and during the collective violence in Poso, Ambon and North Maluku. Once violence was perpetrated along religious lines, police and army troops as well as under-employed young men were drawn to participate in violent acts framed as 'religious community defence'.

Dutch colonial officials introduced Protestantism as the true faith suitable for interior Sulawesi natives who had not been swayed by the foreign Muslim practices of early migrant Arabs or Malays. By contrast, the mixed coastal Sulawesi groups who adopted Islam argued that they were native Muslim 'sons of the soil', free to move anywhere along their trade networks in the archipelago, while Protestants were allied with foreign Western religion and imperial masters. Both rationales for religious nativism can be constructed by selecting among historical data concerning migration and religion in the Indonesian Archipelago. Therefore, rather than one set of 'victims' turning into 'killers', as in the Rwandan case, both Indonesian

12 Mamdani 2001a, 2001b. I use the terms 'native' and 'indigenous' here recognizing that they are constructed, fluid, and contested political categories. Both connote such varied ideas as: 'original people' (*orang asli*), 'sons of the soil' (*pribumi*), current residents, newly contacted isolated groups, and descendants of local people described in the first European records who have no other known origin.

Muslims and Christians had grounds to see themselves as victims, and they took revenge upon each other during various phases of the Poso and Maluku conflicts. When these conflicts escalated, moreover, they did so because the attacked were able to attract financing, weapons, military agent support, or militia personnel from migrant and trans-national religious networks who saw these local conflicts in grander national or universal religious terms (see Aragon 2005).

As Central Sulawesi's narrow coastline rises sharply to interior mountains, Muslim traders initially remained within a few kilometres from shore (Adriani and Kruyt 1950, II). Other than Chinese traders, pre-colonial migrants to Central Sulawesi were mostly Muslims, and many intermarried with native women. Indigenous coastal groups in the Poso area who became Muslim include Tojo, Bungku, and Togian. Muslim migrants include Gorontalo, Bugis, Makassar, Mandar, Kaili, and Javanese people. Earlier migrants formed an elite business class in Poso City, while later migrants more often assumed roles as labourers. After New Order bureaucratic reforms of the 1970s, outsider Muslims, usually Javanese, Gorontalo, or Bugis, were installed as civil servants. During the past decades, especially as the Trans-Sulawesi 'highway' was cut through Poso during the 1980s, large numbers of South Sulawesi migrant farmers entered the interior in search of land for cash cropping.

Sulawesi highlanders, viewed by earlier Europeans as 'pagans' eligible for Protestant conversion, were sorted by language and then lumped together by colonial authors as various kinds of 'Toradja'.[13] Ethnic identities that emerged during the colonial period in the Poso region include the mostly Protestant Pamona, Mori, Napu, Besoa, and Bada. Other Protestant converts, including Minahasa from North Sulawesi and Sa'dan Toraja from South Sulawesi, were sent to the area as preachers and teachers. Until the end of the New Order when migration shifted the demographic balance in Muslims' favour, Protestant Pamona communities maintained significant political representation in the Poso District.

Most Poso District residents either are Muslim, the unmarked national majority category, or Protestant, the unmarked highland category. But a small percentage of migrants are Catholic, Hindu, or Buddhist. Either a common religion or length of residence in a particular area can be invoked to minimize interpersonal differences based on the other criterion. Protestant Pamona and Muslim Tojo speak virtually the same language and may consider themselves more alike than do Muslim Tojo and Bugis (or Javanese) migrants. By contrast, self-consciously Muslim Tojo may consider any of their fellow Muslims as more like them than any non-Muslims.

Indigenous versus migrant statuses in Sulawesi are relative categories that

13 Adriani and Kruyt 1950; Aragon 2000; Kaudern 1925; Kruyt 1938.

can elide both time and space, meaning the duration of present residence and its distance from an original homeland. In reality, the families of some Arab or Malay Muslim migrants became earlier Poso City residents than some migrant families from Protestant highland areas. Moreover, descendants of 'original' groups living near the coast became Muslim through conversion or marriage to early Muslim traders, especially Bugis who elevated this integration strategy to a fine art. Struggles for control over resources among these earlier and later populations, whose ethnic identities were entangled with religious affiliations, animated the Poso conflict yet their ideological divisions initially were more messy than Messianic.

During the past ten years, most anthropologists have focused on the constructed, political, or contextual aspects of ethnicity.[14] Indonesianist scholars rejected 'primordialist' or essentialist notions of ethnicity, the monolithic stereotypical views that were drawn from colonial ethnography and later reified by the New Order government in its cultural programs. What appeared in their place, especially following John Pemberton's book (1994) on 'Java', was a view of ethnicity as artificially constructed by the discourse of state power apparatuses. For Central Sulawesi, Albert Schrauwers (2000) makes this argument about the Pamona, who are a post-colonial amalgam of scattered pre-colonial highland communities around Lake Poso.

Yet new 'opportunity structures' have contoured more ethnic changes from the late New Order to the present. For example, the Javanese generally do not pursue migration, but the Soeharto regime brought them to Central Sulawesi in significant numbers, first in the capacity of trans-migrants to open wet rice fields, and second as Jakarta-appointed civil servants.[15] In the first case with insufficient resources to stay at home, they had little choice but to become 'Sulawesi people'. In the second case, Central Sulawesi was considered a hardship post. Some department heads in the 1980s routinely asked for bribes in the form of round-trip airline tickets to Java. These bureaucrats remained firmly 'Javanese', scorning Central Sulawesi and its natives. But their children are different. The grown daughter of an army officer stationed in Poso could not speak Javanese and had rarely been to Java. She called herself a Poso person (To Poso), speaking only Indonesian with friends who included Muhammadiyah Muslims from Tojo, Gorontalo, and South Sulawesi, as well as some Protestant Pamona.[16] These varied migrants are not the kind of Javanese that either Geertz (1979) or Pemberton (1994) described.

14 An excellent dissertation discussing 'messy' and changing identities in Luwu, Sulawesi is Roth (2003).

15 Some Central Sulawesi people, both Muslims and Christians, have interpreted transmigration (*transmigrasi*) as 'Javanization' (*Javanisasi*). Roth (2003) observes this also in South Sulawesi.

16 K. Robinson (2000) also notes that many poor Javanese women have emigrated to become domestic servants in the Middle East, Malaysia, and Hong Kong.

The national and global economies have had novel effects on their class-stratified cultural patterns and ethnic consciousness.

Bugis migration patterns had an even greater effect upon Poso. Bugis are renown for their cultural inclination to *rantau*: to seek their fortune through migration in order to return with capital, buy land, and raise their status at home. But in Central Sulawesi, as in other regions, many Bugis migrants have little interest in returning 'home'. Political disturbances in South Sulawesi, land shortages, ascribed status restrictions, and under-employment inspired many to emigrate. Ample opportunities awaiting Bugis in Central Sulawesi have included development projects desiring migrant labour, unplanted forests (often long-term fallow swiddens), and some government officials willing to sell customary village land (*tanah adat*) or conservation lands.[17]

Another pathway opened for South Sulawesi migrants from conjunctures in the global economy, ecology of cacao, and the unevenness of Sulawesi's regional development. When the price of cacao (*coklat*) rose dramatically in the 1990s, South Sulawesi farmers already were familiar with its cultivation from government outreach programs, or earlier technology transfers from Sabah. Most Central Sulawesi farmers, by contrast, were not yet familiar with cacao horticulture. The Indonesian monetary crisis (Krismon) made cacao cropping for export more profitable than wage work or subsistence farming. Suddenly, local people who quietly had sold or otherwise lost access to their ancestral land through various development processes wanted that land back, and resented the many new migrants who had profited in their stead.

Yet, what looks to some like Bugis or general migrant aggression and greed for land appears to others as admirably industrious, government-supported entrepreneurship in the nation's booming agricultural export sector. Javanese became less uniformly 'home bodies' under New Order politics, transmigration, and global economy shifts. Bugis too, following new roads and economic frontiers, often migrated voluntarily on a permanent basis. Both these Diaspora populations retained strong ethnic constituencies 'at home' willing to lobby for, and defend them during post-Soeharto violent conflicts (K. Robinson 2002).

By contrast, Pamona ('Bare'e speakers') were subsistence rice farmers when the Netherlands Indies government began tinkering with their societies after 1905. The Dutch mission provided some of them education and opportunities for ministry or local civil service, but not for entrepreneurship, which remained in the hands of Chinese and Arab-Malay populations. 'Bare'e speakers' living in the coastal area of Tojo, east of Poso City, formerly

[17] Aragon 2002. As Acciaioli 2004 notes, Bugis cultural motivations to migrate are not strictly economic, but are contextualized within a broader set of behavioural and cosmological values. Those important nuances, however, are beyond the range of the arguments made here.

also were labelled Pamona, but they intermarried with incoming Bugis and Gorontalo settlers and generally converted to Islam. By the 1990s, most eschewed the ethnic label 'Pamona' for its Protestant connotation and began to consciously identify themselves as Tojo.[18] Tojo, Bungku, Gorontalo, and Bugis ethnic associations in many major towns suggest a new, multi-sited ethnic consciousness born from local expansions of political opportunity.

Muslim leaders were at the vanguard of anti-colonial movements, and they see their entrepreneurship as responsible for Central Sulawesi's recent development. As part of Indonesia's Muslim majority and, by the 1990s, a demographic majority in the Poso District itself, they argue that they are entitled to dwell anywhere in the district and control its political and business fortunes.[19] This last scenario in fact existed when violence in the Poso District began and the political families described below took power. During the 1980s and 1990s there was an addition of roughly 90,000 trans-migrants from Java, Bali and Nusa Tenggara, and a perhaps equal number of voluntary migrants, mostly Muslim Bugis, Makassar, and Mandar people from South Sulawesi. By 1998, over 60% of the Poso District's roughly 350,000 residents were registered as Muslim while less than 36% were recorded as Protestant (Arianto Sangaji 2003:13).

Thus, many factors besides bureaucratic corruption, including ethnic inequities, migration patterns, land alienation, changes in global markets for cash crops, religious proselytizing, and partisan media narratives played significant roles in fostering communal distrust in eastern Indonesian regions such as Poso (Aragon 2001, 2005). Resentments about past inequities were cultivated during the competitive 1999 election campaigns. With Golkar's success no longer automatic, candidates needed to attract both wealthy sponsors and the electoral action of the masses. Playing the cards of religious identity politics among sensitive ethnic constituencies brought predictable votes, but also uncontrollable violence.

[18] In 2004 I tracked archival documentation of this identity shift in the Central Sulawesi Museum. A wall map of 'Ethnic groups of Central Sulawesi', which was installed in the mid-1980s, includes only Pamona, Lore, Mori, and Bungku groups in the Poso region. The ethnic area now called Tojo is still identified under the Pamona label. The Bugis, Gorontalo, Javanese, Minahasa, and other migrants – now powerful residents of the region – do not appear on the map, which thereby erases the political and cultural realities of the province.

[19] Mindanao is a useful comparative case because it offers a mirror image to Poso's ethnic, nativity, and national political religious dynamics. In the Christian-majority Philippines, minority Muslims identified as native to Mindanao described to me how they resent being demographically overrun by Christian migrants seeking fertile land. By contrast, Christians told me that migrants should not be blamed because the land formerly was 'wasted' by Muslim groups who live by trade rather than 'more productive' farming.

Family affairs: Tojo ascendance

George Junus Aditjondro (2003, 2004a) and his Central Sulawesi NGO activist collaborators, including Harley (2004) and Arianto Sangaji (2003), suggest that violence was intentionally provoked by incumbent Poso District leaders to mask and facilitate their corrupt governmental practices. These pro-reform investigators have done significant research into the less savoury aspects of Sulawesi politicians' financial activities. Yet, district corruption in Indonesia was not confined to those areas succumbing to collective violence. If patrimonial politics and 'rent capitalism' had been a sufficient condition to precipitate post-Soeharto conflicts, most Indonesian districts would have followed the known cases.[20] They did not. Rather, additional circumstances affecting group relations were required to promote violence. Such caveats aside, the politics of institutional corruption was integral to the Poso conflict's emergence as well as its perpetuation.

Poso district heads' bribery and nepotism practices, from the Soeharto to the post-Soeharto era, evince more continuity than radical change. The district head (*bupati*) for ten years before the Poso conflict governed for the maximum two terms (1989-1994, 1994-1999). Born in Poso City during the Japanese occupation, he identifies as ethnically Tojo. Tojo names the site of a colonial era Muslim kingdom (Atkinson 1989; Kruyt 1930), and now a coastal area east of Poso City influenced by Bugis and Gorontalo migrants. Tojo and Pamona dialects are nearly identical (Noorduyn 1991) although, in the past twenty years, the categories have diverged as ethnic identities, distinguished by coastal versus interior locations and respective conversions to Islam and Protestantism.

The Tojo district head affiliated with the second largest Indonesian Muslim organization, Muhammadiyah, known for its relatively strict, modernist stance. He developed his career as an enthusiastic Golkar activist beginning in the early 1970s, part of the 'native sons' Muslim response to Christian bureaucratic dominance in the province. By the late 1980s he had consolidated authority among his fellow Tojo and also among Poso's Muslim migrant communities by becoming head (*ketua*) of the Poso District branch of the Indonesian Association of Muslim Intellectuals (ICMI). He thereby became a leader of both Poso City's 'old' migrant labourer community from Gorontalo, as well as 'newer' Muslim migrants from Java and South Sulawesi.

The former district head's triple affiliation with ICMI, Muhammadiyah,

20 In an eye-catching comparative example of judicial exposé, virtually the entire West Sumatran Legislative Council (DPRD) was convicted in court in Padang, a relatively conflict-free area, of embezzling Rp 6.4 billion (US$ 711,111) from the 2002 provincial budget (*Jakarta Post* 18-5-2004).

and Golkar, all favoured by Soeharto's last vice-president and successor B.J. Habibie, was a winning political package for the late 1980s and 1990s.[21] This trend among ambitious civil servants embodied a modernist Muslim political ascension, despite the fact that, historically, party politics in Indonesia have been linked more to the favoured deliverance of resources than to strong commitments on debatable ideological issues (H. Schulte Nordholt 2003). But perhaps it is exactly this added declaration of pious 'purity' to what had been the more oecumenical attraction of pay-offs through affiliation with the previously nationalist Golkar party that is a novel element in the religiously polarized conflicts of post-Soeharto Indonesia. Golkar itself became factionalized with the Habibie wing of Golkar becoming allied to the Muslim United Development Party (PPP, Partai Persatuan Pembangunan; Malley 1999; O'Rourke 2002:344). This national factionalization of Golkar affected Sulawesi's district politics in 1998 as well.

Prior to the Poso violence, or even the success of the 'triple affiliation package', corruption was firmly entrenched in Central Sulawesi's bureaucracy among both Protestant and Muslim civil servants. In the 1980s, Soeharto and his family presented a model of personal enrichment followed through the governorship to the district level (George Junus Aditjondro 2003:xxviii). To win his first district headship in 1989, the Tojo candidate reportedly paid the Central Sulawesi governor 250 million rupiah to secure the appointment (Harley 2004). To win a second term, he reportedly paid 350 million rupiah to the same governor, plus bribes to the staff of the Minister of the Interior, who would finalize the selection, and to members of the district parliament (Dewan Perwakilan Rakyat Daerah I, DPRD I), who needed to support his nomination to the governor. Why was winning the district head position worth so much?

Upon assuming his post, the district head assigned his wife to represent all other district civil servants (*wakil sekretaris* Korpri Kabupaten Poso). Then she was promoted to be head of all the district's civil servants (*kepala bagian pegawaian*), and put in charge of hiring, promotion, and firing decisions. In that capacity, she could receive bribes from those who sought profitable bureaucratic positions.

Another member of the wife's family was given the contract to produce Poso District residency or identity cards (KTP, Kartu Tanda Penduduk).

21 In the 1990s, Arabs of Hadramaut origin claiming descent from the Prophet became increasingly influential in high government circles (Mona Abasa 2004). Residing in Yemeni quarters of Jakarta, they made business connections with President Soeharto, Vice President Habibie, and the 'Green' or pro-Muslim army generals. Habibie's preference for Harmoko to lead Golkar reflected the increasingly pro-Muslim activism of Golkar (see Hefner 2000). Although the idea behind ICMI was to create a 'think tank' to rival earlier Christian-led ones, ICMI branches in provinces such as Sulawesi were more pro-Muslim political organizations.

Beyond the routine monitoring of new migrants to the district, citizens' identity cards, which mark name, village, and religion (but not ethnicity) played two important roles in the Poso violence. First, they were inspected by vigilante groups 'sweeping' vehicles and neighbourhood roads for religious enemies. Second, many new identity cards became needed after the 2001 Malino ceasefire accord. Members of militias, displaced persons, or undocumented migrants then sought legitimate residency in certain villages, either for safety, or in pursuit of land or humanitarian aid allotments.

The district head's younger brother was hired as director of district public construction (*kepala bagian pembangunan*), and assigned to build modernist Muslim junior high schools (*madrasah tsanawiyah*).[22] Other family members were invited to take lucrative contracts for district projects such as building roads. Civil servants or police who did not cooperate with this nepotism program were transferred or demoted. Most simply took the perquisites offered.

The district head's administration worked with some non-kin business cronies who were awarded construction projects known by the percentage of their kickbacks as 10 percent or 20 percent projects (George Junus Aditjondro 2003:xxxiii; Harley 2004). Some of these partners were from the older Chinese or Arab elite of Poso. Others were members of the provincial or district parliaments. These politicians often sold the building contracts onward to subcontractors. Equipment from the district's Public Works Department was provided or sold to preferred contractors. As a result, many district roads, bridges, and clean water projects were not built, or else were built poorly with diluted cement or inferior materials.

I had observed such badly built, corruption-related infrastructure in Central Sulawesi since the mid-1980s. Most urban residents were aware of these 'transaction costs' for local projects although they might not know the exact details or extent of mismanagement. Such activities were characterized as 'not good' (*tidak baik*), but they also were accepted as 'business as usual' (*bisnis biasa saja*). The national model for this kind of contract shorting was early set and symbolized by Soeharto's wife, Ibu Tien, widely known as 'Ibu Tien Persen' (Mrs Ten Percent), or sometimes even Ibu Lima Puluh Persen (Mrs Fifty Percent).[23]

The most unseemly money diversion exposed during the early Poso con-

22 That brother later was convicted of creating leaflets that slandered his father's Protestant rivals in 1998.

23 President Megawati's corruption was mocked with the name 'Ibu Mega Persen' (Mrs Gigantic Percent), while Soeharto's grown children and business partners only multiplied the excesses.

flict was the district head's mismanagement of the Kredit Usaha Tani (KUT, Farmer's Credit Program). Although the ostensible aim of the loan program was to help farmers cope with seasonally high planting costs, the district head used the funds from Jakarta to pay his political supporters. Many supporters were lobbied through the Partai Daulat Rakyat (PDR, Islamic People's Sovereignty Party) to support the 1999 presidential bid of Adi Sasono, one of President Habibie's ministers. Organized into regional Muslim NGO groups that were supposed to administer the farmers' loan funds, these supporters were supervised by district head partners who also took cuts of the money (George Junus Aditjondro 2003:xxx-xxxi). Moreover, the lists of needy farmers reportedly were padded by names of fictitious farmers.

An ethnic Minahasan PDI-P (Partai Demokrasi Indonesia Perjuangan, Indonesian Democratic Party of Struggle) member of the district parliament was murdered in 2000 as he began to expose the KUT fund improprieties. When the Javanese police chief in Poso investigated the case, his transfer from the area was demanded by a group of the district head's partners (Aragon 2001:65). By that point, the ethnic Tojo district head had stepped down, his brother was implicated in the 1998 Poso violence, and the ethnic balance of power shifted from Tojo to Bungku rule.[24]

Bungku ascendance and limits to corruption

As the 1999 elections approached, the ethnic Tojo head of Poso District was reaching the end of his two-term limit. The first phase of Poso violence occurred during the campaign, where his second in command, a Protestant Tojo Golkar candidate, competed with his preferred successor, a Muslim party (PPP) Una-Una candidate. The Protestant had been selected as district secretary (*sekwilda*) by the prior governor in order to train him to become the next district head. A slanderous leaflet that accused the district secretary and one of his Protestant Pamona sponsors of planning to kill the incumbent district head was circulating when the first Poso street fight began on 24 December, 1998. The Pamona associate was an ebony business competitor and political rival of several of the district head's supporters. The handwriting on the leaflet, which led to demands that both Protestants be hanged, was traced to the district head's brother. Reportedly, the leaflet was planned at a meeting convened by the incumbent, which included his business associates

[24] When the Farmer's Credit Program was investigated thoroughly, it was discovered the loans were in arrears by 5.7 billion rupiah (George Junus Aditjondro 2003:xxxv). One of the prosecuted killers of the parliament member was freed while another received four years in prison (S. Sinansari Ecip, Darwis Waru and Alip Yog Kunandar 2002).

and a Poso District Ministry of Religion official.[25]

The leaflet's accusations, the fighting between Muslim and Protestant factions associated with the candidates, and investigation of the brother's leaflet tarnished the reputations of the ethnic Tojo incumbent and the top two candidates. After the 1999 elections, when Habibie's Golkar machine fared better in Sulawesi than in Java, the governor eliminated both top contenders from the nomination list.[26] As George Junus Aditjondro (2004a) has calculated, the retiring district head and his family moved quickly and comfortably to Yogyakarta with luxury automobiles and trillions of rupiah in visible holdings, while Poso was abandoned to a state of escalating violence.

The remaining candidates then made payments to parliamentarians who would select the new Poso district head. By late October 1999, well-compensated members of the Golkar party chose, and the governor installed, a new district head. Reports claim he paid 5 million rupiah in advance, and promised 35 million rupiah to each parliamentary supporter (Rinaldy Damanik 2003:13; *Surya* 10-11-1999). Another long time Golkar activist, the new district head had been Assistant Rector at Tadulako University in Palu. Despite his outsider status in Poso, his candidacy was heavily supported in Palu through the Islamic Students Union (Himpunan Mahasiswa Islam), whose members sought positions as Poso department heads. He also received support from business contractors who had worked with the prior district head, based on his willingness to continue mutually profitable relationships. In fact, many members of the district parliament (DPRD) who chose the new district head owned businesses that received contracts from the district head office (Harley 2004).

The winning district head was from the coastal Bungku region, over 200 kilometres southeast of Poso City. Muslim Bungku politicians, who were ICMI members and Golkar activists during the prior regime, then gained control of several key Poso District posts including deputy district head (*wakil bupati*), head of transmigration, and speaker of the DPRD. They also had lobbied successfully for a new Morowali District to be split off from the southeast of the Poso District. In fact, Morowali was one of the first new districts announced in September 1999 under Habibie's Regional Autonomy Laws, suggesting the closeness of Muslim Bungku ties to the power centres of Jakarta.

The Poso district head shift, along with Bungku success in governing

25 George Junus Aditjondro 2004a. At a later stage the same official from the Department of Religion was instrumental in supporting the entrance of outside Muslim militias into Poso (ICG 2004).

26 The Una-Una Muslim supported by the incumbent continued to mobilize supporters, however, and made a 2004 comeback as head of the new Tojo Una-Una District (see below).

the new Morowali District, perturbed non-Bungku Muslims as well as Christians. Although several Bugis held important posts in the new government, a Bugis sociologist based at Tadulako University in Palu described the new political trend in Poso as 'Bungkuism' (Sulaiman Mamar 2001:121). A Central Sulawesi joke claims that PBB (Persatuan Bangsa-Bangsa, United Nations) no longer stands for the United Nations, but instead for the United Bungku People (Persatuan Bungku-Bungku).

This regional ascendance of Bungku people is not historically unprecedented, although Bungku's glory dates back about 200 years. J. Vosmaer (1839) described the area as a fortified settlement and trading centre that operated independently from the Bugis and Makassar traders who sought sea slugs (*tripang*) collected by Bajo seafarers (Velthoen 1997; Velthoen and Acciaioli 1993). By the 1850s, however, Bugis involvement in the area led to a Bungku conflict with the Sultan of Ternate who destroyed the Bungku settlement. Bugis merchants then gained political influence over eastern Sulawesi, including Bungku. In the early 1900s, the Netherlands Indies Government classified Bungku as a vassal of Ternate, then claimed it as a Dutch holding under administration from Makassar in 1908, and then from Manado in 1924. Bungku was of little prominence during the twentieth century, until its untapped timber and other natural resources could be extracted via new roads built in the 1980s. Then Bungku leaders including the future district head became successful provincial politicians by networking through Golkar and the Islamic Students Union.

Although some observers of the Poso violence have spoken about pre-conflict religious 'power-sharing' in district politics, most of the post-colonial district heads have been Muslims from coastal Sulawesi or from Java.[27] The ethnic Bungku district head was championed by the new governor who was grateful for his help in mobilizing Golkar supporters during the 1999 campaign. The governor also responded to pressure from Muslim Al-Chaira'at organization leaders in Palu to install an ethnic Arab in Poso's district secretary post.[28] The Arab was a close associate of the prior district head of Poso, and one of his in-laws is a Saudi weapons parts manufacturer with business ties to Pindad, the government munitions factory whose products appeared

[27] What is noted accurately is that when past Poso district heads were Muslim, regional secretary or other executive offices often were given to Protestants to make for a more balanced district government than those beginning in 1989. See Suriadi Mappangara 2001 and Rinaldy Damanik 2003.

[28] Al-Chaira'at (also transcribed Al-Khaira'at or Al-Khaerat), which runs a large and popular network of *madrasah* and other Muslim schools in eastern Indonesia, was begun by a mixed Bugis-Hadrami migrant, Al-Habib Sayyid Idrus ibn Salim al-Juffrie, who settled in Palu in 1930. Photographs of the founder are displayed in many Muslims' homes, and the founder's son directs the headquarters, which remains in Palu.

in later phases of the Poso conflict.[29]

The new Poso district head kept past corruption unchallenged, while he installed his own relatives into profitable posts. His oldest child owns a building contract firm while a younger one uses leadership of the local Bungku ethnic association (Kerukunan Keluarga Bungku) to facilitate contracting operations in Poso (George Junus Aditjondro 2004a; Harley 2004). One of his children's contracts was to renovate and expand the Poso district head's office building, possibly in anticipation of it becoming their father's governor's office for the proposed new province of East Sulawesi. The district head also placed a first cousin to head the Welfare and Development office (Kesbang) of the Social Services Department (Dinas Sosial), one of the main channels for Poso conflict aid funds. A nephew headed the Transmigration Department. Contractor partners were appointed as directors of government divisions, such as education or transportation, where they awarded their own firms contracts to build new schools or roads. Some of these were chosen from non-Bungku groups, their allegiance to the administration insured by their comfortable placements.[30] The ethnic Arab district secretary's relatives also were put into key positions, making more funds available to lobby for a new Tojo Una-Una District where he hoped to become future district head.

The nepotism described above was business as usual in Central Sulawesi. What began to draw scorn to the new district head's corruption was his willingness to allow embezzlement of humanitarian aid intended for victims of violence, even re-routing some to militias. For example, an in-law of the district secretary assigned to rebuild Poso's ruined infrastructure was investigated in 2002 for selling aid supplies to finance his luxury house, and for giving two tons of 'rice for the poor' (*beras miskin*) to Laskar Jihad troops (George Junus Aditjondro 2004a; Harley 2004).

In late July 2001, soon after the grisly and well-publicized killings of thirteen Muslim civilians at Buyung Katedo Village, Laskar Jihad sent a delegation from Java to visit Palu and Poso. The delegation was publicly received by the governor, the Poso district head, Tadulako University professors, and by Muslim groups such as the Majelis Ulama Indonesia (MUI, Council of Indonesian Muslim Leaders) and the Dewan Dakwah Islamiyah Indonesia (DDII, Indonesian Council for Islamic Appeals). According to an August 2001

29 Sulawesi military officers said the use of Pindad weapons in Poso attacks entail no necessary connection to strategic military involvement, implying that such weapons are sold routinely on the black market; not a comforting claim. Some Muslim web site messages also claim their proud use of smuggled army weapons in Poso.

30 As suggested by Syarif Hidayat (personal communication), certain types of corrupt clientelism such as contracting awards are driven strictly by mutual business interests (instead of ethnic or religious identity) in contrast to many bureaucratic positions, which have more significant political effects.

report in the Palu newspaper *Mercusuar*, the Laskar Jihad leaders asked to bring humanitarian aid to Poso Muslims harmed by the conflict, and to protect them from further attacks. They claimed reconciliation efforts were only weakening law officials' attempts to control and prosecute Christian attackers (S. Sinansari Ecip, Darwis Waru and Alip Yog Kunandar 2002:35-6).

Indeed, during May-July 2000, Poso Christian militias took revenge for previous episodes of violence by killing hundreds of Muslim migrants. Both the new district head and Poso's head of the Department of Religion supported the plans of Laskar Jihad and other militias to supplement government forces. Even then Minister for Security, Susilo Bambang Yudhoyono, voiced this perspective on television although, when the violence worsened with jihad groups' participation in November 2001, he and Jusuf Kalla spearheaded the Malino Accord mediation.

Few besides Protestant leaders publicly objected to politicians' support for Muslim militias. Yet, the widespread aid corruption while sporadic violence continued sparked criticism from both Muslims and Christians. As much as two-thirds of the over 160 billion rupiah designated for post-Malino Accord humanitarian and recovery aid disappeared in the hands of government officials, never reaching the programs or disappointed persons for whom it was intended (Aragon 2004; *Suara Pembaruan* 24-2-2005).

Although the Indonesian verb *proyekkan*, referring to 'the making of a government service program into a personally profitable business', is not yet in the Echols and Shadily or *Kamus Besar* dictionaries, it is used frequently by both Muslims and Christians in Poso. They employ the term (usually in the passive form *diproyekkan*) to describe how rebuilt buildings are destroyed anew, false village census figures are used, and there is no transparency for aid funds. In fact, Poso businessmen well-entrenched in past corruption schemes often changed hats to become Malino Accord signatories, and so were placed into post-Malino fund distribution posts.

A powerful Bugis merchant involved in the Farmer's Credit Program (KUT) scam, who also was a Muslim militia supporter in the district heads' inner circle, was selected as a Malino Accord signatory, and then placed on the Malino Accord Task Force (Pokja Deklama), which administers government aid. Through that position, he received reconstruction contracts, including one for a new Mobil Police Brigade (Brimob) outpost west of Poso City. It was not the conflict of interest that angered Poso citizens, but the shamelessness of the extremely rich stealing from impoverished victims of violence even as they were aiding militias who caused more destruction. Many Poso Muslims and Christians say they no longer trust either their political or religious leaders because too many have joined the manipulation (*ikut manipulasi*) of Poso recovery funds.

One cynical joke about the misuse of Poso aid funds goes, 'while refugees get Super Mie (instant noodles), bureaucrats get Super Kijang (cars)' (*Sementara pengungsi dapat Super Mie, pejabat dapat Super Kijang*). Even Jusuf Kalla, formerly Megawati's Minister for People's Welfare, Malino Accord mediator, and Toyota tycoon was embarrassed to hear reports about the mishandling of aid. He visited Central Sulawesi in December 2003 and lectured officials about how they should not make the plight of Poso refugees into a field of personal profiteering. Kalla himself was involved in a dispute with President Wahid over who had profited from the Bulog scandal in early 2000 (*Tajuk* 7 (25-5-2000); Van Dijk 2001:495, 518-20).

But generally, Kalla's immense wealth as a businessman left most ordinary Sulawesi people thinking that he had no need to steal welfare funds or take sides in any conflict that would interfere with his road-building projects or automobile sales.[31]

Another business arena linked to the ethnic Bungku district head's regime and the prolongation of violence in Poso is the expansion of Indonesia's army territorial command. The dangers of spreading regional violence in areas such as Ambon and Poso gave top army generals a national security rationale to increase deployments and provincial bases (George Junus Aditjondro 2004a; Arianto Sangaji, this volume). Military officers made business arrangements with district leaders to build the bases and assist with troop funding. Given the territorial command structure, the army profits from the transfer of authority from Jakarta to the regions (Mietzner 2003). If only 30-40% of Indonesian army soldiers' deployment costs is covered by the national budget, the remainder must be raised on site, leading to soldiers' coercive involvement in both legal and illegal businesses. These include security checkpoint fees, protection services, aid donation re-sale, munitions diversion, gambling, prostitution, natural resources appropriation, and smuggling.[32]

The temptation for military personnel to 'share' in funds for war-torn Poso is overwhelming. People displaced by violence complain how soldiers, rather than needy local people, were paid to build refugee barracks (Aragon 2004). Even some key Poso District executives, Bungku relatives accustomed to enjoying the spoils of political victory, found newly delivered office equip-

31 Kalla's personification of the ultra-successful Bugis entrepreneur has succeeded the image of B.J. Habibie, raised in South Sulawesi, as representing Bugis national triumphs. During Kalla's 2004 vice-presidential campaign, his Palu Golkar supporters engaged in ethnic identity politics by proclaiming on market banners that 'Honouring Jusuf Kalla (with a vote for his ticket) equals honouring Bugis people'.

32 For example, passing a Poso checkpoint in 2003 cost most drivers Rp 5,000-20,000, even if their licenses were in order. On long trips from Palu via Poso to Luwuk or South Sulawesi, drivers would pass dozens of TNI and Brimob posts, some open and collecting while others might be closed with troops 'on break'.

ment appropriated by army officers they were afraid to challenge. After the Malino Accord in December 2001, a new battalion, Yon 714 Sintuwu Maroso, was created to protect Poso City, plus three companies were added for areas east of Poso. George Junus Aditjondro (2004a) alleges that these deployments were made less to protect Sulawesi people than to suppress uncooperative villagers who resist new investments such as Tomy Winata's planned Morowali District marble mine, or the new 270-kilometer road from Kolonedale to Kendari.

The influx of aid money to Poso creates incentives for power brokers to insure that the conflict never completely ceases. As one displaced person explained bureaucrats' insouciance about continuing violence: 'in a conflict area, there is money to be had' (*di daerah rusuh ada uangnya*). Aside from the theft of aid money, the speaker meant that many are willing to pay for protection or weapons once there is ongoing violence. As in Aceh, Poso people say that soldiers arrive in their area with M16s (assault rifles) and leave with 16M (16 billion rupiah). Christians sometimes view the violence and corruption of government officials as ideologically motivated, basically an extreme form of Muslim clientelism, while Muslims tend to see it as purely economic, simply a matter of personal aggrandizement combined with callous neglect of the population. It may well be some of both. But even if corruption is purely a matter of greedily harvesting political windfalls, its grounding in ethno-religious violence has aggravated regional disharmony.

Motives for new districts

Central Sulawesi politicians' lobbying for new districts reveals ethnic leaders looking for new political units they can rule when their terms expire, or they lose campaigns in their current district. The creation of Morowali and Tojo Una-Una Districts are the direct result of ethnic block politics promoted by allies of the last two Poso district heads. In the Morowali District, further schisms have occurred over the capital of the district. The two main competing groups, Bungku and Bugis, are both Muslim, illustrating an emerging ethnic rather than overarching religious dimension to the competition. The proposal to create a new East Sulawesi Province following the 2004 presidential elections emanated from the combined demographic and political gains of Bungku, Tojo, and Bugis blocks.[33]

Although Central Sulawesi politicians run newspaper advertisements that support proposed districts, most citizens have only a vague sense of why

[33] A freeze on the creation of new political units was set in place in November 2003 prior to the 2004 parliamentary and presidential elections.

new districts are being made, and what impact this will have on daily life. Protestants in both the new Morowali District and the smaller Poso District were disappointed with the initial results of *pemekaran*. Many Protestant Mori had favoured *pemekaran*, thinking a closer regional government in Kolonedale would be more responsive than the distant one in Poso City. But, when only one relatively weak political office (*wakil bupati*, deputy district head) went to a Protestant Mori while most went to Muslim Bungku politicians, Mori felt a continued lack of political representation for Protestant-majority sub-districts (*kecamatan*). The plan to shift the Morowali District capital southeast from the more cosmopolitan city of Kolonedale to Bungku City in 2004 left non-Bungku residents, both Protestant and Muslim, feeling further disenfranchised.

The 2000 splitting of Morowali District from Poso put ethnic Bungku men in charge of both areas, which are rich in ebony, *meranti* and *palapi* (woods used in ship building), oil, marble, and nickel mined by PT Inco Mining Corporation. Illegal logging in Morowali Conservation Park reportedly has increased exponentially in recent years (*Tajuk* 7 (25-5-2000); *Jakarta Post* 13-5-2004).

Bungku leaders' temporary control of both districts gave the Poso district head and his business partners more capital to lobby for a new East Sulawesi Province, while they advanced development projects that may provide few benefits to local populations. This follows both New Order and general decentralization trends, leading to an increasing pace of resource removal for the global market (Ida Ayu Pradnja Resosudarmo 2003).

Law no. 51 authorizing the Morowali District in 1999 contained an ambiguity about what town would become the district capital. The law stated that Bungku would become the eventual capital, but that first Kolonedale would be capital because it already had the necessary governmental infrastructure. By 2003, however, the new Morowali district head, an ethnic Bugis, was so profitably entrenched in Kolonedale that he petitioned the Minister of the Interior to keep the capital in Kolonedale. He recommended splitting the Morowali District again, to make a separate Bungku District with Bungku City as its capital. These plans angered ethnic Bungku and various youth associations, which lobbied for the immediate transfer of Morowali's district capital to Bungku City. Demonstrations by Bungku groups in Kolonedale, and Kolonedale groups in Bungku, led to the burning of government vehicles and ethnic sparring between Bungku and Bugis around Kolonedale. Although the central government has supported the original plan to move the capital to Bungku City and maintain the Morowali District borders as specified, the transfer of the capital is not yet realized.

In addition to ebony in the upland forests, the reported discovery of oil offshore from the Tojo coast made that area attractive for the creation of a separate district. The splitting of mostly Muslim Tojo Una-Una District from the Poso District in 2003, re-elevated ethnic Tojo to control of their own district. The Muslim Una-Una candidate favoured by the Poso district head in 1998 but denied both district headship and district secretary positions in Poso, was installed as the new head of Tojo Una-Una District in January 2004. From one perspective, this was a delayed victory for one of the Muslim leaders championed by fighters in the early phases of the Poso conflict (December 1998 and April 2000). Yet, the creation of Tojo Una-Una District also coincidentally eliminated the Muslim majority in the residual Poso District. For this reason, many non-Tojo Muslims in Poso and Palu resisted the creation of Tojo Una-Una. By contrast, its formation has given Protestant Pamona and Lore residents hope for more future control over the now smaller Poso District. If Poso City becomes its own district (*kotamadya*), then the interior Poso highlands would become a more autonomous, but tiny and weak, Protestant district.

By 2003, a key issue in Central Sulawesi was a proposed new province of East Sulawesi (Sulawesi Timor), to extend from Poso City to the Banggai Islands. Economic analyses of the Regional Autonomy laws explain that provinces are to have a more minor role than during the Soeharto era, basically only coordination and 'backstopping' for any district unable to perform its own governance functions. So, what are the incentives to create new provinces such as East Sulawesi? If an area has certain natural resources potential, then by becoming a new province it will no longer need to share that income with the adjacent districts or original province (Hofman and Kaiser 2002). Thus the motivation to create provinces, as with districts, emanates from a competitive rather than a cooperative view of citizenship. Political leaders of eastern Central Sulawesi wish to benefit from timber, mining, gas and offshore oil deposits without sharing revenue with people in western Central Sulawesi. The push to create provinces also hints that provinces are not expected to become as politically weak as the 1999 laws and the revised autonomy laws of 2004 suggest.

Although both Protestant and Muslim politicians first proposed creating East Sulawesi in early 2000, district boundaries and executives have changed in the intervening years. The districts now usually planned to enter the new province are Poso, Morowali, Tojo Una-Una, Banggai, and Banggai Islands. Throughout 2003, supporters noted that Central Sulawesi was the largest of the island's provinces (14,434 square km), far too huge and rugged to govern effectively. They added that the eastern section needed the economic boost that new province status would bestow. Skeptics, however, suggested that the politicians' true aims concerned greater access to, and military protection for, the region's timber, cacao, oil, nickel, marble, and shrimp.

A rancorous debate concerns whether East Sulawesi should have its capital in Poso or Luwuk. Poso residents argue for their city, saying it is older, centrally located, and – because of the recent violence – already has an army battalion, a prerequisite for all provinces. They note that Poso was the capital of a much larger district before the recent partitions. Only by becoming the capital of East Sulawesi Province, which would reincorporate exactly the same partitioned areas (and Banggai) can Poso City regain or surpass its former administrative stature. But then, one might wonder, what was the point of the whole contentious *pemekaran* exercise of the past five years?

In 2003, some Poso Muslims claimed there would be anger and more violence in Poso if their city was not chosen to become the new provincial capital. By contrast, advocates for Luwuk noted that their city is peaceful and its infrastructure intact, unlike Poso. This debate over the future capital of the proposed province pits the leadership of two western districts – Poso, and Tojo Una-Una – against those of the two eastern districts – Banggai and Banggai Islands.[34] This is a clear case where a 'reunifying' *pemekaran* plan intended to benefit some segments of a population only radiates further inter-regional competition and hostility. The dispute ultimately will be settled by central government authorities, who likely will evaluate future payments or investment deals.

In mid-2004, the East Sulawesi issue was still provoking demonstrations, counter-demonstrations, and angry debate (Arianto Sangaji 2004). A national parliamentary leader (*wakil ketua* Dewan Perwakilan Rakyat, DPR) noted the planned borders of East Sulawesi would make it a larger province than the province from which it would split – a formula technically prohibited in the *pemekaran* rules. He argued that Poso District should remain in Central Sulawesi, disqualifying Poso City from capital status, while the new districts removed from the Poso District would become East Sulawesi. This suggestion aroused further rage, with Muslim-oriented youth groups such as the Forum Komunikasi Generasi Muda Sulawesi Timur (FKGM Sultim, Youth Communication Forum East Sulawesi) lobbying fiercely against politicians unwilling to defend a Poso City-centred East Sulawesi Province (Arianto Sangaji 2004).

Protestant minorities in Poso developed their own Protestant majority district plans, but they never got far in the lobbying process. Some argue that Pamona and Lore people will regain more control within the Poso District now that the Tojo Una-Una region has exited. One Protestant plan for a Pamona-Lore District follows 2001 'wishful thinking' to create a province called Sintuwu Maroso. This plan aimed to reunite the current Poso and Morowali Districts back into what was the Soeharto era Poso District, except the capital of the new province would be the Protestant mission centre of

34 Morowali District leaders split on the issue with the Bugis Morowali district head supporting Luwuk and the deputy district head, a Mori Protestant, supporting Poso City.

Tentena instead of Muslim majority Poso City. The nativist character of the proposed province was stressed by naming it with the Pamona language motto 'Sintuwu Maroso', meaning 'Strongly United'. Given the prolonged violence in Poso, that phrase has become the source of many jokes. Many Poso residents say that *Sintuwu maroso*, 'United we are strong', has become *Sintuwu malonco*, 'United we flee'. As the word play suggests, the Sintuwu Maroso Province plan disappeared along with violence and the loss of Protestant Pamona in any significant bureaucratic positions.

Decentralization and democracy

Decentralization in post-Soeharto Indonesia cannot be equated simply with democratization, but must be investigated in terms of power struggles linked with the revised regional finances specified by the 1999 regional autonomy laws (H. Schulte Nordholt 2003). States like Indonesia routinely operate in part through illegal practices that are rarely prosecuted (Heyman and Smart 1999). Post-Soeharto patterns of corruption in Central Sulawesi, and their entrenchment within family networks and ethnic constituencies, are continuous with Soeharto regime models. What has changed is the greater political and financial autonomy of the district from Jakarta, creating increasingly empowered district heads with a need to attract local voting blocks and develop untapped natural resources. In Poso, this situation became combined with the revised public performance of religious and ethnic identities for the purpose of extending claims to both political power and land rights. In terms of national strategies for resource development, we should consider *pemekaran* as another form of economic 'outsourcing', but one with specific Indonesian socio-political antecedents and local ecological consequences.

District leaders in Poso turned to religious identity politics in 1998, motivated by a combination of ideology and efforts to protect political power and payments. The transition to regional autonomy was coterminous with Poso's collective violence, as district leaders sought to heighten religious tensions to mobilize voters. Only by focusing on district governance are we likely to answer the puzzling question of why escalating waves of violence generally followed the major roads outwards from Poso City, but then, with some recent exceptions, stopped at the pre-conflict district (*kabupaten*) boundaries.[35]

35 The exceptions include 2000 and 2001 Christmas season church bombings in Palu, the killing of a Palu prosecutor on May 26, 2004, a woman minister during a Palu church service on 18 July 2004, and nearly simultaneous shooting attacks on two Palu churches during services on 12 December 2004. All three of the recently attacked churches are branches of the Poso Protestant denomination (GKST, Gereja Kristen Sulawesi Tengah).

Because district and provincial executive posts in the New Order were regulated by choices made in Jakarta, Muslim religious credentials were necessary for 1990s success at the regional level, although native ethnic credentials also were promoted to insure broad local support. The Golkar-Muhammadiyah-ICMI activism by district leaders, who sought support from Muslim migrants and natives, accentuated the region's religious polarization in 1998. An ethnic conflict strictly between Muslim Tojo and Bungku, or between Protestant Pamona and Mori, would never have escalated beyond local interest, or been prolonged for six years by attracting outsider fighting specialists. It was rather the invocation of a bipolar religious divide that turned a petty youth fight and a contentious district campaign into a chronic state of siege and suspicion between deterritorialized religious groups.

When the Poso conflict was nationally mediated in December 2001 after attacked Muslims and Christians fled into different territories, Muslim leaders could lobby the divided ethnic blocks to create new districts for administration and development. Muslim Bungku politicians conceived the Morowali District just before they took control of the Poso District from an ethnic Tojo leader. Bungku politicians then could administer two regions, one in their home ethnic territory and one beyond it. Tojo politicians, in turn, conceived the Tojo Una-Una District as a means to regain a regional centre of power in their ethnic territory. By splitting Tojo Muslims off from the remaining Poso District, however, Protestants returned to a demographic majority in the now smaller district. Pamona leaders hope to regain control in Poso even though Protestants are still too intimidated by violence to return to Poso City, where their old neighbourhoods are occupied by displaced Muslims. The fissiparous process of *pemekaran* not only draws on prior ethno-religious identities, but also cultivates them in new ways to define groups who should dwell in separate political territories.

Poso District administrations crossed the line of 'routine corruption' when they began to use conflict aid funds to buy personal luxuries and support militias instead of helping the displaced. Regional NGOs in Central Sulawesi have worked hard to expose government malfeasance and cultivate local unity. Yet, populist activism like that in Jakarta makes slower headway in provincial outposts where intimidation and state suppression exist beside new media and imported products as 'the natural features of a landscape of power' (Tsing 2003:215). In this landscape the terms and conditions for receiving 'democracy' often look much like the New Order terms and conditions for receiving 'development', that is, they involve the attrition of local group autonomy and environmental control. Any upgrade in the political status of one's locality may entail a trade-off of little understood resource rights. Poso District's non-elite groups are unsure about the impact of *pemekaran* although many Muslim and Christian urban dwellers hope that new districts will deliver bureaucratic jobs that they might win despite the patterns of 'unequal buying'. *Pemekaran* in Central Sulawesi unquestionably is aimed towards the elite pursuit of forest and shoreline resources. Whether profits from those development projects will be shared more widely and equitably to fulfil needs of the diverse populace is still unclear.

The Soeharto government created a symbolic map of the Indonesian nation in its famed Jakarta theme park Taman Mini, where every province had its own ethnic groups and all groups were theoretically equal as portrayed by their material culture displays. Religion was relegated to the background. In the actual provinces, however, ethnicity was more complex, often nascent, mobile, or entangled with religious identities. The dominance of Java could hardly be hidden, although inequities among other groups largely were. Political economy inequities emerged from a combination of demographic, geographic, and state policy differences dating from the colonial period forward.

Soeharto's regime then fostered new movements of these diverse peoples across the provinces, through transmigration, road construction, and development projects attracting labour migrants. The Soeharto regime's increasing regulation and prioritizing of religion over ethnicity and custom had additional consequences for district leadership success, as well as the development of local identities and inter-religious tensions. The post-Soeharto regional violence, religious territorialization in places like Poso, and initiatives for the ethnic partitioning of districts after 1998 can be seen as a culmination of these policies, where unequal opportunity buying still exists largely unexplored and unchecked by either national or local social institutions. Future leaders, both national and local, may want to consider this history and the potential for greater harmony among a diverse citizenry.

The true bright blooms in Central Sulawesi's 'blossoming' process, which need to be emphasized in closing, are the impressive efforts made by several Central Sulawesi NGOs and international investigators to bring Poso conflict aid embezzlement and continued violence to national attention. With President Susilo Bambang Yudhoyono's initial public push against bureaucratic corruption, Central Sulawesi NGOs seized the moment to speak out about Poso's continued troubles. In both local and national newspapers, NGO directors have demanded that local bureaucrats, their hired hands, and even military personnel, be investigated and prosecuted for their misdeeds (*Kompas* 31-5-2005; *Suara Pembaruan* 29-4-2005). Some police authorities also are rising to the challenge, despite continued killings and bombings such as those in Tentena on 28 May 2005. These nationwide efforts, and the direct elections in June 2005 for new district heads in Poso and elsewhere, remind us of the possibilities for democratization and accountability that, at least ostensibly, set the decentralization wheel in motion.

MYRNA EINDHOVEN

New colonizers?
Identity, representation and government in the post-New Order Mentawai Archipelago

Sedang bicarakan situasi politik di kepulauan ini [...] boleh dibilang bisnis seperti biasa. Dulu kami digigit kucing, sekarang digigit anjing, rasa sakitnya sama aja.

Talking about politics with regard to this archipelago [...] it may be said it is business as usual. In earlier times we were bitten by the cat, now we are bitten by the dog, both are equally painful. (Liong Hamid Satoko, December 2002, Saibi Samukop.)

Introduction

Even before Law no. 22/1999 on decentralization of the state administration became operative the then-president Habibie granted the Mentawai Archipelago full independent district status at once.[1] As a result of intense lobbying on the part of various local non-governmental organizations (NGOs), the Mentawai Archipelago finally detached itself from the mainland district of Padang-Pariaman on 9 October 1999 (*Mimbar Minang* 14-10-1999). The Mentawaian case, a pioneer project within the pan-Indonesian process of administrative fragmentation or *pemekaran*, is foremost the result of activities by local elites entangled in a contest for political positions. The whole process is characterized by intense political turmoil and all kinds of exclusionisms on the basis of various ethnic sentiments.

The detachment of the Mentawai Archipelago from the mainland district Padang-Pariaman marked a long awaited shift in political power over the ar-

1 Most of the data used in this chapter have been gathered during extensive field research in Indonesia in 2002-2003 and late 2004. Earlier versions have been presented during the EUROSEAS Conference 2004 in Paris and the Renegotiating Boundaries workshop 2004 in Jakarta. I would like to thank the Renegotiating Boundaries workgroup and Juniator Tulius for their inspiring comments and valuable additional insights.

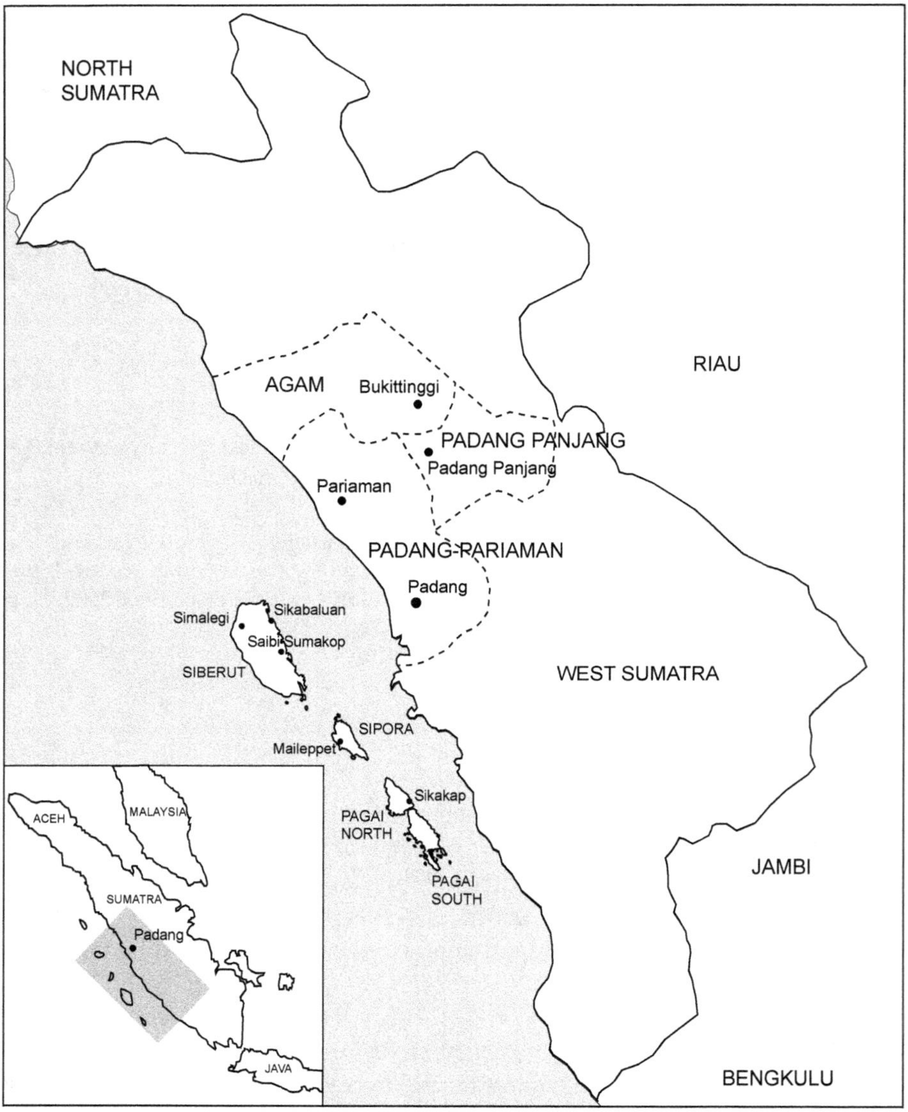

Map 3. Mentawai archipelago and West Sumatra

chipelago. Local elites have been able to take over the political power from the mainland Minangkabau who had been ruling the archipelago for decades. The Mentawaians were euphoric now that they finally saw themselves freed from their 'colonization' by the significantly different – in cultural as well as religious senses – mainland Minangkabau. Now that the initial excitement over the new district has died down, new patterns of power and representation have become visible, but at the same time old modes of representation and familiar administrative styles suggest a strong continuity with New Order politics.

The processes of decentralization currently taking place in Indonesia are believed to empower local communities and stimulate greater accountability by local governments, and have therefore often been equated with democratization and the strengthening of civil society (Aspinall and Fealy 2003:1-14; Antlöv and Cederroth 2004, see also H. Schulte Nordholt 2003). Closer investigation of the experiences within the Mentawaian communities, however, raises the question of whether and to what extent these new power constellations and reformulated modes of representation fulfil the aspirations of the Mentawaian constituencies.

During the shift in local power relations, the notion of identity has been politicized. The term *putra asli daerah* (literally: autochthonous sons of the region) is omnipresent in negotiations over political positions (*Puailiggoubat* 4(March 2002):2). It is only *putra asli daerah* that should control local governments, because only they are believed to be able to secure privileged access for their communities in the allocation of economic resources and government positions (Aspinall and Fealy 2003:6). Regional autonomy and decentralization have also resulted in a renewed interest in *adat* (tradition, custom). Local NGOs have taken up the notion of *adat* to voice their claims for greater recognition of certain local traditions and *adat*-based rights over natural resources (Acciaioli 2001). Placing *adat* in the middle of the decentralization discussion is a powerful political act, because *adat*, in public discourse, is considered to originate from below. During Soeharto's authoritarian, top-down New Order regime, *adat* was 'domesticated' and de-politicized by the state (Schefold 1998). Only its aestheticized 'peaks' were enlisted to contribute to the process of nation-building (Picard 1997). Recently, however, *adat* has required new symbolic and rhetorical importance which fuels political activity related to the administrative changes and political interests.

While these processes have certainly opened up new opportunities for some, others stand to lose their grip on the political process. While local elites are engaged in political negotiations it appears that local communities do not seem to be able to fully partake. Those prominently involved advocate *adat* and the privileges due to the Mentawaian community, but at the same time they view the new opportunities from a variety of interests, trying to find structures most sympathetic to their own interests. Ordinary people are at best spectators, informed only when major decisions have already been taken. Common people thus easily develop cynical views about the political rhetoric which emphasizes *adat* and the bottom-up character of the whole decentralization process (Von Benda-Beckmann 2001).

Local NGOs tend to play a Janus-faced role within the whole process. Harbouring the majority of the local Mentawaian elite and having access to both the financial and the infrastructural means, many local NGOs have been recently transformed into political strongholds, bypassing their intermediate civil society function (Eindhoven 2002).

This chapter starts with an overview of the situation in which Mentawaians found themselves while the archipelago was still part of the district of Padang-Pariaman. I will address the problematic inter-ethnic relations between Mentawaians and Minangkabau people. I will also briefly discuss government policies with regard to the Mentawaians as a typical group of people in Indonesian society. In the next section I shall discuss the genesis of a critical elite among the Mentawaians and what kind of activities they deployed under the banner of the local organizations IPPMEN and Yayasan Citra Mandiri. The third section explores the creation of the district of Kepulauan Mentawai and the rush for *putra asli daerah* that ensued. This will be followed by an account of how members of the Mentawaian elite have taken up their new role as politicians. I then discuss the role and position of both local NGOs and local communities. The chapter will conclude with an overview of the political situation in the Mentawai Archipelago now that the initial turbulence raised by *pemekaran* has died down.

Mainland colonizers

Both geographically and administratively the Mentawai Archipelago is part of the province of West Sumatra and was until late 1999 part of the district of Padang-Pariaman. The Mentawai Archipelago, consisting of four larger islands (Siberut, Sipora, North Pagai, and South Pagai) and several smaller islets, is situated in the Indian Ocean approximately 100 kilometres off the west coast of Sumatra. The autochthonous Mentawaians form a majority within their own territory, with an estimated 70,000 people. A still insignificant number of migrants from West and North Sumatra, Java, and Nias reside mostly in the harbour villages.

While Mentawai was still part of Padang-Pariaman district, the archipelago covered nearly 80% of the territory of the district and was responsible for almost three quarters of the district's total revenue – the export of dried coconut, rattan, and especially timber being the most important sources of income. Although insignificant in number, migrants almost completely controlled trade on the islands. It was they who enjoyed the surplus, leaving the Mentawaians as ill-paid suppliers of rough materials only. With the migrants having their family and business interests abroad, most of the proceeds generated on the islands never returned to Mentawai. This, together with the unequal redistribution of taxes and reforestation budgets, turned Mentawai into an area where exploitation was rife while structural investments were absent.

Within Padang-Pariaman district, political power was invariably in the hands of the Minangkabau – the dominant ethnic group in West Sumatra. Due to a lack of education, experience, and ambition, the Mentawaians have not been able to take up positions in the administrative machinery. Nor was there ever any real attempt to interest Mentawaians in these functions (Persoon 1994:227). One had to be a Muslim in order to be able to apply for the function of civil servant, and this made it virtually impossible for most Mentawaians to apply for government positions. Being Christianized since the beginning of the twentieth century, most Mentawaians nowadays see Christianity as an integral part of their identity.[2] There are several cases known where Mentawaians have converted to Islam – or at least changed their Christian names into Islamic ones – in order to qualify as a government employee. However, the number of Mentawaians involved in local government remained low, and where they were granted the opportunity to take up a position in the bureaucracy they did so at the lower administrative levels.

Government offices were located on the Sumatran mainland, so all administrative matters for the Mentawai Archipelago had to be arranged on the mainland in either Padang, West Sumatra's capital city, or Pariaman, some 60 kilometres north of Padang. In earlier days a trip from one of the Mentawai Islands to the mainland took at least a fortnight and involved transportation costs and maintenance that were beyond the reach of most Mentawaians. This left many Mentawaians without proper administrative evidence of their citizenship like birth certificates and marriage documents, leading to problems when travelling, seeking higher education or marriageable partners outside the Mentawaian region.

As part of its ideology of national development, the Indonesian govern-

2 Compared to Protestantism, both Islam and Catholicism were rather late in targeting Mentawai. While the first German protestant missionary disembarked at North Pagai in 1901, Islam did not enter Mentawai until 1952 (Persoon and Schefold 1985:xv) and Catholicism started activities only in 1954 (Coronese 1986:29). In 1954 the local religion, *arat sabulungan*, was prohibited. During the so-called Rapat Tiga Agama (meeting of the three religions) it was decided that every Mentawaian had to forswear *arat sabulungan*, and had to embrace either Islam or Protestantism (Sihombing 1979:99). Later Catholicism was added as an official choice. Islam among the Mentawaians has taken a flight with the organized activities by Dakwah Islamiyah Indonesia (pan-Indonesian organization responsible for the spread and maintenance of the Islamic religion within the Indonesian Archipelago) which started in the late 1960s (H. Mas'oed Abidin 1997). The Islamic initiatives have been particularly influential on the island of Sipora and to a lesser extent on the Pagai Islands.

ment has identified certain groups of people as backward and lost from the mainstream of national progress and development. Their isolation was supposed to be the main cause of their backwardness and also the reason why these people became known as *masyarakat terasing* (isolated communities). The government has developed various development and assimilation programmes to modernize these people and turn them into proper Indonesian citizens. Mentawaians affected by these government policies have learned to understand themselves in mainly negative terms. As *masyarakat terasing* the Mentawaians have been stigmatized as a social, religious and agricultural problem (Persoon 1994:67-120), practising a lifestyle that should be done away with as soon as possible.

With the responsibility for governing the Mentawai Archipelago in the hands of the Minangkabau, it was to a large extent also the Minangkabau who were responsible for the implementation of these special development and assimilation programmes. Convinced of their cultural and religious superiority, these mainland civil servants were eager to implement the government's development and civilization policies amongst the Mentawaians. But the implementation met with practical obstructions. The abundant free-roaming pigs, harsh environmental conditions, and a population perceived to be unfriendly and potentially dangerous turned the Mentawai Archipelago into a very unwelcoming place for the predominantly Islamic Minangkabau. Consequently not many Minangkabau traders dared to expand their businesses into the hinterlands of the islands and Minangkabau civil servants were rarely present on the Mentawai Islands and were ruling the archipelago primarily from the Sumatran mainland. Development projects in the fields of infrastructure, agriculture, and education were finished in haste, completed with inferior materials, prematurely abandoned, or even never implemented. In practice the development of the area was tuned in to the needs of the Minangkabau community residing on the islands. Physical development was confined to the construction of sub-district level government offices, mosques, schools, healthcare facilities, and basic infrastructural facilities in the harbour villages. This led to enclaves of migrants residing in the harbour villages surrounded by poorly serviced local communities.

Critical voices

During the late 1980s growing dissatisfaction emerged among a small but growing number of Mentawaian intellectuals. They started to question the ongoing erosion of their cultural identity and the incompetent and corrupt governmental practices of Minangkabau officials. Eventually they started a lobby for more Mentawaian involvement in local politics.

Due to various religiously based initiatives, opportunities for education within and outside the Mentawai Archipelago have increased significantly since the early 1960s.[3] As a result an ever increasing number of young Mentawaians managed to finish higher levels of education. When transportation facilities between the Mentawai Islands and the Sumatran mainland improved during the 1980s, the number of Mentawaian students seeking education on the mainland increased rapidly. However, once arrived on the mainland, they encountered many problems: poor housing facilities in the city of Padang, the general shortage of finances, the fear of being Islamized,[4] the emergence of drug abuse amongst some of the young Mentawaians, and the omnipresent disdain for their being Mentawaian. With their substantially different culture and lifestyle, the Minangkabau tend to look at the Mentawaians with a mixture of repugnance and fear. Convinced of their own cultural and religious superiority, the Minangkabau tend to perceive Mentawaians as a pagan, primitive and dirty people, still in close contact with nature and the spiritual forces it may encompass. This leads to the belief that Mentawaians have control over certain potentially dangerous spiritual powers. The Minangkabau therefore prefer to avoid open conflict and overt aggression with regard to the Mentawaians. The idea of the Mentawaians being dirty is foremost based on their habit of keeping pigs and eating pork, which is *haram* (prohibited) in Islam. The Mentawaians in turn generally perceive the Minangkabau as religious fanatics. Moreover, the Mentawaians consider Minangkabau to be an unreliable and murderous people. Minangkabau are known for their ability to inflict disease and even death upon weak or unprotected persons. As a result of these interethnic animosities, many young Mentawaians have long denied their own cultural background in order to be successful in the Minangkabau-dominated environment on the mainland.

The ecology of the city, together with the growing analytical capacities of the Mentawaians residing in Padang, made these people more sensitive with regard to notions of ethnic identity. Resulting from this increasing ethnic consciousness, the growing group of Mentawaian students and scholars residing in Padang started to cluster together and organize themselves along ethnic lines. Detached from their families, their wish to organize themselves was in the first instance the product of their feelings of uneasiness, loneliness

3 Protestant and Catholic missionaries have upgraded the education system and offered possibilities for higher education elsewhere. Islamic organizations increasingly also try to get a grip on the Mentawaian community through education programmes.

4 Mentawaians generally perceive Islam and processes of Islamization as dangerous forces from outside, from which one has to abstain in order to avoid detachment from the Mentawaian self. Mentawaians adhering to Islam are, of course, not similarly convinced of this loss of 'pure' Mentawaian identity. Though growing at a considerable rate, the number of Mentawaian converts is still small and they generally have a hard time to publicly defend themselves as equally Mentawaians.

and uncertainty over their lives and futures, but soon political dimensions emerged as well.[5]

In 1982 IPPMEN, short for Ikatan Pemuda Pelajar Mentawai (Association for Mentawaian Youth and Students) was founded by a group of Mentawaian students residing in Padang. Initially IPPMEN was meant as a forum through which Mentawaian students could gather in order to discuss, process and analyse their lives in Padang. In the early 1990s, however, IPPMEN began to comment on government policies regarding Mentawai and the position of Mentawaian individuals as citizens in the broader Indonesian society. In several letter campaigns IPPMEN criticized the Padang-Pariaman bureaucracy for its unwillingness to develop the Mentawai Archipelago. While agreeing with the commonly accepted idea that the Mentawaians were engaged in a struggle through which they tried to escape from their backwardness (*keterbelakangan*), ignorance (*kebodohan*), poverty (*kemiskinan*), and general state of misery (*kemelaratan*), IPPMEN also stated that these features should not be understood as an intrinsic part of Mentawaian culture, but were a result of imperfect, inappropriate and ill-adapted government policies, especially with regard to education and economic development of the Mentawaian region. The Minangkabau administrators were simultaneously accused of perceiving the Mentawai Archipelago as an income-generating area where the existence of a distinct ethnic group was only a disturbing factor in the exploitation of the natural resources. Somewhat impressed by the actions undertaken by these young intellectuals, the government of Padang-Pariaman started to formalize its relationship with IPPMEN in 1992, as a result of which IPPMEN received some financial aid in order to finance their activities.[6] In the early 1990s the Padang-Pariaman administration even installed an assistant district head who was burdened with the pressing issue of development in the Mentawai Archipelago. However, due to a general lack of direction, a crisis in management, mutual distrust, and the contested involvement of some of IPPMEN's leaders in the logging sector, IPPMEN has over time lost most of its initial significance and credibility. But it cannot be denied that IPPMEN was the cradle for a new generation of self-conscious Mentawaian individuals. Through their involvement in IPPMEN many young Mentawaians learned to organize themselves, to put their personal experiences into words and to negotiate their collective wishes and constraints with those in power. The dignity of Mentawaian culture and identity and their exclusion from sharing the revenues generated

[5] Ikatan Pemuda Pelajar Mentawai (IPPMEN), Padang, Voorstel voor internaat en secretariaat, project proposal, 1989.

[6] This money is part of the so-called Dana Pembinaan Pemuda dan Karang Taruna (Youth Development Fund), which is money directly received from the central government for sport and other recreative activities among the younger generation within the district. Until IPPMEN explicitly asked for the Mentawaian share of this money, Mentawai had never received any of it.

through the exploitation of the natural resources present in the Mentawai Archipelago are recurring central points in these negotiations.

These critical voices tuned in nicely with international movements promoting the conservation of the world's cultural and natural heritage. In contrast to the government's point of view, international agencies perceive of the Mentawaians as another example of a marginalized indigenous people entrapped in a hostile nation state that is held responsible for the destruction of the natural habitat of these peoples. From the late 1970s onwards several international organizations have been active on the Mentawai Islands. Amongst others, more established organizations like Survival International, World Wide Fund for Nature (WWF), UNESCO, the Asian Development Bank (ADB), and Conservation International (CI) have been – and some of them still are – running various programmes and projects in Mentawai (see also Persoon 1998).

Due to increased contact with these large international organizations the Mentawaian elite learned to present themselves as a genuine indigenous people living in an endangered tropical rainforest. While making use of this internationally accepted discourse on indigenous peoples and nature conservation, the Mentawaian intelligentsia has been able to generate considerable amounts of money from international donor agencies involved in nature conservation and the empowerment of indigenous peoples. Especially during the late 1990s the Mentawaian elite has institutionalized itself in various local organizations; one of the most prominent being Yayasan Citra Mandiri (YCM, 'Vision for Autonomy' Foundation).

In July 1995 Kortanius Sabeleake' and Yudas Sabaggalet, both formerly active in IPPMEN, founded Yayasan Citra Mandiri (YCM). It focuses on advocacy and economic development of the Mentawaian communities through just and competent use of the natural resources within the Mentawai Archipelago. YCM aims at empowerment of the Mentawaian community through collective, community-based agricultural activities supported by technical assistance, advocacy, education, training and credit facilities. YCM's goal is not only to empower the Mentawaian communities in a material sense, but also to awaken Mentawaian ethnic consciousness through its activities. According to YCM 'the empowerment of *adat* communities lies in the understanding of one's rights and duties, not only as a member of the local community, but also as a citizen within the context of the Indonesian nation state'.[7] The use of the word *adat* (custom, tradition) is clearly a political statement. Instead of using the much-contested terminology *masyarakat terasing*, YCM already in 1995 started to use the term *masyarakat adat* (traditional, indigenous com-

7 See also http://www.lp3es.or.id/direktori/data/sumbar/sumbar_005.htm (last accessed 22 August 2006).

munity), which is considered more respectful. After Yudas Sabaggalet left the organization in 1998, Kortanius Sabeleake' became the executive director of YCM, a position he occupied until late 2004 when he became head of the district parliament (Dewan Perwakilan Rakyat Daerah, DPRD). Over time YCM has been working with an ever-changing staff of some 20 persons, of which nearly a third work in the main office in Padang, another third in the editorial office of the newspaper *Puailiggoubat*, published by YCM, while the last third is active in the field. YCM has been involved in a great variety of activities, among which we can find advocacy with regard to land disputes, mapping of traditional territory, agroforestry, pilot studies and more in-depth research. Unlike IPPMEN, YCM's activities are almost solely determined by their sponsors (UNESCO, German Embassy, Forestrade) and more powerful counterparts like Lembaga Riset Advokasi (LRA, Institute for Policy Research and Advocacy) and Wahana Lingkungan Hidup Indonesia (WALHI, Indonesian Forum for the Environment).

In 1997 YCM made a start with the creation of a local council of experienced *adat* leaders, the *dewan adat*, an idea that they copied from the more experienced, Kalimantan-based organization Pancur Kasih.[8] By late 1997 YCM had established *dewan adat* in several villages on Siberut. The *dewan adat* is supposed to strengthen the position of local *adat* communities vis-à-vis government institutions, and to lobby local government bodies with crucial impulses from the bottom level of Mentawaian society (*Puailiggoubat* 6(May 2002):8). In the beginning of 2002, however, the idea of *dewan adat* still had not found general acceptance yet. The *dewan adat* in the villages mentioned earlier where still struggling with their legal position. There was little to no cooperation between *dewan adat* and local NGOs other than YCM, and in the mean time the *dewan adat* were still waiting for its official acknowledgement by the local government. At the time of writing the factual implementation of *dewan adat* seems to have completely failed (*Puailiggoubat* 49(1-14 June 2004):5). Although in theory government officials support democratic strengthening and bottom-up strategies and activities, they tend not to be enthusiastic about such things. Government officials do not recognize the *dewan adat* as a serious initiative, but as another vagary by YCM, initially leading to disappointment and later to indifference on the part of those involved.

Since 2001 YCM is closely linked to the Rainforest Foundation Norway (RFN).[9] The cooperation with RFN has significantly influenced the position of

8 See also Tanasaldy in this volume for more information about Yayasan Pancur Kasih.

9 The Norwegian Rainforest Foundation, active in Indonesia since 1997, is an environmental as well as an aid organization that works for the protection of the rainforests and its rich resources for coming generations. To achieve this goal, the Rainforest Foundation supports indigenous and forest peoples that live in and off the forests in their struggle to protect the environment and attain respect for their human rights. (http://www.rainforest.no.)

YCM. The Rainforest Foundation is not only a prestigious international partner, but also a generous donor. The Rainforest Foundation Norway has more than doubled the budget for YCM from US$ 50,000 in 2001 to US$ 110,000 in 2002.[10] Lately YCM has invested considerable amounts of money in the bureaucratic expansion of the organization. In the second half of 2002 a new office was opened in Maileppet on the island of Siberut and a start was made on the building of another new office in Tuapeijat on the island of Sipora, which was operational at the time of writing. There are still plans to open a third office on the Mentawai Islands in Sikabaluan in the northern part of Siberut Island. Late in 2002 the editorial office of *Puailiggoubat* detached itself from the main YCM office in Padang and took up residence in an office in the vicinity. Especially the new office in Maileppet has raised negative publicity. The fact that the office seemed ready for use for several months, yet was still not operational on a day to day basis at the end of 2002, set evil tongues wagging. Malicious suggestions that YCM actually did not know what to do with the money they collected in the name of the local communities, that the money had been invested in a useless expansion of real estate, which was probably only meant to benefit the personal interests of YCM members, were much in the air. Besides, a considerable number of people involved in YCM campaigned quite intensively during the latest elections for district parliament. Although there is no direct proof for this accusation, local communities strongly believe that the RFN funding has largely been used for these personal political campaigns. Just like IPPMEN in earlier days, YCM is now generally believed to create fame and personal gain by selling the image of indigeneity and endangered natural environments to large donor organizations, without ever really taking local communities into account. In other words: the credibility and accountability of YCM is under increased questioning, not only among local government officials, but also – more alarmingly – among local communities on the Mentawai Islands.

The rush for putra asli daerah

After the fall of Soeharto's authoritarian New Order regime the initial, somewhat concealed, lobby for more Mentawaian political involvement changed into a blatant request for the rigorous detachment from Padang-Pariaman district as a completely new district. When the Mentawai Archipelago was eventually granted district status in October 1999, people immediately started falling over each other in order to guarantee the most profitable positions for either themselves or their protégés. In contrast with what the Mentawaian elite had been lobbying for, the governor of West Sumatra installed Badril

10 http://www.rainforest.no.

Bakar, a fellow Minangkabau originating from the Sumatran mainland, as interim district head for the new district Kepulauan Mentawai. Local NGOs and several politically engaged individuals were disappointed by the installation of this interim district head. For the majority of Mentawaians, still traumatized by non-indigenous, Islamic Minangkabau rulers, it was obvious that their district head should be a Christian and above all a *putra asli daerah* (indigenous person). Being a Muslim and a member of the commonly distrusted Minangkabau, Badril Bakar was the first target for the local NGOs. Their hostility towards him withheld him from a more energetic performance and was definitely among the several reasons why he was dishonourably dismissed in April 2001 and sent back to the mainland.

With Badril Bakar gone, the governor appointed a second temporary district head. This time he was a Mentawaian, Antonius Samangilailai, former sub-district head of South Siberut, originating from Sipora. Although a Mentawaian, his Islamic image and the fact that Antonius was widely believed to be the timber companies' right hand man made his appointment controversial as well. Many considered Antonius and the governor hand-in-glove when it came to logging matters in the Mentawai Archipelago.[11]

Soon after Antonius was appointed interim district head, elections for the DPRD were announced. This became the moment when the political turmoil came to a climax, because the new members of the DPRD would be responsible for the constitution of the local government and the election of a permanent district head. A feature of striking importance in these political negotiations was the omnipresent call for *putra asli daerah* to take up this most influential position. The use of the term *putra asli daerah* is to be interpreted in ethnic terms, primarily differentiating between the Mentawaians and the Minangkabau. Whereas the initial lobby for more local political involvement was directed against the unreliable and corrupt Minangkabau administrators, it was a common wish that local politics now also had to be taken over by sincere and trustworthy local persons, *putra asli daerah*.

Who is considered *putra asli daerah*, is, however, a matter of highly local perspective. For many local communities, notions of belonging – rather than ethnicity – lie at the heart of their experienced identity. Mentawaians tell a myth in which at a certain moment the population on Siberut became involved in a serious dispute, which after some time had all the features of a real civil war. After a great wave of violence, people tended to stay out of sight of possibly violent individuals as far as possible. Some even fled as far as the southern Mentawai Islands. Since the clash, the population from

[11] The governor of West Sumatra, once district head of district Padang-Pariaman himself (therefore pretty well informed about the potential natural resources available within Mentawai), is known as an advocate of logging concessions on the Mentawai Islands.

the southern Mentawai Islands refer to the inhabitants of Siberut as Sabirut. The population on Siberut in turn refer to the people on the southern islands as Sakalagat. The people on the Pagai Islands again differentiate between themselves and those on Sipora, calling them Sakalelegat (those we left on the island of Sipora but are still of our kind) or Sakobou. All are categories that come along with negative stereotypes. Sakalagat are the cowards (they migrated from Siberut in earlier ages), the ones who were driven away, the losers, the ones from whom we have to fear black magic, the ones who eat *gette'* (taro – regarded as inferior), the ones who are *maju* (developed or modern) but who forgot about their culture and identity, the ones who became more or less similar to the Minangkabau. Sabirut in turn, of course, are described by others as the ones who stayed, the passive ones, the ancient (*kuno*), outdated, old-fashioned and conservative part of the Mentawaians. They are rude, harsh, traditional and savage. The Sabirut like to kill. They are known for cutting your head off for no particular reason. While people might refer to themselves according to the above mentioned categories, all prefer to call themselves Simattaoi (Mentawaians).

The political translation of these intra-ethnic animosities is done with the help of the term *putra asli setempat* (people originating from a certain as yet unspecified place). While *putra asli daerah* only differentiates between Mentawaians and *sasareu* (literally: those from afar; outsiders), *putra asli setempat* differentiates quite precisely among Mentawaians themselves. For people in search of political constituencies, the heterogeneous constitution of the population within the Mentawai Archipelago is thus a problematic issue. Which person is likely to get the broader support of society is a delicate question. Putting a Satoko clan member, originating from Saibi Samukop (South Siberut), forward in political negotiations might guarantee the support of fellow clan members in Saibi Samukop, but not automatically the support of broader society in South Siberut, let alone in North Siberut or, even more unlikely, of those on the southern Mentawai Islands. Candidates in the first DPRD elections therefore often had to campaign against the odds. The elections, which were fought along party lines, led to an overwhelming victory for Partai Demokrasi Indonesia Perjuangan (PDI-P, Indonesian Democratic Party of Struggle), followed by Partai Damai Kasih Bangsa (PDKB, the Love the Nation Democratic Party) and Golkar. As soon as the DPRD was finally installed in late June 2001, negotiations over the position of district head began. PDI-P and PDKB clustered together and put forward two candidates for district head: Edison Saleleubaja, a Protestant clergyman originating from Sikakap (North Pagai), and Alexander Lukman, an ethnic Chinese with a Catholic background. Alexander was eager to take up the position of district head. He had far-reaching ideas about opening his own logging company on the islands. He had an elaborated political plan written even before he was officially listed as a candidate for the position of district head. By contrast, Edison was not at all eager for the position. Many of his friends, however, whom he had known from his years in the local NGO Yayasan Kondisi,[12] were now involved in the logging sector in Mentawai and they thought it very convenient to have a close friend occupying the influential position of district head. Financially supported by his friends, Edison became a political puppet in the hands of the logging sector.[13]

Besides Edison and Alexander there was a third serious candidate for the position of district head: former interim district head Antonius. Together with his equally Muslim running mate, Ridwan Siritubui, originating from Simalegi (North Siberut), they formed the Islamic pole in the elections. They could count on the votes from Golkar and the smaller Islamic parties in the DPRD. Not unlike the two other candidates, Antonius and Ridwan also leaned heavily on financial support from the logging sector.

In a close finish between Antonius and Edison Saleleubaja after two rounds of elections, the latter was finally elected as the first district head of Kepulauan Mentawai district. The story goes that Edison's camp had spent Rp 1.3 billion (€ 130,000) to buy the crucial vote within the DPRD.

Edison was officially installed in August 2001, soon after which he appointed the various heads of the local government departments. All departments were now invariably headed by Mentawaians, most of whom were friends or close relatives of Edison. Edison's old position of head of DPRD was taken up by his brother-in-law. Ridwan Siritubui, the former running mate of Antonius was asked to take up the important position of district secretary. Although Ridwan's qualifications were officially not adequate to take up the position of district secretary – a point over which the deputy district head Aztarmizi was to fall at a later stage – Edison preferred to install fellow Mentawaians over the undoubtedly more experienced and better qualified outsiders.[14] Edison was clearly reluctant to give the newly gained power back into the hands of the far more experienced Minangkabau administrators, who were also eager to take up some of the vacant positions. Interestingly, only the strategic position of head of the Department of Forestry was given to a Minangkabau. According to Edison himself he did so because he considered this position to be far too

[12] Under the leadership of Edison Saleleubaja, Yayasan Kondisi started as an evangelistic organization aiming to empower the Protestant population on the Mentawai Islands. After only a short time, however, they found themselves involved in the logging sector.

[13] Bakrial, involved in the logging company PT Mundam Sati, active on Sipora and the Pagai Islands, even pushed Edison as far as taking up Aztarmizi, the former assistant district head and close relative of Bakrial, as his running mate. Edison, lacking any experience in governing a district, thought it a good idea to link up with the experienced Aztarmizi.

[14] At the moment Ridwan became district secretary he had achieved the rank (*pangkat*, according to level of education and working experience) of 3D, while 4A is officially required to take up the position (*Puailiggoubat* 16(15-31 January 2003):3).

contested to be occupied by a Mentawaian. Due to this decision, Edison found himself immediately under fire by local NGOs on the one hand, who demanded the conservation of what was left of Mentawai's tropical lowland rainforest, and by the financial supporters of his political campaign on the other hand.[15]

Dealing with development

Whereas the Mentawaian lifestyle has long been stigmatized as *terbelakang* (backwards), two key words in the discussions about the past, present and the future of the Mentawaians and their environment are *pembangunan* (development) and *kemajuan* (progress). The word *pembangunan* has its origin in the word *bangun*, which means 'to construct', but also 'to wake up from a state of unawareness'. In the latter meaning we can find a connection with the New Order government's point of view that the *masyarakat terasing* should be brought back into the mainstream of national progress.[16] *Kemajuan* implies a forward motion towards modernity. The local understanding of modernity comes in a multitude of variations. Depending on the circumstances modernity might imply having asbestos-roofed houses, schools, roads, prestigious infrastructure, churches, plastic kitchen utensils and western clothes, but also cars, bicycles, motorcycles, outboard motors, computers and mobile telephones. The term *maju* is used in an interrelated sense for a way of life which foremost involves using manufactured goods and having the knowledge that pertains to them. Travelling by motorcycle for instance is considered *lebih maju* (more modern) than paddling along the river in a dug-out canoe. In order to progress and develop one should thus leave behind the old ways of life and start adhering to a more progressive, consumptive lifestyle.

Completely in tune with these ideas about progress and development, the newly installed local government launched several prestigious development projects. They were financed by the Dana Alokasi Umum (DAU, General Allocation Fund), an annual allowance from the central government in order to set up administration, transportation and infrastructural facilities. Transportation facilities between Mentawai and the mainland have improved considerably since 1999 and there is even a plan on the drawing board to rehabilitate the airstrip on the Island of Sipora and construct a small airport. In accordance with the 2001 development plan for Tuapeijat a complex of completely new government offices was to be built in Tuapeijat on the Island of Sipora.[17] Another important activity in the development of the archipelago is

15 Especially the local NGO Yayasan Citra Mandiri has been very vocal in this respect.

16 See Ariel Heryanto (1988) for a more elaborate discussion of this topic.

17 The choice for Tuapeijat as the new political centre of the district was not a deliberate one. While Muara Siberut – the main harbour village on Siberut – would have been a much more likely choice, under the guidance of interim district head Antonius it had already become clear

the construction of various roads. These are often old dirt roads and already existing trails within and between villages that are to be repaired and refurnished with a cement top layer. Elsewhere, often hand in hand with small scale logging concessions, completely new connections over considerable length are being realized. Contractor companies – almost invariably in the hands of local DPRD members – are eager to get their hands on these projects because the additional revenues from the lumber that must be removed from the trajectory is considerable. In order to collect as much timber as possible, roads from one village to the next often do not run in a straight line, but tend to meander tremendously. These practices not seldom lead to conflicts with intervening local communities who often see part of their gardens destroyed by the advent of the road. In the meantime the local government does not seem to be very eager to act against these practices because they might then get into conflict with befriended persons or family members within the DPRD.[18] Besides, the government generally perceives the forest as a realm that accommodates practices which contradict the local understanding of progress and modernity. The forest and all the cultural and natural diversity it contains is not perceived as something valuable in itself, as promoted through Western notions of nature conservation and cultural survival. The forest and the lifestyle of its inhabitants are more often than not perceived as disturbing obstructions to the swift and sound development of the region.

Since early 2003 the DPRD has tried to push through the idea of upgrading the number of sub-districts from four now to eight and more recently ten in the near future (*Puailiggoubat* 4(March 2002):11). This *pemekaran wilayah* is considered important for the development of the district. Ten sub-districts will lead to a considerable increase in the budget for development received from the central government, subsequently leading to an increase in local development projects, which is very much in the interest of several members of the DPRD and the local government. Local communities also seem to be enthusiastic about the plans. Most people can already imagine how the quality of their lives will improve after the creation of the new sub-districts that will undoubtedly translate into more facilities such as schools, medical centres, harbours, police offices, and telecommunications. While several local communities have already made part of their lands available for the construction of these facilities, the government wants local communities in each of the planned sub-districts to make at least 100 hectares available. These negotia-

---

that no other communities elsewhere within the archipelago were willing to hand over their land to the government. Besides, the limited availability of clean water suitable for consumption has seriously delayed the operability of the new offices in Tuapeijat. At the time of writing, problems with water are still not completely solved.

[18] Members of local government are generally believed to be bribed by contractor companies often in the hands of DPRD members.

tions over land is probably one of the reasons why the implementation of the ten sub-districts has been delayed. Since sub-district facilities can be built on 5-10 hectares of land, the government's request for at least 100 hectares is considered absurd. From a governmental point of view, however, this demand does make sense. Plots of at least 100 hectares that need to be cleared for different purposes can first be handed out as an IPK logging concession, which could in turn generate income for the district in the form of taxes.[19] Whereas the land in Mentawai is now commonly considered to be in the hands of local communities, the local government has to negotiate with local communities over land on which they wish to realize the development projects. Since most land in Mentawai is owned by a great variety of clans, these negotiations are invariably extremely complicated and lead to great confusion among all parties and sometimes even to serious conflicts among clan members and the government, and among clan members themselves.

So far the development of the archipelago has been handled mainly in terms of physical development. While the construction of new offices and infrastructure might be called overwhelming, ideas for a more structural approach with regard to development are suspiciously absent. Problems in the critical sectors of education, healthcare and economics are barely addressed. Although medical centres and schools have been erected at various locations in the archipelago, there seems to be no planning for their actual operation. Teachers and medical personnel are still absent. Besides, facilities like these are still extremely poor in the more remote areas of the archipelago. Local politicians seem to lack a development perspective that goes beyond physical development only. The former New Order rhetoric and practices with regard to development are still very much in use. The dependency on the development budget from the central government remains extremely high. Local income generating activities are – apart from several small private enterprises paying taxes – generally absent. So far the local government has not been able to break the foreign monopoly over the vibrant surfing industry in the Mentawai Archipelago, has not been able to stop the illegal exploitation of the Mentawaian waters by foreign fishing fleets, and – even more surprisingly – has not been able to generate a substantial income from the logging sector active in the archipelago. Hopes for the future are set on foreign investments in the tourist industry, but with tourism in Mentawai focussing on surfing (monopolized by mainly Australian businessmen) as well as on the forested environment and its adherent local cultural practices, the current attack on the natural environment and the swift vanishing of the forest on the islands does not seem to be very constructive.

[19] So-called IPK logging concessions (Izin Pemanfaatan Kayu, Wood Utilization Permit) are issued to clear forested lands for other purposes such as infrastructure or plantations.

Tricks of the trade

With the district itself not gaining from the logging activities, the question arises why then the logging sector seems to be more vibrant than ever before. Though in 2004 at least 20 new permits for small scale logging concessions were issued for a total area of more than 30,000 hectares, the local administration was not able to collect any retribution fees from the timber companies involved (*The Jakarta Post* 24-3-2005). It is generally believed that both members of local government and the DPRD are subject to bribery from the logging sector. Besides, Edison himself was widely believed to have received payment for the smooth and unquestioned issuing of the smaller IPK licenses.[20] When Kortanius Sabeleake' in late 2004 – he had just been elected head of the DPRD – publicly confronted Edison with these accusations during a meeting between local government and DPRD on the issue of revenues generated within the district (*pendapatan asli daerah*), Edison suspiciously fell acutely ill and had to leave the meeting prematurely.[21] While we might never find out what was precisely going on and how much money was involved here, it is a fact that the Mentawaian administration and Mentawai's natural resources stand to lose while some individuals quite clearly enrich themselves over these practices.

It is especially in the awarding of the currently plentiful development projects to the executive parties that a lot of corrupt practices ensue. Many local politicians have lately founded their own contractor company – whether capable of the factual implementation of the projects or not – through which they are able to lay their hands on the money allocated for the projects. As a result the projects are transferred through various befriended contractor companies before they are finally implemented. By that time only half of the initial budget for the project may be left, which then results in projects that are only half finished or completed with inferior materials because after the various transfers there is not enough money left to finish the project properly (*Puailiggoubat* 6(May 2002):8). These practices are often referred to as *diproyekkan*: making something into a project in order to get access to (part of the) project funding.

Collusive practices also emerged in the selection procedures for civil servants. After Edison Saleleubaja was installed district head, a large number of members of the Saleleubaja clan were accepted as civil servants. Although an official examination must be passed before one is able to become a civil servant, a personal recommendation from the district head makes the examination a mere formality. Those people not in the privileged position to obtain a personal recommendation from the district head himself often simply buy the

20 Until 2002 IPK concessions up to 100 hectares could be issued by the district head personally. See also McCarthy in this volume.

21 Edison was hospitalized several days after this incident. In Indonesia, sudden illness is often a device to avoid embarrassing situations for politicians and high officials.

position for either themselves or their protégés. It goes without saying that for those without the financial means or a personal relationship with some higher government official, the much sought-after civil servant positions are difficult to obtain.

KKN, the Indonesian triad of corruption (*korupsi*), collusion (*kolusi*), and nepotism (*nepotisme*) has been and still is a major issue in Indonesian politics. While Mentawaians are now part and parcel of these practices it is difficult to point an accusing finger at anyone in particular. It is rewarding to behave as unobtrusively as possible in order not to attract negative publicity. What did, however, lead to a public outcry was the presumed corruption of the district secretary, Ridwan Siritubui. His name became a substitute for blatant corruption when Rp 7.6 billion (€ 760,000) of government money allocated for reforestation was transferred to the 'wrong' account number. Even before the money could be returned, local NGOs and the media had blown up the story to huge proportions. Ridwan was openly attacked by the deputy district head, Aztarmizi, who also accused him of illegally transferring Rp 8.2 billion (€ 820,000) of development money to the various departments. On the basis of oral agreements with Edison and the various heads of departments, Ridwan did indeed lend them a total sum of Rp 8.2 billion – money that was to be returned at a later stage. Aztarmizi, who on the basis of Ridwan's insufficient qualifications felt politically bypassed by Ridwan, not only accused him of corruption, but also questioned his professionalism and experience. Annoyed by Aztarmizi's accusations, Ridwan struck back at Aztarmizi by stating that Aztarmizi and his fellow Minangkabau friends had been in power long enough in the Mentawai Archipelago and that it was time for them to let go of their superior attitude. Since Ridwan had been brought up within the Minangkabau community, he seriously offended many with this statement. Aztarmizi, with the financial support of his close relative Bakrial, mobilized some of the Mentawaian civil support organizations to demand a close investigation of Ridwan's activities. This triggered counter demonstrations by other parts of Mentawaian society who believed in Ridwan's sincerity. The situation began to get out of hand when Ridwan refused to cooperate with the investigating team. Ridwan was convinced of his innocence and stated that the financial transactions had been done with the oral approval of Edison. Both Ridwan and Edison disappeared. Some weeks later police arrested Ridwan in the city of Bukittinggi on the Sumatran mainland (*Puailiggoubat* 28(15-31 July 2003):3).

Ridwan was brought to trial, but it experienced serious delay as the most important witness, the district head, remained untraceable. When at length Edison had been heard – he saved his own skin by stating that he had never given his consent – Ridwan was sentenced to five years jail.[22] Ridwan, however,

22 *Puailiggoubat* 49(1-14 June 2004):3. Here we should remember that Edison was indebted to Bakrial, who had earlier paid for Edison's political campaign in the race for the position of district head.

took the case to the high court, which exonerated him. At the time of writing Ridwan was waiting to be reinstalled as district secretary. However, with the relationship between him and Edison under severe pressure, Ridwan's future position within the Mentawaian administration is a highly uncertain one.

Whether corruption and money politics have increased or not is difficult to assess. Money politics and corruption were also perceived as a considerable problem when the Minangkabau were practising them and Mentawaians were excluded. Now that fate has given the advantage to the Mentawaians, corruption and money politics seem to have decentralized as well. Ordinary citizens are now, much more than under the Minangkabau administration, able to profit from ethnically instigated patron-client relationships with their government.

Where have critical voices gone?

With the Mentawaian politicians entangled in all kind of conspiracies, and local communities left out of the political negotiations, the question arises why there is not more protest against these forms of exclusion. Where have local NGOs gone and why are they not able to fill the gap between local communities and their government?

Politics (*politik*) and politicians (*politikus;* sometimes replaced by the more friendly term *politisi*) have always been something of a dirty category. The word *berpolitik* (politicking) is for instance also used to describe peoples' sneaky strategies to push through their own interests. And indeed, the Mentawaian political elite is – like their Minangkabau predecessors – often accused of acting in their own interests only. Not unjustifiably, local communities feel that most of the political debates and decision-making processes occur beyond their realm. They have only the weapons of the weak (Scott 1985), of which gossiping, nasty insinuations, and the threat of using black magic are the most common. Most local communities are, however, less informed, less involved, sometimes even ignorant and this makes them more passive, quick to develop cynical attitudes, and sometimes believing that politics is something not applicable to them.

In the more remote areas of Mentawai (the west coast of Siberut Island and the Rereiket area) where the majority of the population is still illiterate, news only trickles down on an irregular basis. Many people in these areas are still in the dark about the significant shift in political power that has taken place. Though some people in these areas are aware of the fact that Mentawai has obtained district status with its own district head, some people do not perceive Edison as their political leader because he originates from Sikakap, which means that he is a member of the much distrusted Sakalagat and should therefore not be considered capable of supporting their interests.

Nevertheless, regardless of the omnipresent corruption and money politics, the majority of Mentawaians believe the current political constitution to be much more promising than that of the previous Minangkabau administrators. With fellow Mentawaians in power it has – at least for some part of the population – become easier for local communities to communicate with their political leaders and to get privileged treatment for their businesses, while opportunities to enter politics have increased significantly. Corrupt and collusive practices are certainly not a new phenomenon. But they were perceived as more disturbing during the Minangkabau administration, because the Mentawaians were excluded from them. Though annoying for those not able to partake, bribery and corruption of this kind is a commonly accepted form of politicking.

The sometimes prestigious infrastructural developments that the local government has implemented have also mitigated any negative public opinion. Regardless of the disturbing side effects of these development projects – of which not everyone is equally aware – people tend to perceive of them as positive and above all adding to their modernity. With local communities themselves involved, they gain directly from these projects by receiving payment on a daily basis. This stands in complete contrast to the way in which such projects were implemented in earlier days, when projects were almost invariably implemented by outsiders. The fact is, local communities often lack a more long term perspective with regard to certain developments. As a result local communities often only start complaining when the negative impacts of certain practices have become completely visible and irreversible.

While the empowerment of civil society is at stake and hopes are high that local NGOs will raise political awareness and push through measures of political accountability, they do not seem to be able to put their theoretical potential to full use (see also Collins 2003; Bob Sugeng Hadiwinata 2003; McVey 2003). The reason for their poor performance lies in the fact that the majority of local NGOs have recently become political strongholds themselves. While most of the Mentawaian elite were until recently involved in local NGOs and support organizations, various individuals within these local organizations now see no other option than to use their organization as a platform from which they can easily jump over to institutionalized politics. This leaves civil society basically without actors who do not have a double agenda. The shift to politics by Kortanius Sabeleake', the former director of YCM, is just one example of this. However, Kortanius' case is interesting. Having been the founder and the acting director of YCM since 1995 and the driving force behind the local newspaper *Puailiggoubat*, he created a lot of support for himself personally.[23] While YCM claims (for reasons of transparency) to have cut off all official

[23] So far *Puailiggoubat* is the only local newspaper made by Mentawaians meant for the Mentawaian public.

affiliation with Kortanius since he was appointed head of the DPRD late in 2004, it cannot be denied that he still enjoys considerable support from YCM and he is also, not unimportantly, able to influence the local media.

As far as local NGOs and village councils are involved in the monitoring of local politics they do not do so on a structural basis. Often the constitution of these organizations coincides with the emergence of a particular political issue they might favour or dislike. Not seldom, public demonstrations by these groups are instigated (and paid for) by people in the higher political echelons in search for an outcome sympathetic to their interests.[24] While these public demonstrations thus do not necessarily ventilate the popular will, they do add to the general confusion and certainly influences the way in which the issue appears in the media.

New colonizers?

The decentralization process in Indonesia has led to an important shift in local power relations in the Mentawai Archipelago. The Mentawaians have been able to liberate themselves from what they saw as cultural repression and political colonization by the mainland Minangkabau. The question remains, however, whether this shift has indeed also led to a more democratic political system at the local level. It turns out that the local government has been captured by a local elite, which does not equally represent all levels of society. On the basis of selective ethnic sentiments, differing ethnic groups living in the Mentawai Archipelago are consequently excluded from political participation. *Putra asli daerah,* not necessarily more competent, are being privileged over *sasareu* (non-Mentawaians). Besides, there is also still that part of Mentawaian society living in the more remote areas of the archipelago that is still unaccounted for. These people, most of them illiterate, do not take part in the politicking that takes place mainly outside their realm. So far there have been few initiatives to incorporate these people into the local political system. Moreover, in the opinion of the local government, these people can only be incorporated within the development process if they let go of their old fashioned forest-based lifestyles. In this respect local politicians seem to have slipped back into the former New Order rhetoric with regard to *masyarakat terasing,* which can be regarded as a definite step back in the empowerment of local communities. Apart from this disquieting development, it is striking to see how easily the new political elite is able to let go of their former ideals and rhetoric with regard to their rights to self-determination and to access natural resources; a rhetoric through which they in earlier days linked themselves to powerful, mainly overseas donor organizations campaigning on behalf of

24 See also Vel in this volume for a description of similar events.

indigenous peoples and nature conservation. It appears that opportunistic behaviour on the part of the local elite, losing all interest in the wellbeing of the communities on whose image of indigeneity they have been preying for decades, is the rule rather than the exception. A situation has been created in which eventually all stand to lose.

JACQUELINE VEL

Campaigning for a new district in West Sumba

Crowd cheerfully welcomes the new district in Sumba

Thousands of people gathered on the plain of Laikaruda in the middle of Sumba on the 31st of January 2003 to celebrate the new district of Central Sumba.[1] Trucks and small buses had gone early in the morning to the villages gathering passengers and spreading the word that a delegation from Jakarta was coming to inaugurate the new district. It would be a feast, with gong music and meals with meat. The honoured guests from Jakarta received traditional gifts, such as beautiful hand woven cloth. Traditional dance performances stressed the local population's commitment and the strong culture and tradition of the area that was to be a district by itself. Banners over the road proclaimed the creation of Central Sumba as an act of pure democracy – *Vox populi, vox dei: Suara rakyat adalah suara Tuhan* (The voice of the people is the voice of God) – and the slogan would locally be interpreted as a sign of (the Christian) God's blessing over the campaign.

The crowd only learned afterwards that this was just one step in a very long process of creating a new district. They had been mobilized to assure the visiting delegation of the Central Parliament in Jakarta that Central Sumba above all rested on the genuine wishes of the people *(aspirasi masyarakat)*.

This chapter is about *pemekaran,* the creation of a new district out of old (sometimes called 'redistricting') in West Sumba.[2] Current proposals aim to split the present district of West Sumba into three: Central Sumba, West Sumba and Southwest Sumba. Throughout Indonesia, the campaigning rhetoric always mentions three main reasons for creating a new district: it brings the government closer to the people, it will be beneficial to economic prosperity, and it is the wish of the people to have their own district. A new

1 I would like to thank the International Institute for Asian Studies in Leiden for the affiliated fellowship that enabled me to work on this article.

2 See the Introduction to this volume.

district will have its own bureaucracy with a budget to spend according its own priorities, which is one good reason for new candidate bureaucrats to create their own district. Setting up a new district bureaucracy promises a large number of jobs for well-educated but presently underemployed locals.

Pemekaran is a long process, involving campaigning on Sumba, lobbying to the institutions and people who will take the ultimate decisions in Kupang and Jakarta, and lengthy bureaucratic procedures. Although the efforts for *pemekaran* in West Sumba started in 2000, four years later the campaign has not yet been successful.

The case of Sumba presented here is an example of how new laws and institutions created at the national level are taken as opportunities by members of the local elite, who adjust them to local political culture and use them to strengthen their positions or interests.

In some areas of Indonesia, the struggle for a larger share of the benefits from exploitation of the area's natural resources is the main driving force behind *pemekaran*; in other areas persisting religious conflicts or ethnic distinctions make *pemekaran* an obvious opportunity to separate 'us' from 'them'. On Sumba, none of these conditions seem to be present. Then what were the social forces behind the campaign? How would the identity justifying the new district be constructed? Why was there so little opposition? How is this case specific for Sumba? Why has the campaign not been successful, or at least, not yet? Does the case of *pemekaran* on Sumba support the thesis that local aristocracies in the Outer Islands of Indonesia survive all changes in national politics and remain in power locally (Magenda 1989:61-2)? How does this case study contribute to understanding the processes that accompany decentralization?[3]

This chapter describes the campaigns for two of the three new districts proposed in West Sumba, namely Central Sumba and Southwest Sumba.[4] Alongside these empirical parts it presents a framework to understand the opportunities that decentralization offers. This starts by stressing that Sumba is a resource poor island and that the state bureaucracy is the most important economic sector, receiving over 90% of its budget from Jakarta. Creating a new district needs actors who engage in political struggle to reach this goal. These people are connected to each other through networks deploying shared histories and cultures. For the purpose of lobbying for their cause – Central Sumba in this case – they create a shared political identity. Two important

3 Jacqueline Vel's forthcoming monograph *Uma politics; Democracy and contemporary political culture on Sumba* will include the sequel in the Sumbanese democratization process: the 2005 direct elections for regional head (*pikalda*), in which some of the main actors in this chapter play a prominent role again.

4 The Indonesian names of the proposed districts are: Sumba Tengah, Sumba Barat and Sumba Barat Daya.

elements of this political identity are the boundaries that separate 'us' from 'them', and the stories about those boundaries (Tilly 2003:32). The third section provides an overview of the various ways in which Sumba has been divided administratively in the past, since the currently proposed division uses arguments of historical precedent.

The fourth section answers the question who the local rulers are, and concludes that they are still usually members of the Sumbanese aristocracy, who are well educated and have a successful professional career as well. Campaigning for *pemekaran* is part of competition between factions of the local elite. In this competition, elite factions have to create their own constituency. The fifth section discusses the problematic role of religion and ethnicity on Sumba as ingredients for creating political identity, as labels to distinguish 'us' from 'them'.

Campaigning for a new district requires strong rhetoric and attractive theatre. Being a successful politician on Sumba is largely a matter of being the best orator. The sixth section goes into this phenomenon using examples of the campaign for South Southwest Sumba.

Creating a new district is not a completely local affair. It involves actors, institutions and decisions on all levels, from the grass root up to Jakarta. Studies on these decentralization practices can therefore not be limited to the local context. The practices on Sumba in the campaign for a new district show the importance of networks as vehicles in political campaigns. Religious networks, alumni networks, kinship and marriage alliance networks create – much like political parties do – connections between people who can provide reciprocal services. The seventh section describes three successful Sumbanese men who reside in Jakarta or the provincial capital Kupang and who play a very important role in the attempt to create a new district in their home island. They link the region with the centre.

The economic importance of the state on Sumba

Sumba is an island, about 210 km long and 65 km wide, located southeast of the line Bali – Lombok – Sumbawa – Flores. It is part of the province of East Nusa Tenggara, one of the poorest in Indonesia, where between 1996 and 2000 on average only 0.65% of the Indonesian national gross domestic product was generated.[5] Sumba is divided into two districts, East Sumba and West Sumba. Both districts are resource poor and the economically most important sector is the state.

5 BPS Statistics Indonesia at http://www.bps.go.id/sector/nra/grdp/table4.shtml, accessed 5-8-2004.

Table 1. Sumba in figures.[6]

Indicator	West Sumba	East Sumba	Nusa Tenggara Timur	Indonesia
Population 2002 (x 1000)	366	191	3,925	217,100
Per capita income 2002 (in US$**)	116	191	173	3,200
Surface area (in km^2)	4,051	7,000	49,880	1,919,317
Population density (people/km^2)	90	27	83	116

** For comparative purposes the income figures are given in US$, using an exchange rate of 1 US$ = 9,000 rupiah.

The figures clearly show a very small per capita income, but actual poverty of the Sumbanese population is a matter of debate among statisticians and policy-makers (Betke and Ritonga 2004). The macro figures do not include income in kind. The larger part of the population in Sumba has income in kind. Especially food is either a product of one's own cultivation or received through barter trade, which are invisible in the statistics (Vel 1994b:35-8). Despite this addition, Sumba remains a very resource poor island. Cashew nuts, vanilla and cacao are at present the most promising crops for export to other regions. Sandalwood, which used to be the island's major commodity, is officially banned from trade. Informal sources confirm however that illegal logging and trade is finishing off the last sandalwood left on the island, just as in Timor (McWilliam 2001).

The best type of employment with regard to status and monetary income from the Sumbanese perspective, and the common ideal for pupils starting their education, is to be a civil servant. The riots in 1998 in Waikabubak, West Sumba's district capital, were triggered by demonstrations against the district government, which was accused of fraud and nepotism over the results of exams for candidate-civil servants (Vel 2001:154). According to *Sumba Barat dalam angka 2002* (Sumba Barat in figures 2002, see Badan Pusat Statistik Kabupaten Sumba Barat 2003) there are 1,356 official civil servants in West Sumba, and another 3,600 people who work as school teachers or health workers. The total of about 5,000 people who work for the government is 25% of those employed outside agriculture in West Sumba. The only other

6 BPS Statistics Indonesia at http://www.bps.go.id/ and http://ntt.bps.go.id, UNDP Human Development Report at http://hdr.undp.org/statistics, and World Fact Book of the CIA at http://www.cia.gov/cia/publications/factbook/.

sector in which people on Sumba earn a good (monetary) income is trade. This sector on Sumba is completely dominated by Sumbanese of Chinese ethnic origin. Table 2 depicts the structure of the economy in West Sumba according to official state statistics:

Table 2. West Sumba's Gross Domestic Product 2001 and its division over the major sectors of the district economy.

Indicator, for West Sumba 2001	Billions rupiah	Percentage of District GDP in 2001
Gross Domestic Product (current market prices)	482	100
Government expenditures	78	17
GDP produced in Agriculture, of which:	284	61
a. food crops' contribution to GDP	194	42
b. horticulture	34	7
c. forestry	0.8	0
d. livestock	50	11
e. fishery		1
GDP produced in:		
a. trade	14	9
b. tourism	1	0
c. mining	2	1
d. industry	3.5	2
e. building and construction	7	4
f. banking and finance	6	3
g. transport and communication	8	3

Source: Badan Pusat Statistik Sumba Barat 2003.

By far the largest sector is agriculture. In terms of employment – or daily activities of the population – 87% of the economically active population works in agriculture. This figure includes well-educated people who have not succeeded in finding a job corresponding with their education, who constitute an invisible, yet politically important category. The agricultural sector accounts for 61% of the District Gross Domestic Product, and 42% of the GDP is produced in food agriculture. The latter figure is highly fictive because a large part of food production is subsistence agriculture, which means that just a small part of the harvest is sold, while the bulk of it is kept for consumption or enters the barter economy, where food is exchanged for services (Vel 1994a:71). The government is much more dominant in the district monetary economy than these official figures suggest. Just the government routine expenditure is visible in the GDP accounts, 16% of GDP. The district government is the employer of the official civil servants, *pegawai negeri sipil,* and of numerous other employees with a minor status. It is also the institution that issues projects in infrastructure. The district government obtains its revenues – 155 billion rupiah in 2001, or 32% of the GDP – for more than 90% from the central government, through the General Allocation Fund (Dana Alokasi Umum, DAU).[7] A new district would have a new district government with its own share of DAU. The campaigners in West Sumba envisaged great opportunities for themselves and their under-employed relatives.

The past as a source of arguments for pemekaran

In the debate for or against the new district many historical arguments are put forward. What would make Central Sumba a meaningful entity? Administrative practice in the past could provide the answer. The history of administrative boundaries does not reveal what is now considered West Sumba as a natural social or geographical entity. The boundaries involved in the discussion about *pemekaran* were created in the past by state officials, and these boundaries shifted every once in a while.

The most constant type of area in Sumba is the traditional domain. This has always been the area referred to if Sumbanese explain other Sumbanese's identity to a third party: '*orang* Lawonda', '*orang* Loli'. 'Domain' is used in the anthropological literature to refer to traditional regions. Rodney Needham (1987:7) describes the characteristics of a domain on Sumba as follows:

> Its integrating force within a domain is the hegemony of a main village and of the leading clan of that village. This clan owed its power to its ancestral spirits (*marapu*) and the unity of the district or domain was manifested in the attendance at sacrifices and ceremonies performed at the main village by the dominant clan.

From the earliest accounts, Sumba is described as an island with permanent internal warfare. It appears there was strong enmity between the domains. The object of warfare was to capture food, horses and people. In the precolonial era land could have been the subject matter of internal disputes but not the object of warfare between two domains. The sharp borders drawn on maps of traditional domains are imaginary. A domain is defined by its centre and not by its borders.[8]

Taro Goh (1991) registered 16 domains in West Sumba and another eight in East Sumba. Other sources mention more: Meijering, Jongbloed et al. (1927:8) mention 29, whereas Oemboe Hina Kapita (1976:51-3) gives a more detailed sub-division when he describes the history of administrative divi-

7 Badan Pusat Statistik Kabupaten Sumba Barat 2003:252. In 2001 it was 92%.

8 This is the mandala form of polity (Anderson 1990).

sions. While living in Lawonda I noticed that people who originate from the domain Umbu Ratu Nggai still make a distinction between at least four domains within that area, which supports the larger number mentioned by Oemboe Hina Kapita.

What is important within the context of finding stories to support the idea of creating a new district is that districts can be made up of several traditional domains. Stories about the connection between these domains serve as an argument why they should be gathered within one administrative area. In the course of history many different larger administrative units were constructed on Sumba. Consequently, domains shifted from one unit to another.

Under colonial rule, which started on Sumba in 1912, the whole island of Sumba was one *afdeeling* (similar to today's district) of the Residency of Timor within the Dutch Indies administration. The colonial administrators considered the many traditional domains on Sumba, and chose one among the aristocrats *(maramba)* of each area to be appointed as king *(raja)* and this person subsequently acted as indirect ruler *(zelfbestuurder)*, for the colonial government. Sumba was divided before 1915 into three sub-districts, named *onderafdeelingen* (see Map 1). These in turn contained smaller sub-units called, in colonial terms, kingdoms or territories (*kerajaan* or *landschappen*). If one *landschap* comprised more than one traditional domain, the colonial government would appoint a raja from one domain with assistant raja from the other domains. Although traditional domains were autonomous, they were linked in various ways. Cooperation in warfare or protection against slave raiders from outside created bonds. Marriage alliance was the most important traditional way of creating ties between members of various domains. Oemboe Hina Kapita describes how the raja of Lewa Kambera in the mid-nineteenth century was in control of the whole area of central and East Sumba, because of marriage alliances with the aristocracy of all the domains in that area (Oemboe Hina Kapita 1976:33). The first administrative units in Sumba correspond with the area of influence of the major raja at that time. In 1915 West Sumba was split in two after Assistant Resident A. Couvreur studied the social structure in Sumba and decided to create Northwest Sumba and Southwest Sumba (see Map 2). In 1922 the two parts of West Sumba were united again, and what was called Central Sumba in those days merged into East Sumba (see Map 3).

The Dutch Protestant Christian missionaries also divided the island into several territories for their work. In 1930 they decided to subdivide West Sumba into West Sumba-West and West Sumba-East (Wielenga 1949:189), following the linguistic boundary that divides the area where the East Sumbanese language Kambera is spoken from the area of the West Sumbanese languages (see Map 4).

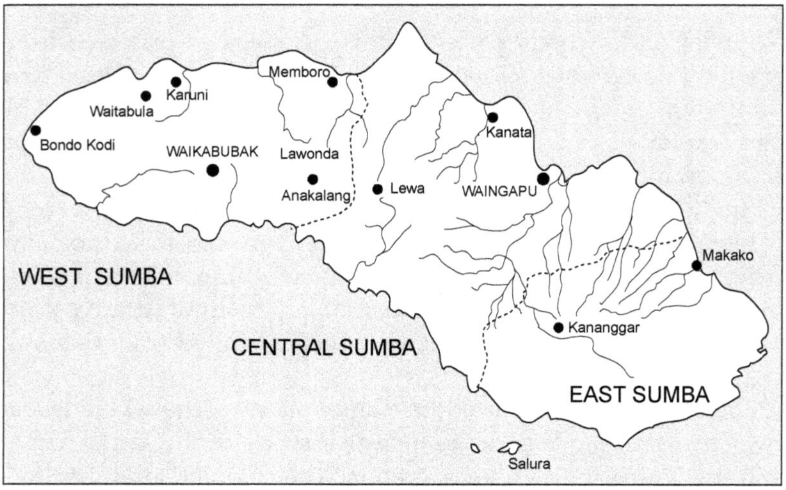
Memboro
Karuni
Waitabula
Bondo Kodi
WAIKABUBAK
Lawonda
Kanata
Anakalang
Lewa
WAINGAPU
Makako
WEST SUMBA
Kananggar
CENTRAL SUMBA
EAST SUMBA
Salura

a

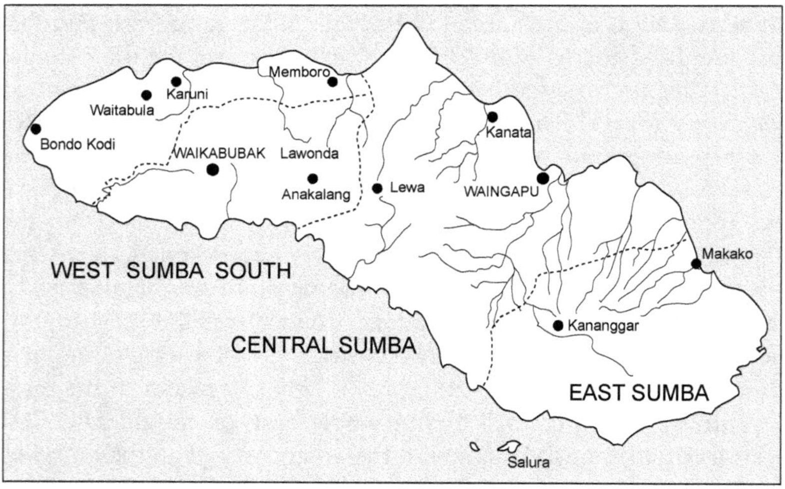
Memboro
Karuni
Waitabula
Bondo Kodi
WAIKABUBAK
Lawonda
Kanata
Anakalang
Lewa
WAINGAPU
Makako
WEST SUMBA SOUTH
Kananggar
CENTRAL SUMBA
EAST SUMBA
Salura

b

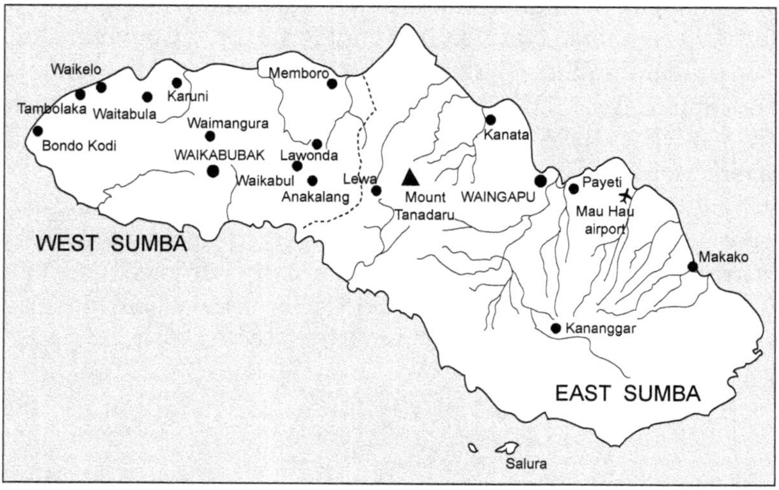
Waikelo
Memboro
Karuni
Tambolaka
Waitabula
Waimangura
Kanata
Bondo Kodi
WAIKABUBAK
Lawonda
Waikabul
Lewa
Anakalang
Mount
Tanadaru
WAINGAPU
Payeti
Mau Hau
airport
WEST SUMBA
Makako
Kananggar
EAST SUMBA
Salura

c

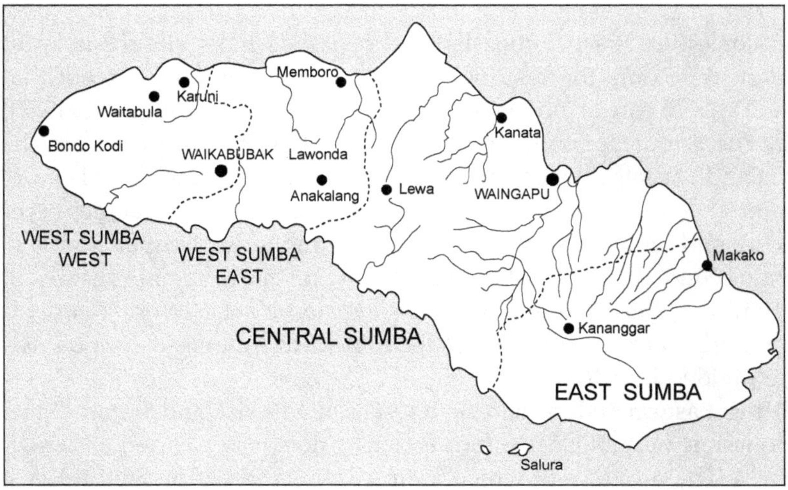

d

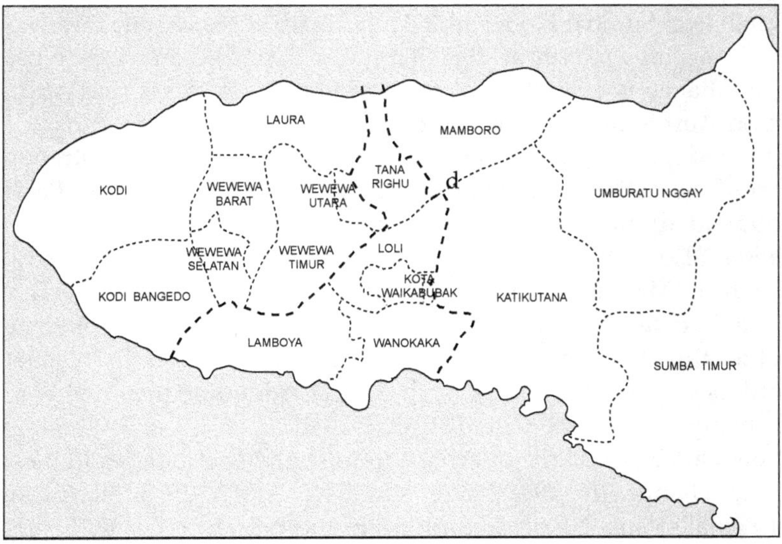

e

Map 4a. Government administration before 1915, 3 onderafdeelingen

Map 4b. Administration 1915-1922, 1 afdeeling divided into 4 onderafdeelingen (Kapita 1976: 620)

Map 4c. Administration 1922-2004, divided into East and West Sumba

Map 4d. Christian mission districts after 1930 (Wielenga 1949): 4 onderafdeelingen, West Sumba divided

Map 4e. West Sumba's subdistricts in 2004, with the boundaries of the proposed three new districts (bold black)

The missions area West Sumba-East corresponds most closely to what was intended to become the district of Central Sumba in 2002, except that sub-district Tana Righu is not included in the plans. Wielenga (1949:43) argued that the linguistic boundary separating West Sumba-West from the rest of the island was also the boundary east of which 'the landscape is more mountainous, sparsely populated, where animal husbandry is the main economic activity and which is less accessible for bringing the Gospel'.

After the Second World War Sumba was one of the 16 member states of the federation of Eastern Indonesian States, created by the colonial government to counterbalance the nationalist movement in Indonesia. Sumba was at that time divided into 16 *kerajaan*.

In 1950 the Eastern Indonesian States ceased to exist and became part of the Indonesian Republic. The former federation was divided into several provinces. The province of which Sumba was part became Sunda Kecil, which was renamed Nusa Tenggara in 1954. The province consisted of Bali, Lombok, Sumbawa, Sumba, Flores and Timor. In 1958 Nusa Tenggara was again divided, this time into three: Bali, East Nusa Tenggara and West Nusa Tenggara. Simultaneously Sumba was divided into two districts (*tingkat II)*, East Sumba en West Sumba, just as it had been before.

In 1962 the Indonesian government introduced a uniform administration in every part of the nation. West Sumba was called Daswati II Sumba Barat and was subdivided into several sub-districts replacing the former *kerajaan* or *landschappen* (also known as *swapraja)*. At first, there were only four sub-districts, of which 'Mau' was exactly what is now proposed as the new district of Central Sumba. Oemboe Hina Kapita (1976:74) writes that 'for some reason or other this division was not making governance easier'. The sub-district's borders were shifted and two sub-districts added, so that Memboro afterwards belonged to another sub-district.

In the New Order period the internal administrative boundaries in West Sumba did not change. In 1999, the six sub-districts of West Sumba were divided into smaller sub-districts, resulting in the present total of 15 sub-districts.

The most recent new administrative division of West Sumba was for the general elections. The general election committee constructed five electoral areas (*wilayah pemilu)*, each combining from two to four sub-districts, from which locally registered representatives would be chosen in West Sumba's parliament.

The fourth election area contains sub-districts that belong to three proposed new districts: Laura and Wewewa Utara to Southwest Sumba, Tana Righu to West Sumba and Memboro to Central Sumba.

A conclusion from this overview of Sumbanese administrative history is that boundaries of administrative territories were constantly changing in history. Therefore the idea of *pemekaran* as part of the decentralization discourse is nothing new. It seems to be just a new name for a practice that has been familiar for nearly a century.

Local rulers and the social forces behind pemekaran

Ancestry is the unifying principle in traditional domains. The ancestral spirits are called Marapu, and this term is also used to indicate the indigenous beliefs and ancestor divination. Spiritual specialists (*ratu*) are the ones who receive knowledge of the ancestors concerning every aspect of life. This knowledge appears in ritual speech, poems of paired sentences, and in rituals. The *ratu* know the procedure for each ritual, have the ability to indicate an auspicious time for each stage, and indicate the objects required to fulfil the ritual.

The *ratu* were not the political leaders of their clans. The nobility, *maramba,* held temporal power within each clan (*kabihu)* (Forth 1981:237), but this leadership was not a hereditary attribute of all noblemen. The leader in charge was someone of noble descent with excellent rhetorical skills (Kruseman 1836, in Hoskins 1993:44), and wealthy enough to be able to organize large feasts.

Traditionally, leaders on Sumba were only leaders within their own domain. This changed with colonial rule, when some of the *maramba* were appointed by the colonial government as raja or assistant raja, placing them into a larger structure and creating a new hierarchy.

> From the earliest contacts, Europeans have taken themselves to be confronted with territorial political units under the leadership of rajas. These regions were eventually consolidated by the Dutch colonial government, in 1928, into nineteen independent administrative districts (*landschappen*); but by indigenous criteria the boundaries of these were artificial and disputable, and within them there were in some instances more numerous territorial sub-divisions which had their own traditional claims to separate recognition. (Needham 1987:7.)

In the area that is proposed as Central Sumba the successive raja from Anakalang and Lawonda are the most famous local leaders. They serve as icons of the glorious past and their careers as proof of the superiority of the people of these domains. Some of their descendants are now active leaders in the campaign for Central Sumba, many others are not, while some even oppose the idea of *pemekaran.*

Umbu Tipuk Marisi is the most famous of the raja Lawonda. He was the first grandson of Umbu Siwa Sambawali, the first *maramba* appointed as raja Lawonda, from 1913 until 1932. Umbu Marisi studied at the Academy for

Government Sciences in Batavia (Jakarta). Upon his return to Sumba after the war he became Sumba's highest government official, chairman of the council of raja, in 1949. He delegated governance over his *kerajaan* Umbu Ratu Nggai to his assistant-raja Habil Hudang, who held the position until the system of governance was changed in 1962 (Oemboe Hina Kapita 1976:51). One of Habil Hudang's daughters is now the 'mother' in the lobbying committee for Central Sumba. The chairman of the committee for Central Sumba is linked to Habil Hudang's family through marriage alliance. Umbu Marisi moved to the provincial capital Kupang on nearby Timor Island in 1958 to become deputy governor (Pembantu Kepala Daerah Tingkat I untuk Sumba). His children did not return to Sumba to be active in politics.

The raja Anakalang's rule was restricted to *swapraja* Anakalang, until 1962, when Umbu Remu Samapati was elected to be West Sumba's district head (*bupati*). He delegated his task as raja to his brother in law Umbu Sulung Ibilona. Both Umbu Sulung and Umbu Remu sent their sons for education to Java. Umbu Sulung's eldest son Umbu Djima was district head in West Sumba for ten years, from 1985 until 1995. Afterwards he was a member of the national parliament for Golkar, until 1999. He is not an active supporter of the campaign for Central Sumba.

Umbu Remu's son, Umbu Sappi Pateduk, came back to Sumba in 1990 from Java. He wanted to live in his home area, to be able to combine his government career with his tasks as leader of his clan. He became the head of the district planning board (Badan Perencanaan dan Pembangunan Daerah, Bappeda) in West Sumba. After the 1999 elections it was the first time since 1958 that district heads were to be elected by the district parliament. He was not successful in the last elections, because he was just one among several Golkar candidates from Anakalang, struggling for the support of the same constituency. Support was divided and in the end the PDI-P candidate from further West in Sumba, Th. Langgar, won the position.[9] Frustration that 'Anakalang has lost power' is among the motives to create Central Sumba district. Umbu Sappi Pateduk was appointed in 2000 as member of the district head's staff (*asisten II*). He is mentioned as the top candidate for district head of Central Sumba, but he does not show official, open commitment to the campaign.

Burhan Magenda (1989:61-62) argued in his study of local aristocracies in the Outer Islands of Indonesia that they survive all changes in national politics and remain in power locally. In the recent literature on decentralization in Indonesia, all cases of *pemekaran* discussed reveal the strong interests of local elites, who act as initiators of the secession process, head the lobby-

9 Previously Th. Langgar was district secretary (*sekwilda*) in the district of North Central Timor, had always been a Golkar member but switched in time to PDI-P.

ing committees, and – if successful – occupy the offices of power in the new provinces or districts (Quinn 2003). Yet a more detailed analysis is necessary to reveal which members of the local elite are involved in campaigns for *pemekaran*, and which are not. The ones active in the campaign on Sumba were actually a small group. Closer analysis suggests that the older participants in the campaign were marginal members of the local elite: with sufficient status in traditional terms to be accepted as a leader, but with positions in government or the private sector that did not satisfy them, or put them outside the decision-making circuit. Leading people in the Central Sumba movement include a village head, a reverend suspended from his church office because of a long history of larger and smaller conflicts, and several retired civil servants. These are supported by a large group of well-educated, unemployed youths, who do not want to work in agriculture. These youths see the new district as an opportunity to get the jobs they hoped and studied for. In the short term the campaigning itself provides them with lots of excitement, which is otherwise hard to get in Sumba. They are very vocal and could become more powerful in their capacity to use violence and enforce social exclusion for political opponents.

The case of Central Sumba shows political action by a different group than the ruling local aristocracy, who are silent or absent in the story. That the campaign – at least until January 2005 – has not succeeded could therefore be an indirect argument in favour of the continuity of the ruling local elite.

Burhan Magenda (1989:50-5) distinguishes two types of regional elites: the commercial and landed aristocracies, of which the latter would fit an 'inland state' such as Central Sumba. This typology is very useful, especially in historical studies, because it pays attention to the great importance of material resources as the source of power. During my fieldwork and various visits afterwards I learned that people in Anakalang and Lawonda use a much more elaborate concept of 'local aristocracy'. In this local concept the raja dynasty is just one family of rulers among several. In the same area there are more noble families, and some of these other families are in no way – except in their historical connection to the government – inferior to the family of the raja. One other clan in Anakalang was famous for its ritual specialists, and at present its best known member is Secretary General of the Protestant Christian Church of Sumba. Yet another clan in Anakalang claims superiority as the clan of first residence, therefore they are the 'Lord of the Land' (Mangu Tana). The present chairman of the General Election Committee in East Sumba, who used to be a university lecturer in Java, is a prominent member of this clan. The local aristocracy, therefore, is not a monolithic institution, but it is a diverse group of local elites, who can either act in unison or compete among themselves. They are all connected through marriage alliances.

The Central Sumba story hints at changes in the criteria for local leadership. The definition in the anthropological literature on Sumba emphasizes traditional social rank and thus defines the local elite as those of noble rank, the *maramba.* Magenda, somewhat differently, defines the local elite in an 'inland state' like Sumba as the landed aristocracy, which evokes a rather static and singular definition of local elite, that focuses on internal sources of power and leaves out ties to other parts of Indonesia and influential connections within other spheres of society. On Sumba, land is no longer the most important source of power. The state has become more important than land. Political disputes are about state offices and funds. A district head has the means to employ thousands of relatives and has access to funds for buying support. Local aristocrats can only survive as leaders if they acquire additional qualities: a good education and a professional career, preferably a good position in the bureaucracy.

This argument leads to the necessity of potential leaders to create a strong political identity among their constituency, because kinship and marriage alliance might not be sufficient anymore.

Cultural and religious arguments for creating a new district

Elsewhere in Indonesia, local identity politics are often played out in terms of religion and ethnicity. In Central Sumba this is not easy to do, because the area is rather homogeneous in both those terms. Instead, as we shall see, local leaders conjure up identities out of less tangible materials. To do that, they need to possess highly refined oratorical skills.

Religious affiliation and ethnicity can both provide strong labels for creating political identity. Studies on violence in Indonesia give many examples of how these labels were used in defining the parties in violent battles (Colombijn and Lindblad 2002). Labels can only be helpful as markers of political identity when they provide a name for the shared characteristic of a group in opposition to other, neighbouring groups involved in contentious politics (D. Brown 1994:29).

Religious adherence as it is registered on the official identity card shows that more than 80% of the population of West Sumba adheres to one of the five religions officially recognized in Indonesia. According to the Statistics Office in West Sumba, 52% of the population was Protestant Christian in 2002, 27% Catholic, 3% Muslim and 18% 'other', which in Sumba means that they are open adherents of the traditional Marapu religion. The history of the Protestant Christian Church dates back to 1880 with the arrival of the first Dutch missionaries, and is rather comparable to that of Central Sulawesi, as described by Lorraine Aragon (2000). In both regions ethnic minorities – as seen from the national perspective – were converted, and the missionaries made major efforts in education and development. A difference between Sulawesi and Sumba however is that in Sumba there is no local Muslim majority, which might have stimulated a distinctive identity for the Christian minority. As a strategy to distinguish oneself from the inhabitants of the neighbouring territory, Protestant Christian identity does not make sense in Sumba. Christianity as a uniting characteristic of modern, educated Sumbanese, who are well connected to the Indonesian state, does make sense. Protestant Christian and later Catholic missions founded schools on Sumba, and the contemporary result is that the educated elite is connected through Christian networks without making a strong distinction between Catholics and Protestants. Catholics are found mostly in the western part of the island. If West Sumba is to be divided into three new districts, Central Sumba will be relatively more Protestant Christian and Southwest Sumba more Catholic. This argument is not used openly in the campaigns.

Ethnicity is a useful concept when Sumba is studied within the larger framework of the Indonesian nation-state. In a similar effort to deal with ethnicity, Aragon (2000:52) speaks of 'the fluid and concentric layering of self-identities'. The further from their homeland, the more ethnic identity is formulated in outsider's terms. But in Sumba it is hard to make external ethnic labels other than 'Sumbanese'. Exceptions to that rule are Muslim immigrants from other islands, and people originating from other islands living permanently on Sumba. For example the Savunese have their own language and in some villages in East Sumba they have their own hamlets, but their ethnic background was in 2004 not (yet) converted into a political identity.

One external definition of ethnicity on Sumba is found in the ethno-linguistic literature. According to an international team of ethno-linguists at the Artha Wacana Christian University in Kupang, who published *A guide to the people and languages of Nusa Tenggara,* there are eight Sumbanese languages, which they associate with eight different ethnic groups (Grimes et al. 1997:67-75). Violence in West Sumba's capital Waikabubak in 1998 took place between *orang* Wejewa and *orang* Lauli. However, these two groups are in the language guide both part of the Wejewa language area, where Lauli is mentioned as a dialect of Wejewa and its speakers consequently are not regarded as a different ethnic group.

Rhetoric and theatre in campaigning for pemekaran

Being a successful politician on Sumba is largely a matter of being the best orator. The style of rhetoric that works best is culturally determined and changes constantly. In 2004, political rhetoric in local election campaigns on Sumba and in the lobby for creating Southwest Sumba – which was in 2003 referred to as Sumba Jaya – was a combination of Christian sanctimonious talk, New Order jargon, quasi-ritual speech, colloquial talk and fashionable television language.

The 'People's congress for Sumba Jaya' on 29 April 2003 was the peak of the campaign for this new district. People from seven sub-districts gathered in Waitabula, West Sumba's second town after Waikabubak, and Sumba's Catholic centre. On this day representatives of all seven sub-districts delivered a declaration supporting and urging the foundation of their new district, Sumba Jaya. They offered the signed declaration to the members of the Jakarta Committee for Sumba Jaya with the request to take this 'will of the people' (*aspirasi masyarakat*) further upwards in the decision-making process.

At the event no representatives from the decision-making bodies – whether in Waikabubak, Kupang or Jakarta – were present, but the ceremony was carefully orchestrated with these people as the audience in mind. The Sumba Jaya committee made a VCD of the event, serving as a modern and lasting proof of the strength of their social movement. The VCD perfectly captures the political symbols and rhetoric that politicians on Sumba use in contemporary campaigns.

The documentary starts with the arrival on 25 April 2003 of the Jakarta delegation at the (only) airport of West Sumba, Tambolaka, which will be an important asset of the new district. The Jakarta Committee consisted of six members, four middle-aged men and two women, who were all born on Sumba – in the area that they hope will become Sumba Jaya. They pursued their education and careers on Java. The committee included an army officer who is a bodyguard of a recently retired general in Jakarta, a private businessman and two university lecturers. It has good strategic access to people in the Ministry of Domestic Affairs.[10] Upon arrival they wore suit-jackets made of West Sumbanese hand-woven cloth that looked so similar that they were as if dressed in 'uniforms of the traditional representatives'. The group set out to Waitabula in a convoy of jeeps, preceded by a cavalcade of motorcycles, a reminder of the traditional horse riders' welcoming escort but also looking like a modern youth gang. The documentary shows that shortly after their arrival the Jakarta Committee, together with the chairman of the local committee for the new district, set up a meeting with representatives from all areas in the new district to explain the strategies and agenda for the People's Congress. They reminded the audience that this was the 50th meeting in preparation of Sumba Jaya, a landmark, and an additional reason why the Jakarta Committee's presence was justified.

When the Jakarta delegation entered the field for the event on the 29th, they wore traditional dress combined with modern shirt. Although in a way

10 The next section gives a short profile of the committee chairman, Markus Dairo Talu.

they were the hosts of the ceremony, they got a seat in front as the guests of honour.

The groups from each of the seven districts arrived in trucks and small buses. Apparently the villagers were asked to come in traditional dress, and each group was preceded by dancers, who danced and shouted as if they were going to war. The official ceremony started with the Indonesian National Anthem. Then a Protestant Christian reverend explained to the audience in the local language that success can only come with the blessing of the Lord, and he said a prayer in Indonesian, in which he asked the Lord for support for the campaign for Sumba Jaya and his blessing on the People's Congress. Representatives of each of the seven sub-districts read their declaration, in Indonesian, after which there were a few minutes for dances and cheers, called *spontanitas*.

The shared summary declaration of pursuit toward the new district of Sumba Jaya was the core of the event. *Pemekaran* is a goal that needs to be established within the framework of the State, and this calls for state-like procedures. A female member of the organizing committee declaimed with the monotonous and theatrical voice of a well-trained Indonesian school teacher. After each part of a sentence she paused and all sub-district representatives and citizens present repeated the words, as if they were saying the Lord's Prayer (Paternoster) in Church.

In line with Joel Kuipers' opening statement in his book *Power in performance,* that on the island of Sumba a vibrant form of ritual speech is required in all ceremonial events (Kuipers 1990:i), the organizing committee of the People Congress in Waitabula invited a specialist in ritual speech to give a performance after the reading of the declaration.

The few Indonesian words incorporated into the couplet-style monologue indicated that the speaker had composed it especially for this occasion, to frame the message of the declaration in the vernacular Wejewa. On the one hand this was rather similar to the complete domestication of traditional culture familiar in the New Order, as it is described by John Bowen (1986) with regard to the appropriation of the concept of traditional self help, *gotong royong*. On the other hand it was also a way to add a type of rhetoric to the ceremony that livens up the audience and increases their commitment. Generally, political leaders rarely win support by rhetorical tactics and strategies that employ reason and rationality. Reason is dull and rarely moves people to action. Instead, according to Frederick Bailey (1983), it is passion that sways people.

The style of ritual speech is that of an 'angry man' (Kuipers 1998:49). Good ritual speech on Sumba is (very) loud, a constant stream of words without hesitation. It is also orderly, as displayed in the paired sentences of ritual speech. The performer at the Waitabula event did not completely succeed in attracting the attention of all. The audience were people from seven areas in West Sumba and from other areas – like Jakarta – so that many did not understand the words. Usually on Sumba, the audience enjoys 'traditional' performance invented especially for the occasion, because the performer mixes in lots of jokes. The Sumba Jaya 'ritual speech' was probably too serious.

Most of all the People's Congress in Waitabula was a display of the grass roots involvement which is formally the primary basis for *pemekaran*. Political leaders prove 'grass roots involvement' by getting a large crowd to attend the event. Leaders everywhere in the world use large crowds as the visible sign of support, to strengthen their political power. Kuipers (1998:74-5) calls this feature in the context of Sumbanese political culture 'the ideology of audience completeness'. Audience completeness confirms the authority of the leader. Conversely, a key image of a leader's social influence, prestige and status is the capacity to create a 'complete audience'. The completeness shows in the number of people who attend, in their evaluation of the way they are received at the event – most concretely measured in how many heads of livestock are slaughtered for the meals served to the audience- and in the volume and number of the verbal responses they produce during the leader's oration.

Campaigning for a new district is partly just rhetoric and theatre, set up by the initiators of the campaign, who need to do this to be acknowledged as leaders. The spectators enjoy it, it provides entertainment, good meals and fun. A people's congress or any other large gathering on Sumba does not necessarily imply that all the people present know what the event is about, let alone that they come because they support the officially stated cause.

Upward mobility and links with Jakarta

The Jakarta Lobbying Committee for the cause of Southwest Sumba is very important in the campaign for the western district. They organize, they initiate, they provide money, they provide campaigning materials, they lobby at the decision-making institutions in Jakarta and they return to Sumba every once in a while. Who are they and why are they interested in a new district on Sumba? Three examples present at least part of the answer.

Dr Manasse Malo lives in Jakarta, where he is professor of sociology at the University of Indonesia. He was member of the national parliament (Dewan Perwakilan Rakyat, DPR) until October 2004. He was born on West Sumba (Wejewa) in 1941 as the son of the first Sumbanese reverend of the Protestant Christian Church. He was a bright student and received a church fellowship first to study at the Christian University in Salatiga, Central Java, and to study theology in Jakarta. He was then lucky enough to get the chance, through international church connections, to study in the United States, and finally he earned his PhD degree at Wisconsin University. His wife is not Sumbanese, but born in Manado.

Manasse Malo has written and spoken widely on decentralization policy in Indonesia (Manasse Malo 1995). In 1998, fired by Reformasi, Manasse Malo was one of the founders of the Partai Demokrasi Kasih Bangsa (PDKB, Love the Nation Democratic Party), a mainly Christian Party, with a constituency predominantly in Eastern Indonesia. He was elected chairman. In the 1999 elections PDKB won three seats out of 35 in the district parliament in West Sumba, and five seats in the national parliament. In 1998, I heard about discussions among the Kupang members of the new party indicating that at that time they were in favour of making Indonesia a federation again.[11] Eastern Indonesia would be one of the member states, including even East Timor, and – according to their hopes or dreams – PDKB would become the largest party.

From 1999 up to the recent 2004 election period Manasse Malo was deputy chairman of the national parliament's Sub-Commission on Domestic Affairs and Regional Autonomy, and a member of the parliamentary committee that deals with regional autonomy. Now he is retired. He is a strong supporter of turning Sumba into a province, and the law requires a province to have at least three districts. He is the main source of information and the gatekeeper to all useful contacts in the bureaucracy in Jakarta. Now that he is retired he would not mind returning to Sumba, and be head of one of the new districts, or perhaps even governor of the Province of Sumba, 'if the people ask me to'.[12]

In 1999 Manasse Malo had a discussion with Umbu Dedu Ngara about their ideas on *pemekaran* Sumba. The latter was staff member of the provincial planning board Bappeda Nusa Tenggara Timur (NTT) in Kupang, and also heading for retirement. His home village is Lawonda in Central Sumba. His family is not the raja's, but certainly noble. The family members of his generation and younger are well-educated, most of them in Java. Umbu Dedu Ngara studied in Salatiga and was a board member of the Gerakan Mahasiswa Kristen Indonesia (GMKI, Indonesian Christian Student Movement), just as Manasse Malo had been.

Umbu Dedu Ngara conveyed the idea to create a new district of Central Sumba to several other provincial officials who originate from central Sumba, and they began together to lobby for it. They put the idea on the agenda at meetings of the Ikatan Keluarga asal Sumba di Kupang (IKAS, Union of Sumbanese residing in Kupang).[13] In the new decentralized structure the

11 Personal communication with Nico Woly, Kupang, december 1998.

12 Interview with Manasse Malo, Jakarta, 16-12-2004.

district has budgetary autonomy, and more decision power over many issues has been transferred to the district level, leaving the province with a mostly coordinating – and less powerful and rewarding – role. So the provincial elite had good reasons for moving one step downwards in the administrative hierarchy. Moreover many Sumbanese who have reached the autumn of their careers look forward to returning to Sumba, where they are cared for by their relatives, appreciated because of their status and relative wealth, and where they can die in peace and be buried in accordance with the prescriptions of tradition.

Markus Dairo Talu is not retired yet, since he is just in his early forties. He is an army officer with the modest position of adjutant, but the rewarding task of bodyguard for a major general, who was his master for many years. With his general, Markus served in the Presidential palace for some years. He is also a freelance security specialist, who acted as bodyguard for businessmen on their request, or as their 'debt collector', and as doorman for a fancy discotheque in Jakarta. This identity is not really known in Sumba. On Sumba, whenever Markus returns from Jakarta to his homeland in 2003 and 2004, he was the benefactor for the campaign for Southwest Sumba, and chairman of its Jakarta Lobby Committee. Sumbanese spectators see his love for the homeland and watch his wealth when he distributes T-shirts, caps and money. His life history is an attractive success story for those who do not belong to the aristocracy. Having lost his father, he lived with his mother and siblings in poverty in Wejewa (Waimangura). He was able to attend the Catholic school, and received a scholarship to attend a course on Java. There he met an army officer who became his mentor and introduced him to the army. In Jakarta he owns 4 houses, and provides housing and work for around 50 boys from his home area in Sumba.

What these three main actors in campaigning for the new districts have in common is that they were born on Sumba, received a good education and, with or without a church scholarship, pursued their education in Java. Consequently they had a successful career, after which they wanted to return to their home island, where they enjoy high prestige and status and social security provided by their relatives. They are connected through various modern networks: the political party, student alumni organizations, the Christian Church or the unions of emigrant Sumbanese in cities outside Sumba.

13 Interview with Manasse Malo, Jakarta, 16-12-2004.

Campaigning for Central Sumba

After Umbu Dedu Ngara and two fellow provincial officials paid a visit to Waibakul,[14] the capital of Katikutana sub-district (Anakalang), local elite members set up an organization to lobby for the new district, called 'Forum Komunikasi Pembangunan Desa' (Consulting Committee on Village Development), usually called simply 'the Forum'. Agustinus Umbu Sabarua, village head of Anajiaka (bordering the sub-district capital) became head of the forum. Its members consist of invited representatives of youth and women's organizations, village and church leaders, in short 'leaders of every segment of the population'. The Forum's tasks was to obtain: a. proof of the *aspirasi masyarakat* (popular wish), and recommendations from; b. the head of West Sumba; c. the district parliament; d. the provincial governor; and finally e. from the national parliament in Jakarta.

The Forum started by inviting representatives of all kinds of civil society organizations and local leaders around Anakalang for a workshop. The Forum's chairman said that the content of the workshop was to 'socialize regional autonomy', and explained the arguments for creating a new district. The main argument was that a new and smaller district would bring government services closer to the people, implicitly suggesting that those new services would correspond better to the population's needs and would be delivered faster and more efficiently. In this first workshop the participants discussed which other sub-districts could be invited to join in the new district of Central Sumba, since regulations at that time required a minimum of three sub-districts per district. The Forum's chairman phrased the main arguments for inclusion as 'a shared culture', which he specified as linguistic unity, and marriage alliances.

To the west the linguistic border is a real barrier dividing the people that speak Kambera from the people who speak the different west Sumbanese languages. But language is not a good basis for demarcating the eastern border of Central Sumba, since eastwards everyone also speaks (a type of) Kambera.

Marriage alliances on Sumba can be regarded as the cement between the (patrilineal) clans (*kabihu*), stating the rules and extent of social, economic and political solidarity (Keane 1997:51-6). Marriage alliances in Sumba are asymmetric, which means that a long chain of clans are tied to each other through marriage bonds. In this chain the bride-givers have special power over their bride-receivers (Keane 1997:54). All present political leaders in west Sumba have a known identity in terms of marriage alliances, and are

14 Umbu Dedu Ngara (Bappeda), Umbu Giku (Livestock Service, Dinas Peternakan), Agus Umbu Sulung (Bappeda) from Kupang. Interview with Gany Wulang, Waihibur, 4-2-2003.

interconnected in this sense. All the Sumbanese actors involved in the lobby for Central Sumba are connected by kinship and marriage alliances, including the campaign's most important man in Jakarta, Manase Malo, whose sister lives in the same village as the chairman of Central Sumba's Forum.

The second step in the process of the 'socialization of regional autonomy' was a workshop to inform and consult the leaders of all four sub-districts, or in the words of the Forum's chairman: 'to see whether they accept the conclusions that we already drew in the first workshop'.[15] The workshops were held in cooperation with NGOs working on democratization in 2001 and 2002.[16] The social work of these development organizations focuses on teaching local government officials and village communities about procedures and rights that the decentralization law has given them. The NGO staff are well aware of the difference between their civil education and the 'political games' of those who primarily seek personal benefit by creating new districts. Yet, local NGO staff are part of local society, and subject to pressure from the local elite.

The third step was a seminar with provincial government officials to assess the feasibility of a new district. The decentralization laws, especially Government Regulation no. 129/2000, specify a set of measurable criteria to decide whether a new district can be created or not. What counts is the availability of both natural and human resources, the number of inhabitants, size of the surface area, economic potential, the presence of civil society institutions and people's political participation, and also the level of infrastructural development and social services.[17] In November 2001, a Sumbanese lecturer at the Satiya Wacana University in Salatiga, Umbu Tagela, wrote:

> Law no. 22/1999 and the Government Regulation no. 129/2000, which provide all the rules with regard to the number of inhabitants and the level of economic growth and the way this should be calculated mathematically, surely leaves no option for splitting up Sumba into several new districts. Yet, if the number of inhabitants is decisive, the Sumbanese could easily fulfil the criteria by just putting off the present family planning policy. [But] would not that be an offence against national policy? And if low economic growth is the reason for not allowing a split-up, would that mean that in terms of politics Sumba is expected to be poor for ever? The real reason [for granting permission to new districts] is whether the ones in power have the political will to support the development of Sumba.[18]

15 Interview with Gany Wulang, Waihibur, 4-2-2003.

16 In the area around Anakalang workshops were organized by Yayasan Wahana Komunikasi Wanita (Waihibur/Waikabubak, Sumba), and Lembaga Bantuan Hukum (Maumere, Flores).

17 See Chapter III of Government Regulation no. 129/2000.

18 *Sabana* 7(10-25 November 2001):5.

In July 2001 the local *Sabana* newspaper opened with headlines reviving the age-old rumour of gold resources in Mount Tanadaru, in the interior of Sumba. The fact that this mountain is situated in Central Sumba made the news favourable to the prospect of the new district. Until this presumed gold reservoir is actually exploited it will do nothing to alter the unfavourable conclusion as regards feasibility of a new district, namely that there is no economic potential for Central Sumba.[19] Only 3% of the government income in West Sumba is derived from local taxes, the rest originates from Jakarta. There is one phrase in Government Regulation no. 129/2000, that can still be of support to the Central Sumba lobby. Chapter III, section 3, which formulates the criteria for the formation of a new district, adds in the final sentence the possibility of 'other considerations that enable the execution of regional autonomy'.[20]

The fact that with such a bad score on feasibility the case was not closed, leads to the conclusion that *pemekaran* must not be considered merely in terms of the administrative execution of a set of decentralization laws, but should be seen as a political activity. In May 2001, the Forum wrote a petition and a proposal, added a large number of supporters' signatures, and sent it to the district government of West Sumba, the Province, and to the national Parliament (DPR) in Jakarta. Manase Malo received the petition and stimulated the campaigners to continue their struggle, adding his advice on how to make the campaign more effective. He seemed dedicated to realize *pemekaran* on his home island. Indeed, rumour said, he dreamed of becoming the governor of Sumba, which would need the creation of another district first and afterwards a separate province. One of his pieces of advice in the early stage of lobbying was that the Forum should pay a visit to Jakarta to convince the commission's members personally of Central Sumba's viability. A group of 25 men and three women of the Forum therefore set off to Jakarta. At home the number of cynics was growing, but the delegation itself was wildly enthusiastic.

Ibu John was one of the three women in the party heading for Jakarta.[21] At 66 years of age she was the mother of the group. She is a daughter of the last raja Umbu Ratu Nggai, Habil Hudang. As a girl she was selected to be educated in the mission's school in Payeti, which was the best education available at the time and a guarantee for membership of the Sumbanese elite. From this group of Protestant Christian youngsters some went for further studies to Salatiga. Ibu John and her husband both studied to be teachers, and after their return they set up the Christian Senior

19 This was firmly stated in an interview with one of Waikabubak's leading Chinese businessmen.

20 *Pertimbangan lain yang memungkinkan terselenggarannya Otonomi Daerah*. Government Regulation PP 129/2000, Chapter III, section 3, pp. 129-200.

21 This section is based on my interview with ibu John (Rambu Moha) in Waikabubak, 20-2-2004.

High School (SMA) in Waikabubak. Many of the current politicians, government officials and members of Central Sumba's Forum are her former pupils, including the present district head. Ibu John has known Manasse Malo since they were young, he is her 'little brother' in the Sumbanese, educated, Protestant Christian elite. More recently, Ibu John and Manasse Malo had been in touch because they were both involved in Malo's political party PDKB. In December 2002 Ibu John attended the congress of this party in Jakarta and spoke about Central Sumba with Manasse Malo. He urged her to join the lobbying party to Jakarta.

They set off on 11 January 2003, first by ferry to Denpasar in Bali. There they went to Rocky Umbu Pekudjawang, a successful tourism businessman born in Anakalang,[22] to ask him for transport money to Jakarta. Ibu John related that upon seeing the tourist coach full of uncles, cousins and aunts, he decided to sponsor more than half of the costs of the trip. The party rested in Semarang, Central Java, where they were received by close relatives living there. They got a meal and food to go and an additional contribution of 2 million rupiah.

In Jakarta Ibu John was invited to give a speech to the members of the sub-commission on *pemekaran*. She told them, dressed in traditional Sumbanese style, about the hardship of the people living in this remote area to be named Central Sumba, and how far they were from essential government services, about their genuine wish to develop themselves, of the great potential of the land, and that the will of God was helping them. Touched by this emotional speech, and assured that their ticket would be paid, the commission members promised that their inspection team would pay a visit to Sumba within a short time.

The parliamentary inspection team from Jakarta visited Sumba on 31 January and 1 February 2003. When they landed in the capital of East Sumba, they were very politely received by the district head of East Sumba. He had already made it clear from the start that Central Sumba could never include part of the present East Sumba district, with the formal argument that *pemekaran* means dividing one administrative unit into two, not recombining bits of two districts. It was his interest to make sure that no part of his territory would be claimed by the new district. Subsequently the team was welcomed by thousands of people in Laikaruda, the event with which this chapter started. The Forum had 'motivated' the crowd to come and offer the best of traditional presents. The crowd's presence reassured the Jakarta team of the local people's wish for autonomy, and in traditional terms it stressed the Forum members' leadership and legitimacy to represent the population.

With the lobby straight to Jakarta, Central Sumba's Forum by-passed and therefore offended the district parliament. Thus one obstacle remained, for the final application procedure a recommendation from all levels was required. Whereas the national parliament's team was ready to give its approval, and the governor and parliament at provincial level were ready

22 Rocky Umbu Pekudjawang was also number one on the Golkar list for the national parliament in Nusa Tenggara Timor (NTT) in the April 2004 elections.

to issue the recommendation, the district parliament and the head of West Sumba were not. In Waikabubak, on 1 February 2004, the offended parliament of West Sumba treated the team very impolitely, without a proper reception, and the district head remained absent, claiming he had been summoned by the governor in Kupang.

In the meantime the West Sumba district government had also received a proposal for *pemekaran* by yet another part of the district. Sumba Jaya would unite seven sub-districts in the western part of West Sumba.[23] This part of West Sumba is the relatively more developed. The capital of Sumba Jaya would be Tambolaka, now known as the location of West Sumba's airport. Sumba Jaya would also include West Sumba's major harbour at Waikelo. The creation of Sumba Jaya would split the ever-feuding domains of Lauli and Wejewa (see Vel 2001), and would imply that very little would be left for the remaining part of the original West Sumba. In February 2003, Central Sumba's Forum was confident that Sumba Jaya's chances were poor, 'since the 15th of October 2002 was the deadline for submitting proposals and they were too late'.[24] Sumba Jaya's lobby appeared to be very strong, though, and if the legal criteria for *pemekaran* were to be used to assess feasibility, this proposal would stand a much better chance. The proposal for Sumba Jaya – whose name was changed to Southwest Sumba in late 2003 – increased the feeling of competition in West Sumba, and behind the stage, the hopes of success in Central Sumba began to decline.

A second complicating factor was protest from Wanukaka, where a movement sprang up to refuse participation in the proposed district of Central Sumba. The official arguments were that there is no history of Wanukaka being part of the same administrative unit with Anakalang, Umbu Ratu Nggai and Memboro. Trade relationships with the town of Waikabubak are strong. Waibakul as capital instead of Waikabubak would make the distance to government services for the population of Wanukaka even longer. This new development created tensions between Wanukaka and Central Sumba's proponents. A new sub-ethnic distinction emerged to explain initial support for Central Sumba by some people from Wanukaka: Wanukaka *atas* (upper) versus Wanukaka *bawah* (lower), where Wanukaka *atas* refers to the 10% of the population residing in the mountainous area adjacent to Anakalang, where marriage alliances are many.[25]

23 The seven sub-districts are: Kodi, Kodi Bangedo, Wewewa Barat, Wewewa Timur, Wewewa Selatan, Palla (Wewewa Utara) and Laura.

24 Interview with Agustinus Umbu Sabaruwa, chairman of the Forum, 5-2-2003.

25 Interview with Muana Nanga, director of STIE in Waingapu, 18-02-2004.

West Sumba's district head Thimoteus Langgar decided to create a committee to guide the *pemekaran* process for the proposed new districts. He appointed his deputy district head as chairman, and former district head Umbu Djima, from Anakalang, as vice chairman.[26] This team invited the Nusa Cendana University from Kupang ('team Undana') to make a feasibility study on the potential for West Sumba to be split into more than one district using the criteria from Government Regulation no. 129/2000 to measure the score of potential new districts. Undana's Team recommended three options for West Sumba. The first option was to split West Sumba into West and Central Sumba, the second to split into West Sumba and Southwest Sumba, and the third was to create all three new districts. Apparently to remain united in one district was no option.

The team formulated positive conclusions, supporting the lobby for creating new districts. However, two economists in Waingapu, Siliwoloe Djoeroemana – born in Anakalang – and Muana Nanga – born in Wanukaka – wrote a very critical review of the feasibility study:

> The team did not assess whether West Sumba fulfils the criteria for *pemekaran*, but instead focused on the new districts, parts of the present district. Government Regulation no. 129/2000 states that already existing data should be used, that are compiled by authorized institutions. Instead, the team gathered many new data, or used data from the sub-districts offices. The data themselves show a remarkable bias, positive towards a sufficient score for ability for splitting up the district. Compared to the official statistics published in *Sumba Barat dalam angka 2000* (Badan Pusat Statistik Kabupaten Sumba Barat 2001) for example the total length of roads has doubled. Also there seem to be 15,000 post offices and the like in Waikabubak only, which gives the impression the team counted the letters and not the post offices.[27]

After a number of demonstrations and a road block, organized by youth involved in the campaign and supported by some Forum members in Central Sumba on 22 May 2003, the West Sumba government finally agreed to give its recommendations, opting for three new districts, in what they called a 'win-win solution'. The district parliament added two restrictions before the recommendations would indeed be issued. Southwest Sumba had to reconsider its boundaries with West Sumba in order to make the division of resources, inhabitants and infrastructure more equal. Central Sumba had to reconcile with Wanukaka, to decide which of the latter's sub-districts would be part of the new and the old district.

26 Decree of the district head of West Sumba no. 379/2002, 31-12-2002.

27 My summary of Siliwoloe Djoeroemana and Muana Nanga, 'Catatan kritis atas draft laporan hasil penelitian Tim Undana tentang pemekaran kabupaten Sumba barat', *Suara Sumba* 3-6:6-7.

By February 2004 it appeared to be very hard to publicly criticize or even question the idea of Central Sumba in Anakalang. Those who did – like the critics of the Undana report – were accused of not being loyal to their place of birth, and in fact were threatened with social expulsion. In Sumba there were not yet – as elsewhere in Indonesia – private militias who are sent to make people change their opinion. Less severe, but just as effective, are exclusion from mutual help services, and bad rumours. Being elite on Sumba makes one by definition dependent on the services of many kinsmen and fellow villagers. Those elite members who live in the capital or even outside Sumba still count on their relatives to provide them with space and material for ceremonies like weddings, and eventually to provide them with a proper grave. Rumours that spread bad stories about alleged illness, accusations of being too old to think positively or being too estranged from Sumba to appreciate *aspirasi masyarakat* are effective to reduce authority. Youth play an important role in spreading these rumours. At the seminar on *pemekaran* in Waikabubak youth delegations openly contested the authority of highly educated speakers who were cynical about Central Sumba. The youth groups in Anakalang are strong because of their growing number. The most active members are unemployed, well-educated – with bachelors degrees from Java or Kupang – who do not want to work in agriculture and cannot find suitable employment. They dream about new districts full of new positions in government service.

In February 2004 it appeared as though the lobby for Central Sumba had turned more Christian. The lobbying group that set out to Jakarta comprised one Protest Christian reverend who said prayers preceding every next step in the process leading to the final positive decision on Central Sumba. Calling the creation of the new district the wish of God (*kehendak* Tuhan)[28] makes critics of the *pemekaran* opponents of the Lord. This is another type of threat and a means of social exclusion in a community where being regarded as a good Christian is similar to being respected. More ritual and Christian rhetoric also increased the theatrical value of the campaign, which could have been a deliberate strategy to compensate for the absence of sound, practical arguments.

On 26 February 2004 Manasse Malo was very pleased to receive a delegation of the West Sumba district parliament, the Forum for Central Sumba, and one for Southwest Sumba, as well several Sumbanese from Jakarta who brought the last requirements for the proposal to create new districts in West Sumba.[29]

Officially these requirements were a number of documents with the recommendations of all the offices involved as well as a description of the process of *pemekaran* written by the district parliament. In practice the

28 Interview with Ibu John (Rambu Moha) in Waikabubak, 21-02-2004.

29 *Sabana* 52(23-28 February 2004):1.

requirements included bribes at all levels. For Central Sumba this was a serious problem. The secretary of the Youth Organization for Central Sumba estimated that up to 23 February 2004 the campaign for Sumba Tengah had spent between 800 and 900 million rupiah on air tickets, food and bribes.[30] For Sumba this was an immense amount of money, whereas by Jakarta standards it was 'just cigarette money'.

The result of the meeting in Jakarta was that the proposal to split West Sumba into three – Southwest Sumba, Central Sumba and West Sumba – was officially put on the agenda for the plenary session of the national parliament to decide.

Unfortunately for the activists from Sumba, the campaigning period for the national election started early that March. The Minister of Internal Affairs dismissed all decisions on matters of regional autonomy until after the new parliament was installed, probably October 2004. In Sumba, as everywhere else in Indonesia, political campaigns from March 2004 onwards concerned the elections. Central Sumba's activists shifted their attention from *pemekaran* and concentrated on the elections for the district parliament in April, some of them being candidates themselves.

A second alarming matter was the revision of Law no. 22/1999. The minimal number of sub-districts in a new district was now raised to seven districts, which had to have existed for at least five years. For some time there was hope in Sumba that the decision for *pemekaran* in West Sumba would be taken before the changes in Law no. 22 took effect. However, the law was changed on 10 May by presidential decree. This makes it hard to believe that Central Sumba will ever be realized, although professor Manasse Malo was still optimistic in December 2004.[31]

The campaign for Central Sumba shows that to create a new district involves a long process, and success is not guaranteed. In the same period, since 2000, many other districts were created, which raises the question why it took so long for Sumba. That so many people and institutions have to provide their recommendation or decision, and the fact that they have to be 'motivated' to do so, is one explanation for the tardiness. Once the law on a new district is passed, the legislative bodies (and persons) have done their task and lose this opportunity for extra income. It would be interesting to see figures that relate the amount of expenditure involved in 'the cost of the campaign' – like the 1.5 billion rupiah of Tojo Una-Una (Cohen 2003:50) as compared to the lesser 900 million of Central Sumba – to the speed with

30 Interview with Adri Saba Ora, secretary of Forum Komunikasi Pemuda Peduli Sumba Tengah, 23-2-2004. For comparison: Margot Cohen reports that the campaign to create the district Tojo Una-Una in Central Sulawesi required 1,5 billion rupiah (Cohen 2003).

31 Interview with Manasse Malo, Jakarta, 16-12-2004.

which the *pemekaran* process took place. The fact that Central Sumba has not yet succeeded in becoming a district by itself does not contradict the opinion that all government decisions in Indonesia are for sale, but it could be interpreted as a sign that a district has a minimum price, which is too high for poor and small areas like Central Sumba to pay.

DIK ROTH

Many governors, no province
The struggle for a province in the Luwu-Tana Toraja area in South Sulawesi

Introduction

Pemekaran, or administrative fragmentation, formed an integral part of the process of decentralization and regional autonomy which unfolded in Indonesia since 1999.[1] *Pemekaran*, which was specified in Government Regulation no. 129/2000, has created new opportunities for political actors in provinces, districts, sub-districts and municipalities. In 2000 alone, the Department of Home Affairs and Regional Autonomy received requests for 13 new provinces and 44 districts.[2]

Decentralization and *pemekaran* are, too often, seen as unproblematic mechanisms of administrative reform, part of a transition towards predetermined structures of governance, contributing to development, democracy, civil society and good governance (see Aspinall and Fealy 2003; Turner et al. 2003; World Bank 2003). Similarly, political actors themselves tend to phrase such complex and contingent processes in terms of mechanistic routines based, of course, on a developmental 'vision and mission' (*visi dan misi*) and rooted in the 'aspirations of the people' (*aspirasi masyarakat*).

Others are more critical. Hadiz (2003b) criticizes mainstream decentralization thinking as belonging to a depoliticizing neo-institutionalist approach to development. Many authors stress that the outcome could also be more chaos, local power play, localized corruption, disintegration, and the emergence of 'little kings' (Hadiz 2003b; Kingsbury and Aveling 2003; McCarthy

1 Research for this chapter was financed with a grant from the Netherlands Organization for Scientific Research (NWO). Interviews with key political actors were held in Jakarta, Makassar, Tana Toraja and Luwu. I feel indebted to all who shared with me their views and opinions. I also thank Diks Pasande for his valuable assistance.

2 GTZ 2001a; Kingsbury and Aveling 2003; Sakai 2002; *Tempo* 28-4-2001; http://www.bps.go.id/mstkab/kab-2004-UU.pdf.

2004). They recognize the importance of analyzing such processes in their specific socio-cultural, political, economic and other contexts (Sakai 2002; Schulte Nordholt 2003). Only in this way a-priori assumptions about purpose, direction, or outcome of *pemekaran* can be avoided.

In this chapter I discuss the struggle for a new province in the Luwu-Tana Toraja region in South Sulawesi. Similar movements elsewhere in Indonesia have been remarkably successful. Bangka-Belitung and Gorontalo, for instance, quickly gained autonomy, while West Sulawesi was ratified in 2004.[3] Other autonomy movements are still struggling, with uncertain outcome. This is also the case with the struggle for Luwu (Raya) Province, which has generated a variety of lobbying activities, proposals, committees, meetings, press briefings, and (self-appointed) spokesmen, but all in vain. The province seems to be more distant than ever before. 'There are many governors, but no province', concluded one of the people involved. Recently the process was compared to 'pushing a broken-down car' (*Palopo Pos* 11-9-2004).

The Luwu (Raya) case is complex: political and economic power and control of strategic resources merge with differing perceptions of history and identity, defined along lines of religious affiliation or customary traditions and relationships. Elizabeth Morrell (2002) and M. Nathan (2003) have analysed the case. Morell is critical of the proliferation of autonomy movements, and regards them as symptoms of dissatisfaction that need to be taken (more) seriously. Nathan (2003:38) approaches *pemekaran* in terms of the 'original goal' of 'bringing the government closer to the people' and is too optimistic about decentralization, *pemekaran*, and the role of local elites in these processes.

Based on the Luwu case I will stress three points. First, *pemekaran* cannot be simply interpreted as the next step in a process of establishing a more democratic, transparent and development-oriented society. The struggle for a separate province is a multi-dimensional power struggle involving different actors and interests. Second, *pemekaran* should not be approached in an a-historical manner by isolating it from its socio-historical context. Instead, it should be analysed as a continuation of long-term processes of socio-political change under the new political conditions created by Reformasi. Third, the struggle for a province is not exclusively about political and economic power but is also related to processes of ethno-religious identification. These form legitimizing arguments in such power struggles but have, at the same time, their own social and historical meaning and dynamic. In the following section I will sketch the socio-historical context of the case and discuss earlier attempts to establish a province. Then I describe and analyse the recent emergence of a movement for Luwu (Raya) Province and two contending

3 Law no. 26/2004. See Morrell 2005; *Kompas* 25-9-04.

factions operating within it. In the next section I discuss the dynamic interaction between different agendas for administrative change both at district and provincial level. Finally, I zoom in on the hidden agendas of the conflict between the two factions in the movement and discuss the role of ethno-religious interests.

South Sulawesi, Luwu and Tana Toraja: a short history

South Sulawesi Province covers the south-western peninsula of Sulawesi. In 2003 it covered 62,482 km^2 (42% of Sulawesi) with a population of 8 million. It harbours four major ethnic groups: Bugis, Makassarese, Toraja and Mandarese. With more than six million people Bugis and Makassarese are the largest groups who live primarily in the southern part of the province. Mandarese live in the northwest and Toraja in the northeast of the province.[4] In the course of history, religion became a crucial ethnic marker. Common adherence to Islam among Bugis and Makassarese created an increasingly common identity. Bugis and Toraja identities, on the other hand, were deeply influenced by the different paths of socio-cultural change. The Toraja remained largely animist until the establishment of colonial rule and the arrival of Dutch Protestant Reformed Mission (Gereformeerde Zendingsbond) in the early twentieth century, and then massively converted to Christianity. Since many centuries Islam became a major formative element of Bugis-Makassarese identity. Relationships between Bugis and Toraja became dichotomized in terms of a contrast between 'pagan' and 'primitive' upland Toraja and Islamized and 'civilized' inhabitants of the Bugis lowland, and later of Christian Toraja and Islamic Bugis (Bigalke 2005; Pelras 1996; Volkman 1985).

Until 1959 Luwu was a kingdom governed by a *datu* (king) and is widely regarded as the cradle of Bugis culture. Though associated through myth and history with the Bugis world, Luwu is not an exclusive Bugis area. Court culture and language in Luwu was Bugis, but the majority of the population of Luwu speak Tae', the Toraja language. Based on kinship and shifting political alliances rather than on fixed territoriality, Luwu's relationships with other areas were dynamic and flexible. Luwu used to cover large parts of current Central Sulawesi (Poso), Southeast Sulawesi (Kolaka) and South Sulawesi (including parts of current Tana Toraja District and the southern Bugis lowland). Around 1605 the Luwu nobility converted to Islam and from the seventeenth century onwards the power of the kingdom declined.

4 Recent migration has changed these patterns. The Mandarese in West Sulawesi are no longer part of the province of South Sulawesi.

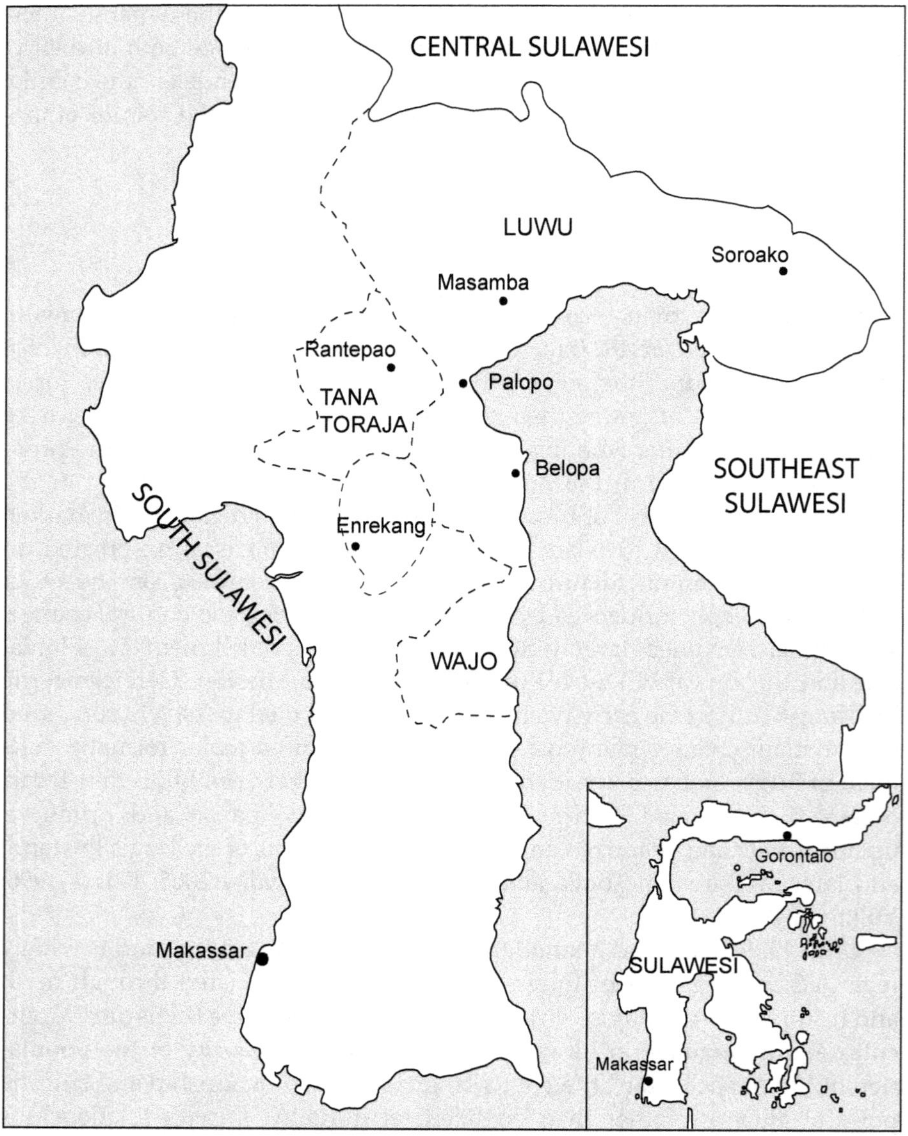

Map 5. South Sulawesi

Luwu and the Sa'dan highlands (current Tana Toraja District) are connected through sociocultural, political, and economic ties. The character and scope of these ties – expressed in myths of the divine and common origin of the early kingdoms of South Sulawesi: Luwu, Goa (Makassar) and Sangalla – varied between regions and historical periods. However, Luwu's claims of power over the highland population were not recognized everywhere (Bigalke 2005; Volkman 1985; see below). In 1905 Luwu was subdued by the Dutch and became a 'self-governing territory' (*zelfbesturend landschap*) under colonial administration. The kingdom was deeply affected by these changes: some existing ties with other regions were severed (for example with Wajo in the South and Poso in Central Sulawesi), while others were artificially created or strengthened. The Sa'dan (Toraja) highlands were incorporated into Luwu and divided into the sub-disctricts Makale and Rantepao. Thus, the Dutch had frozen the dynamic and shifting power relations in the area into a fixed structure of territorially defined administrative units.

In the 1940s and 1950s the administrative status of 'Makale-Rantepao' had shifted between greater dependence on and relative autonomy from Luwu. In the 1950s the area had lost its previous autonomous status. The tensions between Luwu and the highlands were sharpened by the outbreak of the Darul Islam rebellion. Under the leadership of Luwu-born Kahar Muzakkar, Darul Islam developed into a separatist revolt that held South Sulawesi in thrall between 1950 and 1965. From 1953, the movement shifted from a communist towards an Islamic ideology. The killing of Kahar in 1965 marked the end of the movement (Van Dijk 1981; Harvey 1974; Velthoen 2004). Recent developments in South and Central Sulawesi, like the spread of Islamic extremism, the entry of Kahar's sons into politics, and the emergence of the *sharia* movement indicate a possible link between the 1950s and recent developments of decentralization and *pemekaran*.

From 1953 onwards, tensions between the mainly Christian highlands and Islamic lowland increased and formed the context in which a broadly supported movement in the Toraja highlands demanded autonomy from the Luwu Kingdom. Highland autonomy from Luwu was finally granted in 1957 and effectuated in 1959.[5] Luwu and Tana Toraja emerged from this process as separate districts (*kabupaten*) of South Sulawesi.

Luwu has a special position in South Sulawesi. It is characterized by a complex mix of socio-cultural influences and ethnic identifications. Administratively it belongs to the Bugis-Makassarese world of South Sulawesi and is widely regarded as a Bugis area. However, historical ties with the highlands of current Tana Toraja have also formed Luwu culture, language and identity. Economically, Luwu is important for South Sulawesi.

5 Emergency Law no. 3/1957.

Before Luwu was split up in 1999, it was the largest of 21 South Sulawesi districts, covering almost 25% of the province. It is relatively sparsely populated, but rich in natural resources for agriculture, fisheries, forestry and extractive industries. These resources have attracted many migrants: Bugis and Makassarese from the lowlands and Toraja from the highlands.

A major cash earner in (East) Luwu is PT International Nickel Indonesia (PT INCO). In 1968 it was given a 218.529 hectare concession, more than 50% of which is situated in South Sulawesi while the remainder is located in Central and Southeast Sulawesi. In 1996 the contract was extended until 2025.[6] In 2003 the company produced 70,000 tons of nickel. With a growing world demand its economic prospects are bright. The regional income generated by INCO is a major trophy in connection with the politics of *pemekaran*. Currently the proceeds flow to South Sulawesi. However, if Luwu becomes a province, INCO proceeds will stick there. It will be clear that the province of South Sulawesi is not very enthusiastic about this prospect.[7]

During *pemekaran* of Luwu District, the nickel mines changed hands several times. In 1999 North Luwu split off from Luwu, gaining control over INCO. In 2003, East Luwu split off from North Luwu, taking over the mines (Nathan 2003). Mining, with INCO as the largest contributor by far, provided a considerable share of the Gross Regional Domestic Product (PDRB) of North Luwu in 2001: 57.86%. In the same year, INCO contributed Rp 4,8 billion in taxes. Morrell (2002) mentions a Rp 10 billion contribution to the South Sulawesi economy from INCO royalties in 2001. Though an estimated 60% flew back to North Luwu (where the mines were located then), the remainder was still of considerable importance.

In contrast, Tana Toraja is economically not as important as Luwu, but it is the main symbol of South Sulawesi culture to the outside world, and the main reason for tourists to visit South Sulawesi.

Decentralization and pemekaran

Government Regulation no. 129/2000 stipulates the criteria for administrative change in the framework of regional autonomy.[8] Formal objectives are: better government service, democratization, regional economic develop-

6 *Kompas* 7-1-2004. See K. Robinson 1986, 1999.

7 Morrell 2002; Nathan 2003. Nathan puts the importance of mining in perspective. In 2002, North Luwu received 20% of its revenues from local resources (90% of which INCO taxes and revenues). Central government allocations (Dana Alokasi Umum, DAU) contributed almost 60% of district revenues (Nathan 2003).

8 Government of Indonesia 1999, 2000. Government Regulation no. 129/2000 distinguishes between *pembentukan daerah* (the formation), *pemekaran daerah* (splitting), *penghapusan daerah* (abolishing) and *penggabungan daerah* (merging) of regions.

ment, better use of regional capacity, more security, and more harmonious relationships between centre and regions. It also mentions the preconditions for such changes according to various categories: economic, regional capacity, socio-cultural, socio-political, population, geographic area, and 'other considerations'. It specifies that a new province should consist of minimally three districts and/or municipalities (*kotamadya*). A new district should consist of minimally three sub-districts.

Recently, Law no. 22 and Law no. 25/1999, as well as Government Regulation no. 129/2000 have been revised and replaced with Law no. 32 and Law no. 33/2004. Throughout Indonesia lobbying movements emerged for new administrative regions, which were driven by the ambitions of local elites and did not automatically result in good governance. By posing stricter criteria, the revised Law no. 32/2004 reaffirms central control by throwing up barricades to this seemingly unlimited process of *pemekaran*. It does so by increasing the number of districts and/or municipalities minimally required for establishing a province (five), and the number of sub-districts required for establishing a new district. It also sets new time limits to prevent the acceleration of *pemekaran*: new provinces may split up after ten years, new districts after seven and sub-districts after five years.[9]

These quantitative criteria cause *pemekaran* processes at various levels to be interdependent and interlocked. Thus, *pemekaran* of sub-districts create the necessary conditions for district *pemekaran*. Increase in the number of districts can, in turn, form the basis for a new province. The dynamic interaction between these processes at various levels is also crucial in understanding the shifting political options, preferences, and choices in the struggle for a province in the Luwu-Tana Toraja area.

Sulawesi was also deeply affected by *pemekaran*. In 2000, Gorontalo Province split off from North Sulawesi,[10] while in South Sulawesi several movements for regional autonomy emerged.[11] The strongest demands came from the north-western and north-eastern parts of this province. In 1999, the districts of Mamuju, Majene and Polewali-Mamasa demanded autonomy from South Sulawesi and aimed to establish a separate West Sulawesi Province.[12] Around this time, the movement for establishing a province in the Luwu-Tana Toraja area also started making its demands.

9 Law no. 32/2004, chapter II, articles 4-5. Law no. 32/2004 was ratified on 15 October 2004. On the other hand, the law provides the new possibility for regions (whether province, district, or municipality) to attain the administrative status of *kawasan khusus* (special region).

10 Law no. 38/2000.

11 *Kompas* 28-10-1999 and *Tempo* (28-4-2001) mention five initiatives. See Morrell 2002.

12 Morrell 2002. Formally ratified by the national parliament on 22 September 2004. With more than one million inhabitants, it covers 16,796 km^2, 26.87% of the original province (*Kompas* 23-9-2004, 25-9-2004). Other initiatives emerged in the southern part of the province: Sulawesi Timur and Ajatappareng (Morrell 2002, 2005) 'Sulawesi Timur' was coined by three different

Luwu and Tana Toraja were also affected by *pemekaran*. In 1999, North Luwu District (Kabupaten Luwu Utara) split off from Luwu.[13] The new, reduced district of Luwu, with Palopo as capital, covers 3,247.77 km^2 with a population of 403,931 in 2001.[14] North Luwu, with Masamba as capital, covered 14,447.46 km^2 with a population of 442,267. In 2002, Palopo gained the administrative status of municipality (*kotamadya*).[15] Shortly after the establishment of North Luwu, lobbying started to establish a separate district of East Luwu (Kabupaten Luwu Timur) in the north-eastern part of the initial district. In 2003 this district split off from North Luwu and currently harbours INCO.[16]

Even relatively small Tana Toraja (3,205 km^2; 400,000 inhabitants) became the object of demands for *pemekaran*. Panitia Pembentukan Kabupaten Toraja Utara (PPKTU, Committee for Establishment of North Toraja District), representing seven sub-districts in north Tana Toraja, was formed in 2002. In September 2002, the request for a district was supported by the district head and parliament of Tana Toraja.[17] This initiative was soon followed by political lobbying for yet another district: West Toraja (Toraja Barat). Under the revised law of 2004, the outcome of these initiatives is uncertain.

When Luwu started splitting up, the movement for a separate province emerged. In 1999 demonstrations for Tana Luwu or Luwu Raya Province were held in Luwu.[18] According to press statements, Luwu (Raya) Province was intended to unify the area covered by pre-1999 Luwu and Tana Toraja. Unification of these areas would create a province covering 20,901 km^2 with a population of 1,189.757.[19] The emergence of this movement did not signify tensions between Jakarta and the regions but rather between the districts involved and the province of South Sulawesi (Morrell 2002).

political movements in South and Central Sulawesi: one in southern South Sulawesi (mentioned here); another in the north-eastern part of this province exploring political support for a province covering Luwu, Tana Toraja and Enrekang (see below); a third in Central Sulawesi, covering the eastern part of this province (see Morrell 2002).

13 Law no. 13/1999.

14 The capital of Luwu will shift to Belopa. Palopo is the intended provincial capital.

15 Law no. 11/2002 (10-4-2002).

16 Law no. 7/2003 (3-5-2003).

17 Keputusan DPRD no. II/KEP/DPRD/IX/2002 and Surat Bupati no. 136/1063/PEM/UM, 26 September 2002, tentang persetujuan pemekaran Kabupaten Tana Toraja.

18 The land of Luwu; Greater Luwu Province.

19 This equals 33.45% of South Sulawesi (62,482.54 km^2) before the establishment of West Sulawesi, and 15.56% of its 7.647,492 population. Badan Koordinasi Pembentukan Propinsi Luwu (BKPPL) Jakarta, Pembentukan Propinsi Luwu Raya, 2000.

Earlier provincial ambitions: Toraja Raya and Lutat

The current struggle for a province in the Luwu-Tana Toraja region and the various competing options involved did not simply fall out of the blue. Political ideals of establishing a province have a history that goes back to the colonial period. The recent political processes can only be understood if they are placed within this broader regional historical context. In this respect, two political movements stand out: Toraja Raya (Greater Toraja) and Lutat.[20]

Toraja Raya refers to political ambitions emerging in the context of changes related with the colonial period, revolution and decolonization, Darul Islam, the demise of the Luwu Kingdom and the fixation of administrative boundaries that remained in place until the late 1990s. Toraja Raya had its roots in colonial transformations in the Luwu-Tana Toraja area, especially in connection with the Dutch Reformed Mission (Gereformeerde Zendingsbond). While lowland Luwu had been under Islamic influence since the early seventeenth century, the highlands of current South and Central Sulawesi had an animist population. The colonial government stimulated missionary activity in the highlands out of fear for 'advancing' Islam, which required the formation of a Christian 'buffer' (Bigalke 2005). Such a buffer zone was established through an administrative unit covering the highlands of current South and Central Sulawesi called Grooter Toradja (Greater Toraja). From the 1930s, this idea took root among a Dutch-educated, Christianized section of the population of current Tana Toraja, who increasingly identified as 'Toraja people'. Gradually, they took up positions in the colonial and post-colonial administrative system and became politically active. Affiliated to the Toraja Church (Gereja Toraja) and the regional branch of the Indonesian Christian Party (Parkindo), they were active propagators of a Toraja identity. In the 1950s, the political ideal of Greater Toraja continued to influence regional politics. In its post-colonial form, 'Toraja Raya' was also an expansive movement associated with the search for Lebensraum, or land for densely populated Tana Toraja, and greater political influence in Luwu. Another major political objective was (mainly Christian) highland autonomy from (mainly Islamic) Bugis southern Sulawesi domination (Bigalke 2005; Roth 2002, 2003, 2004).

Lutat refers to attempts in the early 1960s to establish a province combining Luwu and Tana Toraja. The Lutat concept had been developed by Java-based intellectuals from these districts. Its political objective was also gaining provincial autonomy from South Sulawesi. It was based on a similar awareness of the mutually supportive and complementary resources of Luwu (land, other resources) and Tana Toraja (labour, educated people). However, where Toraja Raya had been the product of processes of ethnic identification

20 Lutat is short for Luwu Tator. Tator is short for Tana Toraja (Roth 2002, 2003, 2004).

along the dividing line of religion, Lutat stressed common socio-cultural and historical ties between highland and lowland populations across existing administrative boundaries. The Jakarta-based people behind Lutat were of a younger generation and less influenced by Lebensraum-politics.

Lutat enjoyed broad support among the Luwu and Toraja elites. In the early 1960s the movement mobilized ample political support from the region and resolutions supporting Lutat were prepared in both districts. The movement stressed the non-separatist character of Lutat and clearly distinguished the movement from regionalist movements like Darul Islam. Andi Jemma, last Datu of Luwu and *pahlawan* (hero) during the revolution, became the figure head of this movement. In 1963, President Soekarno had even expressed his sympathy and support. However, Lutat did not materialize, due to the political turmoil of the 1960s and probably also because of South Sulawesi's resistance (Roth 2002, 2003, 2004).

Luwu (Raya) Province: shared political ideal or bone of contention?

The political changes after 1998 sparked off provincial ambitions in Luwu. But the boundaries of the new province were highly contested and the movement was eventually deeply divided. The issue of inclusion or exclusion of Tana Toraja was the cause of this disagreement, and I will analyse the organizations lobbying for one option or the other at different locations: Jakarta, Makassar, Luwu and Tana Toraja. I will also discuss the contrasting narratives used to legitimize the different options for the province and relate them to the regional context.

According to a Luwu newspaper, Luwu Raya should encompass Luwu, North Luwu and Tana Toraja as 'these three districts form from a cultural-historical point of view still a unity. In geographical terms, the districts were once united in the Luwu Kingdom.' The newspaper also stressed that demography, human potential and natural resources support its formation (*Sawerigading Pos* 1-11-1999). Early 2000, the Front Penuntut Pemekaran Kabupaten dan Pembentukan Propinsi Luwu Raya (FPPDP-LR, Front for the Demand of District Autonomy and Formation of Luwu Raya Province) was established in Palopo.[21] It stressed the need for *pemekaran* and the formation of Luwu Raya within the old boundaries of the former Luwu Kingdom. The document refers to earlier attempts by Andi Jemma in the 1950s to establish a special area (*daerah istimewa*), and in the 1960s to form a province. It says that Luwu Raya should comprise the districts emerging from *pemekaran* of pre-

[21] Front Penuntut Pemekaran Kabupaten dan Provinsi Luwu Raya (FPPDP-LR), Rencana wilayah Propinsi Luwu Raya, wilayah Kerajaan Luwu 1918-1957, project proposal, 2000.

1999 Luwu.[22] In a formal request for provincial autonomy FPPDP-LR defines the province as 'consisting of the districts of Luwu and North Luwu, and the Municipality of Palopo, separated from South Sulawesi but still under protection of the beloved unitary state of the Republic of Indonesia'.[23] The proposal also contains several letters of support. One 'Deklarasi Provinsi Tanah Luwu' is signed by the Makassar-based chairman of the Kerukunan Keluarga Luwu (KKL, Association of Luwu People) and Ikatan Pelajar Mahasiswa Indonesia Luwu (IPMIL, Indonesian Association of Luwu Students).[24] Another one, which uses the term 'Luwu Raya' rather than 'Tanah Luwu', is signed by the Datu, the district heads of Luwu and North Luwu, the chairmen of the Luwu and North Luwu parliaments, and (again) the chairman of KKL in Makassar. The letter states that the former Luwu kingdom, defined as covering pre-1999 Luwu, should be the basis of Luwu Raya.[25] Other letters, in the name of political parties, NGOs and other organizations in Luwu also base their support for 'Luwu Raya' on this 'narrow' interpretation.[26] The regional press also regularly covered the campaign for a new province. Usually it defined the province as consisting of post-*pemekaran* Luwu and North Luwu, and East Luwu and Palopo (the latter two still to be formed then) (*Fajar* 4-11-1999, 7-2-2000; *Palopo Pos* 1-5-2000).

Thus, Tana Toraja was hardly mentioned in the first statements which favoured the new province (*Kompas* 26-2-2001). Luwu had just been split up into two districts, and the province stood a real chance under the new political conditions. The first priority for reaching this objective was to further increase the number of districts. Primary candidates were East Luwu and Palopo. At this stage, the struggle for a province and lobbying for another new district and a municipality were mutually supportive dimensions of the political agenda of FPPDP-LR.[27] The *pemekaran* of Luwu was assumed to create ideal conditions for establishment of Luwu Province.

22 Letter 27-1-2000. In this letter and another one dated 27-4-2000, Tana Toraja is not part of the plans.

23 Letter FPPDP-LR-Palopo dated 1-7-2000. Tana Toraja was not part of the proposed province.

24 The KKL chairman became closely associated with the movement that rejects Tana Toraja (see below). IPMIL is a political lobbying organization with an Islamic identity in which Makassar-based Luwu students are organized.

25 The name of the Datu under a letter giving this narrow interpretation is remarkable. Attempts to replace it with a broader one including Tana Toraja led to a conflict within the movement; see below (letter 22-1-2000).

26 Letters 22-1-2000, 22-5-2000 and 25-3-2000 respectively.

27 Later, contradictory interests became visible; see below.

The Jakarta-based movement

A different conceptualization of the province was being developed in Jakarta. As in the 1960s, Luwu Raya was buzzing around among the Jakarta-based Luwu and Toraja communities after 1998. The older generation is still quite prominent: some of the current political activists had also been involved in the Lutat movement. The Luwu and Toraja elites in Jakarta were mainly guided by a vision of a province that resembled Lutat: a vision that included Tana Toraja. The Jakarta-based movement became organized in the Badan Koordinasi Pembentukan Propinsi Luwu-Raya (BKPPLR, Coordinating Body for the Formation of Luwu Raya Province).[28]

In 2001 the Jakarta group presented its plans for Luwu Raya (including Tana Toraja) (*Suara Pembaruan* 1-4-2001; *Media Indonesia* 1-4-2001). The declaration, on behalf of the Datu, was historically legitimized by reference to the Luwu Kingdom as an administrative unit under colonial rule which included current Tana Toraja and the historical ties between the areas. Further, it stressed that the movement emerged from the aspirations of the people of Luwu, North Luwu and Tana Toraja. The new province was to comprise of six districts and municipalities.[29] If realized, it would combine a high potential of natural and human resources with other economic assets like tourism. It would have (in 2001) a locally raised revenue (Pendapatan Asli Daerah, PAD) of Rp 45 billion, cover 20,901 km^2 (33.5% of South Sulawesi), and have a 1.189,775 population (15% of its 2001 population). A Jakarta-based spokesman with a Luwu background stated:

> The source of inspiration for Luwu Raya is the history of the Luwu Kingdom and the dedication of its Datu, Andi Jemma, to the ideal of turning Luwu into a special region or a province. He wanted to keep the kingdom together as much as possible. Even in the fifties he had conveyed his ideal to the president. Later, the Lutat-movement continued this struggle in the name of Andi Jemma. With the existing districts and municipalities we can create a province to make this come true. Another ideal of Andi Jemma, a nationalist, was not to discriminate on the basis of ethnicity or religion. If we want a province based on former *afdeeling* Luwu, both Luwu and Tana Toraja should be included.

In Jakarta there was a more broadly shared vision among Luwu and Toraja people. Consensus had more or less been reached on issues like the name,

28 Formally the coordinating body of the regional organizations in Makassar, Luwu, Tana Toraja and North Luwu. Its working programme assumed establishment in December 2001.

29 'Deklarasi pembentukan Propinsi Luwu Raya', Jakarta, 31-3-2001. Andi Achmad Opu To Addi Luwu, Pemangku Datu Luwu; 'Pernyataan Andi Achmad Datu Luwu', Makassar, 12-3-2001.

capital, and regional background of the first governor of the province. But even here such issues proved to be sensitive. Like in South Sulawesi, competition between Luwu and Tana Toraja and anxieties associated with religious identities played a role in the capital as well. According to one person 'it took us a year to reach an agreement about the name of a province, which was still beyond reach'.[30]

The region: Tudang Sipulung

On 17 October 2001 a so-called Tudang Sipulung meeting was held in the 'palace of the king of Luwu' in Palopo.[31] It was attended by district heads and other government representatives of Luwu, North Luwu and Tana Toraja, chairmen of the parliaments, and representatives of various groups in society, NGOs, students and youth organizations. Some Jakarta-based supporters were also present. The Datu opened the meeting:

> *Afdeeling* (the administrative unit) Luwu covered part of Southeast Sulawesi (Kolaka) and Central Sulawesi (Poso). In South Sulawesi, it covered current Luwu, North Luwu and Tana Toraja. Law no. 22/1999 and Government Regulation no. 129/2000 give as a criterion for the formation of a province a minimum of three districts or municipalities. Consisting of Luwu, Luwu Utara and Tana Toraja, former *afdeeling* Luwu certainly fulfils these criteria [...] That is why three district heads and chairmen of the regional parliaments of the districts that cover the area [...] are present at this Tudang Sipulung to sit together in a familiar atmosphere of togetherness and equality, and discuss the strategic steps to promote the idea of the formation of a province. As a person who feels the pulse of struggle, I do not want the land of Luwu to be torn into pieces only because of certain group interests.[32]

Though most participants were in favour of including Tana Toraja, some youngsters openly voiced their objections. One young attendant objected because of the Christian background of the Toraja population. According to some participants, the opponents had been instructed by the Makassar-based group struggling for Luwu Province, and were students of Makassar universities, known as *tukang protes* (protest experts). Despite these critical voices, the document summarizing the decisions states, among others, that agreement has been reached on formation of Luwu Raya Province consisting

30 Naming options: 'Lutat' expresses inclusion of Tana Toraja. 'Luwu Raya' can be interpreted in contradictory ways (Greater Luwu/Luwu Toraya). 'Luwu' is Luwu-biased. Geographical names create confusion (for example Sulawesi Timur).

31 Tudang Sipulung is Buginese for 'sit and discuss together'.

32 Pidato pembukaan Pemangku Datu Luwu (Andi Achmad Opu To Addi Luwu) dalam acara Tudang Sipulung di istana Datu Luwu, 17-10-2001.

of Luwu, Luwu Utara, and Tana Toraja.[33]

A similar meeting had been held in Tana Toraja. In June 2001, a statement had been sent to the Tana Toraja parliament, mentioning socio-cultural and historical arguments (Lutat; the Toraja as one of twelve ethnicities of the Luwu kingdom) in favour of the formation of a province together with Luwu and Luwu Utara.[34] It also pleaded for a name that clearly reflects the role of Tana Toraja. It mentioned two possibilities: first, Luwu-Tana Toraja (Lutat); second, Luwu Raya, in which the 'Raya' stands for Tana Toraja.[35]

Thus, the Tudang Sipulung process yielded a widely but not fully supported decision about Luwu and Tana Toraja merging into Luwu Raya Province. Point of departure was a specific vision of the history of the kingdom under colonial rule, as an administrative division that included current Tana Toraja.

Heading for conflict: 'Committee' and 'Front'

Around 2001, struggle for the establishment of the province was taken up by a group of Makassar-based people with a Luwu background, mainly intellectuals active in KKL (see above). At the initiative of the KKL, a Makassar-based committee was established: Komite Pusat Pembentukan Provinsi Luwu (KP3L, Central Committee for the Formation of Luwu Province).[36] A spokesman stressed in this context the specific Luwu ethnic and cultural values, and the need to protect them. Another spokesman, closely affiliated to KKL and rector of the Universitas Muslim Indonesia (UMI, Muslim University of Indonesia), also stressed the Luwu identity of the new province and added that 'from a socio-cultural point of view, the people of Luwu are indeed disappointed with South Sulawesi'.[37]

So, the issue whether to include or exclude Tana Toraja started to divide the movement. The establishment of KP3L was a turning point for it no longer assumed a role for Tana Toraja as its spokesmen tend to use the terms 'Provinsi Luwu', 'Tana(h) Luwu' or 'Wija To Luwu' (the people of Luwu) rather than

[33] Tudang Sipulung rakyat Luwu Raya (rakyat Luwu, Tana Toraja dan Luwu Utara); Keputusan musyawarah, Palopo, 17-10-2001.

[34] Badan Koordinasi Pembentukan Propinsi Luwu Raya Wilayah Tana Toraja, 3-6-2001. See also Musyawarah Pembentukan Propinsi Luwu Raya; Aspirasi masyarakat Kabupaten Tana Toraja tentang pembentukan propinsi baru 'Luwu Raya', Tana Toraja, 15-10-2001.

[35] The document stresses that '"Raya" is a recognition of the existence of Toraya'.

[36] *Kompas* 26-2-2001. Though called 'central', KP3L is Makassar-based.

[37] *Kompas* 26-2-2001; *Tempo* 28-4-2001. The Luwu-based section of KP3L is the Komite Pembentukan Provinsi Luwu (KP2L). In 2003 another section was formed in Palopo, also supporting exclusion of Tana Toraja. Panitia Deklarasi Provinsi Luwu, Palopo, 28-6-2003.

'Luwu Raya' (which is used by those who want to include Tana Toraja). In reaction to the emergence of the Makassar group ('the Committee'), the Front Perjuangan Pembentukan Provinsi Luwu, (FP3L, Front for the Struggle for Formation of Luwu Province or 'the Front') was established in Palopo in 2003, in support of a province that includes Tana Toraja.[38] Here follow accounts of a Makassar-based KP3L representative, a Luwu-based Committee spokesman, and a Front spokesman. First the Makassar based KP3L member:

> Our point of view has to do with the past. In the fifties, the Toraja separated themselves off from Luwu. Now the Luwu people do not want to join with them. Representing the aspirations of the people, we have to listen to their opinion. In Jakarta it is different: they broadly agree that Luwu has to join with Tana Toraja [...]. We have already discussed the issue with the people in Luwu, and they simply do not want it. They say 'Luwu is Luwu only' [...]. For the old generation, Luwu and Tana Toraja are indeed one. But for younger generations things are quite different. It is a pity that there is this political background, of the Toraja stabbing their own brothers. Though we are regarded as ethnically the same, the people have a different perception of that as well. But it is not a religious problem.

The Luwu-based spokesman of the Committee:

> Looking at the history of Luwu [...] we must stress that its name was the Luwu kingdom. This must also be the basis for the new province, there is no alternative. We must consider Luwu's possible future as a province, and its advantages [...]. But the process should not only involve people associated with the kingdom and its past. This should be a more comprehensive discussion, involving religious leaders, leading persons in society and politicians. Nobody has more rights to speak than others; the spirit of change and struggle for the province are shared by all. The Front bases itself on the Tudang Sipulung, but this meeting did not accommodate all components. The Committee has gone down to the grassroots [...] Luwu should be the basis of the province. Luwu can build a province on its own. We are four now: three districts and a municipality. Later, if they wish to join the province, let them apply. Did anyone order them to separate themselves off from Luwu in 1957? We did not tell them to do so; it was their own wish to leave us!

A Palopo-based Front member:

> The Committee stresses that three districts is enough for a province. But there are other reasons and motivations behind it. The difference in religion is very important. The issue of religion, though never openly mentioned, was introduced by the Makassar-based Committee and their Luwu-based supporters. Further, those who support the Committee are afraid that well-educated people from Tana Toraja will beat them in the competition for power, positions and resources. Counting the number of Toraja people in Tana Toraja and Luwu, they fear Toraja political victories in future elections for crucial positions in the province.

38 Front Perjuangan Pembentukan Propinsi Luwu (FP3L), Palopo, 9-8-2003.

Thus, a fission emerged between Committee and Front. There is common ground in the use of historical arguments to legitimize a new province, whether including or excluding Tana Toraja: the glorious past of the kingdom, promises by President Soekarno, and the role of Andi Jemma. A respected nationalist, he represents the kingdom, nationalist values, and the ideal of Luwu Province. The stress on his nationalist spirit and values is crucial in the current struggle. It is no coincidence that the lobbying for formal recognition of Andi Jemma as a national hero (*pahlawan nasional*) coincided with the struggle for a province.[39] Presenting regional political ideals in a nationalist spirit of cooperation with other provinces and Jakarta rather than in terms of separatism is crucial, especially for South Sulawesi and Luwu, former basis of Darul Islam and current setting of Islamic political and military activism.

Another shared historical argument in favour of a new province concerns the neglect, exploitation and discrimination by South Sulawesi. While Luwu contributes considerably to the provincial income, little has been done for its development. Educated people from Luwu and Tana Toraja are never given a chance to develop a government career and climb to leading positions in Makassar (see Nathan 2003). These problems are largely blamed to 'BOSOWA', the regionally powerful political and economic elites of the Bugis areas in South Sulawesi.[40] The new province would create new opportunities for the population and speed up development by shortening the lines of governance.

Beyond these general legitimizing and, to some extent, unifying stories, the differences between Committee and Front stand out. Both parties actively engage in inventing and re-inventing history. The Front bases its view on the Luwu Kingdom as a colonial administrative unit that included Tana Toraja. Thus, the colonial definition of the kingdom, once resisted in the highlands, is now idealized and mobilized to support Luwu Raya. The Committee, however, stresses not so much common bonds and shared values, but rather factors that have come to divide both areas and their populations. Arguments about differences in culture and a history of competition for resources merge with an interpretation of history in which the struggle for administrative autonomy of Tana Toraja from Luwu in the 1950s is presented as a stab in the back of the Luwu people.

Early 2004, the Badan Koordinasi Perjuangan Pembentukan Provinsi Luwu (BAKOR-P3L, Coordinating Body for the Formation of Luwu Province)

[39] In 2002, Andi Jemma became a national hero. Muslim Massewa 2002; *Suara Merdeka* 9-11-2002.

[40] BOSOWA stands for Bone Soppeng Wajo, Bugis districts in South Sulawesi.

was established in Palopo to bridge the gap between Front and Committee.[41] Little has changed since then, and no serious steps towards reconciliation have been taken. The BAKOR-P3L clearly awaited the new government regulations for *pemekaran*. Its chairman stresses that the cultural and historical relations between Luwu and Tana Toraja should be taken into account in discussions about the province, if only because otherwise the movement would lose support from the Jakarta-based group.

In October 2004, the revised law on regional autonomy was ratified. The BAKOR-P3L took a pragmatic stance, adapting to these new legal realities. Recently, *Fajar* quoted its chairman stressing the need for unification of the two contending groups into one organization representing all parties, including Tana Toraja. He pleaded for a re-opening of discussions between Front and Committee (*Fajar* 1-12-2004). Towards the end of 2004 it seemed that the integrative vision was gaining ground. The chairman was quoted stating: 'The problem whether Toraja joins or not needs not to be debated any longer. It has already been solved. Toraja is part of Luwu, and therefore it cannot be separated from the province' (*Palopo Pos* 25-11-2004). However, the future prospects of the province remain highly uncertain (*Fajar* 23-1-2005).

Keeping all options open

Luwu (Raya) was not the only regional option for a province. Spokesmen in Tana Toraja stress that they are not willing to join Luwu at any price. In 2000, the Badan Perjuangan Pemekaran Propinsi Sulawesi Timur (BP3ST, Body for the Struggle for Pemekaran of East Sulawesi Province) was established to lobby for a province encompassing Luwu, North Luwu, Tana Toraja and Enrekang (a district bordering on southern Tana Toraja and Luwu).[42] Political activists in Tana Toraja and Enrekang formed the core of the movement, which was to expand to Luwu and Luwu Utara. The plans of the movement created not only political controversies but also confusion about the name of the province (*Palopo Pos* 3-11-2000; see note 12).

At that time the movement for a separate province of West Sulawesi emerged. When discussions about Luwu Raya were stagnating, for people in Tana Toraja West Sulawesi became an attractive alternative, and talks between

41 Nathan (2003:44) concluded that 'plans for Luwu Raya have been abandoned in favour of Luwu province and campaigners are confident that Luwu province will be formed before the 2004 elections'.

42 Badan Perjuangan Pemekaran Propinsi Sulawesi Timur (BP3ST) wilayah Tana Toraja, Enrekang, Proposal tentang pembentukan wadah perjuangan pemekaran Propinsi Sulawesi Timur, 2000.

representatives of West Sulawesi and Tana Toraja were initiated. In Luwu, there was much resistance against the idea of merging Luwu and North Luwu with Tana Toraja and Enrekang into a province of East Sulawesi which implied the disappearance of the name 'Luwu Raya'. Initiators of the East Sulawesi plan, who had also made eyes at a part of the intended province of West Sulawesi that has close socio-cultural links with Tana Toraja, were accused of having too strong ties with Tana Toraja. One Luwu politician expressed the fear that the difference in natural resource endowments between Luwu and North Luwu on one hand, and Tana Toraja and Enrekang on the other, would lead to 'increased exploitation of the natural resources of Luwu by the strong human resources from those areas'. East Sulawesi received a cool reception in Luwu and was also rejected by the Enrekang elites.[43]

Thus, although many prefer Luwu Raya, debates in Tana Toraja about *pemekaran* were not restricted to this option only. Some older-generation Toraja even nostalgically mention 'Toraja Raya' as an alternative choice, which does not stand a great chance but most closely matches an identification with Toraja. After ratification of Law no. 32/2004, Tana Toraja can even pursue a new option: acquiring the status of special region (*kawasan khusus*) on the basis of its cultural heritage and potential for tourism.[44]

Legitimizing pemekaran

Debates on splitting up Tana Toraja were rooted in the different histories of its northern, southern and western parts. The issue gained in importance in connection with the possible formation of a new province in 2001. Toraja political actors stressed that the bargaining position of Tana Toraja would be stronger if it had more districts and political leaders, *adat* leaders, and youth organizations started to discuss *pemekaran*. After discussions in seven northern sub-districts, the Committee for Establishment of North Toraja District (PPKTU) was formed. In October 2004, proposal and positive recommendations by the district head, parliament and governor were awaiting the installation of a new parliament of the province of South Sulawesi in order to continue the procedures.[45]

A similar movement started demanding *pemekaran* of West Toraja. This demand will almost certainly not make it beyond the first feasibility studies.

43 *Fajar* 27-10-2000, 31-10-2000; *Palopo Pos* 14-10-2000, 28-10-2000, 2-11-2000, 3-11-2000, 9-11-2000, 10-11-2000, 13-11-2000, 15-11-2000.

44 *Fajar* 23-11-2004.

45 Keputusan DPRD no. II/KEP/DPRD/IX/2002 and Surat Bupati no. 136/1063/PEM/UM, 26-9-2002, tentang persetujuan pemekaran Kabupaten Tana Toraja; SK Bupati Tana Toraja no. 22/III/2003 8-3-2003. There were also protests; *Fajar* 25-1-2003.

Its establishment would probably become an economic burden rather than an opportunity for development. Some people expressed the fear that *pemekaran* may even lead to the breakdown of Tana Toraja. According to such a scenario, West Toraja could join West Sulawesi, while South Toraja and North Toraja could either stay with South Sulawesi or join Luwu Raya. Especially the Tana Toraja elites in Jakarta regard this as a disaster. Apart from creating economically weak administrative units, it would mean the disappearance of Tana Toraja as the administrative unit that represents Toraja identity. Instead many Toraja in Jakarta prefer incorporation of Tana Toraja into Luwu Raya.

District pemekaran versus provincial interests

Pemekaran is an extremely sensitive political process that may involve contradictory interests at various levels. Tana Toraja has not yet been affected by *pemekaran* so far. However, it could become a key area in connection with the establishment of a new province. In the sensitive relationship between South Sulawesi and the Luwu-Tana Toraja region economic interests are important. South Sulawesi risks losing income and strategic resources. Therefore, it wants to block the formation of new provinces. Formally, there are no restrictions to *pemekaran* as long as the preconditions specified in the law are fulfilled; *pemekaran* is based on 'the aspirations of the people'. However, the North Toraja case shows that lower-level political interests in district formation can be played off against higher-level interests in establishing a province.

Demands for *pemekaran* are dependent on the willingness of higher authorities to deal with them. Therefore, relationships of dependence and power differences are crucial. This contradicts simplistic views of *pemekaran* as facilitated and stimulated at all levels of governance to create a more democratic society based on 'the aspirations of the people'. However, in the case of *pemekaran* of North Toraja the South Sulawesi governor demanded a formal statement from the Tana Toraja parliament stating that *pemekaran* will not be used as a basis for the formation of another province.[46] However, nobody regarded the document as a constraint on future political choices for joining any provincial movement.

46 Keputusan Dewan Perwakilan Rakyat Kabupaten Tana Toraja Nomor: 1/kep/DPRD/I/2004 tentang pernyataan sehubungan dengan pemekaran Kabupaten Tana Toraja, Makale, 8-1-2004. It says: 'The parliament of Tana Toraja states that *pemekaran* of Tana Toraja is in no way related, and will not lead, to the formation of a new province'. Though the statement is not specific about which province is meant, people commenting upon it primarily associated it with the possible contribution of new districts to Luwu Raya.

Contradictory interests in Luwu

Another example of the complex ways in which the agendas at district and provincial levels can be competitive is the establishment of East Luwu District. North Luwu came primarily into being as a result of frictions between two candidates for the position of district head in Luwu in 1999: Kamrul Kasim and Luthfi A. Mutti. Luthfi had the support of Andi Hasan, a member of the eastern Luwu elite, who had built a strong power base as Golkar leader in Luwu during the New Order. His support for Luthfi was in vain: Kasim won by default because of a split in the votes (see Nathan 2003) and became the new district head. Andi Hasan was disappointed and started putting his political bets on North Luwu.

Pemekaran of North Luwu in 1999 had not caused great political tension, though it drained Luwu from the most qualified part of its administrative apparatus. *Pemekaran* had (passive) support among the North Luwu population. However, it was the product of the political lobbying of elite networks rather than of participation and democratic processes. Luthfi, its first district head, was closely related to the Directorate General of Regional Autonomy through Ryaas Rasyid. This seems to have been an important factor in establishing North Luwu. According to one account, 'after the Luwu district head election had been lost by Luthfi, Rasyid just decided to divide Luwu. It happened in a few months, without a local political movement, mass pressure, or much NGO influence. One could say that Luthfi was given his own district and dropped there.' Despite all this personal lobbying, there were important and widely recognized improvements in North Luwu under the Luthfi administration (*Fajar* 26-4-2005; Nathan 2003).

The elites from northeastern Luwu had supported the establishment of North Luwu and Luthfi's appointment as district head. However, they also had their own agenda of *pemekaran*. The ink of the signatures under the document that formalized North Luwu was still wet when they started demanding the formation of a separate district of East Luwu (Nathan 2003). As Luthfi was initially unwilling to give up this resource-rich part of his new district, the issue generated much tension and even threatened to escalate into violent conflict in 2001 and 2002. According to sources in Luwu, violence between supporters of Luthfi and groups demanding the new East Luwu district could barely be avoided by mobilizing the kinship networks through which the contending elites are all related.

The establishment of North Luwu in 1999 and, later, East Luwu and Palopo brought the formation of a new province within reach. In this context the participation of Tana Toraja was no longer indispensable. However, rather than speeding up the formation of a province, *pemekaran* in Luwu generated contradictory interests. When the movement for a province emerged, North

Luwu had already been established but East Luwu had not yet been ratified. Andi Hasan represented the northeastern elite with its interests to control the INCO mines through the establishment of East Luwu District. The plans for Luwu Province were not very popular with either the former or with the current governor of South Sulawesi (*Fajar* 27-6-2003, 16-2-2004).

As the fate of East Luwu was still dependent on cooperativeness of the governor, it was not in the interest of the elites from eastern Luwu to support the plans for a new province at that moment.

In late 2004, when the Luwu movement was in dire straits and the law revised, blame for postponement of Luwu Province was laid with the North Luwu parliament and especially its former chairman, Andi Hasan from East Luwu, who had failed to issue a recommendation.[47]

Hidden agendas? Politics of religious and ethnic identity

Contested control over resources explains processes of *pemekaran* in Luwu only to some extent. It does not clarify the rift in the movement for a new province and the fault lines along which this has become manifest. In order to understand why the movement split, we should focus on processes of ethno-religious identification and the ways ethno-religious sentiments are mobilized.

The history of Luwu and Tana Toraja relationships and especially earlier attempts to establish a province bear witness of the sensitive role of ethno-religious identifications. During the 1940s and 1950s tensions increased as a result of decolonization and the Darul Islam movement, when ethnic and religious frictions determined the dividing lines along which conflicts unfolded. Though never openly debated under the New Order, these tensions never disappeared, and often played a mobilizing role in violent conflicts between migrants from Tana Toraja and the local population in lowland Luwu.[48] These tensions also informed the struggle for a new province.

After the fall of the Soeharto regime, Sulawesi was hit by Islamic radicalism and inter-religious violence. From 1998 onwards, massive violence between Christians and Muslims struck Central Sulawesi (ICG 2001a, 2004) while several bomb attacks hit Makassar in 2002. Luwu experienced communal conflicts (Roth 2002; Nathan 2003). As before, some of these conflicts took shape along ethno-religious lines dividing people from Luwu and Toraja. In

47 *Fajar* 10-10-2004. A Makassar Committee spokesman severely criticized the parliament. *Palopo Pos* 11-9-2004.

48 Nathan 2003. See also *Kompas* 15-9-1998, 14-1-1999, 15-1-1999; *Suara Merdeka* 16-1-1999, 11-2-1999.

addition, Luwu also had its share of Islamic extremist violence as illustrated by a bomb attack in Palopo early 2004.[49] Arrests of suspects of the Makassar bomb attacks even yielded evidence for the existence of military training camps in Luwu.[50]

The establishment of the Komite Persiapan Penegakan Syariat Islam (KPPSI, Preparatory Committee for the Upholding of Islamic Law) in 2000 caused unrest in Sulawesi.[51] Its main objective was special autonomy for South Sulawesi in order to facilitate the introduction of *sharia* law. In December 2001 KPPSI announced a draft law on the introduction of *sharia* in South Sulawesi, and proposed to give the province a status similar to Aceh. The political agenda of KPPSI and the links with extremist Islam have given rise to a growing concern about the ambitions of political Islam in Sulawesi (ICG 2002a; Dias Pradadimara and Burhaman Junedding 2002). The Makassar meeting of KPPSI was strictly guarded by a paramilitary group called Laskar Jundullah (Army of God), which had become the regular security force of KPPSI.[52] When linkages between Laskar Jundullah and violent Islam extremism became publicly known, KPPSI distanced itself from the organization.[53]

The emergence of three children of the legendary Luwu-born Darul Islam leader Kahar Muzakkar on the regional political scene is in this respect interesting, as they are also involved in debates on the administrative status of Luwu. This fits in with a revival of the political agenda of Darul Islam and Kahar (Velthoen 2004), which is referred to as neo-Kaharisme. These developments are closely related to the emergence of KPPSI in South Sulawesi politics. A KPPSI spokesman has stated that many members regard this movement as a continuation of Darul Islam by constitutional means (ICG 2002a:17).

Dias Pradadimara and Burhaman Junedding (2002) have identified the social basis of the movement that supports KPPSI as male, urban (Makassar)-

49 *BBC Indonesia* 10-1-2004: http://www.bbc.co.uk/indonesian/news/story/2004/01/040110_palopoblast.shtml; *Kompas* 11-1-2004; *Suara Merdeka* 11-1-2004.

50 ICG 2003a, 2004. Near Enrekang and in East Luwu. Another camp was in Central Sulawesi (ICG 2004).

51 KPPSI was founded after introduction of the regional autonomy laws in 1999. It was formally established during a meeting of the Islamic Congress in Makassar in October 2000, after an earlier congress in Yogyakarta of the Majelis Mujahidin Indonesia (MMI, Council of Mujahedeen for Islamic Law Enforcement). Later, KPPSI became KPSI.

52 Headed by Agus Dwikarna, it had been established in Makassar in September 2000. Dwikarna was member of the executive committee of MMI. He was arrested in the Philippines in 2002 on the charge of possessing explosives and belonging to an Al Qaeda-related network (ICG 2002a; *Kompas* 20-3-2002).

53 ICG 2003a, 2004; Dias Pradadimara and Burhaman Junedding 2002; see Van Bruinessen 2002. Laskar Jundullah is also associated with the military training camps found in Luwu and Central Sulawesi, and has been accused of recruiting Muslim troops for and bringing weapons into Poso. Laskar Jundullah also executed violent 'sweepings' in Makassar (ICG 2001a; *Jakarta Post* 22-4-2002).

based, highly educated. Members tend to support Golkar and a New Order type of modernization, and are often affiliated to universities. Through their academic networks they mobilize support for political Islam, especially from young South Sulawesi males.

There are strong links between KPPSI and the Makassar-based Committee that advocates a Luwu province. Important activists of the Committee are Islamic people with a Luwu background, who are affiliated to a Makassar university. They are closely linked to other Makassar-based organizations like KKL and KPPSI. The chairman of KKL and leading figure and main spokesmen of the Committee is also member of the advisory board of KPPSI. The secretary general of KPPSI is also secretary of KKL, actively involved in the Committee and one of its spokesmen. The secretary of the Committee, one of the sons of Kahar Muzakkar, is a vocal supporter of KPPSI in Sulawesi Selatan. The chairman of KPPSI has an advisory function in the Committee. There are also Committee linkages to Luwu. A Luwu-based spokesman for the Committee, who recently died, former rector of Andi Jemma University in Palopo, was also affiliated to KPPSI. Other active Committee members in Palopo, among which the rector of the Sekolah Tinggi Agama Islam Negeri (STAIN, National Islamic High School) and secretary of the Palopo branch of the Committee, are also members of the advisory board of KPPSI in Makassar. Thus religious identity plays an important role in the struggle for Luwu Province.[54] A Committee spokesman:

> The Committee wants to build something with a specifically Luwu identity. Luwu will get lost in a province with Tana Toraja. We must defend the specific characteristics and values of Luwu and Luwu-ness (*keluwuan*). That is the ideology of the Committee. There are people who cry out 'that is Islamization' but that is not true. Our basis is idealism for Luwu, not only religious idealism. This is a struggle for the people of Luwu; an ethnic, not a religious struggle.

This opinion is criticized by an Islamic member of the Jakarta-based group from Luwu:

> Some people have a narrow-minded opinion on the province. If you ask them about their stance they stress that they are 'nationalists' and want good relationships between religions. But practice is different: they discriminate along lines of religion and ethnic identity. They use vague arguments about history, cultural differences or habits like drinking and gambling, but what they mean is differences in religion. They differ widely from those who want to include Tana Toraja in the new province, and who know the history of the kingdom. People from the Luwu

54 This does, however, not imply that there is a link with radical Islam. Several people have stressed that, whatever struggle may be involved, it will be a constitutional and legal one (*Republika* 1-4-2005).

> nobility are much more tolerant towards other religions. The group of intolerant people is small but potentially dangerous. They never speak their minds, and get mad if you call them extremists. But they do not accept a province which comprises of Christians and Muslims. What will this extremist thinking lead to? It damages our religion and obstructs the province movement.

The province as a symbol of Luwu ethnic identity

The struggle for a new province has turned into a struggle about ethno-religious identity in which ethnicity and religion are intertwined. There is no formally recognized ethnic group, or '*suku* Luwu'. The term 'Luwu Raya' refers to a province including Tana Toraja, whereas the terms 'Tana Luwu' and 'Provinsi Luwu' exclude Tana Toraja. Terms like 'Wija To Luwu' (the people of Luwu), '*keluwuan*' ('Luwu-ness') and '*kejayaan* Luwu' (the greatness of Luwu) denote attempts to construct a specifically Luwu identity that contrasts rather than overlaps with Toraja identity, and that ties Luwu to South Sulawesi or legitimizes a separate administrative status. This discourse is used by the Committee.[55]

Attempts to construct a distinct Luwu ethnic identity are not new. During the late New Order the (re-)construction of Luwu identity was expressed in terms of the history of the Luwu kingdom – the heritage of Andi Jemma and Lutat – and manifested in the 'royal palace' in Palopo. In this reconstruction of 'the kingdom' ties with Tana Toraja took a prominent place. And this representation of history was propagated by the Front in its struggles for Luwu Raya.

In opposition to the Front, a restricted conception of Luwu-ness is advocated by Committee. Many motives are involved here: the wish to give the new province an Islamic identity (to facilitate the introduction of *sharia*), fear among the Luwu elite for well educated and dynamic Toraja who might occupy key positions in the new province, and the ambition to reinforce a Luwu identity that has been marginalized by Toraja who have successfully put their own culture on the map and attracted tourists, while the memory of the glorious past of the Luwu kingdom withered away.

History, again, serves as source of legitimacy. On 23 January 2004, Luwu celebrated its 737th birtday (Hari Jadi Luwu) with military and *adat* ceremonies. The day vaguely refers to a mix of anti-colonial struggle, the coming of Islam (stressing the Islamic character of Luwu identity), and the origins of Luwu kingship. The celebration emphasizes the unity of Wija To Luwu and the mayor of Palopo stressed in his speech that Tana Luwu still forms

55 *Kompas* 26-2-2001.

an inseparable unity and that 'its glue is the circulation of the blood of the people of Luwu'.[56]

Conspiracy theories surround the province struggle as well. It is said that the Committee is an instrument of the South Sulawesi political elites to divide the Luwu movement in order to obstruct the formation of a new province. This theory was underscored by the close relationship between Jusuf Kalla (a Buginese, and known to be not very enthusiastic about *pemekaran*) and prominent Committee members, but further evidence is lacking. A competing Buginese definition of Luwu identity, which represents the political interests of the current province of South Sulawesi, focuses on Luwu as the core of Bugis culture, implying that Luwu belongs to South Sulawesi and that restoring the greatness of Luwu as a kingdom (*kejayaan* Luwu) within the confines of South Sulawesi is more important than province politics. According to the governor of South Sulawesi, Amin Syam,

> the formation of Luwu Province [...] will mean separation from South Sulawesi [...] During his speech [...] he asked elements of Luwu society to restore the greatness of Luwu when it was a kingdom, hundreds of years ago. In front of thousands of inhabitants of Luwu [...] Amin recalled the past greatness of Luwu. He mentioned Sawerigading as the human figure able to turn Luwu into a cultural barometer of South Sulawesi.[57] Presently, according to the governor, Luwu will be able to rediscover its greatness [...]. Yet the governor did not spend a word on Luwu Province, he only talked about 'restoring the greatness of Luwu'. (*Fajar* 14-2-2004.)

In this section I have related the province struggle to issues of ethno-religious identity in Luwu and South Sulawesi. The characteristics and affiliations of key actors in the Committee against the background of South Sulawesi politics and the conflict about Tana Toraja make it likely that the province struggle merges with, and is captured by, broader agendas and objectives of political Islam. The province movement is also related to attempts to construct specific images of Luwu and to use these either as the basis for a new province or to legitimize the status quo.

56 *Fajar* 23-1-2005. In the late Soeharto period, when it was introduced, the district government tried to increase its legitimacy by using such symbols of Luwu's past. After *pemekaran* the celebration ceremony reflects fragmentation by exhibiting dances from the new administrative regions: Luwu, North Luwu, East Luwu and Palopo.

57 Hero of the I La Galigo epic which relates the origin of the Luwu Kingdom and Bugis culture.

Conclusion

In the preceding pages I have described the struggle for Luwu (Raya) Province and the conflicts it has generated. Supporters of the restricted option are organized in the Committee, while those favouring the inclusion of Tana Toraja have formed the Front. While the Luwu and Toraja communities in Jakarta tend to support the Front, the Committee reigns in Makassar. At the district level, Front views are prominent in Tana Toraja, while Committee and Front are competing for power in Luwu. A mixture of motives and interests play a role, including competition for political positions and economic resources, ethno-religious identity politics, historical nostalgia for the old kingdom, and resentment against South Sulawesi, as well as a genuine concern for a more equitable, socially just, and democratic society.

Until now the province has not materialized. This does not mean that there are only losers, because the winners are South Sulawesi Province and the provincial elites in Makassar with an interest in the status quo. Two factors came in handy: first, the rift in the Luwu movement, and second the revised Law no. 32/2004 which created a new blockade.

The failure to establish a new province clearly illustrates the three points mentioned in the Introduction. First, rather than a pre-planned turn to democracy, transparency and good governance, *pemekaran* is a struggle for power, influence and resources between elite groups. 'New' values like 'aspirations of the people' and 'development from below' are not the driving forces but merely legitimizing arguments.[58] The rift between Front and Committee shows that processes of *pemekaran* can be captured by particular interest groups.

Second, to understand these processes it is crucial to take the historical context into account. The re-awakening of the province movement, the rift between Front and Committee, the historical arguments used to legitimize conflicting viewpoints, and the sensitive relationships between the districts and Makassar as well as between Luwu and Tana Toraja can only be understood in a broader socio-historical perspective. *Pemekaran* is, to a large extent, the continuation of a long history of changing administrative relationships between Luwu, Tana Toraja, and Makassar, and of shifting boundaries and identifications.

Third, the role of ethno-religious identifications is important. It is not possible to accord to the factors of ethnicity and religion the place of either merely ideology and legitimizing narratives, or of one of the 'real interests' in the struggle. While acknowledging the crucial role of political control over

[58] Note that, in a way, *pemekaran* is counter-developmental, as it usually involves redistribution of resources from poorer to richer areas.

strategic positions and resources, I would not go as far as seeing issues of identity merely as legitimizing language that hides the 'real' interests, as Vedi Hadiz (2003b:13) seems to imply. Rather than merely being secondary to strategic material interests, identity politics became a major issue that has even caused the movement to split. Perhaps we have identified the main root of the struggle: conflicting views of the moral and normative basis of society.

Shadow states and the black economy

JOHN F McCARTHY

Sold down the river
Renegotiating public power over nature in Central Kalimantan

In April 2004 a timber broker in Banjarmasin described joining a timber shipment down the Barito River earlier that month. An actor known as an *ekspedisi* took responsibility for a huge raft of timber complete with custom built shelters for those taking the three week trip along this major river. The shipment itself was also often known as *ekspedisi*. Stretching over two kilometers long, and comprising of 123,000 m^3 of timber, the *ekspedisi* required several tug boats to pull the logs, each costing 60 million rupiah to hire. Three hundred gangsters (*preman*) armed with machine guns protected it. To entertain brokers accompanying the timber shipment, *preman*, rogue officials (*oknum*) and others occupying key posts along the watercourse, the actor behind the shipment provided prostitutes, marijuana, ecstasy and other drugs. These *ekspedisi* shipments are extremely expensive to operate, and given their size and the length of their journey, difficult to hide from local officialdom. Yet, the *ekspedisi* only had documents for 30,000 m^3 of timber.[1] Like virtually everyone active in the resource sector, the *ekspedisi* necessarily negotiated its way in the twilight zone between legality and illegality.

The *ekspedisi* system came to the attention of the national press in May 2002. At this time, in the district of Barito Selatan, a team of provincial police confiscated a consignment of 200,000 m^3 timber – over 54,000 logs worth approximately 100 billion rupiah (approximately US$ 10 million) – being shipped down the Barito River without a full set of official documents (*Kompas* 20-6-2002). Press reports focused on the illegality of the *ekspedisi*, carrying allegations of collusion between the district governments found along the river and the *ekspedisi* (*Banjarmasin Post* 30-5-2002). For the newspapers at

1 Interview with a timber broker, Banjarmasin, 26-4-2004. The most common meaning of *ekspedisi* is as in English, an excursion undertaken for a specific purpose, but it is also a technical term for (a business that does) cargo forwarding, such as sending parcels by ship.

least, these stories were confirmed when the head of the district issued post-facto transport permits (SKSHH, Surat Keterangan Sahnya Hasil Hutan or *susulan*) and a letter (*surat sakti*) to the head of the provincial police requesting the release of the timber. However, rumours in the district contended that the police only confiscated the timber because the head of the provincial police deemed that the payments from the *ekspedisi* were insufficient. Finally, amid further insinuations of behind the scenes intrigue, the governor supported the district lobbying, even though releasing the timber in this fashion was technically in contravention of forestry regulations. To intimidate the police, or possibly provide a legitimate reason to release the logs, the timber interests behind the *ekspedisi* mobilized 1,500 'demonstrators' who descended on the shipment. In face of this show of force and a letter from the governor, the police finally allowed most of the logs to proceed (*Kompas* 13-6-2002). In a symbolic nod towards laws for processing 'illegal timber', the police auctioned a small amount of the logs.

While this story pointed to the struggle over access to the extensive benefits to be gained from this province's extensive forest resources, it only touched upon the extent and unremitting nature of this struggle. In addition to the district government agencies and the police, business interests, *preman,* indigenous entrepreneurs and remote villagers vied with or accommodated each other in attempting to maximize their benefits. While this struggle sharpened as Indonesia embarked upon a rapid decentralization process in 1999, it shifted with subsequent political, economic and legal changes, reaching a turning point when, after 2002, the central government recentralized areas of administration, especially with respect to forest management.

This chapter examines how decentralization and the subsequent recentralization affected the exercise of public powers over nature in Central Kalimantan. As actors attempted to shape these fluctuating conditions for their own ends, some actors have managed the transition well, others have seen the initial gains of 1999-2000 washed away. The central analytical problem requires analyzing the connection between changes in the modes of resource control under regional autonomy and the changing patterns of political representation, participation, and power. This involves connecting recent theoretical understanding of the mechanisms, the structures and the processes at work in the control of natural resources and the wider literature concerned with civil society, the state and power. My objective is to draw some conclusions concerning the functioning of civil society, the state and the exercise of power and the prospects for successful decentralization in this particular context.

This chapter advances two related arguments. First, the turn to and away from decentralization in the forestry sector over 1998-2004 involved a struggle over resources that reveals the particular course of politico-legal change over this period. During the high season of regional autonomy pre-existing localized modes of exchange and accommodation became more autonomous of the previously dominant centralized mode of resource control. As these decentralized modes of access flourished under regional autonomy, rents were more widely spread. While this allowed a wider range of strategically situated local actors to benefit, due to the structural disadvantages they faced, poor rural actors only gained short term and limited benefits. Over time the older system became more apparent: as corporate interests adjusted, they incorporated district elites and administrative structures as well as key rural actors into their processes of resource access. Just as colonial regimes inevitably incorporated local elites, predominant economic interests found ways to cooperate with and incorporate local strongmen, administrative and village elites. In this way the decentralized modes of resource extraction which have received so much bad press articulated with still dominant centralized modes.

Second, the constellation of actors benefiting from this system of resource access was highly changeable as the system was subject to shifts in power, political position, and legal authority. As district and upriver actors depend on personalistic, clientalist ties to officials occupying positions in various state agencies and to outside financiers and timber interests, they are particularly vulnerable to legal-administrative and political changes, particularly those that affect state based patrons in an administration under transition. The nature of these changes over 1998-2002 led to considerable changes in the constellation of actors benefiting from the system. While district actors and administrators had exceptional opportunities to gain benefits during 1999-2002, since 2002 the pendulum has swung back the other way as central government has slowly reconstituted its authority. This began when the police gained authority to apply sanctions in the forestry area. Under a command structure, still under the control of the central government, they increasingly deployed this against nonconforming district administrations. At the same time the Ministry of Forestry successfully recentralized areas of forest administration with Government Regulation no. 34/2002. Central government authority was again confirmed with the passing of a new regional government act (Law no. 32/2004) that stressed the authority of provincial governors just at the time when the political system was consolidating under the new president Susilo Bambang Yudhoyono and his vice-president Yusuf Kalla. These changes meant that once again actors with strong links in Jakarta and reaching down to governors and provincial police chiefs are once again in the best position to benefit from resources. While they have lost many of their formal powers they enjoyed over 1999-2002, state based actors in the local domain still retain an informal capacity to manipulate other actors access to market.

In discussing developments in Central Kalimantan, I will analyse how the mechanisms, structures and processes at work in the control and maintenance of access to benefits have changed (Ribot 1998). For convenience, I will do this by dividing up the discussion into three sections, covering, first, the period immediately before regional autonomy, second, the high season of autonomy (2000-2002), and third, tracing developments from 2002. But first, I will discuss some theoretical considerations.

To understand the impact of regional autonomy on patterns of resource use, the concept of 'access' is central. Access has been defined as the ability to derive benefits from natural resources (see Ribot 1998:308). As actors struggle to benefit from the productive use of natural resources, they make use of a range of social, economic, and legal mechanisms. Legal frameworks, institutional power, group membership, social or ethnic identity, social status, the dynamics within a resource-controlling group, access to the state, to capital, to material resources, to customary authority, to markets, to knowledge and the ability to use institutional mechanisms are all factors that affect the process of gaining access to resources (Berry 1989; Ribot 1998; Ribot and Peluso 2002).

The main point is not whether access is considered legal or extra-legal, or legitimate or illegitimate according to various normative views (Ribot 1998). Access primarily depends on an actor's ability to dominate or influence other actors. Patterns of resource access can ultimately be understood in terms of how power is allocated and exercised within a society (compare Berry 1989). Central to this analysis then will be an analysis of how regional autonomy in Central Kalimantan has affected relations of power, encompassing both the legal and de facto loci of control. This means it is important to trace first, the changing prescriptions of law regarding property, permits, licenses and titles and official structures of authority, and second, changes to the whole ensemble of mechanisms shaping access – 'the structural and relational forces' – that exist 'prior and parallel to' socially recognized sets of rules (Ribot 1998:310).

Consequently, we need to understand how the changes associated with decentralization or regional autonomy have affected the structure of political, economic and legal relations that govern conditions of access. For, as the dominant discourses and the structures of power change, institutionalized mechanisms governing resource access are adjusted. When the existing institutional arrangements and social relations are restructured, new modes of identity and action are created, and new categories of people may rise to pre-eminence (Berry 1989:43-4). Yet, such a structural analysis needs to be supplemented by an actor oriented approach, because, within the changing patterns of political representation, participation, and power under regional autonomy, actors take up new strategies. As they attempt to shape conditions for their own ends, this in turn affects patterns of access and use.

The late New Order

The New Order system of governance has been analysed in terms of horizontal and vertically integrated networks of power and interest largely financed with extra-legal revenues, including those derived from the timber sector.[2] Under this system powerful politico-bureaucrats pursued entrepreneurial activities and extracted rents where possible, either for self enrichment, to command the loyalty of others both within and outside the pecking order, and/or to sustain the political interests of the institutions in which they were embedded.

This was particularly apparent in the forestry sector where an apparently centralized state system controlled access to resources. Under the Basic Forestry Act (no. 5/1967) the State – namely the Ministry of Forestry and its line agencies – controlled access to benefits via a concession licensing system (McCarthy 2000). As is well known, actors with access to key decision-makers within the regime, such as top military officials or cronies of the president, obtained legalized timber concession permits (Hak Pengusahaan Hutan, HPH). Given the close relations between the politico-bureaucrats controlling access and the corporate actors mining the forests, during field operations the legal strictures pertaining to state control over forest access remained primary to obtaining access. In parallel with these legal rules there existed a well established but unwritten set of rules regarding how the benefits of resource access were divided in the process of obtaining various licenses and permits, in working forest areas, in transporting logs downriver, and exporting timber overseas.

During this time Central Kalimantan became, as a local academic described it, the 'kitchen' of the concession system. To open the area to exploitation, a state forest mapping exercise (Tata Guna Hutan Kesepakatan, TGHK) classified 75% of the province's surface area (20.2 million hectares) as national forest estate (*kawasan hutan*) and some 9 million hectares of this area as 'production forest'. Disregarding indigenous property rights in these areas, the ministry of forestry granted 108 timber concessions (HPH) of 20 year duration to exploit these areas. Accordingly to one estimate, concessions operating in these areas at one point supplied an estimated 40% of national log supply each year (*Kompas* 18-6-2001).

At this time companies holding timber exploitation licenses paid the cost of processing the required licenses and permits and the formal taxes and duties that needed to be paid on legal timber. Even if they processed the requisite permits, they still faced the expense of making well-established

2 For discussion of this phenomenon, see C. Barr 1998, 2002; Robison and Rosser 1998; Robison 2002; MacIntyre 1994.

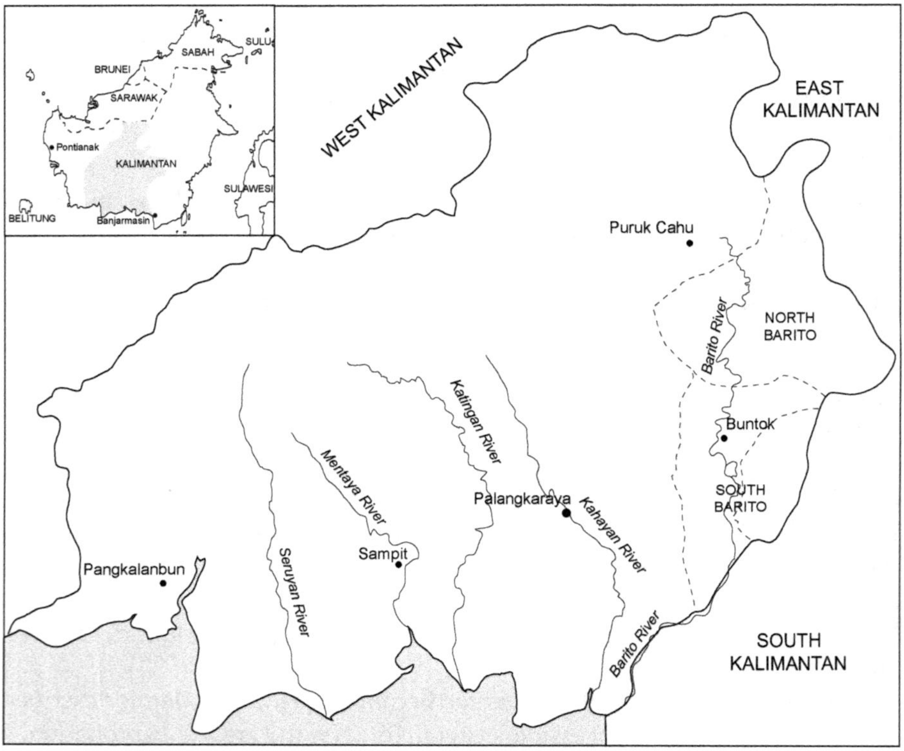

Map 6. Central Kalimantan

payments to police, military, forestry and local government officials whose concurrence was needed for smooth operations in the field or along the river as they transported timber to market. To maximize profits, timber operators sought to minimize formal taxes and duties and the cost of obtaining permits. Mostly they extracted timber beyond their legal quotas and in areas adjacent to their legal areas. This meant that they needed to transport timber downriver well in excess of the amount for which they had documents.

Under the concession system, companies with official HPH concession licenses along the Barito River usually ran integrated operations that encompassed logging large areas, transporting timber downriver, and finally exporting sawn timber or plywood. However, the actor holding a concession license might also sub-contract various functions to other operators. In parallel with the vertically integrated concession system, other actors sold their services to concessionaires, such as shipping timber downriver. According to sources involved in these shipping operations, if the concessionaire had full documents for a shipment, they would use company barges (*tongkang*). However, if the shipment lacked full documentation they would engage the services to what had become known as *ekspedisi*, a sub-contractor shipping timber downriver. On average, *ekspedisi* would only obtain permits for approximately 30% of the timber they transported. Given the significant taxes thereby avoided, ample funds were left over to make the payments required to navigate the informal system.[3]

In parallel with the institutional order working down from Jakarta, as I have described elsewhere (McCarthy, forthcoming), during the New Order a system of resource extraction operated in outer island Indonesia that demonstrated the primary institutional arrangements characteristic of these areas. These consisted of self-regulating networks of exchange and accommodation that determined access to and use of key local resources which formed the most serious obstacle to the operation of formal state policy at least as it appears in policy documents and laws. The logic of this system is clear: over long periods of time state decision-makers in distant Jakarta have developed nation wide organizational rules pertaining to the local domain – specifically with regard to state forest. Yet, these rules failed to accommodate the interests of diverse actors and the variety of situations found in the local area (see Ostrom 1992). These interests included the extra-budgetary needs of local political actors and officials to maintain the local state apparatus, to sustain political loyalties, and to meet their personal economic ambitions. The state order also failed to meet the ambitions of local entrepreneurs disadvantaged by regulations that privileged those able to obtain forest exploitation per-

3 Interview, Buntok, 24-7-2002.

mits in distant Jakarta, as well as the requirements for labour and economic opportunities for villagers disadvantaged by a state concessions system that allowed the logging customary lands in a fashion widely held to be unjust and inequitable.

Under the localized system of resource extraction that emerged, local entrepreneurs handled quasi-legal timber operations, sometimes in cooperation with outside concessionaires. They could do so as long as they conformed to a system of reciprocities that involved extra-legal gifts, payments and political support and other exchanges with key local politicians and state functionaries. These systems of extraction worked under the blind eye of local officials who were otherwise loyal to the regime. As they evolved, they grew into encompassing webs of exchange and accommodation that included forestry staff, army personnel and other key local functionaries while reaching out into the wider society to encompass village and *adat* heads. In many cases local bosses with access to capital and contacts and kinship relations within state agencies, with the agents of centralized concession operators and local police and military officials played key roles within these arrangements. While legal state sanctions would not be applied against those conforming to the reciprocities regulating this system, the legal domain of the state and those empowered by it remained central to the system. Officials within these networks derived their power from their capacity to issue permits, enforce state regulations and apply state sanctions. While this involves state power, these arrangements are not coincident with the state. Within complex evolving situations, to varying degrees the institutional arrangements governing access to resources both reflected and refracted customary local notions of rights, clientelist patterns of exchange and accommodation, and state laws within an institutional matrix working in an overlapping, and complicated fashion across these three institutional orders (McCarthy, forthcoming). Consequently, as Barbara Harriss-White (2003) has noted when discussing similar systems in India, the precise boundaries of the state remain blurred. Viewed from this angle, the state appears as a system or a set of bureaucracies 'that resists straightforward analytical closure' (Gupta 1995:392). Thus, the power of actors occupying positions in the state lies in their ability to manipulate other actors' access to market (see Reno 1995).

This became particularly evident in Central Kalimantan during the 1990s, when Soeharto pushed a peat project, the notorious Peat Land Development Project (Project Pembangunan Lahan Gambut, PLG). As this mega-project aimed to convert one million hectares of peat swamp forest in southern Central Kalimantan to rice and other crops, it allowed for the wholesale clear felling of the peat swamp forests of southern Central Kalimantan. During this process, timber brokers connected to companies with valid permits to log particular areas would provide advances to loggers in the form of food or cash, or buy the timber directly from villagers working in surrounding areas. After purchasing logs, they would sell them on to sawmills that opened along the banks of the major rivers, or directly down to Banjarmasin, the major port for South-Central Kalimantan and the seat of major plywood and timber exporting factories, making considerable profits along the way. This system was operated by financiers from the timber companies who had placed orders with the local entrepreneurs and brokers, organizing for shipments of logs to be sent to Banjarmasin or further a field to Surabaya and Jakarta. These transactions occurred in collusion with district and provincial forestry staff, local military officers, the police and other local government staff. These officials received extra-legal payments on a regular basis. This meant that loggers received early warning of law enforcement, and cases of illegal logging were 'solved' in local coffee shops.[4]

With the police still under the armed forces, ABRI (Angkatan Bersenjata Republik Indonesia, Indonesian Armed Forces) was a leading agency in these processes. According to one source, the regional commander (*danrem*) appointed individual district commanders (*kodim*), taking into account their promises regarding the amount of money they would 'store' upwards to the military command. This was just one of the unofficial ways the military obtained additional income. In Central Kalimantan well before regional autonomy, well-connected entrepreneurs and local timber interests at the district level in the interstices of the New Order state.

Regional autonomy

Even before the key autonomy law (Law no. 22/1999) had come into effect, district governments had gained greater legal authority in the forestry sector. They were, for example, entitled to grant small scale logging licenses.[5] Under regional autonomy districts set up district forestry offices (*dinas*) that were accountable only to the district head and these now operated according to new district regulations (*perda*) rather than the directives of the Ministry

4 Tim Pemantuan Kawasan Konservasi Air Hitam, Kabupaten Barito Selatan, Kalimantan Tengah, lindungilah ekosistem air hitam dari ancaman Proyek Lahan Gambut (PLG) satu juta hektar di Kalimantan Tengah, laporan lapangan pemantauan kawasan konservasi air hitam di Kecamatan Dusun Hilir dan sekitarnya, 1997.

5 In 1999 a Ministry of Forestry initiative encouraged community groups to form cooperatives to obtain thirty-five year 'community forestry leases' (Hak Pengusahan Hutan Kemasyarakatan, HPHKM) which could be issued by district governments. A government regulation (no. 6/1999) also established the concept of Forest Product Harvest Concessions (Hak Pemungutan Hasil Hutan, HPHH), giving the *bupati* power to issue permits for HPHH in areas of 'production forest' of up to 100 ha.

of Forestry in distant Jakarta. These formal changes, combined with the discretionary powers gained by district administrations following regional autonomy, meant that districts gained a large degree of de facto control over the way resource policy worked in their districts. From 1999 onwards district administrations in Central Kalimantan began to issue timber licenses to local people operating in their own name or in the name a community group incorporated into a cooperative or 'farming group' (*kelompok tani*). District entrepreneurs also began to formalize their operations by obtaining more extensive licenses for timber mills which had until then to various degrees worked outside the law.[6]

Under this system, the national forestry department lost its capacity to operate as a vertically integrated agency with full technical responsibility for forests.[7] In this way, regional autonomy entailed a significant change in the locus where those wishing to gain access had to invest, pay a fee or exchange a service. To the mortification of the Ministry of Forestry, after 1999 district officials became important gatekeepers governing access to forest resources found in their district.[8]

Yet, many permits could still be obtained from provincial and central government agencies, ensuring that decentralization led to the diversification of control over access to forest areas and markets. Competition intensified between different agencies and different levels of government to control access, as well as between actors who had invested in relationships at a particular level.[9] Consequently, the state was less able to maintain the pretence of operating as a unitary actor, as it had now emerged in a more plural guise (McCarthy 2004).

In Central Kalimantan the New Order had acted like a predatory state, extracting large rents from the province's forests, despoiling the patrimony of the indigenous people while providing very little in way of collective goods, especially in remote rural hamlets.[10] After the demise of Jakarta's author-

6 For descriptions, see McCarthy 2001a, 2001b.

7 Under Law no. 22/1999 the provincial forestry office (*kanwil*) were abolished and, after the formal commencement of regional autonomy in 2001, the *dinas* at the district level became primarily responsible to the district head. For, as Article 4 of the new law stated, autonomous regions 'shall respectively be independent and shall not have a hierarchical relationship to each other' (Law no. 22/1999, Article 4). As the *dinas* at the district level no longer reported to *dinas* at the provincial level, the Ministry now had to rely on the *dinas* at the provincial level to pursue their objectives.

8 See McCarthy 2001a, 2001b.

9 See McCarthy 2004.

10 This is exemplified by the poor infrastructure in the new district of Gunung Mas. While the extensive timber resources found here were extracted for decades, the state had yet to develop the most basic communications, transport, health and other facilities. In 2001, virtually all villages lacked electricity or telephone, and there were only 23 kilometres of sealed road in the

ity in law and public discourse, rural people and district elites alike openly challenged the mining of the forests by outside actors. Now local group membership, social and ethnic identity became more important in determining who could legitimately gain access to resources in the local domain. For a long time villagers had resented the way outside interests – especially timber and mining companies close to the regime – had extracted resources without respecting their *adat* property. In villages across the province anger at the way outside interests had over-ridden *adat* property rights, at the role of in-migrants in extractive industries, and at the minimal benefits enjoyed by local people boiled to the surface (ICG 2001b; McCarthy 2001a, 2001b). In numerous disputes in remote areas those claiming *adat* rights exerted physical control over particular areas. These *putra daerah* ('children of the region') sentiments worked against outsiders exploiting resources subject to *adat* claims. Villagers asserted *adat* claims over local resources via demonstrations, blockades, and the threat of physical violence and asserted physical control over access to resources in areas around their villages, swiddens and forest gardens.

At the same time local elites railed against the way Jakarta based actors had over-stepped the local administration in gaining permits, and the fact that the lucrative process of resource extraction occurred without providing sufficient funding for the development of local infrastructure, while failing to allow local entrepreneurs to gain sufficient benefits from resource extraction. Antipathy against outsiders holding key positions within the local bureaucracy translated into moves to indigenize key positions in the bureaucracy. Local politicians used '*putra daerah* resentments' to legitimize decisions that were seen to favour local interests. District elites, who felt they had not enjoyed a fair share of resource extraction during the New Order, now saw this as their turn to benefit.[11]

Those *putra daerah* close to officials or with the means of winning their favour gained prominence, using kinship, village or other contacts in the administration, exchanging favours and offering money to obtain small scale exploitation permits, permits to transport timber and sawmill licenses. District regulations (*perda*) and policies explicitly or implicitly favoured people with *putra daerah* status in granting formal exploitation permits.[12] If these brokers and small scale entrepreneurs could work with groups of villagers, helping them to incorporate as cooperatives or merely enlisting their names

---

whole area of 10,804 square kilometres (McCarthy 2001). In contrast, one of the first acts of the new district of Gunung Mas was to build an effective road link down to the provincial capital of Palangkaraya.

11 This phenomenon was also found in other areas of Kalimantan. See for good example 'Rencana Menhutbun tidak disetujui wakil rakyat Kutai', *Suara Kaltim* 20-11-2000.

12 McCarthy 2001. See Peluso and Harwell 2001.

on permit applications, they could process small scale timber concessions in the name of village collectivities.

With the explosion of resentment and demands by villagers upriver against conglomerates, a large number of disputes emerged between concessionaires and villagers. As concessionaires and outside financiers faced increased threats from local actors, with regional autonomy, timber conglomerates found they needed to renegotiate renewed access to resources. At least formally, they could still obtain permits in the old way, but it was no longer sufficient to just obtain exploitation licenses via the central government. Having gained more extensive powers under regional autonomy, assertive district heads began to issue short term exploitation permits to local interests inside concession areas, typically favouring *putra daerah* with kinship affiliations, or with political or economic ties, from the same area. In these and other ways, district heads could put pressure on conglomerates to negotiate access via district administrations. In Central Kalimantan, working with local businessmen, many concessionaires began to invest in other extraction strategies. Extending the system that had operated during the PLG period, conglomerates worked with local businessmen and brokers, with informal support from district heads and the governor.[13] For example, Djajanti, one of largest timber conglomerates in Central Kalimantan, allowed local companies to harvest its concession areas, according to one of its commissioners, 'on the condition that they only sell to us'.

> We worked out what our costs would have been if we had been working the areas ourselves. And that's what we've paid the companies now working our concessions', said Sudrajat. Sudrajat decided to take this course of action because it seemed more advantageous than having to strong-arm it with the district head. With their current powers, it is very difficult to get the district heads to back down. (*Tempo* 46, 24-7-2001.)

The conglomerates also needed to negotiate taxation and levies – formal or otherwise – imposed by the local government (*Kompas* 16-8-2001). The system had the virtue of raising significant district taxes (Pendapatan Asli Daerah, PAD) that benefited local government. Given corruption and collusion in the way the system operated, unofficially it also enriched those occupying key positions in the district administration.

Apart from incorporating district elites and administrative structures into their processes of resource access, entrepreneurs and outside companies also sought to integrate key rural actors. They preferred for instance to operate through a villager, a local cooperative registered with the district government,

13 Timber interests also contributed large amounts of funds for the governor of Kalteng at the time of the last elections (McCarthy 2001a, 2001b).

or a community group who could obtain operating permits from the district government. In Central Kalimantan ethnic identity had become important: belonging to a particular village, ethnic or *adat* group gave an actor a sense of entitlement. By operating behind a person or group with *putra daerah* status, outside actors could more readily legitimize their operations. This also had an added advantage: with many villagers recruited into timber operations in one way or another, many benefited under this system, and this tended to dissipate many emergent 'vertical' conflicts. In a number of cases individual villagers worked as the front men of concessionaires, operating cooperatives in villages areas without involving fellow villagers or making sufficient compensation for exploiting their *adat* property. Conflicts between companies and villagers were often transmuted into conflicts between villagers engaged in cutting timber in their *adat* territories and those who felt left out.[14] If extra-legal activities were involved, the actors behind the permit protected their good name and avoided the risk of legal sanctions. If the actor behind the permit was an official, a person with several permits, an outside concessionaire, or someone who might wish to disguise the extent of their operations, this strategy helped to avoid scrutiny.

The system offered additional economic advantages. Government agencies found it difficult to effectively tax informal logging operations that did not have an office and were not formally registered as a company. Village logging teams, or those acting in the name of communities, did not pay central government taxes such as the PSDH.[15] Yet, as their timber lacked official documentation necessary to take it to market, they would have to sell it to the first available buyer, usually 'bosses' such as owners of small sawmills or timber collectors. While these operators might be able to obtain documents that would enable them to transport timber within the district, they lacked the documentation necessary to market the timber outside the area. As timber without a full legal status had a lower price, conglomerates that could use production permits obtained from the central government to render the timber legal, could buy the timber cheaply from poor villagers, making considerable profits in the process. Further, given the long-standing over the harvesting of timber inside concession areas, concessionaires faced difficulties meeting their production targets (Kompol Eddy Hermanto 2004). By subcontracting village teams to log surrounding areas, concessionaires could avoid the appearance of illegality, access other sources of timber subject to *adat* rights, and co-opt villagers all at the same time. Consequently, villagers remained in a weak position after regional autonomy. Even if they could

14 Interview Dinas Kooperasi, Kapuas, 27-4-2004.

15 Provisi Sumber Daya Hutan, Forest Resource Royalty. Interview, Dispenda, Kuala Kapuas, 27-4-2004.

muster the money to obtain forest exploitation permits from the district government, they needed to obtain exploitation or transportation permits, and these expenses were cumulatively beyond the means of village actors and small time brokers. Local brokers and villagers lacked the capital required to use heavy machinery, run a saw mill, or obtain the permits required to transport the timber to the market.[16] Villagers might log village areas under exploitation permits granted by district administrations in the name of individual villagers or cooperatives set up in the name of community groups. Yet, this logging took place under the coordination of brokers financed from outside, or on behalf of concessionaires. Even after decentralization, those with control over capital and permits that allowed them to take timber through key nodes in the commodity chain where value was added, accrued the largest share of the profits (Zerner 2000).

We can see these changes affecting the operation of the *ekspedisi* discussed earlier. By 2000 the Barito River had become an insecure place. With up to 30 gangs of river pirates operating along the river, timber shipments faced the hazard of hijacking. At the same time government agencies were competing more extensively to extract benefits from the system. By 2004 there were 480 posts from Puruk Cauh down to Banjarmasin. A variety of state agencies including Polsek, Koramil, Forestry, local government revenue collection agencies (*dispenda*), village posts, and the River Police, the police unit for ports and the navy ran these posts to levy 'taxes' on passing timber.[17]

Faced with an uncertain business environment, these interests found it easier to mobilize local strongmen to organize operations upriver. Timber companies now more extensively used *ekspedisi* who could guarantee the arrival of timber downstream, which involved sharing profits to minimize risks.

The actors running these operations required considerable skills and audacity, with the amount of profit depending on how they handled these risks. This encompassed arranging all the payments and negotiations with the various administrative areas found along the river. The amount of money involved was not trivial: an *ekspedisi* might provide hundreds of millions of rupiah to the head of the security forces in a riverside district each time the *ekspedisi* passed (Kompol Eddy Hermanto 2004). The reasons for this were clear: law enforcement authorities who felt affronted by the level of payment had the capacity to seize a shipment or arrest the *ekspedisi* leader. District government leaders also derived large profits from *ekspedisi*. They could hold

16 Even under regional autonomy, those wishing to obtain a permit required considerable capital. In 2002 a recommendation for a HPHH permit could (informally) cost 10 million rupiah. In addition, other investments were required, for example to pay for aerial photographs and field surveys.

17 Interview with a timber broker, Banjarmasin, 26-4-2004.

up a shipment, for instance if payments were not made. Shipments could therefore only proceed with the tacit agreement of district leaders.

Moreover, if the timber was confiscated, district heads could arrange for it to be processed according to the legal fiction that it had no owner and 'auction' it back to the *ekspedisi* (Kompol Eddy Hermanto 2004). Alternatively, as a shipment could be lost to hijackers or fall prey to an extortion racket run by a rival underworld gang, payments were required to rival *preman* working along the river. On occasion disputes led to casualties, if for instance the armed *preman* protecting a shipment became involved in a shoot out with river pirates, or the police and river *preman* engaged in a gun battle.

Given their capacity to bridge this crucial space in the commodity chain *ekspedisi* accumulated large amounts of capital. By 2002, in addition to working for concessionaires and Banjarmasin based timber mills, *ekspedisi* carried timber for freelance brokers who went upriver to place orders. Further, *ekspedisi* worked as entrepreneurs in their own right, overseeing timber operations upriver and taking timber from scores of local timber brokers. At the peak of the *ekspedisi* system, shipments could be over 3 kilometres in length (*Banjarmasin Post* 8-7-2002).

The risks involved in the system meant that only the strongest *ekspedisi* could survive. In 1995, according to one source, there were approximately six actors working as *ekspedisi*. By 2002, only four key figures straddled the link between local timber operators and buyers upriver and the market downriver in Banjarmasin, thereby becoming the key players in the forest sector for this area. As this process of 'natural selection' proceeded, in 2004 only two continued to work the river.

Power, civil society and accountability under regional autonomy

There are further issues to consider with respect to this system, the first of which concerns the nature of power in this out-of-the-way and long neglected province. Under regional autonomy the local administration had gained authority over licenses and permits, while the police retained power to enforce the law. At the same time, entrepreneurs, brokers and agents of Jakarta based conglomerates maintained a hold over productive processes through their control over capital and access to outside markets. While the wheels of this system were oiled by a range of accommodations and exchanges between actors, these arrangements extended way beyond simple transactions between the actors involved. If the system was to continue to operate with such a high degree of corruption and illegality, it needed to protect itself from unwanted scrutiny. Exposure outside the province could lead to law enforcement activities from external actors, or the demand for payments in exchange for turning a blind eye. With a national campaign against illegal logging, those with most to lose from the exposure of their operations were prepared to intimidate or take violent action against actors who might expose it. Consequently, in Central Kalimantan power is often naked in its expression.

In 2002, when I visited an upriver area with a large number of timber operations working outside the law, thugs (*preman*) followed my movements. Here an NGO activist described how some of these *preman* had tried to kill him by running his motorcycle off a remote road into some trees. While it is possible to discover who is benefiting and how, it is not always good for one's health or career to unravel the connections between modes of resource control and political power.[18]

Villagers remained relatively disadvantaged under decentralization. Yet, the system that flourished at this time led to a much wider distribution of benefits than the earlier centralized system. Ironically, this wider distribution of benefits also encompassed the key agents of what is often considered civil society. This became apparent when a reporter told me how all journalists in the provincial capital, Palangkaraya, received monthly payments from a major timber mill not to report on their activities. When villagers had burnt down the mill after a long festering dispute, the local press failed to carry the story.[19] During a journey upriver, another journalist told me of a range of illegalities and corrupt activities he had uncovered in the area. After he left, others present described him as a 'journalist without a paper' (*wartawan tanpa surat kabar* or WTS, a word play on the Indonesian term for a prostitute). This freelance journalist travelled around with a press card uncovering illegalities and extracting blackmail money in exchange for suppressing publication. According to one report, a timber operator could face forty journalists visiting his office, asking for one hundred to two hundred thousand rupiah in exchange for not exposing illegalities. In a district along the Barito River, each time an *ekspedisi* passed, the *ekspedisi* would be given a list of the names of journalists who would need to be paid between five hundred thousand and five million rupiah not to report the *ekspedisi* (Kompol Eddy Hermanto 2004).

District officials and journalists also discussed a similar phenomena among NGOs, which they jokingly referred to as 'organizations that like to make requests' (Lembaga Suka Minta, a wordplay on the Indonesian term for NGOs, LSM or Lembaga Swadaya Masyarakat). With hundreds of NGOs

18 These realities also prevent the type of commodity chain analysis advocated by Ribot (1998), making it difficult to quantify the division of benefits from resource extraction pre- and post-decentralization.

19 Interview, Palangkaraya, 22-4-2004.

emerging after the end of the New Order period, many NGOs in the province also collected information in upriver areas, extracting money from those involved in exchange for silence.[20] According to a DPRD (Dewan Perwakilan Rakyat Daerah, District Assembly) member interviewed in Buntok, the capital of Barito Selatan district, every time an illegal timber shipment passed through Buntok, several NGOs received a payment.

NGOs and the press may be considered the key protagonists of modern civil society. Yet, rather than acting as the torch bearers of 'a moral community, a legitimate political order' (Khilnani 2001), many of the key actors in civil society acted like just another group of rent-seekers. With journalists and NGOs often in the pockets of commercial interests, it was hard to envisage the press taking on a critical role. There are also obstacles to the healthy development of what Jürgen Habermas (1992) has called a 'public sphere' – where public opinion formed through free discussion in the press informs and controls the activities of the state.

If democratic decentralization is about devolving powers to downwardly accountable actors (Agrawal and Ribot 1999), we can understand outcomes in terms of the way accountability relations encompass local government. Indeed, the main mechanisms of accountability set out in both Law no. 22/1999 and Law no. 25/1999 operated primarily through elected district assemblies (DPRD) that have the capacity to hold executive accountable.[21] The underpinning assumption seems to have been that the legislative would use mechanisms at its disposal to police and punish government officials – including the head of the region – who misbehaved. But, with only a weak link between DPRD members and their constituencies through a poorly designed electoral system. According to DPRD members interviewed in the course of this research, collusion between elected representatives and the chief executive office, under the laws of 1999 still elected by the legislative, has distorted the operation of accountability mechanisms.

These problems become particularly evident at two key moments each year. In order to enhance the monitoring of executive behaviour and hence improve government performance, Indonesia's decentralization laws provide the DPRD with the power to reject the annual accountability report of the head of the region. In theory, if this report is not accepted, the district head

20 According to informants, only a few NGOs and journalists in Palangkaraya remained free of these corrupt influences.

21 Law no. 22/1999 speaks of the 'role of the DPRD in performing its function as the monitoring body in the implementation of regional autonomy', and the DPRD is meant to monitor and to improve government performance. For example, the head of the region is accountable to the DPRD (see Law no. 22/1999, Article 44 and 45), and the DPRD has the authority to reject the accountability report of the head of the region and even dismiss the regional head (Law no. 22/1999, Article 3).

can be forced to resign.[22] According to a number of accounts from Central Kalimantan, the district heads pay money to members of DPRD to ensure the acceptance of their accountability report. Within the system of exchange that dominates district politics, the accountability report becomes a lever to extract business and other concessions from a district head, with DPRD members refusing to pass reports until agreement is reached regarding how district projects will be divided out.[23] Expensive deal making also affects the arrangement of the annual budget. The head of the district assembly, the district head, the secretary of the district (*sekda*), heads of district agencies (*kepala dinas*), and heads of factions in the DPRD, are the major players in arranging the budget (RAPBD), obtaining projects worth millions of rupiah. In return for their acquiescence, DPRD members obtain projects and sums of money allocated 'for lobbying'.[24]

According to a disillusioned DPRD member interviewed in 2004, a career in the DPRD has become an object of accumulation both for personal and political ends. Candidates for the legislature need to invest in the party to become a candidate, and once a candidate is elected they need to earn money for the party to support re-election.[25] To this end, they need to obtain lots of projects. Consequently, 'people are very disillusioned with politicians, they just see them as being after their own interests'. Given the dominant power of the executive in policy processes and the way collusive practices have corrupted the DPRD, community aspirations fail to be taken up by DPRD. It is hardly surprising that villagers have little expectations and, according to one DPRD member, they are not interested in meeting DPRD members visiting their constituencies.[26]

Members of the DPRD have also been involved in the timber trade, using their status within networks of exchange and accommodation encompassing the executive to provide operations with a degree of immunity from law enforcement. DPRD members have provided recommendations for timber to pass through their districts or supported the statements of timber interests in the name of the DPRD. More directly, it has been estimated that more than 60 DPRD members in Central Kalimantan have been directly involved in tim-

22 In late 2004 Law no. 32/2004 took away the power of the DPRD to hold the district head accountable in this way.

23 Interview, 11-8-2002. Interview DPRD member, Palangkaraya, 24-4-2004.

24 Interview DPRD functionary, Kapuas, 27-4-2004.

25 Under this electoral system, the position of a candidate on the ballot paper determines the likelihood of obtaining a seat in DPRD. Candidates who failed to gain a seat typically complain of collusive, corrupt practices determining the position the party allocated them on the ballot paper.

26 Interview DPRD functionary, Kapuas, 27-4-2004; Interview DPRD member, Palangkaraya, 24-4-2004; Interview NGO employee, Palangkaraya, 23-4-2004. Yet, given the lack of transparency, it is very difficult to know the political deals that take place, how projects are divided up, and how much an accountability report costs to get through the legislative.

ber enterprises.[27] This points to the reality that formal mechanisms of public participation and representation bear little resemblance to the actual mechanisms determining who gains access to resources and how they do so.

Post autonomy: changes after 2002

From 2000 two significant changes occurred that were to have far reaching consequences after 2002. First, in July 2000 Abdurrahman Wahid separated the police from the armed forces, a decision that took effect as of 1 January 2001 (ICG 2001b; Kompol Eddy Hermanto 2004). Prior to the restructuring of the military, the military and police were integrated into a unitary command structure. As the military was the lead agency, 'the police could be leant on by ABRI, and so they weren't so brave'.[28] After the reforms the police reported directly to the president under a national police chief. As the head of the provincial police (*kapolda*) now had a rank of brigadier general while the head of the local military command (*danrem*) remained a colonel, the local police commander was superior in rank. Yet, like the military, the police remained under-funded and, according to one report, obtained only 30% of their operating budget from the government. At the same time the central government made no steps to improve accountability within the force, and – despite regional autonomy – there was no formal means of holding police downwardly accountable to the local population.[29] To be sure, the provincial police chief (*kapolda*) remained accountable upwards to the central government. As the *kapolda* could be moved if Jakarta was dissatisfied with his performance, he remained in a subordinate position to the governor, the representative of Jakarta in the regions. Yet, with the governor's support, Jakarta reappointed the same person to the position three times, suggesting that the governor and the *kapolda* had worked out mutually agreeable arrangements. Consequently, as long as the *kapolda* tied in decisions with the governor, the district police chief (*kapolres*) could operate on his behalf outside the matrix of district accountability relations.[30]

27 The decision was formalized with the promulgation of the new police law in January 2002; Undang-Undang Republik Indonesia Nomor 2 Tahun 2002 Tentang Kepolisian Negara Republik Indonesia.

28 Interview, Forestry Official Kuala Barito, 25-4-2004. Within the regional hierarchy, the head of the regional military command (*dandem*) was a colonel with a higher rank (class c) than the head of the provincial police (*kapolda*) who was colonel with a rank of class g.

29 USINDO Open Forum Challenges to Police Reform in Indonesia, with Adrianus Meliala, lecturer at the University of Indonesia, 26 September 2002, Washington DC. Http://www.usindo.org/Briefs/Police%20Reform.htm.

30 Interview, Palangkaraya, 22-4-2004.

In 2000, an institutionalized committee (the Muspida) that included the local head of the administration, the local military and police chiefs – with the forestry agency handling operational matters – used to coordinate district policy as well as the distribution of revenue across agencies. At this time, given the history of military pre-eminence, a number of timber businesses still operated in this region under military protection.[31]

After 2002, making use of their new powers, the police began to work more autonomously of district civil and military commands. As the technical agency concerned with forests, forestry agencies had long competed with the police to control law enforcement in the forestry sector. While forestry officials had investigatory powers, they needed to report infringements of forestry law to the police whose responsibility it was to process the case until it reached court.[32] Armed with their extended authority, now the police increasingly came down to confiscate timber without involving district forestry agencies. Although this left district forestry agencies primarily in control of permits and licenses, there was little district administrations could do. As district forestry agencies – and the wider district administration – saw the police usurping their authority and the revenue that followed from its application, jealousy increased between the police and the other agencies, including the military and the district forestry agencies.

The second change occurred when the Megawati administration began to reassert the control of Jakarta over far-flung provinces. Responding to the competition over control of forest resources, the national government moved to reassert vertical control with a key regulation that effectively worked against district timber regimes. In July 2002 the central government issued a new Government Regulation (no. 34/2002) pertaining to the forestry sector. Before this time, the authority of the ministry of forestry had been disaggregated. With a political struggle occurring in the centre, the laws pertaining to natural resource use and regional autonomy remained uncoordinated, inconsistent and contradictory.[33] During this time there were serious dis-

31 McCarthy 2001a, 2001b. Primarily the Muspida (*musyawarah pimpinan daerah)* at the district level, but also the Muspika (*musyawarah pimpinan kabupaten*) at the sub-district level.

32 According to the criminal law (Law no. 81/1981), the police had the primary investigatory powers (*penyidik tunggal*). However, forestry laws (such as Law no. 41/1999) gave forestry officials investigatory powers for forestry related matters. These areas of law set the scene for long standing institutional competition between police and forestry officials.

33 In January 1999 a government regulation (no. 6/1999) established the concept of Forest Product Harvest Concessions (Hak Pemungutan Hasil Hutan, HPHH), giving the district head power to issue permits for HPHH in areas of 'production forest' of up to 100 hectare. On 13 November 1999, the new Minister of Forestry attempted to reverse the implementation of this policy. In 2000, another ministerial decision (Kepmenhut no. 051/Kpts/2000) once again gave regional governments the power to allocate concessions licenses. Kepmenhut no. 541/Kpts-II/2002 then cancelled this earlier decision. Finally, in 2002 with the passing of a more binding

putes within the districts and among central and provincial authorities over natural resource decision-making. Finally, the Forestry Ministry regained control over the permit system, timber transport licences, and the collection of taxes on forestry activities, effectively rescinding district authority to issue 100 ha exploitation permits and raise district taxes in the sector.[34] While the central government did not immediately repeal district regulations that contradicted the new regulation, district heads who continued with earlier policies faced legal sanctions.

With a national campaign against illegal logging, the police began to make law enforcement efforts that also made for excellent public consumption. Raids by the police concentrated on small scale sawmills and timber shipments run by local entrepreneurs and brokers, along with larger timber operations and some *ekspedisi* operating without full legal documents. Over time the police and the provincial courts began to act more aggressively against 'illegal logging', leading to their effective control over the forestry sector. District officials involved in administering district regimes were faced with arrest by the police for breaking national law. In a well known case, in 2003 the head of the forestry agency, the district head, the head of the DPRD in the district of Barito Utara all faced legal charges for providing transportation documents to an *ekspedisi* containing uncertified timber. They allegedly issued the documents according to a district decision in contradiction of national forestry laws that provide that timber without documents should be confiscated and auctioned. Provincial rumour held it that the case involved political competition and unhappiness regarding the division of revenues with other actors. Meanwhile, two senior officials in a neighbouring district faced charges for the fictive auctioning of timber, and the deputy head of the forestry agency in a third district also faced charges (*Banjarmasin Post* 3-3-2003).

Yet despite this apparent crackdown, according to one forestry official on the Barito River, 'if timber passes through with "the flag of *kapolda* on it", no-one is brave enough to touch it'. 'Police can arrest us', he said, 'but we can't do anything to them'.[35] According to a number of sources, a broker close to the provincial police chief was now the key gatekeeper in the province. Only

Government Regulation (no. 34/2002) did the Ministry successfully begin to curtail the capacity of districts to allocate concession licenses, but not before some districts granted a cache of new 10,000 hectare IPHK licenses within their territories.

34 The most stringent restrictions introduced by Government Regulation no. 34/2002 were that districts could only give permits for up to 20 m^3; at the same time the provincial forestry agency tightened procedures for transporting timber, in effect taking back over timber transport permits. Interviews in Kapuas during 2004 revealed that, taken together, these changes stopped districts independently issuing new permits and made timber operations uneconomical for local businesses.

35 Interview, Forestry Official Kuala Barito, 25-4-2004.

timber syndicates linked and making payments to this broker and with the informal blessing of the provincial police chief could continue to operate. This had led to a further round of 'natural selection', with actors lacking an excellent working relationship with this gatekeeper, or either failing to make speedy or adequate payments, facing legal sanctions.[36]

These developments led to several changes in the field. Before, with competition between the police and the forestry agencies, law enforcement remained somewhat unpredictable. But now, the extraction of timber became easier and more 'manageable' for the few syndicates that now were able to operate. Second, the district bureaucracy could no longer guarantee access to resources as they used to. With small scale timber licenses (HPHH) expiring, many small scale district operators found that they could no longer negotiate new permits. Third, after Government Regulation no. 34/2002, in a similar fashion as before regional autonomy, permits needed to be processed at the provincial level and in Jakarta.[37] This increased the dependence of local operators on actors who could process permits (HPH with valid licences) or guarantee taking timber out. Fourth, as districts could no longer apply district regulations, a number of administrative practices for raising PAD (Locally Raised Revenues) and laundering timber could no longer be used.[38] Accordingly, district revenues from the forest sector fell into decline. And so the high tide of regional autonomy in the forestry sector ebbed.

36 Interview journalist, Palangkaraya, 22-4-2004.

37 Interview second assistant district head, Kantor Bupati, 25-4-2004.

38 For example, prior to Government Regulation no. 34/2002, districts had at least two ways of dealing with timber. Timber lacking the required permits could be 'caught' and handled according to a legal fiction that it had no owner. It would be 'auctioned' and sold on, and if the actor behind the shipment could negotiate this, the timber would be sold back to them. As the administration then issued legal documents, the timber (known as *kayu temuan*) then had a legal status. Alternatively, if an actor did not make these arrangements in advance, the timber could be confiscated (known as *kayu tangkapan*). Although the person making the shipment would be listed in the legal documents (*berita acara*), after sufficient lobbying with the district administration, the timber might be released to the owner, and legal documents would be issued after payment of district and (perhaps) central government taxes. Typically, the case would not proceed because of 'lack of evidence'. In the rare occasion that a case was taken to court, the offender would usually be instructed to pay PSDH without the application of criminal sanctions. While these methods generated revenue, they in effect laundered timber lacking the required documents. After Government Regulation no. 34/2002, the *kayu temuan* practice ended, while *kayu tangkapan* continued if the actor concerned could not make speedy and sufficient payments, or otherwise secure their operations via the dominant timber syndicates.

Conclusions

Under the New Order cliques of politico-businessmen and their crony capitalist partners with access to the highest levels of the regime could deploy considerable power encompassing finance and business opportunities in far-off places. For instance, actors wired into networks of power in Jakarta could work concessions for themselves, fixing things upriver in due course. In doing so they could rely on the vertically integrated command-and-control structures that existed within state agencies such as the Ministry of Internal Affairs, the Ministry of Forestry and the Military which found their apex in the circle around Soeharto. This vertical integration, together with the enduring nature of the regime and the rewards offered to those who remained loyal to the system, gave the New Order a sense of corporate coherence and autonomy seen as characteristic of developmental states (compare Evans 1995).

At the same time, before regional autonomy there were well established localized modes of resource control. As exemplified by the PLG project in Central Kalimantan, exchange relationships between district level officials and law enforcement agencies, entrepreneurs, brokers and strongmen formed a 'decentralized' system of resource access and control. In facilitating the extraction of forest resources from the area and its transport to markets controlled by financiers and corporate interests in far away Jakarta, this 'decentralized' mode of resource control articulated with the centralized mode.[39]

After the passing of the key decentralization law (Law no. 22/1999), political competition and conflicts over policy undermined horizontal ties within the state in Jakarta. At the same time, the decentralization laws hewed at the vertical connections within the state (McCarthy 2004). Between 1999 and 2002 district governments were freed from the command-and-control structures that had held them (to varying degrees) accountable upwards under the old regime. Institutional arrangements within the state became fragmented and contested, which reduced the capacity of the centre to set the rules and to enforce them.

Yet, despite the apparently drastic changes in the system after 1998, there was a great deal of continuity in the modes of resource access and control. Political decentralization had merely rearranged pre-existing 'decentralized' ways of organizing production and allowed them to flourish. With larger groups of actors involved in production and enjoying benefits, routes of access initially became more diverse.

To avoid the risk and hassle involved in running a business under these unpredictable conditions, outside financiers and business interests increas-

39 See Obidzinski (2003) for an extended analysis of how this mode of resource extraction operated over a long period of time in another area of Kalimantan.

ingly subcontracted elements of their operations to local brokers, financiers and entrepreneurs. Given the importance of ethnic identity, these tended to be either *putra daerah* themselves, or actors who could involve *putra daerah* to arrange permits or operations in the villages and smooth relations with district elites. Over time local strongmen who could help guarantee the field operations of downstream conglomerates became more prominent, dominating the transport of timber out of the area. These figures gained a key role as intermediates between small scale brokers, entrepreneurs and loggers upstream and the financiers and industries downstream. Over time this led to a local centralization of control and benefit distribution around these strongmen. Ironically, decentralization had led to local centralization of this key node of resource control, a process which became more explicit after 2002.

A series of changes in the structure of state authority began to affect this system from 2001. With the strengthening of the status and institutional position of the police, the provincial police chief (*kapolda*) became more powerful. This allowed district police to operate under central control outside the matrix of district accountability relations. As the national government pushed for more rigorous law enforcement against 'illegal logging', the police began to apply the law against district and provincial actors involved in the sector. Yet, there were exceptions: a few syndicates with ties – via discreet gatekeepers – to the provincial police command continued to operate. At the same time, with the transition to the Megawati presidency, the central government wished to iron out the fragmented and contested state institutional arrangements. With a stated interest in reviving the unitary state, the administration set out to address some of the problems that had reduced the capacity of the central government to set the rules. In this context, the administration passed a key government regulation that reasserted the role of the ministry of forestry. This signified the end of effective district authority over forest permits. Consequently, the system for extracting resources became ever more centralized. These changes mark the re-establishment of a more vertically integrated system, where financiers and timber interests could expect greater predictability.

Over the 1998-2004 period, local actors faced a very fluid situation. Entrepreneurs, brokers, license holders and sawmill owners who had risen to prominence during the PLG period had to ride successive waves of legal, economic and personnel changes if they were to continue to prosper. After regional autonomy, change in politics and economics affected the personal situation of official sitting in the public sector agencies. The restructuring of the district and provincial agencies, changes in leadership, and the creation of new districts, were accompanied by a high degree of mobility in the public sector and changes in the authority and relative power of military, forestry, district and police agencies. This led to a process of 'natural selection', where only the strongest and most capable figures could survive. Those actors who could adjust, such as key local strongmen, needed to be able to use their multiple assets to insulate themselves from any particular change in the legal-political constellation.

Even if the logic of state action had been undermined during the messy process of implementing the decentralization reforms, the state remained important. Within public discourse, the application of state power still needed to be legitimated through the law. Yet at this time the legal system was contradictory. Consequently, state agencies at different levels of government relied on different areas of law within an inconsistent, rapidly changing legal framework. Here legality was first a matter of interpretation and perspective, which (as ever) was shaped for personal and institutional ends. The meaning of a law was coloured by shifting and contested interpretations of state regulations between competing agencies within a bureaucracy that was no longer so vertically integrated.

Localized matrices of power relations characteristic of these regions primarily regulated access and use of resources. The local state in its changing relations with provincial and centralized state authority remains primary to these networks. Above all, this is because those with the capacity to use state power locally necessarily will have to play the prominent roles within these networks of exchange and accommodation. Yet, given the informal nature of these institutional arrangements, they are best considered as neither coincident with nor independent of the local state.

Beyond the question of legal interpretation, a state agency – such as a district government, the ministry of forestry, or the police – needed to impose its interpretation in the field. A law could be used – through the threat or application of legal powers by a state law enforcement agency – to extract payments, to force an accommodation, to render an operation uneconomical, or to shut it down altogether. This depended on who had the authority or capacity to issue, obtain or manipulate documents, and who had the will or ability to enforce regulations at a particular time, and when, why and how they chose to do this. These applications of power in the field effectively regulated actors' capacity to extract resources from the system. By using this power, state actors in various ways controlled other actors' access to market, to various degrees accumulating revenue and enriching themselves in the process.

Initially district administrations set up district regulations that creatively used the centrally created legal system. At the high point of regional autonomy, well positioned district entrepreneurs and brokers improvised within the framework provided by these rules and the way they were applied, gaining windfall profits. The de facto control of villages over surrounding territories in the field meant that, for the first time in many years, conglomerates and financiers had to pay those claiming customary rights for access to resources.

Moreover, the development of a permit system that allowed local people to legally extract resources gave upriver actors a chance to market timber resources within the law for the first time. To be sure these benefits were unfairly distributed in villages, and the rural poor remained disadvantaged. Nonetheless, the allocation of permits to local actors combined with the de facto control of villagers over surrounding areas strengthened the bargaining position of villagers, contributing to a wider sharing of benefits. This increased the relative value that local people gained from the mining of their forests. For villagers, entrepreneurs and district officials the legitimacy or illegitimacy of the system of resource extraction depended on its capacity to distribute benefits, rather than to any abstract notion of accountability or state legality. Here political, legal or physical activities of actors focused on ensuring their own participation in the clientelist system for distributing benefits rather than on the formal policy-setting functions of government.

Like the New Order before it, local government during the regional autonomy period set about raising revenue and extracting as much benefits from the forests as possible for political and other reasons while ignoring the ecological limits of Central Kalimantan's forests. Unfortunately, regional autonomy reforms also failed to establish the rights of local users in any enduring way (see Ribot and Peluso 2002:163). Consequently, with changes in state laws from 2002 onwards, recentralization abolished these district regimes and the capacity of a range of local people to benefit. The new decentralization laws (Law no. 32/2004 and Law no. 33/2004) further institutionalized this direction. The high season of regional autonomy had ended.

Acknowledgements

A heartfelt thanks to all those people who have helped me so much with this work in Central Kalimantan. For obvious reasons, sadly I am reluctant to thank you by name. Thanks to the participants of the KITLV project 'Renegotiating boundaries; Local politics in post-Soeharto Indonesia' for their comments. Initial research was carried out in Central Kalimantan for the Australian Centre for International Agricultural Research (ACIAR) funded research project for the Centre for International Forestry Research (CIFOR) concerned with the evolution and impact of the decentralization of policy-making on forests and other sectors. I carried out further research in Central Kalimantan under a fellowship from the Van Vollenhoven Institute, Leiden University, during 2001-2003, and finally for the KITLV project 'Renegotiating boundaries; Local politics in post-Soeharto Indonesia'. The article was written under an Australian Research Council grant at the Asia Research Centre, Murdoch University.

ERWIZA ERMAN

Deregulation of the tin trade and creation of a local Shadow State
A Bangka case study

Introduction

Can tin swim to Singapore by itself? This was the angry question of a local journalist from *Bangka Pos* about smuggling tin-bearing sands. Smuggling of Bangka's tin sand, known as 'Bangka coffee' (*kopi Bangka*)[1] has increased since the deregulation of the tin sand trade was withdrawn and a ban was imposed on its export by the Minister of Trade and Industry, Rini Soewandi, in early June 2002. Tin may only be exported in smelted form or tin bars, which are far more profitable both for Regionally-Generated Revenue (Pendapatan Asli Daerah, PAD) and for the business operators. Even so, the smuggling of tin sand has never stopped; the government finds it difficult to control this mafia.

The deregulation of the tin trade that accompanied the introduction of regional autonomy in January 2001 signalled a new era in the history of Indonesia's tin mining management. The region's response to the transfer of authority for tin management from the centre to the regions, and its search for sources of regional revenue, were both rapid and radical. Regional autonomy actually brought about new conflicts, which were business and power conflicts rather than cultural or political ones.

This chapter will attempt to examine how power was transferred from the old tin regime to the new, and to what extent the practices of the tin business are under the control of the local government. What benefit does this business bring the people of Bangka? Why did the tin smuggling mafia

1 'Bangka coffee' is the term used by the Bangka tin sand mafia in Singapore. When ships carrying *kopi bangka* arrive in Singapore, the receivers of the smuggled goods (mostly ethnic Chinese), who are often also lenders to the small tin miners in Bangka, handle it right away (Interview with smuggler BY, 7-6-2004).

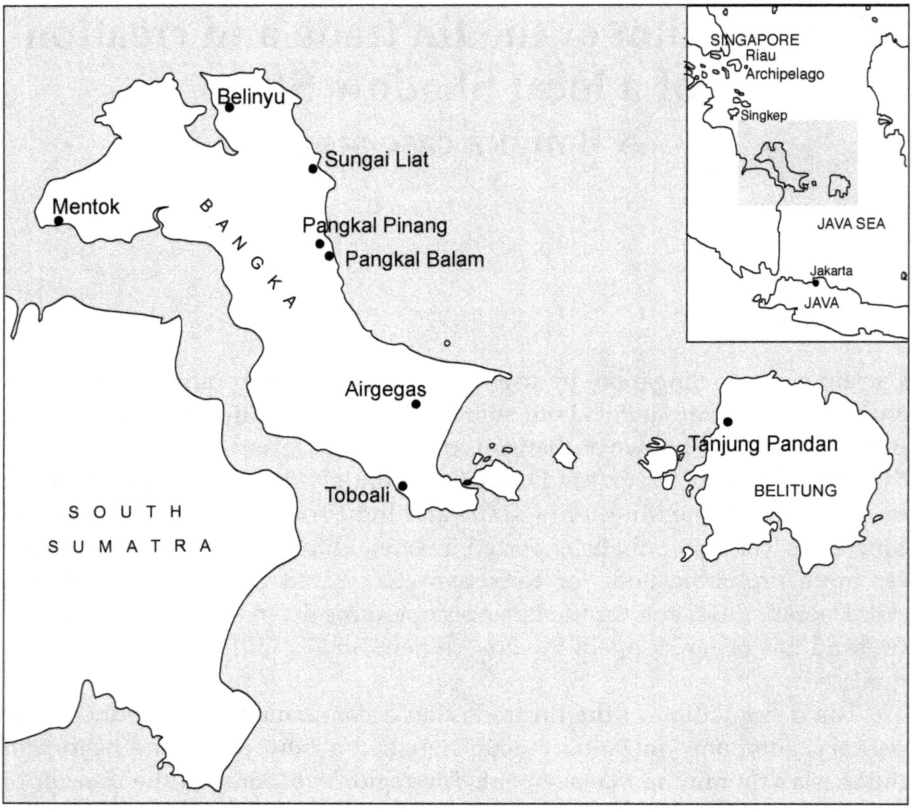

Map 7. Bangka Belitung

emerge, and why is it so difficult to prevent? To what extent are local state actors involved?

Mining tin is not terribly difficult. From its simplest form to its most technologically advanced, it can use a simple pan, other non-mechanical methods, pumps powered by 20 HP engines, or dredging ships that operate offshore. Once the tin has been dug up, it is washed, either with the panning system in the river or using spraying machinery, to separate the tin sand from the soil. The tailings, a yellowish mud, flow into the rivers, which are so important for the residents' day-to-day needs. If the mines are located along the coast, the sea water is likely to become turbid.

The old tin mining regime

Monopoly and centralization were the earmarks of Bangka's tin industry throughout its long history, from its eighteenth century beginnings in the time of the VOC (Vos 1993), throughout the Dutch colonial period, and continued by the government of Indonesia, both the Old Order and the New Order (Erwiza Erman 1995). The profits flowed to the centre, whether in the Netherlands, Batavia, or Jakarta. This placed the local government elite and the community in a disadvantageous position, except in terms of certain facilities that were built.

Development of the administrative and governmental region of Bangka was closely tied to, and highly dependent upon, the expansion of the tin mining area and the presence of a labour force. The Dutch state companies were nationalized between 1953 and 1960. From that time, Indonesia's tin mining region – the islands of Bangka, Belitung, and Singkep – was combined under a state company called PN Tambang Timah. The Indonesian government, both in the Old Order and the New Order, followed the mineral policy of the colonial government, which considered tin, like coal and oil, a strategic commodity that had to be supervised by the state, both in its exploitation and in its trade (Erwiza Erman 1994).

During the New Order era, the government reorganized and restructured state companies to become more efficient and free of corruption. This was done during the oil boom (1973-1981) and the early collapse of oil prices (1982-1985) (Mari Pangestu 1996:67-96; Robison and Hadiz 2004:9). In 1976, PN Tambang Timah Indonesia became a Limited Company called PT Tambang Timah (Persero). This was intended to eliminate corruption; it was also hoped that the new company would be financially more independent. The New Order government also invited foreign investment. In 1973, the Australian Kajuara Mining Company joined with PN Timah to establish PT Koba Tin. PT Tambang Timah produced 10% of the world's tin output in 1983, the largest in the world.

During the period of collapsing oil prices (1982-1985), when the government no longer had funds to subsidize the state-owned companies, there was a new policy: privatization. In the coal mining industry, privatization was signalled by the opening of Kalimantan to private foreign and domestic companies under several generations of Contracts of Work. PT Tambang Timah Indonesia did the same, by entering into contracts with private parties to carry out mining in the less productive regions and in smaller mines, with their production surrendered to the parent company. These mines were called Contract of Work Mines (Tambang Kontrak Karya, TKK) or simply Work Mines (Tambang Karya). In 1985, there were 152 TKK operating under contracts with PT Tambang Timah, 87 of which were on the island of Bangka (*Tambang Timah* 1986:8). Most of the contractors were ethnic Chinese, and half of the state's mining production came from TKK. Some of this production was smuggled to Singapore. A rough estimate states that around 3,000 to 5,000 tons of tin concentrate arrived in Singapore each year from these mines in the late 1970s and early 1980s (Baldwin 1983:176). One source from Tambang Timah claimed that small-scale panning tin miners tended to engage in this smuggling. The calculation is that these TKK produced 26% to 32% of the total tin production from 1983 to 1986, using spray mining.

Despite liberalization, the government continued to treat tin, like coal and oil, as a strategic commodity whose mining and trade were supervised by the state. Jakarta's control was tight. PT Tambang Timah used the military to protect mining areas, and prohibited local residents from mining tin, from keeping it in their homes, even if only one kilogram, and especially from trading it to outside Bangka. Anyone who violated these regulations would face an immediate prison sentence.[2] The incident when many village residents were arrested and shot by the military because of tin smuggling near the town of Jebus remains covered up. The harsh regulations of the New Order regime made the populace mere spectators of the PT Tambang Timah tin business.

Excessive bureaucracy and centralization were the main characteristics of the tin industry during the New Order era. The procedure for private investment was complex; it required approval from the Minister of Mining and Energy, the Investment Coordination Agency (Badan Koordinasi Penanaman Modal, BKPM), the People's Representative Assembly (Dewan Perwakilan Rakyat, DPR), and the President. The local government had no authority, and tin royalties went to the centre and to Palembang, rather than to Bangka. The local government was in a weak position, while PT Tambang Timah, as an extension of the central government, was all-powerful.

2 Interview with Sugono, 6-6-2004.

Decentralization and the new tin mining regime

The 1997 economic crisis and the post-Soeharto period brought important changes in the political system, in the management of tin mining, and in the status of Bangka. The most basic change was the local (district or city) governments' claim to authority over management of mining with the introduction of regional autonomy in early January 2001. Local governments now felt that they had the authority to issue mining permits to private parties, or to manage tin through local government companies. In fiscal terms, this reform provided a better allocation for the regions, even though the authority remained with the central government. Mining companies pay royalties to the government that grants their permits, that is to say the central government. Of the 80% of the royalty that is passed to the province where the mine is located, 32% is split between the districts/cities within the province, 32% goes to the district that actually produces the commodity, and the remaining 16% goes to the provincial government. This does not yet include the various taxes, such as land lease, property tax, and other taxes. But it seemed that the central government, in this case the Department of Mining and Energy, wanted to retain its authority. This is evident from a statement by the Minister that the mining industry would remain under Jakarta's control for the coming five years.

Bangka had long been keen on regional autonomy. The struggle to establish a province of Bangka Belitung, separate from South Sumatra, goes back to 1956.[3] Starting in 1999, the Bangka district government demanded ownership of shares in PT Timah Bangka, first 10% and later 25% from the 65% state share of the company's stock (*Bangka Pos* 15-2-2001, 16-2-2001). This struggle continued until 2001, and was eventually discussed in Jakarta by Commission VIII of the DPR-RI (Dewan Perwakilan Rakyat Republik Indonesia), then chaired by Darmansyah Husein, now district head of East Belitung. The demand even got as far as President Abdurrahman Wahid, but failed. The struggle for share ownership became even fiercer in early 2001, when there was a rumour that PT Tambang Timah was to be privatized, as one of the requirements from the International Monetary Fund (IMF) when the Indonesian government signed the Letter of Intent in January 2001. The demand for share ownership then shifted to a demand for replacement of the company's Director, a Javanese, Erry Riana Hardja Pamungkas, with a 'native son' (*putra daerah*), a common tendency in many regions in the era of regional autonomy. There were also criticisms about the lack of transparency in the

3 See Sakai 2003a. The province Bangka-Belitung was established in 2000 and has seven districts (*kabupaten*): Bangka, Pangkal Pinang, Belitung, Bangka Barat, Bangka Tengah, Bangka Selatan, and Belitung Timur.

company's management and the insensitivity of PT Tambang Timah Bangka toward the interests of local residents.

The efforts pioneered by the district head of Bangka to obtain shares in PT Tambang Timah were aided by Bangka *preman* (small-time hoodlums) and social organizations such as NGOs, mobilized by, among others, a Bangka *preman* and descendant of pirates, Johan Murod, who exposed cases of manipulation and corruption within PT Timah. He then mobilized the masses to demonstrate for the replacement of Erry Riana Hardja Pamungkas with a native son.[4] The outcome was that the struggle to obtain shares in PT Tambang Timah failed yet again, but the 'native son' issue succeeded, as Thobrani Alwi was appointed as Director of PT Tambang Timah. Under pressure from the local government, PT Tambang Timah granted several relatively uneconomical mining concession areas to the local government. In July 2001, the local government also established a Regional Company operating in the tin mining business, Bangka Global Mandiri (PT BGM), with a total mining concession area of 10 hectares. This company also has a subsidiary, PT Bangka Multi Niaga (PT BMN), which exports tin. The share ownership in PT BMN is 30% from PT BGM and 70% from PMK Niaga Jakarta. The implementation of regional autonomy was the start of a new tin mining regime in Bangka, which in turn created complex social and economic problems that persist to this day.

The new tin mining regime was signalled by deregulation of the tin trade. Decree of the Minister of Trade and Industry no. 146/1999 was issued by Minister Rini Soewandi in 2001.[5] It declared that tin was no longer considered a strategic commodity whose mining and trade had to be supervised by the central government. This was an important decision, because it weakened a monopoly the state had held since colonial times. It reflected the Indonesian government's increasing commitments, since the 1998 economic crisis, to IMF free market ideology (Robison and Hadiz 2004).

Not only tin, but also other commodities such as sugar and rice, were deregulated through the trade policies issued by this Minister. The local government seized on tin deregulation as an opportunity to issue licenses, to regulate export, and to stipulate a decentralized management system. The district head of Bangka issued District Regulation no. 21/2001 (8 May 2001) on implementation of general mining in Bangka, and District Regulation no. 2/2001 (1 July 2001) permitting the export of tin sand. According to the district head, these local ordinances were intended to increase locally-generated revenue (PAD). Local revenues from pepper exports were declining, as the price of pepper fell from Rp 90,000 per kilogram during the 1998 economic

4 *Bangka Pos* 6-6-2001; interview with Johan Murod, 13-2-2004.

5 'Chaos rebuffed', *Far Eastern Economic Review* 18-2-2001.

crisis to Rp 30,000 in 2001 and then Rp 19,000 in April 2005.

It was now possible for anyone to engage in tin mining or trade. There were soon 21 companies operating there, in addition to the Regional Company and PT Tambang Timah. Most businessmen were former owners of Contract of Work mines contracted to PT Tambang Timah, mostly ethnic Chinese. Business was good, prices were high, and they were able to eliminate the marketing bureaucracy. The difference between the price paid by PT Tambang Timah for tin sand and the price on the open market in Singapore, was high, around Rp 24,000 per kilogram of tin sand.[6]

The small-scale mines called 'unconventional' or 'informal mining' (*tambang inkonvensional*, TI) that had already emerged since the start of reform in 1998 became even more numerous, with financing from capitalists in Pangkal Pinang (Bangka), Jakarta, or even from Singapore and other areas, using trusted counterparts. These financiers are known as *cukong*. The *cukong* have an extensive tin marketing chain that runs from the city of Pangkal Pinang down to the villages. The fall in the pepper price to below the cost of production (Rp 12,000 per kilogram) in early 2003 caused many residents to switch from pepper farming to tin mining. With mining, cash was available immediately, as soon as the tin sand was collected, unlike when cultivating pepper plants, which requires extraordinary patience. These tin miners were not just residents of Bangka, but also newcomers from other regions who came to seek their fortunes in the new province. Informal tin miners received cash immediately when they handed their tin sand over to the village *cukong* (*cukong desa*) or the 'city tin collectors' (*kota kolektor timah*) who came from the city to buy the sand directly on site (Erwiza Erman 2003).

According to a rough calculation in December 2001, there were around 1,320 informal mining operations with business entity status, plus another 4,671 individual businesses (*Kompas* 10-12-2001, 18-12-2001). Another calculation, from January 2002, indicated around 10,000 units of unconventional mining machinery, and an estimated 130,000 miners (*Kompas* 6-1-2002). By way of comparison, according to findings by PT Timah in October 2003, in the district of West Bangka there were around 871 units of informal mines (*Detik.com* 16-12-2003). By early 2004, the number of informal miners had risen by 400% compared with the previous year. Although there are still no firm statistical data, this huge increase can be extrapolated from the fact that dealers in Chinese-produced mining machinery have opened branches in every city in Bangka, and even down to the district level throughout the island (*Bangka Pos* 27-4-2004).

6 This price difference was the main reason mentioned by smugglers and others in Bangka when discussing the smuggling of tin sand. Interview with former tin sand exporter Hongky Listiadi, 13-2-2004.

As the district head hoped, the new tin mining regime seemed to provide a greater contribution to Bangka's PAD. The contribution from January to September 2001 came to Rp 9 billion, far greater than the Rp 2 to 3 billion per year contributed to the regional government by PT Tambang Timah Bangka (*Bangka Pos* 16-9-2003). On the other hand, the presence of informal miners and new tin sand exporters created new competition for PT Tambang Timah, because the tin production from the informal miners was far greater. PT Tambang Timah no longer had a monopoly in Bangka. PT Timah held that this excessive supply of tin sand from the informal miners was responsible for the fall in the tin price on the international market. According to data from the Central Statistical Bureau (Badan Pusat Statistik, BPS), tin sand exports were 8.26 thousand tons, with a value of US$ 9.8 million, in 2001, and rose to 8.79 thousand tons, with a value of US$ 12.5 million, in 2002. The state company blamed the district regulation and the Decree of the Minister of Trade and Industry for its collapse. Discussions on the collapse of PT Timah were carried in the capital's mass media to the end of 2001.

PT Tambang Timah's balance sheet from July to December 2001 showed a deficit of Rp 250 billion. It would lose Rp 50 billion per month as long as the tin price did not improve (*Kompas* 20-12-2001). To try to overcome this problem, the company undertook an efficiency strategy. Around 1,440 dredging vessel personnel were laid off, because 13 of the 20 operational units were no longer in operation. In early December 2001, the company was forced to lay off 3,000 employees. This led to a decline in money in circulation from PT Timah employees' salaries, which came to Rp 10 billion per month, of which 50% was spent in Bangka Belitung. The company had debts of Rp 9.3 billion, comprised of property taxes, tin export fees, and other fees owed to the district. Another efficiency strategy was to limit the electric power supply in the Belinyu area to 10 hours per day. The caretaker governor calculated the losses suffered by Bangka at Rp 470 billion per year, compared with if tin sand were exported in the form of metal (that is, if it were first smelted and then exported in the form of tin bars).

Although they were not the only cause of PT Tambang Timah's near-collapse, sharp criticism was directed by PT Tambang Timah, the caretaker governor, and the members of the level I and level II local assemblies (DPRD I and DPRD II)[7] from the Golkar Party and Partai Persatuan Pembangunan (PPP, Unity and Development Party) at the district regulation, the Decree of the Minister of Industry and Trade and at the informal miners (*Bangka Pos* 1-8-2001). The governor, PT Tambang Timah, and their allies made efforts with the central government to cancel the tin sand export licenses.

7 Dewan Perwakilan Daerah Rakyat, Provincial assembly (DPRD I) or District assembly (DPRD II).

However, others attacked the Director of PT Timah, including criticism from within the profession itself. Ladjiman Damanik, former Chairman of the All-Indonesia Association of Mining Engineers (Perhimpunan Ahli Pertambangan Seluruh Indonesia, PAPSI), explained that the damage to the state company was due not only to the widespread illegal mining and exports and the sharp fall in the tin price, but even more to portfolio manipulation and the company's lack of concern for local communities. The portfolio manipulation had been going on for around five years. Profits were seldom reinvested in tin mine exploration as capital for the future, but were put into other activities. Ladjiman also condemned the company's New Order-style approach, which tended to use security actions, rather than a humane and persuasive approach, in dealing with informal miners (*Kompas* 8-12-2001).

From October 2001 to January 2002 members of the DPR-RI and officials from the Department of Trade and Industry visited to see for themselves the severe environmental impact caused by informal mining.[8] These meetings resulted in an agreement to urge the Minister of Trade and Industry to withdraw the deregulation of the tin sand trade. However, the district head and his allies in the party Partai Demokrasi Indonesia Perjuangan (PDI-P, Indonesian Democratic Party of Struggle) dug in their heels. They argued that the district regulation was important to the local economy. *Preman* gangs, groups humorously known as the 'alliance of the misled' (*perkeliruan*), some NGOs, as well as PDI-P members in the regional assemblies (DPRD I and II) again questioned PT Tambang Timah's miniscule contributions to development of Bangka's economy, and mobilized the masses of the miners to demonstrate.[9] This was, indirectly, an ideological conflict between Golkar, represented by the old regime of PT Timah, the governor, and his allies, against the PDI-P, represented by the district head and his allies, including the *preman*.

Finally, a regulation prohibiting tin sand exports was issued by the Minister of Trade and Industry on 17 April 2002 and came into force from 1 June 2002 (*Bisnis Indonesia* 21-5-2002). Tin sand must first be smelted on the island. Tin exporters must have mining concession areas. The period from April to June 2002 was a grace period granted by the central government to the region to implement the new regulation. The local government demanded an extension of the grace period, claiming that financiers and tin exporting companies were building tin smelting plants in Bangka. However, as of the end of 2003, no one had actually established such a tin smelting business.

This ban on tin exports met with resistance from the district head's allies, who based their argument on issues of the 'people's economy'. The President Director of the Regional Company Bangka Global Mandiri, Yusuf

8 Interview with Abrun, 13-2-2004.

9 Interview with Johan Murod, 12-2-2004.

Faisal,[10] said that the decree cancelling tin sand export licenses created great unrest among the 11,000 smallholder miners. Dasuki, a PDI-P member of the Provincial DPRD, and also a tin businessman who was no longer in partnership with PT Tambang Timah, also stressed the ban's negative impact on the people's economy.

The ban on tin sand exports lasted only six months. In January 2003, the district head of Bangka issued Inter-Region Trading Licenses, or SIPAD (Surat Izin Perdagangan Antar Daerah), through District Regulation no. 20/2003. According to the district head, the intention of issuing the SIPAD was to reduce the amount of tin sand smuggling to Singapore and Malaysia. Basically, it gave tin exporters the opportunity to trade in tin between regions, provided that the exporters had mining concession areas and sent the tin sand to another region where there was a tin smelting company. Exporters must also pay a tax on each kilogram of tin sand traded between regions. A total of 98 SIPAD were issued by the local Industry, Trade, Cooperatives, and Investment Service (Dinas Perindustrian Perdagangan Koperasi dan Penanaman Modal, Indagkopem). Of these, 51 were issued to three companies: CV Basuki, CV Bayu Mandiri Pratama, and PT Kranji Jaya Utama (KJU) (*Bangka Pos* 28-9-2003). The other 41 SIPAD were issued to CV Donna Kembara Jaya.

CV Basuki is owned by Hendrie Lie and his two younger brothers, Bangka Chinese who live in Jakarta. He is known as a 'strong man' in Bangka, a smuggler king, owner of an airline (Sriwijaya Air) and gambling venues, but also a philanthropist who donates to social organizations, both Chinese and non-Chinese. CV Bayu Mandiri Pratama is led by H. Eling Sutikno, a native of Bangka, a former journalist in the capital with strong ties to the bureaucratic and political elites in Bangka and Jakarta. CV Donna Kembara Jaya is owned by Ernawati Rebuin, sister of the Mayor of Pangkal Pinang, Syofyan Rebuin.

The two types of SIPAD that were issued have yielded production of 4,689 tons, and the regional government has reaped revenue of Rp 561,494,700, derived from the fees collected under District Regulation no. 20/2001 (*Bangka Pos* 16-12-2003). Examining more closely, we find that of the four companies holding the district head's SIPAD, CV Bayu Mandiri Pratama made the greatest contribution, Rp 323,500,000. CV Basuki and PT Kranji Jaya Utama, in contrast, stopped exporting tin sand in May 2003, due to lack of raw material.

Just like the earlier district regulation on tin export licenses, the SIPAD also created a new conflict between the district head and his allies on the one hand, and PT Timah and the new, definitive governor of Bangka Belitung

10 Yusuf Faisal, also Chairman of the Mineral Industry Association (Asosiasi Industri Mineral) in Bangka, is from Sulawesi. This association was founded after the issuance of the district head's district regulation on export of tin sand from Bangka. Most Bangka tin sand exporters are members of this association. Interview with Pak Abrun, 12-2-2004.

on the other. Accusations from the district head's foes came fast and furious, from members of the Golkar and PPP factions at both the district and the provincial levels. In meetings at the Provincial DPRD, efforts were evident by Golkar representatives to corner the district head, for example by Mustadja Santoso (Golkar), and Taufik Rani, who is in the tin business with PT Timah. They said that the district head's SIPAD were being used as an excuse to increase tin sand smuggling and unlicensed tin mining. These accusations were rebuffed by the district head's clique, including an officer from the Trade and Industry Service. He said that tin smuggling was already widespread long before regional autonomy, and could be traced back to the time of the VOC.

HA Hudarni Rani, a descendant of Mentok nobility and a Golkar party member, who was chosen as the first elected governor of Bangka in early 2002, started to take over regulation of the tin business at the provincial level, arguing the districts were incompetent. With the partitioning of the district, effective from February 2003, the debates on regulation of the tin business never yielded any decision, and the problem actually became even more complex, as there was now the added issue of regionally-generated revenue (PAD) for each of the districts, and a struggle between them for their economic interests.

Starting in October 2003, the issue of the district head's SIPAD was taken up at the provincial level. Mustadja Santoso, from Golkar, was chosen to head the Special Committee on the Draft District Regulation on Management of General Mining (*Bangka Pos* 21-2-2004). This Special Committee worked until January 2004, when a district regulation was passed by the provincial DPRD and came into force. This district regulation was more complex, regulating export taxes, reclamation, mining exploitation, transportation, smelting, and trade in tin both within and between districts. Under the new procedure, mining concessions were not simply issued by the Mining Service but also required approval from the DPRD. To prevent abuse of this regulation, and so that various agencies would not blame each other, integrated control involving the various related agencies was established in January 2004. Control over mining locations, use of heavy equipment, and the payment of taxes on tin sand that was to be smelted in tin smelting plants in Bangka, was much stricter than before. But will this tighter control produce higher local revenue and reduce the illegal trade in tin to outside Bangka? It is difficult to answer this question without first examining the methods used to control mining and the marketing system. The Deputy Chairman of the Bangka district DPRD, Samsumin Sagap from the Golkar Party, said that the more complex the regulations were, the more smuggling there would be, and the less responsible the mining system.[11]

11 Interview with Pak Samsumin Sagap, 14-2-2004.

The deregulation and subsequent reregulation of the tin trade, both by the central and the local governments, showed, first, a rapid response from the region to the transfer of authority over tin mining and the tin trade from the centre to the regions. The district head of Bangka played an important role in issuing district regulations, both the first one that gave form to the deregulation of the tin trade by the Minister of Industry, and the later district regulation on SIPAD. Even though the old regime operated from Jakarta seemed to have the formal powers to prevent an irresponsible and environment-unfriendly mining system, this regime was unable, or failed, to exercise this power, because the informal market, or black market, continued to operate. And although the governor has taken over duties from the district head and regulated the tin business in greater detail, the stricter the regulations, the more the smuggling. The next section will examine the emergence of the Shadow State at the local level and how it operates, making the black economy in Bangka so difficult to prevent.

The tin business and the emergence of a local Shadow State

The district head has become the centre of a new tin mining regime and has the authority to control natural resources in Bangka. The old tin centralized management regime has been unable to maintain its authority and its formal powers, because even though regulation has now been reimposed on tin sand exports, a 'black economy' has emerged in Bangka. The district head is a graduate of the military university, Universitas Veteran ABRI (Angkatan Bersenjata Republik Indonesia – Indonesian Armed Forces) in Yogyakarta. He received a naval military education and last served as a lieutenant. He has also received a master's degree from a university in Australia. He was at first a member of Golkar, but – according to several Bangka political figures – was not greatly involved in politics. In the run-up to the 1999 election, he switched to PDI-P and served as district head for the 2000-2004 period. He was a vocal figure in the struggle to establish the new province, and collected Rp 2 billion in funds from smallholder miners and from PT Tambang Timah Bangka and PT Koba Tin. He also arranged navy warships to carry residents from Bangka to attend the official inauguration of the new province. When candidates for governor of the new province of Bangka-Belitung started to be nominated in early 2001, the district head was nominated in a meeting of the PDI-P's Bangka and Belitung branch in Tanjung Pandan in May 2001. He was a strong candidate; but he later seemed reluctant to give up his position as district head and withdrew. But since January 2004 he began gathering support to run for governor in 2007. Many in Bangka still see him as the only strong candidate. Since then, there has been an undercover struggle between the district head and the governor. Whenever there is a demonstration against the district head by the public and NGOs, there is a counter-demonstration against the governor and his clique, as we will see.

To examine the practices under the district head's tin ordinances, this section will analyse two cases, involving people known in Bangka as the Tin Kings (Raja Timah); here I refer to them as Tin King I and Tin King II. We will see how their business practices involve bureaucrats, politicians, the police, the military, *preman*, and NGOs. This collaboration has created a 'Shadow State'. There are many definitions of the Shadow State, for example those in William Reno's study (1995) in Sierra Leone, and in Barbara Harris-White's (2003) in India. Reno said that the existence of the Shadow State was inseparable from the practices of the jewel smuggling market and the informal market. This occurred because of erosion of the functioning of formal state institutions. This situation becomes even worse when this erosion coincides with a serious economic crisis (Reno 1995:2-3). This spurs state actors to build alliances with various elements in society to gain short-term economic and political advantages through the informal market. State actors invite investors to join in the shadow state network they build, and provide them with protection using their formal authority. Barbara Harris-White prefers the term 'informal economy' to 'informal market' when examining the practices of the Shadow State. This refers not to the small-scale economic sector of the common people, but to the use of formal institutions (public and private) for private ends, including tax lenience, abuse of public authority, corruption, collusion, and forced privatization of state assets (Harriss-White 2003:6). This second form of 'informal economy' belongs to the 'big guys' and large business operators. A study by Pasuk Phongpaichit (Phongpaichit et al. 1998) examined the smuggling of weapons, women, and illegal drugs – or the 'black market' – in Thailand. In the case of Indonesia, Henk Schulte Nordholt (2003:579) has shown that the process of administrative decentralization has created opportunities for regional leaders, or 'bossism' as in the Philippines, to operate through an alliance between bureaucrats, the bosses of business-oriented parties, the military, and criminals. Such alliances are also found in Thailand (Phongpaichit et al. 1998; McVey 2000).

Tin King I is an important businessman from Jakarta, whose business contacts cross national boundaries and who has diversified into many sectors. Tin King II is a typical local businessman at the district level with long experience in the tin business as a partner of PT Tambang Timah. Despite the difference in scale and business networks between these two businessmen, the methods through which they do business are similar: collaboration and informal actions in formal business.

Tin King I

At 2.00 a.m. on 13 February 2003, residents of Sadai village captured trucks carrying around 42,750 tons of tin sand, packed in wooden crates which were covered with sacks of pepper. This tin sand was to be taken to Java on the passenger ship Tri Star via the port of Ciwandan, Cilegon, West Java (*Bangka Pos* 13-2-2003). The tin sand belonged to CV Tin King I, a local tin company owned by Tin King I, a Bangka Chinese in Jakarta who was looking for business opportunities in Bangka. CV Tin King I is located in Sungai Liat, in the area of his birthplace, the capital of Bangka Induk district, and the turf of the district head who issued the district regulation on tin sand exports. The tin sand was to be sent to PT Tambora Mandiri in Jakarta, and to a tin smelting company in Surabaya with an unclear address, to be smelted. The shipment was made after the district head's SIPAD permits were issued.

Just as CV Tin King I's trucks were about to unload the tin sand at the port of Sadai, Toboali, they were stopped by PT Timah's security unit, and then the NGO Lintas 99 brought village residents to help impound the tin sand that was about to be shipped. Several in the crowd threatened the employees of CV Tin King I and tried to force CV Tin King I to pay a ransom of around Rp 500 million to the Sadai village community to release the tin. Bargaining between CV Tin King I and the local community ensued. At first, a number of people claiming to speak on behalf of the community demanded a contribution from CV Tin King I to the residents of Sadai village. After tough negotiations, CV Tin King I eventually donated Rp 30 million to Sadai village (*Bangka Pos* 14-2-2003), and the sand was released. Even so, apparently some data were manipulated, as only five of the nine trucks that were carrying the tin sand were in fact exported to the destinations. According to an activist of Lintas 99 in Toboali, the district head's Decree was legally flawed, as it conflicted with the ban on tin sand exports issued by the Minister of Trade and Industry (*Bangka Pos* 16-2-2003). Following the interrogation of the PT Timah security guards and three employees of CV Tin King I (*Bangka Pos* 19-2-2003, 23-2-2003), several NGOs in Toboali agreed to send letters to various Jakarta authorities to check whether the tin sand shipment was in line with the provisions of the district regulation on SIPAD (*Bangka Pos* 20-2-2003).

CV Tin King I had complied with all the formal requirements of the district regulation on tin exports, such as holding a 200-hectare Mining Concession at Air Gegas village, South Bangka. Tin King I was called a 'strong man of Bangka' and a smuggling and gambling king, but he also helped many social activities, for both the ethnic Chinese and the Malays of Bangka. He had other businesses in the transport and plantation sectors, in Bangka and elsewhere. Together with his two younger brothers, he even had a new airline, Sriwijaya Air, of which the local government was very proud.[12] Tin King I was at first close to the governor of South Sumatra, and was known to be unenthusiastic about establishing a new province. But once the new province was established, he became close to the district head. When the definitive governor of Bangka-Belitung was appointed, from Golkar, he again changed his clique to the governor and contributed funds to support the governor's campaign in the 2004 election. Tin King I is also known to be close to one of Bangka's top lawyers, a figure in the PDI-P, who has defended him in his tin smuggling cases.

As soon as the district regulation on tin sand export licenses came into force, CV Tin King I started business. We do not know how business operators may have influenced the district head's ordinance. It is also not possible to obtain accurate figures on the tin exports, as some of it is done legitimately and some through smuggling. But when tin sand exports were licensed, the data on official tin sand exports was as follows. From January to February 2002, the company exported 100 tons of tin sand abroad (*Bangka Pos* 13-2-2003). After the ban on tin sand exports came into force on 1 June 2002, CV Tin King I still obtained a permit to export 135 tons of tin sand on 2 June 2002, complete with export license documents, although this shipment was the subject of much criticism from local government officials (*Bangka Pos* 3-6-2002). PPP and Golkar members of the district DPRD therefore say that CV Tin King I's business is somewhere 'between official and unofficial'.[13]

Since the ban on tin sand exports came into force, nothing more has been heard of the company's business activities. Nevertheless, from reports in both local and national newspapers and interviews with several informants in Bangka, it is known that Tin King I continues to export tin sand abroad, but now through smuggling. The local mass media carry reports on his smuggling trade, but the reporters are never transparent about this; they always refer to the company's owner by using initials.[14] Furthermore, the cases of the tin sand that was impounded have never been taken to court for trial, and so the cases of tin sand exports to Jakarta and Surabaya as quoted above have led to protracted debate in the DPR.

CV Tin King I used its district head's SIPAD permit as justification for

12 According to one local source, after his success in tin sand smuggling, Tin King I established a consortium of Chinese *tauke* (bosses) for the legitimate business of Sriwijaya Air and arranged a strategy for the various losses and profits from their smuggling business. He was then able to persuade the bank to give him a loan, which was used to rent used aircrafts, then named Sriwjaya Air, for Rp 300 million per month. He is the official owner of Sriwijaya Air. The inauguration of the airline's maiden flight was attended by all Bangka's top officials. He has now become a respected citizen in Bangka and plans to add to Sriwijaya Air's fleet in the near future. Interview with informant X, Pangkal Pinang, 19-2-2005.

13 Interview with member of the Bangka District DPRD, 12-2-2004.

14 Interview with *Bangka Pos* journalist, 8-8-2002.

exporting tin sand outside Bangka. The case was examined in sessions of the DPRD-II. A special committee was then formed, with the task of investigating the case of tin sand exports by CV Tin King I to Jakarta and Surabaya involving PT Timah.[15] The results of the investigation revealed that in the destination locations, the companies that received the tin sand did not in fact have smelting plants. The tin sand shipments were also not found in the records of the officers of the ports of Tanjung Priok and Merak (*Bangka Pos* 7-3-2003, 9-3-2003). Tin King I, when invited to give evidence about the smelter in Surabaya, did not attend the meeting of commission B of the district DPRD; he sent a deputy instead. From this, it is evident that Tin King I, as a powerful figure in Bangka, has greater authority than the members of the legislature (*Bangka Pos* 9-3-2003). Furthermore, the PDI-P members of the DPR, like the district head, who was also being investigated, chose to remain silent during the sessions on the CV Tin King I case. In contrast, the representatives from Golkar, PPP, and Partai Amanat Nasional (PAN, Party of the National Message), the big parties in Bangka, continued to try to corner Tin King I and to make an issue of the district head's SIPAD.

The case of the tin sand exports by Tin King I, which were protected by the regional police chief and the district head, were in fact an instance of business rivalry between PT Timah and CV Tin King I, and at the same time of political rivalry between the district head, from PDI-P, and his legislative opponents. In April 2003, the district head had to present his accountability report to the DPRD, a critical time that provided an opportunity for the district head's political opponents to try to bring him down. Criticism of informal mining came fast and furious to corner the district head. This included the case of the impounded tin sand, heated discussions in the DPRD about CV Tin King I's tin sand exports, the strong reprimand from the governor to the district head of Bangka about the uncontrolled mining by informal miners, and counter demonstrations and letters to the editor both supporting and attacking the district head and PT Timah. It became clear that the interests of the most vocal parliamentarian, named Osfindinar, lay with those of PT Timah and the governor, while the district head's interests were in line with those of CV Tin King 1, which was protected by the regional police chief.

Among the district head's other allies were the NGOs and *preman* in the '*perkeliruan*' group.[16] They mobilized the masses to demonstrate at the DPR

[15] As well as its investigation of the CV Tin King I case, the special committee also conducted a similar investigation of tin sand exports using SIPAD permits to Tanjung Pinang. The result was the same; there were fictitious manipulations in the sand exports.

[16] The word *perkeliruan* is derived from the word *keliru* meaning 'mistaken, confused, erroneous'. I have not been able to discover why they are called this. The term appeared with the start of reform (Reformasi) in Bangka. This group consists of *preman* and NGO members, who are outsiders, relative to the bureaucracy and the representative institutions. The members of the

in support of tin sand exports by CV Tin King I and mining by informal miners. The *preman*, led by J.M., found it easy to mobilize large numbers of people, because he had been the chairman of numerous associations – for karate and other sports, and fishermen's associations – and was also close to the regional police chief.[17] Coffee shops became important venues for meetings between actors from state institutions, businessmen, *preman*, and NGOs to discuss the 'projects' they planned to undertake. Close relationships were forged there, thus shaping a genuine local Shadow State, a *negara perkeliruan*, if we may be allowed to use a term that has been popular in Bangka since the start of regional autonomy.

The business and political opponents of the district head and CV Tin King I also had allies. Demonstrations against the district head and CV Tin King I began with the NGO 99 in Toboali Selatan. This NGO attacked CV Tin King I, the district head's SIPAD permits, the behaviour of the regional police chief, and the informal miners who were destroying the environment. But counter-demonstrations in support of the district head were just as strong. In March 2003, 200 residents of Toboali, Mentok, and Kelapa districts, and former tin workers joined together in the Perhimpunan Pengelola dan Pekerja Tambang Timah Rakyat Bangka (P3TTRB, Association of Bangka Small-Scale Tin Miners and Operators) came to the Bangka DPRD building.[18] They demanded the mining concessions that PT Timah had not yet granted to the local government. Threatening posters were displayed with slogans such as 'Closing informal mines is murdering us', and 'Return tin mining concessions to the state to be managed by the people'. P3TTRB's Deputy Chairman Tito Rahadi said that the mining community would 'do a calculation' if the governor's letter to the district head to close the informal mines were implemented (*Bangka Pos* 30-3-2003). Evidently the issue of the common people was being used to maintain the tin business, a common trend since Reformasi, especially in the sector of small-scale mining financed by shadowy *cukong*. At the same time, university students in the Gerakan Mahasiswa Nasional Indonesia (GMNI, Indonesian National Student Movement) also demonstrated in front of the DPRD office, demanding that the DPRD reject the district head's Accountability Report for 2002. But then a number of housewives from the Pengajian Al Mafiroh prayer group in Sungai Liat, in which the district head's wife was active, also swarmed into the DPRD office courtyard and demanded that the members of the Bangka DPRD act fairly.

perkeliruan have been able to expose the corruption of government officials and lend their support to certain groups within the bureaucracy.

17 Interviews with J.M., 8-10-2003 and 12-2-2004.

18 It should be noted that the district head was very firm in struggling for the demands of former tin employees against PT Timah, the Minister of Finance, and the Minister of Mining and Energy for their severance payments that they had not received.

Arguments broke out between the two groups of demonstrators.

The case of CV Tin King I has never been resolved. While the CV Tin King I case was being debated in the DPRD, Tin King I was formulating a new strategy: to request a permit from the local government to build a tin ore smelting plant that could handle from 100 to 200 tons of tin sand (*Bangka Pos* 6-3-2003). A permit was quickly obtained. This CV Tin King I tin smelting plant would be the second privately-owned one in Bangka Belitung, as there was already one owned by PT Koba Tin. Oddly, at the same time, a proposal from PT Koba Tin to build an additional smelter did not receive a permit from the government. It remains unknown exactly what kind of lobbying Tin King I did with local government officials, such that even while his company was being attacked by members of the legislature and he was clearly engaging in manipulation by using the district head's SIPAD permit, he was still able to obtain a permit from the government to build a smelting plant. Tin King I owns four tin smelting plants, which are operated by his younger brother C.L., with the actual management done by Malaysians.

We can draw several conclusions. First, it is evident that the business was protected by the police, and that there was secret cooperation in the granting of the district head's SIPAD permit. Second, the way that the CV Tin King I case was taken up in the DPRD illustrates the concurrent business and political conflicts between Osfindinar and his allies against the district head and his allies, and between PT Timah and CV Tin King I. In this conflict, the serving district head came out the winner, because his accountability report in May 2003 was accepted by the DPR.

Tin King II

Tin King II is also well known in Bangka, although he is still relatively young. He was born in 1970 in Mentok, West Bangka, to an ordinary ethnic Chinese family. His father was a truck driver, and his mother a housewife and mother of nine. Because of the family's difficult economic circumstances, he did not finish school; he only went as far as the second year of junior high school in Mentok. He then worked in the shop of a Bangka Chinese family in Jakarta that sold automotive equipment. Returning to Mentok, Tin King II tried many different types of business: he traded in corn and in livestock feed, was contractor for a pipe factory, and eventually went into the tin business. Tin King II now has a luxurious house in Mentok and spends his free time playing with his pet dogs.

He first became interested in tin mining in 1994, when he saw the tin panners in the rivers in Mentok, which was operated by PT Koba Tin. He learned the ins and outs of tin mining, from finding locations to assaying the tin content of the ore obtained. He then went into partnership with PT Timah, using the name of a friend's company. He claims that he succeeded in changing PT Timah's prohibition on keeping tin at home, something that was strictly prohibited by the New Order government, although he did this unofficially at first. His tin business grew swiftly, from eight employees at the start to 70 employees. He established his own company, called CV Wijaya, and paid his employees an average of over Rp 1 million a month. The company has branches in many small towns throughout Bangka. In addition to the tin business, he also operates buses and a bottled gas business. Bangka people call him the 'strong man of Mentok', whose business interests are unshakable, even though his mining area encroaches on protected forest. The authorities can do nothing to stop this, nor can the environmental NGOs. And the small-scale miners who are mining in the prohibited areas declare that their mines are legitimate, because they have paid 'tribute' to government officials.

Tin King II did not actually have much capital when he entered the tin business. His main capital was the trust he received from many sectors, from businessmen in Jakarta to bureaucrats in Bangka. He is known to be close to the district head. Two months before the district head issued the district regulation on tin sand exports, Tin King II terminated his contract as a partner of PT Timah. When the district regulation was issued, he was the first person to export tin sand, officially recorded as 4,000 tons, and contributed Rp 4.8 billion in taxes to Bangka district coffers. When the ban on tin sand exports was imposed, he joined with the district head and the new director of PT Timah, a native of Bangka, to build a tin smelter at Liat. According to an unconfirmed rumour, the capital for its construction was embezzled from the Regional Budget (Anggaran Pendapatan dan Belanja Daerah, APBD).

When PT Timah and local and central government officials started to raise criticisms of the negative impact of the district regulation in the form of environmentally irresponsible mining activities, Tin King II was no longer exporting tin officially. In late 2001, he smuggled 600 tons of tin sand through Singapore, which was then seized by the police, together with another 500 tons of tin sand owned by two other businessmen. He and the other two smugglers were taken into custody. An interview with a *Bangka Pos* journalist revealed that before engaging in smuggling, he would first survey the safe and strategic locations from which to smuggle tin sand. He contacted the customs and excise service, obtained a recommendation, and 'reported' to port officers and other related agencies, including the security forces. Apparently, the smuggling was safer when it was witnessed by the security forces.

Was this arrest then processed in the courts? All three cases simply faded from public view. The tin that had been impounded was returned to Tin King II's warehouse for safekeeping, because the police could not afford the Rp 150 million warehouse bill, as was the tin belonging to the other two businessmen.

The arrest of Tin King II and the seizure of the tin sand he was smuggling had a strong impact on the price of tin sand, and therefore on the informal miners. The price of tin fell sharply from Rp 18,000 to Rp 12,000 per kilogram, and marketing tin sand became difficult. The miners grew restless, and held demonstrations against the local government. The miners depended heavily on Tin King II, not only because he controlled the marketing of the tin sand from the miners, especially in West Bangka, but also because of his social work for the poor. He donated to many social activities and provided scholarships to Bangka families that could not afford their children's school fees, regardless of whether they were Chinese or Malay. Tin King II's arrest also led the *perkeliruan* group to exert pressure by issuing several statements that basically strengthened the position of Tin King II in the eyes of the public. There was a rumour that funds of Rp 1.5 billion were ready to ensure that Tin King II's case would not go to court. The impounded tin would remain 'safe', in the sense that Tin King II himself and other parties who guarded it would receive a 'share' (*Bangka Pos* 6-1-2002). Another rumour spread by the *perkeliruan* group was a defiant attitude with the comment that 'right after the raid at Pangkal Balam, the very next day we exported that tin sand to Singapore' (*Bangka Pos* 6-1-2002).

These two cases illustrate the practices of the new tin mining business regime under the authority of the district head of Bangka. Actors from government agencies, whether from the local government or the legal apparatus, are involved. Government actors issue permits, provide protection, and manipulate data, as in the tin sand export case of CV Tin King I. Unfortunately, I have had difficulty in uncovering the actual transactions between the actors from local-level state institutions and these two Bangka Tin Kings, such as what rewards were received by bureaucrats, politicians, the military and police, and other state actors involved in the business, whether directly or indirectly, and what these profits were used for.

The level of protection provided by law enforcement officials seems to vary, in line with the interests of the business operators. In the tin sand export case of CV Tin King I, the territorial police chief (*kapolres*) immediately claimed that the tin was legal, while in the case of Tin King II, the police arrested the owner and seized the tin sand that was being smuggled. But this turned out to be a charade, since the impounded tin sand was later returned and Tin King II's tin sand smuggling case has never gone to court.

The protection from law enforcement officials for the tin sand smuggling cases, which has never ended, is an open secret on this island of tin. A smuggler who could be categorized as a mid-level Tin King related his experiences when he needed protection. He said that tin smuggling on shore is not that difficult, because he can get through by handing out money to certain persons. Furthermore, he knows exactly what locations along the coast are not monitored. For example, two kilometres from the pier, the smuggled tin will slip through, because the security forces do not operate 24 hours a day.[19] At sea, smuggling is done in two ways. The first is to use boats owned by Buton fishermen, who are not connected to the onshore tin business network. These Butonese know the routes to use to evade detection by navy patrols. The second is to 'entice the officials to play in the open seas'. This method involves chartering a larger ship, but with a cargo of only two tons, while also renting five smaller ships from Buton fishermen, with a total cargo of 50 tons of tin sand. He knows that the Bangka navy patrol is very limited and can only catch one or two smuggling ships. According to this smuggler, the security forces are also pleased when they can catch one or two ships. The capture of one big smuggling ship with a relatively small cargo is not a problem for the smugglers, as they still make a good profit from the others. If a ship with a large cargo is caught, then the smugglers ask the security forces to protect them and not arrest them, by offering them a 'share'. If the security forces refuse to grant such protection, there is an understanding that everyone involved in smuggling will remain silent during interrogation. This is unlike the top ranks of smugglers, who require the protection of the security forces, whether army or navy, who escort the smuggled tin from the port in Bangka to the edge of Singapore waters.[20] It is therefore not surprising that one often hears in Bangka: 'How can Bangka be safe and secure when even the security forces are involved in the mafia with the Chinese *cukong*?'

And this protection, collaboration, or even active involvement in the tin business is not entirely denied by the law enforcement officials. Their low salaries encourage them to seek additional income from such enterprises. Furthermore, the security forces' impotence in deterring smuggling is a reflection of the general weakness of state institutions, with limited numbers and quality of personnel, facilities, and compensation (*Bangka Pos* 2-7-2002). At the same time, there are demands for the law enforcers to act swiftly and firmly in preventing and handling violations. It is in this condition of a weak official state that 'people's justice' sets an ultimatum demanding firm action from the government apparatus.

How do these practices affect the community and the environment? It

19 I would like to thank Zaiyardam Zubir from the Faculty of Literature of Andalas University, Padang, who helped in observing the tin smuggling process at night, at the time of the first round of the presidential election. After quite a long approach, he was eventually accepted and allowed by the smugglers to follow the tin smuggling from the land, navigating rivers at night, and then pushing the motor boat off from the coast. The smuggled tin sand was taken offshore by motor boat and then transferred to a waiting ship. The *kopi bangka* was then taken to Singapore.

20 Interview with a smuggler, 4-6-2004.

is generally acknowledged that the new tin mining regime has made an extraordinary contribution to locally-generated revenue, and has created new jobs for the unemployed, especially those who were dismissed from PT Tambang Timah Bangka and PT Koba Tin, pepper farmers who were suffering losses due to the low pepper price, and even newcomers just arrived in the new province. However, it has had a grave impact on the public and on the environment, which the district head could never have imagined. The district head faced the aggressiveness of money, greed, and violence in the new tin mining business. The 'people's economy' that he had hoped to encourage was buried by a vicious economy interested only in short-term profits with no concern for the living conditions of the miners or the serious environmental impact on Bangka. This aggressive economy has given rise to numerous conflicts, between the public and the government, and within and between the mining and non-mining communities.

The characteristics of the informal miners' economy can be seen from their total lack of concern for regions that, according to the government, are off limits to mining. Hoping to reap immediate profits, financiers and *tauke* (foremen), tin collectors, and the miners themselves are racing to find tin deposit areas, whether on land, in the rivers, along the coast, or in the middle of the ocean. On land, the miners encroach on protected forests on the slopes of mountains, residential areas, plantations, near public facilities such as roads, bridges, and public water processing plants, and right next to local residents' rice fields. The informal miners also encroach on the former mining locations of PT Tambang Timah that have been reclaimed. At sea, the informal miners, called 'floating informal miners', work the whole area, starting from the coasts of Sungai Liat and Blinyu, and now along nearly the entire coast of the island.

Although the district regulation contains a provision requiring reclamation, this is apparently never done. Areas that have been mined out are simply left as gaping pits. The exact number of these pits remains unknown, but is clearly rising steadily. According to research by Sriwijaya University, Palembang, in 1998/1999 there were 887 pits in the province of Bangka-Belitung, 544 of which were on Bangka, with an estimated area of 1,035.51 hectares, or 1% of the total land area of Bangka (*Kompas* 27-6-2001). Obviously we cannot claim that these pits were created solely by informal mining; PT Tambang Timah is also responsible for many pits that have not been filled in.

The encroachment of informal mining into prohibited areas has had a tremendous impact on the residents of Bangka. Fishermen have lost their livelihoods, since they cannot catch fish in the coastal waters contaminated with tailings. This is why around 1,120 residents of Air Anyut village, Sungai Liat district, made an agreement to reject the presence of informal miners in their region, because they damage the river waters. The community asked the government not to grant any permits, and the district head summoned the mining operators, but there was no response (*Bangka Pos* 18-9-2003). Operators of service industries, such as hotels, which were expected to help raise PAD, now complain that the beaches that were previously tourism attractions have become dirty (*Bangka Pos* 3-10-2003). Village residents complain that clean water from the rivers has become scarce. The rivers can no longer be used to soak pepper, and the water can no longer be used for daily needs. The municipal water supply (Perusahaan Daerah Air Minum, PDAM) is also starting to become contaminated, or even shut off entirely, as was experienced by the residents of Toboali, South Bangka (*Bangka Pos* 11-11-2003). The Rangkui River, which flows through the provincial capital, Pangkal Pinang, is also polluted from informal mining that takes place upstream. Residents of Rias village, where the government was increasing Bangka's food self-reliance through rice planting, complain that the water for the rice fields is polluted. Owners of palm oil plantations complain that their areas are riddled with small pits. Forests are disappearing, because even the pepper farmers have converted their pepper plantations into 'tin plantations'.

Protests from fishermen and housewives to the DPRD II (district level) have not gone unheeded. Public officials have responded quickly; they have visited mining locations, and innumerable discussions have been held in the legislature, but the results remain unsatisfactory. The problem is not a simple one. First, there are problems with control over, and the penalties to be imposed on, the uncontrolled mining, because the agencies involved – the forestry, agriculture, and mining services, and the various local governments (village heads, sub-district heads, and district heads) – are all pulling in different directions. Second, the government faces a dilemma: closing the informal mines without providing alternative livelihoods will have bad consequences, especially when the pepper price is low; but on the other hand, leaving the informal miners to operate uncontrolled brings even greater risks.

The government also faces a range of social problems emerging within the informal mining community itself. Problems with alcohol, gambling, and women are inevitable. This has been so since the colonial era. Competition to obtain mining areas often turn into mob violence between one group and another. Reports of crimes such as fights between tin bosses, between groups of miners, and even between villages, and cases of tin theft, have become commonplace among the informal mining community in Bangka. Informal mining is full of violence.

The government has made some efforts to set things in order, from warnings to repressive action against informal miners that are damaging the environment. For example, in November 2003 a formal notice was issued to halt 'floating' informal mining activities along the coasts of Rebo, Teluk Uber, and

Rambak, Sungai Liat district, following previous oral and written warnings (*Bangka Pos* 4-11-2003, 12-11-2003, 24-11-2003). The owners of the informal mines ignored these warnings. An integrated team of 72 personnel, comprised of army, navy, police and officials of the relevant agencies, then seized the illegal mining operations, using force when necessary. Some of these efforts to restore order have succeeded, while others have not. Demolition of informal miners' machinery and equipment has, for example, been done successfully along the coastal areas of Tikus and Rambak, which are in the territory of Bangka Induk district.

In early 2004, law enforcement was taken over by the provincial government. This was done in connection with the partitioning of districts in the province of Bangka-Belitung. However, large numbers of informal miners continue to violate the regulations.

Efforts to put the mining business in order are executed in various ways. Aside from often being discriminatory, mine clearance efforts are also complex, because of the involvement of state actors in the mining business. The territorial police chief says that even before the officers go into the field, the plans for the raids have been leaked. He says that even within the police force itself, 'it is difficult to tell friend from foe' (*Bangka Pos* 2-7-2004). As a result, the police fail to find evidence of illegal mining in prohibited areas; the equipment has already been removed, and the place is deserted. But the miners swarm back once the team has left. The plans are leaked because the team members themselves own mining businesses. The mining clean-up system used by the government is also discriminatory. The only mines cleared out are those of small-scale miners, and rarely those owned by large-scale informal miners, those owned by the *tauke* (*Bangka Pos* 13-11-2004).

Working conditions for the miners themselves are also far from satisfactory. There are no social guarantees. There are no reliable data on the number of mining accidents that cause injury, disability, and death. Figures collected from local media reports from January to October 2003 mentioned 39 accident cases, with 23 serious injuries (in the sense of requiring hospital treatment) and 16 deaths. Accidents were caused by landslides and by getting caught in machinery, resulting in permanent disabilities (*Bangka Pos* 15-10-2003). Between January and July 2004, 27 informal miners died when they were buried in landslides. Many injuries or deaths are not taken to hospitals, or otherwise escape reporting in the mass media, or are deliberately covered up by the miners themselves. Most of the miners are not mine owners, but either 'sharecroppers' or wage labourers, who work in terrible conditions with no guarantees.

Decentralization, deregulation, and the Shadow State: a discussion

Who holds the dominant power in this local Shadow State? A tin businessman and smuggler said:

> The power in Bangka is not the district head, not the governor, not the members of the DPR, but money, money, money. Its exhilarating scent extends everywhere. The NGOs? They are the easiest – shouting in the morning, just give them some money and they're quiet by the afternoon.[21]

The involvement of state actors in this informal economy is closely related to their need to defend their political power from other competing forces who seek to wrest the authority to control natural resources. The voices for and against deregulation of the tin trade, and for and against the district head's SIPAD, are a reflection of the business and political competition between PT Timah and the local tin companies, between the centre and the regions, between the province and the district, and between Golkar, which wishes to regain power, and PDI-P, which won the 1999 elections in Bangka.

The case of Bangka shows similarities to Sierra Leone, in that the emergence and survival of the Shadow State reflects the weakness of formal state control, evident in the consistent failure to impose order and security in the tin industry, which is concerned only with short-term profits. Although decentralization of power is meant to be an effort to bring the state (central government) closer to the regions (Syarif Hidayat 2003), in the case of Bangka, exactly the opposite is seen. In reality, the district head and his allies are simply carrying on the work of the New Order. Although the people of Bangka are now permitted to mine, in general they remain nothing more than miners (sharing the proceeds, or day labourers in the case of newcomers) in working conditions that are far from satisfactory. The serious environmental damage that has resulted has actually made it more difficult to improve the region's economy. Thus, the new province of Bangka-Belitung or Babel, is re-experiencing the brutal economic practices of the New Order period, operating with a new face.

21 Interview with smuggler X, 7-6-2004.

SYARIF HIDAYAT

'Shadow State'?
Business and politics in the province of Banten

> Our knowledge of the nature of local political leadership in modern democracies based on systematic comparative scholarship is limited. This makes it difficult to generalise across political systems. [...] Political scientists just have been more interested in their own political system, and in interviewing national politicians than in comparative studies of local leaders. (Eldersveld et al. 1995:1.)

> The informal market role in rulers' construction of parallel political authority in the wake of the near total decay of formal state institutions – a Shadow State – is less well known. (William Reno 1995:1.)

Introduction

The quotations above indicate how few comprehensive studies there are on local politics. Observers tend to focus on the national level. Yet in the Indonesian context, local power relations cannot be understood simply through a formal approach, as they also involve informal networks, including relations between power holders and business. Therefore, a fuller understanding requires an approach that can simultaneously comprehend the formal and informal relations.

Motivated by a desire to understand more fully the power relations in the conduct of local governance in Indonesia, especially in the post-Soeharto era, I decided to undertake this research, with the theme 'Business and politics in the province of Banten'. My interest grew when one day I found an article in the 'Nusantara' column of *Kompas* daily (4-7-2003), entitled 'If you're going to Banten, don't forget your black clothes'. The writer, 'Zal', described the influence of the *jawara* in the conduct of local government in Banten.[1] The

[1] Raffles (1965) and M. Williams (1990:45-6) define the *jawara* in Banten as people who do not have fixed jobs and commit criminal acts. I would further describe them as an individual or

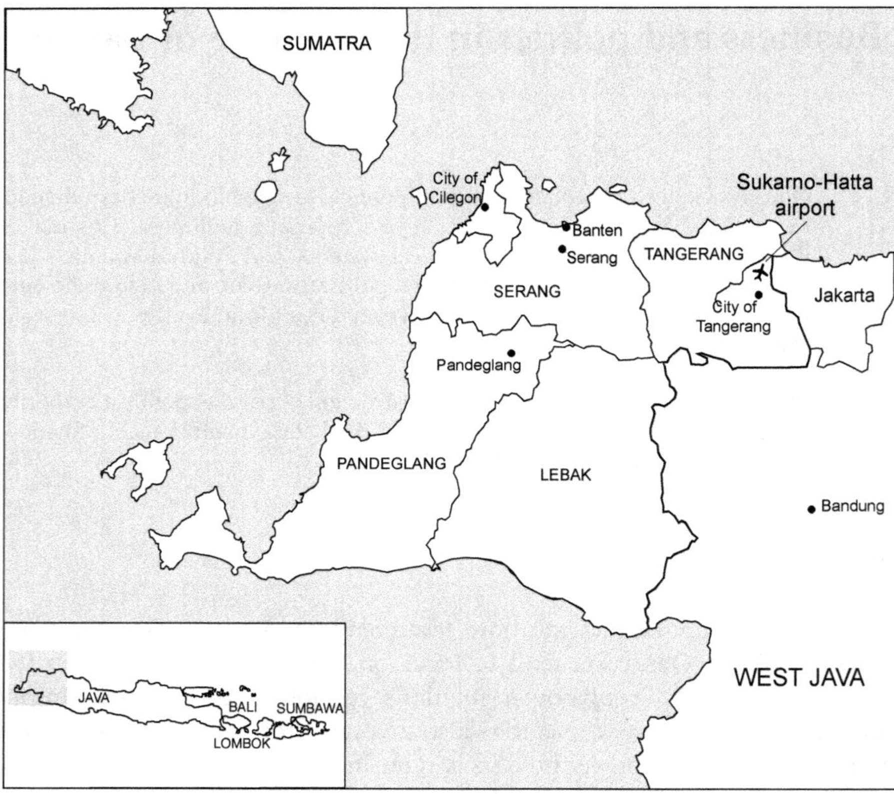

SUMATRA
City of Cilegon
Banten
Serang
Sukarno-Hatta airport
TANGERANG
SERANG
City of Tangerang
Jakarta
Pandeglang
PANDEGLANG
LEBAK
Bandung
WEST JAVA
JAVA
BALI
SUMBAWA
LOMBOK

Map 8. Banten

black clothes that he referred to are the official uniform of the *jawara*, now better known as *pendekar*. These black-clad *pendekar*, Zal wrote, have awesome power and influence. They control projects and intervene in local government policies:

> Black clothes are the favourite of the Chief of Banten's *pendekar*, Chassan Sochib (74). Wherever he goes, this community figure always wears only black. Chassan has dozens of black garments. Banten's public considers him an important local personage and, indeed, an important actor in the province's history. Chassan is seen as having served the development of Banten's infrastructure through his numerous contracting companies. However, he is also often the object of public criticism; he is accused of excessive intervention in local government policy. 'Especially when it comes to projects, nearly all of them are controlled by the (group dressed in) black', says one Banten Provincial Government official.
>
> Chassan denies these allegations. On several occasions Chassan has said that these misguided charges are simply due to jealousy. He claims that his contracting companies and the trust he has gained from the government are thanks to his many years of hard work.
>
> It is undeniable that Chassan is considered a 'strong man' in Banten. Many national figures are known to be close to him, such as General (retired) Wiranto. It also happens that one of Chassan's daughters, Ratu Atut Chosiyah (39), was elected as Banten's first deputy governor, on a ticket with governor Djoko Munandar.

This journalistic information inspired me to examine the role of the *jawara* in Banten in its initial period as a separate province. Not all *jawara* in Banten are 'pure' *jawara*, who rely solely on their martial arts ability and their powers of invulnerability. Some are businessmen, with a tremendous interest in obtaining access to the resources controlled by the local government. They will make maximum use of this dual status. As businessmen, they will maximize their financial resources, and as *jawara*, they can use their resources of force.

The provisional suspicion of the existence of 'dual-status *jawara*' then inspired the writer to develop a number of questions: Is it true that the *jawara* in Banten also have status as business operators? If so, how great is their influence in the conduct of government in Banten? Is there a correlation between their role in the establishment of Banten province (especially in the election of governor and deputy governor) and their role in the post-election period? How was this access to the local government built? And how do these '*jawara*-entrepreneurs' and local government officials interact?

---

group of persons who have a source of physical power (and the supernatural knowledge that accompanies it), who dare to oppose injustice, and who protect weaker individuals or community groups.

Historical background, social characteristics, and economic profile of Banten

Banten is one of five new provinces established since the passage of Law no. 22/1999 and Law no. 25/1999. Banten was the first and opened the door for the creation of the other new provinces through partitioning of existing ones – Bangka Belitung, Gorontalo, North Maluku, and the Riau Islands. Banten had a long history as an autonomous region during the Sultanate (1552-1809). But during the Dutch colonial occupation, with the abolition of the Sultanate of Banten, the area lost its autonomy (in 1817). It became a Residency (Khatib Mansur 2001:531). With the enactment of Law no. 5/1974 on Government in the Regions, the Soeharto regime reduced Banten to one of several regencies under the Province of West Java. This brought with it many disadvantages. Until the end of the New Order, Banten had West Java's lowest levels of education and public welfare. Banten also had a high number of 'backward villages' (Khatib Mansur 2001:166-7). All these things help explain the movement to establish a separate province of Banten, which apparently began in the late 1950s.[2]

After laying buried throughout the New Order, the will to establish a province resurfaced in early 1999. Numerous organizations were established. Three important ones were the Komite Pembentukan Propinsi Banten (KPPB, Committee for the Establishment of the Province of Banten) led by Uwes Qorny; Kelompok Kerja Pembentukan Propinsi Banten (Pokja PBB, the Working Group for the Establishment of the Province of Banten) led by H. Irsyad Djuwaeli; and Badan Koordinasi Pembentukan Propinsi Banten (BAKOR PBB, the Coordination Body for the Establishment of the Province of Banten) led by H.Tb. Tryana Sjam'un. Public figures and other elements of the community including *jawara* and entrepreneurs joined together, and strategies both formal and informal were put in play. The long journey of the people of Banten to achieve their ambition reached its climax on 4 October 2000, when the national parliament (Dewan Perwakilan Rakyat Republik Indonesia, DPR-RI) passed the Law on Establishment of the Province of Banten (Law no. 23/2000).

Moch. Aly Yahya was a key 'figure of struggle' who worked on many levels. As a 'son of Banten', he was a member of the steering committees of several of the organizations in the movement, including KPPB and BAKOR PPB. At the same time, as a young Golkar politician, he sat in the national parliament. It was in his capacity as a DPR-RI member that he drafted the

2 Interviews with Hasan Alayrus, 3-6-2004; Djamaludin, 18-6-2004; and UU Mangkusasmita, 1-7-2004. See also the 'Remarks from a Banten public figure' written by Kiyai-Haji Tubagus Chasan Sochib and the Prologue written by H. Uwes Qorny in the book by Khatib Mansur (2001).

DPR Initiative Bill (Rencana Undang Undang, RUU) on Establishment of the Province of Banten, which was later passed as Law no. 23/2000.

The new province of Banten comprises four regencies and two cities: Serang, Pandeglang, Lebak, Tangerang, the City of Tangerang, and the City of Cilegon. Serang was designated the capital. One unique aspect of Banten is the harmonious relations between *jawara* and Ulama (religious leaders). In most people's understanding, Ulama and *jawara* are two diametrically opposed worlds; yet in Banten they live together in a harmonious synergy. It is therefore quite right when M. Tihami (a historian in Banten), says that 'Ulama and *jawara* in Banten have always worked hand in hand – since the period of the Sultanate, in the struggle to expel the colonialists, and in the period of Indonesian independence'.[3] Yet their roles have diverged in history (M. Williams 1990; Sartono Kartodirdjo 1966; Raffles 1965). The *jawara* have continued to play a dominant role as informal political force, from the time of the Sultanate to the present day, while the official role of the Ulama in the conduct of government affairs has all but disappeared.

Turning now to the economy, three main sectors play an important role. In 2000 the Gross Regional Domestic Product (GRDP) of Banten was divided as follows: 50.41% for the Processing Industry sector; 17.36% for the Trade, Hotel, and Restaurant sector; and 9.49% for the Agriculture sector, with several other smaller sectors.[4] Thus, around 50% of Banten's economy is dominated by manufacturing, which includes textile, finished clothing and leather, chemicals, and metal goods. However, this does not position manufacturing as the main target of the government development programs. As a newly established province, over the past four years (2001-2004) most of the development programs in Banten have been geared toward upgrading economic infrastructure and basic services, especially in Education and Health. In 2001 the budget allocation for construction of roads/transportation facilities and other physical structures came to around Rp 116 billion (54.7% of the total Regional Budget (Anggaran Pendapatan dan Belanja Daerah, APBD)).[5] In 2002, this rose to Rp 130 billion (30%),[6] in 2003 to Rp 150 billion (34%),[7] and in 2004 to a phenomenal Rp 216 billion (49%).[8] The execution of these large-scale physical construction projects has become one of the main objects of attention from business people in their 'informal economy' practices with local government officials.

3 Interview, 24-6-2004.

4 Badan Perencanaan Daerah Propinsi Banten 2002. Similar figures can be read for the years 2001 through 2003 (Badan Perencanaan Daerah Propinsi Banten 2003).

5 Results of Discussion of Bill on Revision of the Banten Provincial Budget, 2001.

6 Banten Provincial Regulation no. 37/2002 on Revision of Banten Provincial Budget for 2002.

7 Banten Provincial Regulation no. 10/2003 on Revision of Banten Provincial Budget for 2003.

8 Banten Provincial Regulation no. 3/2004 on Revision of Banten Provincial Budget for 2004.

'*Jawara*-entrepreneurs' is one of the terms popularly used among observers in Banten to label those businessmen, whether individuals or groups, who now have such a dominant influence over the provincial government's top officials.[9] 'Tuan Besar', who will be the chief protagonist in this study, is an important figure in this *jawara*-entrepreneur network.[10] He has been a businessman of the first rank, especially in construction, since the 1980s. Before Banten became a province, Tuan Besar had many dealings with the West Java Provincial Government and was frequently entrusted to handle large-scale construction projects. At the same time, Tuan Besar's status as a prominent *jawara* is another, but inseparable, side of his identity. This status is not simply hereditary; for he was the founder of one of Banten's foremost *jawara* organizations. Tuan Besar is also a senior politician in Golkar.

Formal and informal governance: empirical reality and the approach of this study in Banten

As soon as Banten was established as a province, several steps were taken to complete its formal government apparatus. In early March 2001, the Panitia Pengisian Keanggotaan (PKK, Committee to Select the Membership) of the Banten Dewan Perwakilan Rakyat Daerah (DPRD, Provincial Parliament) was established, under the chairmanship of Hassan Alaydrus.[11] This committee, later known simply as the Banten PPK-DPRD, or the Team of Five, was appointed by the Minister of the Interior in Jakarta. The team's main duties were to determine the numbers of seats attained by each political party in the provincial DPRD, based on the results of the June 1999 election; to draft, establish, and announce the Daftar Calon Sementara Baru (DCSB, Provisional List of New Candidates); to accommodate and follow up on public objections to the DCSB; to draft, establish, and announce the Daftar Calon Tetap Baru (DCTB, Definitive List of New Candidates); and finally, to designate the selected candidates. The PPK-DPRD worked quickly. Less than a week after it was established, the PPK-DPRD had set out its working agenda (Agus Sutisna 2001:48). By July 2001, only two months later, it had completed

9 This information was obtained from interviews with Iwan Kusuma Hamdan, 1-6-2004 and Boyke Pribadi, 7-6-2004, among others.

10 Tuan Besar is a nickname I am using to protect his privacy. *Tuan* is an honorific term of address roughly equivalent to sir, boss or master, while *besar*, literally 'big', indicates his influence.

11 The establishment of the Committee to Select the Membership of the Provincial DPRD was stipulated through Decree of the Minister of the Interior no. 162-35/2001 dated 2 March 2001. Hasan Alaydrus, who was appointed as the Committee's Chairman, was a leading figure in the struggle to establish the province of Banten.

the last item on its agenda, the selection of the definitive candidates for members of the Banten provincial DPRD.[12] The Banten provincial DPRD has 75 seats, but 8 were allocated to the military (Tentara Nasional Indonesia, TNI) and police (Kepolisian Republik Indonesia, Polri). Thus, the total number of seats to be allocated among the political parties was only 67.

The Banten provincial DPRD for the 2001-2004 term was headed by Dharmono K. Lawi (Chairman), a politician from Partai Demokrasi Indonesia Perjuangan (PDI-P, the Indonesian Democratic Party of Struggle). The three deputy Chairmen were Muslim Jamaluddin (Golkar), Infantry Col. Rohman (Tentara Nasional Indonesia – Angkatan Darat, TNI-AD, the Indonesian National Army – Ground Forces), and Mufrodi Muchsin (PPP, Partai Persatuan Pembangunan, United Development Party).[13] Thus the DPRD was dominated by three major political parties: PDI-P, Golkar, and PPP. Of the 67 seats, 24 seats were held by PDI-P, 12 by Golkar, and 12 by PPP. The DPRD was not dominated by one party. In such a situation, it was virtually unavoidable that informal practices such as lobbying and compromises would colour decision-making processes.

The next step, and the first duty of the DPRD, was to elect the governor and deputy governor for the 2001-2006 term. The election process began on 16 September 2001 and ended on 3 December 2001, when the ticket of Djoko Munandar and Ratu Atut Chosiyah was elected as the winner.

Djoko Munandar is a native of Solo, Central Java. His most recent position was deputy mayor of Cilegon. When he registered as a prospective candidate for governor of Banten, Djoko allied himself with the PPP. Ratu Atut Chosiyah is a businesswoman from Serang and daughter of Kiyai Haji Tubagus Chasan Sochib.[14] Atut was nominated for deputy governor of Banten by Golkar.

The institutional apparatus was now complete. Hopes for the immediate creation of a more prosperous, democratic, and religious Banten were concentrated on these two important provincial institutions, and particularly on the newly-elected governor and deputy governor. Similar hopes at first accompanied me when I began my research in Banten in April 2004 (three months after Banten was established). But during the first two months I was surprised by the attitudes of a majority of the informants, who tended to be

12 The chronology and dynamics of the process of selecting the membership of the Banten Provincial DPRD are described in detail in Agus Sutisna (2001:43-54).

13 Decree of the Minister of the Interior no. 161/2001 dated 24 August 2001 on Inauguration of the Leadership of the Banten Provincial People's Representative Assembly.

14 Chairman of the Indonesian Association of Champions of Banten Martial Arts, Art and Culture, Persatuan Pendekar Persilatan dan Seni Budaya Banten Indonesia, PPPSBBI; senior politician in the Golkar Party; and Chairman of the Banten Chamber of Commerce and Industry (Kamar Dagang Indonesia, Kadin) (Iwan Kusuma Hamdan et al. 2004).

pessimistic when evaluating the performance of the provincial government, and seemed unenthusiastic about the future.

Several of my informants said the provincial government was almost 'totally crippled' in carrying out its formal functions, because informal forces were able to control the governor.[15] HOS, a member of the provincial DPRD, said Banten had a sort of 'private government' headed by the Tuan Besar mentioned previously.[16] This private government had tremendous influence over the provincial government's economic dealings. He alleged it monopolized nearly all local government projects, and pressured the provincial government to accommodate its interests when drafting the annual project development budget. Even more interesting information was put forward by BOB, an academic at Tirtayasa University.[17] Agreeing with HOS, he also described informal practices within the local bureaucracy. BOB tried to persuade me of Tuan Besar's power in determining bureaucratic transfers. Ayip Muchfi was the first district secretary (*sekretaris daerah, sekda*) of the Province of Banten. He was appointed immediately after Hakamudin Jamal was appointed acting governor of Banten. But once Djoko Munandar and Atut Chosiyah became governor and deputy governor, Ayip was dismissed, without going through the proper procedure. Apparently, BOB continued, the replacement of the regional secretary was related to a long-standing personal conflict between Ayip and Tuan Besar.

The initial indications suggest that informal political and economic forces dominate local governance in Banten. In studies of state-society relations, such practices of informal governance, or Shadow States, are nothing new. In the Indonesian context there have been few critical analyses of Shadow State practices. But Henk Schulte Nordholt (2003:558, 579) explicitly mentioned Shadow State practices in connection with the decentralization and regional autonomy policies in the post-Soeharto period:

> New ways of looking at 'the state' are necessary in order to trace continuities in patrimonial patterns and to incorporate various arrangements that link formal institutions with informal networks, which help to undermine artificial distinctions between 'state', 'society', and 'market'. [...] Decentralization in Indonesia does not necessarily result in democratization, good governance, and the strengthening of civil society at the regional level. Instead, we witness a decentralization of corruption, collusion, and political violence that once belonged to the centralized regime of the New Order but is now moulded in existing patrimonial patterns at the regional level. [...] On the whole, regional leadership may take the shape

15 Among the informants interviewed were HKI (academic and NGO activist), 1-5-2004; MUM (member of the Banten Provincial DPRD), 30-5-2004; TNT (high Serang Regency official) 14-5-2004; and MAA (Banten journalist), 15-5-2004.

16 HOS is a member of the Banten Provincial DPRD. Interview, 9-5-2004.

17 Interview with BOB, 7-5-2004.

> of what John Sidel (1999) has called bossism, which operates in regional shadow regimes characterized by alliances of bureaucrats, party bosses, businesspeople, military, and criminals.

Barbara Harriss-White has provided a more comprehensive theoretical and empirical discussion about the informal economy and Shadow State practices in India. According to Harriss-White, there are at least two definitions for the term 'informal economy'. First, business activities of an individual, and/or of a company not registered with the government, for which taxes are not paid. Second, the behaviour of formal institutions (public or private) to evade regulatory control. The forms of this second type of informal economy include tax exemptions, abuse of public policy, corruption, collusion, and forced privatization of state assets (Harriss-White 2003:4-6). It is clear that the first type of informal economy is the arena of 'the little guys' (small farmers and small business operators), while the second is the domain of 'the big guys' (large-scale business operators and state officials).

Barbara Harriss-White has applied an approach called 'social structure of accumulation' (SSA), in which social structures are one of the determinant factors for economic accumulation. She identified four such dimensions of social structure: class, caste, gender, and space. A majority of economic transactions in India take place through the informal economy. They proceed in a familial atmosphere, based more on reputation than on formal law, but also often with elements of (the threat of) violence:

> Some roles in the 'shadow' state are played simultaneously by the bureaucrats of the official state; for instance, accepting tribute, patronage and/or clientelage. Other 'shadow' state livelihoods are a form of self employment, although they depend on state employees, politicians and other interested social forces for their incomes; for example, private armies enforcing black or corrupt contracts, intermediaries, technical fixers, gatekeepers, adjudicators of disputes, confidants, contractors and consultants. Hence the real state, including its shadow, is bigger than the formal state, and has a vested interest in the perpetuation of a stricken and porous formal state [...] By the end of the 1990s in some parts of India, notably Bihar, up to 40 percent of the development budget was said to be creamed off by contractors. The 'shadow' state spills spatially into the lanes surrounding state offices and into the private (some would argue, the 'female') domestic space of officials' residences. This must be the most vivid image of the blurred boundaries between state and society. (Harriss-White 2003:89.)

We can note four general characteristics of the practices of the informal market and the Shadow State. First, they develop as a consequence of the decay of the formal (state) institutions, especially when accompanied by an acute economic crisis. Second, accumulation of short-term political and economic benefits outside the framework of formal regulations is the primary aim of transactions through the informal market. Each party maximizes its resources to then trade on them in the informal market. Third, the modus operandi, or working mechanisms, of the informal market and the Shadow State fall into two categories: manipulation of public policy, and use of networks of individual alliances or institutional alliances. Fourth, the actors involved come from both the state and society. Among the latter H. Schulte Nordholt (2003) mentions business operators, party politicians, and even criminal gangs.

This approach is relevant for 'reading' the practices of local governance in Banten. The following section will describe the election of the governor and deputy governor, followed by a discussion of the practices of the 'Informal Government'.

The election of the governor and deputy governor

The process of electing the governor and deputy governor revealed the various social, economic, and political forces (especially the *jawara* businessmen) at work. This was obviously an important moment for them.

Several Banten community figures who had earlier been the main players in the struggle to establish the province of Banten disappeared during the election process. Among them were Tryana Sjam'un (Chairman of BAKOR PPB), Uwes Qorni (a pioneer in the movement to establish a province of Banten, and Chairman of KPPB), and Moch. Ali Yahya (drafter and proposer of the DPR Initiative Bill on Establishment of the Province of Banten). In contrast, the previously discussed Tuan Besar (a *jawara*-businessman figure), who during the period of the struggle to establish the province of Banten had played mostly a behind-the-scenes role, emerged as a dominant force.

In technical terms, the election of governor and deputy governor of Banten comprised five stages: initial registration of prospective candidates; screening of prospective candidates, stage I; screening stage II; selection of the definitive tickets of candidates for governor and deputy governor; and finally, the election of the ticket of governor and deputy governor ('D-day').

Initial registration of prospective candidates for governor and deputy governor

The initial registration of prospective candidates for governor and deputy governor began on 16 September 2001. The local political dynamics from the opening of registration to D-day – the election of the ticket of governor and deputy governor – were unpredictable. PDI-P nominated Mamas Chaeruddin (Chairman of the Banten DPD-PDI-P) as its candidate for governor. Golkar put forward Moch. Aly Yahya (member of the Golkar Faction in the DPR-RI) as its candidate for governor and Hj. Ratu Atut Chosiyah (a businesswoman) for deputy governor. PPP nominated Djoko Munandar (Chairman of PPP's Banten Regional Leadership Board) as its candidate for governor. In addition, an alliance of three other parties – the Partai Keadilan (PK, Justice Party), the Partai Amanat Nasional (PAN, National Mandate Party) and the Partai Bulan Bintang (PBB, Moon and Star Party) nominated Tryana Sjam'un (businessman and figure in the struggle for the province of Banten) as their candidate for governor (Iwan Kusuma Hamdan et al. 2004:119-20).

Tuan Besar was not among the prospective candidates. This was part of the game-winning strategy. Rumours had long been spreading that Tuan Besar had ambitions to hold the post of 'Banten Number One' (governor).[18] To disprove this rumour, Tuan Besar did not formally register as a prospective candidate for governor. However, behind the scenes, he had mobilized his resources behind a certain ticket of candidates. As a senior figure in the Banten Golkar Party, Tuan Besar had a clear obligation to support its candidates for governor (Moch. Aly Yahya) and deputy governor (Atut Chosiyah). But he had an even greater interest in ensuring the nomination of Atut, as Tuan Besar and Atut share a very close family relationship.

Little 'money politics' activity was going on at this early stage. But various community elements came out in favour of this or that candidate. A 'Letter of Support' for Atut Chosiyah came from the martial arts association Persatuan Pendekar Persilatan dan Seni Budaya Banten Indonesia (PPPSBBI, Indonesian Association of Champions of Banten Martial Arts) on 18 September 2001 (two days after the opening of registration of prospective candidates for governor and deputy governor). It was signed by the Chairman of PPPSBBI, H.Tb. Chasan Sochib, and its deputy secretary-general, M. Suminta Idris,[19]

> We of the Executive Committee of the Indonesian Association of Champions of Banten Martial Arts, Art and Culture (PPPSBBI), in connection with the Election of the governor and deputy governor of the Province of Banten for the period 2001-2006, feel called [to declare that] it is necessary to select the right leaders, who understand the character and culture of Banten's society and have a sense of the unity and integrity of the people of Banten.
>
> Therefore, we of the PPPSBBI herewith declare our full support for Mrs. Hj. Ratu Atut Chosiyah as candidate for deputy governor of the Province of Banten for the period 2001-2006 in the coming election for governor and deputy governor.

The letter signalled that the *jawara* sided with Atut Chosiyah as candidate for deputy governor, and therefore also with whoever would be the candidate for governor on the same ticket with her. And it reflected an initial form of the *jawara*'s involvement in the election process. Later, their involvement tended

18 Interviews with HKI, 1-6-2004; DLM, 18-6-2004; and HAI, 6-7-2004.
19 The writer has a photocopy of this letter.

towards mass mobilization with the theme of 'protecting and safeguarding' the election, and towards intimidating supporters of other candidates. There are indications that these activities of the *jawara* were closely related to Tuan Besar's winning strategy.[20]

Screening of candidates

The first round had resulted in 22 prospective candidates for governor and 7 for deputy governor. These were now 'screened' to produce 12 candidates for governor and deputy governor of Banten. Up to this stage, the candidates were not yet assigned to pairs, or tickets. In the third round, screening stage II, the 12 candidates were paired up into 'tickets', each ticket being nominated by one of the 6 factions in the Banten Provincial DPRD. In its plenary session on 25 September 2001, through a secret vote, the DPRD designated 12 candidates for governor and deputy governor.[21] In the next stage of screening, the factions in the Banten Provincial DPRD nominated 5 tickets of candidates for governor and deputy governor (Iwan Kusuma Hamdan et al. 2004:122). These 5 tickets were: 1. Djoko Munandar and Ratu Atut Chosiyah (nominated by the Golkar and PPP Factions); 2. Herman Haeruman and Tb. Mamas Chaerudin (nominated by the PDI-P Faction); 3. Ace Suhaedi Madsupi and Tb. Mamas Chaerudin, nominated by the ABK Faction (Fraksi Amanat Bintang Keadilan, Mandate-Star-Justice Faction); 4. Herman Haeruman and Hilman Indra (nominated by the ABK Faction); and 5. Herman Haeruman and Ade Sudirman (nominated by the Al Bantani Faction).

The most striking point to note is the disappearance of Moch. Aly Yahya as candidate for governor during screening stage II. This prominent figure in the struggle to establish the province had received only 28 votes in screening stage I. But there are also strong indications that the disappearance of Yahya's name from the 'market' of candidates was closely related to the political scenario crafted by Tuan Besar and his 'Success Team'. As explained by several informants, from the outset Tuan Besar had a greater interest in the position of 'Banten II' (deputy governor), as this was the position relevant to Atut

20 Interviews with HKI (academic and NGO activist), 1-6-2004; MAA (Banten journalist), 15-6-2004; and HOS (member of Banten Provincial DPRD), 9-6-2004.

21 *Harian Banten* 26-9-2001. The 12 candidates for governor were Herman Saerens Sudiro (53 votes), H.M. Ali Muchtar (45 votes), Endjat Sudrajat (42 votes), H. Ace Suhaedi Madsupi (56 votes), Sagaf Usman (54 votes), Prof Dr Herman Haeruman (53 votes), Azril Azhari (47 votes), Susila Budi Mufreni (50 votes), M. Wasal Falah (37 votes), H. Suhaemi (52 votes), H.M. Aly Yahya (28 votes), and Djoko Munandar (54 votes), while the 12 candidates for deputy governor were Tri Mulyono (62 votes), H. Ade Sudirman (55 votes), H. Abdul Halim Amir (48 votes), Hj. Ratu Atut Chosiyah (61 votes), H.M. Masduki (50 votes), H. Djakaria Mahmud (43 votes), Gusti Bagja Mulyadi (53 votes), Tb. Mamas Chaerudin (42 votes), H. Makmun Suchari (51 votes), Mukhlisin Arief (45 votes), H.M. Sofwat Hadi (50 votes), and Hilman Indra (56 votes).

Chosiyah, whom he was championing. The position of governor was too 'heavy' for Atut;[22] too heavy in terms of her own experience and personal capability, and too heavy for Golkar, which hoped to effect her victory.[23] Yet Golkar had already nominated Aly Yahya for governor and Atut Chosiyah for deputy governor. To resolve this problem, things were 'arranged' so that Golkar decided only to seek the position of deputy governor. This was clearly one reason for Aly Yahya's withdrawal from the race, since from the start he was only interested in being nominated for governor.[24]

The challenge for Golkar, and for Tuan Besar, was to choose another candidate for governor to be paired with Atut Chosiyah. This was a complex job, which required heavy political and economic 'ammunition', as nearly all the candidates for governor who had passed through screening stage I already had partners to run for deputy governor. But in this situation they displayed their skills. After careful calculation, it was decided that Golkar must form a coalition with one or more other parties. The choice was between PPP and PDI-P. PPP had not yet determined the name of its candidate for deputy governor to be paired with Djoko Munandar (its candidate for governor). After various approaches and compromises, a Golkar-PPP coalition was formed, and the PPP's candidate for governor, Djoko Munandar, was paired with Ratu Atut Chosiyah as candidate for deputy governor.[25] It appears that Tuan Besar was the main contributor to finance the election of this ticket.[26]

Selection of the tickets of candidates

The next stage was to determine the three tickets of candidates who would run in the final round, the election itself. On 3 October 2001 the three tickets selected were: 1. Djoko Munandar and Atut Chosiyah (nominated by PPP and Golkar); 2. Ace Suhaedi Madsupi and Tb. Mamas Chaerudin (nominated by PDI-P); and 3. Herman Haeruman and Ade Sudirman (Al Bantani Faction) (see Iwan Kusuma Hamdan et al. 2004:122). The selection of these three tickets of candidates elicited both positive and negative reactions from the public. For example, on the day after the three tickets were selected the

22 Interviews with HAI, 6-7-2004; HKI, 1-6-2004; and THA, 24-6-2004.

23 As explained in the earlier discussion, the Golkar Party had only 12 of the 75 seats in the Banten Provincial DPRD.

24 This decision by the Banten Golkar Party DPD was acknowledged by Aly Yahya when this writer interviewed him. When asked about his feelings regarding the Golkar DPD's decision, Aly Yahya diplomatically stated, 'as a good senior Golkar Party cadre, I had to respect and abide by the DPD's decision' (interview, 6-7-2004).

25 This information was obtained from an interview with HAI, 6-7-2004.

26 This information was obtained from interviews with several informants, including SME (business operator), 9-6-2004; THA (former BAKOR officer), 24-6-2004; HKI, 13-6-2004; BOB (academic), 7-6-2004; and MAA, 15-6-2004.

NGO Aliansi Martabat Perempuan Banten (AMPB, Alliance for the Dignity of Banten Women) submitted a letter rejecting the candidacy of Atut Chosiyah for deputy governor of Banten. Signed by Hj. Ratu Syarifa Usmah Wahid (Chairwoman) and addressed to the members of the Banten Provincial DPRD, it said:

> The presence of the name of Ratu Atut Chosiyah among the candidates for governor and deputy governor of Banten for 2001-2006 is deeply shocking and disappointing to the Alliance for the Dignity of Banten Women. This woman named Ratu Atut Chosiyah is extremely depraved in terms of her morality and behaviour, and unsuited to represent the women of Banten.
>
> In our opinion, Ratu Atut Chosiyah is totally unsuited to represent women in this honoured position in the province of Banten. Ratu Atut Chosiayah is well known primarily as a businesswoman who will use any means to promote the success of her businesses. She is shamelessly having affairs with those she plans to do business with, [...]. Among those who work in the Public Works Service in Bandung, she is very well known. [...]
>
> Therefore, we as the Board and the members of the Alliance for the Dignity of Banten Women herewith 'reject the candidacy of Ratu Atut Chosiyah for deputy governor of Banten'.[27]

The next day (5 October 2001), Perguruan Paku Jung Kulon, a martial arts school in South Banten, responded with a letter of support for Atut Chosiyah's candidacy. This letter, signed by M. Suwarta SMHK (Chairman) and addressed to the Chairmen of the Factions in the Banten Provincial DPRD, said:

> We, from the Community Organization 'Perguruan Paku Jung Kulon' of South Banten, in selecting a candidate for deputy governor of the Province of Banten for the period 2001-2006, follow the call of our hearts in supporting Mrs Hj. Ratu Atut Chosiyah, the daughter of a great Banten personage, as the partner for the governor soon to be elected.
>
> Our reasons for choosing Mrs Hj. Ratu Atut Chosiyah, daughter of this great Banten figure, for deputy governor of Banten are as follows: She is known by the community of Banten; She has extensive understanding of the region and culture of Banten [...]. She has experience in the administrative technicalities of development in and community activities, as a successful national-scale business operator; [...]. She is the one and only 'Srikandi of Banten' who wishes to improve the role of women in the various aspects of development.[28]

27 This statement of rejection is quoted from Statement of the Alliance for the Dignity of Banten Women no. 66/AMPB/X/01, 4-10-2001 (the writer has a photocopy of the letter).

28 This statement of support is excerpted from letter of 'Perguruan Paku Jung Kulon' no. 01/PPJBS/2001, 5 October 2001, regarding Support for deputy governor Candidate Hj. Rt. Atut Chosiyah (the writer has a photocopy of this letter).

Postponement of the election

The waves of support and rejection continued to swell and became increasingly difficult to hold back. Although the DPRD tried to fend off the various demands, protests, and statements of rejection submitted by various elements of the Banten community, it was difficult to cover up the deviations that had occurred in the process. According to Law no. 22/1999 and Government Regulation no. 151/2000, the pairing of candidates for governor and deputy governor should have been done by the candidates themselves, and not by the DPRD factions as had happened here. Another violation had to do with the administrative requirements of Tb. Mamas Chaerudin, the candidate for deputy governor who was paired with Ace Suhaedi Madsupi; it was suspected that he did not actually have a high school diploma or the equivalent, as required by Law no. 22/1999 and Government Regulation no. 151/2000 (Iwan Kusuma Hamdan et al. 2004:122).

To resolve these problems, the Banten Provincial DPRD consulted the Department of the Interior, which felt that the rules used in Banten were in need of correction. So on 12 November 2001 the DPRD held a plenary session to discuss revision of the rules of order for election of the governor and deputy governor.[29] The results of this revision were then submitted to the Department of the Interior for review, and at the same time, informal approaches were undertaken to complement this. It is reported by one member of the Banten Provincial DPRD that Tuan Besar took part in this informal political process by making the most of his personal relationship with the Minister of the Interior.[30] On 24 November 2001 the Minister of the Interior, Hari Sabarno, sent a letter of approval.[31] Consequently a meeting of the Steering Committee (Panitia Musyawarah, Panmus) of the Banten DPRD decided on 26 November 2001 that the final round, the election of the governor and deputy governor of Banten, would be held on 3 December 2001.

'D-day': election of the governor and deputy governor

The long-awaited day finally arrived. The atmosphere was increasingly tense, because even though the DPRD had granted full authority to the police and military to handle security for the election session, and asked them to clear the area within a 4-kilometre radius of the DPRD building of *jawara*, this ele-

29 Invitation Letter of the Banten Provincial DPRD (signed by H. Muslim Jamaluddin), no. 162.4/DPRD/157/X/2001, dated 9-11-2001, regarding plenary session.

30 Interview, 9-6-2004.

31 Letter from the Minister of the Interior to the Chairman of the Banten Provincial DPRD, no. 121/2402/SJ dated 24-11-2001 (the writer has a photocopy of this letter).

ment of the community continued to mobilize its masses. The *jawara,* wrote Iwan Kusuma Hamdan et al. (2004:126), were on guard as early as 06.00 a.m., claiming to safeguard the election process. They were even swarming inside the building in regular civilian clothing.[32] In this rather tense atmosphere, the DPRD held the final election round. Sixty-nine of the 75 assembly members were present. After a vote by secret ballot, the final count showed that the ticket of Djoko Munandar and Atut Chosiyah had emerged as the winners, with 37 votes (Iwan Kusuma Hamdan et al. 2004:126). Apparently,[33] the defeat of the PDI-P ticket was due not only to money politics and intimidation but also to political compromises between the Golkar Party and the PDI-P to allocate the leadership positions in the regional legislature and executive. It must be remembered that the Chairman of the Banten Provincial DPRD, Dharmono K. Lawi, was from the PDI-P.

Among those who were most pleased and able to breathe a sigh of relief after this final round of the election were Tuan Besar and his Success Team. After navigating a highly complex election process that took up great political and economic resources, finally their candidates had achieved victory. The next question was how Tuan Besar would now be compensated for the political and economic 'sweat' expended in the electoral process.

Tuan Besar and practices of informal government: the case of project racketeering

As briefly described in the previous discussion, the cases of 'project racketeering' (*premanisme proyek*) had their roots in the monopolistic practices in the execution of physical infrastructure projects for the Banten provincial government during fiscal year 2003. From the information written in the Dokumen Anggaran Satuan Kerja (DASK, Work Unit Budget Document) of Banten's regional budget (Anggaran Pendapatan dan Belanja Daerah, APBD), it is known that the total value of the construction budget for Banten in fiscal year 2003, both that financed from the APBD and from the state budget (Anggaran Pendapatan Belanja Negara, APBN), was approximately Rp 35 billion.[34] From this budget, the Banten provincial government financed numerous physical and non-physical development projects. According to Presidential Decree (Keputusan Presiden, Keppres) no. 18/2000 on Guidelines for Procurement of Goods and Services for Government Agencies, specifi-

32 Interview with HOS, 18-6-2004.

33 Interviews with HKI, 1-5-2004, and HOS, 9-5-2004.

34 Decree of the governor Banten no. 902/Kep 45-Hak/2003, on Determination of the Work Unit Budget Document (DASK) of the Banten Provincial Budget (APBD). The writer has a photocopy of this document.

cally in Article 12(2), procurement of contracting goods/services and other services shall be done through:

a. Tender, that is, a series of activities to supply the needed goods/services by creating healthy competition among equal suppliers of goods/services that meet the requirements, based on certain established methods and procedures that are consistently followed by the parties concerned, so that the best supplier is selected.
b. Direct selection, if the Tender method is difficult to implement, or will not ensure achievement of the target. [Direct selection] is done by comparing the bids from several qualified suppliers of goods/services through price quotations, or technical and price quotations, followed by competitive negotiations, both on technical aspects and on price, to obtain a reasonable and technically justifiable price.

Indeed in formal terms nearly all the Banten provincial government's development projects during fiscal year 2003 were implemented through tender. However, as indicated by HOS,[35] many of these tenders were simply formalities to comply with the administrative procedures. In reality, HOS continued, the tender winner had already been determined. Tuan Besar played an important role in influencing the Tender Committee and other important personages. His modus operandi varied from informal lobbying with local officials and distribution of 'envelopes' (bribes), to physical intimidation. It is difficult to know the precise value of the projects managed directly by Tuan Besar. He owns several companies not registered in his name, and often uses other companies that he does not own as a strategy for winning tenders. Even so, as HOS pointed out, in general Tuan Besar is interested mostly in physical construction projects. Tuan Besar is among the top entrepreneurs in the lucrative construction sector. In 2003 the total value of physical development and/or construction projects was approximately Rp 18 billion (51.4% of the province's total development budget for that year).[36] Most of these projects were concentrated in six institutions that carry out local government projects: Dinas Bina Marga (road and highway construction and maintenance, around Rp 3 billion);[37] Dinas Cipta Karya (housing, building, and urban development, around Rp 4 billion);[38] the

35 Interview with HOS, 9-5-2004.

36 Decree of the governor Banten no. 902/Kep 45-Hak/2003, on Determination of the Work Unit Budget Document (DASK) of the Banten Provincial Budget (APBD), Books 1, 2, and 3. The writer has photocopies of these documents.

37 Road and Bridge Supervision Projects, and Road and Bridge Planning Projects.

38 Project for Design of the Education and Training Campus of the Province of Banten, Project for Technical Design of Banten Provincial Government Administrative Buildings, Project for

Irrigation Service (around Rp 2.5 billion);[39] the Health Service (around Rp 430 million);[40] the General Services Bureau (around Rp 4.6 billion);[41] and the Equipment Bureau (around Rp 2 billion).[42]

It seems competitors for Tuan Besar were burdened with an extra fee. For projects not performed by Tuan Besar himself or allocated to business operators in his group, a project fee of 10% to 11% of the project value was levied. The percentages of these project fees, by category of activity and source of financing, can be seen in the following table:

Project fees by category of activity and source of funds

Project classification	Project fees by source of funds (%)	
	APBD	APBN
Road and highway projects	10	11
Irrigation projects	11	11
Building construction projects	10	10
Procurement projects	10	10

Source: This information is quoted from a circular letter sent on 12 April 2002 to a business operator who was to perform a project with classification K-1.

How did the issue of 'project racketeering' come to the fore? According to information from several DPRD members who were interviewed,[43] suspicions of malpractice in the management of Banten provincial government projects first arose with an official report from the Badan Pemeriksaan Keuangan (BPK, Supreme Audit Agency) to the Chairman of the DPR-RI on 19 February 2003, which stated:

Housing and Residential Accommodation Development in the Province of Banten (P2P), Project for Development of Residential Facilities and Infrastructure (Technical Assistance for Guidance of Construction).

39 Project to Supervise Execution of the Work of Projects for River Rehabilitation and Normalization Projects, Irrigation Network Projects, and Lakes Overlapping Regency/City Boundaries, Project for Technical Planning of Execution of Pond Construction Projects, Rural Unfiltered Water Cistern Projects, and Water Resource Planning Projects.

40 Project for the Establishment of Malingping Hospital.

41 Project for Rehabilitation of State Buildings, Expansion of General Services Bureau Offices, Employee Offices, Government Bureaus, Rejuvenation and Upgrading of Parks, and Utilization of Bus Parking Areas at the Regional Secretariats; and Project for Facility and Infrastructure Upgrading, 2004.

42 Project for Development of Dormitory Support Infrastructure.

43 Interview with HOS, 9-5-2004.

> The results of the audit revealed 14 findings with a value of Rp 24,207.67 million for Fiscal Year 2002 (through October), which are categorized into indications of losses to the region/state of Rp 5,497.46 million, reduction to regional/ state revenues of Rp 333.33 million, wastage of Rp 10,191.02 million, [in]effectiveness of Rp 8,09.81 million, and others in the amount of Rp 94.05 million (Audit document for the second semester of Fiscal Year 2002, pages 1-2).

The preliminary suspicions of practices of project racketeering then surfaced on 26 August 2003, when the Fraksi Amanat Bintang Keadilan (ABK, Mandate-Star-Justice Faction) of the Banten Provincial DPRD submitted a Faction's Final Note in response to the governor's Financial Note on revision of the Regional Budget for 2003. In presenting the ABK Faction's Final Note, the faction leader said:

> We would also like to express our thanks to all members of the Banten community, as we all share the same perceptions regarding project racketeering. Only by tearing out this loathsome practice by its roots can our beloved province's journey toward development proceed as desired. As long as this project racketeering behaviour persists, no matter how great the budget that is allocated to develop our beloved province, the results will never reach the target. The people of Banten will never be able to enjoy true progress and prosperity.
>
> These project racketeering practices are a form of corruption, collusion, and nepotism (*korupsi, kolusi, nepotisme,* KKN), and eradicating them must be the first priority in this era of reform. Only with sincerity and courage from all parties will we be able to completely eliminate these dirty practices.[44]

Although the text of the Final Note from the ABK Faction did not explicitly state that such project racketeering practices had occurred in the province of Banten, and did not directly accuse any specific institutions or actors involved in this constellation, this oral and written statement from the ABK Faction served as the trigger factor for further discussion of the project racketeering issue within the DPRD building, which later developed into a topic for public consumption. Just one day after the ABK Faction presented its Final Note in the plenary session of the Banten Provincial DPRD, discussion of the practices of project racketeering spread to outside the DPRD building, and a polemic in the mass media between Tuan Besar and the ABK Faction was unavoidable.

On 27 August 2003 *Fajar Banten,* one of Banten's leading newspapers, carried a report with the headline 'Tuan Besar denies existence of project racketeering'. Tuan Besar was reported as saying that the accusations of project racketeering put forward by the ABK Faction were defamatory. The

44 This quotation was excerpted from the text of the Final Note of the Mandate-Star-Justice Faction of the DPRD Banten on governor's Financial Note on Revision of the 2003 Regional Budget (Serang, 26 August 2003). The writer has a photocopy of this text.

statement by the ABK Faction was destructive toward Banten, he continued, and a deviation from Banten's religious culture. Tuan Besar went on to say that the allegations were equivalent to an accusation that all business operators in Banten were guilty of it:

> The statement by the ABK Faction about Project Racketeering will not only divide the community, but will also have the effect of destroying Banten's religious culture. Base accusations such as this will only lead to slander, injustice, and slaughter of the charisma and aims of the community of Banten. Such members of the Assembly (who launched this statement) are unsuited to serve as representatives of the public. Actually, if there is anything lacking in the implementation of development in Banten, (this can) be improved collectively, and if there are any deviations, these can be straightened out through consultation. (*Fajar Banten* 27-8-2003.)

While Tuan Besar and his group were attempting to create a counter-opinion movement regarding project racketeering, support for the ABK Faction continued to flow in. On 28 August 2003 five members of the Presidium for a Clean Community (PCC) visited the Banten Provincial DPRD to declare their support for the ABK Faction. The PCC declared their readiness to work with the ABK Faction to resolve the cases of project racketeering through legal channels. The PCC advised the ABK Faction to submit its evidence to the prosecutor's office and the police (*Fajar Banten* 28-8-2003).

The polemic about project racketeering heated up when Tuan Besar said that the members of the Banten Provincial DPRD were like 'thieves shouting thief':

> We would like to ask the members of the assembly, specifically from the ABK Faction, to point out exactly who they are referring to as (project) racketeers. I see something very odd here: Thieves shouting thief. [...] We have evidence that certain individuals in the legislature (members of the Banten Provincial DPRD) have requested projects from project leaders or from professional associations and organizations. (*Fajar Banten* 3-9-2003.)

The polemic reached its culmination on 9 September 2003, when Tuan Besar, together with around 100 other Banten business operators, came to the Banten Provincial DPRD building to hold a dialogue with the DPRD members, and specifically with the members from the ABK Faction (*Fajar Banten* 4-9-2003). The business operators asked the ABK Faction to show concrete evidence about the existence of project racketeering practices, and to state directly exactly which business operators were involved. They demanded that the ABK Faction withdraw its statement, which they felt had created unrest among the business community and the public. The ABK Faction was asked to make a public apology, to be carried in all the local mass media. If they did not comply, the business operators would go through the established legal channels.

But this dialogue, which went on for around two and a half hours, did not attain the desired results, because the ABK Faction managed to avoid a confrontational stance. It said that 'as an extension of the political parties, we cannot comply with the business operators' demand that the ABK Faction withdraw its statement. We will provide a reply as soon as we have held meetings with the political parties'. This was a sensible response, given the increasing 'heat' of the dialogue within the DPRD building and the presence of a large number of *pendekar*, both inside and outside the building. A report in *Fajar Banten* (4-9-2003), said that there were around 50 black-uniformed *pendekar* Banten gathered outside the Banten Provincial DPRD building at the time.

Next, Bueti Nasir (a member of the ABK Faction from the PBB) said that the ABK Faction would not withdraw the statement it had made about project racketeering. Racketeering (*premanisme politik*) was a relatively polite expression compared with other words with the same general meaning. A similar statement was made by Partai Keadilan Sejahtera (PKS, Banten Justice and Prosperity Party), which said, 'there is no way that the parties will approve the ABK Faction's apologizing and withdrawing its statement about project racketeering, because the statement did not point to anyone (specific institutions or individuals)' (*Fajar Banten* 5-9-2003).

These indirect replies from the ABK Faction brought a strong reaction from Tuan Besar specifically and from Banten entrepreneurs in general. The Banten Chamber of Commerce and Industry (Kadin) issued a 'Summons' (*somasi*) to the ABK Faction through letter no. 149/Kadin-Banten/IX/2003 dated 7 September 2003. The basis given for issuing this Summons was that the term 'project racketeering' implies that unethical practices are used by business operators in Banten to win projects. On this basis, the Summons explicitly demanded that the ABK Faction withdraw its statement about project racketeering and apologize to Kadin and to the public of Banten. If the ABK Faction ignored this demand, the Banten Kadin threatened to report the problem to the police (*Fajar Banten* 8-9-2003).

Responding to this threat, the Chairman of the ABK Faction (Mudjahid Chudori) stated that his side was 'not afraid of the Banten Kadin's threat to report this to the police' (*Fajar Banten* 8-9-2003). The ABK Faction had solid evidence and enjoyed broad support from various parties. After this the polemic faded away. Apparently, it was difficult for the hopes of Banten's public for a thorough investigation to be realized through the ABK Faction. Numerous technical and political obstacles stalled any resolution of the case through legal channels. As noted by HOS (a member of the ABK Faction),[45] even though their Faction had sufficient evidence, to follow up on this through

45 Interview with HOS, 9-5-2004.

legal channels they would really need support from the regional executive, and specifically from the governor. But, HOS continued, they did not obtain this support, even though HOS himself tried to persuade the governor.

For myself, at the end of my field research in Banten, I was left with two questions. Why was the ABK Faction never willing to show or reveal its evidence of project racketeering practices committed by Tuan Besar and his group? And why didn't the governor of Banten give his crucially necessary support to the ABK Faction?

Conclusion

Some academics have responded to situations such as those described in this chapter by suggesting re-centralization of power in the hands of the central government. Such suggestions overlook the fact that not all the problems in the regions are the result of decentralization and regional autonomy policies. It is more accurate to see them as a consequence of the shift in patterns of interaction between state and society in the post-Soeharto era. The public (society) is no longer totally marginalized, either in the decision-making process or in implementation. However, this does not mean that we are now living in a fully civil society, for society is represented mostly by the elite. Decision-making at both the national and the local levels is coloured by coalitions and bargaining of interests between the societal and state actors.

The case of project racketeering in the province of Banten demonstrates that the conduct of regional government is far more complex than has been portrayed in the literature to date. Decision-making and policy implementation in the regions are now flavoured with 'collusion' and bargaining of interests among the local government executive elite and the *jawara*-entrepreneurs. If this empirical reality is related to the shift in patterns of state-society interactions, as mentioned above, then the Banten case shows that post-Soeharto decentralization and regional autonomy has created greater space for societal elites to build and develop informal networks with local state actors. Can the operation of these informal networks be considered practices of a 'Shadow State'? The project racketeering occurred together with a weakness in the formal institutions of local government in Banten. This resembles what William Reno (1995) has referred to as a 'Shadow State'. The governor and deputy governor faced great difficulty in getting the formal institutions of the local government to function properly, partly because Tuan Besar, as the main figure in the Shadow State, played a role as financial and political sponsor in getting these two top leaders elected. Tuan Besar's dominant influence over the conduct of local government represents the 'costs in return' for the political and economic investment he made at the time of the election.

M. ISA SULAIMAN and GERRY VAN KLINKEN

The rise and fall of governor Puteh

This chapter started life with only one author, M. Isa Sulaiman. Four days after presenting it at the authors' conference in Jakarta on 22 December 2004, he was among those who died in the great tsunami that struck Aceh (see in memoriam in this volume). Henk Schulte Nordholt and I decided as editors that the orphaned chapter should pass into my foster-care for the final phase. Isa had lived at our house in Leiden for five months in 2003, where he and I talked often about Aceh. I dare to think he would agree with the way it has been taken forward. He is responsible for all the factual material (drawn from local news clippings and interviews with many of those named). My part has mainly been to step back from it and say why it was important to write this, as well as to make explicit some theoretical understandings that lay hidden between the lines. He was particularly impressed with a chapter on Aceh in David Brown's 'The state and ethnic politics in Southeast Asia' (1994). Some of Isa's masterly command of detail had to be sacrificed in the interests of the less specialized reader.

Gerry van Klinken

Introduction

Understandably enough, most media reporting on Aceh before the tsunami was about the war. It focussed on the two armed parties, Indonesia's armed forces TNI (Tentara Nasional Indonesia) and the Acehnese liberation army GAM (Gerakan Aceh Merdeka). This has also been true of scholarly work on Aceh. This chapter aims to complement these other studies by describing the politics around the civilian administration. Although it retreated to its strongholds in the towns at the height of the insurgency before martial law was declared in May 2003, Aceh's civilian administration has never disappeared. At the time of writing it has once again expanded into the countryside, where it penetrates everyday life to a high degree. Indeed, it has grown. Special autonomy beginning in July 2001 has meant a considerably enlarged budget for the administration. It is important not to leave it out of

1 Aspinall 2002; Aspinall and Crouch 2003; ICG 2003b; Kell 1995, Reid 2003; Robinson and Rosser 1998; Schulze 2004.

account. Studying the administration helps us to understand the continuities with the New Order. Reformasi has not brought as much change to Aceh as might be supposed. The military may come and go, but government goes on forever. Moreover, popular disenchantment comes as much from everyday administrative failures as from acts of exceptional military brutality. We cannot understand the armed resistance movement, the most extreme form of popular resentment, without understanding the corrupt factionalism of the civilian bosses. This chapter suggests that Aceh's main problem lies less in policy emanating from Jakarta than in a pattern of local government that is as deeply rooted in Aceh as it is elsewhere in Indonesia. When government is run along the lines of personalized elite favouritism – technically known as neo-patrimonialism – the resulting nepotism clashes so fundamentally with what people have a right to expect from the modern state that protest is almost unavoidable.

David Brown's (1994:112-57) clear-sighted chapter on neo-patrimonialism in Indonesia, written during the New Order, took Aceh as its case study. Max Weber defined a patrimonial system as one in which 'the object of obedience is the personal authority of the individual which he enjoys by virtue of his traditional status [...] What determines the relations of the administrative staff to the chief is not the impersonal obligations of office, but personal loyalty to the chief'. In today's world, traditional deference of this kind has become rare. People expect to participate in politics and to receive the benefits of economic development. Personal relations between patrons and their clients are still important, especially when state institutions are weak, but the relationship is now more pragmatic. Instead of providing protection in exchange for loyalty, the patron gives money in order to obtain political support. Hence the term 'neo' patrimonialism. One of those who rediscovered Weber was Eisenstadt. His paper, which itself became a classic, quoted Indonesian examples (Eisenstadt 1973:11-8). This approach was then widely adopted by Indonesianists such as Harold Crouch (1979) and Don Emmerson (1983) to analyse the New Order government under President Soeharto. It remains a useful framework for analysis and has been applied to Aceh in this chapter.

A polity run along neo-patrimonial lines is inherently nepotistic, and its politics tend to be communal. This does not have to mean instability is inevitable, but Brown (1994:121) points out that it does face three inherent tensions. First is the tension between a cohesive patrimonial elite and elite factional disunity. The personalized nature of relationships makes it almost impossible to be inclusive, thus leaving dangerously dissatisfied factions on the margins. Second is the tension between the claim to universalistic administration and the practice of political favouritism. People today expect the government to be there for everyone. They become annoyed if it is not. Third is the tension between the concern of the patrimonial elites to exclude mass political participation, and their countervailing interest in mobilizing mass political support without, at the same time, creating channels for oppositionist participation. In other words, patrimonial elites need to mobilize the masses to win their support, but they don't want things to get out of hand. At moments of transition, all three tensions can come together to create instability. The story of the rise and fall of Aceh's governor Abdullah Puteh illustrates the value of these observations.

This chapter begins with a sketch of social stratification in Aceh, which is then used to explain the political restructuring that took place in the 1999 elections. The second part describes the election for governor. This was an occasion for intense competition by local groups. The third part concerns the favouristic conduct of government under governor Puteh. The fourth is about reactions from society, ranging from the provincial parliament, to various marginal groups including the liberationist movement GAM. The chapter closes with conclusions.

State formation and the new middle class

It is a mistake to view neo-patrimonial politics as simply a continuation of pre-colonial patterns. The 'neo' in neo-patrimonial is important. The modern state has had a profound effect on society in the twentieth century. It created a new middle class out of a predominantly agrarian population, one that was highly dependent on the state's resources. This middle class consists of bureaucrats, state-dependent 'contractors', and independent professionals. Only the last group stands somewhat outside the patronage networks of state elites.

The Dutch brought an end to the sultanate of Aceh early in the twentieth century after they exiled the last sultan to Ambon and then to Batavia, where he died in 1903. They retained his princes, the *hulubalang*, because they needed them as intermediaries between government and people. However, these landed aristocrats were destroyed by popular militias led by Tgk Daud Beureueh in 1946 (Reid 1979:135-90; M. Isa Sulaiman 1997:114-64). Commercial plantations and oil wells begun in colonial times continue to be owned by outside capitalists with the support of government. Gas discovered in the 1970s contributed US$ 2-3 billion a year by the 1980s (Dawood and Sjafrizal 1989). Most Acehnese, meanwhile, remain farmers. So the economy is divided between traditional farming on the one hand, and large plantations, timber and hydrocarbon exploitation, and industry on the other. The latter are owned by the state or by large capital outside Aceh. In the absence of local capitalists, a class of businesspeople arose who supplied goods and services including construction as partners with government

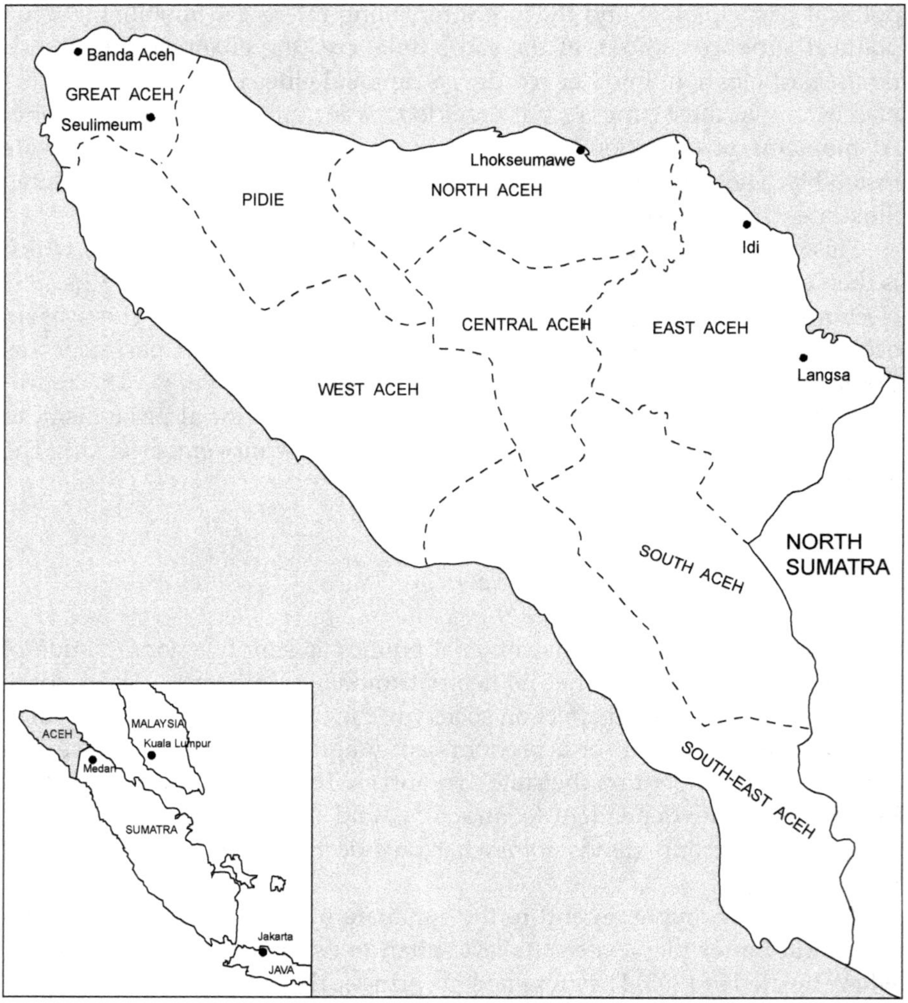
Banda Aceh
GREAT ACEH
Seulimeum
PIDIE
Lhokseumawe
NORTH ACEH
Idi
CENTRAL ACEH
EAST ACEH
Langsa
WEST ACEH
NORTH SUMATRA
SOUTH ACEH
SOUTH-EAST ACEH
ACEH
MALAYSIA
Kuala Lumpur
Medan
SUMATRA
Jakarta
JAVA

Map 9. Aceh

and large capital. Most people simply call them 'contractors, since they are dependent on government contracts. Since most economic resources are controlled by the state and channeled to Aceh through the national budget (Anggaran Pendapatan Belanja Negara, APBN) or the provincial budget (Anggaran Pendapatan dan Belanja Daerah, APBD), it is easy to imagine that these people have a high stake in local politics. Contractors number in the thousands and are found in the provincial capital and every district capital. They have organized themselves into a number of associations.[2] The chairperson of the provincial chamber of commerce (Kamar Dagang Indonesia, Kadin) always comes from their circles. Bureaucrats are also an important category. Like the contractors they come from every layer within society and are found everywhere. Of course they also have an enormous stake in local politics, since their livelihoods depend on the state. Military officers also belong to this group. Retired military were politically influential under the New Order because they controlled the government party Golkar.

As elsewhere, a group of people not dependent on the government has also arisen. Especially since the 1980s they have been conducting advocacy on behalf of the poorer section of the population. They tend to be educated and include lawyers, journalists, and NGO activists. They too have numerous associations.

Religious teachers (*ulema*) occupy a respected position in this majority Islamic area. They are not a closed caste, since the entry requirement looks more to qualifications than descent. Some run religious schools in the village, others are paid by the state as teachers or religious judges. So only some (those who work for the Department of Religion or the *ulema* council Majelis Ulama Indonesia, MUI) depend on the government for a living.

The 1999 election

Despite the state's economic dominance, its institutions are not strong in the sense of being able to impose its will regardless of personalities. Instead the state has built its authority on personal alliances with local elites, who remain factionalized, mainly by district of origin. This became evident when political change – democratization and decentralization – swept Indonesia after the end of the New Order in 1998. First we look at the effect of democratic competition in Aceh. This led to the election of a new governor in Aceh. The governor is extremely important to Aceh's middle class. The election

2 Of the 16 associations, some are local like Asosiasi Kontraktor Aceh (AKA, Acehnese Contractor Association), while others are branches of national associations like Gabungan Pengusaha Konstruksi Nasional (Gapeknas, Federation of National Contractor Enterprises).

procedure demonstrated not only the great skill of the key players at predicting and manipulating outcomes, but also the emergence of district-based alliances that cut across political party lines.

Reformasi offered new freedoms to speak and to organize politically. Since most of the middle class lives in town, while the bulk of the population is rural, they depended on party organizers at the level of the district and subdistrict towns to reach their constituencies. Golkar had been the largest political force in Aceh since the 1987 election. Before that, it had been pipped to the post by the Islamic party PPP. The dominant figure in Golkar's Aceh branch was Maj-Gen (retired) T. Johan (1937-2001), who became provincial chairperson in 1993. He came from an aristocratic family in Seulimeum, Aceh Besar, and had been chief of staff of the Iskandar Muda military area command (1984-1985) and deputy governor of Aceh (1988-1993). From 1997 to 1999 he chaired the provincial parliament, where Golkar had 23 of the 45 seats against PPP's 12. In the 1999 election he stood for the national parliament (*Serambi Indonesia* 18-2-2001).

The national elections on 7 June 1999 were seriously disrupted by GAM. After the government ended the special military operation (Daerah Operasi Militer, DOM) in August 1998, many of its leaders had returned from exile in Malaysia to rebuild the separatist organization amid the new freedoms (M. Isa Sulaiman 2000:165-94). GAM intimidation meant almost no-one voted in the districts Pidie and North Aceh, and only half voted in East Aceh. The government was forced to estimate what the result might have been based on party votes outside these areas. The new provincial parliament formed on 5 October 1999 had 14 PPP (Partai Persatuan Pembangunan, Unity and Development Party) seats, nine PAN (Partai Amanat Nasional, Party of the National Message), eight Golkar, six PDI-P (Partai Demokrasi Indonesia Perjuangan, Indonesian Democratic Party of Struggle), eleven for smaller parties, and six allocated to the army and police.

Clearly, the election had failed to generate an absolute majority. Decisions were bound to be difficult. This immediately proved true when it had to decide who would occupy the chair and three deputy chairs, normally reserved for the largest parties in the election. PAN and an alliance of smaller parties made the first move, one that would have advantaged themselves. But this was cut short by Golkar leader T. Johan, who put together a deal whereby the chair went to PPP, and the deputy chairs respectively to PDI-P, Golkar and the army/police faction. At this, PAN and its allies staged a walkout (*Kontras* 58(10-16 November 1999):12).

The altered composition of the provincial parliament immediately threatened the position of the governor, Syamsuddin Mahmud (1936-). He had just been reelected to a second term by a parliament still dominated by Golkar and the military. Claiming the governor was not doing enough to resolve the

Aceh conflict, lacked reformist zeal, and was corrupt, two PPP members collected enough signatures from fellow parliamentarians to put up a motion on 22 April 2000 calling for his dismissal (*Kontras* 86(24-30 May 2000):8). The motion passed. President Wahid responded by sacking Syamsuddin Mahmud the following month. He appointed a caretaker named Ramli Ridwan (1941-), who till then had been a senior official in the directorate for regional autonomy (Pemerintahan Umum dan Otonomi Daerah, PUOD) in the Interior Ministry in Jakarta.

Governor's election and the communal patron

Having won the chair of the provincial parliament, and having successfully manoeuvred the governor out of office, the once (mildly) oppositional party PPP naturally felt itself in a strong position to win the governorship. That they were to be outwitted by Golkar strongman and former soldier T. Johan had as much to do with district-based patron-client politics in Aceh as with Johan's considerable skills. Aceh in 2000 had eight districts, of which the richest and most populous were these three: Great Aceh (including Banda Aceh), North Aceh (Lhokseumawe), and East Aceh (Langsa).[3] Provincial parliamentarians from each district gathered regularly in a 'caucus' of their own, regardless of party origins.

Of course money played a role in the governor's election. The 'success teams' of each of the three pairs of contenders for the province's highest office spent money particularly to persuade indecisive members. This took place in the greatest secrecy so it is difficult to be sure.[4] However, the key to the successful election of Abdullah Puteh lay not in the money he spent but in the skill with which he was able to play one district off against another. In particular he was able to split the vote from the key district of Great Aceh.

Abdullah Puteh was elected in two rounds of voting at a special session of the provincial parliament held on 4 November 2000. In the first round Puteh and his running mate Azwar Abubakar won 25 votes, just short of the required 50% plus one. The two other pairs won respectively 14 and nine votes, with five invalid votes and one abstention. This disqualified the weak-

3 The others were Pidie, Central Aceh, South Aceh, Southeast Aceh, and West Aceh.

4 My (M. Isa Sulaiman – ed.) interviews with several members and success teams indicate that only one member of parliament refused to accept the money. The amount of money handed out by each success team was between Rp 50 and Rp 150 million per member. Some candidates handed out cheques that could only be cashed after he was elected. Several members received money from more than one candidate. The issue of bribery nearly became big news in Aceh in January 2001 when *Serambi Indonesia* newspaper picked up grumbles from the success team of a losing candidate about the cheques they themselves had given to various honourable members. However, the rumour disappeared after the Aceh Public Prosecutor promised to investigate.

est of the three candidate pairs. In the second round Puteh's vote went up to 33, enough to declare him the winner. His supporters hugged each other in joy, while the losers slumped in their seats, unable to believe what they had just seen.

How did Puteh do it? The rules in the new electoral law (Law no. 22/1999) specified that candidates for governor and deputy governor should go together in one packet, to ensure they could work together. Any two people who satisfied basic selection criteria were allowed to register as potential candidate pairs. The parliamentary party factions then chose from among these potential candidates those pairs they wished to support as candidates. This reduced number of pairs then submitted to a secret ballot in parliament to determine the winning pair. Each pair had a 'success team', normally consisting of politicians, businesspeople and bureaucrats, who would try to lobby the parliamentarians on their behalf at each stage of the process. By the time selection of potential candidates closed in September 1999 there were six names for governor on the table, or five serious names since one (T. Syaukani Markam) lacked supporters in parliament. All five were bureaucrats or former bureaucrats, who had built a following in Acehnese society while in office. They were these:

1. Ir Abdullah Puteh (1948-) from East Aceh, Golkar activist
2. Drs A. Malik Raden (1945-), from Great Aceh, senior Education Department official (Kepala Kanwil)
3. Drs M. Kayosyah (1940-), from North Aceh, PPP activist
4. Ir Iskandar Husin (1946-), from Pidie, secretary-general in the State Ministry of Human Rights
5. Ramli Ridwan (1942-), from North Aceh, acting governor

Only two of the five were active in political parties (the others being prevented by their official positions), but strangely enough this did not translate to greater political support for them. Only PPP and PAN put forward candidates from their own ranks. PPP had the most seats in parliament, and this should have put PPP activist Kaoysyah in a good position. But party support was split along district lines. It failed to unite behind Kaoysyah, who was from North Aceh. Five PPP members from Great Aceh all belonged to the Great Aceh caucus, and they supported Malik Raden, who was from their own district. Another PPP parliamentarian, from East Aceh, supported Abdullah Puteh for a similar reason. Puteh also managed to attract the support of another PPP parliamentarian from West Aceh. Thus the PPP vote was divided among three candidates. Kaoysyah's position was further weakened by Ramli Ridwan, the ambitious acting governor, who also came from North Aceh. Thus the already meagre six parliamentarians from North Aceh divided their votes between two candidates.

PAN, the second largest party in parliament, was bedevilled by similar problems. Too small to aim for governor, this party hoped at least to score deputy governor, and initially prepared four of its members to step forward (later reduced to two). Disagreements developed over which gubernatorial candidate they should be teamed with. Some members favoured Abdullah Puteh, others Kaoysyah, others again Iskandar Husin. District considerations again played the major role. The resulting proliferation of PAN-supported pairs divided the PAN vote the way the PPP vote had also been divided.

PDI-P and the alliance of small parties were too small to take initiative but supported Abdullah Puteh, Malik Raden, and Iskandar Husin.

Golkar members similarly supported different candidates depending on their respective district of origin. Some wanted the acting governor Ramli Ridwan, others the Education Department official Malik Raden. But provincial Golkar chairperson T. Johan supported Abdullah Puteh, and took advantage of his own party's divisions to pair Puteh with a deputy gubernatorial candidate from his own district of Great Aceh.

The chances of the other candidates were imperilled by the same district-based considerations. Malik Raden, for example, would have won friends by giving facilities to contractors and politicians through his position at the Education Department, and he had been active in various Islamic organizations in the 1970s. But the fractured PPP vote, and the presence of two other Great Aceh candidates, weakened his support. Iskandar Husin, too, had a wide network through his earlier work in the Transmigration Department and his social involvement as chairman of the provincial football association among others. But his Pidie support base of only six Pidie parliamentarians was too narrow for success in a parliament numbering 54.

All this worked in favour of Abdullah Puteh. Puteh was born into a commoner family in Idi, East Aceh. He graduated from the prestigious Bandung Technical Institute (Institut Teknologi Bandung, ITB) and had been living in Jakarta since he became chairman of the government-minded youth organization Komite Nasional Pemuda Indonesia (KNPI, National Indonesian Youth Committee) in 1984-1989, where he succeeded the later Golkar strongman Ir Akbar Tanjung. Between 1992-1997 he served in national parliament as representative of Golkar for his birth district. In 1998 he became deputy secretary-general of the national Golkar executive. He had a business in Jakarta recruiting workers to send overseas, and another together with Abdul Ghafur developing oil palm in West Aceh. These ventures generated a wide network of connections. He had challenged for the Aceh governorship in 1998, but Syamsuddin Mahmud won a second term instead. However, he nurtured relations with an array of people from various districts who were dissatisfied with Syamsuddin Mahmud. The East Aceh caucus also supported their local boy. And Akbar Tanjung was able to lean on Golkar's Aceh members to give Puteh a hand. This last source of support became decisive when T. Johan swung behind Puteh, as we shall see.

At its first pleno session on 30 September 2000, parliament voted on the five pairs of potential candidates led by the names above, in order to select three pairs. Kaoysyah and Ramli Ridwan were eliminated in this round. This left Abdullah Puteh, Malik Raden, and Iskandar Husin, each with their partner. They enjoyed the most cross-party support. Five of the six factions voted for Puteh (the military/police abstained), while only four and three voted for the other two respectively.

Ramli Ridwan, the disappointed acting governor, at this stage tried to use his powers to persuade the Interior Minister and the President to cancel the next round of voting, on the grounds of irregularities in this round. As a result President Wahid told a visiting parliamentary delegation on 23 October to postpone the gubernatorial election and concentrate on a negotiated peace with GAM (*Serambi Indonesia* 24-10-2000). But the other parliamentarians objected angrily that no peace could be built by a governor lacking legitimacy, and parliament went ahead with its next meeting on 4 November as planned regardless of the President's feelings (*Serambi Indonesia* 30-10-2000; *Kontras* 109(1-7 November 2000):13). This latter course of action would have been impossible under the New Order, when provincial parliaments merely rubber-stamped President Soeharto's wishes as conveyed along military and Golkar channels.

Puteh already enjoyed the strongest cross-party support, but now T. Johan's strategy of selecting a running mate for Puteh began to pay off. First, this deputy gubernatorial candidate came from Great Aceh, thus pulling in votes from other Great Aceh members regardless of party affiliation once the field had narrowed. Second, both he and Johan himself were retired soldiers, and this won the support of the assembly's military and police members. Combined with the various contradictions that made life difficult for the other remaining candidates, this ensured Puteh's quick success on 4 November.

The administrative structure that governor Puteh had to work with was quite different to that of his predecessors. Regional autonomy laws (Law no. 22/1999 and Law no. 25/1999) gave greater powers to districts than the province, separated the legislative from the executive and thus from the governor's control, and passed more control over money to the regions. The conflict in Aceh had also given rise to two special laws for Aceh (Law no. 44/1999 and Law no. 18/2001), which returned greater powers to the province, and increased the influence of religious *ulema* on local government. These laws also increased Aceh's oil and gas receipts by respectively 55% and 40% over the provisions in Law no. 25/1999, though only for eight years.

Scholars have doubted whether giving greater powers to districts has made them more effective and democratic. A district head with more control over money can become a 'little king' if they can strike a deal with the local parliamentary chairperson, business, and military commander (H. Schulte Nordholt 2003:572). Syarif Hidayat (2002:47) has shown in Riau, Banten and West Nusa Tenggara how the regional autonomy laws have primarily benefited local elite interests. Hadiz (2003c:603) similarly showed that democratic institutions in mayoral elections in Medan and Jakarta in 2000 were hijacked by parasitic interests incubated by the New Order government. How would Aceh fare, where autonomy was focussed more on the provincial level?

Officials and their affiliations

Governor Abdullah Puteh and deputy governor Azwar Abubakar were sworn in by the Interior Minister on 25 November 2000. The deputy's role was restricted to disaster relief (Satuan Koordinasi Pelaksana Penanggulangan Bencana Alam, Satkorlak), and otherwise mainly ceremonial, though he did have a say in the distribution of important positions. The governor's first task was to reorganize his administrative structure in accordance with the new laws, as well as to make fresh appointments in the bureaucracy. He owed his 'success team' a favour, especially T. Johan. When the incumbent provincial secretary retired, Puteh replaced him with one of the assistant provincial secretaries, a man from Great Aceh, Johan's home district. He also embraced his political rival Malik Raden, the gubernatorial candidate from Great Aceh, by appointing him as head of the provincial training board (Badan Pendidikan dan Pelatihan, Badan Diklat). Malik Raden would otherwise have retired from his position at the Education Department, which was to be dissolved in favour of a provincial Education Service. Several of Raden's former Education Department colleagues, one from Great Aceh and one from East Aceh, were also given positions. Thus governor Puteh, himself from East Aceh, built an alliance with the Great Aceh elite, and with the Islamic network Pelajar Islam Indonesia (PII, Indonesian Islamic Students Organization) by placing Malik Raden's followers in some important posts. These allies were essential if he was to face up to his challengers. His other key appointments, made in the course of 2001-2003, mainly came from his own district of East Aceh, as well as from those in other districts who had supported his election.[4]

[4] For example, the provincial planning board (Badan Perencanaan dan Pembangunan Daerah, Bappeda) went to economist Prof. Dr T. Iskandar Daud, university lecturer from East Aceh, while the Assistant for Aceh Specialness was filled by Drs Zainudin Saman, formerly at the religion office (Kanwil Departemen Agama Aceh) and also from East Aceh.

Favouritism in development projects

Financial autonomy took effect the month after Abdullah Puteh took office. Whereas in the New Order most government money passed down to the regions through provincial offices of central government departments, now all but two of these offices were dissolved in favour of provincial services (*dinas*) or boards under the control of the provincial governor. (The exceptions were Religion and Justice.) The governor was compensated for the extra salary burden through an annual block grant of around Rp 300 billion (Dana Alokasi Umum, DAU, General Allocation Grant), while special tasks such as education and health were funded through another grant (Dana Alokasi Khusus, DAK, Special Allocation Grant).

Of the greatest importance were oil and gas receipts, which increased enormously under Law no. 25/1999. As a result, the provincial budget (APBD) more than doubled to Rp 542 billion between 2000 and 2001 (see Table 1). Law no. 18/2001 added even more to these hydrocarbon receipts, reaching Rp 2.1 trillion in 2002 and Rp 2.3 trillion in 2003.[6] The latter were divided up between the province and various districts, especially the two producing districts North Aceh and East Aceh. Governor Puteh placed 30% of it into a provincial education fund. This meant that the provincial budget in 2002 went up nearly three times again in 2002 over the previous year, and it reached Rp 1.573 trillion in 2003. Most of this came from oil and gas. Of course Aceh also still received funds from the national budget (APBN) through the remaining offices of the national departments. But most of this large pot of money was under the control of the governor.

Table 1. Provincial budget (APBD) and national budget (APBN) spent in Aceh (billions of rupiah)

	1993/1994	2001	2002	2003
APBD	4,058	542,753	1,572,094	1,579,000
APBN*	460,358	760,000	888,000	1,024,000
Inpres	145,313	–	–	–
Total	659,729	1,302,753	2,460,094	2,603,000

* In 1993/1994 sectoral projects funded out of the national budget APBN were generally spent by the relevant provincial office (Kanwil) of the national department, so-called 'vertical' units. Since 2001 only about 15% of these funds were still spent by the vertical unit, namely Religion, Justice, Police, Public Prosecutor and the State University. Source: Biro Keuangan and Bappeda.

6 *Serambi Indonesia* 20-3-2001; T. Rivolsa Ismail 2004.

The huge increase in funds at the governor's behest did not go uncontested. Especially the district heads of East Aceh and North Aceh (who themselves also enjoyed vastly increased budgets) questioned the size of the amount held back at the province for education. Puteh silenced them by promising the money would still be spent in the various districts. Nevertheless, this tremendous increase in financial autonomy, unbalanced by a proportionately tightened control regime, turned the governor and his team of officials into veritable money-spending machines. One consequence was the questionable electricity project described below. The governor and deputy governor also allocated themselves greatly increased 'routine expenditure' budgets (Table 2).

Table 2. Routine Expenditure Budgets (billions of rupiah)

	2001	2002	2003
Governor	2,245	4,090	6,560
Deputy governor	1,230	1,750	2,960
Total	3,475	5,840	9,520

Source: Aceh parliament secretariat.

The pyramidal power relations between the governor and his heads of services (*kepala dinas, asisten, biro,* and *badan*) allowed the governor to intervene in large projects carried out by these subordinate agencies and turn them to his own personal advantage or that of his cronies. Law no. 18/2000 permitted the governor to directly allocate projects, that is, without tendering. He made use of that to allocate billions of rupiah worth of contracts in 2001 and 2002. One example of a project that fell to his cronies was a printing machine worth Rp 4.2 billion for the Infokom Service. The contract went to a brother of Rusli Bintang, a contractor from Great Aceh who had supported Puteh. Tragically, the machine turned out to be second-hand, whereas the price had been marked up even above the real new price (*Modus* 19 (January/February 2003):6; *Serambi Indonesia* 28-2-2003). All these facilities bought Puteh valuable loyalty against his rivals.

It would take too long to describe all the instances of collusion one by one. Here we will only take two cases, namely the airline PT Seulawah NAD Air, and the development 'NGO' YPAB Nur Raudha. In both cases we will see how public interests overlapped with personal ones, how unclear the boundary was between the 'formal' and the informal in the conduct of government, and how a symbiotic relationship grew up for the mutual protection of governor Puteh and his closest officials and business colleagues.

PT Seulawah NAD Air

From this moment, things began to go wrong. Or rather, at first they went very well, before taking the inevitable nosedive. Troubled security after mid-1999 repeatedly disrupted road travel between Aceh and the outside world. The New Order had made Aceh nothing more than a 'hinterland' for Medan in North Sumatra. The cheapest safe alternative routes to Medan were the thrice-weekly Pelni ship, and the once-daily Garuda Boeing 737-300 flight. Seats on the flight to and from Medan were always hard to get. From Medan onward, flights were numerous. Wanting only the best for his region, Governor Abdullah Puteh took the option, not of opening the Medan air route to some private airline – though Bayu Airlines had already made an offer – but of setting up a provincial air carrier. His close colleague Sam A. Walean, an adventurous businessman from Menado who lived in Jakarta, in mid-April 2001 introduced Puteh to Datuk Mat Safuan, owner of Safuan Group Bhd. in Kuala Lumpur. Puteh talked to him about investing in an Aceh air service. Datuk Mat Safuan initially responded enthusiastically. He imagined not only flying Banda Aceh-Medan-Jakarta and Banda Aceh-Penang-Kuala Lumpur, but also taking Acehnese *haji* to Mecca, of whom there are more than 5,000 every year.[7] Governor Puteh then instructed his confidante and Assistant for Finance and Development, Ir Usman Budiman, as well as Sam A. Walean and a contractor named Ramzi Tharfi who had supported him in hard times, to start building the company.

On 28 June 2001 PT Seulawah Air was registered in Jakarta with the notary Mrs Chairunnisa Said. The name was derived from Mount Seulawah, which rises up to form a backdrop for the provincial capital Banda Aceh, flanked on either side by Great Aceh and Pidie, the birthplaces of Acehnese culture. It was also the name of the Dakota aircraft the Acehnese people donated to President Soekarno representing the Indonesian government during the national revolution in 1948, and which is still regarded as the beginning of Garuda Indonesia Airways. Seven months later, on 28 January 2002, it officially changed its name to PT Seulawah NAD Air, for unclear reasons except that Safuan Group was no longer part of the project. Its initial capital had been planned to consist of six million shares with a nominal value of Rp 10,000 each. But the official announcement only mentioned about a million shares owned by the Aceh provincial government (NAD, Nanggroe Aceh Darussalam), 700 thousand by Sam Walean (director of PT Wawasan Sakti

7 Sam Walean said Datuk Safuan put down Rp 2 billion in July 2001 as an initial investment for PT Seulawah Air (*Modus* 3(14-24 May 2003):10). In fact the annual *haj* is organized through the Department of Religion, so Datuk Safuan's hopes of using Seulawah aircraft for this purpose were unrealistic.

Informindo Nusa), and 300 thousand by Ramzi Tharfi (director of PT Benzi Prima).[8] Abdullah Puteh appointed Usman Budiman chief commissioner of the new airline. Provincial secretary Thantawi Ishak became a commissioner. Executive director was Sam Walean, with his office in Astha Building, Kebun Sirih, Jakarta. Ramli Tharfi was deputy director.

The next thing to do was obtain an Air Operation Certificate from the Transport Department, do a feasibility study, recruit 27 cabin staff, and find an aircraft. Since Safuan Group Bhd had withdrawn, they rented a Boeing 737-300 from Transmile Group Bhd, based in Kuala Lumpur (*Kontras* 251(30 July-5 August 2003):15).

In September 2002 the Transport Department issued an operational certificate. Governor Puteh felt it was time to present his achievement to Aceh's parliament as the representatives of the people. The problem was that in accordance with its deed, the one million shares or Rp 10 billion the provincial government had invested had to come from the provincial budget. By September 2002 Rp 6 billion of that amount had already been put in. But the law does not allow the governor to invest in a private company. The governor may invest only in a state-owned regional company, which can only be formed by parliamentary legislation. But PT Seulawah NAD Air was a private company. Two of the commissioners were key provincial officials, but the identity cards quoted in the charter only listed them as private individuals, not in their official capacity. So while Puteh announced on 23 September that he had taken Rp 6 billion out of the provincial budget for the carrier, a few months later it appeared that the government shares were listed in the name of the Aceh Regional Development Company (Perusahaan Daerah Pembangunan Aceh, PDPA) (*Serambi Indonesia* 24-9-2001).

With parliament satisfied, governor Puteh set about organizing the inaugural flight from Blang Bintang airport Banda Aceh. A spectacular ceremony on 25 September 2002 included 300 dancers to welcome President Megawati, who had come to cut the tape. Five hundred invitees from all over Aceh and beyond came in their traditional finery. Governor Puteh felt he wanted to make up to President Megawati, because on her first visit on 8 September

8 This statement by Usman Budiman is not consistent. In an interview on 3 December 2001, before the official name change, he said the Safuan Group Bhd owned Rp 20 billion in shares, the Aceh province 20%, and a private company 20% (*Kontras* 168(12-18 December 2001):13). But in the public presentation at the Infokom Hall on 23 September 2002 he no longer mentioned Safuan Group Bhd, but said the province owned 1 million shares, Transmile Group Bhd 1 million, PT Wawasan Sakti Infonusa 700 thousand, and PT Benzi Prima 300 thousand shares (*Suara Aceh* no. 174(15-30 September 2002):4). Later, when disagreement had broken out with Sam Walean, he never again mentioned shares owned by Transmile Group Bhd. Sam Walean said that Usman Budiman, witnessed by Abdullah Puteh, asked for 25% of the shares owned by PT Wawasan Sakti Infonusa, but Sam Walean refused to give them to him (*Modus* 3(14-24 May 2003):11).

2001 she had grown furious when someone in the audience had interrupted her. Being so highly dependent on the goodwill of government at the centre made regional officials bend over backwards to preserve harmonious relations. So it was not surprising to see a huge banner over the stage with the words: 'Mbak Mega... Smile, for you have brought 'Seulawah' back again'. The ceremony cost hundreds of millions of rupiah, perforce taken by governor Puteh from other projects since this was an unbudgeted activity.

Commercial flights commenced two days later, twice daily to Medan Aceh and twice weekly to Jakarta. Tickets were priced a little under those of Garuda. The rush for cheap tickets made Seulawah NAD a sought-after name among Banda Aceh travel agents. Agam Patra, a contractor and close colleague of governor Puteh, was soon awarded the sole agency on Seulawah NAD ticket sales in the provincial capital. This was the beginning of trouble with Sam Walean, whose promises to another business to make them sole agents had to go unfulfilled. Indeed the haste and untransparent collusion with which the company had been set up soon began to cause more conflicts. Passengers turned up with the same seat number. Shareholders began to grow suspicious of each other. For of the three shareholders, only the provincial government had actually put money into the venture, whereas the board of directors was dominated by a private company led by Sam Walean. On 31 October 2002, barely a month after operations had commenced, governor Puteh wrote Sam Walean effectively asking him to transfer his ticket sale funds to the private account of himself and that of Usman Budiman, at Bank Bukopin Jakarta account no. 1015736.01 55. Sam Walean apparently took no notice of the letter, so governor Puteh organized a meeting with the commissioners and directors at the Jakarta Hilton Hotel three days later. Participants were invited only by phone, but the meeting turned into a Shareholders General Meeting, which decided to terminate Sam Walean as executive director and replace him with former Garuda director M. Suparno, who knew governor Puteh well. Suparno soon fired Sam Walean's closest associates in the company, thus locking Walean out (*Modus* 1(16 April 2003):4).

Infuriated and claiming his rights as shareholder and founder had been abused, Sam Walean took Usman Budiman and Thantawi Ishak to court in Banda Aceh for falsely identifying themselves in the company's official charter as privately employed and not as civil servants. He also accused Abdullah Puteh and Usman Budiman of illegally ordering company money to be transferred to their private accounts, and alleged that the Shareholders General Meeting fell short of the requirements of commercial law.

This was a great embarrassment to governor Puteh and his cronies, and made them afraid. They sprouted loud rhetoric and began to lobby. They revealed that of all the shareholders only Aceh had put money on the table, while the identity card business had been the lawyer's oversight.

They privately asked Sam Walean to withdraw the case (*Modus* 1(16 April 2003):6). Feeling the wind in his back, Sam Walean evidently asked for Rp 3 billion compensation to settle out of court (*Modus* 9(29 August-9 September 2003):22). Whether there was a connection with his suit against the top provincial officeholder is unclear, but at the end of November 2002 police broke into Sam Walean's hotel room in Banda Aceh and arrested him for fornication (*Serambi Indonesia* 25-11-2002). Anyhow, Sam Walean's suit did intimidate governor Puteh, because after a meeting in Medan on 11 March 2003 both sides agreed to stop legal proceedings, while Sam Walean and Ramzi Tharfi, who had still not paid for their shares, were reinstated in the company (*Serambi Indonesia* 25-11-2002).

In Suparno's hands the carrier grew even more inefficient than it had been under Sam Walean. The wages bill blew out from Rp 150 million to Rp 450 million a month, while Ramzi Tharfi failed to store about Rp 200 million in Medan ticket sales. The company also faced intense competition on the Medan-Jakarta route. By early March 2003 outstanding payments to Transmile Group Bhd for aircraft lease and to Pertamina for fuel reached almost Rp 10 billion, despite parliament having earlier agreed to inject an additional Rp 4 billion (*Serambi Indonesia* 25-11-2002). As a result, Transmile Group Bhd took its aircraft back and Seulawah NAD ceased to fly after only six months in the air.

Stung by the crisis, parliament called the company management to give an accounting of itself on 20 March 2003. Sam Walean, strangely, was not called to testify. Since he knew more than anyone, the report presented to parliament was in the nature of an internal review, not an audit. The director of the Aceh Regional Development Company (PDPA), when asked to explain how Seulawah NAD shares came to be on its books, denied all knowledge of it. This in turn made governor Puteh and Usman Budiman all the more irate. They said PDPA was just an extension of the provincial government (*Kontras* 251(30 July-5 August 2003):16).

Clearly Seulawah NAD Air was now too debt-laden to operate again. It also still owed compensation to Sam Walean for dropping the court case against Abdullah Puteh and co. Nor was it possible any more to shift the billions of rupiah in debt to the provincial budget, as had happened earlier. Parliamentarians, and Abdullah Puteh's rivals, had run out of patience with the company. PT Seulawah NAD Air was bankrupt.

One avenue that did remain open was to charge the debt to some special or emergency project. This should be easy to do, since two of the commissioners, Thantawi Ishak dan Usman Budiman, held key positions in the provincial bureaucracy. Signs in that direction became evident when Usman Budiman took the 'eternal fund' of the Naval Commander's Institute (Lembaga Panglima Laut) worth Rp 8.4 billion in the government's possession and put it up as a guarantee for the Pertamina fuel bill. However, this came to nought when the institute and outside critics got wind of it (*Kontras* 251(30 July-5 August 2003):16).

A similar manoeuvre seemed to lie behind the emergency electricity supply project, undertaken by the provincial government to raise the supply by 12 Megawatts in 2003 at a cost of Rp 30 billion. Aceh gets much of its electricity from Medan via a high-tension line, but GAM militias repeatedly attacked the pylons carrying the cable. This was another opportunity to close the Seulawah NAD debt. After several meetings with governor Puteh, William Taylor from electrical supplier CV Sari Alam generously agreed to 'lend' Rp 3 billion via Usman Budiman to Suparno, the director of the bankrupt air carrier. William got a contract to supply 25 generators, but 14 of them were second-hand and three were seriously inoperable.[9] As a result, Banda Aceh's on-again off-again electricity supply did not improve despite the generators project. This provided more material for Abdullah Puteh's rivals, who used it to demand that he be sacked.

YPAB Nur Raudha charity organization

Marlinda Purnomo (1964-), Abdullah Puteh's second wife, felt she must not sit idly by but should help her husband and do something for the people of Aceh. She felt the formal positions she held, as chairperson of the Family Welfare Program (Program Kesejahteraan Keluarga, PKK) and of the Provincial Handicraft Council (Dewan Kerajinan Daerah), did not give her enough room to 'do more' to help relieve the suffering of this afflicted society. As a woman, she was moved by the plight of women and children, initially those who lived around the governor's official residence. She talked about her ideas with colleagues within the same powerful circles. Of course they welcomed them, and soon she had declared a movement of concern for the nation's children. This was on 27 January 2001, when the wife of the Interior Minister installed her in the PKK and Handicrafts positions (*Serambi Indonesia* 28-1-2001). To give it concrete shape, she set up a legal body called the Yayasan Peduli Anak Bangsa Nur Raudha (YPAB Nur Raudha, Nur Raudha Foundation of Concern for the Nation's Children). The name was that of her daughter by Abdullah Puteh and meant 'light of Raudha', where Raudha is a holy place in Mecca in which prayers are surely answered. Linda Purnomo took the chair, and she was assisted by a number of provincial officials or (mainly) their wives (*Kontras* 167(5-11 December 2001):9).

For security reasons, and to bring the governor's palace closer to the

[9] *Media Indonesia* 2-5-2004. Questioned by the police, William acknowledged he had negotiated with the governor several times to obtain the electricity project (*Serambi Indonesia* 4-6-2004).

people, the NGO opened an office just behind the governor's complex. A service centre and health clinic was set up for mothers and children to attend every Monday and Thursday. At first it aimed only to help those from the two *kampong* next to the governor's complex. Operational funds came from the flood relief fund chaired by deputy governor Azwar Abubakar (Rp 220 million), from the Industry Service (Rp 50 million) and from the Women's Empowerment Bureau (about Rp 50 million) (*Kontras* 167(5-11 December 2001):7). Pretty soon many people heard about the social work being done by YPAB Nur Raudha, and requests for funding assistance began to flow in from various directions. This naturally inspired Linda Purnomo to increase her fundraising efforts, and to expand her service network to more people. Using her position of influence, she lobbied heads of services and contractors to donate or make facilities available. District heads and mayors were asked to open branches of the organization in their respective districts and towns.

In July 2001 she auctioned paintings before government officials and contractors to raise funds for her foundation, and at her birthday party on 15 October 2001, in front of officials, she installed the wives of 12 district heads and mayors as heads of YPAB branches in their respective districts and towns (*Serambi Indonesia* 16-10-2001).

In short, donations in kind and in money soon became a steady stream into the foundation's coffers. Some of these were government programs transferred to the foundation, among them the mass circumcision for 1000 boys worth Rp 100 million from the Aceh Disaster Relief Fund (Satkorlak), the gift of an ambulance worth Rp 60 million from the Health Service and the handicraft skills course for school drop-outs worth Rp 25 million from the Education Service.[10]

Linda Purnomo's activism through YPAB Nur Raudha demonstrates clearly how fuzzy the boundary was between official and private business. This drew criticism from NGO activists with long experience at the grass-roots. Moreover they learned that the mass circumcision exercise, which should have been for 1000 people, was only given to 400 (*Kontras* 167(5-11 December 2001):5-11, 20). When they exposed what they knew through the mass media, it not only angered Linda Purnomo but also her husband Abdullah Puteh. He accused the newspaper that carried the expose of slandering his wife's organization (*Serambi Indonesia* 9-12-2001). The criticism did have an influence on YPAB Nur Raudha. Its secretariat moved to a humbler

10 It is difficult to know exactly how much money YPAB Nur Raudha obtained by means of government transfers or from contractors. The anti-corruption NGO Samak estimated Rp 9 billion worth of government projects in the 2001 provincial budget were implemented by YPAB Nur Raudha. Marlinda denies the figure is as high as this (*Kontras* 167(5-11 December 2001):7; *Kontras* 168(12-18 December 2001):24).

address in Tgk.Chik Di Tiro Street, and its social welfare activities were drastically scaled down from those of its first eight months. All the district branches closed down.

Collaborating with parliament

Governor Puteh's corruption and abuse of office could really only continue because Aceh's parliament exercised weak control. Although the recent legislative changes had given parliament greater powers, in other respects it continued to be burdened with the legacy of the New Order. Parliament remained a collective entity that lacked an opposition as is normal in a democracy. Even PAN and the alliance of small parties, despite walking out at a critical stage, still took their place on important commissions. Decisions were also still taken in a hierarchical fashion, beginning with the Leaders Consultative Body (Badan Musyawarah Pimpinan) then down through the commission and factional meetings. Governor Puteh often made use of this hierarchy to ask parliamentary leaders to approve his 'emergency' or 'urgent' measures, including the PT Seulawah NAD company and the helicopter purchase to be analysed below. At the end of 2000 he obtained 'in principle' agreement letters from the parliamentary speaker for the next year's budget and for the supply of new cars, even though parliament had not yet debated the budget. Moreover parliamentarians abused their power of veto over the governor's annual report to wring concessions out of him, thus building collusive links between governor Puteh and parliamentary speaker Muhammad Yus.

Parliamentarians are not rich, and they also have to contribute to party coffers out of their own salaries. The large increase in the provincial budget following special autonomy gave parliament a lot more money to spend on itself. Routine parliamentary expenditure more than tripled to Rp 18.9 billion over the three years to 2003. The speaker's house, only built in 1998, was expensively renovated in 2002 at a cost of Rp 800 million. Each new project was an opportunity for commission chairpersons and their contractor friends to siphon money into their own pockets. Governor Puteh knew how to turn these material temptations into support for his own plans. The electrical generators scandal, for example, involved a 'loan' of Rp 750 million to the deputy speaker at that time, T. Bakhrum Manyak, as 'thanks' for services provided (*Serambi Indonesia* 28-1-2001).

When a small number of critical parliamentarians tried to challenge this collaboration between the speaker and the governor, they paid for it dearly. In November 2001 several members from the smaller parties tried to put together a motion of no confidence in the speaker Muhammad Yus. They had enough signatures, but Muhammad Yus crushed it by simply refusing to put it on the agenda (*Serambi Indonesia* 6-12-2001). They then tried another tack, namely to propose that direct elections for governor be implemented immediately. A new law (Law no. 18/2001) envisaged direct elections in five years time, but did permit a faster implementation (*Kontras* 224(8-14 January 2003):14). When, under public pressure and with sufficient numbers in parliament, it was finally discussed in January 2003, Muhammad Yus rejected the proposal as un-Islamic, and the military/police faction said Aceh was not safe for elections (*Serambi Indonesia* 7-1-2003; *Kontras* 226(22-28 January 2003):3). It took more than a year before a direct elections measure was approved, by which time Aceh was no longer ahead of the rest. For their trouble, the two parliamentarians who had been most vocal in their opposition to Speaker Muhammad Yus were evicted from parliament. They were Mukhlis Mukhtar and Hasbi Bustamam, both members of the PPP of which Muhammad Yus was provincial chair. Thus parliament was robbed of two of its critical voice.

Reactions from GAM and other marginal groups

In this section we see another of David Brown's three tensions, namely the tension between the claim to universalistic administration and the practice of political favouritism. There are always going to be those for whom nepotism and collusion are completely unacceptable. The anger such practices generate lies at the heart of the oppositional agenda. Indeed one might say the emotions around corruption allegations are the main resource used in inter-elite competition in Indonesia. At the extreme end of the oppositional spectrum stood the separatist movement GAM. At its other end stood a group of critical professionals who remained engaged with the game played by the establishment.

Unlike the bureaucrats, politicians and contractors, GAM remained entirely cynical about the special autonomy package offered by the central government. GAM spokesperson Sofyan Daud said in July 2001 that special autonomy was merely a trick to turn the area beyond Java into an Indonesian colony. The oil royalties, too, were no extraordinary generosity, since the government had long enjoyed Aceh's riches while returning only about 1% to Aceh (*Kontras* 144(4-10 July 2001):5; *Kontras* 163(7-13 November 2001):5). GAM wanted a referendum on Aceh's future association with Indonesia (*Serambi Indonesia* 28-2-1999, 20-2-2000). GAM had no interest in who became the next governor, and its commanders were satisfied merely to collect revolutionary taxes (*hak sabil* and *pajak nanggroe*), especially from government offices, contractors and politicians, in order to finance their struggle. Recalcitrants faced terror or intimidation. Since GAM effectively controlled most of the countryside at this time, all candidates for governor took care to make personal contact with its leaders in order to avoid intimidation. A bomb caused some damage at parliament house on 11 September 2000, just as candidates were being selected. Neither as candidate nor as governor did Abdullah Puteh dare to confront GAM. He always said diplomatically that GAM activists were not enemies but 'our brothers', though there remained some differences between them about Aceh's status within Indonesia.[11]

With most local elites having been co-opted, social control over the government passed to 'liberal' professionals whose livelihoods did not depend on the government, especially NGO activists, lawyers and journalists. They included journalist Kamal J. Farza and Akhirudin, who both coordinated Sorak (Solidaritas Rakyat Anti Korupsi, People's Anti-Corruption Solidarity), human rights activist Dr Humam Hamid, his younger activist brother Farhan Hamid who taught at Syah Kuala University, and M. Saleh who wrote for the national weekly *Forum Keadilan* and led the local *Modus* tabloid. Some were new to the political arena, others supported alternative gubernatorial candidates in 2000. This 'critical group' (*kelompok kritis*) raised issues such as dishonesty in the gubernatorial elections, abuse of office, illegality and corruption under governor Puteh. Sometimes they mobilized the masses to protest outside the provincial parliament, and they took corruptors to court.[12]

Puteh was not an easy target to bring down. He had such a close relationship with parliament that the activists' colleague Mukhlis Mukhtar there was kicked out, as we saw. He had the power to veto the appointment of Public Prosecutor and Police Chief, and plenty of money to spend on renovating the Prosecutor's home. Unsurprisingly therefore, the Public Prosecutor rejected the corruption suit they entered on the grounds that it was unproven (*Serambi Indonesia* 19-11-2002; *Modus* 3(14-24 May 2003):4).

Blocked at home, the critical group then took their demands to the national level, since they too had elite connections in Jakarta. A 2002 decision of the People's Consultative Assembly (MPR, Majelis Permusyawaratan Rakyat) on the implementation of special autonomy in Papua and Aceh (TAP MPR-RI no. IV/2002) said government had a responsibility to bring peace to Aceh. They took this as their legal basis to demand Abdullah Puteh be sacked. Kamal Farza took a petition signed by 40 Acehnese NGOs to the Interior Minister. The effort got a hearing from an influential 'Team of Five for Aceh', and from President Megawati herself on 4 September 2002, briefly turning it into a national news item.[13]

11 *Kontras* 121(24-30 January 2001):22-3. Acting governor Ramli Ridwan also met secretly with GAM in the interior of Great Aceh between June and November 2000.

12 For example, *Serambi Indonesia* 8-10-2002.

13 It consisted of Muhammadiyah chairperson Syafii Maarif, MUI chairperson KH Ali Yafi, Islamic intellectual Nurcholis Majid, former Interior Minister Suryadi Sudirja, and former Foreign Minister Ali Alatas. Syafii Maarif supported the petition (*Forum Hukum dan Keadilan* 22 (15 September 2002)).

Although Abdullah Puteh responded defiantly and threatened to stop anyone who disturbed his government (*Serambi Indonesia* 16-11-2002), the issue continued to gather momentum in Jakarta. It was noticed by the new Aceh Desk at the office of the Coordinating Minister for Politics and Security (Menko Polkam) Susilo Bambang Yudhoyono. One of the staff there was Kaoysyah, the candidate for governor who lost out to Puteh. A high profile workshop on conflict resolution in Aceh at the prestigious Indonesian Academy of Sciences (Lembaga Ilmu Pengetahuan Indonesia, LIPI) on 23 April 2003 included a recommendation to replace the governor (*Modus* 3(14-24 May 2003):20). Minister Susilo Bambang Yudhoyono was about to bring these considerations to a cabinet meeting when they were brought into the open by a Metro TV news item on 25 April. Governor Puteh swung into action and began phoning his Golkar contacts. As a result Golkar chairperson and House of Representatives Speaker Akbar Tanjung declared that governor Puteh had been democratically elected and the central government had no right to intervene (*Serambi Indonesia* 27-4-2003). Back in Aceh, Puteh's loyalists in parliament and the bureaucracy also spoke out in his support (*Modus* 3(14-24 May 2003):19). Mixed signals from Aceh led Jakarta to take a middle course. On 28 April 2003 Interior Minister Hari Sabarno said no decision had been taken on dismissing governor Puteh but he would send a team to investigate the corruption allegations (*Serambi Indonesia* 29-4-2003, 3-5-2003, 4-5-2003).

Governor Puteh had won a reprieve. He issued some rather general statements in his defence, for example reminding his hearers that only a quarter of the money from Jakarta stayed at the province while the rest flowed to districts beyond his control, but avoided addressing specific issues (*Kontras* 226(22-28 January 2003):9). Indeed, the promised corruption investigation against him had to pass through one of two official finance watchdogs, but only after receiving permission from the governor. This as good as guaranteed that the investigation would fail.[14] For public consumption, governor Puteh moved Usman Budiman, of the PT Seulawah NAD Air scandal, sideways into another job. He also sent his closest cronies to plead with the senior journalist M. Saleh, who had exposed one scandal after another, to ease up on the governor, while offering to 'help out' his lightly funded *Modus* tabloid. In July he took the lecturer and activist Farhan Hamid to court in Jakarta for defamation over a story about a road in the Mount Leuser National Park, demanding Rp 100 billion in compensation (*Kompas* 27-3-2003; *Serambi Indonesia* 22-7-2003; *Modus* 6(20-30 July 2003):10).

In the midst of these elite tussles the central government declared a

14 The two agencies were BPKP, authorized to audit projects funded from the national budget, and Bawasda, for provincial projects.

military emergency on 19 May 2003. The Iskandar Muda military area commander Maj-Gen Endang Suwarsa became martial law administrator, while governor Puteh was a member of his council. Fifty thousand police and soldiers began operations to hunt down GAM and seize back territory. Hundreds of NGO activists from the critical group fled the province. Bureaucrats, parliamentarians and contractors warmly welcomed the operation, because it relieved them from GAM intimidation and extortion as well as from annoying criticism by the liberals. Thus governor Puteh, who had previously spoken about GAM as his 'brothers', told a meeting in his native East Aceh he was offering a Rp 50 million reward for information leading to the arrest of the controversial GAM commander Ishak Daud, something he would not have dared to do earlier. He now stood shoulder to shoulder with the military to eliminate GAM (*Serambi Indonesia* 3-8-2003).

The third tension of neo-patrimonialism, according to David Brown, is the risk associated with mass mobilization. Governor Puteh had to take this risk, since GAM and the critical group had been doing the same beyond his reach. But he was always cautious in this regard, choosing to address audiences on cultural and religious themes rather than social ones. A week after becoming governor he held a Quranic celebration in his official residence, inviting religious teachers from all over Aceh. On 19 December 2000 President Wahid himself came to Banda Aceh to declare the implementation of Islamic law (*syariat* Islam), which was later followed up with several institutional innovations. A good portion of the windfall oil and gas money passed into these new religious institutions, to keep them busy with various activities.[15] In short, religion and custom were manipulated to support the government's conflict resolution strategies, while the elite was smothered with money and facilities to keep them on side. Satisfied he had won the upper hand, governor Puteh reminded his rivals to be patient until he completed his term in office. 'The desire to be governor is natural and legitimate. Do not let it stoop to unhealthy means [...] It's a good thing my 'martial arts' are up to the job, otherwise I would have been finished long ago. When a blow comes from the left, I know exactly how to avoid it.' He described his rivals as 'mere learners' in the martial arts arena (*Kontras* 242(21-27 May 2003):12-3).

However, governor Puteh's rhetoric was not sufficient to silence the critical group. They argued that the martial law operation was not merely about military matters but about upholding the law, and asked Maj-Gen Endang

15 In July 2001 the Indonesian Ulema Council (MUI) was replaced by a less Indonesian-sounding Ulema Consultative Council (Majelis Permusyawaratan Ulama), and a provincial Syariat Islam Service (Dinas Syariat Islam) was established the year after. The Dinas received Rp 42 billion from the special educational fund in 2002, and the MPU increased its budget manyfold to Rp 4 billion.

Suwarya to process corruption cases such as the purchase of the printing machine, the purchase of helicopters, and the electrical generators project. Activists who had fled to Jakarta joined forces with anti-corruption groups there such as Indonesia Corruption Watch.[16] Whether moved by these criticisms or not, Maj-Gen Endang Suwaryo interrogated William Taylor, the electrical supplier, in mid-April 2004, and along with him several associated officials. The issue was that some of the generators had been second-hand, and the supplier had paid project money to the bankrupt PT Seulawah NAD director M. Suparno. William Taylor, Usman Budiman and another official were even detained for a while.

Aware he was the real target of these investigations, governor Puteh flew to Jakarta, contacted a famous lawyer, and once more complained to Golkar's Akbar Tanjung. As a result he was invited to meet with an important parliamentary commission on 30 May 2004. Akbar Tanjung and some other politicians said the martial law administrator was going beyond his authority in pursuing Puteh.[17] On 5 May, national parliament advised the government to downgrade martial law in Aceh to a 'civil emergency' that would restore governor Puteh's powers (*Serambi Indonesia* 25-4-2004, 6-5-2004; *Media Indonesia* 2-5-2004; *Kompas* 29-4-2004). President Megawati followed this advice on 19 May 2004. Feeling vindicated, Puteh repeated his earlier assertions to the press that he had always acted within the bounds of the law.[18] Although the corruption cases taken up by the martial law administrator were not dropped, Puteh felt confident enough to strike back with a corruption case of his own against one of the martial law officers. It concerned 17 vehicles, which had been smuggled in as part of a humanitarian assistance shipment. President Megawati ordered the police to investigate (*Serambi Indonesia* 22-6-2004).

In the meantime the critical group did everything in their power to press the government to persist with the corruption allegations against Puteh raised by the martial law administrator. So President Megawati on 27 May 2004 gave the police and the Corruption Eradication Commission (Komisi Pemberantasan Korupsi, KPK) permission to examine governor Puteh. The allegation only focussed on a smaller problem, namely a project to purchase a Russian MI-2 PLC Rostov helicopter at a price of Rp 12.6 billion.

16 Others were Gerakan Rakyat Anti Korupsi (Gerak, People's Anti-Corruption Movement) and Persatuan Bantuan Hukum Indonesia (PBHI, Indonesian Legal Aid Association).

17 According to rumour, governor Puteh's cronies attempted to strike back at Maj-Gen Endang Suwayro by means of a sex scandal. A month earlier Metro TV aired an exclusive interview with a beautiful actress in Bandung who said she had been given a Mercedes with an 'NA' number plate (from Sabang, Aceh) by an important military officer in Aceh.

18 Exclusive interview with Abdullah Puteh in *Media Indonesia* 2-5-2004 and *Kompas* 20-5-2004.

KPK found that the contractor directly appointed by governor Puteh, Bram Manoppo from PT Putra Pobiagan Mandiri, had marked up the helicopter's price (*Media Indonesia* 2-5-2004; *Serambi Indonesia* 20-7-2004). The electrical generators case proved difficult to bring to court, since the transfer of Rp 3 billion to M. Suparno of PT Seulawah NAD looked like an inter-company loan, although the contractor had only done it under pressure from Puteh. Nevertheless, the KPK investigation was sufficient to make Puteh a suspect, and President Megawati was forced on 20 July 2004 to instruct Abdullah Puteh to hand over his responsibilities to the Coordinating Minister for Politics and Security.[19]

Still, Puteh was not out of friends. The Coordinating Minister for Politics at this time was Hari Sabarno, who also held the Interior Ministry, and he had declared a year earlier that Puteh could only be removed by means of the normal legal, administrative and political channels. He viewed the Presidential Instruction as valid only during the investigating phase.[20] Akbar Tanjung too (himself also a corruption suspect) tried hard to protect Puteh, saying he should not be relieved of duties until convicted (*Kompas* 21-7-2004; *Serambi Indonesia* 20-7-2004, 21-7-2004).

Yet the law was taking its course. In September 2004 Susilo Bambang Yudhoyono, who as Coordinating Minister for Politics and Security had listened to Puteh's critics, was popularly elected president on an anti-corruption platform. A special Anti-corruption Court had been established in the last months of Megawati's presidency, part of a package with the Anti-corruption Commission. This now became the main instrument for implementing Yudhoyono's election promises. On 11 April 2005 the court convicted Abdullah Puteh of corruption and handed down a ten-year suspended sentence. At the time of writing (May 2005) it seemed possible the sentence would be overturned on appeal. Puteh's lawyers argued that the Anti-corruption Court had no retroactive powers, while the alleged offence had occurred before the court was established. Nevertheless the decision was widely praised as adding to the credibility of the new government's anticorruption drive.

Conclusion

The sharp and sometimes dirty competition during and after the governor's election in Aceh in 2000 has demonstrated all the characteristics of a conflict among district-based communal patrons for access to the governor's office.

19 Inpres no. 2/2004.

20 See the explanation of Hari Sabarno (*Serambi Indonesia* 6-7-2004; *Serambi Indonesia* 28-7-2004).

The issue was local resources, not ideology. Where political parties are supposed to act as a single unit, here they were divided up around a series of communal patrons. These patrons maintained personal ties of loyalty and material obligations with their clients. Thus unlike the money politics and thuggery that coloured local politics in some other places, Abdullah Puteh's victory had more to do with his skills of manipulation, which he used to accommodate dissatisfied elements before his election.[21] After taking office he built alliances with local strongmen in and outside parliament, including with his former rivals, and thus created political stability, at least for a time. He placed around him a set of followers chosen on the basis of personal loyalty rather than merit, so that he sat in the middle of a network of patron-client relations. How parasitic this network was became obvious among others in the PT Seulawah NAD Air and YPAB Nur Raudha scandals. He also built alliances with national elites to protect him against the local attacks that plagued him repeatedly.

Decentralization brought changes in the form of more money from oil and gas and greater independence for parliament, but other structural legacies from the New Order permitted the governor to engage in political criminality. Autonomy has not yet brought more democratic, cleaner and better government to Aceh. The kind of patrimonial politics practised by governor Puteh have been a traditional pattern in Aceh for a long time (Hurgronje 1893-95; Langen 1888; Lombard 1967). The sultan and his *hulubalang* ruled by the use of force, and through personalized cliques in which politics and economics were indivisible. The colonial Dutch introduced administrative renewal once the sultanate was removed, by paying regular salaries to the *hulubalang* and setting up customary courts. But under indirect rule the *hulubalang* continued to exercise their power in traditional ways (M. Isa Sulaiman 1997). Even today, national integration comes less from a unification of economy or culture than from the integration of elites. Communal patrons build alliances with elites at the centre both to gain access to resources and to increase their own legitimacy as local patrons, while central elites need them to gain access to the grassroots.

Of course these bonds of power are not unimportant to the smooth functioning of government, but as long as they remain inadequately balanced by popular participation they become an opportunity for local actors to persist in their destructive patrimonial ways. This in turn increases social inequality and creates unrest. Once a free space for civil society opens up, NGO activists and other reformist movements rise up to fight for the elimination of such patterns. In this context the GAM separatist movement is merely the most extreme form of this negation of an existing pattern of power. The local

21 Contrast the Medan mayoral election observed by Vedi Hadiz (Hadiz 2003a).

communal patrons in Aceh are not as wealthy as the big landowning 'bosses' Sidel (1999) describes in the Philippines, nor as crass as the casino, prostitution and marihuana mafia in Thailand (Ockey 1992; Phongpaichit et al. 1998). Aceh's economy is much more controlled by the state and large outside capital, and its culture perhaps somewhat less abrasive. Yet the upwardly mobile bureaucrats, contractors and *ulema* of Aceh build their followings, and their personal wealth, in similar ways and are thus as parasitic as their counterparts elsewhere in Southeast Asia. The big difference with the past is that today such ways of operating are increasingly under challenge from popular democratic forces.

Fear and the failure of security

ARIANTO SANGAJI

The security forces and regional violence in Poso

Introduction

The term 'security forces' in this chapter refers to the Indonesian national military (Tentara Nasional Indonesia, TNI), the Indonesian national police (Kepolisian Republik Indonesia, Polri), and intelligence institutions such as the national intelligence agency (Badan Intelijen Negara, BIN) – in short, the three institutions that carry out the security and order functions in Indonesia.[1] By 'regional violence', I mean violence that is limited to a particular region within the archipelago. It may take the form of vertical violence, as in Aceh, where we find conflict between the state and people fighting for independence, or of horizontal violence, such as the violence with ethnic and religious dimensions in Ambon and Poso. Ideally, the security forces should carry out their duties in a way that does not conflict with democratic norms and is subject to the authority of the civilian government. The use of TNI forces should be limited to facing threats from external enemies and providing support to the legitimate institution for handling domestic emergencies. It is the police who have the authority to maintain domestic order, while the state intelligence service secretly gathers information to assist the other security forces. Actions by the security forces within these bounds are legitimate and satisfy citizens' expectations of safety. However, quite apart from the various, complex, and possibly mutually contradictory hidden motives of the security forces during Indonesia's current political transition, I intend to demonstrate that the security forces actually reap benefits from the regional violence in Poso by engaging in a series of actions outside the limits of their legitimate functions.

1 I would like to express my special thanks to Gerry van Klinken for his useful criticism and input on this paper.

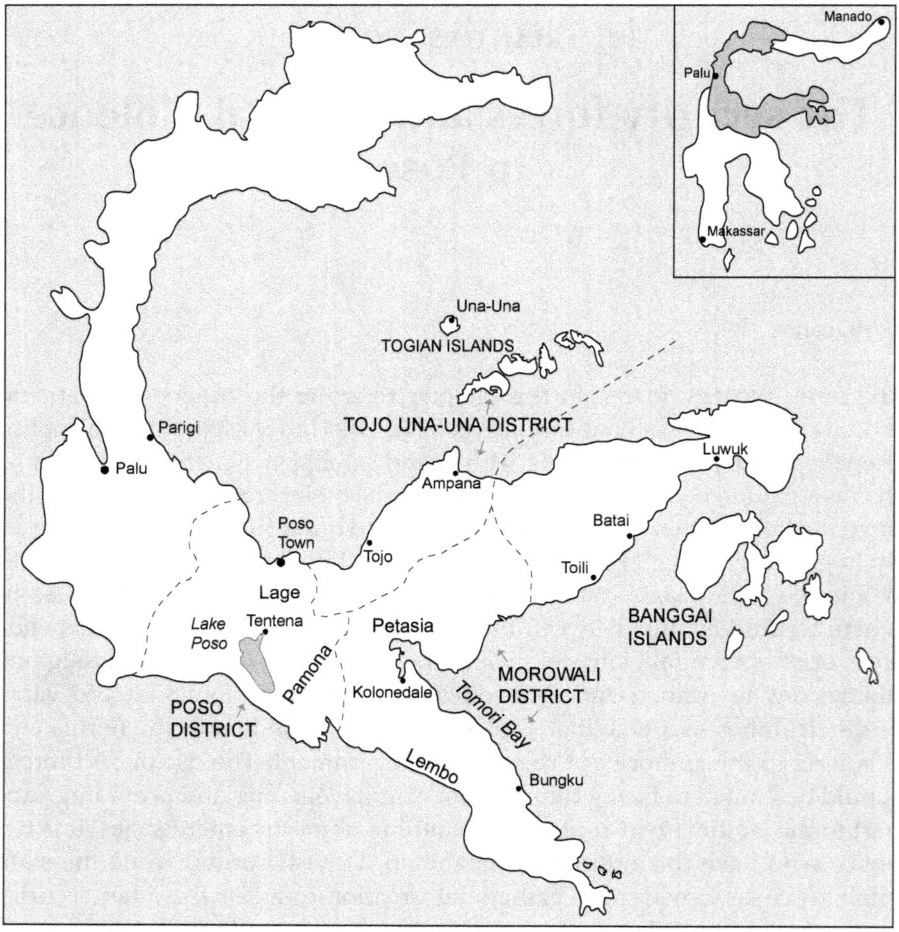

Map 10. Central Sulawesi (2)

The security forces and regional violence

Links between the security forces (in particular the army, Tentara Nasional Indonesia-Angkatan Darat, TNI-AD) and regional violence have been a staple of Indonesian politics since the 1950s. In the cases of the Pemerintah Revolusioner Republik Indonesia (PRRI, the Revolutionary Government of the Indonesian Republic) and Permesta rebellions, the strife was related to internal conflicts within the TNI itself and to the dissatisfaction of TNI commanders in the regions with the central government (Leirissa 1991). The response to this regional violence then provided an entry for the TNI to participate in managing governmental and economic affairs once the state of military emergency was declared in March 1957 (Sundhaussen 1988; Crouch 1978). Using this foothold, and especially after the 30 September 1965 incident, the security forces consolidated their presence in the political and economic spheres, as well as in their legitimate domain of security.

The Reformasi of 1998 was a turning point. The security forces could no longer enjoy the many political privileges they had held during the New Order era. This change was signalled by the elimination of the positions of chief of social and political staff (Kasospol) and chief of territorial staff (Kaster), the elimination of the military's dual function (*dwifungsi*), the liquidation of *kekaryaan* (posting of military personnel to civilian positions) and the social-political function, and the removal of the TNI/Polri factions from legislative institutions by 2009 (Departemen Pertahanan RI 2003:14). The Coordinating Board for Consolidation of National Stability (Bakorstanas) and the Special Investigation Institution (Litsus) were also liquidated through Presidential Decree no. 38/2000. As a consequence, the military's control over political life declined sharply.

Yet Reformasi did not dismantle all the military's privileges. Two important aspects remained untouched. First, despite criticisms, military business activities continued, both 'institutional' and 'non-institutional' businesses,[2] and economic crimes (Singh 2001; McCulloch 2000:28-32). The military has been involved in economic activity since the early 1950s, primarily to earn extra-budgetary income. This activity has included collection of illegal taxes from the business community and more organized activity, such as

2 Institutionally, there are three forms of military involvement in business: First, cooperatives aimed at the welfare of their members and their families; second, business units managed by foundations for the purpose of welfare and education; and third, miltary involvement in state-owned companies, such as Pertamina, Bulog, and Berdikari (Indria Samego 1998:67-8).
The definition of non-institutional military businesses is businesses conducted by retired military personnel, by family of military personnel, or by military personnel themselves outside official channels (for example the other foundations or business entities affiliated with armed forces or the police) (Indria Samego 1998:97).

smuggling. This involvement increased significantly in 1958-1959, when the military acquired control over Dutch companies that were nationalized (Robison 1986:250-1).

Second, the TNI's Territorial Commands (Komando teritorial, Koter), which have existed since the 1950s, were maintained (Sundhaussen 1988:248-50). Even after Reformasi, the Koter, which played a very important role during the New Order era, comprising the Military Area Commands (Komando daerah militer, Kodam), Military Sub-Area Commands (Komando resort militer, Korem), Military District Commands (Komando distrik militer, Kodim), Military Precinct Commands (Komando rayon militer, Koramil), and Village Management NCOs (Bintara pembina desa, Babinsa), were all retained. In the past, these Koter had been the military's main political instrument to rein in citizens' political activity. This situation means that the military still has a strong footing from which to control the life of the citizenry.

The regional violence since the Reformasi of 1998 has, in any case, actually improved the security forces' bargaining position vis-à-vis the civilian government. In response to regional violence, the military has mobilized large numbers of troops from year to year. This implies that the civilian elite has failed to impose civilian supremacy over the military or to provide non-military solutions to solve regional problems (Kammen and Chandra 2003). At the regional level, local governments will again turn to the TNI to find an element that can stabilize the unpredictable political climate, and the military will continue to enjoy access to economic resources in the regions and to maintain its organizational autonomy (Mietzner 2003:256-7).

With reference to regional violence, at the national level the TNI has taken the initiative to force its interests on the civilian government. The proposed Bill on TNI, which was full of 'political' articles, was evidence of TNI's unwillingness to abandon practical politics. The inclusion of a clause on placement of actively-serving TNI personnel in departmental and non-departmental structures is evidence of this.[3] One article in the draft Bill first proposed by TNI headquarters granted the TNI commander the authority to take military action without the president's consent (*Tempo* 16-3-2003). In the end, however, Law no. 34/2004 put the authority and responsibility for mobilizing TNI forces in the hands of the president.

It is generally agreed that the regional violence in Poso has taken place in several episodes since December 1998. The public uses the term Poso I for the incidents that occurred in December 1998, Poso II for April 2000, and Poso III for May-June 2000; Poso IV broke out in early July 2001, and Poso V with the attacks on several villages in sub-district (*kecamatan*) Poso Pesisir in late November 2001 (Ecip, Darwis Waru and Alip Yog Kunandar 2002:8-40). Since

[3] See Article 47 of Law no. 34/2004 on the Indonesian National Military (TNI).

the Malino Meeting in December 2001, sporadic violence has continued in the form of mysterious attacks.

Perpetuation of conflict

I believe that the security forces, both institutionally and as individuals, have sustained the conflict in Poso. This perpetuation of the conflict can be observed in several aspects: toleration of violence, engaging in violence outside the limits of their duties, distribution of firearms and ammunition, mysterious shootings/killings, rivalry between armed units, mobilization of troops, and relations between the security forces and *laskar* (partisan militias).

Toleration of violence

The term 'toleration of violence' refers to situations in which the security authorities do not take the necessary legitimate and professional preventive and repressive action to end conflict. It takes the form of simply allowing open physical contact between disputing parties, or of mobilizing troops to the location of the violence but too late to properly intervene.

The humanitarian tragedy in Poso indicates how deep this toleration has been. In the case of the mass slaughter of Muslim residents in Sintuwu Lemba Village (Lage sub-district) in May 2000, the Crisis Centre of the Central Sulawesi Christian Church (CC GKST) produced a report on the chronology of the case.[4] The report stated that members of the security forces allowed the battle between the two sides to take place. When armed conflict broke out between residents in Sintuwu Lemba Village on 28 May 2000, the security forces who were at the location actually left the scene. However, three sources from among residents who survived the Sintuwu Lemba incident confirm that not all the security forces left the scene of the incidents; some of them were directly involved in the fighting.

If they had wanted to prevent the violence at Sintuwu Lemba, the security forces could easily have done so. The headquarters of Company B, Infantry Battalion 711 (Kompi B Yonif 711/Raksatama) in Kawua is only around 7 kilometres, or five minutes, from the scene of the incident. And the Lage police sector (*polsek*) station in Tagolu Village is only around 1 kilometre from Sintuwu Lemba. Yet it is known that a number of village residents were tortured and killed near the Tagolu village administration building.

The actions of soldiers in the field seem to have reflected the attitudes

4 www.gkst.org (accessed 28-8-2002).

of their commanders. The commander of Korem 132 Tadulako, Colonel Hamdan Z. Nasution, behaved very strangely when an attorney, Karman Karim, brought one of the Sintuwu Lemba victims to meet him. When the victim, Ilham, told of the torture he had experienced, the commander lightly replied, 'Why didn't you resist?' And when Ilham said that a soldier from Company 711 Raksatama just sat and watched the torture of the Sintuwu Lemba residents, Hamdan simply listened cynically (*Mingguan Alchairaat* 91, June 2000).

Toleration of violence also occurred when armed conflict broke out between Muslim and Christian groups at Bridge II between Kawua and Ronononcu Villages in Poso Kota on 12 November 2001. The armed conflict began at around 7.15 a.m., but the security forces only arrived at the location at around 12.15 p.m. Yet much earlier, at 8.05 a.m., Pastor Damanik from CC GKST had contacted Lt. Col. (Inf.) Syamsurizal Harahap, commander of Kodim 1307 Poso, to stop the violence. This is very strange, since it is only around 5 kilometres from the Kodim 1307 Poso headquarters to the scene, and around 1 kilometre from the headquarters of Yonif 711/Raksatama (Damanik 2003:71-2).

Engaging directly in conflict

Security forces are known to have been directly involved in violence in Poso outside their legitimate duties. During Poso III (May-June 2000), in which hundreds died, many army and police personnel are suspected of direct involvement. No fewer than 29 army and police personnel were interrogated by the military police. Of seven individuals identified as being seriously involved, two were army officers with the rank of captain (*Surya* 7-7-2000; *Formasi* 48, July 2000). Then, following investigations, two NCOs and one enlisted man from Kodim 1307 Poso were declared suspects by the Military Police Detachment (Detasemen Polisi Militer, Denpom) VII/2 Palu.[5]

Earlier, the commander of Korem 132/Tadulako, Infantry Colonel Hamdan Z Nasution, stated that the involvement of the military and police personnel was limited to supplying instant noodles and rice (*Detik.com* 23-6-2000). But this statement was only intended to avert a greater responsibility following the emergence of various accusations of involvement by military personnel. In their testimony to the Palu Military Police Detachment, the three army personnel, with the initials MR, CP and AT, admitted supplying ten rounds of ammunition to one of the parties to the conflict in Poso. Furthermore, during the TNI's month-long Operation Love of Peace (Operasi Cinta Damai), the

5 *Fajar* 7-7-2000; *Pedoman Rakyat* 7-7-2000; *Fajar* 21-6-2000; *Surya* 22-6-2000; *Kompas* 21-6-2000; *Fajar* 28-6-2000.

security forces seized thousands of bullets from civilians (*Detik.com* 7-7-2000). Many of these civilians stated that they had received the ammunition from military and police personnel.

Involvement of police personnel is also acknowledged. During the humanitarian tragedy of Poso III, the Central Sulawesi regional police chief (Kepala kepolisian daerah, Kapolda) reported that he planned to take four of his personnel to court, as they were suspected of involvement in the unrest. Two of them, with the initials HP and SS, were members of the Poso police Subregion. They assisted a certain group when it carried out attacks in several places in Poso Pesisir sub-district (*Pedoman Rakyat* 21-7-2000).

From reports of official sources – both Muslim and Christian – it is very clear how deeply army and police personnel were involved. For example, the official publication of Laskar Jihad – one of the Muslim militia groups fighting in Poso – *Buletin Laskar Jihad* (Edition 15, year I) reported that individuals from Army Company B, Infantry Battalion 711/Raksatama in Kawua, Poso abducted and shot dead seven residents of Toyado village. One of the corpses was thrown off a military truck in Ronononcu Village, Lage, clearly to make it appear that the murder had been committed by a Christian group.

Perhaps because they were so blatantly involved in the violence, these TNI personnel were caught by the legal system. The National Human Rights Commission (Komnas HAM) considered their acts to be human rights violations (*Kompas Cyber Media* 11-12-2001). From these cases, the commander of Denpom VII/-2 Palu, MP Lt. Col. Wempi Hapan, later stated that 14 personnel from TNI Company B Infantry Battalion 711/Raksatama had been designated as suspects. Two of them were officers (second lieutenants) and the remainder enlisted men. They were charged with abduction, shooting, murder, and torture and were to be tried in Military Court 17, Manado, North Sulawesi (*Radar Sulteng* 16-7-2003; *Sinar Harapan* 17-7-2003).

On the other side, reports from CC GKST stated that personnel from Brimob – the Mobile Police Brigade, or special combat forces – engaged in shooting on 27 July 2001 that killed three Christian residents. Later, the secretary of CC GKST stated that 17 Brimob personnel attacked Batugencu Village on the evening of 12 August 2002. Following the attack, residents found many cartridge cases from organic weapons (*Suara Pembaruan* 14-8-2002; *MAL*, week II, August 2002). Five persons were killed and 500 houses burned in the attack.

Direct involvement in violence also occurred in the 12 November 2001 incident at Jembatan II, Poso. During armed contact between Muslim and Christian groups, three men in TNI uniforms suddenly appeared on a hilltop and let loose a volley of shots directed at the Muslim forces. Around 15 minutes later, the three came down the hill and left the location by motorcycle, heading toward Lage. Pastor Damanik from CC GKST, who had come to help evacuate residents, witnessed this incident (Damanik 2003:72).

Violence committed by the security forces has taken other forms as well. For example, Brimob Private First Class Zakeus (Jack) Juan (who was drunk at the time) shot at a 'Honda Jaya' intercity bus heading toward Luwuk, capital of district (*kabupaten*) Banggai (6 February 2003), killing a passenger from Toili, the main transmigration area in Banggai district (*Radar Sulteng* 8-2-2003, 30-4-2004).

Distribution of firearms and ammunition

One reason the violence in Poso has been so protracted is the security authorities' loss of control over the spread of small arms. The security forces are completely unable to stem the traffic in firearms and ammunition, whether from illegal sales and barter, smuggling in from abroad, or support from certain parties within the country. In fact, the security authorities are themselves often connected with the traffic in firearms and ammunition.

For the general public, the only satisfactory answer to explain the spread of organic weapons and ammunition into the hands of civilians must be a connection with the official security institutions, since they hold the exclusive right to control the distribution of arms and ammunition throughout the nation. Furthermore, it is the duty of the security forces to investigate the sources for the spread of organic arms and ammunition; a properly conducted internal investigation would surely reveal their origin. No concrete steps have yet been taken to trace the ultimate sources for the spread of arms and ammunition. Consider, for example, the seizure of 2,846 rounds of ammunition sent to Poso on the Pelni passenger ship KM Ngapulu, which arrived from Java at the port of Pantoloan, Palu on 3 October 2002. The plastic ammunition box was labelled PT Pindad (*Kompas* 5-10-2002; *Nuansa Pos* 5-10-2002; *Jakarta Post* 9-10-2002). In this case, the police only arrested the field operators, Farihin Ibnu Ahmad alias Yasir and Anto (*Nuansa Pos* 5-10-2002). The police should have further investigated how the ammunition changed hands from PT Pindad to Farihin and his associates.

Much earlier, in the attack on Sepe Village (Lage subdistrict), on the evening of Sunday, 1 December 2001, a case of 5.56 mm calibre bullets was found. The box, with the PT Pindad logo and a capacity of 1,400 bullets, was labelled 'Poso' in marker and 'B' with paint. It can therefore be surmised that this 25-kilogram case of bullets was allocated to Company B, Infantry Battalion 711 Raksatama in Kawua, Poso, but 'somehow' found its way into the hands of the insurgents in the village. According to the data on the munitions case, the ammunition was made by PT Pindad in March 1989 under contract no. KJB/004/DN/M/1988 dated 12 March 1988 (Aditjondro 2004b:42).

There have been many such cases of distribution of these illicit materials in Poso. In a police operation in mid May 2004 in Poso Kota, Poso Pesisir, Lage, Pamona Utara, and Pamona Selatan sub-districts, the security forces found three crates of 5.56 mm calibre ammunition produced by PT Pindad. They also found 11 homemade rifles, one revolver, 200 rounds of 5.56 mm, 12.7 mm, and 7.76 mm calibre ammunition, walkie-talkies, ski masks, knapsacks, and a bullet-proof vest reading 'Kopassus' (Komando Pasukan Khusus, the Army Special Forces) (*Detik.com* 14-5-2004).

The spread of firearms and ammunition in Poso (and also in Palu) is like an iceberg. The successful sweeps by the security forces uncover only the topmost layer, while below the surface, there is far more that remains unseen. Many residents possess firearms and ammunition, store them in PVC pipes, and hide them underground. Several informants are certain that many business operators in Poso possess illegal firearms.

So where did all these guns come from? It is undeniable that the *laskar* (partisan fighters) who came to Poso brought in some of them. Two separate *laskar* primary sources confirm that they brought various types of firearms into Poso starting in 2000, including revolvers, AK-47s, M16s and SKS.[6] Furthermore, Agus Dwikarna – leader of Laskar Jundullah – said that he obtained four AK-47s from Ambon to be used in Central Sulawesi. Agus revealed this at Darul Jalal mosque on 24 December 2001 and was monitored by BIN (Conboy 2004:228, 231). Another primary source who admitted taking part in the attack on the Brimob headquarters in Tantui, Ambon said that a number of SKS, revolvers, and US army carbines – perhaps he meant US M1 Carbines – were taken to Poso.[7] It is well known that this attack led to the loss of hundreds of organic weapons belonging to the police.

But it is also possible that members of the security forces, both active and retired, sell weapons to civilians. One source in Poso confessed that in March 2001 he had been offered M-16s for Rp 7 million apiece (around US$ 700 at that time), SS-1s for Rp 5 million and FN-45s for Rp 2.5 million. If he agreed, the broker would put him in touch with a source in the security forces.

The most blatant abuse has to do with the traffic in ammunition. Many residents admit that they have obtained various types of ammunition directly from the security forces. A 5.56 mm calibre bullet can be bought from an individual in the security forces for between Rp 3,000 and Rp 5,000. Typically, whenever 'BKO' troops (Bawah Kendali Operasi, Under Operational Control; for example troops brought in from another region) are withdrawn, residents can obtain bullets easily – through purchase, barter for deer antlers, or even for free.

6 Interviews, 29-10-2003 and 8-11-2003.

7 Interview, 28-6-2004.

Not all the firearms and ammunition in circulation come from the security forces or related institutions. Another important source is smuggling from the nearby southern Philippines. Typically, M-16 weapons are smuggled in using the 'leapfrog' method, that is, from island to island in the Sangihe Talaud island chain of North Sulawesi, and eventually brought to Poso (*Radar Sulteng* 27-10-2003). Smugglers also bring weapons from the southern Philippines through Tawao (Malaysia) and then to Nunukan (East Kalimantan), and then on to Poso. When the security situation heats up, the weapons are brought into Poso by sea, often at night using fishing boats. In contrast, when the situation is relatively calm and the security forces slacken their checks of vehicles coming in and out of Poso, it becomes easy to smuggle in weapons by car or even motorcycle.

The smuggling routes through Nunukan and Sangihe Talaud are common knowledge. In early 2000, the North Sulawesi sub-district police foiled an attempt to smuggle weapons on the motor vessel KM Daya Sakti, which sails the route between Bitung (North Sulawesi) and General Santos City (Philippines), in the waters off Pulau Buang, Sangihe Talaud (*Gamma* 28-3-2000). The Philippines' National Security Advisor, Roilo Golez, has acknowledged that weapons are smuggled from the southern Philippines to Indonesia (*Sinar Harapan* 28-8-2001). National police Chief General Da'i Bachtiar stated that the southern Philippines was the source of the weapons used by the armed group that attacked in Beteleme in October 2003 (*Jakarta Post* 3-11-2003). And Nasir Abbas, an accused Jemaah Islamiyah figure, stated in court in Palu on 4 October 2003 that the Jemaah Islamiyah network had smuggled weapons through the Tawao-Nunukan route. All this indicates that the security forces certainly have sufficient information to fight weapons smuggling.

In any case, without efforts to trace the sources of weapons and ammunition, the security restoration operations that take place in Poso are no more than a joke. If nothing is done to investigate, prevent, and crack down on the sources of the weapons in circulation, violence can erupt at any time. As a result, in these operations, the security forces are simply acting as firemen; they come and put out the fire, leave, and get ready to be called again when the violence resumes.

Admittedly, it is very difficult to stem the flow of home-made weapons. And given the protracted nature of the violence, local residents have become increasingly skilled at producing such weapons. Even though tens of thousands of homemade firearms have been seized from residents, it is very easy for them to produce new ones. Workshops in Poso, Ampana, Parigi, Tentena, Kolonodale, and Palu have stepped up their output as producers of locally-made firearms. Home-made arms started to be produced on a large scale during Poso phase III (May-June 2000), when Poso residents suddenly received photocopies containing patterns for guns, both long and short barrel, from an unknown source.

According to the Head of Matako Village, just one day after the attack on the village on 22 July 2001, the commander of the Poso Military Area Command, Lt. Col. Syamsurizal Harahap, came to the village. Speaking to the village head and a number of residents, he advised the residents to arm themselves. The weapons should not be used to attack, but only for self-defence. Residents immediately responded by buying or making firearms. They then obtained ammunition easily by buying it from the security forces posted in their village.

Mysterious shootings/ killings

One dominant form of violence since the Malino Declaration in December 2001 has included shootings, bombings, and murders with sharp weapons by unknown persons. This pattern signals a major change from the previous forms of violence, which were characterized by open attacks involving large numbers of people. For the sake of simplicity, we will refer to these mysterious attacks as 'Petrus' (from the Indonesian *penembakan misterius*, mysterious shootings), a term widely used in Central Sulawesi to describe the events in Poso. However, the term is not limited to shootings by unknown persons and other murders by unknown persons, but refers also to mysterious bombings. The term therefore has a far broader application than the 'Petrus' of the 1980s.[8]

In any case, Petrus has certainly become a frightening spectre for the public, both in Poso and in Palu, the capital of the province of Central Sulawesi. Since 2002, Petrus has claimed many victims (see Table 1). One shocking case occurred on 18 July 2004, when a Petrus attack killed Pastor Susianti Tinulele and injured four of her congregation during services at the Effata Church, Jalan Banteng, Palu municipality.

The Petrus cases always employ more or less the same pattern. The killers use guns (long or short barrelled), knives, or machetes. The perpetrators are small groups of two to four persons. They use motorcycles, usually Yamaha RX King, if the target is in a densely populated or crowded area. In many cases, the shooters/killers wear masks (and are popularly known as 'ninja'), but in other cases they make no effort to hide their faces. Killings have taken place in residents' gardens or fields. Petrus operates both night and day.

The killings are rightly called mysterious, because the security forces

8 At that time, the iron fist of the Soeharto government killed between 5,000 and 10,000 alleged members of criminal gangs. Although this Petrus was related to eradication of criminals, it also signalled a conflict within the elite of the security forces (Cribb 2000:191; Bourchier 1990:186).

never succeed in shedding any light on the Petrus cases. Typically, the police use their standard answers about the perpetrators: 'The perpetrators have been identified', 'The authorities are conducting a hunt', 'From evidence uncovered at the scene of the crime, the authorities know what type of weapons were used', or 'The authorities have blocked all approaches in and out of Poso/Palu'. Or perhaps, slightly better, they may release sketches of the alleged perpetrators. But aside from this, the security forces do nothing.

Table 1. 'Petrus' cases after the Malino Declaration

Period	Shootings Number of cases	D	I	Murders Number of cases	D	I	Bombings Number of cases	D	I
2002	30	21	11	1	1	–	17	5	4
2003	11	7	9	3	4	–	9	–	7
2004	11	7	17	3	3	–	5	6	3
Total	50	35	34	7	8	–	31	11	14

Source: Clippings from local newspapers and Central Sulawesi Regional police
D: Dead; I: Injured.

In mid June 2004, in the midst of the election campaign, the police in Ambon arrested four people who were involved in mysterious shooting cases there. One of them had two identity cards (KTP). On his KTP from Palu, he used the name Rizky, while on his KTP from Batumerah, Ambon, he used the name Salman. As well as ID cards and bullets, the police also seized a Lion Air ticket from Makassar to Ambon dated 31 May 2004 and Rp 500,000 in cash. This man, with a crew cut and athletic build, chose to remain silent during the interrogation (*Radar Sulteng* 15-6-2004). At the very least, this case indicates that the mysterious shooters have high mobility between Poso, Palu and Ambon. Strangely, however, the police did not investigate the possible connections between this person and the several previous mysterious shooting cases in Poso and Palu.

Another form of violence has been attacks by armed groups. Generally, these attacks are done in an organized way, using organic weapons. This was the pattern, for example, in the nearly simultaneous attacks that took place at several different locations in mid October 2003. In Beteleme Village (Lembo sub-district, Morowali district), the attack killed three and injured 20, and the resulting fire destroyed 30 houses, seven motorcycles, and three cars. In this attack, the security forces shot dead some perpetrators and arrested others.[9]

[9] In session on 28 August 2004, the Palu Sub-district Court sentenced 12 of the accused to prison terms from two to four years each, while one other was acquitted (*Radar Sulteng* 30-8-2004).

The most dramatic incident occurred in Saatu Village and Pantangolemba Village, (Poso Pesisir sub-district). In this attack, the armed group killed ten persons. In this case, the security forces were unable to discover the identity of the perpetrators, though a person named Iwan was later arrested in Luwuk, on charges of involvement in the attack. All that was recovered from the field following the attack was 20 5.56 mm calibre bullets manufactured by PT Pindad (*Kompas Cyber Media* 12-10-2003).

The mysterious thing about these two cases is the statement by the deputy head of the BIN, As'at Said. He said that the intelligence personnel in the region knew about the possibility of an attack, but the information was late arriving at the centre (*Tempo Interaktif* 13-10-2003). This statement is not only very strange, but also quite suspicious. How could the security forces know beforehand about an armed attack, yet do nothing about it?

Another interesting point is the strong indications of involvement by the security forces in a number of cases of mysterious shootings in Poso and Palu. The first such incident was the shooting at Bethany Church, Jalan Pulau Kalimantan, Poso on the night of 20 October 2004. This shooting incident, in which Hans Lanipi was shot in the back, was related to the rental of a gun by First Police Brigadier Ray Fendy. A source in the Central Sulawesi regional police stated that Ray had rented his gun for Rp 1.5 million to Andi Makassau, a suspect in a case involving malfeasance in distribution of humanitarian funds for refugees in Poso. The results of ballistic testing showed that Ray's gun was used in this shooting.

Another case involved Deputy Police Commissioner Iskandar Rauf, when there was an attack on the Immanuel GKST Church on Jalan Mesjid Raya, Palu. This shooting and bombing incident on 12 December 2004, which injured Bintijaya, was linked to Iskandar, an officer in the Traffic Directorate of the Central Sulawesi regional police. Central Sulawesi regional police chief Aryanto Sutadi confirmed that the attackers had used a gun that was later identified as belonging to Iskandar. It is not known how the gun fell into the hands of the attackers, because at the time Iskandar was on duty outside Palu.

Thus the sources of the ethnic and religious violence in Poso and Palu are not solely within the community; rather, it is clear that the conflict is also intrinsic to the security forces themselves.

Mobilization of forces

The mobilization of forces for security restoration operations in Poso is officially under the control of Polri. The involvement of TNI troops is part of their assistance function, generally known in administrative terms as mobilization of forces 'under operational control' of Polri. This is in line with the perspective of the national security strategy, in which the Poso violence is categorized as 'low-intensity conflict'. In this situation, TNI involvement is a part of 'military operations other than war' (Department Pertahanan RI 2003:52-3).

The Poso violence was followed by mobilization of large numbers of security troops. Large-scale mobilizations especially began following the violence in May-June 2000. The troops came both from 'organic' (locally based) police and army forces, from the Central Sulawesi regional police and Korem 132/ Tadulako, and from 'non-organic' forces from outside the immediate region. As things developed, the number of troops deployed depended on the level of escalation of the violence.

As usual, the troop mobilizations in Poso used operational code names: Operasi Sadar Maleo, Operasi Cinta Damai, and Operasi Sintuwu Maroso. During the May-June 2000 incident, the Central Sulawesi regional police conducted Operasi Sadar Maleo, while Kodam VII Wirabuana conducted Operasi Cinta Damai, which was under the operational control of the Central Sulawesi police. At that time, the regional police's Operasi Sadar Maleo was led by police Colonel Drs Zainal Abidin Ishak, who was concurrently deputy police chief of the Central Sulawesi regional police. The army's Operasi Cinta Damai Task Force was led by Infantry Colonel Moch. Slamet, who was also territorial assistant of Kodam VII Wirabuana. Later, Zainal Abidin and Moch. Slamet were promoted, respectively, to Central Sulawesi police chief and commander of Korem 132/Tadulako.

After the Malino Declaration in December 2001, the government again deployed a security restoration operation. Code named 'Operasi Sintuwu Maroso', it was to be conducted for a certain period, which could be extended as needed. As things have turned out, Operasi Sintuwu Maroso has now entered Chapter VI; the operation has been repeatedly extended each time new violence breaks out. It seems to have become a regular pattern: each extension of the operation is preceded by a (planned) troop withdrawal. Immediately before or after the withdrawal, new violence occurs – mysterious shootings, killings, bombings, or sporadic attacks. In such cases, the option chosen is to mobilize new troops and/or extend the security restoration operation.

The humanitarian tragedy in Poso has upgraded the status of the army and police presence in Central Sulawesi. Previously, the chief of the Central Sulawesi regional police held the rank of colonel; now it has become brigadier general, because the Central Sulawesi regional police has had its status raised from C to B. In addition, in 2002 the Air Force established a detachment in Palu.

Poso has also become an operational area of Kopassus. Earlier, there were many reports that a number of Kopassus personnel had been posted to Tentena and Poso, but this was difficult to confirm. But after a mysterious shooting that killed Lorenzo Taddey, an Italian tourist, near Pendolo (Pamona Selatan sub-district) on 8 August 2002, Wirabuana Military Area Commander Major General Amirul Isnaeni confirmed that Kopassus had sent 12 security personnel to investigate the presence of foreign citizens living in Poso (*Jakarta Post* 10-8-2002). These personnel had been posted there since mid July 2002 (*Kompas Cyber Media* 15-9-2002). The Central Sulawesi regional police stated that six Kopassus personnel were posted in Tentena and six others in Poso Kota (*Kompas Cyber Media* 4-8-2002). But Kopassus was there not only to investigate the presence of foreigners. An official source at the military's Poso National Unity and Public Protection (Kesbang Linmas) Office stated that the 12 Kopassus Special Mission (Sandi Yudha) personnel were in Poso to conduct an intelligence operation.

Later, following a number of incidents of armed conflict in Palu, two Kopassus personnel were placed there as well. Their intelligence operation activities were not limited to gathering information about the violence, but also extended to other issues, such as cases involving land ownership and misappropriation of humanitarian funds intended for Poso.

Thus, the protracted violence in Poso has led to an increased penetration by the security forces into the community. Such opportunities for penetration are in fact now relatively rare in Indonesia, as the country makes its transition to democracy. Suspicions have therefore arisen among the public, which has had such a long experience with militarization of government, that this penetration may itself have given rise to new violence, precisely so that it can become institutionalized.

Rivalry between armed units

The separation of Polri from the TNI, since 1 April 1999, has led to a type of rivalry between them. The Poso conflict provides an illustration of this. This can be seen from the conflicting statements of the TNI and Polri leaderships in the security restoration operations in Poso. When the Central Sulawesi regional police deployed its Operasi Sadar Maleo starting 1 July 2000, at the same time the Wirabuana Kodam VII began its Operasi Cinta Damai. Strangely, the Central Sulawesi Regional police chief Colonel Drs Soeroso, could not explain the administrative relationship between these two operations. He acknowledged that Operasi Cinta Damai was under the operational control (BKO) of the Central Sulawesi police, but this was done only by telephone. In fact, any such operational control relationship for troops must have a formal administrative basis.

Contradictory statements also appeared in connection with the placement of a Kopassus unit in Poso. The statements by the Wirabuana Military Area

VII commander and the Central Sulawesi regional police chief were completely opposite. It was known that a dozen Kopassus personnel were posted to Poso, under the direct control of the Wirabuana Military Area commander, and not under the operational control of the Central Sulawesi regional police. The Wirabuana Military Commander, Major General Amirul Isnaeni – a former Kopassus general commander – stated that his organization had coordinated this with the Central Sulawesi regional police.

In contrast, the Central Sulawesi regional police chief Brigadier General Zainal Abidin Ishak, stated that there had been no coordination, but only information (*Mingguan Alchairaat*, week II, August 2002). Even stranger, the posting of these Kopassus personnel was not acknowledged by their main force. Kopassus's Head of Information, Captain Farid Ma'ruf, denied that any Special Mission (Sandi Yudha) personnel had been sent to Poso. However, the Head of the Army's Information Service, Brigadier General Ratyono, stated that the presence of this intelligence unit was directly responsible to the TNI commander through the assistant for intelligence and the assistant for operations at TNI headquarters (*Tempo* 25-8-2002).

The commander of Korem 132 Tadulako, Colonel Suwahyuhadji then settled the matter of the Kopassus presence in Poso. He said that at first, these elite troops were brought in without the knowledge of the Central Sulawesi regional police chief, as their arrival was under the direct instructions of TNI headquarters. Later, however, TNI coordinated this with the Central Sulawesi regional police (*Kompas Cyber Media* 4-8-2002).

Differences of views between the security forces on the violence in Poso are also seen on the issue of involvement of international terrorist networks. The Head of the National Intelligence Agency (BIN), Lieutenant General A.M. Hendropriyono, indicated that the Al Qaeda network was involved in the Poso conflict. In an interview with *Buletin Laskar Jihad* (Edition 15, year I), Hendropriyono stated that this information came from Spanish intelligence, from their interrogation of captured Al Qaeda members. The captives said that they had trained in Poso (see also *Kompas* 13-12-2001). But the Central Sulawesi police chief denied this and said that there were no indications of involvement of the Al Qaeda network led by Osama Bin Laden in Poso (*Jakarta Post* 14-12-2001). The commander of Korem 132/Tadulako, Colonel Suwahyuhadji, also rejected speculation about terrorist training camps in Poso (*Kompas* 23-10-2003; *Jakarta Post* 29-10-2002).

Security forces and laskar

The onset of violence in Poso was followed by the presence of *laskar*, or armed militias. On the Muslim side, for example, there were Laskar Jihad and Laskar Mujahidin, and on the Christian side, Brigade Manguni. These groups employed religious or ethnic sentiments, or a combination of the two. They were relatively well trained in the use of various types of standard combat weapons, in bomb making, and in carrying out attacks on their opponents. The presence of the *laskar* signalled an important change in the violence in Poso. Up to April 2000, the conflict still used traditional weapons. But with the presence of the various *laskar*, the nature of the armed violence sharply increased, as signalled by the use of standard combat firearms, home-made firearms, and bombs.

There has long been a relationship between the security forces and *laskar* or armed groups of civilians in Indonesia. The killings of anywhere between tens of thousands and two million people accused of being Indonesian Communist Party (PKI) members or sympathizers following the 30 September 1965 incident is, of course, the most important example of this (Cribb 1990). The cases of East Timor and Aceh provide other examples of how groups allegedly 'sprang up spontaneously' from within the civilian community, when it was obvious that they were in fact deliberately organized, trained, and supported by the military authorities, with the support of the civilian authorities (G. Robinson 2001). The same pattern occurred with the case of the *pam swakarsa* (local security forces), in which the military mobilized civilian groups to face the large protest actions being carried out by students following Reformasi in 1998 (Zen 2004:92-8). Central Sulawesi, and especially Poso, has had a similar experience. During the Permesta rebellion in the 1950s (Harvey 1977), youths united in the Central Sulawesi Youth Movement (Gerakan Pemuda Sulawesi Tengah, GPST) worked shoulder to shoulder with the military in eradicating the rebellion. The Indonesian military trained this militia and supplied it with weapons and ammunition.

This pattern of violence has at least two clear aims. First, it provides a shield for the security forces, enabling them to claim that the political violence that occurs is not connected only to them, but also involves civilian groups who happen to share their political views. Second, the security forces can reap political, and of course economic, advantage from situations of instability.

Unlike in the cases of vertical violence such as in East Timor, when the security forces openly support the militias, in cases of horizontal conflict such support is closely concealed. The logic behind this is clear: in vertical conflicts, the security forces can easily mobilize sentiment based on the ideology of the NKRI (Negara Kesatuan Republik Indonesia, Unitary State of the Republic of Indonesia) to justify their actions. In contrast, in cases of horizontal violence, there is no ideological justification for the security forces to support armed militias. This type of concealed support is evident in the case of the Laskar Jihad. Certainly, from the start, the security authorities tolerated the existence of this armed militia group, for example when the Laskar Jihad conducted its National Joint Training exercise in Bogor in April 2000. There are even reports that Kopassus personnel provided training to Laskar Jihad members (Kingsbury 2003:208). More fatally, the military failed to take any action against Laskar Jihad when the group decided to go to war in Ambon, even though President Abdurrahman Wahid had openly prohibited this (Prasetyo 2002:180-1; Schulze 2002). This is understandable, as it was widely understood that Lieutenant General Djaja Suparman, Army Strategic Command (Kostrad) commander at the time, had created Muslim militias such as Laskar Jihad, and diplomats in Jakarta said that the disappearance of Rp 160 billion of Kostrad funds – of which Djaja's replacement, Lieutenant General Agus Wirahadikusumah, later made an issue – occurred because the money was used to finance militia operations in Maluku (O'Rourke 2002:371).

The same happened with Laskar Jihad's arrival in Poso. Despite the open announcement of their presence, the security forces did nothing whatsoever to prevent, and even allowed, the arrival of these *laskar*. Even with over 2,000 TNI and Polri personnel concentrated in Poso at the time, Laskar Jihad was unrestrained when it carried out its attacks. The authorities should have taken stern action to prevent the arrival of Laskar Jihad, in order to prevent an escalation of the violence. On the other hand, the security forces' failure to protect the Muslim community in Poso was also a problem, as this was the excuse for Laskar Jihad's coming to Poso.

The complexity of the relationship between the security forces and militias can also be seen in the case of Brigade Manguni, which is well known for its role in the regional violence in Poso. The connection with Brigade Manguni was revealed by an army deserter named Sonny Mantiri. A secret written intelligence report from the security authorities about armed groups in Poso stated that Sonny led Brigade Manguni, with personnel strength in Poso of around 600 persons, armed with organic weapons. One influential Christian figure in Poso confirmed that Sonny had trained youths from Silanca Village (Lage sub-district) in warfare.[10] He was constantly travelling to and from Tentena to obtain ammunition from a source he knew there. Oddly, during the attacks on the Christian community in Sepe and Silanca Villages in August 2002, he 'happened' to be in Tentena. While in Silanca, he had close relations with TNI personnel, but not with the police. When he married a young woman from Silanca in 2001, many TNI personnel attended the wedding party. In mid 2004, he died at Tentena Hospital, with foam coming from his mouth, though the doctors there said he was suffering from hepatitis. Previously, his family had refused to have him treated in Palu, due to rumours that he would be the target of an operation by the security forces.

Brigade Manguni was reported to be close to the security forces. It is

10 Interview, 15-9-2004.

reported that hundreds of Kopassus personnel who had deserted from their units were ready to train Brigade Manguni. Lieutenant General (retired) Johny Lumintang, former Army Chief of Staff, even supported the establishment of Brigade Manguni. The relationship between Brigade Manguni and the generals is also evident from the Minahasa Adat Congress held on 9 December 2003. It is reported that a number of active and retired officers originally from North Sulawesi supported the conduct of the congress. They included TNI Lieutenant General (retired) E.E. Mangindaan, TNI Lieutenant General (retired) Prabowo Subianto, TNI Lieutenant General (retired) Johny Lumintang, TNI Major General (retired) W.E. Kanter, TNI Major General Glenny Kairupan, and police Brigadier General Wenny Warouw (*Radar Sulteng* 4-12-2003).

Institutional and personal advantage

Organic troops and territorial commands

The violence in Poso has upgraded the presence of organic combat troops in Central Sulawesi, and especially in Poso. This is indicated by the establishment of Infantry Battalion (Yonif) 714/Sintuwu Maroso, with its headquarters on the border between Ronononcu Village (Poso Kota sub-district) and Maliwuko Village (Lage sub-district). Two companies of its troops have been posted: Company B in Malino Village (Petasia sub-district, Morowali district) and Company C in Pendolo (Pamona Selatan sub-district). It is planned that another company will be posted in Tabalu (Poso Pesisir sub-district). Previously, the province of Central Sulawesi had only one battalion of army combat troops, Infantry Battalion 711/Raksatama, one company of which, Kompi B Yonif 711/Raksatama, is posted in Kawua (Poso Kota sub-district). The commander of Korem 132/Tadulako, Colonel Suwahyuhadji said that the troops were posted for strategic reasons. Because these areas contain natural resource assets, which are vulnerable to disturbances from outside such as looting, and also because of the Poso conflict, these troop postings were more cost effective than bringing in troops from outside (*Kompas* 5-12-2002).

As if it did not want to be outdone by the army, the police also permanently stationed a company of the Brimob (Mobile Brigade) in Poso. A Brimob company headquarters and barracks now sit proudly on the hilltop opposite Pertamina Marketing Unit VII's Poso Depot in Moengko Baru (Poso Kota sub-district). Another Brimob company is to be posted in Korompeeli Village (Lembo sub-district, Morowali district). The headquarters for this Company IV is currently being built.

Following the partitioning of Morowali district and Tojo Una-Una district from Poso district, Polri also partitioned its police sub-regions (Kepolisian resort, Polres). In Morowali, the establishment of the Polres followed the bloody attack on Beteleme Village, on 10 October 2003. At that time, national police chief General Da'i Bachtiar declared that a preliminary Polres would be immediately established in the district (*Tempo Interaktif* 10-10-2003; *Sinar Harapan* 11-10-2003). This plan was promptly realized, when Central Sulawesi regional police chief Brigadier General Drs H. Taufik Ridha inaugurated the Morowali Polres Office and swore in police Commissioner Drs Hanny Sulistyo Arianto as its first Kapolres (sub-region police chief) on 6 December 2003 in Morowali. In Tojo Una-Una, Polri established a separate Polres on 3 March 2005.

On the TNI-AD side, also following the partitioning of Morowali district from Poso district, the establishment of a new Military district Command (Kodim) there was just a matter of time. As a preliminary step, the deputy commander of Kodim 1307 Poso is no longer stationed in Poso, but rather in Kolonodale, Morowali district. The Morowali district government, in its 2003 Regional Budget, spent Rp 57 million to acquire land for the Morowali Kodim and Polres headquarters.

Thus, the violence that has occurred in Poso has provided multiple benefits for the military. Like killing two (or three) birds with one stone, the mobilization of troops to 'restore' security in Poso has in fact served as the entry for posting of organic combat forces, upgrading the quality and quantity of the military presence, and eventually expanding the number of TNI territorial commands, or at least maintaining the existing territorial commands. For example, new Military District Commands are to be established in the two new regencies recently split off from Poso, Morowali and Tojo Una-Una districts. And if the plan is realized to establish a new province of East Sulawesi, partitioned from Central Sulawesi, the possibility will be open to establish a new Military Sub-Area Command (Korem) in this region, and the police will also establish a new regional police (Polda).

This snowball effect will then lead to the establishment of a new Military Area Command (Kodam), separate from Kodam Wirabuana, which has its headquarters in Makassar. The new Kodam would have four provinces under it: North Sulawesi, Gorontalo, Central Sulawesi, and East Sulawesi, and probably have its headquarters in Manado. Kodam Wirabuana, meanwhile, would cover the provinces of South Sulawesi, Southeast Sulawesi, and the new province of West Sulawesi. This would not be new, because from 1969 to 1985, Sulawesi had two Kodam: Kodam XIII Merdeka, with headquarters in Manado, and Kodam XIV Hasanuddin, with headquarters in Ujung Pandang (Makassar). Since 1985, following the liquidation of the territorial commands, Kodam XIII and Kodam XIV were merged into Kodam VII Wirabuana, with its headquarters in Makassar (Lowry 1996:52, 56). A similar scenario of partitioning of Kodam has occurred in Maluku with the continuing violence there. Before the 1985 liquidation, there was a Kodam XV Pattimura with headquarters in Ambon; now, Kodam Pattimura has been revived, separate from Kodam Cenderawasih, which has its headquarters in Jayapura (see also George Junus Aditjondro 2001:114-5).

Appointments and promotions

There is a sort of general pattern that appointments and promotions are enjoyed by those security officials who had authority for security while violence was taking place. This can be seen from the appointments and promotions of numerous high and middle-ranking officers, both within Kodam VII Wirabuana (Military Area Command) and within the Central Sulawesi regional police. This creates the impression that Poso is considered a 'Spartan training' arena to prepare officers for appointments and promotions.

Several commanders of the Wirabuana Kodam later occupied prestigious positions. Among them are Maj. Gen. Suaidi Marasabesi, promoted to TNI Chief of General Staff; Maj. Gen. Slamet Kirbiantoro and Maj. Gen. Ahmad Yahya, who both later became commander of the Greater Jakarta Military Area Command. A former commander of the Operasi Cinta Damai Task Force later became Military Sub-Area Commander (Danrem) 132/Tadulako. And two former Military District Commanders (Dandim) enjoyed promotions to Chief of Staff of Military Sub-Area Command (Korem) 132/Tadulako. Within Polri, appointments and promotions were also enjoyed by several officers. Police Brigadier General Zainal Abidin Ishak and police Brigadier General Taufik Ridha both enjoyed promotions to regional police chief after serving as deputy chief of the Central Sulawesi regional police. Police commissioner Ricky Wakano, Head of the Criminal Investigation Section of the Central Sulawesi regional police was promoted to deputy chief of the Central Jakarta police sub-region, after he succeeded in arresting Pastor Damanik as a suspect in a firearms possession case. After serving as chief of the Poso police sub-region during a time full of violence, Deputy Chief Police Commissioner Djasman Baso Opu was appointed as sub-region police chief in Palu. Finally, Deputy Chief Police Commissioner Abdi Dharma Sitepu was promoted to sub-region chief of police of Poso after serving as acting commander of the Central Sulawesi Brimob unit.

These appointments and promotions indicate that the violence in Poso is not seen as a failure on the part of the security officers; they are absolved of any responsibility for the violence that takes place. In reality, violence certainly is an indicator of failure to maintain security and order in a region. Thus, the violence in Poso has directly benefited, rather than harming, these security officers in their appointments and promotions.

The businesses of the security forces

The presence of combat troops and the expansion of the territorial commands cannot be seen simply as a response to the existence of horizontal violence. It is also very important to note the security forces' business interests – institutional, non-institutional, and criminal. In the case of TNI, one prominent institutional business since the violence first broke out in Poso is the fuel distribution business. The depot of Pertamina's Marketing Unit VII in Poso uses tank trunks owned by the Primkopad (Primer Koperasi Angkatan Darat, Army Primary Cooperative) of Korem 132 Tadulako. But the Primkopad is actually only a 'nameplate' to protect the fuel distribution operations from the Pertamina Depot done by two private companies: PT Kaliwangi and CV Arba Putra (Aditjondro 2004b:146). But the most significant form of business since the start of the Poso violence has been economic crimes, or what Aditjondro refers to as 'grey businesses'. These take the form of extortion by 'certain individuals' in uniform, protection for veiled prostitution operations, cockfighting, security guard businesses, hunting and smuggling of rare plant and animal species, trade in forest products, transportation of goods and passengers using official vehicles, security escort businesses, levies at guard posts, protection for property of certain businessmen or high officials, protection for the operations of businesses with large capital investment, and the illegal trade in firearms and ammunition (Aditjondro 2004b:149-50).

One form of economic crime correlated directly with the violence is, of course, the sale of bullets of various calibres. Members of the security forces on duty in the field regularly sell bullets to citizens. Several sources have stated that 5.56 mm calibre bullets are the ones most often sold. This type of bullet, which is typically used in long-bore weapons of the SS-1, AK-47, and M-16 types, is sold by military personnel in the field for between Rp 2,500 and Rp 5,000 apiece. However, the quantities sold are usually quite small, only one to five bullets at a time.

Another significant form of economic crime is security services: providing security escorts for residents who need to travel around or across Poso when the violence is intense. The fees for this vary, depending on the distance of the journey and the current level of tension. The greater the distance or the more severe the violence, the higher the costs. PT Fajar Bahari, a company operating a road construction project in Bungku Selatan, Morowali district had to spend Rp 10 million for escort services for a single journey in 2001. The money was paid to an officer in Korem 132/Tadulako. In return, around 20 TNI personnel and a military truck escorted the convoy of company vehicles carrying material and an excavator from Palu to Tompira village, Morowali district. A former employee of the company who led the convoy said that the soldiers involved told him they only received pocket money of Rp 150,000

11 Interview in Poso, 16-10-2004.

each. Fees for security escort services are not the monopoly of officers; lower ranking soldiers do it as well. If long distances are controlled by the commanders, shorter distances are controlled by regular soldiers. Residents in the villages in Lage, Pamona Utara, and Poso Kota sub-districts regularly pay fees to soldiers from Company B, Battalion 711/Raksatama, Kawua to escort them by motorcycle into the City of Poso when the tension level is high. For example, a number of candidate civil servants had to do this when they were in their pre-appointment period in the City of Poso in early July 2004. They paid soldiers between Rp 15,000 and Rp 20,000 for security services, following the shooting of a motorcycle taxi driver.

Another dominant pattern is the timber business. As the region is rich in forest products, soldiers on duty in Poso always see the timber business as a way to earn easy money. From the first Poso conflict (December 1998) to the third (May-June 2000), TNI personnel from Kostrad battalions 721, 722, 723, 724, 725 and 726 from South Sulawesi, together with personnel from Company C, Infantry Battalion 711/Raksatama, Poso, were heavily involved in collection of and trade in ebony. In March 2003, the Poso district Forestry and Plantations Service foiled a shipment of 70 cubic meters of undocumented plywood in Pendolo, Pamona Selatan. According to the Head of the Poso Forestry and Plantations Service, the wood belonged to certain TNI personnel in South Sulawesi (George Junus Aditjondro 2004b:153). Around a month later, the Poso Forestry and Plantations Service foiled another shipment of 6 cubic meters of illegal wood owned by a member of Kodim 1307 Poso. It was reported that the logs were being transported using military trucks. TNI personnel even own illegal sawmills (*Poso Post* 27-4-2003, 10-5-2003).

Polri personnel also see the wood business as a source of illicit funds. An informant in the wood business in Poso said that their businesses are often the object of extortion from the security forces, including the police. A number of sawmill operators say they have been extorted by local police personnel. They state that the extortion took place at the Poso police sub-region headquarters and involved the top officers in the local police sub-region. The method used was that, under the guise of Operasi Sintuwu Maroso, officials would stop trucks carrying wood to the sawmills. Even though the vehicles and the logs all had proper documents issued by the Poso Forestry Service, they were still taken to the police headquarters. There they were forced to part with a certain amount of money if they wanted the trucks and logs to be released. Businessman Hengky Tungkanan experienced this; he had to hand over Rp 70 million as a down payment on a total of Rp 100 million to the head of the Poso police sub-region's Criminal Investigations Unit which was witnessed by the deputy police chief. The deputy chief then took the money to the sub-region police chief. Other victims included Toni Hantowo, who paid Rp 25 million, Chi Dewi (Rp 125 million), Hermawan (Rp 25 million), and La'ba (Rp 25 million) (*Nuansa Pos* 26-7-2004, 2-8-2004).

In July 2004, a policeman from Palu who was posted to Poso was involved in transporting undocumented logs owned by a sawmill operator in Mapane village, Poso Pesisir. The five truckloads of logs were transported toward Palu under the policeman's escort. A primary source who was on the journey said that the sawmill owner paid the policeman Rp 5,000,000 for this work. The policeman was also provided with additional money to pay off Polri and TNI personnel at each guard post along the Trans Sulawesi Highway in Poso Pesisir sub-district. He said that the policeman made payments ranging from Rp 50,000 to Rp 300,000 at each post.[11]

In Morowali district, the involvement of the security forces in the wood business is also quite blatant. In December 2003, the local police seized 60 cubic meters of wood that was being transported to Makassar on four trucks, escorted by two soldiers from Company B, Infantry Battalion 714/Sintuwu Maroso. The wood, from Bungku, allegedly belonged to Made Kuswandi, and there were rumours that he had the backing of an army officer in Makassar.[12]

Economic crimes involving the security forces in the violence in Poso have also occurred in the form of robberies and loss of property. During July 2000, many such cases befell residents in Poso. For example, on 11 July 2000, TNI-AD personnel who were searching for sharp weapons in Uelene village took Rp 4,500,000 from Anwar Mbalowo. Earlier, on 8 July 2000, for no apparent reason, TNI-AD personnel took Rp 2,000,000 from Santo Lagi in Beteleme village, Morowali district. And a computer, a voltage stabilizer, an SSB radio, and an alarm disappeared without a trace from the Pendolo Bank Rakyat Indonesia Unit in Pamona Selatan sub-district when TNI-AD personnel were guarding the BRI building on 9 July 2000.[13]

Other serious economic crimes have emerged in cases of diversion of humanitarian aid funds for Poso. The cabals to carry out this misappropriation of humanitarian aid funds have blatantly included the security forces. Anwar M. Ali, Head of the Poso District Social Welfare Service, who was caught up in the aid misappropriation case, alleged that he had given some of the Poso humanitarian aid funds to local security officials. He confirmed that he had given Rp 112 million to Colonel Joko Purwoko, coordinator of the National Intelligence Agency (BIN) Central Sulawesi Region, and Rp 50 million to Deputy Police Chief Abdi Dharma Sitepu, chief of the Poso sub-region police (*Seputar Rakyat*, Edition 03/Year II/2004).

12 Interview with two activists from Yayasan Sahabat Morowali, an NGO involved in natural resource advocacy in Morowali district, in Kolonodale, 14-10-2004 and 15-10-2004.

13 www.gkst.org (accessed 28-6-2002).

In the long term, the presence of combat troops and the expansion of the territorial commands is actually an investment to guard the natural wealth in the eastern part of Central Sulawesi. This presence is needed to provide protection for the penetration of large-scale capital into the area. It is intended to overcome public opposition when their agricultural land is expropriated or disturbed by the presence of extractive industries in the mining, forestry, or large-scale plantation sectors. It is known that many giant companies, both national and trans-national, are either getting ready to or are already extracting natural wealth from the area. Among these is the world's second largest nickel mining company, Canada-based PT Inco, which is preparing to exploit nickel matte in the Bungku area of Morowali district (Arianto Sangaji 2002). There is also a plan to exploit natural gas in Toili and Batui, Banggai district and in Tiaka, Teluk Tomori, Morowali district.

Elections for president and heads of regions

The protracted violence in Poso has provided political advantages to former and active members of the military elite in their competition for political positions. This is clearly seen in the presidential election results in Poso, Morowali, and Tojo Una-una. In the first round of the presidential election in July 2004, two presidential candidates with military backgrounds – Susilo Bambang Yudhoyono and Wiranto – took first and second places in Poso, Morowali, and Tojo Una-una. The same thing happened again in the second round in September 2004, when the ticket of Susilo Bambang Yudhoyono and Jusuf Kalla won. There was a sort of nostalgia among voters to vote for these two candidates, based on a feeling that a president with a military background would better guarantee a sense of security.

This tendency to elect government leaders with security force backgrounds was also evident in the election for district head of Poso in mid 2005. The field of candidates for district head of Poso to succeed Muin Pusadan was full of candidates with 'green' and 'brown' backgrounds. One name often mentioned was police Lt. Col. (retired) Luther Manganti, former chief of the Toli-Toli police from 1993 to 1997 and former member of the Central Sulawesi DRPD (provincial assembly) for the 1999-2004 period. Another name was Lt. Col. Dede K Atmawijaya, formerly commander of Kodim 1307 Poso and Chief of Staff of Korem 132 Tadulako. Others included police Lt. Col. (retired) Piet Inkiriwang, and Lt. Col. (retired) Rudolf Rukka, former district head of Central Maluku, rumoured to be nominated by the Pancasila Patriot Party.

Conclusion

Reformasi, as an entry point to place the security forces under the control of the civilian government, has not gone smoothly. The rapid transition has been coloured by a tense relationship between the civilian government and the security forces, both because the institutions are not properly prepared and because of the tug-of-war between the interests of the political elite and those of the security force elite. One disappointing result of Reformasi is the government's failure to create a sense of security among the populace. Indonesia's security forces, which during the New Order era were so solid and strong, seem to have lost the power to create social order in line with their legitimate duties and functions. Regional violence, such as that in Poso, is one indication of this.

Violence under the pretext of ethnic and religious conflict has actually created an opportunity for the security forces to restore their image and privileges, which had declined sharply since the start of Reformasi in 1998. First, the violence in Poso has given rise to a significant security force presence in the area. The deployment and addition of organic troops, and the expansion of territorial commands or of other security institutions on the same level, all prove that the security forces have succeeded in forcing the civilian government to bow to their institutional interests. This means that the violence in Poso has had a beneficial political impact for the security forces. Second, members of the security forces have benefited not only institutionally but also personally from the protracted violence in Poso – in terms of career advancement, access to economic activity, and political positions in government.

JOHN M. MACDOUGALL

Criminality and the political economy of security in Lombok

Over the past years, Lombok's primary instruments for re-defining community can be found in its anti-criminal militias. Starting in 1998, *pamswakarsa* or local security groups absorbed roughly 25% of Lombok's adult men for the sole purpose of hunting down the island's thieves. Led by the island's most powerful noble houses and Muslim clerics, *pamswakarsa* waged war against long-standing criminal networks. As these groups grew in force, regional and national actors attempted to recruit militia leaders and their masses to support their political or economic agenda. By early 2000, *pamswakarsa* leaders could claim as many as 400,000 trained members and many more voters to support the political causes of their choosing. By 2003, there were already reports of district head candidates recruiting both organized thief-networks and anti-crime militias to demonstrate side-by-side in support of the same candidate's election. In order to understand how, why and under what conditions such contradictory events have come to pass, we need to understand what happened when Soeharto's control over criminality and security was subverted by an economic crisis. How could criminality assume such an important position in defining power and authority in Lombok?

Lombok had always been famous for its long-standing and traditional thief networks. These networks grew more powerful during the economic crisis when remittances sent from Sasak labourers were suddenly worth several times their previous value. Lombok's thieves preyed upon families with remittance-bought commodities creating a crime wave of unprecedented intensity. While traditionally thieves only held stolen goods and returned them to their owners upon receipt of a *tebusan* or ransom payment, the anti-crime militias formed by Lombok's Islamic clerics or Tuan Guru did not attend to the ransom of stolen goods. Instead, cleric backed militias shifted their moral attention away from the traditional return of the stolen article to focus instead the arrest and execution of the unrepentant thief.

Lombok's anti-crime militias have helped to at once redefine political participation for Sasaks and have contributed to the emergence of more broadly

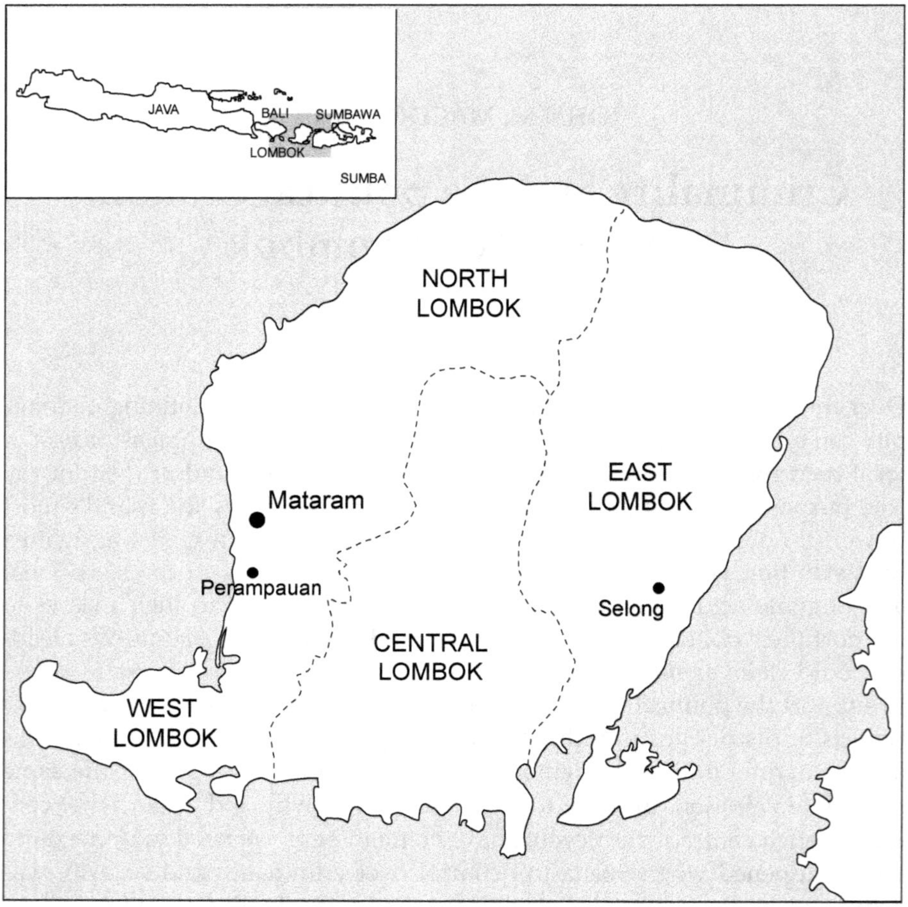

Map 11. Lombok

defined community-level vigilantism. In order to comprehend how these emergent groups were able to grow so quickly we must focus at once on the events of the past five years in Lombok as well as the long-standing cultural and political tensions between rival religious groups, ambitious nobles and the political designs of the regimes that ruled over them. Within these shifting frames of national politics and intra-Lombok competition, various new and old forms of cultural legitimacy have coalesced to redefine self-presentation through theft and vigilantism in post-Soeharto Lombok.

Criminality in a colonial framework

Lombok lies east of Bali and is home to 2.4 million inhabitants. Ethnic Sasak Muslims make up 92% of the population with minorities of some 60,000 Balinese Hindus and 20,000 Sasak Buddhists, mostly in North Lombok. Historically, western Lombok developed closer ties with Bali while eastern Lombok was economically and ideologically (through Islamic affinities) linked to Buginese Muslim kingdoms in Sulawesi to the north and Sumbawa to the east. Since the mid-eighteenth century, two East Balinese royal houses ruled over Lombok until Islamic brotherhoods based in East Lombok revolted against the Balinese colonizers in 1891. Although the Balinese subdued the rebellion, the Muslim brotherhoods asked the Dutch to assist them in their rebellion. After defeating the Balinese in 1894 the Dutch took over control of Lombok, but continuous revolts against the Dutch tax laws plagued colonial administrators until the Japanese invaded Indonesia in 1942.

The Dutch introduced forms of indirect rule that discriminated against Muslim commoners and exalted golden age nobles over counter-colonial leaders. As a result, colonial authorities imprisoned Muslim teachers and disbanded their followings while they rehabilitated Sasak nobility to the position of sub-altern district heads. As district heads and colonial bureaucrats, Sasak nobles re-calibrated their daughters' bride-prices (*aji krama*) according to their contrived claims to golden age descent. Meanwhile, the children of famous Muslim clerics were denied access to colonial schools or patronage.

The Dutch support of golden age legitimacy facilitated the administration of colonial taxation through Sasak nobles but, in so empowering the past against the present, also contributed to the messianic nature of peasant rebellions waged against Sasak nobles. In contrast to the Islamist rebellions against Balinese rule, the messianic revolts of the early twentieth century laid claim to the same golden kingdom of Selaparang that colonial forces used to legitimize the sub-altern nobles of their bureaucracy. Ironically, the Dutch colonial forces were later forced to issue a decree outlawing the use of golden age themes to counter Dutch rule over the island.

Whereas Islamic leaders were penalized and monitored under the Dutch, during the Japanese occupation of Indonesia (1942-1945) Japanese authorities made use of Lombok's Islamic leadership to train Islamic guerrilla units throughout the country to fight the allied forces. Many of Lombok's future political and religious leaders underwent this training. Arab-Indonesian intellectual, Saleh Sungkar was one such figure. Head of Lombok's most important Muslim organization, the Persatuan Ummat Islam Lombok (PUIL, Lombok Association for Muslims), during the Japanese occupation, he became an important reformer.[1] He turned the local branch of Indonesia's largest Islamic party, Masyumi, which he chaired, into an organization that welcomed commoners and nobles alike. After years of political favouritism under the Dutch, Sasak nobles worried that Sungkar's reform would threaten their privileged position. Because of Sungkar's populist policies, many of Lombok's nobles (*mamiek*) left Masyumi to join the Partai Nasional Indonesia (PNI, Indonesian Nationalist Party), where they enjoyed close ties to the military and wealthy Balinese aristocrats.[2]

Saleh Sungkar represented Masyumi in Lombok's district parliament when he was mysteriously murdered in 1952. At the time, he was head of Lombok's district parliament. After his death, several fellow reformers joined Lombok's branch of the Partai Komunis Indonesia (PKI, the Indonesian Communist Party). Muhammed Ba'asyir, a leading Arab member of the Masyumi party under Sungkar, became Lombok's most outspoken advocate of the communist party (PKI).[3] Counter to conventional stereotypes that the PKI was atheistic, modernist Islamic leaders in Lombok joined the PKI as a counter-gesture to Sasak nobles who opposed Masyumi's plans to reform the rice distribution on the island. In November 1965, Lombok's Muslim youth groups, backed by the military, started to kill at least 11,000 Sasak 'communists' for their involvement in land reform and social welfare programs conducted by the PKI in the 1960s.

1 *Satu abad kota Selong* 1998. Lombok's most important religious leaders also founded important *pesantren* during this period. Lombok's largest is Nahdlatul Wathan in Pancor, Selong East Lombok. Others are Nurul Yakin in Praya founded by Tuan Guru Makmun in 1931, Darul Qur'an in Bengkel founded in 1940 by Tuan Guru Haji Hambali, and Assyidiyah in Gunung Sari founded by TGH Jafar.

2 For a more comparative view of post-colonial elites in Lombok and Kalimantan see Magenda 1991.

3 Muhammed Baisir was upset about the political assassination of Saleh Sungkar, who was head of the local parliament for Masyumi at the time. In protest of Sungkar's death Baisir left Masyumi and formed the PKI (Sairul S. Lubis 1962).

The New Order

When the killings were over, Soeharto's political vehicle, Golkar, worked hard to co-opt Lombok's clerics and community leaders. Historically, they had strong alliances to the large Muslim political parties, Nahdlatul Ulama and Masyumi. But in the elections of 1971, one of Lombok's most important Tuan Guru sided with Golkar, reportedly as a sign of gratitude to Soeharto for his role in destroying the PKI. In return, the military and other government officials assisted Tuan Guru in their efforts to proselytize (*dakwah*) in North Lombok's traditionalist hinterland. The primary target of these *dakwah* campaigns were the Wetu Telu communities of northern Lombok. The Wetu Telu posed a hazard to Islamist campaigns because of their unique combination of Sasak ritualism and counter-reformist Islamic priesthoods. Together with sympathetic members of the local military command, Tuan Guru forced many hamlets to replace Wetu Telu tradition with more orthodox forms of Islamic ritual.[4]

Two of the most powerful proselytizers were Tuan Guru Haji (TGH) Mutawalli from Jeroaru, East Lombok, and Tuan Guru Haji Zainuddin Abdul Madjid from Pancor, East Lombok, the founder of the largest Lombok-based religious institution, Nahdlatul Wathan (NW). TGH Abdul Madjid created an impressive network of educational institutions such as Islamic day schools (*madrasah*) and boarding schools (*pesantren*) while TGH Mutawalli was responsible for the conversion programs in northwest Lombok. In addition to his role in the development of educational institutions, TGH Abdul Madjid also undertook attacks against East Lombok's Chinese minority in 1965-1966 (Fathurahman Zakaria 2001). TGH Abdul Madjid's role in the eradication of communist and Chinese merchants in East Lombok attracted the interest of Soeharto's military who later requested him to mobilize support for Golkar among Lombok's religious clerics in the 1971 elections. TGH Abdul Madjid agreed and he continued to serve as Golkar's campaign manager in East Lombok for the 1971 and 1977 national parliamentary elections. Golkar won majorities in Lombok at both elections, and TGH Abdul Madjid represented the province of West Nusa Tenggara in the National Consultative Assembly (Majelis Permusyawaratan Rakyat, MPR).

In 1982, however, at a time when many Muslim leaders were unhappy with Soeharto government policies, TGH Abdul Madjid announced he was

4 For instance, in Tanjung, a sub-district of West Lombok historically allied to Balinese forces, local military officers worked hand in hand with East Lombok's Tuan Guru to destroy sacred sites and ancestral altars as part of a broader effort to dissuade Muslims from performing non-Islamic rituals. As late as 1974, soldiers from Tanjung's military command forced villagers to stand in rows on the community soccer field to profess their adherence to the prophet and holy book of their religion or be considered *kafirs* (infidels) – in effect criminal communists.

leaving it to Nahdlatul Wathan followers to determine their own choice of party.[5] Consequently, his supporters were arrested or intimidated, and government aid to NW schools was cut (Muhammad Nasihuddin Badri 2001:23-25). Largely due to pressure from the military, Abdul Madjid was forced to return to Golkar before the elections of 1987 and remained a supporter until his death in October 1997.

Nahdlatul Wathan grew more powerful than ever under TGH Abdul Madjid's stewardship during the 1990s, but when he died in October 1997, a conflict erupted between his two daughters over who was to replace him, both as head of NW and as a central player in the political dynamics of East Lombok. Less than a year later, Soeharto resigned from office. The end of the New Order and the death of TGH Abdul Madjid left Eastern Lombok without the leadership that had guided their institutions for more than 40 years. In the wake of their father's death, TGH Abdul Madjid's daughters organized militias to fight a battle over legitimate rule of Nahdlatul Wathan. Other leaders took advantage of Lombok's situation to fill the gap in clerical leadership. Guru Ukit and TGH Sibaway, the sons of the aforementioned Islamic proselytizer, TGH Mutawalli, rose to the occasion to form Amphibi, an anti-crime militia that would later become Lombok's largest and most important collective of vigilantes.

The emergence of community-based vigilantism

With Soeharto's regime in shambles, local claims to authority and security stimulated an inward-looking return to the community, while fears of 'phantom' provocateurs operating at the national level imbued local vigilantism in Lombok.

Indonesia's civilian militias are not an entirely new phenomenon. In 1997, the armed forces added to their already extensive arsenal of civilian auxiliaries a voluntary civilian community policing body called *pamswakarsa*.[6]

After Soeharto had stepped down, many provincial governments saw the formation of local *pamswakarsa* as a 'grassroots' security system capable of

[5] He called the choice *ban-bin-bun* meaning respectively *banteng* (bull, the symbol of the Partai Demokrasi Indonesia (PDI), Indonesian Democratic Party); *bintang* (star, symbol of the Partai Persatuan Pembangunan (PPP), Muslim United Development Party) and *bunut* (from the Sasak word for banyan tree, the symbol of Golkar).

[6] Awaloedin Djamin 2002:2. Although this term only became popular after the 1997 legislation it was first mentioned by then Wapang Kopkamtib, Jendral Widjoyo Suyono, when he suggested that a self-funded (*swadana*) and voluntary (*swadaya*) civilian security force be encouraged to provide security for residential areas (*lingkungan pemukiman*) and work environments (*lingkungan kerja*). Kepolisian Republik Indonesia (Polri), Jakarta, Amanat Kapolri, 1-7-1979.

replacing Soeharto's top-down military style of authoritarian rule.[7] Lombok's reformist and conservative leaders welcomed *pamswakarsa* as a new form of 'people's power' capable of taking care of security concerns. *Pamswakarsa* were interpreted as a by-product of regional autonomy initiatives and a quasi-Islamic form of moral vigilantism where citizens were free to impose their own moral sanctions upon their crime-ridden communities.[8]

The economy of theft in contemporary Lombok

Most people in Lombok appealed to local security groups because of the crisis-related crime wave hitting both Lombok's rural and urban communities in 1998 and 1999. The monetary crisis had pushed Lombok's peasantry into destitution. Lombok's poorest peasantry relied on wage labor, and not regular harvests, to support their families. In the village of Pemenang Timur, where I was conducting research, over 60% of the farm land was owned by loan sharks who held ownership over harvests until the often small loan was repaid. During the economic crisis not only did the labourers' wages not go up but the everyday costs of sustaining their households made it impossible to recover their pawned property. Conversely, the crisis weakened rupiah inflated remittance payments sent by Lombok's migrant workers in Malaysia and Saudi Arabia to several times their previous value.[9] For instance, the numbers of formal migrant workers sent by the West Nusa Tenggara (Nusa Tenggara Barat; NTB) Department of Labour abroad doubled from 10,264 workers in 1997-1998 to 20,893 in the crisis years of 1998-1999 most of whom went to Malaysia, the cheapest destination for Indonesian workers to reach. The majority of NTB's workers sent abroad during those years were undereducated, under skilled workers from rural Lombok and Sumbawa. The total remittance payments sent home by these labourers increased even more dramatically. In 1997-1998, migrant workers sent home Rp 37,122,960,000. Twice that number of workers sent home Rp 243,586,395,107 in 1998-1999.

Largely because of remittance-related purchases, criminals were not

7 Regional autonomy Law no. 22/1999 made vague references to the increased autonomy of village authorities in the management of community security.

8 There also developed militias that defended the interests of particular ethnic groups. Lombok's Sasaks had their own version of such an organization called Desak Datu Sasak. Although they were primarily known as an organization prepared to defend any cause that paid, they were regularly involved in pro-Sasak and anti-outsider demonstrations. This was most obvious when they set up roadblocks to check cars for Australian tourists in protest of the Australia's military involvement in the UN peacekeeping forces operating in East Timor.

9 Figures released by the West Nusa Tenggara Provincial Department of Labour Office in Mataram, Lombok.

only making off with cattle but were also stealing valuable goods such as televisions and motorcycles purchased by migrant labourers upon return to their villages.[10] According to one Amphibi militia member, Lombok's thieves were becoming so 'picky' that, after scouring a house for precious goods, the thief left a note for the owner of a black and white television reading, 'get a colour TV and then I'll come and steal it!' Although Lombok's *pamswakarsa* later developed ties to the military, their organizations began with a primary focus on communal security (and not the moral erasure of theft) as the subject of their vigilance.

The rise of anti-crime militias in Lombok was particularly unusual because Lombok was famous for sustaining such a large group of well known and, in many instances, popularly admired criminals. Each of Lombok's districts possesses a village where thieves are not only treated with respect but acquire rank according to their accomplishments. In northern Lombok, for instance, the thieves of Bon Jeruk were famous for elaborate raids on rival communities. A Sasak leader in the West Lombok village of Pemenang, Amaq Nursih, described to me how, after a group of men in a neighbouring village succeeded in killing the criminal attempting to rob them, the thief's family came from Bon Jeruk to retrieve the body.

> They treated the corpse of the man, a criminal, like the body of a hero just returned from war. If we succeed in capturing and killing one of Bon Jeruk's thieves, we have to be prepared to face the consequences. If a Bon Jeruk man is killed in your village, his family will hunt you down until you or one of your kin is dead.

In January 1998, during the height of the crime wave, some of Mataram's young gang members continued to speak admiringly of their thief heroes who were so *wanen* (brave, invulnerable) that they could stop a car full of wealthy tourists with their bare hands.

Despite long and vigorous police campaigns against crime and criminal networks during the New Order, theft in Lombok has always been very persistent. This was especially evident during the post-Soeharto years when unemployment and remittance payments from international migrant labourers dispersed wealth and poverty in uneven and sudden spurts throughout the poorer regions of Central and eastern Lombok. For Lombok's unemployed men few options were available. Those with family assets sufficient to serve as collateral against a loan paid the hefty 'departure' fee required to become a migrant labourer in Malaysia.[11] For them (about 100,000 of

[10] The prices of new motorbikes and televisions inflated much later than staple goods or *sembako* (*sembilan bahan pokok*; nine staple goods that included rice, sugar and cooking oil). This is one of the reasons why remittance recipients purchased TVs and motorbikes.

[11] Tenaga Kerja Indonesia (TKI, Indonesian migrant labourer) or Tenaga Kerja Wanita (TKW, female migrant labourer).

Lombok's 2.4 million residents) their future was relatively bright. Most of Lombok's men had no such assets, however, and they were forced to choose between part-time jobs as labourers or to become criminals.

Many of Lombok's non-criminal men chose to join *pamswakarsa,* which offered forms of masculine and symbolic capital similar to the bravado enjoyed by the island's 'noble' thieves. This similarity presented *pamswakarsa* as more than mere village thugs. Instead, they were brave defenders led by Lombok's Tuan Guru Muslim clerics who equipped them with a mystical invulnerability and an Islamist air of moral righteousness. They could also claim to be among the men responsible for dispelling Lombok of its most cunning criminals. For the other men who chose crime as their means of self-actualization, they had the opportunity to apprentice themselves to Lombok's great thieves and to study the irresistible arts of illusion and deceit.

Reciprocities of theft

Whether respected or not, many of Lombok's criminals are not merely thieves but also ritual practitioners capable of preserving a man's dignity during the ritual theft of his bride (*merariq* or *merangkat*). Many great criminals are also skilled magicians who pass on the arts of invulnerability to their disciples. Great thieves are referred to as the 'Lord of Thieves' (Datu Maling) and are often consulted by politicians and the military. To speak of more practical matters, to this day the best way for a groom to show respect for his future in-laws is to steal his bride, their daughter, from beneath their protective roof.[12] This is not to say that theft in Lombok is culturally sanctioned. Instead, it is important to recognize that Sasak forms of ritual theft evidenced in marital rites and spirit loss (*ketemuq*) are referred to and dealt with in the same way as those who suffer from criminal theft. Spirit loss (*ketemuq*), marriage by theft (*kawin maling*) and criminal theft (*memaling*) are all perceived as forms of partial loss and not 'total' theft. Just as a family loses its daughter to marital theft, or a farmer is deprived of his spiritual vitality (Sk. *semangat*) by an envious spirit, victims of theft in Lombok are rarely fully disowned of their stolen goods. Instead, victims of such thievery are given the opportunity to recover the stolen object. In the case of bride-theft, the thieving son-in-law is

12 I would distinguish Sasak forms of *kawin maling* (marriage by theft) from Balinese or other 'mock theft' marriages (*kawin lari*) practiced throughout the archipelago. In Lombok, the actual theft of a bride is carefully regulated by formal and traditional decrees. In fact hefty fines are levied against the groom if he communicates his intentions to anyone within the girls village, hamlet or even mosque association (*langgar mesjid*). The groom is fined for lack of 'prowess' in his theft. If he damages windows, fences or any other piece of property owned by his bride's kin group, he is fined.

made to repay the family for their loss (of a daughter) in the form of 'prices of tradition' (*aji krama*) or, if the bride's conversion is required, 'the purchase of her religion' (*aji gama*). The victim of soul theft (*ketemuq*) identifies the spirit through hair divination and then pays a ritual ransom (*tebusan*), to the thieving spirit. In a similar fashion, the victim of theft is allowed to communicate with the thief, settle on a ransom price (*tebusan*), and recover the stolen property unharmed.

Criminal networks and tebusan

If a thief in Lombok makes off with someone's motorbike, it does not necessarily mean that the original owner has been fully dispossessed of the bike. For instance, a Sasak friend of mine in Mataram, Gus Par, lost his bike to a band of thieves in 1998 and, within twenty-four hours, he received a phone call stating that the thieves had his bike and they were ready to make a deal:

> In order to get my bike back I had to meet at a pre-arranged location and hand over a *tebusan* payment amounting to roughly 20% of the bike's original value. In less than an hour my bike was back in the same position as when it was stolen. The *tebusan* method has changed somewhat in recent years. It used to be hard for thieves to move motorbikes without the official police papers (Surat Tanda Nomor Kendaraan, STNK) or proof of purchase. After the economic crisis of 1997, bike theft was rampant in Lombok and, regardless of how much the victim offered to retrieve her property, the bikes were being sent somewhere else.

While in the past thieves stole from people's fields and barns, after the economic crisis they preyed on luxury items and motorbikes stored in the domicile. The new dynamics of theft in post-Soeharto Lombok became increasingly clear when I spoke with Asep, an experienced thief who lived on the outskirts of the village of Perampauan, in West Lombok; an area famous for its criminal networks. He explained how in 1998 the ritualized *tebusan* method described by Gus Par had been replaced by another form of non-retributive and export oriented theft. Motorbikes were no longer ransomed by their original owners but acquired new identities and new owners. Asep explained this shift after the economic crisis when local police assisted them in the export of the bikes complete with new engine numbers and legal titles:

> I used to be involved in every aspect of the theft. We would steal a bike, hide it in a safe house and wait for the owner to contact us. If the owner neglected to contact us we would use our contacts to find the owner. We would turn over the bike after we agreed on what we thought was a fair *tebusan* (retributive payment). Now things are different. Most of the experienced thieves don't even steal

anymore. They are middlemen (*penadah*). We don't even have to use the *tebusan* method anymore. Instead, a three-phase procedure allows us to move more bikes more quickly and for more money:

In the first phase, the *pemetik* (literally: picker) or thief will come to us with a stolen bike. We look at the bike and see if it is worth the effort. If it is a high value bike we will accept it and turn over 25 to 30% of the bike's second hand value to the 'picker'. The thieves these days are usually inexperienced high school kids or chumps who, for some reason or another, are forced to steal a bike to make quick money.

The second phase is the *penadah* or 'middleman' phase. The bike arrives in Perampauan after which the mechanics remove the bike's engine number and alter the bike's body and paint job. At this point, the bike is clean and can no longer be traced to any owner, factory or vehicle registration number.

The third, or *penadah II*, or 'second middleman' phase begins after the bike has been fully worked over. At this phase, the police get involved. The military used to be involved in this syndicate but it was taken over by the police when they became more powerful in 1999.[13] At this phase, they make a new engine number so that it is impossible to tell it from an original factory issued number. They then distribute the bike to other areas and issue new motorcycle letters. Nobody even knows that the bike came from Lombok. We have no connection to the bike after this point. It is entirely in the hands of the next phase of bike sellers.

In 1998, a new form of hustle arose to address the needs of bike owners eager to recover their bikes through the *tebusan* method. Asep called the hustle *dangdut* after the Indonesian pop music genre popular in Lombok at the time.

Dangdut is simple. You see, even though we have already erased the bike's engine number and sometimes even impressed a new one to replace it, we still receive requests from the original owner to return the bike for a *tebusan*. When we realized that we could make money off such hopes we cooked up a scheme where, even though the original bike had already been sent off the island, we would keep the bikes original engine number and make a metal facsimile out of old 100-rupiah coins. When requests for a particular bike came in all we had to do was produce an engine number rubbing and force them to turn over the money. Sometimes they wanted the license plate as proof before they turned over the money so we kept those handy too. We usually ask for *tebusan* as large as Rp 4 million (approximately US$ 450.00) for nice bikes. People pay the *tebusan* but their bike can not even be traced to their registration papers anymore.

The use of such 'mock' *tebusan* schemes like *dangdut* forced people in Lombok to take immediate retributive action. Unable to retrieve their bikes, Sasak victims of theft appealed to the police. Even though the victims paid 'opera-

13 In April 1999 the police was officially separated from the military making the police an independent but grossly understaffed and under-funded national security institution (ICG 2001a).

tional fees' or bribes, the police was unable to return the stolen goods to their owners. Villagers grew suspicious. As early as July 1997, villagers wary of police involvement in local theft burned down the police station in Janapria, East Lombok. When the economic crisis struck in 1998, charges of police complicity in crime piqued and local efforts to stave off the crime wave intensified.

Bujak: ex-criminals tracking criminals

At the height of the crime wave in late 1998 and early 1999, reports of a new community-based civilian security militia, *pamswakarsa,* circulated throughout Lombok. In Jakarta General Wiranto had mobilized *pamswakarsa* to protect the Special Session of the People's Congress (MPR) in November 1998. Prior to the MPR meeting in Jakarta, nearly all of Lombok's famous Tuan Guru had gathered in front of the governor's office with the military commander for eastern Indonesia, General Adam Damiri, and Lombok's new governor, Harun Al'Rasyid to show their support for the event and the Habibie presidency (*Lombok Post* 5-11-1998). Two months later, Lombok's anti-crime groups were called *pamswakarsa.*

The first of Lombok's *pamswakarsa* to initiate the war on crime was Pemburu Jejak or Bujak which literally means 'tracker' in Indonesian.[14] Because Bujak consisted of a mixture of ex-criminals and streetwise thugs, they were able to work through contacts in criminal networks to intervene in the *tebusan* arrangements. Bujak mediated in the thief-victim relationship and often brought the *tebusan* cost down considerably. At the time, Bujak was lauded for its ability to protect its client communities from 'total theft' (in other words without *tebusan*).

It is important to note that Bujak's operations focused on the return of stolen goods and retributive money offering (*tebusan*) and not upon the criminal himself. Nevertheless, if Bujak caught a criminal in the act of theft he was often killed immediately. Not to kill or, at least, capture the criminal would be to confess complicit involvement with the crime at hand, which Bujak's former thieves could not afford to risk.

According to many young Sasak men the term *pamswakarsa* sounded too 'Jakarta' to take root in Lombok. Instead, they saw Bujak's emergence as the result of neglected ritual obligations and pointed at the role of Central Lombok's nobility in Bujak's activities as part of the reason for the recent

[14] As early as 1994, Lombok's police force employed Central Lombok's most notorious ex-convicts to form Bujak. At that time Bujak was not a community-based security body but an unofficial group of bounty hunters to help track stolen goods.

death of Lombok's 'noble' thieves (Datuk Maling). As a young nobleman and Mataram 'tough' explained:

> The elders of my household support Bujak with their old weaponry. Each year our ancestors' ritual weaponry (*pusaka*) must be bathed in the blood of a sacrificed cow. The nobles neglected to continue this tradition and, as a result, our weaponry began to call out for human blood. Many of Bujak's noble members carry our ancestral weapons on their nightly rounds for this very reason. When a criminal is discovered in the act of theft the magical weapons fly out of their sheaths on their own accord. They find their victim and kill him without any human involvement. The weapons forced Bujak back into action, not crime.

Bujak's war on crime inspired young men and social groups throughout the island to take the law into their own hands. Nevertheless, for youths who admired many of the thieves being killed by Bujak patrols, it was difficult to accept Bujak's murder of Central Lombok's old and respected thieves. Despite their success in returning stolen goods, Bujak's thuggish reputation contributed to a steady decline in public support for the organization. By August 1998, Bujak was forced to accept the moral supremacy of another militia, Amphibi, based in the Islamic heartland of eastern Lombok.

Bujak and Amphibi

In early 1999 Bujak came under fire. Not only did the organization consist of former criminals but it was also rumoured to be involved in crime against communities that did not join their ranks or pay their dues. Bujak distributed stickers among its clients and, according to residents in Central Lombok in 1999, a stickerless house meant 'fair game' to Lombok's Bujak-friendly thieves. While Bujak owed its resurgence to the criminal complicity of Lombok's police force in the ongoing crime-wave, Bujak's lack of a strong moral leadership inspired the formation of what was to become one of Indonesia's largest militias, Amphibi.

Amphibi was formed in the small town of Jeroaru, East Lombok. Its leaders were none other than the sons of the famous *dakwah* pioneer of the 1970s, TGH Mutawalli. Like their father, both brothers were attributed certain magical abilities. Amphibi was, by August 1999, the new banner of moral vigilance for tens and thousands of East Lombok's Islamic youth. The sudden appeal of Amphibi was only partly due to the re-emergence of Islamic politics and Islamist militias at the national level. Like other militant Islamic groups around the country, it attributed its formation to the moral weakness and criminal complicity of the police in immoral businesses and conflicts. But also, the death of senior religious leader and Nahdlatul Wathan's founder,

TGH Abdul Madjid, only contributed to the mergence of Amphibi and the demand for a new kind of charismatic leadership. For instance, TGH Abdul Madjid's own daughters divided Nahdlatul Wathan into two separate camps as they vied for sole leadership of the organization and formed two separate militias to defend their interests. The combined effects of the separation of the police from the military, the death of TGH Maulana Sheik and the fall of the New Order made room for new forms of religious legitimacy in post-New Order Lombok.

In early 1999, TGH Abdul Madjid's feuding daughters embraced forms of both messianic and modernist legitimacy reminiscent of the early twentieth-century when reformist Islam and messianic rebellions developed side by side. Rauhun, the older sister and committed modernist, evicted her younger sibling, Raihanun, from Nahdlatul Wathan's headquarters. In response to her eviction, Raihanun moved to the mountain village of Anjani, the former home of early twentieth century messianic movements. Meanwhile, Rauhun remained in Pancor, the orthodox center of her father, and watched her followers slowly shift to follow her charismatic sister in Anjani, where, it was told, the visage (*kharomah*) of Raihanun's deceased father displayed post-mortem favour for the messianic daughter and often appeared during Friday prayers at the mosque. Less than six months after Raihanun's eviction, both sisters had amassed large militias.

Amphibi, Lombok's largest *pamswakarsa*, possessed a similar form of religious charisma. Amphibi's leaders, the brothers TGH Sibaway and Guru Ukit, combined archaic Sasak-mysticism and moralistic modernism. TGH Sibaway headed his own *pesantren* in Jeroaru, East Lombok, and was respected for his abilities to draw young 'toughs' into the fold of Islam. His tendency towards more idiomatic Islamic mysticism was reminiscent of his father who employed local idioms and mythology to persuade Wetu Telu to adopt orthodox Islam during the military-backed *dakwah* missions of the late 1960s and 1970s.[15] TGH Mutawalli's other son, Guru Ukit, was less orthodox in his practices. While his bother was known for his devotion, Guru Ukit was believed to have inherited the magical powers of his father. Renowned for his drinking and unconventional behaviour, Guru Ukit's street-wise ways wooed Jeroaru's less than pious toughs to join Amphibi.[16] The brothers, each

15 TGH Mutawalli was famous for his use of magical displays of power to persuade Wetu Telu to adopt more orthodox Islamic ritual. A contemporary of Nahdlatul Wathan's founder TGH Zainuddin Abdul Madjid, TGH Mutawalli, was famous for his use of cultural idioms to persuade traditionalist Muslims to adopt orthodox doctrine (Cederroth 1981).

16 Guru Ukit appears and disappears in mysterious ways. According to one close relation of Guru Ukit's, he has been known to relieve himself almost ritualistically after saying his prayers in the mosque proper. To many of his followers such unusual behaviour suggests that his mystical gifts were even greater than those of his late father. Unlike his brother, Guru Ukit was friend

bearing traces of their father's religious charisma, recruited over a 100,000 members to their ranks only five months after Amphibi became formally active in April 1999.

Localizing national vigilantilism

Amphibi's leaders were by no means estranged by contemporary political and security trends of the post-Soeharto 1999 elections by constructing 'Amphibi security posts' (*pos keamanan* Amphibi) in communities under its care. Painted in bright orange and emblazoned with an Arabic script seal and motto, Amphibi's security posts resembled New Order style 'community guard' platforms (*pos siskamling*) as well as more recent political party stands (*pos partai*). Vigilance was in the air and, whether politically reformist or security-oriented, Amphibi's efforts were not wasted on Lombok's residents.

Amphibi's leaders also combined political fashion with their own notoriety as *simbik*, magically endowed men, when they designed the Amphibi uniforms. During the 1999 election period, Lombok's youth coveted the *rompi*, a multi-pocketed sleeveless vest worn by party paramilitary members (*satgas partai*) and campaign leaders (*jurkam*). Only party-paramilitaries were allowed to use these vests. When Amphibi began recruitment for their night brigade several months after the election, it announced that each of its guards would receive a *rompi* and that every group of 30 men would be given a walkie-talkie for quick coordination 'in the field' (*di lapangan*). TGH Sibaway himself read mystical mantras into the vests to render the Amphibi guard invulnerable. Amphibi became a young man's dream. Not only did its members gain access to moral religious authority derived from a prominent Tuan Guru and his powerful brother (Guru Ukit), but they too would be able to wear the *rompi* and speak through walkie-talkies like the party paramilitaries they saw in action during the 1999 campaign. Sitting astride their motorcycles or lounging at the Amphibi security post the Amphibi guard was the very picture of masculine authority.

In July 1999, Amphibi began to recruit men to become active patrol guards to protect East Lombok's communities. Whereas Bujak relied on bounty payments from the owners of stolen property, Amphibi actually charged its active guard 120,000 rupiah per man for the honour to wear the orange Amphibi vest and hunt criminals in their communities. Bujak relied on ties with criminals to recover lost goods whereas Amphibi used walkie-talkies to coordinate anti-criminal chases in the area. Bujak had the use of sacred weapons from certain noble houses while Amphibi members had mystically

---

to Balinese, Chinese, Christians and Buddhists. Guru Ukit also built a house in the magical forest, Gawah Sukaroh, and gave his sons non-Islamic spirit names (*aran pemalik*) such as Tambing Muter and Sigar Penyalin.

inscribed *rompi* rendering them invulnerable. It was not long before Bujak and Amphibi had a showdown.

Amphibi expansion

On 2 August 1999, Amphibi and Bujak engaged in a full-scale battle on the border between East and Central Lombok. 'The beach, the forest, the fields of the village of Pene, Central Lombok were orange with our colours as we went to battle with Bujak' an Amphibi member said.[17] Although neither group claimed injury nor fatalities, men present at the battle admitted that many people had been killed in the showdown.[18] Amphibi's victory was apparent when it started to open guard posts throughout central, northern and western Lombok. By December 1999, Amphibi had registered 220,000 active members, nearly 10% of Lombok's population and 25% of all adult males in East Lombok.[19] Amphibi's operations targeted middlemen for stolen goods and, unless they confessed to their crimes, killed them publicly. The police could do nothing to prevent Amphibi and Lombok's *pamswakarsa* from taking over their functions.[20]

Unlike Bujak or the other *pamswakarsa* in Lombok, Amphibi developed a modern form of policing criminal networks on the island. Through a combination of religious authority and police methods of surveillance and 'crime prevention', Amphibi drew up lists of 'TO' (*target operasi*) or operational targets which were little more than names of men collected from other thieves interrogated while under Amphibi detention. Amphibi replaced Bujak's ritual *tebusan* scheme, which tended to focus on the stolen property, with a security apparatus bent on the identification and eradication of immoral criminals. Because of this shift in focus and procedure, Amphibi ranks diversified in late 1999. They were no longer loosely affiliated militias but sub-divided into special intelligence divisions broken down into groups of 'trackers' (*pelacak*) and 'hunters' (*pemburu*). 'Trackers' collected information concerning particular criminals, their activities and hideouts, while 'hunters' traced and caught criminals on the run. Amphibi gave captured thieves a choice. If thieves attempted to run, they were killed. If a thief chose not to run he was asked to 'repent' or *mentobat* in the mosque at Jeroaru witnessed either by Guru Ukit

17 Interviews with Amphibi leaders in Jeroaru, East Lombok, October, 2002.

18 One of the difficulties of writing about this conflict is that very few people will admit the number of people who died. According to the *Lombok Post* (3-8-1999) 11 men with injuries and one corpse were sent to the Selong Hospital but Amphibi members claimed that truckloads of victims had been evacuated to be treated locally.

19 National Census Survey 1998.

20 Interview with Amphibi members in Jeroaru, East Lombok, October 2002.

or TGH Sibaway. After their first *mentobat,* criminals were forced to confess the names of their partners in crime, hence the TO list of operational targets. After their second *mentobat* they would be held at Amphibi's jail in Jeroaru. Depending on the crime, TGH Sibaway, the judge (*hakim*) in Amphibi's court, would decide the duration of their sentence. After the thief's third offence, however, the criminal would be considered 'on the run' (*buron*) after which Amphibi's 'hunters' would take over and he would be traced and killed.

The Sengkongo incident

One of the most sensitive cases occurred when Amphibi attacked a Balinese nobleman's family in a Balinese village near Lombok's provincial capital of Mataram. As a nephew of one of Amphibi's victims explained:

> At approximately 1:00 a.m., 18 December 1999, 45 trucks full of Amphibi militia drove from East Lombok to Mataram in search of two Balinese men suspected of fencing goods for thief networks in the hamlet of Sengkongo, Mataram. They were, to use Amphibi's words, TO or operational targets. Upon reaching the village Amphibi demanded the men to surrender themselves. Seeing the presence of over a 1000 armed men in the village, a landless old flute player, I Gusti Made Banjar, struck his *kentongan* wooden slit gong to sound the communal alarm. Upon hearing this, Amphibi guards killed him instantly with scores of deep machete wounds.
>
> After dragging I Gusti Made Banjar's broken body down the road in Sengkongo, Amphibi cried out demands for Si Kentung, the alias of I Gusti Made Padma of the same community. Amphibi suspected I Gusti Made Padma of thievery and cut off one of his upraised hands and severely wounded the other. Amphibi left the community of Sengkongo on the morning of 18 December. Passing by the Mataram market of Beretais, Amphibi made victory rounds waving the severed hand of I Gusti Made Padma who was, after further police investigation, found innocent of the crimes Amphibi claimed he had committed. (ICG 2003c.)

The evening after the Sengkongo killing Amphibi trucks paraded the Lingsar area, the location for the ritual battle-of-rice-cakes between Sasaks and Balinese to be held the following morning.[21] Read as a direct challenge to the Balinese minority on the island tensions rose as Lombok prepared to celebrate Christmas, Balinese New Year (Nyepi) and the end of the Muslim fasting month of Lebaran in the same three-week period. The Sengkongo

[21] The Lingsar rice-cake battle is often explained as a cathartic opportunity for Balinese and Sasak young men to beat up on one another without causing a conflict. In 1999, the Lingsar ritual was run by the police and military and, because it was held during the fasting month, there were very few participants. Interview with Balinese men at Lingsar temple, October 2002.

incident was barely mentioned in the regional press for fear that Balinese would seek retribution against Sasak Muslims in Bali.[22] Over the following month, several meetings between Balinese Hindu leaders and Mataram's mayor did not result in justice for the killing of I Gusti Made Banjar. Instead, Lombok's Balinese were allowed to form their own militia called, Dharma Wicesa (Balinese: Dharma Power). And so militias beget militias.

The Mataram riots

On 17 January 2000, only a month after the Amphibi attack on Sengkongo, over 20,000 Sasak Muslim men crowded into Mataram to hold a religious gathering (Tabligh Akbar) in protest of the violence against Muslims in Maluku. Within three hours, small, organized groups ran through the streets of Mataram targeting and burning Christian homes and Churches and emptying boxes of hymnbooks to be torched in the streets. During the course of the riots, most of the Chinese owned stores and Christian housing complexes located outside of the Balinese protected enclave of Cakranegara were burned to the ground or looted.

Many theories about the riots circulated. A simple economic analysis would reveal that Lombok's peasantry had more than enough reason to target West Lombok's market centres. Since the outset of the economic crisis, Sasak sellers accused Chinese and Arab merchants of taking advantage of the irregular inflation of *sembako* goods for profit.[23] In fact, as early as January 1998, Mataram's Chinese merchants regularly closed their stores in response to rumours that poor Sasaks from East and Central Lombok were preparing to attack markets in the provincial capital of Mataram. Not only were shop owners stockholding goods, but Mataram merchants were buying up gold in Lombok's hinterland at pre-crisis prices. Once peasants became aware that urban merchants were wily destructing their meagre savings, it was feared that they would seek retribution by looting the town's Chinese-controlled market centres.

There were other reasons that contributed to the riots in January 2000. To members of intelligence units the riots came not as a surprise. They had warned the villagers in my research area to avoid Mataram on the 17th of January. By the 15th, scores of trucks were pouring into Mataram in preparation for the event. Riding on the heels of the recent violence in East Timor,

22 Interview with *Lombok Post* and *Bali Post* reporters March 2003.

23 *Sembako* referred to 'nine staple goods' required by most Indonesians to stock their kitchens. The prices of these products, especially rice, sugar and cooking oil, fluctuated wildly according to varying degrees of inflation, stockpiling, and racketeering in Lombok's markets.

it was hard not to assume that a conspiracy was afoot. At the national level, tensions between the recently elected President Abdurrahman Wahid and General Wiranto had piqued since the military backed violence in East Timor had made international and domestic observers wary of Wiranto's counter-reformist intentions. Meanwhile, Wahid's ambivalent stance towards the Christian-Muslim conflicts in Maluku had created an outcry of protest by Indonesia's conservative Islamic groups. A CD-rom tape of the violence in Ambon showing a pregnant Muslim woman and her child being killed was distributed throughout the Muslim communities of Lombok. Also, a fake Christian missionary book was distributed ending with the phrase, 'all Muslims must be exterminated'. It was made to look as if Christians had made the book.[24] Some conspiracy theorists blamed Jakarta-based actors for the Mataram riots and pointed in this respect at the role of Eggy Sudjana, the chairman of the Persaudaraan Pekerja Muslim Indonesia (PPMI, Indonesian Muslim Merchants Association) and associated with General Prabowo Subianto, whose right hand man, Hairul Muslim, was among the men involved in the Tabliqh Akbar meetings of 13 January 2000, before the riots.[25] Eggy Sudjana and friends worked with the Tablig Akhbar committee and agreed that the head of Amphibi would be responsible for security at the demonstration scheduled for 17 January 2000. Strangely, however, on the day of the violence, Amphibi's walkie talkies were not operational, while another group began distributing flyers to all the mosques crying for war against Christians.

After the riots, many of Lombok's academicians, politicians and activists were arrested for their involvement in the Tabligh Akbar held prior to the riots. National actors, most notably Eggy Sudjana, were exonerated for lack of sufficient evidence. By lack of any real explanation of how and why the riots were organized, conspiracy theories gave meaning to violence and reinforced the credence of half-truths regarding the role of Wiranto and his partnership with military-friendly radicals. Conspiracies aside, in a very real way, Amphibi exerted its power over post-riot Lombok without challenge

24 A police intelligence officer in Lombok concurred that, in fact, during the month prior to the riots both the 'anti-Islamic' handbook and the CD-rom coverage of the murder of Moluccan women and children were being circulated throughout Lombok.

25 According to the head of Majelis Mujahiddin Indonesia for West Nusa Tenggara, Baharuddin Anwar, Lombok's Muslim leaders held meetings on 13 January 2000 to prepare for the Tabliqh Akbar protest of violence against Muslims in Maluku scheduled for the 17th of January 2000. A letter was apparently signed on that day and sent to Lombok's Christian community demanding that they write a letter condemning Christian violence on Muslims in Maluku. 'The letter was signed by TGH Sibaway, head of Amphibi and listed as the head of PPMI (Eggy Sudjana's organization) in West Nusa Tenggara. When we contacted him to confirm whether he had signed the letter or not TGH Sibaway denied it' said Catholic leader Remmy Giusnaga.

lending further credence to the theory that Amphibi had anticipated and profited from the insecurity Mataram's riots had produced.

Amphibi's decline

Within two months after the riots, it was not police or the military that were empowered, but instead Amphibi had established branches throughout western Lombok with memberships, they claimed, swelling to more than 600,000. What initially appeared to be a somewhat overzealous approach to neighbourhood crime control had become an island-wide moral movement. Even the governor, Harun Al'Rasyid attended Amphibi ceremonies and the island's businessmen made large 'donations' to Amphibi's headquarters. Villages not included in the Amphibi network formed their own small village-based militias to prevent an Amphibi incursion into their communities.[26] The emergence of counter-Amphibi militias was most popular in villages, such as Perampauan, known to harbour large criminal networks. In fact, the Perampauan-Amphibi conflict of January 2001 showed most clearly how village-based militias were capable of undermining Amphibi's dominance.

As indicated above, Perampauan is famous for its criminals and its 'service' for victims of stolen goods. The Perampauan conflict began with the death in December 1999 of I Gusti Made Banjar of Sengkongo, the Balinese hamlet located in the larger village of Perampauan. The loss of I Gusti Made Padma's hand was due to a larger effort of Amphibi to track down 51 Perampauan thieves. Amphibi insisted that Perampauan village authorities surrender the men or suffer the consequences. TGH Sibaway himself came to Perampauan and swore in about 17 Perampauan residents during the months of March and April 2000. Their TO status remained, however, and over the upcoming months, tensions rose between the neighbouring 'Amphibi village' of Bongor and the 'thief village' of Perampauan.[27] In part to forestall the development of an Amphibi branch in their community, Perampauan leaders developed their own village-based *pamswakarsa* called Perkasa Pengsor. Perkasa Pengsor was limited to simple night security activities and, unlike Amphibi, did not operate outside the village boundaries of Perampauan.

> On 10 January 2001, Perampauan villager Saida and two friends were on their way to the beach when they were ambushed by a group of masked Amphibi

26 Elang Merah (Sakra), Sapu Jagad and Ababil (TGH Bodak) in East Lombok, Perkasa Pengsor in Perampauan (West Lombok), Pemenang Bersatu in Tanjung (northwest Lombok), and Dharma Wicesa for the embattled Balinese minority and Langlang Jagat among northern Lombok's Wetu Telu were all formed as counter-Amphibi militias.

27 Interviews in Perampauan and Bongor, April 2003.

> members. This attack was, according to Perampauan residents, a trap to draw out Perampauan aggression. Perampauan residents and Bongor Amphibi members engaged in full-scale battle in front of the Bongor Mosque using handmade firearms and large fishing bombs. A man from Bongor was killed by a handmade firearm and both sides suffered serious injuries from arrows, machetes and spears.
>
> The morning after the Bongor battle, Perampauan residents stood watch as Amphibi prepared to launch a dawn attack on the village. According to Perampauan residents present during the attack, at 5:30 in the morning 6,000 Amphibi members from East Lombok arrived in Perampauan in open air trucks. The Perampauan religious leader, TGH Mansyur told the villagers to 'protect our village from the PKI (communist party)'.[28] To everyone's surprise, Perampauan's villagers resisted Amphibi's offensive and killed at least 20 of Amphibi's front line militants.

Amphibi's failure to defeat Perampauan was the beginning of the steady fragmentation of the organization in 2001. Amphibi's pan-Lombok appeal and its reputation for *kebal* (invulnerability) were dampened by the news of Amphibi's thousand-man flight from only a few hundred home-village defenders. Wisely, West Lombok district head, Iskandar, had made use of regional autonomy discourse to allow the formation of village-based *pamswakarsa* in Perampauan. With their own *pamswakarsa*, Perampauan residents were portrayed not as criminals and infidels but as villagers upholding the principles of solidarity and autonomy, one of the reformist principles of regional autonomy legislation. After their defeat, Amphibi continued to maintain large branch offices in western Lombok but they no longer obeyed the East Lombok leadership. Instead, Mataram's Amphibi branches began to run petty-extortion schemes to supplement their increasingly localized incomes. Very little of this money was sent to Amphibi headquarters in East Lombok and, according to Amphibi officials, they could do little to control their men in West Lombok.

Regional elections: politicians, clerics and criminals

In mid-2003, heated discussions arose about the election of district heads in Lombok. Especially East Lombok witnessed intense rivalries between competing Tuan Guru and noble camps. Since 1999, each of Lombok's Tuan Guru and militia heads controlled a certain number of seats in the local parliament (Dewan Perwakilan Rakyat Daerah, DPRD). While during the New Order

28 When seen from the perspective of village autonomy, Amphibi's efforts to track and dismember the Perampauan crime-network through forced confessions (*mentobat*) had turned Amphibi into the very embodiment of the 'subversive', a title reserved for PKI and armed separatists under the New Order.

East Lombok's district heads were recruited from the military, the election of civilian Golkar candidate, Haji Syadan, in 1999 depended very much on the support of Lombok's Tuan Guru, the most powerful of which controlled whole blocks of seats within East Lombok's district parliament. In June 2003, however, a couple of 'wild card' candidates decided to buck the trend of following only Tuan Guru and, instead, used Lombok's criminal networks to gain authority among the members of legislature.

For instance, on 1 June 2003 a group of thieves, organized under the name 'The Night Bats Group' (Grup Kelelawar Maling), held a demonstration in front of the district parliament in Selong, East Lombok. Amak Kalep, the head of 'The Night Bats Group' voiced his support for H. Lutfi Mali, one of the candidates for district head of East Lombok. Playing traditional drum sets (*kendang beliq*) and dressed in Sasak ritual clothing the thieves marched beside the members of East Lombok's *pamswakarsa,* Elang Merah, the very militia tasked with hunting down and apprehending the men with whom they now marched. When asked whether he feared arrest or attack after confessing to be the head of East Lombok's largest thief network Amaq Kalep stated: 'All of the members here today have already *nyikep* (carry sacred weaponry with mantras read over them), we are fully prepared'.[29] Commenting on such open cooperation between politicians, thieves, and *pamswakarsa,* a friend from a Mataram-based Islamic lobbying group explained it best:

> It is crucial for a district head candidate to have control over the thief networks in his area. Despite the presence of *pamswakarsa,* each year shows a marked increase in reported crimes. If a district candidate cuts a deal with the thief network he can promise the people that they will be free of crime if he is elected. When people see that the crime has stopped they know that the district head candidate is a man of his word and that he has cut a deal with the criminals. Several of the political Tuan Guru have students in villages known to harbour thief networks. In fact, many of the thieves rely on the Tuan Guru for *kebal* magic and other meditative arts to protect themselves during their stealing raids.

The fact that Haji Lutfi had the authority to recruit both thieves and anti-thief militias to demonstrate at the same event displayed that he knew how closely *pamswakarsa* and thieves actually work in practice. If Lutfi was able to control both groups, he would be able to divert criminal attacks away from communities that supported his candidacy. Of course, Lutfi was not the first candidate to employ such tactics but he was the only one willing to make such an open display of normally behind the scenes moves and political strategy. Despite his efforts Lutfi was never elected.

[29] *Bali Post* 2-6-2003. Amaq Kalep added that the members of his group number 1,791 strong: 'Those are only the heads of the thief groupings. Each head controls anywhere from 10 to 15 subordinate thieves'.

Conclusion

The fall of Soeharto had ushered in profound changes for Lombok. The combined effects of the 1997-1998 monetary crisis, mass-based politics and regional autonomy presented Lombok's leaders and communities with new problems and opportunities.

The demise of Soeharto's authoritarian regime meant that violence, oppression and the right to define 'criminality' would no longer be controlled by the centralized institutions of the state but would be distributed to Lombok's own leaders. Initially, the responsibility to protect one's community was assumed as a reformist duty against the 'provocateurs' and rogue agents of Soeharto's state. This changed when new leaders emerged who established locally defined forms of 'law and order'. In response to Lombok's crime wave, the traditional *tebusan* schemes long employed by criminal networks to hold stolen goods as collateral against bounty payments were replaced by a new style of Islamist vigilance against immoral thieves. It was not long before Bujak's approach to negotiated justice was replaced by Amphibi's much more righteous and unilateral effort to exorcise the immoral criminal from Lombok's communities. Amphibi's reputation for moralist purity over backstreet dealings succeeded to a certain degree and their militia established chapters in virtually every corner of Lombok. The Mataram riots only intensified public desire for community-security and locally defined dominion.

Militias beget militias and by 2001, 'thief villages' (*desa-desa maling*) developed their own counter-Amphibi security posts capable of undermining Amphibi's increasingly bureaucratic and murderous attacks.

As important as it is to look for a Jakarta-based interest behind the Mataram riots, it is even more important to try to understand what local needs Amphibi satisfied in the communities where it thrived. What we discover is not Islamic reformism intent on the implementation of *syariat* law nor a military-backed group of mercenaries, but a heterodox movement full of paradoxes. Lombok's militias are led by charismatic siblings each of whom embody a mutually antagonistic part of Lombok's cultural and political past. Amphibi's Guru Ukit is a drunkard and Sasak mystic while his brother, TGH Sibaway, is an orthodox preacher. Nahdlatul Wathan's feuding sisters are divided in similarly contrasting, but decidedly religious, ways. Rauhun, the elder and more orthodox sister, stands firm in her father's headquarters in Pancor and remains loyal to Islamic rationalism and scriptural purity. Meanwhile, Raihanun the younger sister of the two, fled Pancor to espouse more messianic Islamic themes and relocated her substantial base of followers in the former centre of Lombok's messianic movements, Desa Anjani. H. Lutfi's campaign for district head of East Lombok in 2003 illustrates the nature of the politics of security in Lombok. The Islamic organizations and the various island-wide and local militia groupings embody the particular way in which on Lombok political action has been decentralized. They illustrate the extent to which (anti) criminal action lie at the heart of Lombok's regional autonomy.

How civil is civil society?

DAVID HENLEY, MARIA J.C. SCHOUTEN and ALEX J. ULAEN

Preserving the peace in post-New Order Minahasa

Indonesia has now muddled through six years since the fall of Soeharto, and its economy has grown every year for the last five.[1] East Timor has been liberated, free elections held, repressive laws abolished, and greater autonomy granted to the regions. Yet in the literature concerning the consequences of this Reformasi, pessimism prevails. Decentralization and the end of authoritarian rule from Jakarta, it is pointed out, have led to decentralized corruption, to the emergence of local kleptocracies, to environmental despoliation, and in the worst cases to ethnic strife and the breakdown of social order. Henk Schulte Nordholt and Gerry van Klinken represent a widespread view when they write, in their introduction to this volume, of 'the agony of decentralization' and of Indonesia-watchers torn between 'professional optimism' and 'realistic pessimism'.

But if you happen to go to North Sulawesi, all the pessimism seems rather far-fetched. At the provincial airport the terminal is brand new and the dive tourists keep coming for the nearby Bunaken reefs. The city of Manado makes a more prosperous impression than in the past and boasts a complete new seafront on reclaimed land, with lavish shopping centres and entertainment venues. Loudspeakers on the steeples of numerous churches broadcast sugary evangelical music to match the amplified calls to prayer from the city's many mosques. Well-maintained roads lead up to the mountains and across the tranquil plateau of Minahasa. And this in a mixed but predominantly Christian area not so far from three other Christian enclaves where things have gone badly wrong in recent years: Poso, the North Moluccas, and Ambon. North Sulawesi, since Muslim Gorontalo divorced amicably from it in 2001 and became a separate province, is roughly 70% Christian, as is the

1 This chapter is based on research carried out in North Sulawesi by David Henley in October and November 2003, by Maria Schouten in August, September and December 2004, and by Alex Ulaen intermittently throughout the period since the end of the New Order in 1998. Key interview informants are listed in the acknowledgements at the end of this chapter.

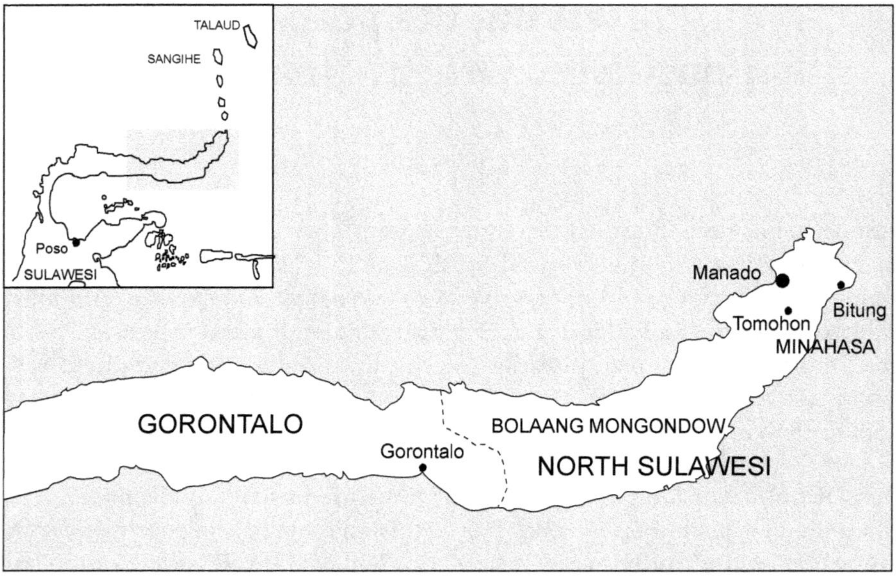

Map 12. North Sulawesi

provincial capital, Manado. In Minahasa, the area which forms the immediate hinterland of Manado and is home to the province's largest ethnic group, the figure is a little over 80% if the city and its port of Bitung are included, or 90% if they are not.

In North Sulawesi the impact of the Asian economic crisis which precipitated the fall of Soeharto was muted, and the subsequent recovery rapid. The provincial economy contracted by a mere 2.4% in 1998 (against 14% for Indonesia as a whole), then grew by almost 6% in 1999 – faster than in 1997 – and has continued to expand at similar rates since. This good performance results partly from the peace and order which has allowed North Sulawesi to benefit from the troubles elsewhere as Christian and Sino-Indonesian refugees (and potential refugees) from the Moluccas and Java have invested money in Manado. Government services still work tolerably well and if administrative corruption has worsened as a result of decentralization and democratization, it evidently has not done so sufficiently to deter inward investment. Neither is there much sign of political conflict or repression. Non-government organizations and political parties flourish, and state propaganda is limited to a softer version of the old Pancasila injunction to toleration of cultural and religious diversity. In an initiative supported by all of the province's significant religious organizations, 2002 was officially designated a Tahun Kasih or 'Year of Love' in North Sulawesi, and the years 2003 and 2004 obtained the same designation. 'Peace, in Manado', as one visiting journalist has noted, 'is something that many people are actively working at all the time' (Lynch 2003:29).

This chapter examines the anatomy of peace in post-Soeharto North Sulawesi, particularly Minahasa. Attention is paid to two spheres, civil society and the state, in which a combination of favourable institutions and prudent decisions has helped to prevent the kind of conflict that has occurred in some other parts of Indonesia, particularly in areas where there is a large Christian population, since the end of the New Order in 1998. Of primary importance here, we argue, is the existence in Minahasa of a rather robust civil society based largely on religious organizations. Potential conflicts, on the whole, have been avoided or suppressed thanks both to the internal discipline of these organizations and to the close mutual cooperation between them, especially at leadership level. A second crucial factor has been the role of a local state which maintains a more or less legitimate near-monopoly over the means of violence, and is able and willing to use this to prevent rather than foment conflict. Besides these political advantages and achievements, economic and demographic factors have also tended to favour the preservation of peace. The local economy has been a stabilizing influence in that it features a relatively egalitarian distribution of wealth, and proved resilient in the face of the international business crisis which struck in 1997. The clear demographic predominance of Christians within the province, and especially within Minahasa, has helped to moderate both Christian fears and Muslim ambitions in regional politics.

The fact that peace and order have so far been maintained by this combination of a strong civil society, a relatively civilized state and a favourable set of economic and demographic conditions, we stress, does not mean that the long-standing tensions between the different religious groupings in Minahasa have been resolved. On the contrary, those tensions have been heightened since 1998 both by outbursts of religious conflict elsewhere in Indonesia, and by policy initiatives from Jakarta which are seen as hostile to Indonesian Christians. The ideological and political effort currently devoted to preserving the peace is in fact a measure of its fragility. At the end of the chapter we very briefly attempt to put the Minahasan experience in wider Indonesian context, and ask whether it offers lessons for other regions and for the future.

Civil society and religion: affinity or antithesis?

In a world increasingly divided by religious conflict, faith often seems the enemy of civility and it can be hard to remember that historically speaking religion has been an important force for integration and cooperation within societies, nations, and civilizations. Under the right circumstances the world religions, by providing institutions and norms of conduct which transcend kinship and local community, can support the development of social capital (networks and trust) and civil society (association and cooperation) among co-believers. This observation, often thought to originate with Max Weber, actually goes back much further. For early modern Europeans, in fact, the truth of it was self-evident: even John Locke, making a famous plea for religious tolerance in his *Letter concerning toleration* of 1689, warned that 'those are not at all to be tolerated who deny the being of a God', since 'promises, covenants, and oaths, which are the bonds of human society, can have no hold upon an atheist' (Locke 1961:93). Besides this link between religious ethics and social integration, the function of religious institutions themselves as buttresses of social order was equally obvious well before Weber and Marx made it a classic doctrine in sociology. Alexis de Tocqueville (1961:154-60), visiting the United States in the 1830s at a time when the federal government was weak and the disintegration of the country seemed imminent, concluded that mass membership of churches and church associations was the main thing still holding American society together.

In the context of modern Indonesia, some have argued that Islam and Islamic institutions play the same kind of role in promoting cooperation and generating a common identity among the members of their huge constituency (Van Bruinessen 2004; Hefner 2000). Jim Schiller, in his contribution to this volume, portrays Islamic teachers, Islamic *pesantren* schools and the Muslim organization Nahdlatul Ulama as guardians of stability and civility at the local level in Jepara (Central Java). In Minahasa, where Christianity rather than Islam is the majority faith, the Christian churches certainly play that role. The churches of Minahasa are among the most impressive examples of non-governmental institutions in Indonesia. The largest of them, the Protestant Gereja Masehi Injili di Minahasa (GMIM), has some 650,000 members, more than three quarters of the population of Minahasa if this is taken to exclude the multi-ethnic towns of Manado and Bitung. The GMIM runs more than 800 schools and a major hospital, and supports diverse charitable and conservation activities. It offers opportunities for social mobility to women – more than half of its ministers are female – and, through its educational scholarships, to the underprivileged. It also owns businesses and plantations, and is very influential in provincial politics: no governor of North Sulawesi, it is sometimes claimed, could attain that position without first cultivating good relations with the head of the GMIM synod.

The organizational discipline of the GMIM is generally held to surpass that of the state itself. Instructions issued by its synod are followed faithfully and quickly by its clergy. Its lay membership is tightly organized into units of 15 to 25 households called *kolom*, meetings of which, held at least once a week, serve both religious and social purposes and are important occasions for the exchange of information. The leaders of the *kolom*, and of each local Protestant congregation as a whole, are lay people elected every five years in a lengthy process which requires the active participation of the local church members. During the New Order, these elections of lay church officials probably came closer to genuinely democratic procedures than did anything in the sphere of formal politics. Another way in which allegiance to church and congregation is expressed is through the sharing of material resources. The GMIM raises at least 40 billion rupiah every year in voluntary funding from local sources. Fund-raising is in fact a major reason for the existence of many church-affiliated associations, although this is never stated openly. The offertories during church services and other gatherings owe part of their success to the opportunities they provide for display. Minahasans consider gift-giving a major virtue, especially when the gift is for the church with its aura of sacredness. A well-publicized religious donation is therefore an effective tool for the enhancement of status, and in contrast with the usual practice in European churches, offertory giving in Minahasa is typically a public procedure. Much of the money collected goes to fund the construction of church buildings: the countless churches of Minahasa, often of a most peculiar architecture, are symbols of prosperity as well as piety, and are there to boost the prestige of their congregations and communities. Another part of the funds, however, is earmarked for social institutions such as schools and health services, which are accessible to members of all faiths.

Similar forms of internal organization extending down to and below the village level, and similar combinations of religious, social, economic and political activities, are to be found among Minahasa's other Christian denominations – most importantly the Roman Catholic church, but also minority Protestant groups such as Seventh-day Adventists and Pentecostals. The GMIM, however, is special not only because of its size, but also for historical reasons. It is regarded as the main heir to the Protestant missions of the nineteenth century which originally converted Minahasa to Christianity. Although the GMIM as such was not founded until 1934, this still makes it one of the oldest institutions in Minahasa. It is also perhaps the most truly Minahasan. Whereas the GMIM has its headquarters in Tomohon, in the heartland of Minahasa, almost all of the other churches are branches of larger organizations based elsewhere in the world. Particularly since Minahasa ceased to exist as an administrative unit in 2003 after falling victim to the nationwide *pemekaran* trend discussed in the introduction to this volume, the GMIM can also be said to form the central institutional focus of Minahasan ethnic identity. Over the last two years the old administrative district (*afdeling, kabupaten*) of Minahasa, dating from colonial times, has been progressively dismembered into three new districts and an autonomous township (*kota*).

Tension between religion and civil society arises when what civility calls for is not solidarity among co-believers, or what Robert Putnam (2000) calls the 'bonding' form of social capital, but rather the 'bridging' form which makes possible tolerance and cooperation between followers of different faiths. A system of cooperation which depends on encapsulating individuals within a more or less uniform institutional, ethical and cultural environment may prove worse than useless when it runs up against another such system with equally universal ambitions. The violent 'clash of civilizations' (Huntington 1996) which, according to some observers, has developed across the world since 2001 exacerbates tensions between Muslims and Christians in Indonesia, encouraging them to see themselves as members of global diasporas in conflict rather than as Indonesian citizens of different religious persuasion. In Minahasa things are not helped by a surprisingly direct identification with Israel: advertisements above Manado streets offer tours of the Holy Land on the same format as those advertising Haj packages to Saudia Arabia for Muslim pilgrims. In response to the threat (real and perceived) from *laskar jihad* organizations based in Java, Minahasan Christians have provided equal proof that social capital has its dark side by using it to create their own paramilitary groups. The most important of these, the Brigade Manguni or 'Owl Brigade' (the owl was an oracular bird in local pagan belief and has also become the symbol of Christian Minahasa), is led by a former

Jakarta gangster and reportedly sponsored by a retired Kopassus general.

Such militias enjoy considerable cultural appeal in Minahasa, where there is a general admiration for forceful people who dare to speak up for themselves. Brigade Manguni, nevertheless, has shown restraint by presenting itself as a critical complement to, rather than an opponent of, the government apparatus. The churches themselves have kept their distance from this and other paramilitary groups, and an attempt in 2002 to set up a militia directly affiliated to the GMIM was quickly disowned by the synod of that church. Moreover, since 1998 the leaders of all the major religious organizations in Minahasa – including, crucially, the Islamic groups, most importantly the local arm of the Majelis Ulama Indonesia (MUI, Council of Indonesian Islamic Scholars) – have cooperated intensively with each other to help prevent any outburst of the kind of religious violence afflicting other parts of Indonesia. When 15 truckloads of Brigade Manguni youths set off for Manado from Tomohon at Idul Fitri in December 2002 to 'help the government' impose order on 'chaotic' (*semrawut*) Muslim street traders, they were prevented from entering the city by local police warned of their approach by the head of the MUI, who had in turn been tipped off by a prominent member of the 'Catholic' militia Legium Christum.

The internal discipline of the individual religious groups and organizations, meanwhile, is used to good effect in preventing inflammatory reactions to events inside or outside Minahasa. The GMIM, for example, has been able to ensure that its preachers, sometimes despite themselves, keep stressing Christ's injunction to turn the other cheek in the face of any provocation. Sermons and meditations at religious assemblies of all denominations frequently include positive references to people of other creeds, who are described as *saudara* (brothers and sisters) worthy of *kasih* (love). An important part of the cooperation to prevent violence has taken place in the framework of the provincial government's Badan Kerjasama Antar Umat Beragama (BKSAUA, Organization for Inter-Faith Cooperation), an institution which was established early in the New Order period but became much more active and important after the fall of Soeharto. The BKSAUA has numerous local branches, even in villages where the only religious divides are between different Christian churches. The leader of a BKSAUA branch committee is typically an elderly, generally respected person. This is not a demanding job, but the prestige attached to the function is evident from the treatment the incumbents receive on formal occasions in the village.

To what extent the contribution of religious leaders and organizations to the preservation of the peace in Minahasa actually rests on religious principles, and to what extent on prudent self-interest, is a moot question to which we will return below. But whatever the motivations behind it, up to now it appears to have worked. A civil society of sorts exists in Minahasa, and there is a good chance that it will continue to exist in the future. But this is not the kind of civil society in which individual citizens interact freely within the bounds of the law, political and associational life is based on secular, rational principles, and religion is a private affair. It is more like Dutch society in the time of *verzuiling* or 'pillarization', when religious orientations (Protestant, Catholic, or secular) determined which schools people went to, which associations they joined, and to a large extent also which political views they held. This is not to argue, as do Deborah James and Albert Schrauwers (2003:59), that the close association which exists between religious and political behaviour and institutions in many parts of Indonesia reflects 'the effects of a Dutch colonial culture'. Nevertheless the situation in the Netherlands half a century ago was similar to that of contemporary Minahasa in the sense that the different religious 'pillars', partly because of their very separation, were able to coexist in peace despite deep disagreements and prejudices, the political balance between them maintained by a constant process of accommodation and compromise between their respective elites (Lijphart 1968). In Holland, it was out of this framework that a more secular form of civil society ultimately evolved. But to expect a rapid secularization of political life in any part of Indonesia today would be unrealistic at best. And in Minahasa, where religious institutions are deeply intertwined with the maintenance of social stability, the provision of public goods, and indeed the redistribution of wealth, such a development would also be undesirable from any realistic point of view.

Conflict management and the social contract: bringing the state back in

Although religious leaders in Minahasa are directly involved in maintaining the peace, when it comes to dealing with potential flashpoints such as the Idul Fitri incident mentioned above they are careful to rely on the police rather than their own followers to nip the trouble in the bud. That coercion and indeed violence will sometimes be necessary for this purpose is frankly acknowledged, even emphasized, by Christian and Islamic leaders alike. Their position, according to a statement issued by BKSAUA members in July 2001, is that any disturbance of public order should be *ditindak tegas* (firmly dealt with), by which they mean little less than that the police should shoot to kill before the trouble can escalate. The special *bimbingan rohani* or 'spiritual guidance' which the GMIM provides to members of the police force is designed not to increase their awareness of human rights, but to give them the courage and resolution to use force if necessary to maintain the peace. It is likely that religious organizations also supply more concrete (financial) forms of support to police personnel. They also work in close cooperation with other organs of the state. Besides the official meetings of the BKSAUA, from 1999 to 2002 a small *rapat kordinasi*, described by some as 'the real DPRD' (Dewan Perwakilan Rakyat Daerah, provincial assembly) and comprising permanent representatives of the Protestant, Catholic and Muslim communities as well as the provincial government, the police, the judiciary and the military, was held at least once every month in Manado to coordinate security policy.

Many informants not themselves directly associated with the state have assured us that in Minahasa there is still considerable public respect for the institutions of government. This respect improves the prospects for peace by making people reluctant to take the law into their own hands. The attitude that only the state has the right to punish disturbers of the peace is found even in the ranks of the Minahasan paramilitary groups. Journalist Jake Lynch, reporting on a 'show of strength' staged by Brigade Manguni in response to the Bali bombing (and the simultaneous explosion outside the Philippine consulate in Manado) in October 2002, was surprised to find that the demonstrators were not bent on retaliating against Islamic terror themselves.

> Their rampage through the streets, hundreds clinging to open-topped vehicles, wearing black t-shirts and shouting at the top of their voices, looked both spectacular and slightly sinister [...]. Listen carefully to these people, though, and they project a sort of muscular communitarianism, which may not be as threatening as their appearance suggests. What would they do, if, for instance, any of their members discovered 'outsiders' in Manado? Why, hand them over to the police, of course. If they keep their word [...] then that would at least represent a step forward from the situation in other, more troubled parts. In Poso, for instance, the trigger incident for the first round of rioting came when a Muslim man, injured in a street brawl with Christian youths, ran instead into a local Mosque to rouse fellow believers to take revenge. (Lynch 2003:30.)

Whether Manado's Muslim youths would take quite the same view is less clear: the composition of the local state in Minahasa, although far from homogeneous, reflects that of the population at large, in which Christians form a clear majority. Certainly it would be naive to assume that public support for the police as guardians of public order in Minahasa results entirely from trust in the impartiality of official justice. Soon after the fall of Soeharto, however, Muslims in the port town of Bitung on the east coast of Minahasa did hand over to the police a number of Islamic agitators who they said had recently arrived from outside the province to sow discord between local Muslims and Christians. And Muslims throughout North Sulawesi know that the police force in the province has since shown itself capable of acting – with the support of church leaders – against threats to the peace from Christian as well as Muslim quarters.

Both the trust which Minahasans still place in the (local) state as guardian of the peace, and the responsible attitude of the local authorities when it comes to fulfilling that expectation, can arguably be traced back to the (by colonial standards) unusually harmonious quasi-contractual relationship which developed between state and society in Minahasa during the period of Dutch rule. By the early twentieth century the special regard in which the Dutch held Minahasans as loyal soldiers and servants of the crown, combined with the lucidity and assertiveness with which Minahasans, thanks to colonial education, were able to raise their grievances, had already created a stable political system which involved reciprocity and representation, and which was widely regarded as legitimate despite its colonial character (Henley 1996:94-107). A widespread familiarity with bureaucratic structures and procedures also developed. In the mid-twentieth century came a long interlude of violence and repression, beginning in 1942 with the Japanese invasion and continuing through the suppression of the Permesta regional rebellion (1957-1961) up to the establishment of the New Order in 1965. The ideal of a benevolent social contract which included the state, nevertheless, survived: Permesta was directed only against the policies of the central government under Soekarno, and did not question the legitimacy of the Indonesian state as such. During the New Order a relatively favourable experience of economic development without severe political repression served to revive that ideal and continues, alongside an idealized collective memory of the region's unique colonial past, to colour Minahasan attitudes to the state today.

It is striking that the trust placed in the civil and police authorities does not extend to the army, which is regarded as a liability when dealing with conflicts because of its continuing involvement in power politics at the national level. While the preference for the police over the army seems to be present in Minahasa among Christians and Muslims alike, it is significant that Christians explain their attitude partly in terms of the support which the army is seen as having provided to Muslim protagonists in the recent Ambon conflicts. While it would be an exaggeration to say that people in this part of Indonesia have any very strong belief in the 'rule of law', all groups involved in preserving the peace in Minahasa have certainly been concerned to ensure that policemen, not soldiers, represent the coercive power of the state in situations where conflict suppression is called for.

The state has many faces and its predatory aspects, so prominent in the recent history of Indonesia, have rightly been the focus of much attention among Indonesianists. But its more or less contractual role in the provision of public goods, the most fundamental of which is peace and order, should not be ignored either. In Minahasa, peace and order have been preserved thanks partly to the local state's prudent and responsible use of the means of violence at its disposal. Among social scientists the contract approach to the state reached a low point of popularity under the influence of Marxism in the 1960s, when Robert Carneiro (1970:733) went so far as to declare that 'no such contract was ever subscribed to by human groups, and the Social Contract theory is today nothing more than a historical curiosity'. Today, however, some are arguing once again that the origins of state power must be sought in the demand for conflict resolution (Stone Sweet 2002; Henley 2004). The evidence of contemporary Minahasa confirms that civil society cannot replace the state, only complement it, and that the kind of state it needs to complement is one which is bound to society by a social contract, yet retains sufficient autonomy to intervene in society with force and impartiality when that is what fulfilment of its contract demands.

> In Indonesia, the culture of civility remains vulnerable and incomplete if it is not accompanied by a transformation of state. This is to say, [...] civil society is not opposed to the state but deeply dependent on its civilization. The state must open itself to public participation. At the same time, independent courts and watchdog agencies must be ready to intervene when, as inevitably happens, some citizen or official tries to replace democratic proceduralism with nether-world violence. As vigilantes and hate groups regularly remind us, not all organizations in society are civil, and the state must act as a guardian of public civility as well as a vehicle of the popular will. (Hefner 2000:215.)

Discussion of decentralization and democratization in Indonesia, it seems to us, should focus in the first place on their implications, both positive and negative, for the endeavour to create a healthy relationship between state and society. On the positive side, these processes should in principle make it easier to check the predatory impulses to which states, given their control of means of coercion, are inevitably prone. On the negative side, closer engagement with society may weaken the state to the point where it no longer has the power to serve the public interest, or subvert its impartiality to the point where it no longer has the inclination to do so. This is not to suggest that the authoritarian states of the colonial or New Order periods acted with impartiality where the interests of their ruling elites were involved. But the centralization of power under those regimes at least meant that many regional issues – the protection of national parks, for instance – involved elite interests less directly than they do today, now that power is more widely dispersed. A related point is that the centralized corruption of the New Order state was at least more transparent and predictable, and hence less disadvantageous for business and investment, than today's decentralized corruption.

Economy and demography: the politics of prosperity and proportionality

Besides possessing a strong civil society and a relatively civilized local state, North Sulawesi benefits from an economic structure which discourages conflict. One of the more prosperous provinces of Indonesia, it also displays a comparatively even distribution of wealth. In 2001, with 11% of its population officially living under the poverty line, North Sulawesi had the fourth lowest poverty rate in the country after Jakarta, Bali and Riau. In the urban areas where its Muslim immigrants are concentrated, the figure was under 9% (*Statistik Indonesia* 2002:593-5). Many households still do endure hardship, and of the Muslims in Manado and the rest of Minahasa, many are labourers and petty traders belonging to the poorer sections of the population. Even so, by Indonesian standards their deprivation, whether measured in absolute terms or relative to other groups, is in most cases mild.

> Income inequality in North Sulawesi is clearly low [...]. The greater part of the population falls within the medium income bracket [...]. One reason for this persistent pattern of even income distribution is that a characteristic feature of North Sulawesi is the small scale of its economic activities in almost every sector. Many actors contribute to economic output, and North Sulawesi effectively has what is referred to as a people's economy (*ekonomi rakyat*) without this having to be promoted by all kinds of plans and slogans. (Vekie A. Rumate 1999:10.)

This unplanned 'people's economy' reduces the scope for jealousy and resentment among the province's religious groups, and provides strong structural disincentives to civil conflict. Even during crises there are relatively few people in North Sulawesi who do not have something to lose, and when times are bad the enhanced fear of losing it tends to make people more rather than less inclined to defend the status quo. It is telling that in this province the financial crisis which began in 1997, and the political uncertainty created by the fall of Soeharto in 1998, fostered conservatism rather than radicalism in political life. After the 1999 general elections the former New Order state party Golkar, with 20 out of 45 seats, was still easily the largest faction in the provincial assembly. In the 2004 parliamentary election Golkar was again the most voted for party in North Sulawesi, and in the first round of the presidential election of the same year Golkar candidate Wiranto obtained more votes in the province than did any of his rivals.

The economic consequences of the Asian financial crisis which precipitated the fall of Soeharto, it is worth repeating, were in any case less serious in North Sulawesi than in some other parts of Indonesia. One reason for this was political stability itself, which made the province an attractive haven for capital belonging to Christians and Sino-Indonesians displaced or threatened by conflicts elsewhere. Other factors, however, had to do with the diverse and partly export-oriented character of the provincial economy. Because the 1997 crisis was East Asian rather than global in scope, it had the effect of making many exports more, rather than less, profitable due to the falling value of the Indonesian rupiah relative to the US dollar. Nutmeg and cocoa growers in North Sulawesi, for instance, experienced boom times, and exports of coffee, fish, wood, furniture, and gold from the province also increased. For a time at the height of the crisis the weak rupiah brought traders from the Philippines, where the peso had lost less of its value, flocking to Manado and Bitung to buy a wide range of suddenly cheap Indonesian products. At the same time employment in the large and growing service and construction sectors enabled many others to share in the good fortune of the exporters, while savings and credit were available on a considerable scale to tide the least fortunate over. Among those worst affected by the crisis, it should be noted, were North Sulawesi's (mostly Christian) civil servants, whose privileged economic position was eroded as their salaries were overtaken by inflation.

If a relatively even distribution of wealth has helped to keep religious tensions under control, when it comes to the crude politics of demography it is precisely the imbalance between the province's Christian and Muslim populations which has been an advantage in terms of preserving the peace. Although a small and sometimes vulnerable minority in the Indonesian nation as a whole, Christians still form a large and fairly confident majority within the confines of North Sulawesi. Their lack of fear of the local Islamic minority inclines them to tolerate that minority and to accept its participation in the public and political life of the province – on a level, that is, proportional to its numbers. If elsewhere the call for 'proportionality' in government is usually a call for the political marginalization of Christians, in Minahasa it is a reassuring recourse for the Christians themselves. At the same time, the awareness of being a minority themselves at the national level is an additional reason for Minahasan Christians to avoid even the semblance of threatening Muslims. Their concern is not only that this would lead to hostile external intervention in Minahasa, but also that it might provoke acts of vengeance against fellow Christians elsewhere in Indonesia. Within Minahasa, the potential vulnerability of the Muslim group inclines its members in a parallel way to prudence and moderation. This situation is intrinsically more stable than one like that of Ambon in which the two groups are more equally matched, so that every economic rivalry from street vendors to construction contractors, and every public appointment from governor downwards, threatens to become an explosive winner-takes-all contest between Christian and Islamic blocs.

Demographic situations, of course, are liable to change. Due to a combination of faster natural increase and slow but steady immigration of Muslims from elsewhere, the Islamic part of North Sulawesi's population has long been growing more quickly than the Christian part. One reason why Minahasans were able to accept the separation of Gorontalo from North Sulawesi in 2001 with equanimity was that within what was left of the province, it restored a Christian majority which by that point had become vanishingly thin.

Percentage of population adhering to Islam in North Sulawesi, Minahasa and Manado, 1970-2002

	1970	1990	2000	2002
North Sulawesi	43.3	46.2	49.8	28.6
Minahasa including Manado	9.3	13.7	18.6	18.6
Minahasa excluding Manado	5.0	5.1	9.6	10.0
Manado city	25.0	28.1	31.4	31.2

Sources: Jones 1977; *Sulawesi Utara* 1991, 2001, 2003.

Preparations for the split began under the presidency of Habibie, whose father was from Gorontalo. Except for some mixed feelings among higher echelon civil servants about the reduced influence of 'Manado', most Minahasans have been almost as content to let Gorontalo go its own way as most Gorontalese have been to see Gorontalo emerge from Minahasa's shadow. North Sulawesi in its new truncated form is solidly dominated by Minahasan and Sangirese Christians, and only its southern division of Bolaang Mongondow is predominantly Muslim. The fact that Gorontalo is a poor area with few natural resources was another reason for Minahasans not to regret its loss, but apparently did not temper Gorontalese enthusiasm for separation. It should be added that in Gorontalo, where 98% of the population is Muslim, the religious factor as such is less often mentioned as a motive for the separation than it is in Minahasa – although some Islamic groups at national level rejoiced that 'the number of provinces with a Muslim basis has grown again' (Yogi W. Utomo 2000:76). Many Christian Minahasans still fear that in the long run, continued demographic change will still reduce them to a minority in their own land. A demagogue of any ability who advocated some form of ethnic cleansing as the only way to avert this fate would no doubt strike sensitive chords in public opinion. So far, however, no Minahasan leader of any description has chosen to blaze this one-way trail to conflict.

Underlying tensions

In some academic commentary on post-New Order conflicts in Indonesia, the religious tensions and ethnic identities involved in these conflicts are interpreted as rather recent by-products of economic competition, or as the results of deliberate attempts by either outsiders or local elites to create political cleavages (George Junus Aditjondro 2001; Van Klinken 2005). In the Minahasan context, however, such ideas are not very useful. Religious divisions in North Sulawesi are too intrinsic to the society to require any conscious construction in political contexts. At the first Indonesian general election almost 50 years ago in 1955, religion in North Sulawesi (at that time also including what is now Central Sulawesi) was already thoroughly politicized. Explicitly Islamic, Protestant and Catholic parties all appealed with success to their respective constituencies and the most successful secular party, the nationalist Partai Nasional Indonesia (PNI, Indonesian Nationalist Party) secured only 13% of the provincial vote (*Pemilu Indonesia* 2000:40).

At least in terms of church attendance and participation in Christian organizations, Minahasa is a Christian country to a degree which is sometimes difficult for Europeans to understand. Accordingly the area's Muslims, who with some exceptions are not regarded as ethnic Minahasans, are constantly aware of their minority status. Within the category of Christians there also exists an important Catholic minority, which forms a distinct socio-religious 'pillar' with its own institutions closely paralleling those of the GMIM. Catholicism, however, has very little to do with ethnicity, and under present conditions there is no potential for serious conflict between Catholics and Protestants in Minahasa. The potential for Christian-Muslim violence, by contrast, is real, and has been increased by alarm among Minahasan Christians at what they see as threats to their safety and way of life.

Most of these threats have originated from outside the region. Perhaps the most concrete of them was successfully averted in 1999 when six busloads (the first 300 of what was said to be an 800-man contingent) of *laskar jihad* militants, sent from Java via South Sulawesi to defend Muslim interests in Minahasa, were intercepted on their way to Manado and turned back by the provincial authorities. But the fact that elsewhere in Indonesia the militants were not sent home, and violence did erupt, continued to exert an unsettling influence. This was partly because of fears that the conflicts in the Moluccas and Central Sulawesi might be contagious, or reflect a nationwide anti-Christian conspiracy. It was also because many of the 80,000 refugees whom these conflicts brought to Minahasa came with such vengeful feelings toward Islam, and so little left to lose, that they were perceived as a real danger to the delicate peace between Muslims and Christians which people in North Sulawesi were working hard to maintain.

When renewed violence broke out in Ambon during April 2004, the police and military in North Sulawesi were kept on standby. The governor, via the medium of other prominent figures, urged the citizens of his province not to succumb to provocation (*jangan terprovokasi*). The disturbances in Ambon, he declared, were related not to religious differences but to the activities of a political group, the RMS (Republik Maluku Selatan, Republic of the South Moluccas). During this episode a Protestant leader in Manado wrote an open letter expressing his feelings, undoubtedly shared by the majority of Minahasans, on the limits to Christian solidarity where non-Minahasan refugees are concerned. Should things come to a Christian exodus from Ambon, he warned, the refugees must not be welcomed too hastily in Minahasa. Those who had arrived a few years earlier from Maluku Utara, he reminded his readers, had become a burden for the regional government and an unwelcome source of economic competition for the poorer part of the Minahasan population. A further large influx of refugees would inevitably lead to public disturbances and the return of Brigade Manguni thugs (*preman*) to the streets. Later in 2004 acts of violence against Christians in Palu (Central Sulawesi) once again raised the tension in Minahasa, provoking angry protests and Brigade Manguni motorcades.

North Sulawesi is a small part of a very big country, and the comfortable predominance which Minahasan Christians appear to enjoy within their own province contrasts with their status as a small and potentially vulnerable minority in the Indonesian nation as a whole. Just as the achievement of Minahasan civil society in preventing clashes between religious groups might be undone by failures of civility elsewhere in Indonesia, so the working relationship between local state and society in Minahasa periodically threatens to be eclipsed by policy initiatives from the centre of the state, Jakarta, which are perceived as hostile to Christians. The parliamentary debate in 2000 over the 'Jakarta Charter', a proposal to make Islamic law the law of the state for Indonesian Muslims, prompted talk of outright secession in Minahasa at the time, and its repercussions are still felt today even though the outcome of the debate was that parliament rejected the idea. Draft bills potentially affecting religious education in schools, and the position of Christian personnel in the health service, have generated similar anxieties and helped to ensure that theories of Muslim conspiracies against Christians remain favourite topics of conversation in small gatherings.

If Christian Minahasans are not particularly afraid of North Sulawesi's Muslim minority, then, they certainly fear the potential implications of Indonesia's Muslim majority both for national politics and for local Christian-Muslim relations, and few have much real respect for Islam in general. Antipathy toward Islam, in fact, is probably stronger in Minahasa today than it has ever been. In Sonder, a rural area in central Minahasa where the

Muslim population is particularly small, people are proud to tell visitors that there is not a single mosque in the subdistrict. Some local academics argue that genuine tolerance toward Islam cannot be expected in the foreseeable future, and that sights should be lowered to a target of what they call *akseptansi* – a contraction of *toleransi* (tolerance) and *akseptasi* (acceptance) which signifies passive resignation in the face of an unavoidable reality. Nevertheless it is against this background of private antipathy that the intensive public campaign for religious tolerance in North Sulawesi must be understood and appreciated. The apparently idealistic character of the provincial elites' joint peace propaganda effort – as part of which, to give just one illustration, Manado's most respected Islamic leader is regularly to be heard on the local Catholic radio station discussing the theme of 'living together in a plural society' – reflects not naivety, but urgent necessity.

Under the New Order the government of North Sulawesi, a province of unusual ethnic diversity even by Indonesian standards, had already begun to develop its own local variant of the national Pancasila ideology of 'unity in diversity'. This featured the slogans *torang samua basudara,* meaning 'we are all family' in the Manado dialect of Malay, and Bohusami, an acronym indicating the unity of the province's (then) four divisions and major ethnic groups, Bolaang Mongondow, Gorontalo (Hulondalo), Sangir-Talaud, and Minahasa. But it is only since the fall of Soeharto and the grim lessons of Ambon, Halmahera and Poso that the ideological campaign for religious harmony in North Sulawesi has really taken off. The new provincial slogan is *baku-baku baik, baku-baku sayang,* 'be good to each another and love one another', and the repeated references to love (*kasih, sayang*) in the campaign reflect a partly Christian inspiration. There are also references, however, to the culture and identity of pre-Christian Minahasa, which are portrayed as inherently tolerant and pluralistic in the same way as Indonesian national identity is tolerant and pluralistic according to Pancasila. In February 2003, an elaborate monument to religious tolerance was inaugurated by governor A.J. Sondakh – himself, needless to say, a Golkar politician – near Kawangkoan in central Minahasa. Called Bukit Kasih or 'Hill of Love', this is a kind of religious theme park, smaller in scale but even more ambitious in its symbolism than Jakarta's Taman Mini Indonesia Indah (Beautiful Indonesia in Miniature), containing juxtaposed replicas of a mosque, Protestant and Catholic churches, and Hindu and Buddhist temples. It also includes statues of Minahasan ancestor figures, and was deliberately built near the Watu Pinawetengan or 'Stone of Division' which marks the origin and ritual centre of Minahasa according to the modern interpretation of Minahasan paganism. In his inaugural speech, Sondakh described Bukit Kasih as dedicated to 'the spirit of the Minahasan people' (Ponsen 2003:63).

Just as Pancasila itself has always embodied a large measure of wishful thinking, so this Minahasan neo-Pancasilaism, with its emphasis on harmony and inclusion, is partly an oblique confirmation that the potential for discord is strong. In 2002, JAJAK (Jaringan Kerja Kasih, the 'Labour of Love Network'), an elite NGO backed by the provincial government and involving diverse North Sulawesi religious and intellectual figures, published a booklet entitled *Kasih mengubah dunia* ('Love changes the world') in connection with the province's official Year of Love. In his introduction to this anthology Suhendro Boroma, editor of the influential *Manado Post* newspaper and himself a Muslim from Bolaang Mongondow, frankly acknowledges the extent to which it is the threat of violence, graphically illustrated by events in nearby regions, which keeps the eyes of people in North Sulawesi focused on the prize of peace.

> The growing challenge we face in 2002 has to do with a weakening in the values of brotherhood and familial solidarity (*persaudaraan dan kekeluargaan*) which have served the Indonesian nation since its struggle for independence. Some areas in our immediate vicinity, including Ambon, Maluku and most recently Poso, have seen discord, conflict, enmity, and killing among fellow Indonesians. This is a concern and a challenge for the government and people of North Sulawesi, who must protect and maintain their own secure, peaceful and harmonious way of life [...]. We have all known the beauty and happiness of an existence built on love, togetherness and solidarity. That existence has enabled us not only to live our own lives and practice our own faiths in peace, but also to pursue all kinds of social and economic activities without hindrance. Government and society have been able to concentrate uninterruptedly on the task of developing North Sulawesi and improving its standards of living. Our foremost aim now must be to [...] maintain and enhance the environment of peace and prosperity [...] in the province. (Suhendro Boroma 2002:7.)

Despite its apparently hyperbolic idealism, then, the ideological campaign to preserve the peace in Minahasa is ultimately founded on a very pragmatic understanding that the price of failure to preserve that peace would be intolerably high for all parties.

Concluding remarks

Before Soeharto it was conventional to assume that the acknowledgement and politicization of ethnic and religious identities in Indonesia was a necessary and inevitable stage in the 'integrative revolution' (Geertz 1963) which would eventually bring about 'national integration' (Liddle 1970) on a democratic basis. The New Order's success in controlling regional and sectarian politics led many commentators to change their minds on this point. Now, however, there is an increasing consensus that New Order policies, particularly with regard to transmigration and the control of natural resources, generated more ethnic and religious tensions than they defused, and in the long run exacerbated those tensions by denying them any legitimate political expression. Whatever their precise triggers, the episodes of violence in Kalimantan, Sulawesi and the Moluccas since 1998 show that ethnic and religious differences remain potential lines of battle in future civil conflicts. By whatever means, the tensions surrounding those differences will clearly have to be dealt with after all. Against this background, the good news from post-Soeharto Minahasa is that even old, deep religious and ethnic divides need not lead to violent conflict provided the society so divided is also a civil society, provided economic and demographic conditions are favourable, and provided the state is able to play its proper role as ultimate guardian of the peace. Religious institutions, moreover, can themselves be supportive, up to a point, of civil society and a civilized state.

Most parts of Indonesia, sceptics will immediately point out, are not much like this. Minahasa's long tradition of contractual reciprocity between (local) state and society, in particular, is all too anomalous in the Indonesian context. It is hard to see how such a relationship, based as it is on trust, precedent, and a specific cultural environment, could be created at short notice anywhere else. Consultation between the leaders of different religious groups might be intensified in other provinces, but unless the leaders in question were inspired by the same level of commitment to peace which has animated their counterparts in Manado, and enjoyed similar degrees of authority over their respective followers, such consultation might still not accomplish much. And that economic equality moderates social conflict is little more than an abstract truism for regions which lack Minahasa's background of smallholder export agriculture developed in the absence of big business. The problem with trying to learn lessons from history is that history, being partly an accumulation of accidents, is seldom very replicable.

A different kind of cause for optimism, on the other hand, may be discerned in the fact that violent social conflict in post-Soeharto Indonesia, despite all journalistic and also academic alarmism, has actually been restricted to rather few and localized episodes, many of them deliberately fanned for political reasons by military interference (George Junus Aditjondro 2001; Liem Soei Liong 2002). This is not to deny that in some of the affected areas violence, as many chapters in the present volume attest, has been both acute and recurrent. The sustained rise of mob justice since 1998 is also a worrying trend (Colombijn 2005:250-1; Van Dijk 2002). Yet given the New Order's legacy of accumulated political tensions and resentments, the additional pressures brought to bear by economic problems and institutional changes, and the weakened and splintered condition of the state in many regions, the level of public order in Indonesia today can actually be described as surprisingly high. While the threat of lynching parties and the presence of mafia-style protection rackets undoubtedly have something to do with this, Indonesia is far from the condition of anomie found in many African countries where the state is weak and at the mercy of interest groups (Van der Veen 2004). If peaceful public behaviour even in the absence of effective state conflict management or law enforcement is anything to go by, then society in many other parts of Indonesia besides Minahasa is more civil than it is usually given credit for. The origins of this pervasive Indonesian civility deserve further investigation.

Acknowledgements

Among the many informants who contributed information and opinions which shaped this piece, the authors would especially like to thank the following: Arifin Assegaf, Stella Boestami, Suhendro Boroma, Nico Gara, Hetty Geru, Audie F.G. Joseph, Jootje Kawengian, Prof Adrian Lapian, Ferry Raymond Mawikere, Dr Arnold Fr. Parengkuan, Fendy E.W. Parengkuan, Jack Parera, Rev. Wempie Pepah, Tiene Pepah-Warouw, Prof. Ishak Pulukadang, Meriam Rau, Paul R. Renwarin, Prof. W.A. Roeroe, Markus Rumagit, Dr Donald A. Rumokoy, Dr Richard Siwu, Shelley Sondakh, Dr Bert Adriaan Supit, Dr Albert O. Supit, Leo Supit, Diana Tampi-Ratulangie, Prof. Hannie Waworuntu.

JIM SCHILLER

Civil society in Jepara
Fractious but inclusive

Introduction

From the early 1980s to the mid 1990s a thriving Jepara civil society emerged alongside a relatively responsive, development-oriented, 'Powerhouse' State. This chapter explores the character of New Order Jepara civil society and then looks at how that civil society has responded to the opportunities and constraints that accompanied the collapse of the Soeharto regime, the rise of the Reformasi movement, and the democratization that followed.[1]

Jepara is a district (*kabupaten*) on the north coast of Central Java with a population of 1 million. Its capital, also called Jepara, is 90 km from the provincial capital, Semarang, and 30 km from any major trunk road. Between its glory days in the sixteenth century and the emergence of a major furniture industry in the 1980s, it was a relatively isolated and under-developed region. Since the growth of that industry it has become one of the most prosperous non-resource rich districts in Indonesia. The prosperity is not equally shared, but many ordinary Jeparans have done well. In 2002, it had the second lowest percentage of families living below the poverty line in Central Java. Jepara is 93% Muslim. Even under Soeharto the 'traditional' Islamic organization, Nahdlatul Ulama (NU), was and is the hegemonic social institution, with considerable capacity to influence society and to confer or deny legitimacy to the state and its actions. While it frequently has accepted state patronage it has also maintained a degree of autonomy from the state. Muhammadiyah – NU's modernist Islamic rival – has a more recent and much smaller presence.[2]

1 Flinders University and the Australia Research Council funded fieldwork in Jepara. My thanks to Achmed Uzair who has been a diligent and capable research assistance. Earlier versions of some parts of this essay appeared in Schiller 2001.

2 Its political party (Masjumi) won 5% of the vote in 1955 and PAN – a post-Soeharto political party with strong connections to Muhammadiyah – won 6% of the vote in 1999. NU won 55%

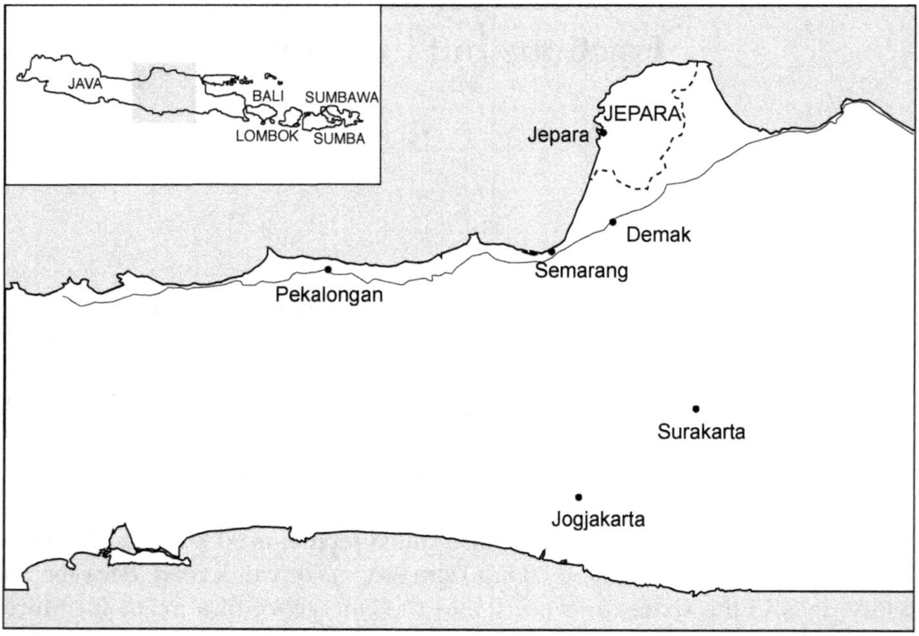

Map 13. Jepara in Central Java

Jepara in the New Order

During the New Order, the strong NU presence, the blossoming of a self-confident, non-crony, indigenous commercial elite around the furniture industry, and the electoral success of the overwhelmingly NU-based party Partai Persatuan Pembangunan (PPP, Unity and Development Party) resulted in a community, and a district assembly, more capable of making demands on local government and uncovering corruption or mismanagement than any other I have encountered. (I have observed and visited with state officials, politicians, civic leaders, and journalists in more than thirty districts and towns.) The commitment of many state officials to development ideology and the reality of a 'people not afraid to shout' (their complaints) led to a relatively more responsive and effective state.

I first studied state-society relations in Jepara in 1980-1982. I found a rather active local assembly (*dewan*), receiving numerous letters and delegations from aggrieved Jeparans, using assembly sessions to embarrass corrupt officials and sometimes modifying legislation to better suit their constituents. Assembly activism was led by PPP representatives who made up 40% or more of the elected members. The PPP representatives were more interested in assembly business than the Golkar majority who mainly had other jobs as state officials. The PPP minority was more willing to attend sessions and committee meetings and more willing to engage in protracted debate to make their point. Ideologically opposed to voting and unwilling to 'waste time', the Golkar forces often compromised with PPP proposals or acted on PPP complaints. As a result Jeparans got a somewhat more diligent, cautious and responsive local government. In today's terminology we would say the Jepara came closer than most districts to achieving 'good governance'.

My explanation for Jepara's activist civil society and developmentalist state was three-fold. First of all, NU had very wide and deep roots in society. NU's hegemony and its web of connections across Jepara and beyond provided those critical of the state with some shelter from official sanctions. NU demonstrated its community standing by winning more than 55% of the vote in the free elections of 1955 and then gathering 40% or more of the Jepara vote campaigning as NU in 1971, while using PPP as its political party in the next four New Order-controlled elections. NU had village elite support in most of Jepara's villages. Its religious teacher, landed elite, and small business leadership, in turn, provided the ongoing organization, patronage and activities, including *pengajian* (Islamic group religious studies) that sustained PPP between elections. It also mobilized financial and popular support for PPP in campaigns.

---

of the vote in 1955 and its constituent parties PKB (Partai Kebangkitan Bangsa, Party of the Awakening of the Nation) and PPP won 56% in 1999.

Secondly, Jepara's economy began to grow as Indonesia's oil boom economy led to mushrooming domestic purchases of Jepara's ornately carved teak furniture. Most of the businessmen involved were Muslim Jeparans with NU connections. After the oil boom ended, national policy promoted non-oil and gas exports and a thriving export furniture industry emerged alongside the domestic industry. Local state officials began to see that support for a business agenda and cooperation with business leaders was essential for success in their careers and could prove lucrative.[3] They also perceived that development projects could be successful if they cooperated with NU landed- and religious teacher-elites. At the same time the materialism of the New Order improved the status of NU landed elites and businessmen who could afford the consumer goods (cars, televisions, motorbikes and so on) that marked higher status. This increased their self-confidence, their influence in society and their sense that they could make demands upon the state and its officials. Like small business entrepreneurs everywhere, most saw themselves as the engine of development and saw the state more as an obstacle than a partner.

The third explanation is reputational and relates to the perceptions and actions of individual government officials. In the entire Soeharto period Jepara never had a military district head *(bupati).* Some retired officials thought that the position of Jepara district head was not lucrative and that moreover Jepara was a hazardous (*rawan*) posting requiring more sensitivity and less coercion. Jepara earned a reputation as a difficult place to be a state official, a place where the people were not afraid to speak out about official misbehaviour. As Jepara's military commander put it: 'The unrest that occurs here is a sign that the people of Jepara are certainly critical [...] Jepara people dare to react to every decision of the regional leadership'.[4] On the other hand its people (or at least its community leadership) were seen as capable of cooperating with state officials for their mutual benefit, if they were treated properly. For example, cooperation with NU community leaders could help keep order and assist in achieving development targets and winning development awards. These awards often led to promotion. The outsider bureaucratic elite that managed Jepara's government – mainly from culturally less Islamic southern Central Java – could have chosen to ride rough-shod over the local, more Islamic commercial and religious elite. Instead district heads

3 The best example of this is New Order elections in Jepara, in which local government officials tried to reduce conflict with local Islamic elites officials by resisting pressure from their provincial and central government superiors to deliver massive Golkar victories. The Golkar vote ranged from 15% to 30% below the provincial average.

4 *Suara Merdeka* 14-7-1999. This idea of Jeparans' critical and vocal character is also described in a series on Jepara identity published in the Jepara local government monthly magazine, *Gelora Bumi Kartini* in 2001.

and other senior state officials often chose to compromise and cooperate with local community leaders.

In short, I saw New Order Jepara as a place with a relatively strong civil society as well as a strong but relatively responsive local state apparatus.

However my research up to Soeharto's fall in 1998 left several unanswered questions about the nature of relations within Jepara civil society and between that civil society and the local state. Did Jepara have a battle-toughened, fractious, and antagonistic civil society? Was it dominated by a strong social organization (NU or the PPP part of it) to which neither the local state nor the society could easily say no? Or was it a civil society that had built up social capital, in the form of civility between social organizations and individuals and civic trust between civil society and the state? Was Jepara's civic culture based more on respect for what cooperation could achieve or fear of what other community leaders or state officials could do to you? The answers to these questions would determine how Jepara's civil society would respond to uncertainty and a changing political, social and economic environment.

Civil society

Robert Putnam (1993) defines civil society as the entire voluntary – not for profit – sector. He excludes the family, businesses and organizations whose main purpose is to win votes and elect politicians. That is a common practice but it seems fruitless to set artificial boundaries between political parties and other social organizations. This seems especially so in a place like Jepara where the hegemonic social organization, NU – surely the core of civil society in Jepara – had its own political party until 1973, and Partai Kebangkitan Bangsa (PKB, Party of the Awakening of the Nation) and PPP competed in 1999 over which party was the legitimate offspring of NU. For the purpose of this essay political parties are seen as a part of civil society. Only families and businesses are excluded. All other non-government organizations – big and small, altruistic or self-interest oriented – are a part of civil society. The focus here will be on how civil society influences politics and how Civil Society Organizations (CSOs) interact with the state.

Civil society is often seen as the key to achieving democracy and to making democracy (and economic development) successful. Unfortunately, civil society is an ambiguous concept. It refers to at least two different circumstances. In the first case strong social institutions deeply rooted in society are able to resist control by authoritarian regimes. This is sometimes called the counterweight concept of civil society. In the second case there is a dense web of social organizations that model or impart civility, cooperation and tolerance and create linkages between sections of society that encourage participation, civic trust, and cooperation. This is sometimes called social capital.[5]

Both of these manifestations of civil society are problematic. If civil society consists of strong institutions able to resist the will of the authoritarian state, what is to stop those same institutions from overpowering democratic processes and capturing democratic systems? Organizations that are powerful enough to resist authoritarian rule may be powerful enough to dominate weak states and to exclude the rest of the population from participating in or benefiting from democratic rule. On the other hand, if civil society is a dense web of social organizations encouraging civic trust and cooperation, how does that dense web come into being and how does the social capital it creates translate into the political cooperation and constraint necessary to make democracy or development work?

The civil society I have seen in Jepara most closely resembles this second, social capital type. Jepara has seldom fiercely resisted the state, rather choosing to bargain with the authorities for its cooperation. Whatever its shortcomings in Jepara, I will argue (as Putnam does for civil society in northern Italy) that it embodies real social virtues.

NU and Jepara civil society

In 1999 I wondered whether or not NU might be able to function as a core institution around which a tolerant but participatory democratic civil society could coalesce. Would it be able to provide a tent large enough to hold its PPP conservatives and its PKB reformers? Would its hold on the state continue to grow and would that diminish its willingness to act as a check on state excesses?

My picture of New Order Jepara depicts local civil society as interacting with national political and economic forces, including globalization, and influencing the actions of Jepara's community leaders, bureaucrats and politicians to create a relatively benign – and yet lively – climate for development and political participation. Here I would like to consider the ways that a CSO like NU can shape civil society and state-civil society relations.

Putnam sees two ways that CSOs may function to create civic trust and encourage civic engagement. Internally, they can instil habits of cooperation, solidarity and public spiritedness in their members. Externally, they can create a model of the pursuit of enlightened – or at least self-limited – self-interest. Under some conditions this can create a dense network of activist groups that have civic competence (that is, the style and skills necessary for public social and political activity), and some empathy for other community

5 This discussion of civil society types and argument about the ambiguity of 'civil society' takes off from ideas advanced by Foley and Edwards 1996.

groups. In other words it can create a culture in which demands are communicated and moderated. In such a climate political participants can afford to be 'good losers' or generous winners. This is much easier when many people belong to diverse organizations, have multiple divided loyalties, or have a world view shaped by a reference group with a diverse range of interests.

Alexis de Tocqueville famously described civic associations as 'free schools' of democracy,[6] in which people learn to cooperate while also competing. This is the opposite of 'amoral familism', which has been described as a way of thinking that emphasizes efforts to 'maximize the material, short-run advantage of the nuclear family and assumes that all others will do the same' (Putnam 1993:18). 'Amoral familism', which Putnam quoted from a study on Italy by Banfield, certainly has a place in Indonesian political culture too. The Javanese concept of *aji mumpung* – taking advantage of one's office – suggests that it is well known. The widespread application to Indonesia of the concept of patrimonialism – a system in which there are no fixed rules and everything depends on the relations between the ruler and the supplicant – also suggests that civic trust is not widespread. Neither the pursuit of short-term material gain, nor unbridled demands on the state when civil society that is too dominated by one world view or one interest group (the inadequate 'counterweight' concept) permits the promotion of healthy social cohesion and common goals.

Jepara NU

What I want to do now is to briefly describe how I think NU as a hegemonic, civil society organization plays a role in shaping civic culture in Jepara. After that I will look at the 1999 democratic election in Jepara and how the election reflected and in turn influenced Jepara's civil society. Finally, I will briefly consider how Jepara's civil society and state are interacting in post-1999 election Jepara. Six years into the 'Reformasi Era' does Jepara more closely resemble an inclusivist, trust-building civil society or an exclusivist, aggressive, civil society?

Jepara NU is a large and complex organization. It is reminiscent of what Alfred McCoy (1993), writing about the Philippines, evocatively called 'an anarchy of families'. Its leadership structure includes a chairman and executive board (Tanfidziyah) and a council of religious scholars (Syuriyah). It has district, sub-district and village branches across Jepara. It has numerous affiliated male and female, adult, youth and student organizations. It has educational foundations – Lembaga Ma'arif and Rabithah Ma'ahid Islamiyah

6 '[G]reat free schools to which all citizens come to be taught the general theory of association' (De Tocqueville 1969:193).

(RMI). Its members manage more than a hundred *madrasah* (non-residential Islamic schools at all levels), dozens of *pesantren* (residential Islamic schools), some Islamic secondary schools, a Timber Technology Academy (Akademi Teknologi Industri Kayu, ATIKA), an Economics Academy (Sekolah Tinggi Ilmu Ekonomi, STIE), and a university, Universitas Islam Nahdlatul Ulama (UNISNU). Its Institute for Mobilizing Human Resources (Lembaga Kajian dan Pengembangan Sumber Daya Manusia, Lakpesdam) runs community development programs and has initiated reconciliation programs between NU and Partai Komunis Indonesia (PKI, Indonesian Communist Party) families who had been victims of the 1965 massacres and mass detentions. The same organization runs forums for poor and marginalized groups. NU members also control numerous small credit cooperatives and a hospital.

Above all, NU provides its members – and many other Jeparans – with a shared religious experience and discourse, including prayer and religious study. Many future Jepara leaders meet through NU schools or youth organization activities. This shared life experience makes communication easier and, under the right conditions, encourages trust. Secondly, NU provides opportunities to develop organizational and leadership skills. Thirdly, success in raising money and completing projects teaches self-confidence and empowers local leaders by demonstrating that there are considerable resources and altruism in the local community. Fourthly, NU provides its members with the opportunity to learn how elections work. This includes the discovery that candidates may need to compromise to win elections and that winners need to consider the desires of those who have lost. (Of course, they may also learn that elections can be rigged!) For the entire New Order period, NU provided a counter-hegemonic model by successfully holding competitive internal national and local leadership elections.

NU also models a decentralized notion of power, with limits on what one faction or individual can control. Its division of power between its council of religious scholars (Syuriah) and its executive board (Tanfidzyah) and between leaders of NU and affiliated organizations means that it speaks with multiple voices and seems to tolerate a wide range of views. It also sometimes acts as a reservoir of trust able to negotiate within society and between society and state.

This sounds very promising for democracy. But Jepara NU also has some weaknesses as a 'free school of democracy'. Banfield's description of 'amoral familism' in Italy describes a world view that also has a place in the NU community. There are frequently problems with lack of transparency, nepotism, collusion and corruption in NU and its affiliated organizations. There is a fairly constant flow of rumours about school budgets being misspent, money for mosque building disappearing, and candidate lists being altered without authority. NU Jepara has never had a woman on its executive board and many of its younger members consider it to be patriarchal. However, there are also a substantial number of reformers in NU that criticize and try to overcome NU's 'weaknesses'.

So how did NU, Jepara's civil society, and state-society relations change amidst the economic and political crises that accompanied the Soeharto regime's collapse?

The economic 'crisis' in Jepara

> Rather, Jepara people felt good fortune because the dollar rose. Because they got a lot of money they prayed for the crisis to continue.[7]

Many Jeparans did well in the economic crisis. At least 80,000 Jeparans are directly employed in the furniture industry, in 1999 worth 400 to 500 million US dollars. The falling rupiah in 1998 actually spurred furniture exports and increased local employment and incomes. At the peak of the Asian economic crisis, the district was full of new furniture showrooms, fully occupied hotels, restaurants, and new shops. In 1998 Jepara sent more than 900 people on the *haj*, three times the number sent by the neighbouring district of Kudus and more than any other locality in Central Java. In 1999 it sent more than 2300, more than any other district in Indonesia. It has more motor vehicles (55,000 in total) than any district or town in Central Java except the capital, Semarang. Commercial and residential land prices are said to be the highest in Central Java and the cost of living comparable to Java's largest cities.

The furniture boom of the 1980s and 1990s continued with some ups and downs until 2000. My point is that economic decline was not the immediate cause of unrest and conflict in the 1998-2000 period. While Jeparans who did not work in the furniture or other export sectors were badly affected by the economic depression and inflation, jobs and wages in the furniture and other export industries increased and Jepara became a place where people moved to look for work.

7 Interview Pak Ali Irfan, NU educator, PKB leader and Deputy Chairman of the Jepara District Assembly, 14-12-1999.

Reformasi and the weakening of a 'powerhouse' state

I have elsewhere described the New Order local state in Jepara as a 'powerhouse' state.[8] A powerhouse state is one that is constantly growing in resources, in the scope of its power (the range of human activity it influences), and the weight of its power (the force and consistency it can bring to bear to influence its people's behaviour). A powerhouse state rests upon its citizens' belief that it will have ever more power and resources and that tomorrow it will have even more patronage to reward or deny you than today. For nearly 25 years the New Order government in Jepara had seen regular growth in its budget, its number of personnel, their salaries, their management skills, and its infrastructure (phones, computers, cars, offices).

How could such a strong state weaken? The answer is that the hopes, expectations and fears that accompany the national collapse of a long-standing authoritarian regime are likely to make for testing times even for its more responsive and competent local state apparatus. Reformasi in Jepara was no exception. It was clear by the end of 1997 that the Soeharto regime was in desperate economic difficulty. By May 1998 Soeharto was gone and the notion that state-society relations would change was widespread. Even before Reformasi, Jepara had a reputation (like much of the north coast of Java) as having a fractious, belligerent society with a history of anti-Chinese rioting, campaign violence, demonstrations, suspicious furniture warehouse fires, and angry deputations to the district government offices. While the local government had been more responsive to its populace than most districts, it had made a number of enemies. Its most divisive actions had probably been its efforts to manufacture election victories by Golkar (the New Order state party) or victories by pro-Golkar village heads.

The euphoria that followed the fall of President Soeharto saw the rise – across Indonesia – of a host of protests and ad hoc organizations, large and small, with reform goals. Jepara's local and village government leadership were targets of demonstrations and riots. Government records indicate that there were 1060 demonstrations (*unjuk rasa*) in Jepara in 1998-1999, peaking in mid-1998.[9] Protests occurred in 95 of Jepara's 192 villages and 120 of 136 village officials targeted were dismissed, placed on the non-active list, or

8 Schiller 1996 I borrowed the term from Geertz 1972, who in turn borrowed it from De Jouvenel 1962.

9 There were only three in 1997-1998 – just before the political crisis – and three just after it in 1999-2000. PEMDA Kabupaten Jepara, Jepara, 'Laporan pertanggungjawaban akhir masa jabatan Bupati Jepara kepada DPR-D Kabupaten Jepara 1997-2002', 2002:90.

reprimanded.[10] I am told that village head elections were held in more than three-quarters of Jepara's villages, many of them to replace unpopular New Order era heads, and to prevent demonstrations in still other villages.

The most important protests were the 5 July 1998 riots in which district government buildings including the library were burnt to the ground. This attack followed the government's decision to ban KH Afifuddin – a fiery, Islamic religious teacher – from leading a public religious lecture (*pengajian*) in Jepara. His preaching had previously been followed by anti-Chinese riots in Pekalongan and Demak. NU and PKB activists had appealed to the local government and local assembly to ban his visit, but PPP supporters were aggrieved by that decision and rioted.

Violence, or the prospect of it, was consistently read by government officials as a warning to lift their own act or face the consequences. Even before the July riots the district head tried to demonstrate his reform credentials by issuing a document entitled 'Report on the implementation of reform in every field'.[11] The report named a committee responsible for Reform and spelled out processes and legal charges for common government services. It warned officials that they would be held responsible for complying with these regulations. The district head also noted elsewhere that a legal system seen as corrupt, unfair and unresponsive was a major cause of discontent.[12]

As in many parts of Indonesia during the most turbulent months of Reformasi, Jepara civil servants feared wearing their uniforms in public or travelling in cars with government license plates. The police disappeared from the streets and the army withdrew from controlling mass demonstrations or riots. Civil service salaries fell in real terms and prospects for local state officials and state budgets did not look good. Civil service morale was at its lowest. For a time the local state almost shut down.

The Jepara government's inability or unwillingness to prevent the looting of its state teak forests, to put an end to violence between villages and against sub-district offices, as well as its failure to prosecute rioters, signalled a government that was no longer dictating to society, and perhaps, no longer in charge of society. In this vacuum, whatever fragile order was to be maintained depended upon the interaction of strong social organizations. It was a time in which mobilization of youth groups, militias and gangs connected to village and local patrons seemed to be increasingly important and the local state authorities, police, forestry police and military increasingly impotent. It was a time in which the civility and tolerance of civil society was tested.

10 Nota Dinas from Kepala Bagian Hukum of Jepara local government to the Jepara district head, 4-9-1998.

11 PEMDA Kabupaten Jepara, Jepara, 'Laporan hasil pelaksanaan Reformasi di segala bidang', 17-6-1998.

12 PEMDA Kabupaten Jepara, Jepara, 'Laporan pertanggungjawaban akhir masa jabatan Bupati Jepara kepada DPR-D Kabupaten Jepara 1997-2002', 2002:28-9.

The 1999 election expectations

It was in this setting, with a weakened state and a strained civil society, that the 1999 election was held in Jepara. This first post-Soeharto election could be expected to be a formative one for the democratization of Jepara. I want to consider what the election tells us about the character and working of civil society in Jepara.

The consensus among journalists, activists, politicians and state officials was that PPP – the old NU-connected party – and PKB – the new, more liberal NU-connected party – would compete for local dominance. Golkar's vote was expected to drop sharply and Partai Demokrasi Indonesia Perjuangan (PDI-P, Indonesian Democratic Party of Struggle) was expected to finish a distant third. The focus of the election watchers was on the contest between PPP and PKB. Would the new PKB party be able to attract votes away from PPP? In 1997 half of the vote had gone to Golkar. Which party would attract most of the 1999 Golkar voters?

Whether it would be possible to implement a fair election, free of violence, was also a matter of public concern. The danger that the election would be a disaster was made clear even before the official campaign began. On 30 April 1999, PKB attempted to establish a branch in Dongos, a poor, overwhelmingly PPP village in the sub-district of Kedung. The PKB supporters clashed with a much larger PPP crowd. It ended with four dead and more than a dozen people hospitalized. A number of houses and vehicles were also burned. The incident was widely reported in national and Central Java papers. The violence resulted in considerable fear that the election might spin out of control in Jepara. Newspaper stories worried that other districts with a potential for violence might be 'Jepara-ized' (*diJeparakan*).

Election results

Twenty-eight parties competed in the Jepara election. PPP (the old party of NU) won easily with 46% of the vote.[13] PDI-P (a successor party to PNI and the party of Megawati Sukarnoputri) came second with 20.2% of the vote. PKB (the new party of NU and Abdurrahman Wahid) was a close third with 18.9%. Golkar was a distant fourth on 8.7% and Partai Amanat Nasional (PAN, Party of the National Message, the Muhamadiyah-connected, coalition of Amien Rais) was fifth with 3.9%.

PPP was the clear winner, coming first in all but two of Jepara's 12 sub-districts and taking in more than double the votes of its nearest rival. PDI-P, despite its splintered organization, did a little better than expected, winning in

13 Election data was supplied by the Kantor Pemilihan Umum Daerah in Jepara.

Keling and Jepara sub-districts and coming second in five other sub-districts. PKB did less well than expected, coming second in Jepara sub-district and placing behind both PDI-P and its main rival PPP in eight sub-districts.

In reality PPP's victory was not as dramatic as it looked at first sight. Its vote only increased about 2% from 1997. The Golkar vote fell 46% from 1997, but only 2% of that went to PPP. PKB and PDI-P each obtained about 20% of the votes lost by Golkar. PPP's share of the vote in urban Jepara district and the furniture industry centre of Tahunan fell by 20% and 12% respectively. PPP actually finished fourth in Jepara town with about half the votes of PKB and PDI-P and slightly less than Golkar. Generally the data suggests that it was in the poorer rural villages near Demak that PPP did best and its vote declines closer to Jepara and to the agriculturally richer and less devoutly Muslim north.

PPP won 18 of the 40 elected seats in the 45-seat district assembly (Dewan Perwakilan Rakyat Daerah, DPRD), PDI-P 8, PKB 7, Golkar 4, PAN 2, and Partai Bulan Bintang (PBB, Crescent and Star Party) 1. The army and police were awarded the other 5 appointed seats. PPP emerged as the largest party in the assembly. However, it fell short of a majority and had to gain the cooperation of one or more parties to pass legislation or elect the assembly leadership.

Jepara perceptions of the election

So how were the campaign and election results received, and what explanations were proposed for the PPP victory and the PKB loss? These narratives on the election suggest a local state and civil society that was bruised by the campaign but still optimistic about the future.

Local state officials were generally enthusiastic about the election and the results. They felt that they had regained respect for their neutral, supporting role in a fair election and that the election result would take them off the hook as being responsible for all of Jepara's problems. As one middle level official put it to me: 'We can now appear in public in our uniforms'. They were also relieved that campaign violence was not as bad as had been feared. While some officials, who had been stung by PPP criticism in the past, would have preferred any other party (even PDI-P or PKB) to be the dominant party they also knew that 12 of the 18 successful PPP candidates – including the leader – had served in the previous assembly. Local bureaucrats may have had some difficulties with the criticisms they had received from the old assembly but there also had been some mutually beneficial cooperation. So, the bureaucracy, for the most part, seemed willing to accept a slightly diminished role and trust the new democracy with greater accountability to a PPP-lead legislature.

Many young community activists, most of whom supported PKB, were despondent about the PPP victory. Unlike the officials, they thought PPP was not too radical but too conservative. One comment was that the 'party which was fierce won'. Another comment in a village where there had been violence was: 'It's just the same, we only changed masters'. Several activists said: 'PPP won, they used the old ways'. By the old ways they meant the coercion, intimidation and vote buying which they believed Golkar had used in previous elections.

In fact, one of the surprises of the election was that there were so few serious incidents after Dongos. However, most people seemed to believe that the impact of Dongos was negative for the liberal NU party (PKB) even though most of the responsibility for the violence had lain with PPP. Dongos was said to have worked against PKB in three ways. Firstly, some NU leaders tried to distance themselves from PKB in order to restore peace in the NU community. Secondly, PKB curtailed its campaign in areas where PPP support was overwhelming and the risk of violence high. Thirdly, in some respondents' eyes, the impunity with which PPP followers were able to attack NU frightened away many waverers who might have been considering supporting PKB. It seemed that only PPP could protect their followers.

PPP was reported to have used strident campaign slogans and stories. PPP banners proclaimed: Islam is my religion, the *kabah* is my orientation, PPP is my choice, *jihad* is my struggle. PKB countered with slogans proclaiming that PKB was the 'sole child' or the 'legitimate child' of NU. PPP reportedly responded by spreading stories that PKB was 'the child of Golkar', 'supported by Israel' and 'supported by America'.

Everyone pointed to the role of *pengajian* (public lectures) in the PPP campaign and many noted the animosity expressed in PPP-sponsored public lectures. The leader of PPP countered that their *pengajian* had started way back in 1997, and argued that PPP activities were simply more popular than NU. A PKB leader noted that as early as 1998 PPP was holding *pengajian* two to three times a night in every sub-district.

Reports on the campaign by the Independent Election Observer Committee (Komite Independen Pemantau Pemilu, KIPP) listed numerous cases of intimidation by PPP crowds or by uniformed militia. The latter were said to be connected to Jepara underworld gangs like Sadigo (an acronym meaning 'a little wrong and I'll kill you'). Very few had been committed by other political parties. PKB leaders claim that religious teachers (*kiai*) associated with PPP banned their villagers from attending PKB rallies, and sent spies to see who went to PKB activities.

Stories about the PPP victory and PKB defeat emphasized the strength of PPP's organization and its hold on Jeparans. In tone this was remarkably similar to a 1997 Golkar analysis of the strong PPP performance in that election which stated that the problem was 'not enough NU *kiai*', meaning too many religious teachers whose loyalty was to PPP rather than NU (even though in reality all PPP *kiai* are also NU members).

Pak Ali Irfan, the deputy district head and a member of PKB, saw the election as a defeat for PKB but a victory for NU, whose elite chaired three of the four major parties: PPP, PKB and Golkar which shared about 70% of the vote.[14] He suggested numerous causes for PPP's strong showing. Firstly, he noted that some popular NU leaders either supported PPP or remained neutral. Secondly, he thought that Jepara's traditional population remained suspicious of change, including the new party PKB. Thirdly, he noted the effectiveness of the PPP campaign techniques and its hold over the population. He thought *pengajian* was more effective than media coverage and campaign rallies that preached to the converted. He said that the PPP hold on some villagers was so strong that, for example, the populace believed stories from their *kiai* that PKB leader (and later president) Abdurrahman Wahid was not really in Jepara or that they shouldn't go to hear him because infidels or Jews would be there. While he mentioned the role of intimidation it was not a major focus of his explanation for PKB's defeat.

PPP leaders saw the election result as due to their superior organization, their political experience and the gratitude of the Jepara people for their decades of standing up to the local government and its Golkar political machine. When interviewed, the PPP head and assembly chairman emphasized the cultural and religious activity of PPP. He said:

> It should have been in Jepara, with an NU absolute majority, yes it should have been that PPP was finished lost badly [...] We used *dakwah* (religious lectures) continuously so that our party activities became the culture of Jepara. [We used our] NU character so that compared to NU activity, there is more PPP activity in Jepara.

Three points are noteworthy about these views of the election results. Firstly, leaders of both PPP and PKB saw PPP's hold over the population through *pengajian* and through the village *kiai* network as central to PPP's victory. Reformist losers of this election, many of whom were involved in education and change-oriented CSOs, might be heartened by the thought that further education, better communications, and social change would weaken the village *kiai*'s hold on the population and ease the way for a more civil, less intimidating future election. In a climate of civility their chances of winning might improve.

14 The Chairman of Golkar was a dean from one of the faculties at UNISNU, Universitas Islam Nahdlatul Ulama in Jepara.

Secondly, the willingness of PKB leader, Pak Ali Irfan, to see an NU victory within a PKB defeat suggests that their NU loyalties might offer losers of future elections a notion that they still had a stake in whatever political coalition dominated local government.

Thirdly, the observations by CSO and community activists about the importance of intimidation and violence in the outcome reflect a liberal impatience with injustice. These reformers are a force for keeping violence – and the state's inability or unwillingness to prevent or punish violence – on the public agenda. Campaign and election violence and intimidation do indicate the presence of combative and exclusive groups in civil society, but the presence of groups and mass media willing to talk about violence might help to make that civil society more capable of compromise and cooperation.

Responses to the election

So far I have been arguing the case that, even though the campaign and election showed signs of suspicion, combativeness and aggressiveness within society, elite perceptions of the elections provided some signs of trust in society and some cause for optimism about future civility in politics. Discussion with PPP and PKB leaders about post-election politics generally supported the argument that there was sufficient trust so that politicians could compromise and work together.

A good example of this was the competition for chairmanship of the new local assembly (DPRD). PPP had won 18 seats but needed 23 votes to guarantee its candidate would win the chair. Pak Ali Irfan, the head of PKB explained that:

> At the time of the selection of the assembly chairman, there was a kind of competition between me and them [PPP]. Some championed me [...] it appears there was an effort to engineer things so I became chairman [...] I didn't like that because the result of the election should not deviate from the composition of the assembly [...]. If I became chairman of the council, while the one who received 18 [seats] became deputy chairman, that wouldn't be fortunate for Jepara.[15]

In the end the PPP candidate for chairman and the PKB candidate for deputy chairman were elected unopposed. Both the PPP and PKB assembly leaders report that afterwards there developed a spirit of cooperation and a combined effort to attend quickly to the many letters and deputations which the 1999-2004 assembly received from its aggrieved or hopeful citizens.

The network of NU friends and respected patrons continues to stretch across party divides. Among the PKB leader's close friends was Pak Jubaedi

15 Interview, Ali Irfan, 4-6-1999.

Ali, an extraordinary NU leader who stuck with PPP in 1999.[16] Pak Irfan said he meets Pak Jubaedi Ali frequently and also continues to meet a number of PPP-politicians on informal occasions. So it seems that the existence of an NU community has enabled Jepara's politicians to trust each other enough to withstand or repair the election damage to civil society.

The 1999 election as a snapshot of civil society

The breakdown of a long-standing authoritarian regime, the uncertain politics of Reformasi and the first democratic election in over 40 years is not an ideal time to see the best face of civil society. Most Jeparans had no experience with democratic elections or resolution of disputes. Many expected that Reformasi and democracy would quickly bring justice, prosperity and opportunity. Many others feared that it would bring revenge and chaos. Given such trying times and given that the election campaign began with massive violence at Dongos, Jepara civil society held up reasonably well. During the campaign there was some small scale violence and some intimidation, but the election was well received, especially by the leaders of the major loser, PKB. Furthermore, the post-election political responses by both the winner, PPP, and by PKB were conciliatory and cooperative.

It appears that at the district elite level there had been sufficient interaction so that both NU-based political parties had enough trust and shared enough civic culture to work together. However, a tolerant, cooperative, trust-building civil society is more closely approximated at the district elite level. At the village level, elite competition seems more severe and civil society more divided along party lines. Usually, the divide is between PPP and PKB but sometimes between those two on one side and the less well-organized followers of the secular PDI-P on the other.

A number of Jeparans described the village level struggle between PKB and PPP as a conflict between *kiai pesantren* and *kiai langgar* (charismatic Islamic teachers who run residential schools and Islamic religious teachers who are paid to give sermons or public lectures at privately owned small mosques). Their argument was that the *kiai pesantren* are less self-interested and more politically naïve, while the *kiai langgar* (called by one activist *kiai bayaran, kiai* for sale) are more worldly-wise and more connected to private interests. Behind their generalization was an important issue, namely the connection between religious identity politics and individual interests. While nearly everyone agreed that the individual interests of competing vil-

16 Pak Jubaedi Ali led NU from the 1960s to the 1980s. He briefly became acting district head in 1966. Pak Jubaedi resigned as district head when forced to give up NU for Golkar. He led PPP in 1982 when they narrowly defeated Golkar in the local election, and stuck with PPP in the 1999 election.

lage-level patrons were a substantial reason for the conflicts that did occur, it was religious and organizational symbols and loyalties that were used to mobilize supporters. PPP used every opportunity to paint its PKB rivals as the instrument of Golkar, or Israel or America, and as weakly committed to Islam. PPP tried to paint itself as on a *jihad* to defend and advance Islam. PKB, meanwhile, tried to portray itself as the official party of NU. One reference in a speech by Abdurrahman Wahid, PKB's leader and affectionately known as Gus Dur went: 'If NU is the chicken, it has two products. PKB is the egg and PPP is the shit'.

Gus Dur's rhetoric aside, what the PKB wing of NU was pushing was a nuanced view of Islam. As Pak Ali Irfan put it, PKB 'looks at people's conduct not their hats'. Its image – as a party that was 'liberal', willing to cooperate with Chinese and Christians, and willing to ally itself with Megawati's PDI-P – didn't work as well in the villages of Jepara as PPP's simpler message that it was the party of Islam.

The 1999 election's impact on civil society

So what effect did the first post-Soeharto election have on Jepara civil society? Did it lay a solid foundation for deepening Jepara democracy? Three aspects stand out.

Firstly, the PPP victory was not as bad for democracy as many have claimed. In victory they could afford to be magnanimous. If they had lost they would continue to be aggrieved. Faced with a share of power over local government they were compelled to do what governments do, to figure out how to make things work. That would make it possible for them either to win or to alienate supporters based on their policies and performance. Either result would encourage voters to offer support to parties based upon perceptions of their interests rather than loyalty to religion or organizational identity. This could be expected to take away some of the heat of identity politics.

Secondly, the role of various members of the NU elite as the main backers of PKB, in the leadership of PPP and Golkar, and as neutral public intellectuals, helped to break down identity politics, and this is likely to increase voters' sense that they do have freedom of choice. In 1955, if you were part of the 55% or so of Jeparans in the NU community, you voted for NU. In 1999 if you were an NU member you could vote for PPP, PKB or Golkar and still believe that you were demonstrating your support for an NU-led party. Divisions within the NU leadership may be worrisome, but one of the things they can do is to teach voters that authority figures can disagree or change their mind and that nothing terrible happens to a voter who makes their own choice, even if their local patron disagrees. As voters come to have multiple and cross-cutting loyalties, civil society will be enriched and campaigns and election outcomes will be less threatening.

Thirdly, while the Dongos incident was appalling, the response by the NU community was generally constructive. The NU and party elites from PPP and PKB seemed genuinely upset by the breakdown of order. The meetings called in response to Dongos by the civil and military authorities and by NU leaders from Jepara and from the province impressed on NU leaders as well as PPP and PKB politicians that violence could easily get out of hand. This led to a winding down of campaign intensity and rhetoric and taught some lessons about civic responsibility. Perhaps PKB retreated further than PPP, but both pulled back from the abyss.

I have argued that in 1999 Jepara's civil society was more inclusive at the district level and combative and exclusive at the village level. To some extent NU has been able to build and sustain a sense of trust and respect between political actors. Reformasi and the 1999 election challenged that inclusiveness. The conflict between PPP and PKB led to violence and considerable tension. However, the response to that violence – and to the election results – by NU and PKB have helped to restore a civic culture in which there is a degree of trust between political party and community leaders.

The 1999 election was the first democratic election in more than 40 years. In the uncertainty and euphoria of Reformasi that followed the fall of Soeharto's authoritarian regime it is not surprising that there was political violence in Jepara. The state party Golkar was clearly going to collapse, but it was not clear whether NU's old guard in PPP or its new, more liberal wing in PKB was going to fill that vacuum. The PPP-leadership felt that they had struggled for decades to represent Jepara's NU community against the Golkar juggernaut. They saw the PKB-leadership as upstarts plotting to harvest the fruits of years of PPP effort.

After the violence in Dongos, despite the invective and intimidation of the campaign, the election occurred without further major incidents. Perhaps civil society having learned from the 1999 election that the winner did not take all would be able to build a growing support base for democracy in Jepara. There were many challenges, for NU, and for the civil society it dominates. NU, its leadership, and its affiliated and spin-off organizations needed to be a source of community activism and remain critical of the state and political parties, while maintaining its capacity to be a conciliatory force. It needed to provide space for liberal critics and conservative religious teachers and party officials alike while maintaining its mass legitimacy.

17 One legislative election in 2004, two presidential elections in 2004 and one district head election in 2003.

2004 and beyond

Six years, four elections,[17] and a lot of political conflict and collaboration have gone by since the end of the Soeharto era. Gone too is the furniture industry boom and the teak forests that made Jepara prosperous. Employment, production and exports fell, largely due to the shortage of quality timber, the shipment of poor quality furniture, and the fear of foreign buyers to travel to Jepara because of Indonesian's terrorist problems. Weakened as well is the Jepara state, no longer such a 'powerhouse', and no longer able to count on rising budgets or selective patronage and repression to attract popular support or ensure community compliance. These have been far more demanding times for Jepara's civil society and state. However, I want to argue that on balance, a more tolerant, inclusive and participatory civil society has emerged. I also want to argue that under some circumstances a civil society that is tolerant, inclusive, and trust-building can contain within it elements that are fractious, critical, and argumentative.

The Jepara state continued to show signs of reaching out to civil society and trying to be more participatory. One sign of this was the Forum Lintas Pelaku (FLP, the Inter-Actor Forum) which brought together many of the district's development-oriented CSOs to implement or evaluate government programs and services. More than 30 organizations and most of the senior state officials attended regular meetings, which were often quite boisterous and critical of the state.

The state's acceptance of the growing role of civil society was perhaps most visible in the 2004 election. Nearly one year before the election the Jepara government appointed a five-member team to choose the Local Election Committee (Komite Pemilihan Umum Daerah, KPUD-kabupaten) nominees. The local government's choice for the selection committee included a lecturer at the NU university, a respected NU leader who was also the head of the Jepara branch of the Majelis Ulama Indonesia (MUI, Indonesia Muslim Scholars Council), a medical doctor, and a Muhammadiyah patron who is a major furniture entrepreneur. The selection committee chose ten nominees from the more than one hundred applicants in a transparent selection process. The provincial election committee (KPUD-propinsi) named the five appointees. Four were from an NU background and three of these were former activists in the NU student organization Pergerakan Mahasiswa Islam Indonesia (PMII, the Indonesian Islamic Student Movement). One KPUD member was a Muhammadiyah leader. Two were businessmen, two were academics and one was a religious teacher. Two had monitored the 1997 elections for the independent election monitor, KIPP and two others had been involved in the implementation of the 1999 election.

The Jepara electoral commission KPUD and its election oversight committee (Panwaslu, Panitia Pengawasan Pemilu) were respected community figures and they managed the campaign and election strictly, even-handedly, and without incident. Parties were provided with clear instructions about where, when and how they could campaign. Parties that violated campaign rules were warned and fined. For example the PKB leader, Gus Dur, arrived late for his scheduled campaign rally and was only allowed to lead a prayer.

The local 2004 legislative and presidential elections showed no signs of the violence and intimidation of the 1999 elections. Competition was keen and the dominant party PPP's share of the vote fell from 44% to 31%. My own analysis of voting patterns in village Jepara shows a large number of competitive villages where no party got more than 50% of the vote and many villages in which the party winning the legislative election did not win the presidential election. This indicates that voters felt a high degree of freedom to make their own choice.

It is interesting that there could be a 13% decline in the PPP vote without a strident campaign and without cries of foul-play from PPP. No one seems to have thought that the elections were won by intimidation or money. No one suggests that religious symbols and identity were important campaign tools. Civil society had guided Jepara through what could have been a stressful election year.

An inclusive civil society

Civil society has been enriched by a growth of reform movements and CSOs concerned with development, social justice, corruption and empowering people. Most of these organizations are led by people with NU backgrounds and degrees from universities in Yogyakarta or Semarang. Some of them focus on advocating the rights of fishermen, forest villagers and salt farmers. Others deal with property development, land rights, and environmental concerns. Several see their task as uncovering mismanagement and corruption in government or law enforcement. Some work together with local government in implementing and evaluating development projects. Others work as part of programs supported by national or provincial CSOs. They raise money from foreign donors, CSO networks, private individuals and the local government.

There is a running debate between 'soft' CSOs that accept state funding, accompany assembly representatives on 'junkets' or privately report corruption or mismanagement to local state officials, and 'hard' CSOs that organize public protest and report corruption to the media or to the prosecutor's office. However, despite the harsh words between them, there seems to be room for both radical and 'co-opted' CSOs in Jepara. Their leaders overwhelmingly share the same lifestyle, the same education, and the same religious, cultural and organizational experience. They also can choose levels of protest in their efforts to influence the state. For example, they fought for a local people's participation law (actually a freedom of information act) by sending letters from their CSO to state officials or the media. For further pressure they can mobilize supporters from several CSOs for public rallies. For example, when pressing for corruption charges against local assembly members they brought in national and provincial CSO dignitaries to their rallies to urge prosecution. Finally, they can gain public support from NU mass organizations and their leaders.

I am arguing that, so far, Jepara's civil society has managed to continue a 'big tent' format. It continues to be an inclusive arena for condemning, criticizing and sometimes cooperating with local politicians and the local state. It seems to have reduced the stridency and alienation of PPP, allowed the PKB supporters to find a role for themselves after defeat (for example as reformers in NU and in other CSOs), and spawned – or at least allowed room for – a new generation of boisterous reformers and radicals.

Those fractious radicals and reformers will pose new challenges for Jepara's NU-led civil society, as will the efforts by the state to coopt would-be critics or whistle-blowers. However, it seems likely that NU's ability to appear to rise above the fray of everyday politics, NU's habit of speaking with many voices, and its place in the community leadership all will sustain a fractious, lively and inclusive civil society.

TAUFIQ TANASALDY

Ethnic identity politics in West Kalimantan

Local politics in West Kalimantan have assumed a strong ethnic colouring since the end of the New Order.[1] Some of this has been conflictual, such as the violence in 1997 and 1999. Since the mid-1990s rifts have developed between the two biggest ethnic groups, Dayaks and Malays, over strategic appointments. Tension over political appointments aggravated after the end of the New Order, involving mass mobilization and sometimes violence. However, ethnicity also functions in quite peaceful ways in West Kalimantan, particularly after 2000. Indeed it can be argued that the politics of ethnic 'power-sharing' now widely adopted at the district level has successfully pulled the sting of the violence and prevented a recurrence of the episodes of 1997 and 1999.

This chapter describes the rise of ethnic identity politics in West Kalimantan and asks to what extent they also offer possibilities of civility (as well as the much better known possibilities of violence). It begins by introducing the ethnic politics of Dayaks and Malays prior to the 1998 reform (Reformasi). Ethnic politics here refers mainly to the politics played or led by ethnic elites to secure greater representation in the executive and legislative branches. The first two sections show that the Dayak political resurgence after 1998 was not an instantaneous movement, but a reaction to a history of repression dating back to the colonial period. The third section discusses how the authoritarian New Order regime retarded local politics and hampered discussion of ethnicity, and the unintended effects of this policy. The last sections discuss how the 1998 reform led to a resurgence of ethnic politics.

1 This chapter has benefited from critical comments made by Myrna Eindhoven, the late Isa Sulaiman, Gerry van Klinken, Henk Schulte Nordholt, Harold Crouch, Jamie Davidson, Melly G. Tan, Vedi Hadiz, and Claire Conway. I am grateful for informants in West Kalimantan who gave me interviews but who wish to remain anonymous.

Map 14. West Kalimantan

Dayak versus Malay: ethnic politics prior to the New Order

Identity formation

West Kalimantan, like many other provinces in Indonesia, has a diverse ethnic population. Based on the 2000 population census, the two largest ethnic groups are Dayaks and Malays, followed by Javanese, Chinese, Madurese, and Buginese (see Table). This chapter discusses only Dayaks and Malays. The Chinese and Buginese, the other important 'native' ethnic groups with long and significant associations with the province, will not be covered in this chapter, because neither of them have an ethnically consolidated movement in contemporary West Kalimantan.[2] Javanese and Madurese have only recently begun to arrive in significant numbers, and they also have not engaged in ethnic politics. Madurese come from Madura, an island off the northeast coast of Java, the most densely populated and politically central island in Indonesia.

Ethnic populations in West Kalimantan

Ethnicity	1930	1971	2000
Dayaks	48.9%*	41%	33.1%
Malays	28.5	39	32.4
Javanese	1.2	2	10.4
Chinese	13.5	12	9.5
Madurese	0.8	0.6	5.5
Buginese	6.6	5	3.3

(Residual 'others' account for totals just under 100%.)
Source: *Volkstelling* 1936; Tjilik Riwut 1979:49; Badan Pusat Statistik Kalimantan Barat 2001:34.
* Combines the categories 'Dayak' and 'unknown' (*onbekend*), who were mostly Dayaks.

The term 'Dayak' was first employed by Bornean Malays to designate native tribes in Kalimantan. It did not include the nomadic Punan. It was then popularized by European explorers through their writings (Lumholtz 1920:23). The encompassing term Dayak was deficient because it described hundreds of heterogeneous tribal groups. These tribal groups were 'united' only by external forces, such as discriminative policies from Malay sultans and Dutch

2 West Kalimantan Chinese played an important role in the region prior to Indonesian independence (Heidhues 2003; Bingling Yuan 2000). The role of the Buginese was also significant during the Dutch colonial era. Mempawah, one of the more influential sultanates in West Kalimantan, was Buginese. Other important sultanates such as Pontianak and Sambas also had ties with the Mempawah Buginese royals.

colonialists, as well as through religion.

Unlike the externally imposed term Dayak, the term 'Malay' was already widely in use before the arrival of Europeans in the archipelago. It described the inhabitants of many parts of coastal Sumatra, Kalimantan and the Malayan peninsula. In West Kalimantan, it initially designated people from Sumatra and the Malayan peninsula who came to West Kalimantan for trade and to spread their religion. Later, the term was expanded to include those Dayaks who had converted to Islam.[3]

Dayaks routinely experienced discrimination under the Malay sultanates and Dutch colonialism. In most sultanates, Dayaks did not enjoy the same rights as the majority Malays, and were not considered citizens (*anak negeri*). Dayaks were not allowed to work under the sultanates. They also suffered social vilification by Malays, which prevented them from participating in social activities beyond their own group, including education. As a result of these obstacles, Dayaks in West Kalimantan were entirely absent from political movements prior to independence.[4]

The rise and fall of Dayak politics

This situation started to change after the end of World War II. The Allied government led by NICA (the Netherlands Indies Civil Administration) established a Dayak Affairs Office in early 1946. It carried out a series of unprecedented reform initiatives for Dayak emancipation, and secured unconditional agreement from the revived sultanates to abandon discriminatory practices against Dayaks.[5] NICA pushed for higher education for Dayaks, facilitated their entry into the bureaucracy, and later the local parliaments.[4] These pioneering policies were of psychological importance to Dayaks. For the first time they were sitting in equal positions with Malay and Sultanate representatives in the government.

Another important actor in Dayak political emancipation was the Persatuan Dayak (PD, Dayak Unity Party), which was established in 1945. PD performed well in the elections in 1955 and 1958 when it won a significant number of seats in both provincial and district parliaments. A Dayak was appointed governor, and four became district heads (*bupati*). Some assumed positions as members of governing councils (Dewan Pemerintah Daerah,

3 Dayaks treated Dayaks who converted to Islam, also known as Senganan, as Malays. This was a consequence of the Senganan's renouncing their 'inferior' Dayak identities. Senganan would usually resettle in Malay villages, assume new names, adopt a Malay way of life, and claim to be Malay (V. King 1985:57-9; Tjilik Riwut 1993:191; Fridolin Ukur 1971:183).

4 This was not the case in Central Kalimantan. See Van Klinken 2004 and Miles 1976.

5 Kantoor voor Dajaksche Zaken, Pontianak, Notulen Vergadering di Sanggau pada antara Dayak dan Landschap, signed by Oevaang Oeray and assistant resident, 10-10-1946, pp. 4.

DPD, and later Badan Pemerintah Harian, BPH), and others took on leadership positions in local parliaments.[6]

As a result of national policy aimed at curbing regional political parties as well as internal rivalries within the party, by the early 1960s the PD had split into two factions. The biggest, led by the Dayak governor Oevaang Oeray and supported by most Dayak civil servants, joined the left-leaning national party Partindo. The other, led by Palaunsoeka and supported mainly by Catholic teachers and church personnel, joined the Catholic Party (Partai Katolik). This party was generally excluded from parliamentary politics in West Kalimantan from the 1960s until the collapse of the Soekarno government.

Dayak politics under a leftist Partindo suffered a significant setback after the 'communist' coup attempt on 1 October 1965. In mid-1965, under the initiative of the local military commander, West Kalimantan's Partindo branch merged into Ikatan Pendukung Kemerdekaan Indonesia (IPKI, League of Supporters of Indonesian Independence), here a small nationalist party dominated by Malays. After the merger, a clash of ethnic interests occurred within the party. The original Malay members felt threatened and were disappointed with the new leadership structure which included many Dayak figures. This culminated in 1968 when Tan Husni, a Malay and chairman of IPKI, expelled all ex-Partindo members from IPKI.[7] Although later annulled by party headquarters, the expulsion left a scar on relations between the two ethnic groups. It was one reason why many Dayak leaders were persuaded to join Golkar in the emerging New Order. Golkar had closely followed the internal friction within IPKI and wished to cultivate Dayak support. Its efforts however, were initially unsuccessful.[8] The patience of the regime ran out in 1971 as the general election approached. In January those Dayak leaders who had refused to join Golkar and who had links with the Chinese association Badan Permusyawaratan Kewarganegaraan Indonesia (Baperki, Consultative Body for Indonesian Citizenship) were arrested.[9] Oevaang Oeray, the former governor, was transferred to Jakarta at the end of March 1971. Without Oeray's presence, some ex-Partindo Dayak leaders yielded to the pressure to join Golkar a month later.[10] In the 1971 election, Golkar won

6 IPKI, Jakarta, Partai IP-KI Kalbar, IPKI document signed by Achmad Sukarmadidjaja, H. Djilis Tahir, 10-2-1971, pp. 6.

7 Davidson 2002:93-101; L.H. Kadir 1993:304-8; H.M. Baroamas Jabang Balunus n.d.

8 IPKI, Jakarta, Partai IP-KI Kalbar, IPKI document signed by Achmad Sukarmadidjaja, H. Djilis Tahir, 10-2-1971, pp. 6.

9 Dokumen Pemerintah Indonesia, Singkawang, Surat Perintah untuk menangkap/menahan sementara, issued by Laksus Pangkopkamtibda KB, Team Pemeriksa Kodim 1202 Sambas, 14-1-1971.

10 Golkar, Pontianak, Pernyataan bergabung dengan Sekber Golkar, signed by A. Djelani, P. Anjiem, I. Kaping, A. Sawa, J.M. Linggie, 17-4-1971, pp. 1.

21 seats in the provincial parliament (Dewan Perwakilan Rakyat Daerah, DPRD) or more than 66% of the total, whereas IPKI and Partai Katolik, the two supposed Dayak strongholds, won only two seats each.

Malay politics: a response

Malay politics differed from Dayak politics in many ways. The Malay outlook was integrated with national politics much earlier than that of Dayaks. Consequently, after independence, Malay politics were more nationalist, pro unitary state, and therefore Jakarta oriented; while the less exposed Dayaks formed their own local party and supported Dutch federalist policies. Most Malay bureaucrats did not at first consider the rise of Dayaks after 1945 a threat. However, ethnic tensions grew when angry Dayaks victimized some Malay elites in the Landak region, and created chaos in the provincial capital. More tension was prevented after Malay leaders in Pontianak backed down from their earlier demand to arrest the Dayak war leaders, fearing it could incite revenge from their followers (Hassan H. Basry 1961:69-70). From 1945 until the dissolution of a pro-Dutch administration in West Kalimantan in 1950, Malay and Dayak elites were at odds because of their different political outlook. Malays and Dayaks were at the brink of open conflict at the end of 1950 in the interior district of Kapuas Hulu. The Dayak rise in the bureaucracy after their successes in the 1955 and 1958 elections also did not go without reaction. In 1962 for example, non-Dayaks accused Oevaang Oeray of practising ethnic preference in recruitment and promotion of civil servants.[11] Allegations that he was creating ethnic fissures led in early 1965 to demands that he step down.[12]

New Order authoritarianism

The marginalization of local politics

The New Order never wanted to have strong local leadership, fearing it would lead to challenges to national leadership and in the worst case to separatism. One way to prevent this was to appoint 'national' civil servants, often from Jakarta, at the local level. Frequent rotation of key officials such as military

11 Dokumen Pemerintah Indonesia, Pontianak, Pokok: Permohonan pindah Sdr. Mochtarroeddin, pedjabat Wedana Putussibau ke Kantor Gubernur Kepala Daerah Kalimantan Barat, letter signed by Oevaang Oeray, 12-1-1962.

12 Surat Resolusi untuk meretul Gubernur Oevaang Oeray, signed by Abi Hurairah Fattah (PNI), Chris F. Hetharia (Parkindo), PF Soedjimin (PK), Ismail Hamzah (Angkatan 45), Pontianak, 8-3-1965, pp. 2.

commanders was intended to prevent them from cementing close ties with local political forces. In 1999, the majority of local department and bureau heads in West Kalimantan were non-locals, although Malays held some positions and Dayaks even fewer.[13] Another way was to centralize the recruitment of future local elites. Together with similar institutes elsewhere in Indonesia, the prestigious local civil servant training institute (Akademi Pemerintahan Dalam Negeri, APDN) in Pontianak was closed and replaced by a single institute (Sekolah Tinggi Pemerintahan Dalam Negeri, STPDN) in Bandung, near Jakarta, in 1992. Since then, the national institute has accepted only around ten students from West Kalimantan annually, which is much less compared to the 50 students annually, mostly locals, who entered the APDN Pontianak.[14] At the end of the 1960s and during the early 1970s, graduates from the APDN Pontianak had been fast-tracked to become sub-district heads (*camat)*. Fewer STPDN local graduates meant fewer locals to assume these strategic posts.

In an effort to ensure that national interests were paramount over regional ones, strategic decisions were made in Jakarta, in a top-down fashion. District head elections illustrate this. Usually, the central government pre-selected the district head prior to the selection process. It then closely monitored the whole process from the nomination until the election. The government had the power to intervene at any stage to ensure that its own candidate won.

The regime's policy was accentuated by a strong military presence. This was not unprecedented in West Kalimantan. The province's long border with Malaysia invited military attention. They were the dominant force during 'Confrontation' with Malaysia in the early 1960s, and even more so during the early New Order while they combated what they called a communist insurgency (Davidson and Kammen 2002). At this time the military took over strategic positions formerly assigned to civilians such as governor, district head, and parliamentary chairperson. Before the New Order there was only one military district head (Hercan Yamani of Ketapang). But by 1968, five of the seven district heads and mayors were military officers. Four district DPRD chairs were also given to military officers.[15] The power of the military was so great that their regional commander undermined the power of the governor. One high-ranking official revealed to me that Soemadi, the governor from 1966-1971 who was also a military officer, was agitated when the military commander bypassed him on several important decisions. Supported by an extensive command and intelligence network from the provincial down to the

13 ' Kemerdekaan, penindasan dan tuntutan merdeka', *Kalimantan Review* 48(1999):5-7.

14 APDN, Pontianak, Meletakkan landasan yang kokoh dalam mengembangkan kiprah organisasi beserta himpunan keputusan hasil Musyawarah I Ikatan Alumni APDN/STPDN se Kalimantan Barat, 1997.

15 Dokumen Pemerintah Indonesia, Pontianak, Laporan Gubernur Kepala Daerah Propinsi Kalimantan Barat dalam sidang terbuka DPRD-GR, Propinsi Kalimantan Barat, 11-3-1968.

village level, military bureaucrats effectively controlled local politics.

The New Order severely weakened once influential local bureaucrats and political parties. During the period between 1965 and 1971, political parties other than Golkar were demonized, repressed, and separated from their constituents, thus losing their influence. All civil servants, traditionally a source of support for political parties, were required to sever ties with these parties in 1970, prior to the general election. Under these conditions, the other parties fared poorly in the 1971 election, and never recovered. The 1973 national party restructuring caused serious internal friction within the parties, particularly during the general elections in 1977 and 1982. Continuous government interventions further crippled the political parties. For example in 1996-1997, the government effectively orchestrated PDI's West Kalimantan branch to oppose the leadership of the oppositionist Megawati, despite her popularity among party supporters.

Nation building and local culture

Particularly once the New Order was over, a cultural discourse emerged that blamed the New Order's promotion of a national culture for the degeneration of local culture. Dayaks in the NGO Pancur Kasih, for example, accused the New Order of dismantling their longhouses. Malays held similar convictions over their culture, saying that only Islamic symbols had survived the New Order.[165] Both cultures had already been in decline long before the New Order. Dayak culture has undergone rapid erosion since the introduction of Islam and Christianity. Indeed, earlier Dayak politicians had in fact asked Dayaks to abandon some 'antiquated' or 'extravagant' traditions in the name of modernity (Davidson 2002:97). Malay culture waned with the declining fortunes of the sultanates, the centre of Malay civilization in the past. The last remnants of the sultanates' administration *(swapraja)* were abolished prior to the New Order. However, the New Order should also share some of the blame, because it did not try to support those declining cultures, or at least did not prevent them from disappearing altogether. Some New Order cultural policies accelerated the dissolution of local cultures by absorbing them into a national culture.

Local icons that might threaten the country's unity and Jakarta's authority were removed. Sultan's palaces were converted into museums or left to decay. Longhouses, powerful symbols of Dayak communal life and unity, were largely annihilated during the New Order era. The regime claimed they were places of free sex and unhealthy living, fire hazards, reminders of headhunting, and, most importantly, media for communism (Djuweng 1996:7; Roekaarts 1985:15). Many functions attached to the longhouse ceased to exist.

16 'Pembangunan hancurkan kebudayaan Melayu', *Kalimantan Review* 48(1999):28.

Communalism and congeniality among Dayaks decreased, oral traditions were forgotten, and arts and performance related to life in the longhouse declined (Djuweng 1996:17, 124; Drake 1982:49-52). Many Dayak youngsters in the city do not speak their own language because they consider Indonesian or Malay to be more prestigious than their own languages.[17] Dayak cultural performances were portrayed as exotic and primitive. Shifting agriculture was held responsible for forest fires from the 1980s. The regime sponsored Christian missions to convert 'animists'.

Traditional authority was also affected by administrative changes. After 1979, traditional village heads were rapidly replaced by a younger but less respected generation of public servants. Robbed of their traditional authorities, villagers were drawn to modern apparatuses such as the police who were backed by state power, and thus they discarded many of their traditions. Reorganization of village boundaries after 1979 further jeopardized traditional leadership.

Transmigration, the expansion of plantations and logging activities added to the pressures on local cultures. Dayaks, who usually lived in small groups, became a minority in transmigration sites such as Seluas, in Sambas district.[18] Many inland villages now have Javanese or even Batak names.[19] Dayak NGO activists said that plantations and logging introduced prostitution and marriages of convenience (*kawin kontrak*). Locals were pushed to cut down trees in sacred forests for logging companies.

SARA and ethnic politics

The New Order opposed all discussion on ethnic or other 'sectarian' issues.[20] The regime feared such issues could lead to social instability or separatism. After 1971 no New Order census referred to ethnic groups. The West Kalimantan government followed instructions closely by not including ethnic information on their employee records.[21]

The regime also exercised strong censorship. The use of the terms 'Dayak'

17 Julipin and Pius 1987. Assimilation toward a more powerful and prestigious culture is often observed. In Norway, for example, the 'inferior' Sami were incorporated into the mainstream Norwegian culture (Eriksen 1993:29).

18 'Masalah kependudukan di Kalimantan', *Kalimantan Review* 19(1996):12.

19 Some Iban villages were given new names such as Toba, Pulau Manak, and Rantau Prapat by a Batak sub-district head in the early 1980s (Lumenta 2001:113). Javanese names were given to many new villages, and to some villages which previously had Chinese names.

20 Issues to be avoided were summarized in the acronym SARA, 'Suku, Agama, Ras dan Antar-Golongan', meaning Indonesian ethnicity, religion, race (that is, the Chinese) and 'class conflict' (that is, Marxism).

21 However, its provincial human resources department blundered by leaving religious information easily available. In West Kalimantan ethnicity can be easily identified through religion. The 2000 census once more included ethnicity as a category.

and 'Malay' in local newspapers was rare.[22] Much reporting on 'Dayaks' was camouflaged with terms such as isolated (*terasing*) or inland (*pedalaman*) groups. In reporting ethnic conflict, the media never disclosed the ethnic background of perpetrators. Its causes were always described as 'not ethnic' but 'common criminal' (for example *Akcaya* 16-11-1979). Ethnic-oriented NGOs were kept under tight control. They themselves often exercised self-censorship so they could continue their activities. Ethnic organizations established before the 1997 conflict, such as Pancur Kasih, refrained from mentioning the ethnic groups with which they were working.

However, the SARA-sensitivity of the regime did not prevent the eruption of several ethnic conflicts, notably between Dayaks and Madurese.[23] All these violent conflicts started with small altercations in which a Dayak was victimized, which triggered a strong Dayak reprisal. Government officials as well as social experts who analysed these events, particularly after 1997, often agreed with Dayaks that Madurese had been culturally insensitive and callous toward their surroundings.

Most ethnic violence involving Dayaks and Madurese in West Kalimantan does not appear to have been politically motivated. However, political elites did try afterwards to take advantage of them, particularly those that evolved into widespread violence such as in 1997 and 1999. Their role only appeared in the middle to later stages, after significant casualties had fallen. One of their motivations to become 'involved' was to secure ethnic concessions. In the conflict in 1996-1997 for example, Dayaks through their customary councils (to be discussed below) were merely intensifying long-standing demands for political positions for themselves.

Open ethnic politics were certainly not entertained during the New Order. However, they continued at a more subtle level after 1966 within West Kalimantan's bureaucracy. These were usually between Dayaks and Malays but also, for example, between coastal (Sambas) and inland Malays. In the early 1980s, Dayak politicians in Sanggau district (unsuccessfully) demanded several top positions. In 1982 they threatened to sabotage a Golkar victory in the district election.[24] In June 1993, several months after a successful national Dayak seminar, three Dayak politicians wrote a letter to the governor and all other related departments including the president, among others demand-

22 Between 1980-1990, the local newspaper *Akcaya* published only six articles on the Dayak (Davidson 2002:261).

23 'Sejarah perang suku di Kalbar', *Kalimantan Review* 50(1999):10; Davidson 2002. The only one of numerous events that did not involve the Madurese as the 'victim' was the conflict in 1967, when Dayaks expelled the Chinese population from the interior of the Bengkayang and Landak regions. Davidson and Kammen (2002) claim that this episode was driven by the military.

24 Golkar, Sanggau, Laporan khusus; Kelompok 11 di Sanggau, signed by Oteng Sukarna, 28-4-1981, pp. 6. [Introductory letter signed by Djalaluddin Latarissa.]

ing at least three Dayak district heads.[25] This demand was probably the entrée for the two most important cases of New Order ethnic politics in West Kalimantan: the district head elections in Sintang (1994) and in Kapuas Hulu (1995).

Sintang district head elections 1994

L.H. Kadir, a Catholic Dayak bureaucrat, was the government-favoured candidate in the Sintang district head election in 1994 (Tammar Abdulsalam 1997:157). The other 'accompanying' candidates (*calon pendamping*) were Abdillah Kamarullah and Abdul Hadi Karsoem, both Malay bureaucrats in Sintang district. Kadir's appointment seemed guaranteed because Golkar and the military faction occupied almost 80% of the seats. On top of that, Kadir also received support from other parties, particularly PDI which had four Dayak members. But the election in February 1994 turned out to be different from the usual scenario. Kamarullah won the election with 21 votes, while Kadir only got 16 votes, and Karsoem got one vote.[26] Malays welcomed Kamarullah's victory because two previous district heads had been Christians. For the Dayaks, Kadir's failure heightened their conviction that there had been concerted efforts to marginalize Dayaks in the bureaucracy. A Dayak head of the Golkar faction calculated that the defeat had been caused by the defection of almost half the Golkar members. I was told he was also convinced that the defectors were Muslim and non-Dayak (see also Davidson 2002:268). The fact that the regime immediately applauded the election result angered Dayaks (*Kompas* 12-2-1994, 2-3-1994; *Akcaya* 1-3-1994, 3-3-1994). It was highly unusual for the regime to celebrate the defeat of its own candidate. Dayak elites and commoners tried to reverse the result by sending delegations to Jakarta (*Kompas* 1-3-1994). Demonstrations were staged in Sintang and Pontianak (Tammar Abdulsalam 1997:161-2), and some Dayak politicians even threatened to quit Golkar if Kadir was not installed (*Akcaya* 1-3-1994; *Kompas* 2-3-1994). Golkar responded by sending a delegation to investigate matters (*Akcaya* 2-3-1994), but the government signalled it would not reverse the decision.

25 The letter dated 21 June 1993 was signed by G.P. Djaoeng, Rachmad Sahuddin, and A.R. Mecer, influential Dayaks. Djaoeng was the first Dayak district head elected in 1958. Sahuddin was involved in the establishment of district and provincial customary councils. Mecer was the 'brain' and one of the founding members of Pancur Kasih Foundation, a respected Dayak NGO. All were members of Golkar.

26 Kadir himself was not present during the election. One source mentioned to me that Kadir was not interested in the position because of family considerations. His lack of interest might have given incentives for the manoeuvres not to elect him.

After a delay to allow tensions to ease, Kamarullah was sworn in as Sintang district head on 5 April 1994 (Davidson 2002:268). The inauguration did not pass without incident. Two Dayak members of parliament, representing Golkar and PDI, interrupted the inauguration. In Sengah Temila, hundreds of kilometres from Sintang, hundreds of Dayaks vented their anger by blocking the main road between Ngabang and Sanggau and smashing windows of passing cars (Tammar Abdulsalam 1997:163; Davidson 2002:268). This event was the first open political opposition from the Dayaks. It showed that even an authoritarian regime could be 'challenged', and it set a precedent of overt ethnic politics for the next district head elections. All this helped to set the stage for a more severe conflict in 1996-1997.

The Kapuas Hulu district head election in 1995

The election of the district head in Kapuas Hulu in 1995 can be seen as a continuation of the unfinished Kadir saga. In order to assuage the upset Dayaks, the governor reserved this post for the middle-ranked bureaucrat Jacobus Layang. He was not the most senior Dayak bureaucrat, but he was certainly one of just a few to have climbed to the middle ranks.[27] His appointment benefited from his close relations with the military, as well as from his appointment as chairman of the newly established Majelis Adat Dayak (MAD, Dayak Customary Council).[28] Taking a lesson from Sintang, the governor had taken serious steps to prevent an unexpected result. Tammar Abdulsalam, Deputy Governor II who was responsible for elections in Sintang and Kapuas Hulu, was temporarily relieved from his duties. The main reason was his failure to deliver Kadir as Sintang district head the previous year. He was replaced by a confidant of the governor, the incumbent district head of Kapuas Hulu. To eliminate ethnic complications in the election, the Minister of Internal Affairs dropped two Malay candidates from the final list. The remaining three candidates were all Dayaks.[29] Finally, a senior Dayak politician, Iman Kalis, was dispatched as the governor's 'envoy' to Kapuas Hulu prior to the election to ensure the election of Layang.[30] The governor's precautions against a Malay

27 The only two Dayaks with higher provincial positions at that time were L.H. Kadir and J. Sotorman. The governor was not comfortable with 'weak' Sotorman, but at the same time he could not offer the position to Kadir, who had earlier been rejected in Sintang.

28 His relations with the military appeared to be more important than his role in the MAD, which had no political significance and little influence within the Dayak community.

29 The names of five candidates were sent to the Minister of Interior for final approval, two Malays and three Dayaks. Knowing that the government would give the position to a Dayak, these two Malay candidates claimed they were 'Dayak Islam' during the election process (Tammar Abdulsalam 1997:165).

30 This information comes from various interviews.

'scheme' proved to be wise. After the failure to get any of their candidates on the final list, the Malay politicians were manoeuvring to elect the 'best' Dayak district head who could serve their interests. They chose the terminally ill St Kupon. They believed his poor health would not permit him to serve for long, and his Malay deputy would soon take over.[31] They planned a narrow win for Layang one day before the election. With this strategy Kupon could win the election with only a small swing in the voting, and the schemers could avoid being blamed for insubordination because in an election small vote swings are always possible. Further, they encouraged sub-ethnic divisions between the Dayak members of parliament. Sensing the manoeuvres, Iman Kalis, the envoy, objected to the marginal winning strategy advanced by the DPRD. He insisted that Layang should have a decisive vote of 18, while Kupon would have only one vote. He also worked behind the scenes to 'unify' the Dayak vote behind Layang. Even after all these efforts Layang won by only a narrow margin, eleven votes to eight votes for Kupon. Thus increasingly confident ethnic challengers were beginning to threaten the central government's ability to appease this or that ethnic faction by manipulating parliamentary 'votes'. The next phase would be to go public.

Reform and the reinvention of ethnic identity

The politicization of ethnicity in West Kalimantan has a long history. It has been practised by the underdog Dayaks rather than the more powerful Malays. Like the Dayak elites, ordinary Dayaks also felt the deprivation and marginalization. The government had converted ancestral forests and lands into transmigration, plantation, and logging sites with the promise that they would benefit local Dayaks. However, many of these projects in fact worsened their living standards. As the problems increased, silent discontent was slowly transformed into more active protests. In the 1990s groups of villagers went to the local legislative assembly to demand justice in the form of compensation. As the government ignored these demands, peaceful engagements transformed into more violent protests manifested in the burning of plantations, confiscation, and blockades of access to plantations (Davidson 2002:264-6). Thus, Dayak elites, enlightened NGO activists, and ordinary Dayaks began to converge from the mid-1990s into an important political force and accelerated their political momentum. The district head elections of 1994 and 1995 indirectly strengthened the Dayak bonds vis-à-vis other groups. As the movements gathered momentum, Dayaks grew more prepared to act. The events of 1996-1997 became the turning point. It became

31 One high ranking official of Malay origin described the scheme to me as a wicked plot or *rencana busuk*.

the most violent conflict between Dayaks and Madurese in the history of West Kalimantan (Davidson 2003:71-6; Human Rights Watch 1997). After a long period of distress and marginalization, this conflict could be seen as a radical self-assertion by the Dayaks, in this case directed against Madurese immigrants (Davidson 2003:320-1).

The Reformasi of 1998 released a flood of contestation that had previously been taboo, also in the area of centre-region relations and ethnicity. Demands for greater autonomy, or even independence, were growing.[32] Other issues were the subdivision of existing districts (*pemekaran*) and the rights of native sons (*putra daerah*), both of which became vehicles for competition between the two main ethnic groups in West Kalimantan (Bamba 2002:6-7).

Peaceful ethnic politics after the New Order

Contrary to the exclusively violent images created by the widely publicized conflicts of 1997 and 1999, ethnic politics have become widespread and 'normal' in West Kalimantan, but also by and large peaceful. Indeed, the ethnic compromises reached in these politics are designed to short-circuit the recurrence of violent conflicts. The following sections describe the dynamics of these peaceful ethnic politics.

The creation of new 'ethnic' districts

The idea of subdividing districts in West Kalimantan was first discussed at the end of the 1950s, but not implemented as national politics took a centralizing, authoritarian turn under Guided Democracy. The issue resurfaced in the early 1990s. In 1996 the governor proposed some divisions (*Akcaya* 28-3-1996), but district heads and district legislatures cautiously preferred to await a firm decision from the top. However, within a year after the end of the New Order two new districts, Bengkayang and Landak, were carved out from the districts of Sambas and Pontianak. Despite government denials, ethnicity became a major consideration in this *pemekaran* process. Landak and Bengkayang were Dayak districts. In Landak, the Dayak population was 79% while Malays made up only 9.7%. The Dayak population in Bengkayang was 52.4%, while the Malay formed a minority of 18.7% (based on the Indonesian Census 2000). After the division, their respective parent districts, Sambas and Pontianak, became overwhelmingly Malay. The government drew the boundaries of the new districts according to ethnic lines. Thus the majority Dayak sub-districts of Mandor, Menjalin and Mempawah Hulu, which were originally to have remained with Pontianak district, were reassigned

32 *Akcaya* 27-11-1999; 'Baiknya kita merdeka sajalah...', *Kalimantan Review* 48(1998):8-9.

to Landak.[33] The government also fast-tracked the subdivisions in conflict-prone areas. Bengkayang, for example, was established earlier than the better-prepared but tranquil Singkawang. The formation of Kubu district (out of Pontianak district), which was proposed together with the formation Landak district but which has experienced no conflict, were delayed. The district subdivision in these cases are mainly about power sharing and gaining access to the bureaucracy. It was a conscious decision by the government to subdivide districts as a result of which Dayaks could have their own areas to govern. The aim was to prevent the recurrence of violent ethnic conflict that had happened in 1997 and 1999. This has so far been proven to be successful as the former hot-spots Landak and Bengkayang have been peaceful.

The election of the Sanggau district head

Under the New Order, district head elections were tightly controlled, and their results were usually predetermined before the elections. After 1998 the central government ceded most of its control to the local parliament (DPRD) (Malley 2003:109). This new arrangement was first tested during district head elections in Sanggau and then in the districts in Pontianak.

Sanggau's election process started in early 1998, still under the New Order. As usual, it proceeded under the strong influence of the governor, who favoured the head of his social political bureau (Sospol), Soemitro, for the job. But previous experience had taught the locals that ethnic pressure could swing the odds in favour of their preferred candidates. Malays had at least two main candidates, Tahir Herita and Setiman H. Sudin. Until the end of the New Order, Sanggau (like Sambas and Pontianak Municipality) had always been reserved for a military officer. This led some Malays at first to rally behind Tahir Herita, who had a military background. When Herita failed to make the shortlist, many switched their support to Sudin. The Dayak candidates were Donatus Djaman, Benedictus Ayub and Mickael Andjioe. For the same reason, most Dayaks rallied behind the military Andjioe. Their strong performance in the ethnic conflict of early 1997 had given Dayaks an enviable bargaining position. Dayaks had also started bargaining through the customary association MAD. Malays showed no signs of ethnic 'awakening' until the end of 1999. Thus the government thought it would be better to make some concessions to soothe the Dayaks.

Unable to diffuse the Dayaks' support for Andjioe, the government eventually gave in. He made it onto the list of five candidates to be sent to the Interior Minister only at the last minute. Still, Andjioe was pressed to with-

33 *Akcaya* 27-6-1997, 3-6-1998. Based on 2000 population census, those three sub-districts have between 70-90% Dayak population, and less than 7% of Malays.

draw from the competition some days before the May 1998 riots broke out in Jakarta. But President Soeharto's resignation in May 1998 had an immediate effect on the election process. The Dayak customary council which had been working hard for Andjioe's nomination stepped up the pressure. On 4 June 1998, the Sanggau DPRD wrote a letter to the governor and the interior minister suggesting that the 'old system' in the election was no longer proper in the era of reform. The 'people' of Sanggau had rejected Soemitro's nomination, the letter went on, and wanted Andjioe to retract his withdrawal.

Realizing the opportunities presented by the reform, Malay leaders who had been disappointed with the earlier developments were once more drawn into the process. Two days after the DPRD issued the letter, Malay leaders asked the DPRD to remain 'neutral' and not be influenced either by (Dayak) 'masses' or by Jakarta's demands. They wanted the DPRD to consider only three candidates in the package who in their view had demonstrated no 'complications' during the process: Donatus Djaman, Benedictus Ayub, and Setiman H. Sudin. They also expressed their respect for Andjioe's decision to withdraw from the competition (*Akcaya* 8-6-1998). Their requests were astutely devised to block the possibility of Andjioe's return to nomination, as well as to downplay the Dayak demonstrations.

However, the new government in Jakarta was responsive to the more forceful lobby and finally conceded to the Dayak demand. The Tanjungpura regional military commander retracted support for Soemitro, and gave his approval for Andjioe in June 1998. Four candidates were resubmitted to the Interior Minister in September 1998: Mickael Andjioe, Benedictus Ayub, Donatus Djaman, and Setiman H. Sudin. Djaman, an influential Dayak bureaucrat who was also the head of local Dayak Customary Council, was eventually dropped from the final list of three. The government probably feared that with influential Djaman in the race, the Dayak votes would be split, endangering Andjioe's chances. Andjioe won the election in early November 1998 with 29 votes, against Sudin's 12, and Ayub's 4 votes. At the end of the month, Andjioe was sworn in as the second Dayak district head of Sanggau, after more than 30 years.

District head elections after 1999 have been largely peaceful, mostly because of conscious power-sharing between Malays and Dayaks.[34] Both ethnic groups had reached an understanding of their respective ethnic domains. In the district with one dominant ethnic group, the district head and the deputy head are both to be from that ethnic group. This has been the case in the Dayak Bengkayang and Landak districts, and in the Malay Sambas and

34 There were some protests after the district head election in Kapuas Hulu (2000) and in Sanggau (2003). These were mostly related to intra-ethnic conflict, and therefore not amenable to inter-ethnic power sharing.

Pontianak districts. In districts with a mixed ethnicity, such as in Ketapang and Kapuas Hulu, mixed leadership is to be expected.

Regional representation

Another arena for ethnic competition has been the selection of Regional Representatives to the National Assembly (Majelis Permusyawaratan Rakyat, MPR). This is the country's supreme legislative body, and thus very prestigious. West Kalimantan was allocated five Regional Representative (Utusan Daerah) seats in 1999.[35] Understanding the possible ethnic tensions in the selection process, provincial DPRD members agreed to informally have the seats divided among the Dayaks, Malays, and Chinese according to a 2-2-1 formula: two for Dayaks and Malays, and one for the Chinese. However, when voting took place on 4 October 1999 the results did not match the formula. DPRD members needed to select five persons from more than 40 candidates. The Dayak vote was divided among four serious candidates. The results of the voting were Oesman Sapta Odang (34), Zainuddin Isman (32), Budiono Tan (29), Ikot Rinding (29), Chairil Effendi (26). This left Dayaks with only one representative, Ikot Rinding.[36] Feeling cheated, Dayak crowds waiting outside the building became enraged. Under this pressure, the DPRD members decided to annul the letter they had just signed, and promised to reconsider the election (*Kompas* 5-10-1999). The DPRD was committed to have two Dayaks, Ikot Rinding and Barnabas Simin. The Dayaks kept up the pressure until some time in November 1999, yet the DPRD failed to reconvene because of the lack of a quorum.

Safety considerations may have kept members from attending, but more likely the members, particularly Malays, were less than interested in giving in to the hardball game Dayaks had been playing since 1997. Most of those who prevented a decision by absenting themselves from the relevant DPRD meetings were from Islamic parties. Their confidence in going against the Dayak may have been the result of growing support from Malays. The latter had gained a tremendous boost of confidence and symbolic strength after their own conflicts with the Madurese early in 1999 (Davidson 2003:320). This had proven that Malays matched the physical prowess of the 'war-like' Dayaks.[37] The conflict had so markedly improved the Malay bargaining position in the new circumstances that it had reached parity with Dayaks. A new

35 Dayaks of Kalimantan were given one seat for Minority Representative.

36 'Politik reaktif di negeri dongeng', *Kalimantan Review* 51(1999):34.

37 The conflict itself was no less cruel than previous conflicts involving the Dayaks. Mutilation and cannibalism, although not part of Malay culture, were widespread during the conflict. In terms of ethnic cleansing, the Malay-led conflict achieved more than previous conflicts led by the Dayaks. Most of Sambas remained free of Madurese.

ethnic equilibrium had been reached. One Malay group, Aliansi Masyarakat Melayu Kalbar (the Alliance of Malay Community of West Kalimantan), issued a strong statement on 8 June 1999 warning Dayaks (though without naming them) not to turn West Kalimantan into another Ambon. Some days before, some Malays had clashed with Dayaks in front of the provincial DPRD, a scene not seen since independence. To back their stance on the MPR regional representative issue, Malay leaders argued that the original composition had satisfied the ethnic formula, since another member-elect, Zainuddin Isman, was also a Dayak, although Muslim.[38] In the end, Dayaks did not get the extra representative in Jakarta until the next round in 2004.

Ethnic identities were also being consolidated in less overtly competitive ways. Sanggau Dayaks, for example, inserted Dayak customary law into a 'village regulation' (Perda Kampung) that was passed by the district DPRD. A similar move is currently underway in Landak district. Malays rejuvenated cultural festivals and revived defunct sultanates. Many of these activities were organized or supported by ethnic organizations such as MAD, YKSPK, MABM, to be discussed below.

The role of ethnic institutions

The history of the Dayak Customary Council (MAD) can be traced to 1985, when a district level council was formed in Pontianak district. A provincial customary council (*majelis adat*) was established almost ten years later in August 1994.[39] Jacobus Layang, one of its founders, became its head.[40] Like other semi-state agencies, MAD's existence was closely linked to the regime. Its founding charter declared that it aimed to help the government relate to customary society (*masyarakat adat*).

MAD's officials were mostly civil servants. As a state-led organization involved in ethnic affairs, it adopted a cautious public profile. The district councils, established earlier than MAD, mostly 'socialized' government policies to the locals. MAD recorded no activities from the time of its inception until 1997, when the Dayak-Madurese conflict erupted.[41]

38 Zainuddin Isman was a second-generation Muslim born in Kapuas Hulu. Many Dayaks did not see Isman as a Dayak since he never admitted himself as a Dayak nor acted as one ('Kita menuntut keadilan', *Kalimantan Review* 51(1999):33).

39 The initiative, I was told, came from two well-known Golkar politicians: Rachmad Sahuddin and Ikot Rinding (see also *Kalimantan Review* 26(1997):22-3).

40 He was regarded as an expert on Dayak customary law. Layang was a visiting lecturer at Tanjungpura State University from 1979-1995. He had written several articles on Dayak customary law, and a book on the Dayak war against the Japanese during the Second World War. Davidson writes that Layang was pushed to form MAD in order to boost his profile as candidate district head of Kapuas Hulu (Davidson 2003:269).

41 MAD, Pontianak, Laporan pertanggungjawaban Majelis Adat Dayak Propinsi Tingkat I Kalimantan Barat Periode 1994-1997, 19-9-1997.

However, the ethnic conflict of 1996-1997 catapulted MAD into prominence. Caught unprepared and shocked by the extent of the conflict, the government turned to MAD for help. MAD mediated between Dayaks, the government, and the Madurese, and participated in government-sponsored peace meetings (see the details in MAD 1997). Understanding that the government could not dispense with its help, MAD seized the opportunity to bargain for political positions. In February 1997, when the conflict was still flaring, MAD organized a meeting to demand political concessions from the government. In the same month it produced a document claiming that Dayak marginalization was one of the main causes of the conflict, and urging serious efforts to remedy the situation. On other occasions MAD asked openly for several vacant bureaucratic positions to be given to Dayaks. Under such persistent pressures, the governor made some concessions. One of the first was the promotion of Ignatius Lyong to head of the provincial human resources in June 1997. After a few successes under this rather receptive governor, MAD became more aggressive. At its first plenary meeting in September 1997, MAD redefined its objectives by explicitly referring to Dayak interests. It changed its name from a generic Majelis Adat (Customary Council) to today's Majelis Adat Dayak. The name change had been suggested by the governor himself. MAD, together with other organizations such as Persatuan Intelektual Kristen Indonesia (PIKI, Indonesian Association of Christian Intellectuals) successfully lobbied the government for two Dayak district heads, in Sanggau and Pontianak District.[42] MAD continued to pursue Dayak interests, although it yielded little result after 1999. The once accommodative governor had become more resistant. He had discovered the Majelis Adat Budaya Melayu (MABM, Malay Cultural and Customary Council) as a counterforce to MAD. Also, internal friction began to weaken MAD and tarnished its image among Dayaks.

The Pancur Kasih foundation

Ethnic politics in the post-New Order period were not confined to elite manoeuvring for district leadership but also involved increased ethnic awareness among ordinary people concerned about their livelihoods.[43] Much of this awareness raising work was done by the Pancur Kasih foundation in Pontianak, a private NGO initially associated with the Catholic Church.

[42] Under its chairman Mian L. Simanjuntak, PIKI was very aggressive in demanding political positions for Dayaks and Christians. He was mysteriously murdered in January 2000. Many Dayaks saw the murder as politically motivated.

[43] Many arguments in this section follow closely Davidson's arguments (Davidson 2003:256-67).

NGOs under the umbrella Pancur Kasih Foundation always opposed MAD's approach. They believed that although MAD's jockeying had opened some opportunities for elite Dayaks, it did not benefit Dayaks in general. Nor had they forgotten that some district level customary councils (Dewan Adat Dayak, DAD) had acted as agents of the New Order to persuade Dayaks to let go their lands and forests (Bamba 2000:41).

Pancur Kasih was formed in April 1981 by several Dayak intellectuals and a pastor.[44] It was part of a network of Catholic institutions and related NGOs in Jakarta, which provided substantial financial support and also introduced its activists to new ideas and to some concerned foreigners.

Some of the most important NGOs under the Pancur Kasih umbrella are the Credit Union which works in the economic area, the Institut Dayakologi (ID) in the social and cultural area, the Lembaga Bela Benua Talino (LBBT, Institute for Community Legal Resources Empowerment) in indigenous rights, and Pembinaan Pengelolaan Sumber Daya Alam Kemasyarakatan (PPSDAK, Strengthening Community Natural Resource Management) in customary land mapping. These NGOs provide financial guidance and assistance, schools and scholarships, as well as more effective and acceptable agricultural practices. They also give legal advice and have equipped Dayaks with critical thinking to face encroaching forces under the name of 'development'. Whereas MAD has tended to be elitist and aimed only at political positions, these NGOs work at the ground level to assist Dayaks to improve their livelihood. This has earned them Dayak respect and support. In January 1997, a group of Madurese attacked one of the Pancur Kasih buildings and wounded two Dayak women. The attack sparked a deadly Dayak retaliation (Human Rights Watch 1997). The chairman of Pancur Kasih, A.R. Mecer, was appointed as the only Dayak representative for the whole of Kalimantan in the National Assembly MPR in September 1999 (*Akcaya* 15-9-1999). The organization's influence among the Dayak grassroots was recently proven again when a member of the Insitut Dayakologi was elected to the Regional Representative Council (Dewan Perwakilan Daerah, DPD) in Jakarta in 2004.[45]

The credibility of these NGOs on issues related to Dayaks, environment and conflicts, extends beyond the Dayak community. The government has consulted with the Institut Dayakologi for teaching materials on local culture. When the Provincial Statistical Bureau was fined by the MAD because of 'mistakes' in ethnic classification, the bureau consulted the institute for a

[44] Pancur Kasih's formal name was Yayasan Kesejahteraan Sosial Pancur Kasih (YKSPK). In 2001, the foundation was renamed as Union (Perkumpulan) Pancur Kasih.

[45] Four DPD members were elected from West Kalimantan, two Malays and two Dayaks. Maria Goreti was a staff member at ID of Pancur Kasih. Though her profile was lower than other Dayak politicians, academics, and priests who also ran as candidates, she won an impressive support, second only to Piet Herman Abik.

solution. Branches of national NGOs such as the Aliansi Masyarakat Adat Nusantara (AMAN, Alliance of the Indigenous Peoples of the Archipelago) and Wahana Lingkungan Hidup Indonesia (Walhi, Indonesian Forum for Environment) were mainly staffed by individuals linked to Pancur Kasih. Pancur Kasih has consistently focused its work at the grassroots level for almost 20 years. It has refused to get involved in parliamentary and party politics. However, some senior members, including A.R. Mecer, the founding member, were convinced they needed to work within the system to create genuine change. Mecer joined the Christian party Partai Pembela Demokrasi Kasih Bangsa (PPDKB, Defenders of Love the Nation Democratic Party) to compete in the 2004 election in West Kalimantan. The PPDKB quickly established itself in West Kalimantan owing to an extensive Pancur Kasih network. The party failed however to pass the national legal hurdles to participate in the election.

The Malay Cultural and Customary Council (MABM)

Malays were initially slow to take up the challenge offered by the growing Dayak assertiveness. West Kalimantan history reveals that Malays lacked the incentive to build formal ethnic organizations, since they already enjoyed their status as a 'ruling' ethnic group. Even during the heyday of the Dayak PD and Partindo in the 1950s, Malays remained the majority in the bureaucracy and parliament.

This all changed in April 1997, when Malays established the equivalent of MAD and named it Majelis Adat Budaya Melayu (MABM, Malay Cultural and Customary Council). It grew out of earlier similar associations in Sambas and Ketapang districts. It aimed to represent Malays at the provincial level. Already since the 1990s, the provincial government had had difficulty in directing a request for Malay participation for regional Malay conferences or meetings. MABM also aimed to restore the standard of living and revive the culture of Malays, which had been in decline after the dissolution of the sultanates and had been subsumed under a national New Order culture.[46] Despite denials from its founders, its birth was closely related to the heightened tension as a result of the ethnic conflict in 1996-1997. Malays needed a 'counter' for the Dayak political movements at that time (Davidson 2003:346). MABM's first few years were spent on consolidation. It set up branches at the district level, and focused on getting acknowledgement from the Malays. It kept a low profile during the period of transition in 1997-1998.[47] None of its

46 *Kalimantan Review* 48(1999):28.

47 From information obtained in various interviews it appeared that this restrained attitude irked the governor, who on several occasions, as if to balance the Dayaks' demand, urged MABM to take a more aggressive attitude.

overt policies posed a direct challenge to the Dayaks. Instead it has tried since its inception to be friendly towards its counterpart. For example, it continued to attend provincial Gawai Dayak festivals and participate in 'reconciliation' forums organized by Dayaks. During the 1998 crisis in West Kalimantan, together with other ethnic associations, MABM appeared repeatedly in the newspapers urging solidarity and unity among the ethnic groups.

Nevertheless, MABM could not prevent tensions between Malays and Dayaks from increasing. MABM started to build Malay Traditional Houses (Rumah Melayu) at the provincial and district levels, and encouraged Malays to wear *telok belanga* dress at festivals and religious events. MABM personnel lobbied the government to incorporate more Malay symbols such as yellow colour and *lancang kuning* (a traditional boat) in the government premises, such as at the entrance gate. Later, the very existence of MABM indirectly encouraged resistance to the Dayaks, such as occurred during the clash over the MPR representatives in October 1999 described above. The MABM profile was also raised when fighting broke out between Malays and Madurese in 1999-2000. The main actor in the conflict was the Forum Komunikasi Pemuda Melayu (FKPM, Union of Malay Youth Communication), a youth organization which had consultative relations with MABM.[48] Although relatively quiet in district elections in 1998 and 1999, MABM has been actively promoting Malay concerns in more recent elections. The MABM in Sanggau issued a 'warning' in the 2003 district head election not to have both a Dayak district head and a Dayak deputy. It suggested a list of Malay candidates for the deputy position, to pair with the Dayak district head candidate. In Landak and Sanggau, MBAM led the challenge to the implementation of Dayak customary law. For MABM, national law should always prevail over customary law, and the latter should apply only to the related ethnic group. To widen its influence, MABM maintained relations with the newly revived Malay sultanates, as well as Islamic organizations such as political parties, forums and universities. The objective was to build a stronger coalition vis-à-vis the Dayaks.

Concluding remarks

Throughout the post-independence history of West Kalimantan, except during the New Order, ethnic politics have been identical to Dayak elite politics. Dayaks were the only segment of West Kalimantan who constantly and overtly played on ethnic sentiments. They mostly wanted greater representation in the bureaucracy, citing a long history of marginalization. Malay elites

48 For the role of FPKM in the 1999 conflict see Davidson (2002:297).

were more inclined to avoid mobilization and engage in internal office politics, where they had a better bargaining position. The end of the New Order saw a resurgence of ethnic politics. Dayak elites, who had begun to challenge the regime in the mid-1990s, were the first to seize the opportunity offered by the changes occurring in 1998. By mobilizing the Dayak masses, these elites and some ethnic organizations were able to pressure the government to appoint two Dayak district heads. Malays, threatened by the rise of Dayak politics, belatedly formed an ethnic organization in 1997. After the conflict between Malays and Madurese in 1999, which gave them a tremendous boost, the Malays started to answer the challenges posed by the Dayaks.

After 1999, political dynamics among the Dayaks have changed. The customary councils that had played such an important role in 1997-1999 started to lose their influence. They lost ground because the key positions, especially the district head offices, were now institutionally shared between Malays and Dayaks. They also received less support from the grassroots Dayaks because of their elitist approach. Many Dayaks felt that supporting and cooperating with Dayak NGOs such as those under Pancur Kasih would bring more results to the people rather than supporting the MAD and DAD. Meanwhile, Malays created an effective counter movement. Malay-related organizations started to germinate after 1999. The nature of ethnic politics has also shifted from elitist 'power sharing' to more popular issues which affect a wider audience and address fairer civil service recruitment. The issues of district head elections, which used to be the paramount issues, ceased to dominate the agenda.

Ethnic identity will continue to play an important role in West Kalimantan politics, but in increasingly peaceful ways. The trend since 1999 shows that high ethnic politicization between Dayaks and Malays has not resulted in open ethnic violence. Instead, the ethnic politics now played consciously by both Dayaks and Malays has not only prevented further ethnic violence but is part of a new democratic and civil process in West Kalimantan.

ANDI FAISAL BAKTI

Family rule in Wajo, South Sulawesi

Introduction

In this chapter I examine the position of aristocratic power holders in the district of Wajo, South Sulawesi, from the late New Order until the elections in 2004. In particular I address the following questions: 1. To what extent was administrative power embedded in aristocratic family rule in the late New Order? Which families were involved, and how did they exercise their rule? 2. What was the impact of Reformasi and regional autonomy in Wajo? What changes can be observed? 3. What was the effect of the elections in 2004 on the position of the aristocracy? 4. Finally, what kind of changes took place in the local power structure between the late New Order period and 2004?

Christian Pelras (1976:314) analysed traditional authority in Wajo in the 1960s. He concluded that members of the aristocracy would remain in power, although in forms which differ from those of the past. Similarly Burhan Magenda (1989:891-2) emphasized with regard to South Sulawesi the survival of the local aristocracy within the administrative apparatus (*pamong praja*). The fact that the *pamong praja* had become the bastion of local aristocrats is not surprising given the fact that the local bureaucracy had grown out of the dynastic bureaucracy of the 'self-governing territories' dating from the colonial period. The decentralization reforms of 1938 brought about the enlargement of the dynastic bureaucracy, accommodating the fruits of expanded educational opportunities and a growing number of aristocrats (Burhan Magenda 1989:896). With respect to the Philippines, Benedict Anderson (1988) described a so-called 'cacique democracy', in which a well-entrenched oligarchy cooperates with a strong central state machine. Anderson showed how Filipino notables learnt to manipulate electoral politics during the Marcos era. In the following pages I will describe how the aristocratic elite in Wajo tried to survive with 'coerseductive' strategies,[1] when the political system to which they were accustomed began to change.

1 Syllogism between coercion and seduction, a communication concept introduced by Rene Jean Ravault (1985, 1986).

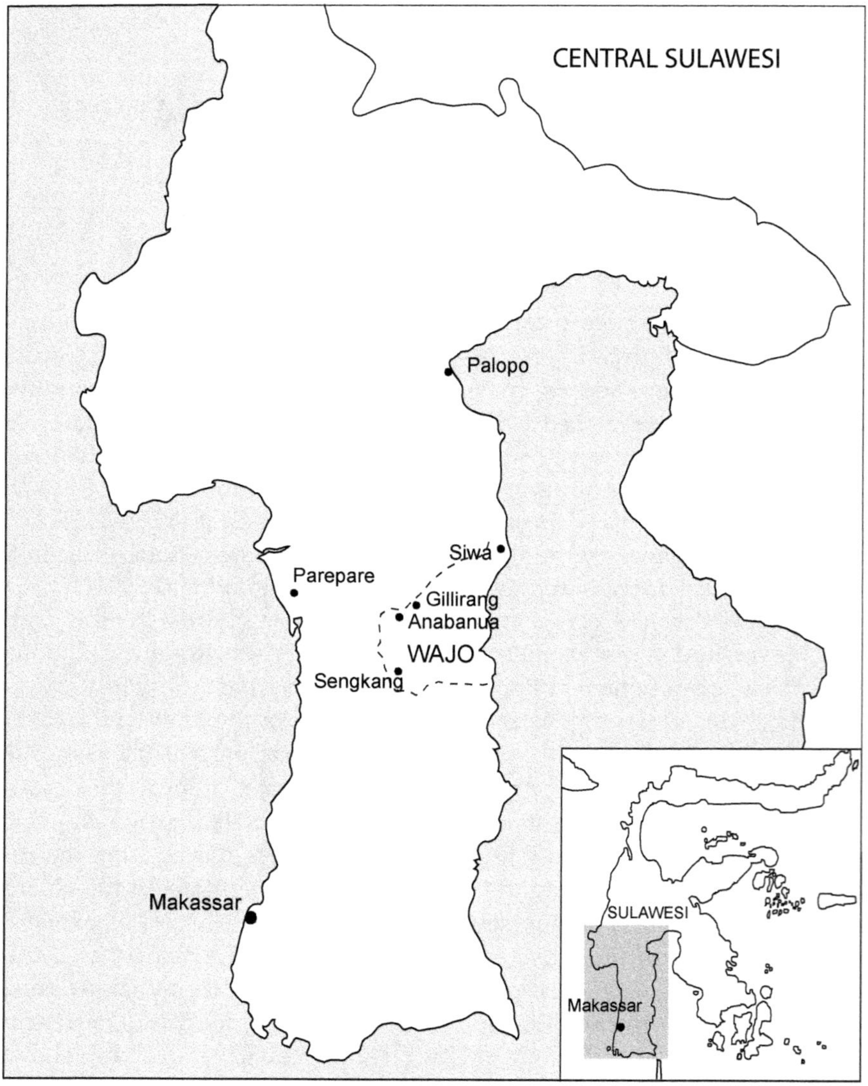

Map 15. Wajo in South Sulawesi

The role of the Wajo aristocracy in the late New Order

In the late 1980s one member of the aristocracy took measures to restore a solid administrative dynasty in Wajo.[2] This action was initiated by a senior Wajorese politician with a military background. I will call him 'the Puang', a term of reference used for Buginese of aristocratic descent. He was born in 1942 in Sengkang to an aristocratic family. After he finished high school he entered the army in 1965, whence he built an administrative career within South Sulawesi. He married the daughter of an aristocratic landowner and cattle breeder from Gilirang, and has four children. In 1995 he was promoted to the rank of Colonel. The Puang started his political career by joining Golkar in 1987 as a member of the Golkar Security and Defence Section, or Wanhat (Perlawanan dan Pertahan Golkar). In the same year he became a member of the Wajo district parliament (Dewan Perwakilan Rakyat Daerah, DPRD). In 1993 he was elected district branch leader of Golkar as well as of the Wajo DPRD, positions he kept till 2004, when we was eventually elected district head.

Although he gained power basically through the military and the Golkar party, he also used and strengthened his network of family connections. He appointed relatives to various strategic and 'wet', or lucrative, positions in the Wajo bureaucracy. Through the so-called 'Jalur Jati' (*jalur,* direction or way, which refers to Jalan Jati,[3] the street where the official residence of the chairman of the DPRD was located), people obtained a position or a promotion, and family members emerged as powerful bureaucrats.

The Puang has paved his way to family rule since 1983, when he was (until 1988) in charge of security at the Wajo district office. He succeeded in appointing his brothers and other relatives to different positions within the district office. In 1989 he showed an interest in becoming district head, but decided to concentrate on his military career instead.

In 1993 the Puang reinforced his power when his brother was appointed Second Assistant to the district head, in the Economy and Development Section, where he was in charge of the budget for development projects. This position is considered very lucrative, as its holder determines prices and expenditures and approves the allocation of projects to various contractors. Two other assistants (assistant one and three) are also related to the Puang. Although these do not directly manage funds, their signatures are required in order to approve projects. As all three assistants are relatives of the Puang, deals are concluded smoothly.

2 In 2002 Wajo had 359,326 inhabitants spread among 176 villages and small towns (BPS Wajo 2002).

3 It also mirrors Jalan Cendana, the street in Jakarta where the Soeharto family lives, which is similarly named after a tree.

In 1998, by which time he was chairman of the district parliament, he tried his luck again for district head, but lost the elections to a financially stronger non-aristocratic Buginese Golkar man who was supported by the central government.

The new district head was, however, to play a marginal role in Wajo politics, as he was soon overshadowed by the Puang. For despite his defeat, the Puang managed to strengthen his position in the years 1998-2004 as the number of bureaucrats related to him increased. A number of departmental heads, sub-district heads, and bureau chiefs were put in place through the Jalur Jati. The position of the Puang seemed beyond challenge, and as his power increased, many prominent leaders in Wajo claimed a family relation with him.[4] Important positions are basically shared amongst his aristocrat relatives and loyal allies. In the mean time, aristocrats not able to use the Jalur Jati are unlikely to be promoted. As one respondent said: 'We know that Jalur Jati is the way to obtain a job, but we do not know who to contact; and if we commit an error while doing so, we will not get a job and lose our bribe money as well. That is the risk.'

Another brother of the Puang is in charge of the Provisions Section (Kepala Bagian Perlengkapan), another lucrative position, in charge of the purchase of all sorts of equipment (television sets, computers, overhead projectors, radios, fax machines, typewriters), tools, vehicles, stationary, furniture (tables, desks, benches), clothes, gifts, and so on. As in many districts in Indonesia, the marking up or duplication of receipts is a widespread practice, and when an inspection is made, the inspector is bribed with plane tickets, hotel vouchers or money deposited in the account of a family member. Another practice is to provide inspectors with letters falsely attesting they have inspected a location (Surat Perjalanan Dinas, SPD), which allow them to claim travel bonuses from their supervisors without having to leave their office. The head of the Provisions Section cooperates with the heads of the Economy Section and the Sub-division of Financial Management and Regional Expenses (Badan Pengelola Keuangan dan Barang Daerah, BPKBD), both of whom are also close relatives of the Puang. Offices (*kantor dinas*) which are considered wealthy, such as Agriculture (the richest), Revenue (the second richest), Transportation, Land, and Information/Communication, as

4 Buginese kinship terminology starts with biological brothers and sisters, then first, second, and third cousins. Fourth and fifth cousins are seen as relatives. The children of these cousins are called nephews and nieces, and their grand-children are called grand-children, and so on. The fathers of these cousins are called uncles, and mothers are aunts, and their grand-parents are called grand-parents too. Thus the system of family ties facilitates a wide circle of relatives. For further reference on the Buginese family, see Millar 1989, Pelras 1976, 1996, 2000, Mattulada 1974, and Andi Faisal Bakti 2004. For an example of the familial way Buginese expand their power in Johore-Riau, see L. Andaya 1995.

well as Forest and Soil Conservation (Perhutanan dan Konservasi Tanah) are led by cousins of the Puang.[5] Furthermore, 10 out of 14 sub-district heads are aristocrats, and they all claim a place in the family tree of the Puang. Four are non-aristocrats, but are connected to the Puang through his relatives.[6]

Since 1988, the Puang had secured the support of members of the aristocracy and wealthy educated non-aristocrats within Golkar. His relatives included the second deputy-chairperson, second deputy-secretary, and third treasurer of Wajo's branch of Golkar. Three out of five section heads are relatives of his, while one of his sisters-in-law was chief of the Women's Affairs section. Apart from relatives, wealthy cronies included the first deputy secretary and the first and second treasurers. Other sections were headed by friends of his.

Although members of the aristocracy formed a minority within Golkar, they still held strategic positions.[7] Non-aristocrats form a majority in the Wajo district parliament, many of whom managed to graduate from Hasanuddin University in Makassar. As students, many had been active in organizations like Himpunan Mahasiswa Islam (HMI, Islamic University Students' Association), Mahasiswa Muhammadiyah (Muhammadiyah Students' Union), or Pergerakan Mahasiswa Islam Indonesia (PMII, Indonesian Islamic University Students' Movement). Usually, having joined one of these organizations, students also joined the Komite Nasional Pemuda Indonesia (KNPI,

5 In the non-departmental sphere a cousin of the Puang heads the Water Supply Agency (Perusahaan Daerah Air Minum, PDAM), where funds are also literally pouring in. Strangely though, the Logistics Depot (DOLOG, formerly BULOG), a lucrative section which manages agricultural products, in particular rice, is led by an individual not related to the Puang family. One respondent explained: 'The head of DOLOG is a Javanese, and is probably placed there by the central government'.

6 Out of 176 *lurah/kepala desa* (mayors/village heads), 59 are aristocrats and relatives of the Puang. While both govern the same village-sized unit, a *lurah* is in charge of a more developed village. *Kepala desa* are required merely to have a high school diploma. However, *lurah* are required to have an academic degree, preferably from a government academy like the Domestic Government Academy (Akademi Pemerintahan Dalam Negeri, APDN). One of these was formerly located in Makassar, before being moved to Bandung and given the status of College of Internal Government Science (Sekolah Tinggi Ilmu Pemerintahan Dalam Negeri, STIPDN). Most *lurah* belong to the aristocracy. Many Wajo bureaucrats, in particular in the district office, sub-district heads and their deputies, graduated from these government institutions. The networks of these state schools were further strengthened in South Sulawesi when Ryaas Rasyid, a 1976 alumni of APDN, became rector of the Institute of Ilmu Pemerintahan (IIP) in Jakarta, which also trains bureaucrats. In mid-1998, during the presidency of Habibie, he was appointed Director General of Regional Autonomy. He was then appointed Minister of Regional Autonomy and drafted the regional autonomy policy in Indonesia. Jamaluddin Santo is a close friend of Ryaas Rasyid, and also, through his wife, a relative of the Puang. Jamaluddin Santo's wife is a daughter of Datu Mungkace, a highly respected noble in Wajo, himself related to the Puang. Santo's wife also graduated from APDN and now works in Bappeda, under the leadership of the Puang.

7 See H. Schulte Nordholt in this volume for a comparable decline of aristocrats in Bali.

Indonesian National Youth Committee), an association affiliated with Golkar. It was considered to be a 'highway' (*jalur tol*) to Golkar membership. These organizations were quite successful in training emerging non-aristocrats in leadership, organization, and management, as well as administration in South Sulawesi, as elsewhere.[8] Some aristocrats were also active in these organizations, but they remained marginal.

The Puang was also deputy leader of ICMI's advisory board in the region through which he played a central role.[9] As the Puang advised on the names of new board members, he had a strong control over the organization. Interestingly, ICMI's treasurer was the same businessman who was also treasurer of Golkar. Another treasurer of ICMI Wajo also headed the Financial Bureau of the district (Badan Keuangan Daerah, BKD). While non-aristocrats are more numerous within the ICMI leadership than aristocrats, interviews show that they greatly respect the Puang.

The Puang also maintained close contacts with businesspeople. All wealthy individuals in Sengkang's central market, such as retailers and store owners, maintain a relationship with Golkar and make regular donations. Apparently, Golkar has a monitoring system to ensure that they remain faith-

8 In order to gain political power in South Sulawesi, one needs to gain access, via HMI and KNPI, to Golkar. This was also seen as an avenue for strengthening the position of modernist Islam. Some of these new emerging Muslims, like Marwah Daud, eventually dominated Golkar in South Sulawesi, and established direct links with party leader Akbar Tanjung in Jakarta, who had been a HMI and KNPI leader in the 1970s. However, during Habibie's presidency, this group was disappointed by Akbar Tanjung who competed with Habibie for the Golkar leadership presidency. Habibie comes from Sulawesi and was the preferred leader to South Sulawesians. After Habibie's defeat, disappointed Muslim Golkar leaders established a regional caucus within Golkar named Iramasuka (Irian Maluku, Sulawesi, and Kalimantan). In the late New Order period, the role of other parties (PDI and PPP) was limited. Only those who strongly believed in political Islam supported PPP, while PDI was basically supported by the Toraja minority of Christians in Sengkang, Bottodongga, Siwa, and Lauwa.

9 ICMI (Ikatan Cendekiawan Muslim Indonesia, Association of Indonesian Muslim Intellectuals) was established in the early 1990s and provided then-Minister of Technology Habibie with a strong constituency. In many cases, governors and district heads became ICMI leaders. ICMI soon branched out throughout the world, in particular in cities with Indonesian embassies and consulates. As a result of ICMI's popularity, ambassadors and consuls almost automatically became ICMI leaders abroad. In South Sulawesi, the retired governor was the advisory board leader of the provincial ICMI branch. A number of former rectors and university professors became deputies or secretaries. In addition, Muslim entrepreneurs, including the spouse of the 2004-2009 elected vice president Jusuf Kalla and her associates were named treasurers.

As ICMI is closer to so-called modernists than to traditionalist Muslims, many among ICMI's board members belong to the Muhammadiyah or HMI. A university professor at the Alauddin Institute (IAIN Alauddin), who graduated from the University of Michigan, became an advisor for ICMI in Wajo and South Sulawesi. He is also the top leader of the As'adiyah Pesantren in Wajo. The Puang supported this *pesantren* financially. While ICMI's board of South Sulawesi mostly includes hajis and non-aristocrats, Wajo board members are mostly hajis and aristocrats with family connections to the Puang.

ful to the party and to consider whether these entrepreneurs should be promoted within Golkar. In fact, one of the biggest businessmen was made treasurer of Golkar.[10] The Puang granted contracts to wealthy entrepreneurs, all Golkar district parliamentarians and who included the treasurer of Golkar, for the construction of district offices and the public transportation terminal in Sengkang. These government projects thus benefited both the Puang and his cronies. As Golkar treasurer, the wealthy Wajo entrepreneur was granted a large number of contracts by the government, including the construction of a road between Ana'banua and Tarungpakkae, a ring road in Sengkang, and a road between Sidrap and Siwa. Apparently, government projects are routinely offered first to state-owned companies (Badan Usaha Milik Negara, BUMN) and then sub-contracted to his company.[11]

Reformasi and regional autonomy (1998-2003)

After Reformasi the Puang further strengthened his position and took advantage of regional autonomy by keeping relatives and cronies in key posts. Even appointments in companies and NGOs which are not under his direct authority ultimately end up on his desk for approval.

As a result of regional autonomy, the district head is no longer controlled by the provincial governor and the central government. The district head is no longer accountable to the provincial governor but to the members of the district parliament. This explains why the Puang is struggling to ensure that these members – and not only his own Golkar people – are loyal to him. Since 1999, the struggle to obtain parliamentary seats is quite open and new parties have mushroomed. Although Golkar and the military (Angkatan Bersenjata Republik Indonesia, ABRI) fractions continued to dominate, the 1999 elections brought change as PAN, PKB, PPP, PDR, PBB and PDI-P each obtained one seat.[12]

10 His business includes ten motorbike dealerships, construction companies, textile production, bookstores, contracting offices, etcetera. He also has branch offices in Makassar and Jakarta.

11 Working closely with the Puang is a Chinese businessman. He owns PT Nei Dua Karya Persada, which deals in real estate, construction/development, car rental, gold and electronic equipment retailing. He has been a Golkar treasurer II (Deputy Treasurer) since 1988, when the Puang recruited him. This businessman has financed Golkar and contributes to Golkar's electoral campaigns. In return he gained access to various government projects.

12 Partai Amanat Nasional (PAN, Party of the National Message); Partai Kebangkitan Bangsa (PKB, Party of the Awakening of the Nation); Partai Persatuan Pembangunan (PPP, Unity and Development Party); Partai Daulat Rakyat (PDR, Islamic People's Sovereignty Party); Partai Bulan Bintang (PBB, Crescent and Star Party); and Partai Demokrasi Indonesia Perjuangan (PDI-P, Indonesian Democratic Party of Struggle).

The power of the Puang was strengthened through his relatives and cronies in the administration from the district to the village levels, as well as in parliament, so that it reached a state of near hegemony. The case of Wajo does, however, not represent South Sulawesi as a whole, where aristocratic hegemony is less evident as only 12 out of 28 district heads belong to the aristocracy.

In 1999, the Puang was elected by the DPRD as chairman for another term. Golkar still dominated the 1999 elections as it won 26 seats. Although the aristocracy formed a minority in the DPRD (with only 10 out of 36 members) the Puang controlled the non-aristocratic members as well. Wealth, education, or marriage into the nobility made it possible for non-aristocrats to become members of the DPRD.[13] They were approached by the Puang to join Golkar and they even constitute the majority in Golkar (19 out of 26).

In contrast to the composition of the DPRD, the top layer of the Wajo bureaucracy is heavily dominated by the aristocracy, as they occupy 90% of the higher positions. They are all believed to have entered the bureaucratic elite through the Jalur Jati.

The general government assistant, simultaneously head of information and communication, and the tax revenue head are uncles of the Puang. The Puang's cousin, formerly a sub-district head, now heads the Environmental Protection Programme, with a significant budget for ecology. While his brother-in-law heads the General Government Administration Section (Kabag Tata Pemerintahan Umum), his cousin, son of a former district head in the 1960s-1970s, was named district secretary. His two brothers remain in their positions, as respectively district government assistant for economy and development, and provisions section head. The Head of the Incomes Section remained under the leadership of his nephew. Two relatives from Gilirang, the town of origin of the Puang, are head of Information and Communication, and Third Assistant (Administrative and Finance). The head of transportation is a close relative of the Puang. Two relatives of the Puang also remained at their posts as head of Agriculture and Forest, and of Soil Conservation. The chief of the Security Bureau is the Puang's cousin. Ten out of fourteen sub-district heads are said to have been promoted through Jalur Jati. The sub-district head of Tempe (Sengkang) is the Puang's cousin. The General Election Committee (Komite Pemilihan Umum, KPU) was also headed by a close relative of the district chief. A son of a former district head (in the 1960s) was appointed head of Guidance and Counselling (*penyuluhan*), while the district secretary is a son of another former district head, and an aristocrat.

The Puang also maintained his grip on the Wajo business community and in particular the small group of Chinese entrepreneurs. Regional autonomy

13 Thirteen members of the DPRD are hajis, which indicates their wealth.

had changed the way in which these entrepreneurs operate. As one entrepreneur explained:

> Regional autonomy facilitates our business and lobbying. During the previous period, the bureaucracy was very complicated and we had to lobby in Jakarta. Now, everything is done here. The DPRD is also independent now, so we can easily lobby each parliamentarian. Under the previous district head [1998-2003], the district government was strong. But, imagine, since regional autonomy and a district head who is an aristocrat [referring to the Puang], government is even stronger now! In addition, under regional autonomy, there is less paperwork and lobbying is easier. I attended the same school as the current district secretary, which makes it easy to have access to the bureaucracy. I am also a close friend of the head of Facilities and Provisions, who is a brother of the Puang. These links helped me join Golkar, and become deputy-treasurer. This position gives me an opportunity to have access to Golkar's leaders. I was even asked to become a Golkar legislative candidate in the last elections, but I declined, as I prefer to do business.

In Wajo, civil society organizations were not able to establish an independent counterweight to the dominance of the Puang. Instead, they were incorporated into his regime.

As'adiyah, the oldest religious school (*pesantren*) in Wajo is affiliated with the Nahdlatul Ulama, but supports Golkar. In return the Puang granted the *pesantren* various facilities, such as a school and a dormitory, mosques, and houses for teachers, and donated Rp 100 million to renovate the *pesantren* leader's house.

Similarly, Muhammadiyah in Wajo is also not very critical. But DPRD members of PAN, the political party most closely related to Muhammadiyah, voiced criticism about corruption and the dominant role of the aristocracy, as a result of which they were eventually isolated by the Puang group.

Among the 400 NGOs in Wajo, only four are perceived as critical. They include AISS (Aku Ingin Sehat Sejahtera, 'I would like to be healthy and prosperous'), and the Sabri Study Club. The leader of AISS complained that many NGOs stopped criticizing government wrongdoings once they were seduced by money or coerced by the Puang. She criticized in particular the Puang, his relatives and followers for monopolizing the leading positions in Wajo. She mobilized people in Sengkang in order to clean up the Muslim cemetery, the dilapidated state of which had been left unnoticed by the government. While some bureaucrats under the Puang have called her mad or strange, she has a growing number of sympathizers, as her actions demonstrated that it is possible to criticize the government without being arrested.

The Sabri Study Club has cooperated with AISS, but its leader's preoccupations basically lie with education and language. He is worried about the fate of the Buginese language, and the reluctance of the government to promote local cultures and Islamic education. According to him, Islam should allow anyone, irrespective of his or her origins, to rule the region.

According to another NGO activist it seems that regional autonomy has made bureaucrats at the district level into warlords:

> District secretaries are very powerful. In addition, all staff members have to 'obey' the district head, which for them represents the aristocracy. They have been coerced to vote Golkar. Individuals are also promised they will keep their positions or will be promoted following the election of a selected candidate. Usually, politicians promise a community or a village they will get a road or a mosque, if they are elected. The government has also given money to opinion makers. A motorbike was promised to each village head (*kepala desa*), while individuals were offered a trip to Mecca as a reward for their support.[14]

In South Sulawesi several cities have their own newspapers. The city of Makassar has *Pedoman Rakyat* and *Fajar*, the most widely read newspapers in South Sulawesi. The *Parepare Pos* is published in Parepare, while Palopo, a city in the north, has the *Palopo Pos*. Sengkang had the *Merdeka Pos*, which was closed in January 2004, after two years in business. Many believe that this latter newspaper was created by the Puang for the sole purpose of supporting his election as district head. After the Puang was elected, the newspaper lost its usefulness and was closed.

Some of the newspapers were quite critical of the misconduct of the South Sulawesi government including the Wajo administration. *Pedoman Rakyat, Fajar, Parepare Pos* and *Palopo Pos* often published articles and letters to the editor on malpractices by Wajo bureaucrats, entrepreneurs, and members of parliament.[15] However, it appears that journalists have also been approached and bribed by government representatives in order not to publish these stories. The practice occurs on both sides. According to an NGO leader:

> We sometimes meet journalists seemingly 'without a press', who have introduced themselves and interviewed us. As we were critical of the Puang administration, they asked us to pay them in order to print this interview, to make the news. However, although we paid, we have never seen that interview published, either because the newspaper for which this journalist supposedly worked does not exist, or because this journalist was bribed further in order for his article not to be published.[16]

14 Apparently, some members of the 'Success Team' of the Puang were brought to Mecca for *umrah* (short pilgrimage).

15 For example the inappropriate involvement of the Puang's cronies in the various projects has been exposed. Quite often, local issues are covered, such as embezzlement of project funds (a Rp 20.3 billion port construction project in Bansalae, North Wajo, see for example *Fajar* 2-3-2005) and the controversy about a rice processing centre in Ana'banua, Wajo.

16 See also McCarthy in this volume.

The elections of 2004: old networks in a new context

Four months before the general elections in April 2004, the Puang was elected by the members of the parliament as district head, and was officially inaugurated in February 2004. His 'opponent', who received only three votes, was an aristocrat from his own family whose candidacy had to demonstrate that democracy is operative in Wajo. The position of district head was the crowning of a long political career, but soon his solid powerbase in the DPRD would be challenged.

During the elections of April 2004 for the district parliament, Golkar had to face a serious decline in popular support as it lost 9 seats (from 26 to 17).[17] As a result, Golkar also lost the majority in the DPRD of Wajo. The decline of Golkar would have been more dramatic without the efforts of the Puang to consolidate the position of Golkar. According to a member of the KPU (the General Election Committee), a letter of the Puang circulated among the members of the KPU and the bureaucracy in which he instructed the lower administrative officials to secure a Golkar victory.

The main challenge to his regime came from two modernist Islamic parties, PAN and PKS (Partai Keadilan Sejahtera, Prosperous Justice Party). PAN managed to win five seats and based its emergence on a substantial Muhammadiyah following. PKS is a new party without a strong local constituency, which nevertheless won four seats. Its rise can largely be attributed to the fact that the party used Habibie's picture on its campaign leaflets throughout South Sulawesi, thus suggesting that Habibie was its presidential candidate (although Habibie was at the time not even in Indonesia).

These changes did not immediately imply that the Puang had lost his dominance in the DPRD. The number of DPRD members with an aristocratic background rose from 10 to 14, the majority of whom were in one way or another connected with the Puang.[18] Also in terms of wealth, representatives of the upper middle class, many of whom are allied with the Puang, still dominate the DPRD of Wajo.[19]

Conclusion

In general, tensions between aristocrats and non-aristocrats seem to have

17 In 1999 the members of parliament numbered 36, but since the military seat was removed after the 2004 elections, this went down to 35. As Golkar won 17 out of 35, its share was reduced to less than 50%, a serious blow to Golkar's popularity.

18 Only 10% of the population belongs to the aristocracy, but this group occupies 40% of the seats in the Wajo DPRD.

19 Fifteen members of the DPRD are haji, and 19 have an academic title.

come to the surface, although they are rarely acknowledged explicitly. Within the aristocracy, competition has also increased as people prepare themselves for a power struggle once the rule of the Puang has come to an end.[20]

The impact of the Puang on Wajo politics has been considerable. Although he was from aristocratic descent it was his career within the New Order state that brought him to power in Wajo. His rise within the army and his move into Golkar provided him with a powerful starting point, from whence he could expand his personal network, the core of which consisted of family relationships. So it was the strong New Order state that initially facilitated his political career in Wajo, but his rise to local power was based on the articulation of institutional power with a wide patron-client network. Together these framed the patrimonial rule of the Puang. Regional autonomy accelerated his career, which eventually resulted in his election as district head in 2004 and gave him the opportunity to establish a hegemonic regime in Wajo. What this case study has shown is that decentralization and regional autonomy have reinforced autocratic rule instead of establishing good governance, transparency and democracy.

However, electoral democracy enabled opponents to gain ground as Golkar lost its majority. The rule of the Puang was primarily based on his ability to control and command the local state and its DPRD. It remains to be seen to what extent this 'cacique democracy' can survive when in the future the new district head will be directly elected by the population.

20 At the time of writing (mid-2005), the Puang's brother, who is now Assistant Two, was being prepared to replace him, in the event of the Puang being unable to continue.

Identities under construction

HENK SCHULTE NORDHOLT

Bali
An open fortress

'Ajeg Bali'

On 16 August 2003 the *Bali Post* celebrated its 55th anniversary with a special edition.[1] It contained an extensive report on a seminar held earlier that month under the title *Menuju strategi ajeg Bali,* towards a strategy for a strong and resilient Bali.[2] The word *ajeg* refers to a discourse about the position of Balinese culture in present-day Indonesia, in particular since *reformasi* and *desentralisasi* had changed the political map of Indonesia. The general feeling at the seminar was that Bali was endangered by a variety of negative external influences and that Balinese culture had to be rescued.

Representatives from various sectors in society voiced a shared concern that uncontrolled building activities and the rapidly expanding tourist sector cause large scale environmental damage, while they also feared that Western influences stimulate criminality, the use of narcotics, and a hedonistic materialistic attitude, at the cost of traditional religious Balinese values. Moreover, the influx of thousands of Muslim migrant workers from neighbouring islands Java and Lombok gave the unpleasant feeling that Balinese are becoming a minority on their own island. In order to counter these negative developments, the need for a spiritual revitalization and the strengthening of cultural self-confidence was felt. Ajeg Bali became the key word in a quest for a new master plan that respected the delicate balance between Gods, men and environment (*Tri Hita Karena*).

1 The information for this article was gathered in 2003 and 2004. I was assisted by Nyoman Wijaya, Slamat Trisila, Ngurah Suryawan and I Wayan Supartha. I would like to express my gratitude to Margreet Bersma, I Nyoman Darma Putra, Gerry van Klinken, Graeme MacRae, Michel Picard, Carol Warren, Adrian Vickers, and the participants of the workshop 'Renegotiating boundaries; Local politics in post-Soeharto Indonesia' (20-22 December 2004 in Jakarta) for their helpful comments.

2 See also Satria Naradha 2004.

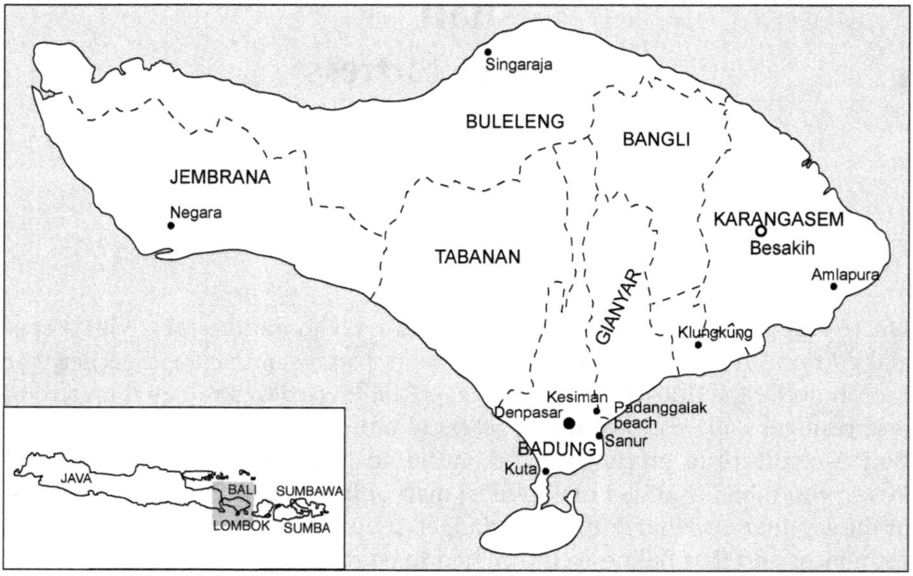

Singaraja
BULELENG
BANGLI
JEMBRANA
Negara
TABANAN
KARANGASEM
Besakih
Amlapura
GIANYAR
Klungkung
Kesiman
Padanggalak beach
Denpasar
Sanur
BADUNG
Kuta
JAVA
BALI
SUMBAWA
LOMBOK
SUMBA

Map 16. Bali

The discourse on Ajeg Bali has a long history, which is closely connected with efforts by outside forces to define the unique (non-Islamic, Hindu) identity of the Balinese. Especially from the 1930s onwards measures were taken to preserve Bali in a steady state of supposed authenticity while at the same time a set of new categories was introduced by which Balinese were invited to think about themselves. In order to preserve the special customary arrangements an institutional distinction was made at the village level between custom (*adat*) and administration (*dinas*). Custom or tradition was framed by religion (*agama*), while later on the notions of culture (*kebudayaan*) and art (*kesenian*) were added. Balinese started to think about themselves in terms defined by outsiders and, according to Michel Picard, they discovered that they had a culture, which was turned into a separate entity that could be displayed, performed, and sold (Picard 1999:16. See also H. Schulte Nordholt 1999; Picard 1996).

Since the 1970s tourism has become a part of Balinese culture. The notion of cultural tourism implied not only the commoditization of culture but also the touristification of society, blurring artificial boundaries between culture (inside) and tourism (outside). Tourism thus contributed to the making of a Balinese culture, which had become a marketable object (Picard 1996, 2003).

The island came increasingly under pressure as Jakarta-based investors and rising numbers of tourists and migrant workers invaded the island from the late 1980s. Were Balinese still in control of their own culture, which formed the backbone of their economy? Two other factors increased a sense of crisis and insecurity among Balinese: first the decentralization laws (Law no. 22 and 25/1999), which promised more autonomy but also brought fragmentation and confusion, and secondly the bomb attack in Legian on 12 October, 2002, which ruined the image of Bali as a peaceful resort isolated from international terrorism. In this context *ajeg* became a catchword to indicate the need for a socio-cultural self-defence. However, apart from the good, but vaguely phrased intentions to strengthen Balinese culture, very few practical solutions were suggested by the participants of the *Bali Post* seminar in August 2003. In the end two dilemmas surfaced: First, how to achieve more regional autonomy vis-à-vis Jakarta, whereas decentralization had produced administrative fragmentation; second, how to get rid of dangerous external influences and unwanted immigrants, while at the same time the Balinese economy needs foreign visitors, investors and labour in order to survive. Bali, the open fortress.

For many Balinese, recent developments have been a confusing experience. It looks as if various seemingly unrelated and diffuse processes are at work with highly insecure outcomes. In this essay I intend to trace some of these processes and investigate to what extent they are interrelated. I will look briefly at recent shifts in economic and political relationships between

Bali and Jakarta, the impact of political reform and administrative decentralization in Bali, and in particular at the effects these had on the politics of caste, the position of regional aristocracies, and the formation of new party-based politics. In Bali decentralization did not stop at the district level but affected the village level as well. What were the implications of these changes in terms of local autonomy and conflict management? In this context it is important to look at long-term trends, which were only accelerated by the recent agony of decentralization and reform. These changes increased a sense of insecurity, which formed the breeding ground of the Ajeg Bali movement.

It would be misleading to focus too exclusively on the special nature of Bali, as 'Baliologists' tend to do. Instead I want to point to some 'Indonesian' phenomena in present-day Bali: ethnic tensions, 'sweeping' of immigrants, the connections between gangs of *preman* (thugs) and politicians, recent election politics, and the role of urban middle class intellectuals in articulating exclusive cultural identities. It is against the backdrop of these developments that the discussions about Ajeg Bali and its post-New Order nature should be understood. And this raises eventually the question of how Indonesian Bali actually is.

Figures of change

One of the key questions regarding the development of tourism in Bali was: how to profit from tourists while at the same time keeping them at a safe distance?[3] Around 1970 it was decided to concentrate mass tourism in the southern tip of Bali. Soon, however, more areas were opened and when in the 1980s the touristification of Bali gained momentum and the deregulation of the banking sector facilitated a sharp increase in domestic investment, tourist areas eventually covered a quarter of the island. In a relatively short period the Balinese economy became increasingly dependent on the tourist industry, which was primarily fuelled by an increase of direct foreign arrivals. In 2000, two million foreign tourists visited Bali compared to one million in 1990 and 300,000 in 1980. Since the early 1990s the number of domestic tourists, who are not included in the official statistics, increased significantly and even outnumbered foreign visitors. It is estimated that in 2001 the total number of tourists was close to three million, which approaches the total population of Bali.

The tourist boom had an immediate impact on the environment, the economy and social relationships. The rise in the number of hotel rooms, from 500 in 1970 to 40,000 in 2002, was accompanied by a rapid increase in restaurants,

3 *Bali Membangun* 2003; *Bali Post* 16-8-2003; *Jakarta Post* 25-5-2003; *Kompas* 12-3-2001, MacRae 1997; Picard 1996, 2003, 2005; Pringle 2004; Putu Suasta 2001.

art shops and so-called *ruko* (*rumah toko*, a combination of a shop and a house, on top of which the house temple is built). As a result every year approximately 1000 hectares of irrigated rice-land disappear and in 2001 there was only 86,000 ha left. The traditional landscape has become a scarce commodity while ongoing erosion and the large quantities of water needed for hotels and golf courses cause serious water shortages for the population of Denpasar.

Bali is no longer a predominantly agrarian society. In 2005 half of the population will live in urban areas. Between 1970 and 2002 the agrarian sector decreased from 56.6% to 21.4% and in 1998 51.6% of the Balinese income was earned from tourism. If related fields like handicraft, garment production and transport are included, 50 to 70% of the workforce depends on tourism.

With an average economic growth of about 8% Bali experienced a transition from an agrarian economy towards an urbanized tourist economy. Social changes included the massive inflow of Muslim immigrants from neighbouring islands, and the rise of a new Balinese middle class for whom the village was a distant icon of 'Balineseness' and the rapid growth of the modern economy and its global dimensions a point of ongoing concern.

Protest

Since the early 1990s external investors have become more and more interested to participate in the tourist economy in Bali, and governor Ida Bagus Oka (1988-1998) proved to be a cooperative go-between, which is why he was also called Ida Bagus 'O.K.' (George Junus Aditjondro 1995). Growing feelings of discontent about the intrusion of Jakarta-based investors culminated in 1993 in the rise of a protest movement against the realization of the Bali Nirwana Resort in Tabanan, close to the holy sea temple of Tanah Lot (*Far Eastern Economic Review* 26-5-1994; C. Warren 1994; Putu Suasta and Connor 1999). The protest was supported by a broad middle class coalition of academics, public intellectuals, students, NGO activists, the regional newspaper *Bali Post* and representatives of the oppositional party Partai Demokrasi Indonesia (PDI, Indonesian Democratic Party). The rallying point of the movement focussed primarily on religious sentiments. It was the proximity of the resort to the temple that mobilized an island-wide protest that embarrassed both investors and government institutions. Resistance was silenced after direct intervention by President Soeharto, and in 1997 Le Meridien Nirwana Golf and Spa Resort advertised its soft opening.

Commenting on the issue, the military commander in Bali, Maj. Gen. R. Adang Ruchiatna stated that 'demonstrators are not part of Indonesian culture' (*Far Eastern Economic Review* 26-5-1994). Public protest was indeed not part of the ideology of Indonesia's New Order, but it was now firmly framed within a religiously informed Balinese discourse of discontent. This became evident when in 1997 another protest was launched against the building of a hotel at Padanggalak beach close to Denpasar. The issue was similar to the Bali Nirwana Resort but the outcome was very different (H. Schulte Nordholt 2001:66-8).

In October 1997 the *Bali Post* reported that at the Padanggalak coast, which belongs to the village of Kesiman, a large tourist resort was being planned and that building activities had already begun without a proper environmental impact assessment. The owners of the project were based in Jakarta but the actual building was done by a local firm in which governor Ida Bagus Oka was indirectly involved. The beach was an important religious site where ritual cleansings (*melasti*) and post-cremation purifications were held. A broad coalition, this time also supported by local villagers, protested against the project. In the village of Kesiman a powerful alliance was formed between villagers, customary (*adat*) leaders and the local nobility. Governor Ida Bagus Oka originated from the village of Kesiman, and the village council decided to ostracize him (*kasepekan*), which implied that the village would boycott his cremation and prevent the proper continuation of the journey of his soul. When he heard about the village verdict, the governor immediately declared that nothing had actually been decided yet about the Padanggalak project, and that the village had, of course, a final say in this matter. With remarkable speed all the building activities at Padanggalak beach were cancelled, and by the end of November 1997 the place had been restored to its former condition. The Padanggalak case showed that a combination of middle class protest and village-based resistance was strong enough to defeat a coalition of external investors and local administrators.

Hubris, shock and recovery

Despite the protests against the boundless expansion of the tourist sector, the ambition of growth prevailed and it inspired sculptor I Nyoman Nuarta to design a 146 meter high bronze statue of the god Wisnu on the Garuda bird. The project reflected a belief in an almost unlimited growth, and symbolized a Balinese sense of hubris. While the economic crisis (*krismon)* hit Java in 1997, Bali suffered less from the crisis. The number of foreign visitors even increased, and optimists speculated that by 2007 seven million tourists would visit Bali.[4]

4 Whereas the national economy contracted by 14% in 1998, the Balinese economy went down by only 4%. Recovery in Bali started in 1999 with 0.5% growth and reached a level of 3.4% growth in 2001.

The new governor of Bali, I Dewa Made Beratha, emphasized that Bali was a safe place amidst the turmoil of ethnic and religious violence in Indonesia. But he also knew that tranquillity on Bali was fragile: 'If a bomb explodes in Bali [...] its image as well as Indonesia's in general will be completely ruined' (*Jakarta Post* 14-8-01). And he was right. The terrorist attack in Legian on 12 October 2002 shattered the image of Bali as an isolated safe heaven. Tourists immediately abandoned Bali and in 2003 the recession in the tourist sector continued due to the SARS epidemic and the Iraq War.

On 15 November a large ritual, attended by thousands of people, was staged on nearby Legian beach to release the souls of the victims and to cleanse the site of the attack from evil forces. It was generally believed that due to this ritual the perpetrators of the attack were soon arrested. Earlier bomb attacks elsewhere in Indonesia had never been solved, but the successful uncovering of the Jema'ah Islamiah network proved, according to this view, that Bali was different from the rest of Indonesia.[5] So, for many Balinese, the ritual gathering in November 2002 marked the successful ending of the tragedy, but the extent to which recovery would succeed depended very much on the political configuration, which had experienced fundamental changes as well.

New rulers

Reformasi came to Bali in the guise of numerous seminars and interactive radio talk shows, but did not bring much reform.[6] There was a brief outburst of (anti-Islamic) 'Bali Merdeka' (Independence for Bali) sentiment in October 1998 when Minister A.M. Sjaefuddin remarked in an interview with *Republika* that Megawati was not a suitable presidential candidate because she worshipped Hindu gods. On 28 October 50,000 demonstrators in Denpasar demanded Sjaefuddin's resignation, but this did not materialize either.

In the early 1990s the oppositional PDI, forerunner of the Partai Demokrasi Indonesia-Perjuangan (PDI-P, Indonesian Democratic Party of Struggle), had been relatively strong in Bali. In the elections of 1992 it won almost 20% of the votes, but the number of seats the PDI acquired in provincial and district elected assemblies was modest compared to the comfortable majority of Golkar and the armed forces. PDI gained in popularity when Megawati

5 The ritual was on strained terms with the desire among foreigners to commemorate the tragedy every year. For why should one invite the souls of the deceased to return after they had been released with care and splendour?

6 Former governor Ida Bagus Oka was accused of corruption and nepotism. In January 2001 he was arrested and brought to court, but in April 2002 he was acquitted of all charges (*Jakarta Post* 13-1-2001, 8-4-2002).

Soekarnoputri became party leader. In 1996, however, the PDI was weakened due to an internal conflict manipulated by the government. Megawati lost her position and the PDI lost most of its popular support. During the elections of 1997 the PDI won only 3.5% while Golkar and the armed forces monopolized the district assemblies.

How strong Megawati's position in Bali still was became clear in October 1998 at the first congress of the PDI-P (PDI's *reformasi*-era successor) in Sanur when 50,000 supporters surrounded the Bali Beach hotel where the convention was held. There was 'an outpouring of emotion and an explosion of energy', one witness wrote.[7] This atmosphere surfaced again during the elections in June 1999, which celebrated both the demise of the New Order and the victory of the PDI-P. The fact that the elections coincided with Galungan – the day when ancestors and gods descend – added to the euphoria.

The elections of 1999 caused a political earthquake in Bali. Golkar fell back from 93.5% to 10% of the votes whereas PDI-P rose from 3.5% to almost 80%. The PDI-P victory was primarily a manifestation of Balinese ethnicity expressing anti-Javanese and anti-Muslim sentiments. These erupted in a violent manner in October 1999 when it turned out that instead of Megawati, Abdurrahman Wahid was elected president of Indonesia. On the evening of 20 October and during the following day riots occurred in Negara (Jembrana), Singaraja, and Denpasar. Especially in Singaraja and Denpasar many government buildings were set on fire while the residences of the (Golkar) district heads were also attacked.[8]

Although the period between May 1998 and October 1999 did not result in fundamental reforms, there was a changing of the guard among the political and administrative elite. In 1998 governor Ida Bagus Oka was replaced by the former provincial secretary I Dewa Made Beratha. He was not a very reform-minded politician but an experienced Golkar bureaucrat and skilful diplomat, who managed to accommodate an overwhelming PDI-P majority in the provincial parliament after the elections of 1999. The provincial and district assemblies were controlled by PDI-P, and in contrast to other regions in Indonesia, where experienced Golkar bureaucrats managed to survive, in most districts new PDI-P leaders came to power.

Apart from a shift from Golkar to PDI-P, the position of the nobility within the administration was also challenged. Until 2000 the majority of the

7 E-mail Rucina Ballinger, 10-10-1998.

8 *Bali Post* 21-10-1999, 23-10-1999; Couteau 2002: 243-5. The attacks were not a spontaneous expression of popular anger. Unidentified trucks coming from Java left a trail of damage in north Bali, while in Denpasar 'unknown people' played a leading role in the riots, which were over as soon as Megawati was chosen vice-president on 21 October.

district heads in Bali still belonged to the nobility, but by 2004 commoners prevailed.[9]

The demise of aristocratic rule was accentuated by the defeat of Bali's most famous royal lineage during the elections in Klungkung in 2003. The previous district heads had come from the royal house of Klungkung and maintained close connections with Golkar, but this time the old royal family was defeated by a commoner who represented a new type of politician. I Wayan Candra was a successful independent entrepreneur, who was supported not only by the PDI-P grassroots but also by various Pasek groups, large non-aristocratic kinship organizations. He had mobilized both anti-Golkar and anti-aristocrat sentiments and terminated the administrative rule of Bali's oldest dynasty (*Bali Post* August, September, November 2003; *Jawa Pos* 24-11-2003).

The fall of Golkar was accompanied by a general decline of aristocratic power. The extent to which Golkar had been intertwined with the aristocracy is reflected in the composition of the provincial assembly. Especially in the mid-1980s Golkar hegemony coincided with a strong aristocratic dominance. In the 1990s, however, a gradual shift in favour of commoner representatives occurred. It seems as if it was no longer necessary for Golkar to rely on the nobility. Instead, the party had nurtured its own bureaucratic cadres most of whom were of commoner descent.[10] In 2004 the ruling elite of the New Order had been replaced by a new group of district heads: four of them were entrepreneurs, two were politicians, one was a dentist, one had a mixed background in education and martial arts, and only two had a bureaucratic background.[11]

Changing caste relationships and religious reform

Leo Howe (2001) has pointed out that in pre-colonial times Brahman priests and noble rulers maintained an ambiguous relationship. Under Dutch colo-

9 In 1970 six districts heads belonged to the nobility and two were commoners; in 1990 the relationship was 5:3 and in 2004 3:6.

10

Composition DPRD Bali:	Non Balinese	Nobility	Commoners
1982-87	10	22	8
1987-92	9	21	15
1997-99	8	12	25
1999-04	4	16	35

This development was not unique for Bali. Michael Malley (1999) has shown that elsewhere in Indonesia Golkar started to rely more and more on its own regional cadres.

11 In 1980 four district heads came from the military, two from the police and two from the bureaucracy.

nial rule caste hierarchy was reinforced, but royal dynasties lost most of their power while the superior status of Brahmans was confirmed. Strong externally imposed states tended to reinforce caste hierarchy and especially the position of Brahmans, whereas periods of weak states (1945-1966 and 1998-) coincided with the emergence of egalitarian tendencies in Bali.

Since the mid-1920s an emerging group of commoner intellectuals, who advocated a status system based on achievement and merit, had challenged the aristocratic colonial elite who maintained that Balinese culture was based on caste hierarchy. While both groups sought to achieve modernity, representatives of the aristocracy emphasized the Balinese nature of their religion, which was rooted in *adat* and caste hierarchy, whereas their opponents pointed to the universal nature of modernist Hinduism, which was more egalitarian in nature (Picard 1999; Ramstedt 2002, 2004). It was along these lines that hierarchy was to be contested or defended during the next 80 years.

In 1958 Balinese Hinduism was recognized as one of the national religions in Indonesia. Balinese had to prove that, if their belief was a religion, it had a god, prophets, a holy book and a daily prayer. External criteria derived from Christianity and Islam started to determine the parameters of religion in Bali, and external sources of inspiration helped to institutionalize Hinduism in Bali as young Balinese intellectuals visited India where they were inspired by new modernist Hindu ideas (Bakker 1993). Modernist ideas caused a gradual shift from ritualism to scripturalism, from magic to ethics, and from a collective to an individual experience of religion (Howe 2001:148). The emphasis on personal merit and individual daily prayers facilitated more egalitarian ideas in which achievement instead of birth determined one's position, while caste could be separated from religion.

The gradual development of these new ideas was increasingly constrained by the rigid bureaucratic structures of the semi-government organization, Parisada Hindu Dharma. In 1986 Parisada was renamed Parisada Hindu Dharma Indonesia when it became a nationwide organization with the task of supporting the Indonesianization of Hinduism. The ongoing bureaucratization of the organization as well as its orientation towards Hindu communities outside Bali facilitated the rise of commoners within the ranks of Parisada. Just like Golkar, Parisada offered commoners the possibility of challenging aristocratic dominance. This was accentuated even more when the national headquarters of Parisada moved to Jakarta in 1996.

The rise of commoners within Parisada strengthened the influence of commoner groups which were organized in quasi clan-based organizations. High on the agenda of these commoner groups, or *warga*, was the recognition of their own priests at the same level as Brahman priests, or *pedanda*.

In 1999 *reformasi* in Bali took the shape of caste conflict and was focussed on one of the largest island-wide cleansing rituals, the so-called Panca Wali

Krama which would have its climax at the all-Bali temple of Besakih (I Gde Pitana 1999, 2001). A massive alliance of commoner groups demanding that *warga* priests should act at the same level as Brahman *pedanda* caused heated public debates and complex bureaucratic intrigues. Facing each other were conservative aristocrats supported by Golkar and Parisada leaders, and reform-minded intellectuals plus commoner organizations that threatened to boycott the ritual at Besakih. Governor Dewa Made Beratha understood the signs of the times and helped the commoners to gain a victory, but conservative aristocrats were not yet defeated.

Soon caste conflict manifested itself within Parisada Hindu Dharma Indonesia. Since the early 1990s Parisada had lost a great deal of government subsidy as President Soeharto started to support the newly established organization of Muslim intellectuals, ICMI (Ramstedt 2002:160-1). Meanwhile growing numbers of Muslim immigrants accentuated the 'rise of Islam' in Bali. Alarmed by the invasion of both Muslim immigrants and Jakarta-based investors, and convinced of the need for a revitalization of Balinese culture, Balinese intellectuals criticized Parisada for its lack of inspiration and inability to protect the Hindu community. Shaken by decreased government protection and external criticism, the aristocratic cum bureaucratic power holders in Parisada had become vulnerable.

At the Parisada congress in 1996 in Surakarta, criticism was raised concerning the intellectual poverty of the organization and its emphasis on bureaucratic procedures. But attempts to separate Parisada policy from Golkar interests and to increase the number of commoners in the board of the organization failed (I Gede Ngurah Bagus 2004). However, at the next congress in Sanur in September 2001 the opposition succeeded in toppling the Brahman hegemony within Parisada. A newly elected board was dominated by commoners and *warga* priests formed the majority of the advisory board.

Whereas modernist Hindu ideas had gained ground in the national Parisada, a powerful group of conservative aristocratic dissidents in Bali remained loyal to old concepts of hierarchy. When these dissidents refused to obey the decisions of the new national board, Parisada in Bali split into two opposing factions, the so-called Parisada Campuan and Parisada Besakih. Tensions ran high when in November 2001 the aristocratic opposition planned to hold its own convention and supporters of the national Parisada tried to prevent this and besieged the house of the governor of Bali to force him to side with them. The governor tried to remain neutral but many people suspected that he sympathized with the conservative Parisada Campuan. Whereas Parisada Besakih criticized the 'feudal' nature of caste differences, the Campuan group criticized the 'Indianization' policy of the modernists of the Parisada Besakih, which would in their eyes eliminate Balinese culture.

The dissident Parisada Campuan can still count on substantial popular support, as its chairman, Ida Pedanda Made Gunung, is a very popular public figure who has an influential daily talk show on Bali TV. Moreover, many commoners are reluctant to give up their long-standing relationship with their Brahman priests, which could bring illness and other disasters.

Hierarchical relationships have changed considerably over the last decades and changes have accelerated since 1998, when caste conflicts formed the core of *reformasi* in Bali. The different external concepts introduced in the course of the 20th century in Bali have led to fundamental changes in the way culture, religion and custom were represented as separate categories. In the use of language and in ritual practices there is a tendency towards egalitarianism. At the same time there is an increase of ritual activities.

Modernist religious ideas advocate modest rituals, which enable more people to participate, especially since public transport has made it possible to visit virtually every temple all over Bali. As a result Bali has become more Hindu than before, while religion is no longer exclusively framed in caste hierarchy.

Administrative fragmentation

The relatively small province of Bali is – with its provincial administration, eight districts and one administrative town – rather over-administered. Since decentralization has transferred funds and administrative tasks to the district level, the districts are often called 'little kingdoms' whose leaders prefer to ignore the coordinating capacities of the provincial government. Officials at the provincial level complain that they have more expertise on a variety of matters but they are no longer consulted because inexperienced district administrations pursue their own policies. District heads often send low-ranking staff members to meetings convened by the governor about matters of common interest where he intends to arrive at a coordinated approach. As a result pressing problems concerning irrigation, the supply of drinking water, and a balanced development of tourism remain unresolved.[12]

A key issue in the relationship between the districts concerns a more equal distribution of administrative funds and locally raised taxes. The amount of money from the centre (Dana Alokasi Umum, DAU) forms in most districts the bulk of the incoming funds. In 2002 DAU covered about two-thirds of

12 Although from time to time efforts were made to put the issue of special autonomy for the province on the agenda, discussions never materialized in concrete political decisions (*Kompas* 8-2-2000, 22-11-2004, 13-1-2005).

13 In 2002 Bali received Rp 1,539 billion DAU from Jakarta; the total income was Rp 2,362 billion, and Rp 1,145 billion was spent on salaries.

Bali's total government income and two-thirds of the DAU was spent on salaries.[13] Overall income increased, but expenditure rose as well. While 2001 still showed a surplus, this evaporated in the following years due to '9/11', SARS, the Iraq war and the 'Bali bomb'.

At the district level the amount of local taxes makes the difference. Eighty percent of the so-called Pendapatan Asli Daerah (PAD) is derived from the hotel and restaurant tax, Pajak Hotel Restoran (PHR).[14] Already during the New Order, rich districts like Badung, Denpasar and, to a lesser extent, Gianyar generated large sums of money, while poor districts like Jembrana and Karangasem produced next to nothing in this respect. Although some adjustments were made to redistribute the PHR from the affluent tourist centres to less prosperous regions, major differences in wealth continued to exist and no structural changes occurred after decentralization.[15]

Regional autonomy reinforced the tendency among districts to give priority to their own interests, as a result of which differences in wealth between regions did not decrease. At the same time there was an uneven distribution of funds between government sectors. As elsewhere in Indonesia, large sums of money went into new prestigious government offices, while, for instance, the educational sector was by and large neglected (*Bali Post* 13-8-2003, 4-9-2003). After decentralization the district budgets show not only that differences in wealth between districts are maintained but also that Bali remains to a large extent financially dependent on Jakarta.

Fragmented autonomy: from desa dinas to desa pakraman

Decentralization in Bali was not restricted to the district level but affected the village as well. Dutch colonial rule introduced a distinction in the 1930s between administrative (*dinas*) and customary (*adat*) rule at the village level. This construction was designed to keep Balinese religion and culture (*adat*) in a supposed authentic state, while modern administration would form 'a thin layer of modernity' touching village Bali only superficially. This *adat-dinas* divide was to survive well into the New Order, when the state penetrated deeper into village affairs and the *desa adat* was increasingly subordinated to the *desa dinas*. Various government regulations stipulated that *adat* was

14 In 2001 PAD in Bali totalled Rp 563 billion, Rp 420 billion of which consisted of PHR.

15 Since the 1970s Badung was required to pay 30% of its PHR and Denpasar 10% to the other districts (Picard 2003; *Kompas* 12-3-2001). In 2002 the district assembly of Badung wanted to reduce its contribution to the other districts from 30 to 15% of the PHR. Governor Made Beratha needed all his diplomatic skills to reach a compromise. In July 2003 it was agreed that Badung would pay 22% and Denpasar 10% of their PHR to the other districts but not to Gianyar and the province.

16 Peraturan Menteri Dalam Negeri no. 11/1984; Perda no. 6/1986 and no. 12/1988.

but an instrument in the pursuit of development and needed state guidance and supervision.[16] *Adat* remained, however, a contested field and on some occasions became a bastion of resistance against unwanted government intervention.

Reformasi and Law no. 22/1999 on decentralization opened the way for a revision of the relationship between the *dinas* and *adat* spheres.[17] It was in the *adat* domain where fundamental changes would take place.

In 2001 the provincial government of Bali issued a regulation on the role of the *desa adat* (Perda no. 3/2001). It reflects in many respects the concerns of urban middle class Balinese who believe that Balinese culture should be protected against the evils of globalization. Since Balinese culture is in their eyes rooted in the *desa,* and the *desa* is based on *adat,* it follows that *adat* forms the cornerstone of Balinese culture. In order to emphasize the authenticity and the autonomy of the traditional village, the word *adat,* which was considered to be too colonial, was replaced by the term *pakraman,* taken from ancient inscriptions.[18]

Perda no. 3/2001 gives the *desa pakraman* full authority to run its internal affairs and makes the village council the highest authority. The *desa pakraman* has authority over village land, which may not be sold and is not subject to government taxation. Illustrating their newly acquired autonomy, some *desa pakraman* requested from the provincial government a larger profit from the tourist 'objects' such as temples, which are located within their borders. Other villages even demanded money from nearby hotels for the view on the authentic village their guests enjoyed.[19]

Whereas under the New Order the *desa dinas* formed the main channel of government funding into the village, after decentralization the provincial and district governments in Bali prefer to subsidize the *desa pakraman.* In June 2001 the provincial government announced that it would donate every *desa pakraman* Rp 10 million and a tax-free Honda Supra motorbike for the village head. According to the announcement, local *adat* had to be reinforced because 'Bali was seriously ill'.[20] District governments also decided

17 Within village administration the advisory board (LKMD) was replaced by a representative assembly (Dewan Perwakilan Desa) with representatives from each hamlet or *banjar* that would control the village head. However, in Law no. 32/2004, which replaced Law no. 22/1999, provisions regarding new democratic village assemblies have been deleted.

18 The word *krama* refers to customary practice as well as the village council (C. Warren 2004; *Sarad* 36, 2003). Unlike the situation in West Sumatra where the *nagari* has replaced the New Order village, in Bali the *desa dinas* has not disappeared. It still provides basic services such as the issuing of identity cards and so on.

19 *Bali Post* 20-3-2002; C. Warren 2004. The new regulation also reinforced the possibilities for the *desa pakraman* to provide credit, set up local businesses and attract investors.

20 *Radar Bali* 7-6-2001. In 2003 and 2004 villages received Rp 20 and Rp 25 million (*Bali Post* 25-3-2004).

to support the *desa pakraman*. Depending on district wealth, villages in the eastern district of Karangasem received only Rp 5 million per year in 2002, whereas villages in the rich tourist area of Badung were given Rp 100 million each.[21]

Officially Perda no. 3/2001 has been effective since March 2002, but its practical implementation remains uneven (C. Warren 2004). Many Balinese appreciate the new flow of funds, which supports temple restoration and ritual activities and strengthens a sense of community. But the Perda was also criticized because it is based on Dutch colonial ideas about the autonomous and republican nature of the Balinese village while reflecting a romantic desire for cultural authenticity.[22]

The invention of traditional police

The new village autonomy was accompanied by the establishment of a brand new traditional police force at the local level, the so-called *pecalang*. Already in 1996 and 1997 village policemen in Sanur and Kuta were active under this name. However, the place were this police force was truly launched was not the traditional village but the founding congress of PDI-P in Sanur in October 1998 (*Sarad* 31, 2002; *Suara Merdeka* 10-7-1997; ICG 2003c). The armed forces were present with more than 3000 men, but there was widespread suspicion that they were pro-Golkar and might cause riots instead of maintaining order. PDI-P had organized its own security forces comprising of 1200 men. The story goes that when tension ran high one man dressed in *adat* clothes managed to stop a crowd that was almost in a trance and persuaded them to sit down. The PDI-P congress proceeded in an orderly manner and it was clear that invisible (or *niskala*) forces had been at work here. Since then militias dressed in traditional attire have served as security forces at other big gatherings, while all over Bali villages established their own groups of *pecalang*. In June 2000 the provincial department of culture organized a seminar about the phenomenon in an attempt to impose some uniformity, and in 2002 a booklet was published in cooperation with Parisada in which tasks, func-

21 Law no. 34/1999 stipulates that 10% of the Hotel and Restaurant Tax has to be redistributed among the villages. In Bali the *desa pakraman* received these funds. Due to the effects of the 'Bali bomb', income from tourism declined and in 2003 villages in Badung only received Rp 50 million.

22 I Gde Parimartha 2003. Another criticism concerned the status of immigrants. Informed by the same modernist ideas, which separate caste from religion, Perda no. 3/2001 separates religious and social spheres of interaction in the village. Hence immigrants are only expected to perform social duties, which are relatively light in comparison with the ongoing flow of religious obligations (*Sarad* 39, 2003; *Bali Post* 27-5-2004).

tions and dress of *pecalang* were explained (Nyoman Widnyani and I Ketut Widia 2002). Within less than four years a moment of charisma had been transformed into a new island-wide and village-based institution.[23]

Perda no. 3/2001 recognizes *pecalang* as a traditional security force (*satgas keamanan tradisional*), especially with regards to *adat* and religion. Their uniform consists of a *destar* or head cloth, a flower behind one ear, a t-shirt on which the word *pecalang* and the name of their village is printed, a safari jacket without sleeves, a black and white chequered *kampuh* over a sarong, and a *kris* which has been blessed in the temple, plus a hand phone, while tattoos are taboo. Thus attired they are supposed to represent traditional authority, which must be seen in contrast to the corrupt practices of an external and often absent police force.

Although some *pecalang* have acted as well-paid and well-equipped security guards, while others have been involved in criminal activities, in most villages the new village policemen play a modest role. The most visible – and often also rather annoying – manifestation of their authority is when they block entire roads and redirect traffic during temple ceremonies and other rituals, for which commercially sponsored traffic signs are used.

Social volcanoes

Far-reaching decentralization, village autonomy and the establishment of a village police increased violent conflicts within and between villages. Since regional autonomy was put into motion, the coordinating power at the provincial level and government authority as such have weakened. As a result, administrative institutions are no longer capable of managing many – sometimes long-lasting – local conflicts. Under the heading *kasus adat* – which is seen as a legitimate form of violence – land and border disputes as well as conflicts about caste and status claims within villages easily explode into large-scale violence, often conducted by groups of unemployed youths. The Balinese journal *Sarad* estimated that between 1997 and 2003 almost every month a *kasus adat* resulted in mass violence (*Sarad* 44, 2003). It seems as if villages show less tolerance toward deviant behaviour, while the implementation of social sanctions has become more violent.

Due to a combination of population growth and rising market prices for land, conflicting claims on land easily result in violent confrontation. According to Indonesian law the village is not a legal body, but according to local *adat* villages do own land. In many disputes, conflicting parties refer

[23] In the old days *pecalang* did not belong to the village sphere. In nineteenth century Mengwi they were agents/spies acting on behalf of the royal centre (H. Schulte Nordholt 1996:150).

either to national law or local *adat* to legitimize their claims (*Sarad* 49, 2004). Apart from land disputes within the village, there are also an increasing number of confrontations between villages involving claims on land and contested borderlines.

Although many *kasus adat* have an economic background, others are rooted in caste conflicts or long histories of rivalries between villages, which tend to generate their own dynamics. Regularly caste conflicts within villages come to the surface when villagers boycott or even prevent cremations of aristocrats who ignored local *adat* rules. Increasingly, conflicts between villages, and between hamlets within the same village, are reinforced by political antagonisms. In most cases government administrators and the police are rather powerless. Meanwhile the government itself has also become the target of popular anger. In several instances police offices were the prime targets of popular discontent at the local level. Taken together, the long list of conflicts also demonstrates that the newly created *pecalang* were not able to prevent the regular outbreaks of violence at the local level.

Sweepings

Since *adat* was seen as the cornerstone of Balinese culture and the ultimate stronghold against the evils of globalization, it follows that *pecalang* were seen as the guardians of this culture. Degung Santikarma (2001a) has argued that, under the New Order, culture was conceptualized in material terms. As a commodity, culture could be reproduced and sold, but it could also be stolen, as was evidenced by a series of temple thefts in the mid 1990s, which were attributed to 'Javanese'. It was therefore not only the task of *pecalang* to protect their village from narcotics and the like, but also to keep their territory free from suspicious strangers.

In the late 1990s a steady flow of immigrants looking for jobs suddenly began to increase, as conflicts and crises drove people from Eastern Indonesia and Java to Bali. Most immigrants concentrated in South Bali, where they tried their luck in the tourist sector. The 2000 census counted about 250,000 Javanese and Madurese immigrants in Bali, out of a total population of 3.1 million people.[24] Apart from a small group of well-to-do entrepreneurs, the majority of immigrants provide cheap labour in the construction and agrarian sectors, furniture and textile production, and in hotels and restaurants.[25]

Muslim immigrants came to embody social pollution, which threatened

24 *Penduduk Indonesia* 2001, Seri L.2.2: 10.9, 11.1.

25 ICG 2003c:8; *Bali Post* 3-1-03. Construction workers from Lombok earn Rp 25,000 per day, whereas Balinese are paid Rp 50,000.

Balinese culture. These feelings were eloquently summarized by the deputy mayor of Denpasar in April 2002:

> Most of these people are jobless, they create a problem. They are criminals. There are problems with housing and traffic jams are getting worse. These people produce a lot of waste; they make slums. (*South China Morning Post* 3-4-2002.)

Although the terrorist assault on 12 October 2002 did not result in a violent cleansing of Muslims, the immigrant population of Bali experienced physical and administrative repression. Immigrants who returned from Java after the fasting month were screened and intimidated by a combined force of regular police, administrative police and local *pecalang*. These forces also conducted razzias on a regular basis in Denpasar and other places in South Bali in search of illegal immigrants. In the administrative sphere especially the municipal government of Denpasar took strong measures to reduce the number of immigrants by applying a 'shock therapy'. In order to obtain an immigrant identity card (Kartu Identitas Penduduk Pendatang, KIPP or Migrant-ID) the immigrants had to show letters from their home village and their employer and landlord in Bali, while the official costs of the card increased to Rp 400,000 per year, to which a similar amount in bribes often had to be added (ICG 2003c; *Sarad* 34, 2003). In January 2003 the governor of Bali and the district heads reached an agreement to issue a uniform rule, according to which non-Balinese immigrants had to pay Rp 200,000 per year for their permit, and immigrants from other places within Bali only Rp 20,000 (*Bali Post* 11-2-2003).

During a meeting of *adat* village leaders in Gianyar early in 2004 emotions ran high about the supposed 'take-over' of Bali by immigrants. Public intellectual Prof Luh Ketut Suryani did not hesitate to depict a gloomy future, in which Hindu Balinese might become a minority on their own island (*Taksu* May 2004). Many villages put up signs forbidding 'scavengers' from entering village territory, and *pecalang* were depicted as vanguard troops defending Balinese culture (Nyoman Widnyani and I Ketut Widia 2002).

The answer to the threat of Western decadence and Islamic intrusions was found in the intimacy of the *desa pakraman*. But the 'revival' of the *desa pakraman* and *adat*, with its conservative, male-biased and exclusive ethnic attitudes, are not in line with the requirements of national citizenship and democracy.[26] It is, moreover, difficult to determine the borderline between legal authority and legitimized violence on the one hand and the criminal activities on the other of semi-official groups who act in the shadow of formal state institutions and political parties.

26 See Connor and Vickers 2003:177-9.

Preman and party politics

Apart from immigrants and ethnic conflict, other aspects of 'Indonesia' penetrated into Bali as well. The rise of PDI-P in Denpasar and Karangasem was accompanied by the formation of gangs of allied *preman* who provided public support in exchange for political protection and room to manoeuvre in the criminal sphere. The genealogy of the biggest gang in Denpasar can be traced back to the 1970s when Ngurah P., a former leader of a PNI militia who had been involved in the killings of 1965, established the Armada Racun. This group wanted to protect Denpasar against the so-called 'Anak Sudirman', or non-Balinese military from the Kodam Udayana, who tried to control the entertainment centres in Denpasar and Kuta. In order to gain protection from higher authorities the Armada allied itself in later years with the thuggish pro-Golkar youth group Pemuda Pancasila.

According to well-informed people in Denpasar, there is a direct link between the Armada Racun and the Forum Peduli Denpasar (FPD), which was established in September 2002.[27] Whereas the name of the Armada (army) Racun (poison) reflected aggression, the new Forum Peduli Denpasar (Forum Caring for Denpasar) presented itself in the guise of a NGO dressed up in a civil society discourse. Supported by intellectuals, politicians, artists and entrepreneurs, the FPD stated in its 'vision and mission' that it aimed to enhance the security and cultural unity of Denpasar and that it would fulfil this task in the spirit of the Puputan Badung – the heroic suicidal resistance of the king of Badung against the Dutch in September 1906. In his opening speech the chairman of the FPD, I Made Sutama Minggik, emphasized that FDP advocated a bottom-up approach to development, resulting in a clean city, with less traffic jams, where people would obey the rule of law. In order to reinforce regional culture he promised to fight drugs and secular marriages.[28]

From the start the FPD maintained a special alignment with the mayor of Denpasar, Anak Agung Puspayoga, who acted as the patron of the organization. Through the person of Puspayoga the FPD was also allied with the PDI-P and puri Satria, the old ruling dynasty of Denpasar. At first sight the FPD manifested itself as a decent organization. It offered assistance to the victims of the bomb assault in Legian in October 2002, for which they received a prestigeous award from the national chief of police Dai Bachtiar during a big event at the Hotel Borobudur in Jakarta. However, the FPD also harbours a variety of illegal activities, from which police, politicians and *preman* benefit.

27 See also ICG 2003c:10.

28 *Bali Post* 30-7-2002, 12-8-2002, 22-8-2002, 20-9-2002, 23-9-2002; official documents of the establishment of Forum Peduli Denpasar 20-9-2002.

It has its basis in the transport sector of Denpasar and controls entertainment areas and gambling spots. It also showed its less friendly face when it became deeply involved in so-called anti-immigrant 'sweepings'. In July 2003 the FPD operated as strongmen protecting the interests of their patron, mayor Puspayoga, when the group attacked one of his political opponents.[29] Commenting on this incident a colleague from Universitas Udayana lamented that in the early days of *reformasi* he was often invited to participate in discussions convened by the mayor, 'but now Puspayoga seems to rely on *preman* to solve his problems'.

Unstable party rule

The intertwining of administrative interests, party politics and criminal activities does not only occur in Denpasar, but also in the small town of Amlapura in the eastern district of Karangasem. Here the political influence of the local dynasty ceased to exist in the mid-1980s. After a period of military district heads, a new PDI-P politician became the new administrator in 1999. He had a degree in public administration but more important was his network in martial arts (*pencak silat*) circles that helped him to win the elections. Just like the mayor of Denpasar, the new district head of Karangasem was supported by a 'civil society' organization, the Dewan Perwakilan Massa (DPM, Council Representing the Masses). The DPM is headed by Kari Subali, a tough guy with a big beard and a moustache, every inch a strong man, who can easily mobilize 200 to 300 men to underline the point he wants to make.

As a new player in the political arena in Bali PDI-P had a weak basis in the administrative bureaucracy, which was still dominated by old Golkar networks, and the party had not much experience in controlling decision-making processes in the district assemblies. Auxiliary forces like FPD and DPM were therefore helpful to support the interests of newly elected administrators.

Apart from the marriage between party bosses and *preman*, the sudden rise to power of the PDI-P was accompanied by spectacular internal conflicts. In the districts of Jembrana and Buleleng *reformasi* and decentralization offered ample opportunities for clever political entrepreneurs to seize power, while tensions between party headquarters in Jakarta and regional branches played an important role as well.

In August 2000 a new district head was elected in the region of Jembrana in West Bali. With 17 out of 30 seats PDI-P dominated the district assembly and it seemed as if the party was in full control of the electoral process.

[29] *Bali Post* 28-7-2003; *Denpost* 26-7-2003, 27-7-2003, 28-7-2003, 29-8-2003, 5-9-2003, 6-9-2003; *Fajar Bali* 26-7-2003.

The party candidate had the blessing of the national headquarters and was expected to gain an easy victory. But due to a miscalculation he was unable to obtain the required 50% plus one of the votes and a second round was needed. To the astonishment of the PDI-P he was then defeated by an outsider, Dr Gede Winasa, who had managed to buy – as many believe – the votes of a majority of the assembly, including a number of PDI-P members. Anger and frustration among PDI-P cadres led to violent attacks on the party office of Jembrana (ruined) and the house of the PDI-P chairman of the district assembly (burned).[30] In July 2003 Gede Winasa also succeeded – against the wish of party headquarters – in gaining control over the regional branch of the PDI-P.[31] Despite his contested rise to power Gede Winasa did achieve remarkable results as an administrator. Although Jembrana is known as a poor district, he managed to increase the local budget and provided both free education and free health services, so that the Indonesian weekly *Tempo* called him 'a record breaking district head'.[32]

Unstable party politics in Jembrana had facilitated the rise of a new strong man. A similar but more complex process occurred in the northern district of Buleleng.[33] Here the position of the district head I Ketut W. Sindu came increasingly under pressure after the elections of 1999.[34] After the elections of 1999 PDI-P had gained a majority in the district assembly and Sindu's room to manoeuvre was seriously restricted. He had to make deals with the leader of the PDI-P, I Nyoman S. Duniaji, whose star was rising rapidly in Buleleng. Duniaji had been headmaster of a high school and a travel agent. While his father had been secretary of the Soekarno-era party PNI in Buleleng, he himself had been a fierce supporter of Megawati when she was ousted from the PDI in 1996. Supported by party headquarters and representing a new generation of reform-minded politicians, Duniaji was in 1999 elected chairman of the district branch of PDI-P in Buleleng. In 2000 he became chairman of the district assembly (DPRD) of Buleleng, while a close friend of his, D.K. Astawa, succeeded him as chairman of the party branch.

The career of Duniaji was resented by an older party cadre, Wayan Dangin, who had lost the elections for party leader and speaker of the district

30 The official inauguration of the new district head had to be postponed when a mob of angry PDI-P supporters of the defeated candidate disturbed the ceremony and several people were wounded and one man was killed. (*Kompas* 15-8-2000; *Apakabar* 28-8-2000).

31 *Denpost* 21-7-2003, 26-7-2003, 14-8-2003, 8-9-2003, 20-9-2003, 23-9-2003.

32 *Tempo* 28-12-2004. I was told that Gede Winasa maintained good relationships with a group of Japanese investors.

33 See Lay 2002:Chapter 3; Savirani 2004:Chapter 4.

34 Sindu was an old and loyal Golkar administrator who had been active in the so-called 'Golkarization' campaign in Buleleng during the 1970s, which had to erase the grass roots support for the leftist wing of the nationalist PNI. In 1993 he had become district head and served now for a second term.

assembly. Dangin wanted revenge. Meanwhile Duniaji's power increased. As chairman of the assembly he made deals with district head Sindu, who depended on him for support. He organized overseas trips and cars for his fellow PDI-P assembly members and influenced decisions regarding infrastructural projects and the appointment of high-level officials. Towards the end of 2001 he felt strong enough to start a campaign to replace district head Sindu. Ironically Sindu was now supported by Dangin, who opposed Duniaji's ambitions. But to no avail. In January 2002 district head Sindu was forced to step down, immediately after which Duniaji started a campaign to be elected as the next district head of Buleleng.

Because Dunaji was confident that he would win the elections, he started to ignore his local power basis. He rejected his political friend and ally Astawa (the local PDI-P chief) as running mate because he preferred a candidate with more education. Actually Duniaji looked down upon most of his fellow PDI-P men in Buleleng and considered them backward and ignorant. Although supported by party headquarters, Duniaji ran the risk of isolating himself.

Suddenly a new candidate appeared, Putu Bagiada, a businessman with a background in private banking in Jakarta. Bagiada was warmly supported by Duniaji's enemies. And as a businessman Bagiada had ample funds to finance his campaign. When the district assembly convened to elect the new district head, Duniaji presided the meeting in his capacity as chairman of the assembly. When he realized that he was losing the elections he tried to postpone the meeting halfway the election procedure, but he failed. Bagiada was elected with 27 out of 45 votes. Shocked by this unexpected defeat Duniaji mobilized his supporters and staged demonstrations against the supposedly fraudulous election. However, in early July 2002 Bagiada was officially inaugurated as district head, while Duniaji remained a relatively powerless chairman of the district assembly.

In the end an alliance between old local party cadres with external money had defeated an alliance between a high-handed leader and party headquarters in Jakarta. Party headquarters was very unhappy with the fact that it had lost control over the party branches in Jembrana and Buleleng. The other district heads in Bali were also worried. The consequence of electoral democracy – fuelled by money politics – was that the PDI-P faced uncontrolled processes of decentralization within its own organization. This offered outsiders an opportunity to penetrate into powerful positions. And this would also have serious repercussions for the election of the governor of Bali in July 2003.

Rising tensions

Meanwhile, campaigns for the national elections of 2004 started in Bali as early as July 2003 and caused violent confrontations between PDI-P and Golkar. Supported by its own militarized youth organization AMPG, Golkar made a modest but self-conscious come-back in the political arena after the devastating defeat of June 1999.[35]

In many places throughout Bali, tensions between PDI-P and Golkar or between PDI-P and its dissident offshoots increased. Especially in Tabanan, Jembrana and Buleleng numerous small incidents were reported.[36] Towards the end of October tensions increased even further when Golkar planned to hold its 40th anniversary in Bali, while PDI-P announced it would celebrate the national commemoration of the 'Youth Oath' with large parades and other manifestations. On Sunday 26 October 2003 a PDI-P parade near Singaraja in Buleleng was attacked by Golkar supporters. Not long afterwards a PDI-P mob retaliated and lynched two members of the youth organization of Golkar. Violence continued during the next two days around Singaraja and consisted mainly of attacks on Golkar offices (*Jakarta Post* 27-10-2003; *Bali Post* 27-10-2003, 29-10-2003).

These incidents caused a lot of concern among party leaders in Jakarta. If the pattern in Bali was to set the tone for the national elections, what would happen in other parts of Indonesia? Both government officials and party bosses put pressure on the local branches of their parties in Bali to refrain from further violence. They succeeded, but many people feared violence might flare up when the real campaign would start in April 2004.

Ajeg revisited

Lack of administrative coordination, violent *adat* cases, internal party turmoil, confrontations between parties, immigrants, *preman* and other aspects of 'Indonesia' illustrate that the old dichotomy between an isolated Bali and its fragile culture on the one hand, and the evils of the outside world on the other, no longer held true. Bali has of course always been open to outside influences, and has long been an inseparable part of Indonesia. But since regional autonomy was set in motion the moral dichotomy between Bali (innocent) and the outside world (evil) was difficult to maintain. For it could

35 Golkar hijacked the slogan 'Bali aman, turis datang' (When Bali is safe, tourists will come), and changed it into 'Golkar menang, turis datang' (If Golkar wins, tourists will come).

36 *Sarad* 44, 2003; *Bali Post* 28-5-2003, 4-8-2003, 27-8-2003, 5-9-2003; *Denpost* 28-8-2003, 8-9-2003.

no longer be denied that 'evil' was now part and parcel of Bali itself (Connor and Vickers 2003). However, the main sources of the evil forces within Bali were still located in the outside world: globalization and, after the terrorist attack in Legian, international terrorism. The threat of globalization – in the guise of a free movement of trade, capital and labour as well as the demoralizing impact of drugs and decadence – motivated concerned urban intellectuals to participate in countless seminars. A telling illustration of these gatherings was a prestigious symposium held in July 2000 on cultural heritage conservation, which was sponsored by the World Bank and Unesco. Here old discourses about the uniqueness of Bali (commonplace since the nineteenth century) and efforts to preserve Balinese culture (since the 1920s) resurfaced in empty 'newspeak'. Since the uniqueness of Bali, its environment and cultural traditions were under challenge, the recipe for sustained development should consist of the empowerment of governance of local communities, the revitalization of historic towns, the adaptation of tradition and the renewal of the cultural fabric by keeping living cultural practices alive.[37] It was along these lines that 'Balinese move into the future by returning to their past, and embrace modernity by re-acquainting themselves with old traditions', as Leo Howe observed (Howe 2001:83). This approach was both inward-looking and conservative.

It was in this context that the new leader of the independent Bali Post Group, Satria Naradha, launched his Ajeg Bali campaign in 2002. The son and heir of Ketut Nadha, founder of the *Bali Post* in 1948 and its chief editor until his death in 2001, Satria Naradha became the self-appointed leader of a moral movement that claimed to protect and strengthen Balinese culture.[38]

During the late 1990s and especially under Satria Naradha the *Bali Post* became a powerful provincial media concern which now includes a local TV station, four radio stations, the well-respected newspaper *Bali Post* itself, the daily *Denpost*, which covers primarily criminality, and several other newspapers and magazines. Although the Bali Post Group has no monopoly – *Jawa Pos* with its imprint *Radar Bali*, *NUSA* and commercial TV stations are alternative sources of news – Satria Naradha is well-equipped to determine to a large extent the political agenda. If necessary, he is willing to impose censorship.

In an interview Satria Naradha claimed that he received his inspiration to launch the concept of 'Ajeg Bali' already in the 1980s, as he was meditating as a high school pupil. 'I received the idea, but I could not yet give it a

37 Announcement of the symposium in *H.SEASIA* 6-6-2000.

38 The *Bali Post* is one of the oldest independent newspapers in Indonesia. It started in 1948 as *Suara Indonesia* (Putra Dwikora and Wayan Supartha 2000). Ideologically the newspaper has always been close to PNI and PDI(-P).

name, but when in the 1990s I saw large billboards in Bali mobilizing people to safeguard Bali, I suddenly knew what it should be'. Others think that the modernist Muslim and Hindu movements of the 1990s, when he was studying journalism in Surabaya, formed important sources of inspiration for his later activities as a cultural activist.[39]

Ajeg Bali was launched at the opening of Bali TV in May 2002, when the governor of Bali, I Dewa Made Beratha urged his audience to *mengajegkan* Balinese *adat* and culture (I Nyoman Darma Putra 2003). *Ajeg* stands for strong, upright, and is in a way a stronger version of the notion of *kebalian*, or 'Balineseness' (Picard 1996). Related terms like *ajeg-ajeg* and *ajegang* refer to village regulations and locate the term in the centre of Balinese culture (I Nyoman Darma Putra 2003). The notion of *ajeg* consists of a loose category that offers different groups of people a comfortable way to talk about Bali. Although many of my middle class intellectual friends dislike the conservative tone of the *Bali Post*, the dull programmes of Bali TV, and the post-New Order nature of the Ajeg Bali discourse, many ordinary Balinese like the concept:

> '*Ajeg* means that we should go back to the origins. Back to the pure and peaceful Bali, when things were orderly and true.'
> '*Ajeg* means that Bali is safe and can resist terrorists.'
> 'Ajeg Bali offers us an answer to modernization without substance.'

They also like the way Ajeg Bali is communicated on local television. Local news and the prime time live horror show *Sekala dan Niskala* address familiar topics, and Balinese soap series offer a welcome alternative to the Jakarta-based *sinetron* situated in an air-conditioned upper class world largely unfamiliar to many Balinese. Although the rather folkloristic formats of talk shows on Bali TV look rather clumsy and guests are expected to appear in full *adat* dress, the messages have an impact. Especially in the talk show *Ajeg Bali* Balinese culture is presented as a homogeneous and relatively static thing, which is essentially religious and rooted in village *adat*.

Balinese culture is also increasingly presented as exclusively Hindu. This is achieved by emphasizing contrasts with Islam and, ironically, by imitating Islamic formats at the same time. In contrast to the Islamic salutation *assalam'alaikum* anchormen, reporters and talk show hosts start with a solemn *Om Swastiastu*, and conclude with *Om Shanti Shanti Shanti Om*, while they bring their hands together in front of their face. When most national

39 Couteau 2002. Whereas Satria Naradha claims the sole 'authorship' of Ajeg Bali, others (Agung Alit 2004) argue that the leader of puri Satria and mayor of Denpasar, A.A. Puspayoga played a major role in conceptualizing the idea. Helen Creese informed me that the term *ajeg* was already used in 1993 in the context of the conservation of Balinese culture (Nyoman Sukartha et al. 1993:4).

networks broadcast the Islamic evening prayer (*adzan magrib*), Bali TV broadcasts a Hindu prayer (*puja trisandya*) at six o'clock that follows the Islamic format and uses phrases derived from Protestant prayers. A televised series of 285 episodes imported from India reminds the Balinese that they are part of a huge civilization that is much older than Islam.

One of the most popular programmes is the daily talk show *Dharma Wacana* (sponsored by Toyota) presented by Ida Pedanda Made Gunung – chairman of the conservative Parisada Campuan – who discusses religious topics and their practical moral implications. He is a witty man and his audience often laughs about the points he makes. Although he is not openly hostile to immigrants the following message is clear enough:

'Many Balinese sell their land in order to eat lots of *sate*, but don't forget that many immigrants sell *sate* in order to buy a lot of land'.

Although many public intellectuals supported the notion of Ajeg Bali, a minority criticized the top-down character of the campaign and compared it with the compulsory Pancasila courses from the New Order period. They feared that Ajeg Bali, because of its vagueness, could be used to silence critical voices, while the magazine *Sarad* warned against the return of 'feudal' attitudes (*Sarad* 43, 2003).

Satria Naradha's prime intention was to unify Bali through his Ajeg Bali campaign. His political agenda was focussed on various issues. He was anxious to prevent the spread of political violence (*Bali Post* 12-9-2003). He was also concerned about the absence of administrative coordination and urged district heads to cooperate more closely with the governor. At the launching of Bali TV he invited these administrators to together hold one torch, symbolizing the unity of Bali. In order to gain support and legitimacy for his campaign Satria Naradha invited administrators and high-ranking guests to sign so-called *prasasti*, stone inscriptions through which they endorse the intentions of Ajeg Bali. In doing so he 'revived' an ancient royal tradition of issuing stone inscriptions and continued a New Order habit of commemorating official events with an inscribed signature of a state authority. All senior administrators of Bali, national politicians and the sultan of Yogya signed these *prasasti*, which were gathered in the *Bali Post* headquarters. In January 2005 Satria Naradha proclaimed ten Ajeg Bali Heroes, while the Ajeg Bali campaign targetted schools and became part of the curriculum, including competitions for the best *ajeg* teacher, *ajeg* pupil, *ajeg* performance, *ajeg* prayer etcetera.[40] Meanwhile the term *ajeg* appeared almost everywhere, in newspaper articles, on banners during public meetings, and in casual '*warung*

40 *Bali Post* 5-1-2005. The heroes included freedom fighters, nationalist and religious leaders, a dancer, a painter, an architect, an environmentalist and one foreigner, the American Catholic priest Shadeg who was honoured for his study of the Balinese language.

talk'.[41]

The Ajeg Bali campaign is instrumental in emphasizing an exclusive ethnic profile of Balinese culture and religion. Ethnic unity was in turn based on religion.[42] When I met Satria Naradha he talked about Ajeg Bali in terms of a 'cultural renaissance', but when my assistant asked him casually what this meant in practice he immediately put the sweeping of immigrants on top of the agenda. This reveals, despite the flexible vagueness of Ajeg Bali, its rigid ethnic agenda. Since the position of the aristocracy is weakened and caste hierarchy is contested, Ajeg Bali offers urban intellectuals and middle class officials an opportunity to represent Bali as a homogeneous culture able to face external threats. At the same time the Ajeg Bali discourse erases conflicts concerning class, caste, religion and ethnicity, while it legitimizes violence (by *pecalang*) in the name of culture.

Gubernatorial elections and Ajeg Bali

The connections between the *Bali Post*, politics and the Ajeg Bali campaign became visible during the re-election of governor Dewa Made Beratha in august 2003. The election showed how party politics and media interests were closely intertwined and how the Ajeg Bali campaign was used to cover up corruption within the PDI-P.

The election of the governor should be understood within a broader context of national politics. President Megawati and her PDI-P sought to strengthen support among governors and district administrators, who were expected to help her win the presidential elections of 2004. A series of controversial elections – in Jakarta, Lampung, Central and East Java – occurred during which local PDI-P candidates were ignored in favour of strong 'non-cadre' favourites of party headquarters in Jakarta. Alerted by the stubbornness of local party branches in Buleleng and Jembrana, PDI-P leaders in Jakarta approached the provincial leaders of the party in May 2003 to 'synchronize' the strategy for the upcoming election of the governor of Bali.[43] It turned out that party headquarters preferred the re-election of governor Dewa Made

41 During the commemoration of the Puputan Badung on 20 September 2003 a banner had the slogan: Dengan semangat puputan kita kokohkan persatuan dan kesatuan demi ajegnya Bali (With the spirit of the *puputan* we reinforce the totality and unity for the sake of the strength of Bali).

42 Bali's police chief Mangku Pastika stated in this respect that 'Ajeg Bali has to be Ajeg Hindu' (personal communication Ngurah Suryawan).

43 It is interesting to see how terms like 'synchronization', 'anticipation', 'coordination' and 'operation', which formed the military grammar of the New Order bureaucracy, are still practiced.

Beratha and rejected the local PDI-P candidate Cokorda Ratmadi. Ratmadi was district head of Badung while his brother, A.A. Puspayoga, was mayor of Denpasar. Both come from puri Satria Denpasar, an old and respected PNI/PDI(-P) stronghold. Megawati preferred Made Beratha, who had a Golkar background, because he had facilitated the founding PDI-P congress in Bali in November 1998. Megawati's counted on the loyalty of 'her' people in Bali and tried to gain extra support in Golkar circles by choosing Made Beratha. This was a serious miscalculation.

When rumours leaked out in May 2003 that PDI-P headquarters did not support the local candidate, panic spread in party circles in Bali. In late June all PDI-P members of the provincial assembly were invited to Jakarta where they were told to support Mega's candidate. For the time being the provincial PDI-P decided to support two candidates: Cokorda Ratmadi and Dewa Beratha.[44] On 21 July party headquarters ordered the provincial PDI-P to drop the candidacy of Cokorda Ratmadi and to vote for Made Beratha. This letter caused a revolt among party cadres, who screamed that the ideals of the party were crushed and that it was now an all-out fight between them and Jakarta (*Bali Post* 22-7-2003, 24-7-2003; *Denpost* 23-7-2003). Three days later Megawati visited Bali and told Cokorda Ratmadi 'If you want to disgrace me, go ahead'.

Emotions ran high, confusing conflicts erupted over procedures, and pressure on Ratmadi increased. Eventually on Monday 28 July Ratmadi announced in front of weeping supporters that he had withdrawn his candidacy.

From then on the *Bali Post* played an active role as a reconciling mediator. Instead of presenting Cokorda Ratmadi's withdrawal as a defeat, he was praised as 'Sang Pahlawan Ajeg Bali', the Hero of a Strong and Unified Bali, who had sacrificed his personal interests to serve a higher public cause. In order to emphasize harmony Satria Naradha staged a reconciliation ceremony in puri Satria, which was directly broadcasted on Bali TV and received front page covering in the *Bali Post* (29-7-2003, 3-8-2003). Reconciliation was underlined by signing yet another *prasasti*, which symbolized the peace between Made Beratha and puri Satria and the pledge of all parties to support Ajeg Bali. The demonstrations by PDI-P supporters against Dewa Made Beratha which took place outside the frames of the cameras were not mentioned, but large scale riots did not occur.

Although the leader of the *Bali Post*, Satria Naradha, had been close to puri Satria, he had his own reasons to support Made Beratha. His television

44 *Radar Bali* 29-5-2003; *Bali Post* 24-6-2004. The running mate of Made Beratha was Alit Kelakan, a young PDI-P cadre who had actively supported Megawati when she was expelled from the PDI in 1996.

station was in jeopardy because it had started broadcasting before the new law on local television (Law no. 32/2002) was in operation. Therefore Bali TV was strictly speaking illegal, and Jakarta could close the station down. Satria Naradha needed Made Beratha's mediation in Jakarta to stay on air, which eventually succeeded.

The role played by the *Bali Post* illustrates that the local press is not always the best agency to reveal background information about local conflicts and other sensitive issues because of their proximity to the issues. On the contrary, often these agencies become involved as interested parties, either by taking side, or by playing an active role of their own.

It seemed as if most of the tension was over after the withdrawal of Ratmadi and the public reconciliation in puri Satria. On the 3rd of August the PDI-P members of the provincial assembly went on pilgrimage to the temple of Besakih and the next day they were locked up (*dikarantina*, quarantined) in Hotel Bali Cliff where they would stay till the election of the new governor on 6 August.[45] The *Bali Post* then covered the re-election of Dewa Made Beratha as governor with 31 votes (out of 55 assembly members), as a 'victory of Ajeg Bali'.[46]

Meanwhile other media revealed that bribery had occurred on a large scale shortly before the election (*Tempo* 18-8-2003; *Radar Bali* 19-8-2003; *Jakarta Post* 23-8-2003, 29-8-2003). Two PDI-P members had confessed they received Rp 50 million from a representative of PDI-P headquarters, who had visited them in Hotel Bali Cliff. Another amount of Rp 100 million would be transferred after the election. The *Bali Post* only reported that allegations about bribery were denied by provincial party leaders (*Bali Post* 13-8-2003). The fact that Bali Corruption Watch, the Legal Aid Foundation and the Pemuda Hindu Bali demanded an investigation and lodged a complaint with the Administrative Court in Denpasar was silenced by the *Bali Post*. The court rejected the allegation.

When Dewa Made Beratha was inaugurated on 28 August, the building of the provincial assembly was heavily protected by police, army and PDI-P militia. No incidents occurred. The re-election of the governor was decided in favour of 'Jakarta' and marked the defeat of regional autonomy. But it had a price. According to a detailed reconstruction by the magazine *Sarad*, 38 PDI-P members of the provincial assembly had received Rp 5.5 billion from their party.[47] Bali's police chief Mangku Pastika stated however that no bribery

45 *Bali Post* 4-8-2003, 6-8-2003. Mobile phones were collected to guarantee that the 38 PDI-P members were isolated from the outside world.

46 *Bali Post* 7-8-2003, 11-8-2003. Apparently seven PDI-P members had defected.

47 *Sarad* 41, 2003. Money from the office of the governor was first transferred to PDI-P headquarters in Jakarta and then distributed among PDI-P assembly members. Taken together the assembly members have probably received a total amount of more than Rp 13 billion from all the candidates involved.

had occurred because the case had not caused a loss to the state. Moreover, he added: 'There is no term for "money politics" in our laws' (*Jakarta Post* 29-9-2003).

Beyond Ajeg Bali: trans-national challenges

Decentralization has resulted in administrative fragmentation, which undermines regional autonomy. A paradoxical development is that Balinese middle class intellectuals tend to stress their regional authenticity and deny their Indonesian identity, but they do both in a very Indonesian way, because throughout the archipelago differences are increasingly expressed in similar terms.[48] Therefore one may wonder how Indonesian the whole *ajeg* campaign actually is.

The dilemma of Bali as an open fortress cannot be solved because an open economy and a closed cultural identity are not compatible. In contrast to the dominant view that defines Balinese culture as essentially Hindu and anchored in village *adat*, Degung Santikarma (2001b:22) wrote:

> Living in the midst of the trans-national traffic jam that is Bali can be an exhausting experience. For gloBALIzation has not just shipped bamboo wind chimes and leering wooden cats out to the boutiques of Berkeley and Brisbane, or seen Bill Clinton and Bay Watch battling for television airtime in the *banjar*, but has opened new markets for that most precious commodity of the new cultural capitalism: authenticity.

The problem with concepts that express hegemonic ambitions like Ajeg Bali is that they are based on post-colonial models that refer to closed and homogeneous societies and cannot incorporate notions of change and agency. Perhaps the need to discuss these issues will fade away as soon as an increase of tourism brings renewed prosperity to Bali, but it seems that growth will slow down. Therefore one of the biggest challenges of Balinese administrators and intellectuals will be to develop a more dynamic idea of their culture, which offers room for hybridity and trans-national dimensions. For how long and to what extent can a concerned urban middle class emphasis on authenticity and a rigid defence of an exclusive ethnic profile of Bali be compatible with the ongoing formation of a new trans-national urban corridor stretching from Bangkok, through Kuala Lumpur, Singapore, Jakarta, and Surabaya to Bali?[49] It is challenging to imagine what an open-minded, self-confident and well-regulated Bali, as a cultural counterpart of business metropolis Singapore, would look like in the future.

48 I borrow this phrase from Bayly 2004:2; See also Vickers 2002:94.
49 Dick 2005; Connor and Vickers 2003:168.

FRANZ and KEEBET VON BENDA-BECKMANN

Ambivalent identities
Decentralization and Minangkabau political communities

Introduction

After the fall of the Soeharto regime, Indonesia has embarked on a large scale process of renegotiating its administrative, political and social boundaries. A body of legislation laid the foundation for this negotiating process, loosening the boundaries between the central state and the regions and shifting power to lower administrative levels, most notably districts.[1] However, the process of redrawing boundaries that ensued extends far beyond the devolution of power to lower levels of administration. This chapter explores two separate but closely related consequences of the decentralization policies characteristic for West Sumatra that have important implications for the drawing of social boundaries.[2]

The first concerns the reorganization of village government. The Law on Village Administration of 1979 put into effect in 1983 in West Sumatra had introduced a nation-wide unified village structure based on the Javanese *desa*. The West Sumatran villages called *nagari* were much larger than the average *desa* in Indonesia. To avoid financial disadvantage for the region the *nagari* were split up in smaller administrative units now called *desa*. From its incipi-

1 See Kingsbury and Aveling 2003; Sakai 2002; Holtzappel, Sanders and Titus 2002; Aspinall and Fealy 2003; Schulte-Nordholt and Asnan 2003; Avonius 2004; Fanany 2003; Turner et al. 2003; F. and K. von Benda-Beckmann 2001, 2005.

2 The research on decentralization which we have conducted since 1999 was carried out with the assistance of Alfan Miko, Aidinil Zetra and Indraddin of the Studies Centre for Development and Socio-cultural Change (SCDev) and in cooperation with Andalas University in Padang. We gratefully acknowledge the help and stimulation of Abdul Aziz Saleh, Alfan Miko, Erwin, Syahmunir, Sjofjan Thalib, Narullah Dt. Parpatiah nan Tuo, Takdir Rahmadi and Tasman. We thank John McCarthy and the other authors of this volume for their thoughtful comments and engaged discussions during two seminars.

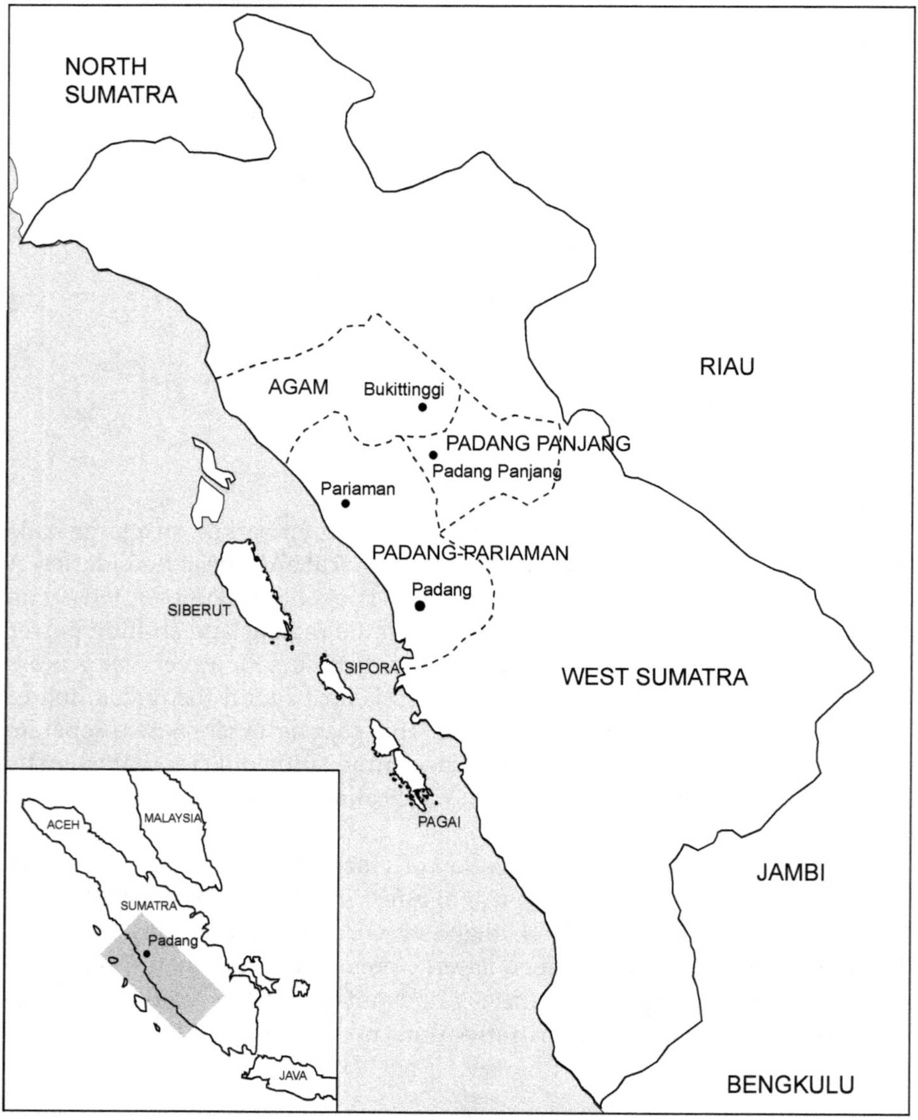

Map 17. West Sumatra

ence the *desa* system and the splitting up of *nagari* had been heavily criticized in West Sumatra and some reunification of *desa* took place during the 1990s. However, it was not until the decentralization policy was put in place that a more fundamental redesigning of the village administration became feasible. With Provincial Regulation no. 9/2000 on the village administration, village boundaries were redrawn and the neo-traditional village communities within the geographical boundaries of the former *nagari* re-emerged. This 'going back to the *nagari*' kindled interest in *adat* and *adat* institutions, and districts designed different ways of incorporating them into the new village governmental structures. As we shall explain in more detail below, this renewed interest in *adat* and its institutions should not be understood as merely populist, nostalgic and backward looking; it has some clear practical and future oriented reasons as well.

The second consequence concerns the reconsideration of Minangkabau identity in the larger Indonesian polity. While other regions in Indonesia show a similar heightened interest in their regional identity, Minangkabau identity seems to be uncommonly ambivalent. Minangkabau used to pride themselves with a prominent political presence before and immediately following Independence, but this position declined during the Soeharto regime. Today, many Minangkabau regret having been reduced to a middle range position of relative insignificance. Coming to grips with their lost superior position and understanding why this happened and what it means for their position within Indonesia is for many as much part of the general discussions about decentralization and the restructuring of village communities as are the more concrete issues of control over resources.

Renegotiations of social, political and administrative boundaries occur in many different but connected arenas and permeate political processes at all levels within the region, and included the urban and rural population in West Sumatra and migrants alike. They have to be understood against undercurrents of *longue durée* in the history of West Sumatra with its ambivalent and shifting relation between three main moral and normative structures of *adat*, the state and Islam.

In this chapter we will focus on the negotiations of the boundaries and political organization of villages. We suggest that control over natural resources is crucial for understanding the tensions and contradictions between *adat* and *adat* structures and the new village administration. Then we turn to the issue of Minangkabau identity and the tensions between *adat*, Islam and the state involved and discuss the various arenas in which debates about these issues are carried out and how the various arenas of negotiation are interconnected. We shall finish drawing some conclusions about the extent to which Minangkabau villages are embedded in larger political structures.

From nagari to desa

When the Dutch incorporated West Sumatra in the beginning of the eighteenth century, during the Padri War between islamicist groups that tried to establish an Islamic theocracy and those in favour of retaining a political structure based on *adat*, the colonial government based their system of indirect rule on the government structure of the *nagari*, the Minangkabau *adat* village, while suppressing Islamic structures. *Nagari* were largely autonomous territorial political units. Leadership, group affiliation and property relations were based on a matrilineal kinship structure. The *nagari* were governed by the heads of matrilineages, called *panghulu*. Over a period of more than half a century the Dutch reshaped the village political order substantially. They introduced a head *panghulu* as mayor and fixed the number of recognized *panghulu*. The council of lineage heads reconstituted in 1915 as the *nagari* council laid the foundation for a dualistic village structure, that in various forms were to characterize village government till today.[3] On the one hand there was the regulated *nagari* government, with the head *panghulu* or mayor and a Village Council or Kerapatan Nagari (KN), which included some but never all *adat* leaders. On the other hand, there remained a *nagari* government 'according to *adat*', albeit not officially recognized by the Dutch. The council of lineage heads, Village Adat Council (Kerapatan Adat Nagari, KAN)[4] or Council of Panghulu remained the highest village institution in terms of *adat*. Most *nagari* had a complex internal structure, consisting of several settlements or wards under different names. These wards were to become the basis for the structure of village administration introduced during the last decades of the Soeharto regime.

In 1979, the Law on Local Government was passed introducing a nation wide uniform village structure. In West Sumatra the law was only implemented in 1983.[5] The law introduced a new type of administrative organization, called *desa*, a purely administrative model with no provision for *adat* matters or leadership as the earlier local government regulations in West Sumatra had done. The other major change regarded the geographical boundaries of the *desa*. In theory the province of West Sumatra could have opted for converting each *nagari* into one *desa*, but mainly for financial

3 See for the history of village government, Westenenk 1918; F. von Benda-Beckmann 1979; Manan 1984; Kahn 1993; Sjahmunir 1996; F. and K. von Benda-Beckmann 2005. See further Kato 1982; Oki 1977; Dobbin 1983.

4 We shall use the abbreviation KAN throughout this paper. As we shall see later, Provincial Regulation no. 9/2000 speaks of Lembaga Adat Nagari (LAN), Adat Law Institution, but in many *nagari* it is common practice to continue to use the term KAN. We shall only use the term LAN when specifically referring to Regulation no. 9/2000.

5 See for more details Sjahmunir 1996.

reasons, it preferred to divide the *nagari* up. The new law allocated a fixed yearly development grant (*bantuan desa, bandes*) to each village, irrespective of its size or population. As the *nagari* were substantially larger than villages elsewhere in Indonesia, West Sumatra would financially be severely disadvantaged had they simply converted each *nagari* into a *desa*. In the first phase, the government chose the simplest way and converted all wards into *desa*. This multiplied the amount of funds from the central government by nearly seven. However, many of the new *desa* proved to be too small. From 1988 onwards a process of reunification set in directed by the provincial government which reduced the number of *desa* by half.[6]

Information on the *desa* period is rather scarce.[7] Mayors and village councils were rather strictly controlled by the district and sub-district administration. This was not new, but as long as the state did not provide many services to the *nagari*, the state's actual control on social and economic and village political issues had been limited. By 1983, state support in the form of structural development grants (*bandes*) and especially development projects had vastly expanded and with that its control over the new village functionaries. During the last decades of the Soeharto regime *bandes* was more and more replaced by project funding. The *kepala desa* became the central figure in attracting project funding from the central and provincial government.

The *nagari* had ceased to be an official administrative unit. However, the provincial government realized that total abandonment of *adat* structures might cause problems. Provincial Regulation no. 13/1983 therefore allowed for the *nagari* as '*adat* law community' and acknowledged the KAN as the institution representing this community. The various implementing regulations that followed gave detailed instructions for the council's constitution and how it was to exercise its main tasks: strengthening traditional values, maintaining the unity of the *nagari* population, and settling disputes on *adat* matters, and managing the *nagari*'s wealth. Thus, paradoxically, the *nagari* as *adat* law community and the KAN were formally regulated, but as 'informal law and institutions'. These new KAN, however, were more Golkar controlled and more bureaucratic than their predecessors of the 1970s, and representation of clan and lineage heads declined. Although they did not function as intended in many villages, the KAN still had considerable influence in village politics. It seems that *adat* leaders and KAN continued to exert authority over lineage land, people, and in dispute management. Conflicts between the KAN and *adat* leaders or *desa* heads seem to have been common. Their role in managing village land (*ulayat*) was contested by the *desa* administration,

6 Thus, the 543 *nagari* in West Sumatra (including the islands of Mentawai) initially split up into 3516 *desa*. After some reshuffling approximately 1700 remained.

7 Sjahmunir 1996; Van Reenen 1996; Biezeveld 2002; Damciwar 1990.

though hardly any *ulayat* was left. Many villages had distributed their *ulayat* land among the lineages long before, while *ulayat* of other villages had been put under the authority of the Departments of Land and of Forestry. Some lineage heads were said to have taken part in shady dealings of expropriation for logging or plantation concessions. The *adat* leaders' authority in marriage and divorce affairs and their authority over the allocation of fees and village development funds were hotly disputed. The period was characterized by a gradual decline of *adat* and *adat* leadership in the villages and the transmission of *adat* knowledge from (*adat*) teacher to pupils virtually came to a halt. There were structural reasons within the villages that contributed to this decline, among them a misfit between *desa* administration and *nagari*. *Desa* authority was based on territorial residence in the *desa*. *Adat* authority was based on the political localization of a person's matrilineage and property. According to the Minangkabau rules of post-marital uxorilocal residence, men resided on the land and in the houses of their wives' matrilineage (F. and K. von Benda-Beckmann 1978). Here they were only *urang sumando* (in-laws) and had no right to speak in *adat* matters. Their own place of authority in *adat* terms was where their matrilineage was localized, quite often in a different *desa*. In addition, *desa* heads often had a weak *adat* position in the *desa* which they headed in their capacity as village head, because they had no status in *adat* there. However, for the majority of the population these tensions were unimportant, and they adjusted relatively smoothly to the *desa*. They had conducted their main daily life and business within their ward anyway. If anything, they enjoyed the fact that the village administration had come closer to their home.

Preparing the ground for a return to the nagari

During the 1990s, public debates among *adat* leaders and urban elites were dominated by negative accounts of the *desa* structure. It was generally held that the *desa* system was not functioning well, that it had destroyed *adat* and the unity of the *nagari* population and that it had eroded the authority of the elders over the young. At a seminar held in 1989, Hasbi (Hasbi et al. 1990) concluded that the predictions of many Minangkabau experts had become true, that the decision to divide *nagari* into *desa* had deleterious social, economic and cultural effects. The *desa* administration had proven unable to mobilize villagers for the common good. Moreover, the state did not provide any significant financial compensation for *desa* heads. While the KAN had been acknowledged by the government, it had become an inefficient institution without real authority (Hasbi et al. 1990:30; Mochtar Naim 1990:60). And it was deplored that there was hardly any cooperation with or support from migrants, because they identified with the *nagari* and not with a *desa*. Mochtar Naim (1990:48) – a well known Minangkabau academic and politician – noted that *nagari* and *desa* did not just differ in size and administrative structure, but that they also represented different world views and philosophies. The *nagari* were the political micro-cosmos of the wider Minangkabau way of *adat* governance, in line with the basic fundaments of *adat*, matriclans, and language, while the *desa* was the lowest unit of the bureaucratic state. 'What we need', Mochtar Naim (1990:60) concluded, 'is a village government rooted in earth and with its head up in the air, and not, as the *desa* system, with the roots in the air and the head below'. Discussing the problems of the *desa* system, Abdul Aziz Saleh (1990:88) – professor of Social Science at Andalas University in Padang – concluded 'that for the time being, the best alternative is to return to the *nagari*, even if we shall have to call this *nagari desa*'. There were also more critical voices. For example, Damciwar (1990:75) – a lecturer at Andalas University – pointed out that 'it was not the fault of the Local Government Law no. 5/1979 that the wards instead of the *nagari* had been declared *desa*, but our own, because we put the financial considerations higher than the social and cultural ones. So we should not be surprised if the *desa* did not develop well'.

Once the possibility of revising the village government structure had become concrete and the laws of 1999 were to be implemented, attitudes in West Sumatra shifted remarkably from a predominant scepsis that had been dominant during the early 1990s, to widespread acceptance among both politicians and the wider population. In 1998, the governor had initiated research on the opinions and attitudes in rural areas. The researchers, under the guidance of professor Syahmunir of the law faculty of Andalas University, concluded that the majority of the rural population preferred a *nagari* over a *desa* structure. Thereupon the governor decided in 1998 that West Sumatra should return to a *nagari* structure and he set out to convince the political field in Jakarta and in West Sumatra. After intensive discussions within and outside the provincial parliament, consultations with non-governmental *adat* and Islamic organizations, influential Minangkabau migrants in Jakarta and discussions in the local newspapers, Provincial Regulation no. 9/2000 on Village Government was enacted. Within a very short period of time the governor had managed to create a broad consensus at the provincial level.

The prospect of going back to the *nagari* had generated quite passionate political discussions circling around two separate issues that often were confused. The first issue concerned the appropriate territorial basis for the new village. The second was about the organizational model to which the village should 'return': a pre-colonial, a colonial, an Old Order (Orde Lama) or an New Order (Orde Baru) model. The images about the *nagari* government before the introduction of the *desa* and the role of the KAN that circulated in the media and many public discussions were based on a shallow knowledge of Minangkabau history and had little to do with historical reality. Rather they reflected the hopes and expectations of the participants in the struggles.

Optimists, among them many *adat* leaders, argued that going back to the *nagari* would solve all problems the *desa* were facing. They hoped it would revive respect for *adat* and *adat* leaders as the legitimate village government and holder of village property, and as the guardians of family histories. These voices were supported by the Lembaga Kerapatan Adat Alam Minangkabau (LKAAM, Minangkabau wide Association of Village Adat Councils). The LKAAM had been established in 1966 after Soeharto had come to power, its main function being to contain political aspirations of *adat* leaders. Though it had always taken a critical stance to the governments' attempts to further registration of lineage land, it developed into a rather complacent organization and became increasingly involved in the Golkar party. Towards the end of the Soeharto regime, the LKAAM dissociated itself from Golkar and took more independent positions. In the Reformasi period, it withered an opportunity for *adat* leaders to recover some of the power they had lost during the *desa* period and became one of the most vocal critics of the government.

More sceptical voices, among them many university teachers and other urban intellectuals as well as most of the acting *desa* heads who feared loosing their position, pointed out that a return to some nostalgic past would not remedy any evils of the *desa*. In their eyes, the main reason why the *desa* did not function well was lack of adequate financial resources and qualified personnel. In their view, *adat* leaders were not a remedy; they were part of the problem, because they often refused to cooperate with the *desa* administration. Moreover, it was claimed, they themselves had contributed to the destruction of *adat* and *adat* authority, because they no longer really knew *adat*, did not develop the KAN into a functioning institution and manipulated whatever control they had over *nagari* assets to their own personal advantage. Among the youth that had grown up under the *desa* system very few saw the necessity or advantage of a *nagari* system of which they had no knowledge at all. During a discussion at the Law Faculty of Bung Hatta University in 2001, students complained they would be subjected to a system that would strengthen the position of old men instead of relying on young, dynamic, well educated persons. Yet others predicted that the local government reform would simply change the name of the village unit and would not fundamentally change the political and economic relationship between farmers and the state administration, or between provincial and national politics. Most common villagers and urban people did not have a clear opinion one way or another, but remained ambivalent, at times almost schizophrenic, towards *adat* and *adat* leadership. On the one hand, a return to *adat* values and governance seemed to hold great promise for improving the social, cultural and political conditions in the region. On the other hand, *adat* and lineage heads were seen as weak, autocratic and old-fashioned.

The land issue

A central issue in the debate concerned the question of control over village land (*ulayat*). The question of who rightfully controlled such resources and could legitimate their exploitation had been a source of conflict between village governments, lineage elders and the Land and Forestry Departments of the State ever since the Dutch had issued the Domain Declaration for West Sumatra in 1874. Villages claim – on the basis of *adat* – that they should control their *ulayat* land. The state claims its superior rights on the basis of national law. While West Sumatra never had a large plantation sector, during the last decades of the Soeharto regime much land and forest had been expropriated with inadequate compensation, yet sometimes in close cooperation with lineage elders. Most of these lands had been given as concessions or licenses to persons or enterprises close to the regime for logging or plantations.[8]

The new political freedom and the public emphasis on anti-corruption, transparency, and good governance had given many the hope that some of the worst injustices could be redressed. More generally, many saw a 'window of opportunity' to settle the still contested *ulayat* issue in their favour and to have it recognized.[9] The central government in 1999 issued a Ministerial Regulation concerning the Recognition of Village Land in order to resolve the *ulayat* problem.[10] However, this regulation only recognized *ulayat* land that 'continues to be held as in the past by the *nagari*, and where the relationships between the *adat* law community and *ulayat* have not been severed in the course of time'. The regulation thus validated all actions on *ulayat* land taken by the government, including the transfer of former Dutch plantations to the state. In the state interpretation, *ulayat* land, once it has been given or taken as license or concession under state law, remains state land after the license expires. A provincial draft regulation on *tanah ulayat* based on this interpretation has been under discussion for the past four years. It has led to many protests and demonstrations, and an alliance was formed between farmers and fishermen, urban intellectuals and NGOs and the LKAAM, claiming that the status of village land cannot extinguish by these acts of government. The

8 See Oki 1977:114; Kahn 1993:202; F. and K. von Benda-Beckmann 2004.

9 Compare Sakai 2002 for examples elsewhere in Indonesia.

10 Between 1994 and 1999, a World Bank sponsored research looked into the possibilities of recognizing and registering communal land rights in Minangkabau and some other regions (Slaats 1999).

LKAAM in particular has become an outspoken critic of the government's draft regulation. It proposed its own draft regulation according to which land concessions after expiration resume their status of *ulayat* land. Some staff of the faculty of law at Andalas University, notably Syahmunir and Narullah, have relentlessly lobbied for recognition of villages' *ulayat* rights, to the growing irritation of the provincial government. Given the contested nature of these land rights questions, the issue of *tanah ulayat* was left out of the Provincial Regulation on Village Government no. 9/2000. Early 2005 the issue was still pending.

The *ulayat* issue became a central factor in the discussions about the role of *adat* in the new village structure, because land claims directed against the state or investors had to be based on *adat*, and in the name of *nagari*, clan and lineage leaders. It became all the more prominent because it was expected that the state would gradually lower its funds for villages and require the *nagari* to generate their own funding. Despite disagreement about the specific form the return to the *nagari* should take, there was general agreement among the rural population that *ulayat* should be under village control. Some of the district heads with personal logging and plantation interests were said to resist a return to a *nagari* structure, because they feared that this would foster claims to *ulayat*. They were slower in responding to the new village structure than those without plantation and logging interests. Despite the fact that the issue has not been resolved, the very idea that *ulayat* in the future may form an important source of revenue for villages convinced many initially opposed of the importance of returning to the *nagari*. *Nagari* could what *desa* never could accomplish: lay a claim on *ulayat* legitimated in *adat*.

The administrative structure of the nagari

Provincial Regulation no. 9/2000 provides for an initial return to the *nagari* in their territorial boundaries of before 1979 and sets a general framework for local government, leaving the details to the districts.[11] The village government consists of an elected mayor, his staff, and an elected legislative body. The mayor represents the *nagari* internally and externally and is accountable to the village parliament which discusses and enacts village regulations and the village budget, and controls their implementation. According to the provincial regulation, the village parliament consists of members elected by the *nagari* population in general and free elections. The district regulations

[11] There is considerable variation in the district and village regulations, both in terms of institutional set up and in terms of election rules. For more details, see F. and K. von Benda-Beckmann 2001; Alfan Miko et al. 2005.

require that the village parliament represent the important categories of persons constituting the *nagari*, including the three classical categories, the *adat* elders (*ninik mamak*), religious leaders (*alim ulama*) and intellectuals (*cerdik pandai*) and '*adat* women' (*bundo kandung*) and 'the youth'. This not only resonates *adat* but perhaps even more the functional groups (*golongan karya*) of the Old Order and the New Order.

Mayor and parliament together form the official village government. In addition, two further institutions are provided for. An Adat and Religion Consultative Council advises the mayor and village parliament on *adat* and religious matters. Moreover, all villages are to have a Village Adat Institution (Lembaga Adat Nagari, LAN) which mediates in disputes relating to lineage property and protects *adat* in general, but which is not part of the official *nagari* government. By choosing the term Village Adat Institution (LAN) instead of Village Adat Council (KAN) provincial parliamentarians wanted to emphasize their intention of dissociating this body from the KAN of Soeharto's New Order. But districts and *nagari* could opt for another name, and five out of eight district regulations have reverted to the term Village Adat Council, KAN. The KAN (and LAN) maintained their ambiguous position in the new village governance structure. It is not a body of the official *nagari* administration, yet it is regulated and its functions are officially regulated in quite some detail.

The politics of changing boundaries

The provincial regulation prescribes that the villages return to the territorial units of the *nagari* before the introduction of the *desa* system. Fusions and divisions of *nagari* are not excluded, but referred to a later stage. A *nagari* may be split up only after consultation of the whole *adat* law community and common deliberation (*musyawarah*) between the KAN and other social leaders. If consensus is reached the decision is forwarded to the district administration and has to be confirmed by decision of the district head. The regulation also provides for the establishment of a new *nagari* with its own administration, while remaining under the KAN of the mother *nagari*. By early 2005, 32 *nagari* had split and it is generally expected that eventually there will be around 800 *nagari*, considerably more than the pre-1983 543 *nagari*.

In most cases the *desa* agreed to reunite, but some of the old *nagari* simply had grown too large and agreed to split up. Some *desa* had once been a separate *nagari* and were fused by the state administration sometime in the past, as had happened with Padang Luar. These *desa* decided to establish a separate *nagari* again, such as Sungai Tenang did early 2005. Such splits have not been problematic.

In two situations the redrawing of boundaries has caused serious problems. One is where *desa* have been caught up in the expansion of municipalities trying to incorporate neighbouring *desa* as municipal districts (*kelurahan*). For example, the mayor of Bukittinggi has unilaterally incorporated some adjacent *desa* of *nagari* belonging to the district of Agam. This has created protracted political fights among the district head of Agam, the mayor of Bukittinggi, the respective parliaments, the media, former *desa* heads and current mayors and *adat* representatives of the *nagari* concerned supported by mass demonstrations of the village population, and included the governor and the central government. Other expanding municipalities such as Padang Panjang and Pariaman face similar problems. By early 2005, these conflicts were still unresolved.

The other problematic constellation concerns *desa* that had originally been settlements of newcomers (*orang datang*) or descendants of slaves (*kemanakan dibawah lutuik*). Most of these settler groups are Minangkabau themselves and have lived there for more than a century. But they may also be traders or Javanese transmigrants who have settled relatively recently. They enjoy only inferior political and economic rights under *adat*. The territory on which these communities live is usually part of the inherited property of original clans who had 'given' it to the newcomers according to *adat*. While this property has the status of inherited property (*pusako*) for the newcomers, it remains under some residual rights of control of the original *pusako* or *ulayat* holders. Some of these groups live in a more or less separate ward of the old *nagari* and were a *desa* of their own. Under the *desa* system such newcomer-*desa* enjoyed a greater degree of autonomy, cherished by these settlements and resented by the old lineages. Newcomer-*desa* are afraid that under the new regime the heads of the old lineages, who mainly reside in the older parts of the *nagari* and who dominate the KAN, will reassert their rights, and for that reason insist on forming an independent *nagari*.

These struggles are an indication of the resilience of *adat* principles and old *adat* status differences and their legal implications. In contrast to equally important social distinctions on the basis of education, the *adat* status differences between newcomers and original *adat* citizens are ascribed, implying a legal status with differences in rights and obligations. The fear among many urban intellectuals that former inequalities, which had been largely balanced out under the *desa* regime, would re-emerge under the new system is more realistic than the *adat* protagonists like to concede.

Contesting nagari resources

One of the major problems in the new *nagari* is the question of who controls the village resources: the mayor representing the village government and its citizens, or the KAN as the representative of the *adat* community? This issue has substantive grounds. Under the New Order an investor wanting to exploit gravel, sand, coal or forest had to negotiate with the provincial or even central administration. District and village authorities simply had to carry out the instructions from above and villages usually received little or no compensation. Today investors have to negotiate at many levels and can no longer neglect village and district administrations. Markets were an important source of income for districts, but today villages want their share and claim control over their markets. Though not many markets have in fact been handed over to villages, most villages expect this to happen in the not too distant future. Village control not only means potential income for the village to use for village development; it also means a source of potential corruption for persons in leading positions. It is in particular this potential illegitimate income that makes the internal struggles among village administration and *adat* institutions so intense. The experience of corruption is so ingrained that distrust among the villagers and their leaders is rampant.

Compared with the period before 2000, the KAN's role in the management of *nagari* resources has changed. The *desa* heads, having no basis in *adat*, could not lay claims to *ulayat* or other *nagari* property, but the mayor as the head of the new *nagari* government now competes with the KAN as the holder of traditional *adat* authority. Somewhat paradoxically then, the return to the *nagari* has formally strengthened the position of the mayor vis-à-vis the *adat* government. The governor's Circular Letter (Surat Edaran) of 2003 prescribes that the riches of the *nagari* are to be managed (*dikelola*) by the Village Government. In some villages, the authority has officially been handed over by the chairman of the KAN to the village government, but many mayors have difficulties to take over actual control over the resources from the *adat* elders or the KAN. In other *nagari*, compromises have been negotiated. There are also examples of fruitful cooperation between the mayor and the chairman of the KAN.

Adat, Islam, the state and Minangkabau identity

In the process of redrawing of villages' geographical, social and administrative boundaries, the relationships between the three major normative orders are also being renegotiated. Going back to the *nagari* not only preoccupies the minds of many Minangkabau because of the details of village government and land rights. Equally important is the feeling that it restores an essential element in Minangkabau identity, namely their geographical, social and political roots. These processes have also revitalized discussions about Minangkabau culture (*kebudayaan*) in general and in particular with respect to the other half of Minangkabau identity – of being Muslim.

Minangkabau identity has always been strong and ambivalent, multi-layered, full of contradictions and tensions. The historically oldest layer is rooted in *adat*. But *adat* has been joined, partially superseded but never replaced, by other worldviews, symbolic universes and legal orders. While the extent to which Minangkabau embraced or rejected new knowledge and values varied considerably, they rarely relinquished the earlier ones. Over time, Minangkabau developed a pronounced self-understanding and cultural – and later ethnic – identity that implies an uneasy and shifting reconciliation of these normative orders. The titles of three recent books by Minangkabau writers indicate this growing concern of Minangkabau with their own ethnicity: *Etnis dan adat Minangkabau* (Ethnicity and *adat* Minangkabau, 2002), H.Ch.N.Dt. Bandaro Latief; *Masih ada harapan; Posisi sebuah etnik minoritas dalam hidup berbangsa dan bernegara* (There still is hope; The position as one ethnic minority living with people and state, 2004), S. Bahar and Mohammed Zulfan Tadjoeddin; *Utopia nagari Minangkabau* (The utopia of the Minangkabau *nagari*, 2003), Hasrifendi and Lindo Karsyah. In each of these publications discussions of the new *nagari* implies a discussion of Minangkabau identity.

Minangkabau *adat* is very elaborately expressed in oral histories, proverbs, stories, and songs. It has sparkled the imagination of foreign observers from the early nineteenth century on and in the Dutch writings on *adat* and *adat* law in Indonesia, sources on Minangkabau occupy a disproportionally large space. Yet as Joel Kahn (1993) has shown, 'constituting the Minangkabau' has never been an affair of colonial Dutch or Indonesian state officials of non-Minangkabau origin only. Many Minangkabau writers have actively contributed to debates on the relations between *adat* and other world views.

The relationships between *adat* and Islam, and later between *adat*, Islam and the state, have varied historically.[12] In pre-colonial times Islam was largely adapted to matrilineal *adat*. This changed in the Padri War, when Islamists offered their own blueprint for social, economic and political organization. It changed again when the Dutch intervened and supported *adat* against Islam. The duality of *adat* and Islam has remained a central and constitutive point of identification for most Minangkabau. The inseparable unity of *adat* and Islam is expressed with the saying '*Adat* is founded on the *syarak*, the *syarak* is founded on the holy Koran' (*Adat basandi syarak, syarak basandi kitabullah,*

12 Taufik Abdullah 1966; F. and K. von Benda-Beckmann 1988.

usually abbreviated as ABSSBK). While this saying has a long history,[13] in recent years it is on everyone's lips. Between 2002 and 2003 three conferences were held and several publications appeared on ABSSBK.[14] The conviction that *adat* and Islam are inseparable, that values of both must govern the lives of Minangkabau, and, given their decline, must be revitalized, has also found its expression in another 'return movement', the 'return to the *surau*'. *Surau* were the sleeping places for unmarried Minangkabau men who had no place to stay in their maternal homes under the system of matrilineal social organization and post-marital uxorilocal residence. They were also the place where instruction in *adat* and Islam was given.

The Dutch and later the Republican governments introduced new social and political worldviews of modernity and development. While many Minangkabau had no difficulty in adopting these new ideas, matrilineality and modernity were often seen as mutually exclusive. Yet Minangkabau persistently occupied a prominent position in the political landscape of the emerging Indonesian state. Minangkabau politicians were represented in the leadership of all political parties and they were disproportionally present in first governments of the Republic. 'Modernity' later gave way to the struggle for independence and, once that goal had been reached, for a democratic Indonesian state.

After the regional rebellion Pemerintah Revolusioner Republik Indonesia (PRRI, the Revolutionary Government of the Indonesian Republic) had been put down by the armed forces of the Republic, Minangkabau's educational head-start dwindled away and most intellectuals became complacent under the increasingly authoritarian and centralist regime of Soeharto's New Order. There is a deep and widespread sense of frustration in Minangkabau of having lost its prominent position in Indonesia.[15] Navis (1995:19) speaks in this respect of an 'intellectual disaster' (*musiba intellektual*).

Discussions of Minangkabau identity since the downfall of the Soeharto regime are mostly inward looking. While in former times the Minangkabau had operated jointly with others against a common enemy (the Dutch during the colonial period, and the Javanese during the PRRI) and had been the centre of the strong and resource-rich Province Middle Sumatra, today they stand rather alone in negotiating their relationships within the national state, and their weak economic position gives them little leeway. Richer provinces within Sumatra such as Riau and Aceh redefine their position within the

13 Until the late 1970s, the relationship was commonly expressed as *adat basandi syarak, syarak basandi adat*. See Taufik Abdullah 1966; F. and K. von Benda-Beckmann 1988.

14 LKAAM 2002; PPIM 2003; Salmadanis and Samad 2003. See also Ade Chandra et al. 2000; Erizal 2000a, 2000b.

15 Taufik Abdullah 1995; S. Bahar and Mohammed Zulfan Tadjoeddin 2004.

Indonesian state from a strong economic position and show no inclination to share their wealth with Minangkabau who have little to offer in return. The enthusiasm for the return of the *nagari* should therefore also be seen in the light of a general frustration of finding Minangkabau in a position among neighbours who are much stronger and richer than West Sumatra. Despite their critique and disillusion most Minangkabau still identify strongly with the Indonesian nation-state. There is no discussion about secession in the region.

The diminished political and ideological pressure from the centre has stimulated an outburst of formerly suppressed Minangkabau-ness, which finds its expression in *nagari*, *adat*, and ABSSBK. Questions that emerge include: how to fill this space, what is *adat*, who knows *adat*, what do *nagari* government and ABSSBK according to *adat* mean? Globalization offers additional frameworks in which identities can be formulated (for example ethnic minority, indigenous people) while at the same time neo-liberal pressure poses challenges that are held to threaten Minangkabau values. With regard to Minangkabau a number of international organizations support the process of decentralization and the return to the *nagari*. Minangkabau as well as outsiders from within Indonesia, foreign anthropologists and development agencies assisting the decentralization policy such as the Ford Foundation, the UNDP (United Nations Development Programme), the GTZ (Gesellschaft für Technische Zusammenarbeit), largely use a global rhetorical repertoire, and local agents increasingly adopt the same language. A striking illustration is the report on a seminar on the return to the *surau*, held in Padang in 2001. It warns of the dangers which the globalization of science, information technology and lifestyles bring for Minangkabau identity and ABSSBK values, but then goes on to frame the issues in globalized language: *partisipatif, dialogis, demokratis, transparansi* and *akuntabilitas, sinergi, efektivitas, efesiensi*.[16] Thus, the normative order represented by the state and transnational normative notions are as much part of the Minangkabau identity as *adat* and Islam, but in contrast to the relationship between *adat* and Islam, there is not much debate about the ensuing contradictions.

Arenas and actors

Discussions and struggles about identity occur in different, interdependent arenas, in villages, among district and provincial political elites, in parlia-

16 'Pemda Sumbar dan ICMI, Padang, Pedoman gerakan kembali ke surau di Sumatera Barat, Kembali ke surau di Sumatera Barat', outcome of seminar and workshop, in Hotel Buni Minang, on 27-28 June 2001. See for Bali, Henk Schulte Nordholt in this volume.

ments, and in circles of development agencies, and among Minangkabau migrants in Medan, Jakarta, or Bandung. Workshops, seminars, books and local TV and newspapers are the main channels of information. Return to the *nagari* and ABSSBK also mean different things for different people in different positions. The debate about the *nagari* has been focussed on the glittering past and has created much nostalgia.[17]

Debates among intellectuals

After a period of relative neglect in the 1980s and early 1990s, *adat* and Minangkabau society are enjoying lively interest among intellectuals, university lecturers, journalists, and migrants.[18] Illustrative are the books published by the Foundation Genta Budaya which came out of workshops held in the 1990s, in which the predicaments of Minangkabau are critically discussed.[19] A series of school books on *adat* and history have been published for use in primary and secondary schools (Yulfian Azrial 1994). With the return to the *nagari*, the search for *adat* knowledge intensified further. Publications on *adat* have increased and older books and booklets on *adat* have been reprinted. The LKAAM publishes books and teaching materials and for some time a *Buletin Seri Alam Minangkabau* in Minangkabau language. It also offers training courses in *adat*.[20] Members regularly publish in local newspapers and appear on TV (*Semangat Demokrasi* 16-19 March 2002). Today the LKAAM is only one organization out of many claiming a greater role for *adat* and interpreting and extolling the significance of ABSSBK. It has been joined by new organizations such as the Pusat Pengkajian Islam dan Minangkabau (PPIM, Centre for Studies of Islam and Minangkabau). Feminist organizations organize meetings on the role of Minangkabau women; NGO alliances fight for *adat* rights and organize seminars and workshops. Migrants write books and pamphlets on Minangkabau *adat* and on problems of ethnicity and identity and organize meetings and seminars

17 Taufik Abdullah (1995:8) characterized this attitude as narcissistic and warned against utopian expectations.

18 Until the 1970s the representation structure of *adat* was relatively simple, consisting of some recognized all-Minangkabau *adat* experts such as Rasjid Manggis Dt. Rajo Panghoeloe (1971) and Idrus Hakimy Dt. Rajo Panghulu, the LKAAM and some *adat* law teachers, social scientists and historians such as Taufik Abdullah, Mochtar Naim, Imran Manan, Amelioes Sa'danoer and Abdul Aziz Saleh.

19 See M. Hasbi et al. 1990; Edy Utama 1995, 1996a, 1996b; Abdul Aziz Saleh and Van Giffen 1990; Idrus Hakimy Dt. Rajo Panghulu 2001.

20 LKAAM, Padang, Lembaga pemberian bekal adat alam Minangkabau (Babekal Alam) LKAAM Sumatera Barat, 2001.

in West Sumatra.[21] The migrants' organization Gebu Minang in Jakarta has founded a book club and in 2001 started to publish a series of short pocket booklets (*buku saku*) dealing with selected aspects of Minangkabau *adat* and history.

There is subtle and not so subtle negotiating about who is entitled to speak about and for *adat*. The LKAAM always emphasizes that it covers both *adat* and religion, in the spirit of ABSSBK, and tries to capture the back to the *surau* discourse. According to them, the all-Indonesian Islamic organization Majelis Ulama Indonesia (MUI, Council of Indonesian Islamic Scholars) is expert on religion only and is therefore not entitled to speak about *adat* or about the relationship of *adat* and Islam. NGOs have no say in *adat* matters either according to the LKAAM. The LKAAM itself is also under critique and its abolition has been repeatedly demanded in the local media. It is criticized for its Golkar past, and other organizations doubt its legitimacy to represent *adat* (*Singgalang* 28-4-2003). NGOs in particular see no reason for the existence of such an institution.[22] Others argue that there is no need for an LKAAM because *adat* is rooted in the *nagari*; there are no *adat* institutions on the provincial level. Moreover, *nagari* leadership should not consist of *adat* elders only. The LKAAM defends its position and history in the media and in seminars. It explains that it was not founded in 1966 by the regional government but by the KAN of all Minangkabau *nagari*. It would accept critique only from those KAN. Moreover, the LKAAM had always claimed that land in Minangkabau was *tanah ulayat* and not government land.[23]

Activist groups such as the Lembaga Bantuan Hukum (LBH, Legal Aid Bureau) or the Forum Peduli Sumatera Barat (FPSB, Forum of Concerned West Sumatrans) take a similar position as the *adat* champions in the *tanah ulayat* issue. The NGO alliance Paga Alam for instance adopts an approach to *adat* and *tanah ulayat* that is even more radically *adat* minded than that of the LKAAM.[24] But while the members of the LKAAM fully identify as *adat*-

[21] M.S. Amir 1999, 2005; H.Ch.N.Dt. Bandaro Latief 2002; H.Ch.N.Dt. Bandaro Latief et al. 2004; S. Bahar and Mohammed Zulfan Tadjoeddin 2004. S. Bahar organized a live discussion of his controversial book (S. Bahar and Mohammed Zulfan Tadjoeddin 2004) on Padang TV. The migrants' organization of Solok district organized a large meeting on *adat*, the position of women and *suku* management in January 2005. The Minangkabau Women Congress planned for 2005 and for a discussion of the agenda with Minangkabau migrants from Java, local NGO activities and the provincial branch of the Indonesian Human Rights Commission.

[22] *Semangat Demokrasi* 16-19 March 2002. See A.R. Rizal in *Singgalang* 6-7-2002; Mochtar Naim in *Singgalang* 4-5-2003.

[23] *Singgalang* 29-4-2003. LKAAM, Padang, Hubungan dan eksistensinya Lembaga Kerapatan Adat Alam Minangkabau (LKAAM) dan Kerapatan Adat Nagari (KAN) di Sumatera Barat, no date.

[24] Paga Alam Minangkabau, Padang, Siaran Pers no. 01/S-Pers/PALAM/IX/2004 tentang Ranperda Pemanfaatan Tanah Ulayat, 2004.

champions, other organizations fight for recognition of *adat* rights without implying an extensive role for *adat* leadership. According to them, government according to *adat* is not democratic but has a feudalistic ring. They differentiate between the substantive rights embodied in *adat* (considered more just than land rights embodied in state legislation) and the organization entitled to claim these rights. Yet others claim that struggles for political and economic rights of the population could better be entrusted to uncompromised civil society organizations. *Adat* rights are supposed to support the interests of the population and not to strenghten feudal positions of corrupt *adat* leaders.

The government and provincial politics

The provincial government is an important and active player in the regional arena. It successfully pre-empted and controlled the politics of decentralization. When it became probable that the Soeharto regime would not last and an era of Reformasi appeared at the horizon, the emphasis on Minangkabau-ness and revaluating the characteristically Minangkabau *nagari* became a means to show distance towards Jakarta and the 'Javanese' village organization of the *desa* which 'Jakarta' had imposed in 1983. Emphasis on Minangkabau-ness also served to reassert local economic interests against domination by central authorities in Jakarta. When the West Sumatran political elite fought against the centre to keep West Sumatra's only large industrial enterprise, the Cement Factory in Padang, under local control, West Sumatran authorities strongly emphasized the specific status of Minangkabau *tanah ulayat* which according to *adat* cannot be sold (Sakai 2003b). As we have seen, this does not prevent the same authorities from insisting that once licenses or concessions have been given for such land, the land remains state land.

The provincial government continues to subsidize most of the organizations engaged in discussions of *adat* and Minangkabau culture. There is hardly any publication without a preface by the governor. The debates between organizations operating at the provincial level such as the LKAAM, the PPIM, and the MUI about the role of *adat*, the position of Islamic authorities, ABSSBK and the return to the *surau* are not only a discussion about values and morals, but should also be understood as a competition for government funding and for advisory services to the government.[25] While this gives the

25 Thus when the LKAAM criticizes the provincial government for not caring about *adat*, this probably is a veiled critique that the government has given too much subsidies to a newcomer in the *adat*-Islam-culture field, the PPIM. See the critical exchanges in the newspaper *Semangat Demokrasi* 23-26 March 2002, (LKAAM) and 20-22 March 2002 (Governor's office).

government a means to sanction certain views, it cannot prevent organizations such as the LKAAM or university staff from criticizing provincial politics. Some other organizations operate more at a distance from the government, as they are supported by migrants or foreign NGOs.

A major topic in the regional political discourses concerns the Minangkabau form of democracy. Most Minangkabau take great pride in Minangkabau democracy with its strong emphasis on common deliberation and consensus and consider it superior to the 'western style 50 plus 1 voting democracy'. It is not just the traditionalist *adat* lobby that is in favour for introducing Minangkabau principles of democracy, many politicians and public figures such as the rector of Andalas University praise Minangkabau consensus democracy as well.[26] Such statements, however, do not prevent the provincial and district governments from overloading villages with regulations and bureaucracy.

Various international, national and regional donor agencies also participate in these debates, following their own agendas and trying to promote their political issues. Thus, the GTZ advises several villages and districts and organizes training courses on the organization of a *nagari* structure, emphasizing issues of transparency and administrative responsibility.[27] Both proponents of *adat* and 'modern' democracy play to the ears of donor agencies. The former emphasize that *adat* is indeed development from below, participatory, community based. The latter stress the value of free elections and democratic decision-making processes. The donor agencies themselves are ambivalent how to evaluate the competing principles of democracy. The Minangkabau consensus type appeals to their notion of participation and community based development (see Asia Research Centre 2001). With their interest in *adat* they want to emphasize that they are not introducing foreign or 'Western' ideas into Indonesia. A brochure of the UNDP Partnership for Governance presents the Minangkabau *nagari* as good governance avant la lettre, indicating that the present good government offensive is nothing new but intended to restore traditional values (UNDP 2001:6). The partnership organizes and finances workshops and small research projects on the progress of the local government reform, carried out by local NGOs or university research and development institutes.[28] These workshops are important events not only because they bring villagers into contact with issues discussed in wider social and political contexts; they also are important meeting places for village offi-

26 See the rector of Andalas University in *Haluan* 8-6-2001.

27 The Friedrich Naumann Stiftung supports anti-corruption training; The USAID-sponsored Perform Project has been active in some districts and some projects are supported by the Ford Foundation. The UNDP partnership for governance has sponsored meetings with villager leaders about democracy and open society in the *nagari*.

28 On the activities of donor agencies, see GTZ 2001b; Turner et al. 2003:129-35.

cials, who learn about each others' experiences. From the discussions we had over the past five years with representatives of foreign donor organizations it seems, however, that the initial enthusiasm for local level democracy has given way to more sober assessments.

These discussions also serve to renegotiate the relationship between *adat* and Islam. Under the rhetorical unity of *adat* and Islam, old struggles over the relative superiority of one over the other continue. The greater autonomy of districts have allowed district heads to make their imprint on the village structure, thus contributing to regional differences within the province. Some district heads clearly favour *adat* dominance in internal village affairs, while others have created a sharper division between *adat* and religion by introducing a separate Council of Religious Elders parallel to the KAN. The return to the *nagari* and especially the issue of land rights are clearly issues that upgrade *adat*. For most local politicians, village leaders and NGOs, the relevant 'community' under debate is the *adat* community of the *nagari* (*masyarakat hukum adat*), not the Islamic community of believers. Initially 'the return to the *surau*' discourse (later called movement) was an answer to the return to the *nagari* discourse. In contrast to the discourse on *adat* with its political and economic overtones, the discourse on Islam stresses the importance of Minangkabau moral values, and the need to defend them against cultural and economic globalization. Islamic pressure in the Provincial Parliament, for example, led to the adoption of a hotly discussed regulation (no. 11/2001) on 'social illnesses' (*penyakit masyarakat*, PEKAT), such as gambling, prostitution and drug abuse. This regulation has great symbolic value but no-one expects any practical relevance. Thus, while *adat* has acquired greater prominence in political and economic terms, Islam is mobilized for specific moral issues.

Villagers

The depressed sense of identity is primarily a problem for the Minangkabau elite witin and outside of West Sumatra, where the discussion about the relation between *adat* and Islam is the most pronounced. However, it rubs off on the rural population as well, because these arenas are linked to rural areas. Many participants mainly engaged at the regional level occupy an *adat* position or are otherwise actively involved in their village of origin. The LKAAM and MUI have their links with villages, as have political parties. Political parties are not allowed to play an open and active role in village elections, but through the organization of workshops for villagers they supported the process materially and made their views known. Moreover, with the new *nagari* many (often retired) migrants, who had lost interest in village affairs, have taken a renewed and active interest in their village or origin. Some have taken on office as *adat* leader, as official advisor, or even as mayor. Wearing several hats at the same time, neither a real insider nor a real outsider, they contribute to the construction of Minangkabau identity and to the more mundane concerns of village administration and politics.

While urban elites discuss *adat* in general terms, villagers tend to discuss it in connection with concrete issues of the structure and procedures of village government, control over resources, and lineage and property histories. This requires knowledge about the actual functioning of the *nagari* government in the past and of the embodiment of *adat* in the political and economic *nagari* constitution. That knowledge remains oral and is, if at all, transmitted within the lineages. However, many of the newly installed young *panghulu* have been elected because of their high education and good connections with the government. They lack authoritative knowledge about the history of their *nagari,* the composition of its *suku* and lineages, the history of *suku* and lineage land and lineage splits, which is necessary to be a successful village leader (Agus Indiyanto 2005). But they are reluctant to ask the old men and women who may know more, because that does not accord with their status and might undermine their authority. More often than not essential knowledge has been lost for ever and the lineage history is being recreated from scratch by young lineage heads without any training in *adat*. The many books and booklets on *adat* are of little help, because these reproduce Minangkabau *adat* and history, as expressed in *adat* proverbs and maxims, but are far removed from contemporary affairs. Knowledge of this type may help the youth to develop a stronger identification with *adat,* but such books do not provide clues as to how *nagari* in the sense of *adat* organizations might be developed or fruitfully accommodated within the state structure.

Likewise, the relationship between *adat* and Islam has different connotations for urban elites and the rural population. While some Minangkabau migrants in Java find it difficult to reconcile the two systems of belief, villagers generally have no problem identifying equally with *adat* and Islam. They are critical of the political elites in West Sumatra who took the issue as an opportunity to debate whether villages should or should not have Religious Councils, for these councils were said to be an entry point for political influence from which political parties were legally barred. Wealthy migrants financed prayer houses and mosques for their family or lineage back home as a public sign of religiosity and of family support. But many villagers regarded these prayer houses as a threat to the *nagari* community, undermining the rule that a *nagari* community shares one mosque, and thus undermining the unity of *adat* and Islam. On the other hand, many villagers have readily embraced the new slogan of 'going back to the *surau*', as a counterpart to the movement of 'going back to the *nagari*'. Few take it literally, but see it as a necessary reconsideration of Islamic morals and values, that are threatened to be eclipsed by the *adat* hype. The rapid spread of Islamic dress requirements for women must be seen in this light. Though it certainly is part of an Indonesian wide development, it has only taken off in West Sumatra since the debates about *adat* had evoked an Islamic response.

Critical voices

Adat and *adat* leadership are not unanimously supported in Minangkabau. Critique is partly directed at established *adat* leadership, and partly at the lifestyle *adat* seems to stand for. Many among the younger generation of urban intellectuals, hold at best ambivalent feelings towards *adat* leadership. *Adat* elders in the *nagari* are frequently perceived as indeed old, old fashioned and backward, not in line with modern life, and lacking good formal education. They are therefore considered incapable of governing the *nagari*. They are also blamed for having given in too easily to the pressures and temptations of the administration and investors during the Soeharto government. They are reproached for having abandoned *ulayat* too easily and of having pocketed compensation without sharing it with their *kemanakan* (matrilineal relatives). Urban intellectuals, on the other hand, are held to be lacking solid knowledge of *adat*. Many leading civil servants of the provincial and district governments in West Sumatra now carry the *datuk* title of a *panghulu*. Since they do not live in the *nagari*, they are seen as useless for day to day village government. While mobile phones have considerably bridged temporal and spatial distance and are indeed frequently used for inter-local communication they cannot replace day to day physical presence and availability.

Finally many Minangkabau have self-critically commented on the flowery but virtually empty rhetoric of *adat* virtues, ABSSBK and the return to *nagari* and *surau*, and depicted Minangkabau as 'champions in slogans' (*juara slogan*), spending hours '*ber*-Minang-Minang', engaged in being Minangkabau. These critics do not trust the regular declarations that the values are good, and that only the people have forgotten them. And they do not believe that once the return to the *nagari* and the *surau* is 'socialized' (*disosialisasikan), adat* values and the authority of knowledgeable elders and their matrilineal kin will automatically be restored and the *nagari* will function as it should.

The return to the *nagari* thus is a lively issue discussed in many arenas at different levels. Each of these arenas has its own political constellation and concomitant preoccupations. However, the arenas are not insulated from each other, but form permeable, overlapping fields. Urban Minangkabau, participating in regional or national debates and at the same time being an *adat* leader or participating in *nagari* matters in another capacity, play a crucial bridging role. But perceptions of the *nagari* certainly are different for people living in the *nagari* and for outsiders. From the outside and from the perspective of migrants living far away, the *nagari* may be a small and intimate community, the incarnation of *adat* and *adat* leadership through *adat* elders in the Adat Village Council, inviting nostalgic feelings and supporting romanticized notions of *nagari* and *adat*. Seen from the inside *nagari* are not cosy communities but complex social organizations divided along many lines.

Conclusions

Decentralization has evoked a process of renegotiating social and political boundaries in West Sumatra in various interlinked arenas each with its own specific focus and concerns. While the province has receded somewhat to the background, districts self-confidently emphasize their autonomy vis-à-vis the province and the central state. The same autonomy allowed districts freedom to redesign their relationship with villages and to define the boundaries of authority. Despite widespread initial scepticism about the wisdom of returning to the *nagari*, it was soon accepted throughout West Sumatra. Much of the debate then addressed the particular form the *nagari* was to take. These debates were carried out in urban centres, in the regions, as well as in each village, while Minangkabau migrants outside West Sumatra took an active part as well. Important links between these arenas were formed by members of urban elites who had become actively involved in village politics as *adat* official or in other capacities. For some it provided a return to their own values which had been oppressed by the autocratic Jakarta regime. For others it provided a populist platform for local politics. A main factor, and not only for *adat* leaders, was the promise of more control over village resources, so vital for a future with decreasing funding from the central government. Such claims only had a chance to be recognized if based on *adat* by *adat* communities, which *nagari* were but *desa* were not.

Decentralization and the return to the *nagari* was much more than just a geographical and administrative reconfiguration. They allowed for considerable differentiation among the districts and villages. Territorial village boundaries were renegotiated under legislation that allowed *desa* to go back to the *nagari* territory and prevented *desa* from establishing their own *nagari*. And it forced the rural population to redefine internal village relationships. In that process, social and economic boundaries that had become more or less obsolete during the *desa* period, such as between original settler lineages and lineages of newcomers or descendants of former slaves were reinforced, causing much tension within villages with a major population classified as newcomers. On the other hand, old social and economic relationships based on common clan-membership of persons living in different *desa* relations that had weakened during the *desa* period now become closer and stronger again. To some extent the new village structure also blurred their boundaries, as migrants living in the urban centres within West Sumatra or outside became more involved in village matters, taking *adat* offices or positions in the village government. Thus the geographical boundaries are not so problematic as such, but because of what they imply for social differentiation and political control over economic resources such as village land and markets. The *nagari*, then, are complex social and political communities, with diverse and ambivalent administrative structures, and with more internal social boundaries and differentiation than during the last decades of the Soeharto regime. Externally they have become somewhat more independent from the central and provincial administration, yet as the lowest level of state organization, heavily regulated and predominantly funded by the districts, they remain deeply embedded in the wider Indonesian political, financial and social structures.

The decentralization policies have stimulated debate about the relationship between *adat*, Islam and the state. This has not only had ramifications for the structure of village government, but also for Minangkabau identity and their position within the Indonesian state. While tensions between *adat* and Islam have marked Minangkabau history from the beginning of conversion, this relationship has gone through phases of great tension as well as relative relaxation. The last decade of the Soeharto period was characterized by general disinterest in *adat* and a rise of Islam. The new political freedom and the decentralization policies increased identification with *adat* even among the urban elites and pushed Islam temporarily more to the background. The return to the *surau* movement must be seen as an attempt to balance out the relationship between *adat* and Islam. Most Minangkabau identify as much with the Indonesian nation-state as with *adat* and Islam and leave no doubt that they see their future within Indonesia. Urban elites are used to combine a modern lifestyle and strong adherence to Islam and with a heightened interest in *adat*, despite the numerous discussions about Minangkabau identity. For villagers state institutions have been part of their everyday life and they have been so accustomed to bureaucratic procedures that it has even rubbed off on *adat* institutions. Even the most adamant proponents of *adat* only strive for a larger role of *adat*, not for retreat from the Indonesian state. The relationship between *adat*, Islam and state has shifted, but the Minangkabau still derive their identity from the three normative orders in conjunction.

Postscript: the revised decentralization laws of October 2004

The revised decentralization laws of October 2004 mark an end to the decentralization policies as discussed in this chapter, paving the road for a partial reversal of decentralization. Given the dynamics of Indonesia's political and economic development it is not easy to predict what this will mean for the internal dynamics within the region, but a few things can be said. During our last field visit in February 2005, officials of the district administration were fully aware of the changes to come. They showed great concern, because it would mean a shift in the power relationships back towards the province and central government, at their expense. The concern among the district officials contrasted starkly with the matter-of-fact attitude we found in villages. In this reshuffle the village structures are of little importance though they will not remain unaffected. The new laws bring considerable change in the degree of village autonomy. The mayor and the village secretary will come under more district control, while within the villages their power will increase in relation to other village institutions, notably the village parliament. However, to many *nagari* the autonomy has proven to be more of a burden than a blessing anyway, because autonomy means more tasks without proper funding. To lose some of this autonomy therefore may be less important than the question how much funding can be expected from the state. There is thus far no indication that the *nagari* will be abolished and replaced by something like a *desa* structure. Politicians at higher levels are fully occupied with their fight for power with the political and administrative centre where villages do not play a role.

CAROLE FAUCHER

Contesting boundaries in the Riau Archipelago

The fall of the New Order and the implementation of the regional autonomy laws have provided fresh opportunities for the local elite to promote and consolidate their own sphere of influence. As has already been the case in a number of provinces and districts, instances of conflict have spread, often in the context of power struggles and highly complex social and political restructurings (H. Schulte Nordholt 2002). In many cases, these conflicts are popularly articulated through the language of ethnic and religious identity politics. Similarly, ethnic and religious sensitivities which were consciously repressed during the period of the New Order, are now exposed. The Riau Archipelago (or Kepri from Kepulauan Riau) had been so far largely spared from acute tensions and mounting violence. However, among the urban middle class and between generations ideological polarization has taken place. The different attempts to conceptualize 'Masyarakat Kepri' – the society of Kepulauan Riau – by politicians and public intellectuals seems to demonstrate how an increasing emphasis on regional identity has gradually superseded a more general concern with the nation. The discussion about the character of the newly formed province of Kepri has oscillated over the past years between the aristocrats' ideal of reverting to the era of the sultanate, and an image of an industrial oriented pluralistic society, advocated by business people, which is strong and autonomous enough to compete economically with Singapore and Malaysia.

The proximity to Malaysia and Singapore has created an interesting paradox. On one hand, Singapore and Malaysia have been a source of identity for the Malays in the Riau Archipelago as important economic and cultural power bases. On the other hand, precisely because of the geographical proximity to Malaysia and in particular to Singapore, the islands of Batam, Bintan and Karimun have attracted the highest number of Indonesian migrants of the whole archipelago, to the point now that Malays are there in minority. Tanjungpinang's population has grown dramatically in the past years – from 98,871 in 1998 to 134,940 in 2004 – which resulted to a dramatic urbanization

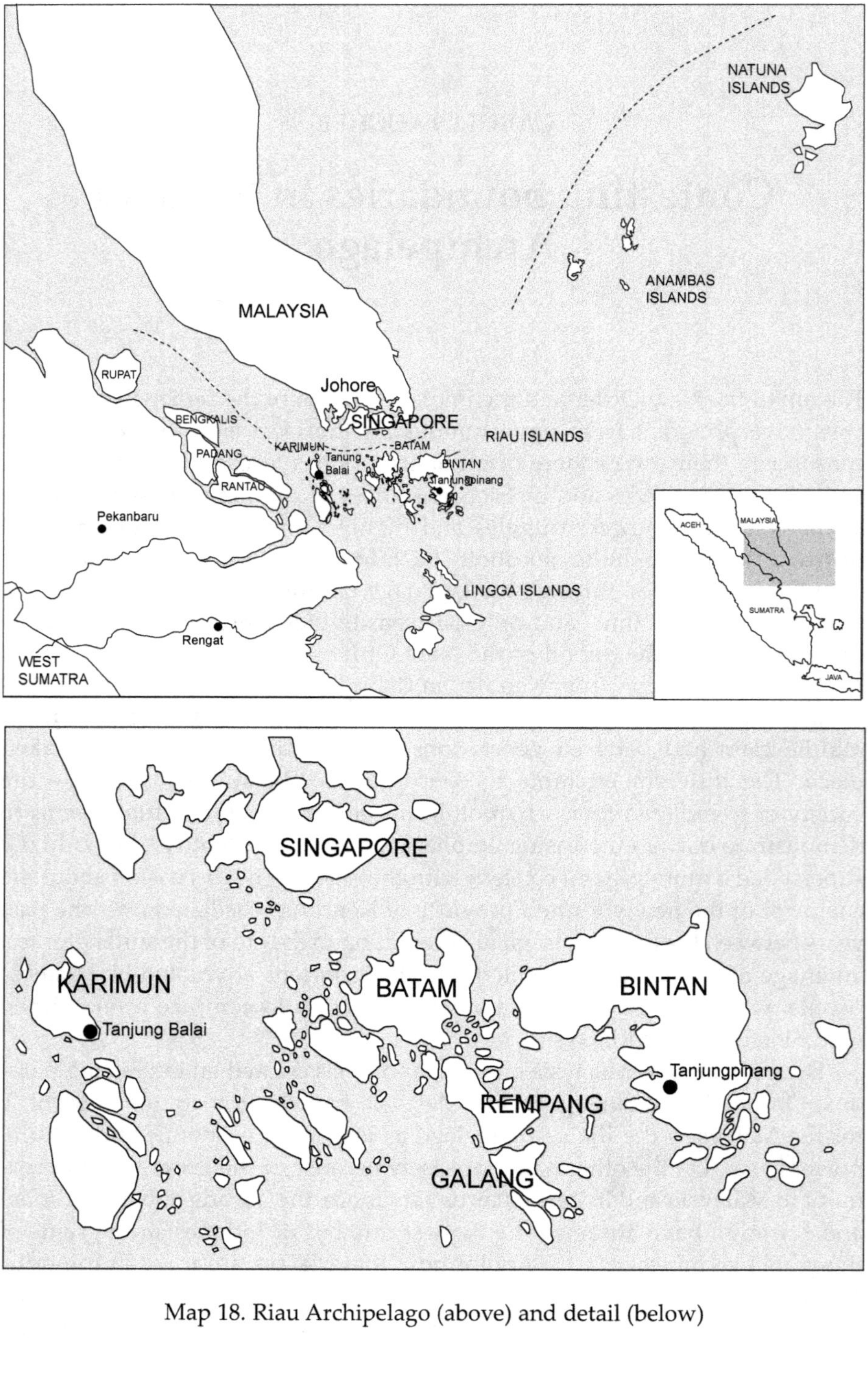

Map 18. Riau Archipelago (above) and detail (below)

and incorporation of large groups of immigrants.[1]

This chapter investigates how the idea of 'Masyarakat Kepri' is imagined whith a specific focus on the role of the urban middle class. I first examine the recent political developments which have resulted in several cases of *pemekaran* (or administrative fragmentation) since the fall of the New Order, at both district and provincial levels. Then I explore the problems different groups encountered in trying to formulate a model that would foster a sense of belonging to the Kepri province. Finally I look at the role of education and the efforts put forward to revive ethnic pride within the context of a wider Malay identity. To what extent is the young generation ready to accept a historically rooted sense of Malayness? Or does it prefer a modern and globalized identity which is linked with nearby Singapore? I will focus on the city of Tanjungpinang on Bintan Island because it has been the most important administrative centre of the Riau Archipelago. It also comprises the greatest number of Malay-Bugis aristocrats in the archipelago and forms as such a centre of Malay identity politics.

From Kepulauan Riau (Kepri) District to Kepulauan Riau Province

Until the formation of a separate province, Kepri was a district consisting of a cluster of islands located at proximity of Singapore, including the islands of Bintan and Karimun but excluding Batam. Tanjungpinang on the island of Bintan was until 2001 the district capital. Soon after the fall of Soeharto and the beginning of the decentralization process, the *pemekaran*-virus affected local leaders in Tanjungpinang as well, where the first thoughts of a split between mainland Riau, with its capital Pekanbaru, and the Riau Archipelago were articulated in public.

Soon Tanjungpinang became an autonomous city (Kota Otonom) and the district of Karimun, which covered the western part of the Riau Archipelago was created. These stimulated stiff competition between the two districts of Kepri and Karimun and the two municipalities of Tanjungpinang and Batam in order to develop economic relations with Singapore and, to a lesser extent, Malaysia. During the same period, Huzrin Hood, then district head of Kepri district, launched his idea of forming a distinct Malay province in the Riau Archipelago. The governor of Riau, Saleh Djasit, opposed the project at a number of occasions. Interestingly it was his most vocal critic, Tabrani Rab – who was also known as the leading figure behind the Free Riau movement – who criticized the idea of a separate province of the Riau Archipelago because he saw it as a strategy by the government to weaken the independ-

1 www.kotabestari.net.

ence movement of larger Riau (in other words mainland and archipelago) (*Jakarta Post* 21-5-2003).

His strong stand against the split of Riau was primarily directed at Huzrin Hood whom he publicly accused of nepotism and corruption. Despite protest from mainland Riau the bill that established the new province was passed in September 2002 by the Indonesian Parliament, but it took almost another two years to see its official implementation. After almost six years of heated debates and intensive lobbying, the new Kepri province became eventually finally operative on the first of July 2004 when H. Ismeth Abdullah, chairman of the Batam Industrial Development Authority (BIDA), was appointed caretaker governor. In 2004, just after the official nomination of the caretaker governor, it was the turn of Lingga to form a new district.[2]

But by that time Huzrin Hood was officially no longer in function. In November 2003, he was sentenced to two years in jail following a Rp 4.3 billion corruption charge.[3] Apart from being district head of Kepri, Huzrin Hood was at that time also the chairman of the Badan Perkerja Pembentukan Propinsi Kepulauan Riau (BP3KR, the Working Committee for the Development of Kepri Province) and the most likely candidate for the position of caretaker governor. Huzrin's arrest was publicly displayed as part of a new policy to show that reforms were really taking place, even far away from Jakarta.

Old dreams, new concerns

For many local Malays regional autonomy offers an opportunity to revert to the period when Tanjungpinang formed the heart of the Malay world and it was well entrenched in the regional economy. The act of breaking away from the provincial control of mainland Pekanbaru by forming a new province that only consists of the Riau Archipelago seemed, at the first glance, to be the best response to a long-standing ideological divide about Malay identity (B. Andaya 1997; Adhuri and Rachmawati 2004). Although it looked at first sight as if Huzrin Hood and his allies wanted to create a province along ethnic lines which would benefit the Malay, in reality a large part of the population of the islands of Batam, Karimun and Bintan consists of migrants. It is therefore even more difficult to emphasize local Malayness as an identity marker for the new province. In order to overcome this problem

2 For a couple of months following this last *pemekaran,* the district head of Lingga was hesitating between remaining in the Riau (*daratan*) province and joining the new Kepri province. He finally opted for the second option.

3 Huzrin Hood was first sentenced to six years. This sentence was reduced to two years after appeal and then to one year in jail and one year under city arrest.

the Malay elite and local academics in Kepri try to revive a trans-national Malay solidarity, or *serumpun.* This elite consists to a large extent of high ranking bureaucrats of Bugis-Malay aristocratic descent who enjoyed many privileges during the Soeharto era.

At the same time, however, mixed marriages are extremely common, especially in urban areas, making questions of ethnic identity even more complex. In public high schools of Tanjungpinang, for instance, the number of students of mix parentage outnumbers the ones who claim belonging to a particular ethnic group. Taken together the ethnic make-up of Kepri is very uneven. While the Malay form a majority in the rural areas – 85% in Lingga – in urban areas, such as Tanjung Balai and Tanjungpinang, they do not count for more than 40%. In Tanjungpinang Javanese form the second largest group with 25%, while ethnic Chinese make up the third largest group with 13%.[4] If we add to this picture the recent inflow of migrants one could argue that at least in Tanjungpinang a multi-ethnic pluralistic framework had been created at the eve of decentralization. The dominant image of Kepri being predominantly Malay was a New Order construction – meant to serve both the interests of the Malay elite and the state – which was mobilized and manipulated when regional autonomy required a reordering of regional relationships.[5]

Despite the fact that the Dutch and the British had already in 1824 officially divided their respective territories in the Malay world, the Riau Archipelago remained until recently a relatively open border zone.

During the Japanese Occupation, the Riau Archipelago was placed under the administration of Singapore and many Malays, including aristocrats, were taken to Singapore to join the Imperial Army (B. Andaya 1997).

During the 1950s and until the *konfrontasi* in 1963, the Riau Archipelago was a duty-free zone where the Strait Dollar of British Malaya was the main currency (Wee 2002; Lufti et al. 1977; Faucher 2005). Tanjungpinang constituted for Indonesians the principal port of entry into Singapore. Migrating to Tanjungpinang was, in fact, the most difficult step; anyone who intended to do so needed a local sponsor. The proximity of Singapore and the use of the Strait Dollar were no doubt important incentives for Malays from mainland Riau to migrate to the Riau Archipelago. Once residing in Tanjungpinang, it

4 Adhuri and Rachmawati 2004. This paper cannot account for the Lingga and Natuna perspectives because this research concentrates mostly on Bintan. However, informants born in Lingga pointed out to me that the islands of Lingga and Singkep have always suffered from lack of support and from disregard of the part of Malays in Bintan.

5 An emphasis on 'Malayness' also helped to erase the role of the economically strong Chinese in Kepri.

6 Jobs in the civil service and education were given to Malays or at least to individuals who would identify themselves as such (Faucher 2005).

was possible to travel to Singapore without passport.[6] Even up to 15 years ago, it was still relatively easy to travel to Singapore but the situation has significantly changed over the past years.

Since the mid-1990s, there have been accounts of Malays from Kepri who were refused entry permits by Singapore immigration officers. Based on these experiences many people in Kepri assumed that any first attempts to enter Singapore were automatically bound to fail. According to respondents the sentiment of alienation from Singapore and Malaysia could be traced back to the early 1990s when the SIJORI Growth Triangle, was implemented, which links the economies of Singapore, Johore and the Riau Archipelago. The agreement between Singapore, Malaysia and Indonesia suggests an open zone which facilitates free interaction. Instead the Growth Triangle embodies a new trans-national hierarchy in which Singapore capital takes the lead and the Riau Archipelago forms, as a provider of cheap labour, the bottom (Perry 1998:87).

The Riau Archipelago was incorporated into Singapore's global project through the opening of two major industrial parks operating under Singapore management, Batamimdo in Batam and Bintan Industrial Park on Bintan Island. Compared to the 1950s, when the same currency was used in the whole region the Growth Triangle is an unequal configuration. Furthermore Christopher Tremewan (1994:43) argues that:

> the implication that the Singapore-Batam-Johor triangle is a relationship of mutual growth is called into question by the absence of substantive mutual investment between Batam and Johor. Rather than triangular, the initiative is more likely to develop as two bilateral relationships with Singapore, leaving one side of the triangle missing.

Thus, the agreement gives Singaporean firms access to cheap supplies of land and labour in Indonesia. In 2002 the Singapore influence over Kepri's economic relations was reinforced through the signing of a free trade agreement with the USA that involves part of the Riau Archipelago as well.[7]

Since the implementation of the Growth Triangle, social representations of Kepulauan Riau have become more and more disparaging in popular discourse in Singapore and Malaysia. The term 'Indon', which has been used as a derogative term for Indonesian migrants in Malaysia during the 1950s, is now used again to refer to any Indonesian in Malaysia and Singapore and appears relatively frequently in the print media of these two countries.

[7] This FTA should largely benefit Singaporean firms because under this pact, components – such as electronics, made offshore of Singapore – which means in Batam or Bintan, will be regarded as if they originate in Singapore, which means that the final products will also qualify as Singaporean (*Far Eastern Economic Review* 18-12-2002).

The increase of criminality in Singapore has been attributed to Indonesian crime syndicates whose members are believed to enter Singapore via the Riau Archipelago.[8] For these reasons, and due to the more recent terrorist threats following 9/11 and the Bali bombings, immigration procedures in Singapore with regard to Indonesians have been tightened.[9] Yet, the bulk of Indonesian visitors entering Singapore through the ferry terminal checkpoints are Malays or ethnic Chinese from Riau who visit their relatives. The tightening of immigration procedures is perceived as offensive by the Malay, even more so since the Singapore immigration officers who are Malay themselves have the reputation of being harsher with them in comparison with immigration officers of other ethnic background. As a result, Malays from Kepri feel that they are cut off from their relatives and alienated from a world they were supposed to be part of.

Relationships between Malaysia and Indonesia came under pressure when the Malaysian government initiated operation Tugas in order to evict some 100,000 illegal Indonesian workers, while the two countries had also a dispute over two rock islands in the oil rich Sulawesi Sea.[10] The harsh portrayal of Indonesia that has been circulating in the Singapore media since the beginning of the Reformasi has further affected cross-border relations and foster a climate of mutual distrust. These tensions made many Kepri Malay ponder about their loyalty towards the wider Malay world. Part of the idea of the autonomous province Kepri was the desire to be treated as equal partners and full control over its own resources. As summarized by the secretary of a local NGO who is a fervent supporter of the *serumpun* ideology:

> We are Malays and should continue to promote and foster cultural and economic relations with Malays in Malaysia and Singapore. However, it is also important to understand that we have our own identity. We need to be diplomatic, but if a *konfrontasi* would happen again, I would definitely side up with Indonesia.

The impact of being portrayed as criminals and the experience of being subordinated to Singapore's economic interests have incited new hopes and ideals which are not exclusively restricted to notions of regional autonomy. For, 'Singapore' and 'Malaysia' are currently the geo-political entities against which a sense of national pride is rapidly emerging in the urban settings of the Riau Archipelago. For people in Tanjungpinang, regional autonomy

8 According to James Warren (2003), these crime syndicates often operate from Batam under the leadership of Chinese from Hong Kong or Singapore.

9 The arrest in early 2003 of Mas Selamat Kastari, the head of the Singapore branch of Jama'ah Islamiyah in Tanjungpinang further aggravated the reputation of Kepulauan Riau as a source of criminals and terrorists (*Jakarta Post* 6-2-2003; *Strait Times* 6-2-2003).

10 Meanwhile Singapore and Indonesia had a conflict over the transfer of sand from Kepri meant for construction work in Singapore.

ideally implies better control over relations with their closest neighbors, especially Singapore, which would ideally prompt greater respect for them. The Reformasi, however, has also brought new hopes for fresh vitality and strength within the boundaries of the Indonesian nation-state. Paradoxically, as I will elaborate below, especially urban youth of Kepulauan Riau seems to turn itself towards the nation, when leaders in many provinces and districts are trying to redefine their identity on the basis of an exclusive regionalism.

Often cultural politics are considered to be marginal compared to 'hard core' issues concerning purely political and economic interests. However, Joel Kahn (1998:1) correctly reminds us that 'contrary to the impression generated by the majority of observers of contemporary Southeast Asia – of a region whose peoples are dedicated entirely to the single goal of economic development – matters cultural are never very far down anyone's agenda'.

As part of the decentralization process, each region is expected to enhance its own exclusive traits. This is accelerated by the process *pemekaran*, which requires a further exclusive emphasis on difference in terms of *bahasa* (language), *adat* (customary laws and customs), *budaya* (culture) and *pahlawan daerah* (local heroes). At the basis of these particularities is often a territorially defined notion of ethnicity. In Kepulauan Riau leaders promote a consensus that 'Malayness' is the basis of its territorial identity. As I have indicated above, in the urban context of Tanjungpinang this notion is being contested by migrants form other regions and local Chinese, but also by young middle class Malay who do not want to be portrayed as belonging to the bottom of the socio-economic hierarchy in the region.

Speculating on the Riau leaders' agenda following the beginning of the decentralization process, Vivienne Wee (2002:12) once asked 'Who owns Riau?' According to her, 'the cultural revitalization movement sustained the idea of the Riau Sultanate as a cultural reality within a temporal past-in-the-present. This further legitimated the everyday practice of customs and rituals derived from the time of the Sultanate' (Wee 2002:15). As I have argued elsewhere, the revitalization of the Riau sultanate in the Riau Archipelago has been frowned upon by commoner Malays all over the Riau Archipelago (Faucher 2005). The question of Riau's 'ownership' is complex in the sense that political leaders cannot restrict themselves to an exclusive Malayness, if they do not want to alienate large sections of the non-Malay population. It is particularly the case in the Riau Archipelago. Therefore there have been lately some attempts to redefine the Kepri identity within a non-ethnic framework. This approach primarily defines Kepri as a 'maritime province' and tries to link economic activities with issues of identity. In this context, ideas to further develop industrial fishing and bio-marine research – with investments from Singapore and Hong Kong – are currently subject of discussion which was also stimulated by Huzrin Hood.

The territorial aspect of the common identity is underlined by recent attempts to knit the archipelago closer together by the building of expensive and prestigeous bridges. In 2004, a series of bridges linking the islands of Batam, Rempang and Galang was completed. The region is now known as 'Barelang', reminding us of 'SIJORI', which also refers to an economic linkage between these islands. A few months after the completion of the Barelang bridges, an even more ambitious project has been announced: The so-called 'Babin' bridge – estimated costs Rp 3 trillion, offering employment to 5,000 workers and planned to begin in January 2006 – will link the two politically and economically strong islands of Batam and Bintan.[11] Regional autonomy has increased internal competition between Batam and Tanjungpinang over the question where the new provincial capital will be located. Batam holds a negative reputation in the popular imagery of Tanjungpinang middle class dwellers and the prospect of the Babin bridge raises fear that criminals and prostitutes of all sorts who are believed to plague Batam will now be given the opportunity to carry their activities to Bintan.

Masyarakat Kepri, Malayness, putra daerah and the Chinese

The use of the Indonesian concept of *masyarakat* suggests that Kepri is populated by a social and cultural coherent group of people, and Masyarakat Kepri seems to refer to Malayness. In practice, however, this Malayness is only accepted when it is expressed in artistic terms, that is to say culture as performance. Ironically, however, one of the prominent Malay performing arts groups in Tanjungpinang, counts in fact only one local Malay among its 70 members. And when the mayor of Tanjungpinang supported the festival for the Revitalization of Malay Culture (Revitalisasi Budaya Melayu) in July 2004 she was criticized by the Chinese in Senggarang for ignoring the pluralistic nature of Tanjungpinang, and in particular the Chinese presence. In response a special event took place in Senggarang, called 'Revitalisasi Budaya Pluralistik', which included performances by non-Malay groups like Balinese and Chinese opera performances (*Kepri Pos* 25-7-2004).

Hence, a hybrid 'Masyarakat Kepri' and a mixed 'Budaya Kepri' are the blurred but sensitive issues local political leaders try to deal with.

The economic priority of the new province was from the very beginning focussed towards industrial development in Batam, Bintan and to a lesser degree Karimun, while the other districts of Natuna and Lingga, where the

11 *Media Kepri*, April 2005. Both projects have been initiated by BIDA (Batam Industrial Development Authority) in a bid to facilitate the transport of natural gas, water, and electricity between the islands.

majority of Malays actually live received less attention. In Lingga job opportunities remain rare and poverty is wide-spread. However, as a Malay high school teacher remarked, the district of Lingga is seen as a region where Malay traditions and *adat* are still strong and where the Malay heritage is truly preserved. However, it is also widely believed that Malay traditions do not co-exist along with development and urbanization. In other words, where Malayness is strong, economic developments remain stagnant. Consequently, defining Masyarakat Kepri in terms of Malayness is met with ambivalence in urban circles as it is associated with economic stagnation.

There are a growing number of non-governmental organizations in Tanjungpinang which openly challenge the way ethnic classifications operate in Indonesia. These organizations advocate that a more inclusive notion of Malayness should provide the framework for a Masyarakat Kepri identity. One of the most outspoken organizations, Kekerabatan Keluarga Besar Melayu (KKBM, The Extended Family of Malay Kin), promotes a Malay identity which resembles the Malaysian idea of *bumiputera*. In order to be included as a 'Malay' in their own Masyarakat Kepri ideal framework, one has to speak Bahasa Melayu, be a Muslim and follow the *adat* Melayu. This interpretation offers room for many local politicians who advocate a revitalization of Malay traditions but who are themselves not from a 'pure' Malay background.[12] However, the chances that the Malay identity of Kepri will be officially recognized are small because Indonesian legislation prohibits the kind of ethnic categorization which is practised in Malaysia and Singapore.

Meanwhile, aristocrats have been reluctant to give up ideas of Malay revivalism which is connected with the old sultanates. Regional autonomy has in many parts of Indonesia been acompanied by a revival of local aristocracies and this was the case in Riau as well (Pratikno 2005). As I said before aristocrats occupied influential positions during the New Order and enjoyed considerable privileges. In an effort to restore their former glory members of the Malay-Buginese aristocracy were initially among the most prominent supporters of the establishment of a separate Kepri province. They were especially attracted by the idea of a regional autonomy defined by ethnic and territorial boundaries. In their view nobody can refer to Kepri as a Malay province without referring to the local rajas of Pulau Penyengat. Moreover, members of the aristocracy are well respected for their scholarship, especially in relation to history and to the Malay language (Faucher 2005).

Defining Masyarakat Kepri according to a strict Malay identity framework will be opposed by the economically strong Chinese minority, which appears less inclined to remain politically passive in the new administra-

12 This interpretation of Malayness was also articulated by Tabrani Rab when he addressed the issue of an independent Riau (Colombijn 2003).

tive setting. In October 2004, Bobby Jayanto (alias Bu Hui) of Partai Patriot Pancasila was elected as the chairman of the DPRD (Dewan Perwakilan Rakyat Daerah, Regional Parliament) of Tanjungpinang for the term 2004-2009. This election was vehemently opposed by various groups, among others the Islamic Forum Komunikasi Masjid Mushola (FKMM, Masjid Mushola Communication Forum). This group organized a series of demonstrations and exposed Bobby's business activities related to gambling and prostitution.[13] The fact that Bobby Jayanto was elected came as a surprise for many and was shocking for Malays. Only a few months later he was put under house arrest pending his trial in a murder case. The election of Bobby J., however, illustrated the potential role of the Chinese on the political scene in 'Malay' Kepri.

Allthough Huzrin Hood and the mayor of Tanjungpinang have always been keen to acknowledge the multi-ethnic aspect of Kepri and Tanjungpinang, the public role of the Chinese are still by and large ignored. But, Chinese-ness could also be incorporated in the 'maritime' identity of the region due to the longstanding role they have played in trade networks (see J. Warren 2003). Today, most of the hotels, golf courses and expensive restaurants in Bintan alone are owned by local Indonesian Chinese, or in partnership with Chinese Singaporeans. Interestingly however, in the narrative of their common dream of reverting to the prosperous 1950s, my aristocrat and commoner respondents unanimously omit the presence of the *taoke*, the Chinese middlemen who played a crucial role in the circulation of trade goods between Kepulauan Riau and the Singapore port (*Kepulauan Riau* 1999).

Educating identities in the context of decentralization

The political rhetoric of a cross-border Malay identity framework would have the potential to survive and expand in Kepri only if it was truly able to replace – or at least to compete with – the state discourse in the local school system. It is therefore interesting to investigate to what extent administrative decentralization offered more autonomy to educate particular regional identities, and what forms this took in Kepri. Decentralization of education was officially implemented in 2003 but this occurred only in 2004 in the Riau Archipelago.

Decentralization caused major changes including the implementation

13 *Batam Pos* 1-11-04. Bobby Jayanto has been one of the suspects in the murder of the local treasurer of Partai Amanat Nasional (PAN, Party of the National Message) in 2001. In 1999 he was suspected of harassing a *Tempo* journalist who was investigating the Singapore-based gambling ring, Elephant.

of the new school curriculum, Kurikulum Berbasis Kompetensi (KBK, Competency Based Curriculum), which involves completely new ways of teaching and learning, as well as the decentralization of funding. Provincial governments are expected to play an active role in terms of monitoring, among others, the providing of teaching materials and the organization of training courses, while educational management, local curriculum development, planning, funding, maintenance, and appointments are under the responsibility of the district government (Asian Development Bank 2001).

Seen from the perspective of headmasters and teachers decentralization results in a complex situation. In general they still see themselves as part of a highly centralized bureaucracy, which involves a curriculum that emphasizes national unity. At the same time, however, headmasters are confronted with district committees and local leaders, whose agenda is determined by regional priorities. Hence contradictory claims are laid on teachers. Standards of competence are still evaluated in Jakarta. This means that an adequate syllabus must be designed according to national norms, detailed by Puskur (Pusat Kurikulum, Curriculum Development Centre), and that an emphasis on regional autonomy is necessarily limited in scope as the curriculum must primarily promote national unity. According to the guidelines of the Kurikulum Berbasis Kompetensi 'the nation has become even more important in the larger context of globalization, information, communication and technology and free market' (Puskur 2002).

Within this centralized framework three subjects of 'local content' (*muatan lokal*) are allowed to be included in the curriculum. These three 'local subjects' are decided on by the district and are compulsory for all students. At the SLTP and SLTA in Tanjungpinang these subjects are 'Computer Science',[14] 'Home Economics' and 'Arab Melayu'. The first two subjects are new but Arab Melayu had already been an elective at the SLTA level under the former curriculum. We see here that decentralization has not led to regional autonomy in education.

Due to the limited scope of the 'local curriculum' very little attention is paid to local Malay history. Moreover, textbooks that deal explicitly with the local Malay heritage are scarce as well. Recently a few history textbooks dealing with local history and written by Malay aristocrats are used on a modest scale at some SLTP and SLTA. It must be emphasized here that in this case alternative histories do not represent the voice of the powerless. As Gregory Forth (1994) remarks, alternative cultural representations and historical narratives often represent elite perceptions, be it in a regional context. This is illustrated by the textbook for the SLTP, *Kedatangan Upu Tandru Daeng Rilaka*

14 SLTP: Sekolah Lanjutan Tingkat Pertama, Junior Secondary School; SLTA: Sekolah Lanjutan Tingkat Atas, Junior High School.

ke-Riau (The arrival of Upu Tandru Daeng Rilaka at Riau), which was first published in 2002. The book traces the journey of the Buginese ancestors of the Riau rulers, who left Sulawesi to join the Melayu royalty and form the Johore-Riau-Lingga realm. Throughout the textbook, the Indonesian character of these ancesors is emphasized. During their journey they visited various Indonesian ports, including Batavia, which is illustratred by the Syair, poems, written by Raja Haji Ali, one of the most prominent historical figures of Bugis ancestry.[15] This text reinforces a more general idea that Malay language and culture belong to the founding elements of Indonesia. Students have already learned in school that the Malay language is at the origin of the current Bahasa Indonesia, and that the local national hero (*pahlawan nasional*), Raja Haji Fisabilillah (1727-1784) was a fierce warrior who resisted Dutch colonialism (Barnard 1997).

Whereas the presence of the local is weak, the impact of the nation-state is strong. SLTA students in Tanjungpinang have all been thoroughly socialized through the centralized Indonesian education system. They are also the first generation which is fully exposed to Indonesian media, notably television and popular music. When I asked SLTA students why they prefer to watch Indonesian television programmes, they answered that Singapore and Malaysian channels were boring and moralistic, that they cannot identify with them and that, most of all, the language used (Malay) was foreign to them. This is not surprising as the Bahasa Melayu spoken by the older generation in Kepri is different from the Malay used in the Malaysian and Singaporean media. But, speaking local Malay is a symbol of backwardness, and only students from the surrounding small islands and fishing communities are said to use it in their daily conversations. Yet, as the Javanese headmaster of a primary school in Penyengat mentioned to me, only two years ago he had great difficulty in understanding his pupils but since Indonesian popular culture and the Indonesian media have reached the island, things have changed very rapidly. According to him, many of them now can speak Indonesian and even prefer to talk Indonesian with their classmates.

What significance does Malayness have for the youth? An SLTA student remarked that she was at a loss about what Malay culture (*kebudayaan*), apart from literature and performing arts, could mean. Malayness in Kepulauan Riau and, particularly, in Tanjungpinang represents a number of different meanings varying from a folklorized representation of literature and arts to political interpretations that fit particular territorial claims.

Barbara Leigh (1999:37) wrote that 'the spirit of Reformasi is allowing young people greater freedom to legitimately explore what were previously

15 Because of its costs and the limited space for local content in the curriculum this relatively 'innocent' book is not widely used.

taken as 'out-of-bounds' thoughts. This process is in turn making transparent boundaries that were previously unacknowledged'. In actual practice, however the production of homogenized national knowledge remains the ultimate goal of primary and secondary school education throughout Indonesia. The space of contestation remains extremely limited, even in the new context.

Apart from the fact that local history emphasizing Malayness does not reflect the actual ethnic make-up of Kepri, local and national history are to a large extent intertwined, which makes it difficult to identify with a particular local history. Moreover, schooling under the New Order has moved students' orientation away from family, home and village towards the prosperity and comfort of modern Indonesian city life (Parker 2002). Indonesia is for many young people in Tanjungpinang synonymous with Jakarta and represents an urban culture. Singapore, in the other hand is a familiar place where many relatives live, but it represents also a regional hierarchy in which Kepri is situated at the very bottom end. Students pointed out that, although they speak Malay at home, they cannot properly understand television programmes from Singapore. Tuning in to Indonesian media does not pose this problem. As a result the cultural taste of most young people in Tanjungpinang navigates between Tanjungpinang and Jakarta and disregards the wider Malay world, including Singapore.[16]

Conclusion

In the preceding pages I have argued that it is extremely difficult, if not impossible, to define a persuasive provincial identity for Kepri. Elitist Malay notions based on the history of the old sultanates is not supported by commoner Malays, while more in general the idea of Malayness is contested by Chinese and various groups of immigrants, and undermined by strained relationships with the surrounding Malay world, that is to say Malaysia and Singapore. The irony is that the 1950s facilitated more coherence in the Malay world compared with the SIJORI growth triangle in which Kepri labour was subordinated to Singapore capital. An interesting and often ignored aspect of decentralization is that the school curriculum is still to a large extent focussed on the unity of the nation state. Together with education the recent penetration of Indonesian mass media in Kepri invited young people in Tanjungpinang in search for a comfortable and accessible modernity to turn

[16] Chinese students on the other hand eagerly consume Chinese popular culture produced in Singapore, Taiwan and Honkong, but they also share the desire to move away from Singapore's dominance.

to Jakarta. The irony is that, whereas the older generation tried to revive, invent and rephrase notions of Malayness which served their interests in the framework of regional autonomy, the younger generation recently discovered Jakarta as a source of identification.

JAAP TIMMER

Erring decentralization and elite politics in Papua

Introduction

In this chapter, I focus on certain members of the bureaucratic elite in Papua as influential actors in determining the future of the region. Amid a wave of recently established new provinces and districts, these leaders adopt strikingly creative ways to gain both popular and central government support, all characterised by marked regional differences. The chapter begins with a substantial historical introduction describing the territory's tumultuous passage from being the last holdout of Dutch colonialism in Asia in the early 1960s, through the history of suffering (*memoria passionis*) that followed integration with Indonesia, and culminating in the Papuan Spring of 1999-2000. Contrary to some other accounts of it, that history was marked by both Papuan collaboration and resistance. Set against this background the chapter examines the strategies adopted by various Papuan elites to make the most of the opportunities offered by Special Autonomy and the redrawing of administrative boundaries (*pemekaran*), while at the same time keeping faith with the popular mistrust of a state that has failed them in so many ways.

For a number of reasons ranging from Dutch nationalism, geopolitical considerations, and self-righteous moral convictions the Netherlands Government refused to include West New Guinea in the negotiations for the independence of Indonesia in the late 1940s.[1] At the same time, the Government in Netherlands New Guinea initiated economic and infrastructure development as well as political emancipation of the Papuans under paternalistic guardianship. In the course of the 1950s, when tensions between the Netherlands and Indonesia grew over the status of West New Guinea, the Dutch began to guide a limited group of educated Papuans towards independence culminating in the establishment of the New Guinea Council

1 Lijphart 1966; Huydecoper van Nigtevecht 1990; Penders 2002:55-177; Vlasblom 2004:124-86; Drooglever 2005:141-74.

(Nieuw-Guinea Raad) in 1961. In addition, a flag, the Bintang Kejora or Morning Star flag, was designed to be flown beside the Dutch flag and a national anthem was adopted to be played and sung during official occasions after the Netherlands national hymn.

After a twelve-year dispute that was reaching its peak with the threat of open military conflict, this policy had to be aborted. In December 1961, President Soekarno issued the Trikora (Tri Komando Rakyat or 'People's Threefold Command') for the liberation of Irian Barat (West Irian). At the heart of this massive mobilization was Operasi Mandala, an Armed Forces of the Republic of Indonesia (Angkatan Bersenjata Republik Indonesia, ABRI) campaign designed to put pressure on the Netherlands government. The United States and Australia were not willing to support the Dutch military forces.

In an international climate of decolonization and after President Soekarno's sustained pressing of Indonesia's claim to the territory, the United States sponsored negotiations between Indonesia and the Netherlands about the future of West New Guinea under the auspices of the United Nations. The resulting New York Agreement of 15 August 1962 outlined the transfer of Netherlands sovereignty over West New Guinea to an interim United Nations Temporary Executive Authority (UNTEA) from 1 October 1962 to 1 May 1963, to be followed by a second phase during which the intervening administration would hand over full administrative responsibility to Indonesia. The agreement formulated the provision that the people of Irian Barat would exercise free choice over their future relationship with Indonesia before the end of 1969.

The victory over what had now become the Province of Irian Barat was a boost to Indonesian nationalism and became portrayed as the final chapter of decolonization.[2] The Indonesians, ruling the new province under the banner of the Trikora mobilization, were triumphant while elements of the Papuan elite empowered by the Dutch began to complain about what they saw as a blunt Indonesian takeover. Feelings of being marginalized by Indonesian bureaucrats and immigrants from other Indonesian islands filling job and business opportunities arose mainly among urban Papuans. Some of the educated Papuan elite were arrested or sidelined as 'collaborators with the Dutch' while others continued to play a role in the administration.

A plebiscite called Pepera (Penentuan Pendapat Rakyat, 'Act of Free Choice') was held in July-August 1969 during which 1020 cautiously chosen representatives from eight regions voted overwhelmingly for integration with Indonesia.[3] Protest was heard, dissonant speeches delivered, desperate outcries in the form of written notes were delivered to the United Nations

2 Soekarno 2000.

3 *Pepera* 1972:82-3; Vlasblom 2004:479. For an account of the Pepera based on archival materials and concluding that it was a sham, see Saltford 2000.

observers, and demonstrations in Sukarnopura (former Hollandia, now Jayapura), Biak and Manokwari were dispersed swiftly by the Indonesian military. Over the following decades, the faith in self-determination as linked to the undemocratic implementation of the Pepera became a key ingredient in a variety of Papuan nationalisms.

In response to the 'Indonesian occupation' of their land a liberation organization called the Organisasi Papua Merdeka (OPM, Free Papua Organization) emerged as a local movement in Manokwari in the 1960s and from there spread over the Kepala Burung (Bird's Head region). It soon became a fragmented network of dispersed groups of guerrilla-fighters.[4] Its access to weapons was limited and popular support scant. Very few elite Papuans joined the armed struggle and the vast majority of people living outside the urban centres did not feel the sense of belonging to a nation that had been invaded by Indonesia. Nevertheless, disillusion with the Indonesian government began to grow widely among those who had enjoyed the fruits of the accelerated development effort of the Dutch government since the 1950s.

President Soeharto's New Order regime (1966-1998) put much effort into developing the province and it received more funds than all other regions of Indonesia. But the implementation of largely top-down development programs often failed. At the same time, an ever-growing but relatively poorly funded military (Tentara Nasional Indonesia, TNI), supporting a network of alliances for both political control and predator business, has lead to the dislocation of Papuans. On top of that, Butonese, Buginese, Makassarese and Javanese immigrants began to fill manual labour and seize small business opportunities. As a result, frustration about limited access to opportunities in modern Indonesia intensified tensions between 'Papuans' and 'Indonesians' in particular those who have arrived in Papua through so-called transmigration programs or the larger waves of spontaneous migration.[5] Furthermore, in terms of governance, the region is amongst the most poorly developed in Indonesia while economic and ethnic and differences play a significant and sometimes alarming role in land and resource politics (Timmer forthcoming).

Following the fall of Soeharto in 1998 and the presidency being handed over to his Deputy President, B.J. Habibie, a spirit of 'democratic reform'

4 A reconstruction of the origin and development of the OPM can be found in Vlasblom 2004: 469, 486-636. Less thoroughly researched is the Indonesian-language account by Djopari 1993.

5 Since the Indonesian government began to stimulate economic development in the region, an older Dutch colonial programme of population distribution from highly populated regions such as Java and Bali to Papua and other less populated regions was continued. Among policy-makers, this so-called *transmigrasi* ('transmigration') was seen as a way to boost the development of Papua, but the programme proved to be largely unsuccessful (Pouwer 1999:173-4).

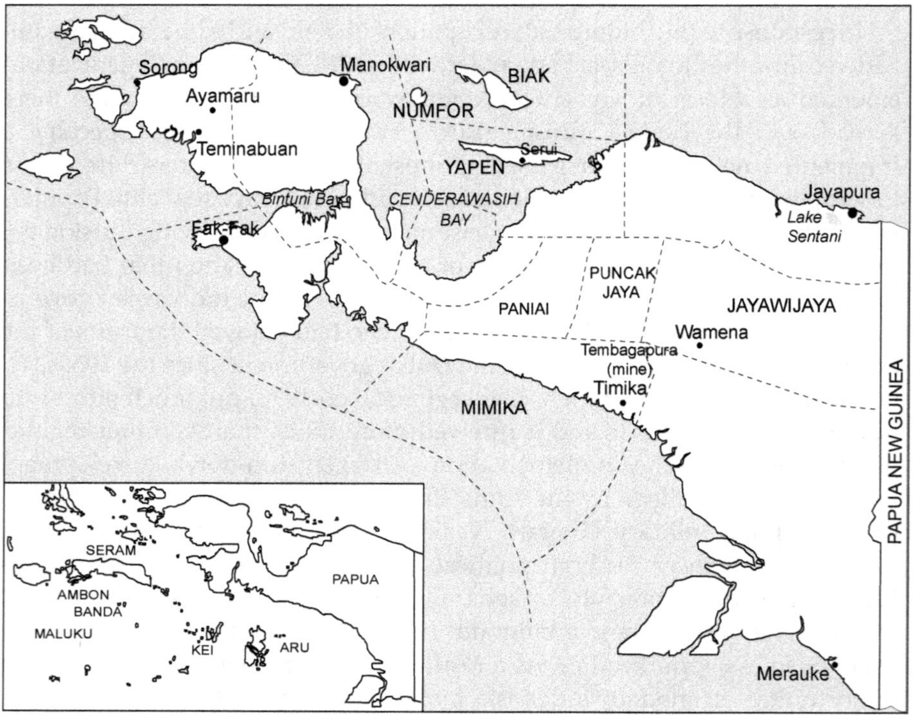

Map 19. Papua (Irian Jaya)

(Reformasi) swept across the archipelago. In Papua it led to what has been duly called a 'Papuan Spring' during which Papuan leaders from all over the region carefully sought to balance representations from coast and highland in a wave of national Papuan actions and the establishment of Papuan organizations (Van den Broek and Szalay 2001). At massive gatherings all over the region during which heated debates over the history of Papua and its possible future ('autonomy' or 'independence') were held, the Papuan Spring 'took the form of the indigenous Papuan people demanding *merdeka,* or independence, from Indonesia' (Agus Sumule 2003a:353; Chauvel 2005:11-20). Before I discuss the Papuan Spring it is necessary to briefly elaborate on what kinds of meanings *merdeka* has assumed in the history of Papua.

Merdeka and Memoria Passionis

The Indonesian nationalist revolutionary understanding of *merdeka* dates back to the mid-1920s growth of the nationalist movement followed, after promises during the Japanese occupation, by the Indonesian revolution of 1945-1949. During the late 1940s, *merdeka* became the battle cry with which the citizenry was summoned to support the cause, the salute with which revolutionaries would greet each other, the cry of solidarity at every mass rally, and the signature at the end of every Republican document' (Reid 1998:155). As Anthony Reid (1998:156) points out, *merdeka* meant national independence to the revolutionaries but the people experienced it as a far more immediate and personal freedom. Later, during Soeharto's New Order government, *merdeka* became part of the military ideologies and plainly came to mean 'the independence' that was proclaimed on 17 August 1945 and ritually celebrated every year since.

In Papua, primarily urban educated Papuans began to absorb the idea of *merdeka* as national independence since the late 1950s, when President Soekarno became determined to incorporate Netherlands New Guinea to complete the nationalist struggle and resistance amid the Papuan elite against the Dutch government grew (Grootenhuis 1961). Before that period, only a limited number of educated and politically active Papuans cherished ideas about *merdeka*. For example, in Serui on Yapen Island, Silas Papare established the Partai Kemerdekaan Indonesia (PKI, Indonesian Freedom Party) in 1946 of which members read sections of Republican papers in village churches on the island, while outside the churches people exercised the exclamation of *merdeka*. Papare was a charismatic leader and the pro-Indonesian movement on Yapen got seriously crippled when he left for Indonesia in 1949 (Vlasblom 2004:162; Chauvel 2005:71).

Around the same time, also as part of a struggle against the Dutch government, Lukas Rumkorem, a Biak assistant patrol officer, established the Partai Indonesia Merdeka on the island of Biak (Vlasblom 2004:163). In Hollandia as well, 'enthusiasm for "red and white" (the colours of the Indonesian national flag) got hold of a number of schooled Papuans' (Vlasblom 2004:163, my translation). The *merdeka*-leader there was Marthen Indey who was raised in Ambon, Maluku, and had been posted to Banda Neira where he got inspired by the prominent nationalist Mohammed Hatta who was exiled there. In 1946, Indey joined the Komite Indonesia Merdeka (KMI, 'Indonesia Freedom Committee') led by the Manadonese government medical doctor, Ms Gerungan. KMI advocated the independence of Indonesia, including West New Guinea through all legal means (Vlasblom 2004:164).

As Richard Chauvel (2005:6) concludes, the nationalism of this period had a narrow base and the nationalists 'were culturally isolated from the great mass of Papuans'. The majority of Papuans had very little knowledge of Indonesia and its *merdeka* struggles. After the incorporation of West New Guinea into Indonesia, people throughout Papua began to learn about *merdeka* as one of the chief dictums of the New Order government. At the same time, resentment began to grow due to the failure of development promises to crystallize and due to the unrelenting military operations, and *merdeka* began to take on meanings that were part of a struggle to secure freedom against a tyrannical state.

While the OPM and a number of Papuans in exile tried to keep the ideal of *merdeka* alive, for most Papuans it became a principle that is suggested to be in the hearts of all Papuans. When asked bluntly about 'OPM', Imyan people of the south-western Kepala Burung, while having no clear ideas about its organizational structure and strategies, tend to suggest that the OPM will eventually complete the struggle for *merdeka*. Further scrutiny of their worldviews, however, reveals that many take the view that Jesus Christ will perform the role of bringing *merdeka*. He will bring wealth and prosperity to their community (not 'Papua') and He will re-establish the just, original order in the world. Imyan refer to this order in terms of Toror or Baimla, a mythological world during which the Imyan were at the centre of the world and possessed all the knowledge and power (Timmer 1998, 2000a, 2000b:302; compare Rutherford 2005 and Golden 2003).

Taking into account the immense variety of cultural traditions in Papua, it should be no surprise that peoples' ideas about *merdeka* are diverse. Moreover, there are also divisions within Papuan communities. Imyan villagers, for example, tend to divide between two groups: one that is inclined to withdraw into autonomy (related to ideas about a past community of male initiates retreating in the forest to engage with powerful sky beings), and another that seeks to benefit from unique opportunities offered by 'Indonesia' by engaging with the government and its promises of development. What the two divisions share is a versatile but persistent concern with effective knowledge that they believe is held among foreigners and considered indispensable for bringing about change that Imyan people themselves can control. These beliefs are expressed in terms of a felt need for relative autonomy from state control when the government's administrative grid discords with local realities and people's aspirations (Timmer 2004b:121-4; compare Maclean 1994).

This concern is in fact a crucial part of a larger and still more intrusive concern with denied identity and lost certainties (Timmer 2004b:130). The Imyan share this concern with most other Papuan communities and it can be said that a possibly shared *merdeka*-aspiration in Papua is thus, in general terms, about deferential treatment as human beings, and in principal irrespective of the political or national context. In these ontological ideas about sovereignty and dignity (*harga diri*), *merdeka* is thus chiefly a response to decades-long denial of the people's competence in learning and performing in modern colonial and post-colonial contexts. This partly explains the unrelenting search for understanding of the suffering of the Papuans, preferably through a democratic dialogue with 'Jakarta' that was so effectively expressed during the Papuan Spring. But the idea of having one's own state, right now and for all times, is seldom on the minds of most Papuans, as it is a construct far from the more intrusive largely individual and communal concern with sovereignty and *harga diri*.

During the 'Papuan Spring' (1999-2000), *merdeka* took on the *harga diri*-meaning when throughout the territory numerous raisings of the Bintang Kejora flag (which was prohibited until 1998) and concurrent praying sessions were organized.[6] The Papuan Spring was a period during which President Abdurrahman Wahid allowed the Papuans to name their province Papua and to raise their national flag along the Indonesian flag. Hundreds of prominent leaders from all over Papua found the space to organize a broadly supported front. They developed political strategies during two large gatherings: MUBES (Musyawarah Besar or 'Grand Gathering for Discussion') in February 2000, and the Kongres Papua (Papuan Congress) in May-June 2000 (Agus Alua 2002a, 2002b). These gatherings proceeded undisturbed and while the political agenda demanded independence of Papua, the strategies developed favoured a dialogue with Jakarta short of violence. The focus was on the suffering of the Papuans and numerous discussions revolved around human rights. 'HAM' (Hak Asasi Manusia, Human Rights) became a widely used term taking on a variety of meanings in different contexts but generally referring to lack of respect for the Papuans.

6 See Van den Broek and Szalay (2001) for an overview of the turbulent events in Papua from 1999 to 2000.

Expressions of independence for Papua were articulated by the Presidium Dewan Papua (PDP, Papuan Presidium Council) that was established during the MUBES. Under the combined highland-coastal leadership of Thom Beanal and Theys Eluay, the Presidium formulated Papua-wide supported resolutions that were adopted during the Kongres. The resolutions include the claim that Papua had in fact become independent with the establishment of the New Guinea Council in 1961 and rejected the New York Agreement because Papuans did not take part in the negotiations. In addition, the resolution states that the Act of Free Choice was not conducted properly (Agus Alua 2002b:96). More widely shared was the opinion that 'the land of the Papuans' had become the plaything of international and capitalist forces and that its people had become marginalized in Indonesian society.

Underlying a strong wish for increased sovereignty with predominant millenarian characteristics, the rise of Papuan nationalisms at all levels of society also called into question any extent to which Papuans had become Indonesians. The differences between 'Papuans' and 'Indonesians' were, however, only rarely expressed. Both the symbolic and explicit messages broadcast during gatherings, manifestations, prayer sessions and flag raisings, emphasized the living memory of distress that in human rights activist circles in Papua is typified as *memoria passionis* (or in Indonesian: *ingatan penderitaan*) in circles of human rights activists in Papua.[7] *Memoria passionis* refers to the memory of trauma due to general social and economic marginalization, frequent denial of dignity, and sometimes outright terror. Since the dawn of this period *memoria passionis* began to be expressed as a shared Papuan history of suffering and was flung in the face of 'Jakarta' when a team of 100 leaders (Tim 100) from all over Papua presented a clear demand for independence to President Habibie on 26 February 1999. Next, a fact-finding team of the Indonesian House of Representatives was sent to Irian Jaya in July 1998, leading to a wave of enthusiasm among virtually all sections of society about a dialogue.

The dialogue was expected to lead to at least formal apologies for human rights violations, end impunity for the armed forces, and increase respect for the *harga diri* of the Papuans. At the same time, it also unleashed often very political expressions epitomized in such as expressions as OFM (resonating with OPM) meaning: Otonomi – Federasi – Merdeka, indicating people's hope that discussion about increased autonomy for Irian Jaya would lead to the establishment of a Federal State of Indonesia which would eventually

7 J. Budi Hernawan and Van den Broek 1999. The concept of *memoria passionis* was introduced into Papua by the Office for Justice and Peace (Sekretariat Keadilan dan Perdamaian) of the Catholic Diocese of Jayapura and is also the title of a series of annual reports on the social and political situation in Papua (www.hampapua.org).

culminate in independence for West Papua. What followed in reality, however, was an overall well-intended Papuan response to President Habibie's offer to contemplate on independence aspirations and, within the term of reference, establish a dialogue between 'Jakarta' and 'Papua'.

The dialogue was continued during Aburrahman Wahid's presidency but a ban on flag raisings and a number of bloody military attacks on protesters discouraged most Papuan leaders to continue seeking understanding of the situation in Papua amid policy-makers in Jakarta. The Presidium was declared illegal and the detention of its leaders on charges of treason and subversion, and the brutal murder of the chair of the Presidium, Theys Hiyo Eluay in 2000 marked the end of the Papuan Spring. The killing of Eluay was orchestrated by Kopassus (Komando Pasukan Khusus, the Army Special Forces). The counterinsurgency practised by the TNI began to form a major threat to most attempts to organize people to defend their rights and to continue pressing Jakarta to seek solutions to past and present injustice and feelings of disenchantment. By the close of 2000, 'the developing atmosphere of a 'Papuan Spring' [...] had been replaced by widespread fear, silence, and renewed anger' (Van den Broek and Szalay 2001:91. At the same time, people began to distrust the remnants of the Presidium and its regional branches because of rumours about the Presidium accepting money from big companies in Papua and frustration about its leaders travelling abroad all the time while neglecting the issues faced by local communities.

Special autonomy and new blossoms

Among the most promising developments in this Reformasi period was the granting of a so-called Special Autonomy (commonly referred to as Otsus, from Otonomi Khusus) for the province of Papua in early 2001. Otsus matches an earlier law for the province of Aceh but was drafted by people in Papua and establishes provisions that surpass the autonomy conditions for other provinces. Otsus envisions enhanced autonomy for Papuan communities and their institutions, as well as a greater share of revenues from resource extraction projects in Papua, including 70% of the oil and gas industry and 80% from mining ventures. On top of that, Otsus entails special funds for the improvement of health services, education facilities, and infrastructure that benefit rural communities for a period of 20 years (Agus Sumule 2003b).

Otsus was a Papuan political choice that indicated a willingness to cooperate with the central government. It was envisioned as a necessary step towards justice for the neglected people of Papua (Maniagasi 2001; Agus Sumule 2003a). A technical assistance team comprising intellectuals from Papua whom the Governor of Papua, Jaap Solossa, had appointed drafted the bill in early 2001. After extensive lobbying by the team and a number of influential Papuans, it was accepted as Law no. 21/2001 that was to be implemented as of 2002 (Agus Sumule 2003a). This initially positive answer from Jakarta was one of an insecure central government after the 1999 ballot in East Timor during which a majority voted against autonomy within Indonesia.

Apart from a few hard-line voices demanding *merdeka*, people in Papua expected positive developments from Otsus. But public interest in Otsus dwindled when people saw that implementation of the Otsus was slow due to the lack of capacity of legislators and that the establishment of the Majelis Rakyat Papua (MRP) or Papuan People's Assembly did not receive support from Jakarta. The MRP is an essential element of Otsus as it envisions the protection of the rights of the Papuans. It would assemble people from customary groups, religious institutions and women groups and grant them extensive political powers. The Ministry of Home Affairs delayed the establishment of the MRP because elements in Jakarta saw that the powers it granted to Papuans could endanger the stability in Papua (Chauvel and Bhakti 2004:38). In the mean time, people in Papua began to question whether Otsus was yet another hollow promise made by 'Jakarta'. Others remained hopeful that with assistance of and pressure by foreign governments and international NGOs Jakarta would eventually grant the MRP to Papua.

These hopes basically faced a dead end after President Megawati Sukarnoputri promulgated a decree on 27 January 2003 on the expedition of the implementation of Law no. 45/1999 regarding the creation of two new provinces (West Irian Jaya and Central Irian Jaya), three new regencies (Paniai, Mimika, and Puncak Jaya), and one municipality (Sorong). The envisioned plan behind the decree is labelled *pemekaran* ('blossoming' or administrative fragmentation). While the division of Papua was also part of the Otsus Law it outlined the procedure that it could only be implemented after deliberation of the MRP and approval of the provincial parliament (Sullivan 2003).

Then Deputy Governor John Djopari stressed that the idea of *pemekaran* was not new but that it had been proposed in 1999 by the then Governor, Freddy Numberi, and his three Deputy Governors: Djopari, Herman Monim, and Abraham Atururi (ICG 2003d:3). Soon it became clear that Monim and Atururi were frustrated because they had been promised governorship for the new provinces but that never materialized. Djopari later became Ambassador for Indonesia to Papua New Guinea and Monim retired. Atururi, however, was still interested in the establishment of a new province.

In contrast to Otsus, the *pemekaran* decree was issued without consultation with the provincial government. Local communities or leaders of religious and other civil society organizations in Papua were also not involved in the decision-making process. While Otsus had been poorly socialized among the people it met with support because it came from people whose dialogue with Jakarta intended to benefit the development of Papua. Supporters of Otsus saw the presidential decree as a sign that the political climate in Indonesia was reverting to a New Order-style government. Many began to speculate that it was an attempt by Jakarta to 'divide and rule' the Papuans. Distress in Papua grew when people learned that the initiative for the policy had come from disgruntled elements in the Papuan elite in cooperation with policy-makers in the central government – the Ministry of Home Affairs and the National Intelligence Board (BIN, Badan Intelijen Negara) (McGibbon 2004:55).

The International Crisis Group (ICG 2003:8-9) points out that BIN involvement in the revival of *pemekaran* may have commenced with the lobby by Jimmy Ijie, a Papuan from the Sorong region. Ijie heads the so-called Irian Jaya Crisis Centre (IJCC) in Jakarta and in that capacity he sent a letter to BIN urging that Law no. 45 be implemented immediately. According to him an administratively undivided Papua would foster Papuan nationalism (ICG 2003d:8). In late 2002, Ijie formed a team called Tim 315 consisting of people from the Sorong and Manokwari regions and a number of Papuan students residing in Yogyakarta and Jakarta to support Atururi to negotiate the plan with BIN and the Ministry of Home Affairs. Apparently, a large amount of money (approximately U$ 320,000) was involved and a number of financial rewards were promised to officers in the Ministry of Home Affairs and to Ijie's IJCC.[8]

A possible other motive for the partitioning of Papua is that the creation of new provinces and districts will imply a significant increase in the number of troops in the territory. Each separate province may get its own Military Resort Command (Komando Resort Militer, Korem), with its own network of District Military Commands (Komando Distrik Militer, Kodim). A potential stronger military presence aroused suspicion as it may not only increase repression but also facilitate connections with local business in which the army is involved. As a result, much of the goodwill that was created among Papuans during the dawn of Reformasi turned to disappointment. At the same time, the awareness that elements of the Papuan elite were involved in the *pemekaran* policy nourished already widespread distrust of those Papuans who are making careers in the formal sector or the armed forces 'infecting them with the Indonesia virus', as the popular expression runs. This virus of Indonesia refers to untrustworthy behaviour of Papuan legislators that is also captured under another popular expression, KKN or Korupsi, Kolusi, Nepotisme (Corruption, Collusion and Nepotism) which dates back to the

8 Muridan Widjojo, personal communication, 7-5-2005.

New Order period. Swiftly the previous expression 'OFM' developed into 'OPM', now referring to a new sequence: Otonomi (autonomy), Pemekaran (blossoming), and eventually Merdeka (independence).

Ideally, the devolution of power entailed in the *pemekaran* policy should be a promising move as it can enhance good governance at the local level. Currently, government officials in the region are inclined to acknowledge local demands to become *tuan di atas tanahnya* ('the ruler of one's own country') but they also tend to be hungry for power after decades of curtailing bonds to the centre. Elite politics and the responses among local people largely revolve around these issues. Decentralization leads to a diversification of political concerns that are connected with local identities which on their turn tend to become more extreme. The resulting condition may be labelled as 'erring decentralization', after the discussion by Netherlands New Guinea's penultimate Governor Van Baal of 'erring acculturation' among Papuans. Van Baal pointed at the counterproductive transformation in people's attitudes to life due to their confrontation with the Western world, or, more precisely, the process in which acculturation goes astray and 'development turns in a direction harmful to the realization of the intended aim' (Van Baal 1960:108). In the remaining part of this essay, I elaborate the characteristics of 'erring decentralization' in Papua in more detail.

Papuanization and adaptation

Present-day conflicts in Papua include disputes over natural resources and economic and political power struggles, and frictions between different ethnicities, religion, and immigrants and locals (ICG 2002b; Amnesty International 2002). Studies of 'the conflict in Papua', however, commonly focus on Jakarta policies and armed forces operations. Most reports produced by Papua watchers portray developments in Papua mainly in terms of violations of human rights by 'Jakarta' which is opposed by 'Papuan resistance'. This resistance is often depicted as a single actor with a uniform ethnic identity driven by a uniting national consciousness. Papuan identity is then presupposed to exist in a bounded cultural and racial sphere defined as 'Melanesia' as opposed to 'Indonesia' or 'Asia'.[9] This is hardly conceivable considering the vast variety of cultural backgrounds and centuries-old histo-

9 See for example, Budiardjo and Sioe Long 1983; Osborne 1985; Sharp 1994; Walsh and Rouch 1999; J. Barr 2002; Martinkus 2002; P. King 2004; and contributions to a special edition on Papua of the *New Internationalist* (Volume 344, April 2002). By and large, these works follow one basic line of argument which suggests that Papua will or should become a second East Timor and that Papuans are the victims of genocide or deliberate, well-organized terror, obscuring the fact that Papuans are (and have always been) divided.

ries of connections between Papua and the Moluccas (see below). Only a few recent anthropological and historical studies of Papuan communities relate to these histories and include discussions about the integration of Papuans into Indonesia and its concomitant internal tensions.[10] Danilyn Rutherford (2003:4), for instance, points out that the high degree of integration of the Biak-Numfor region into Indonesia illuminates 'a socio-cultural economy that stands cheek by jowl with the discourses of Papuan separatism and Indonesian nationalism, yet radically undercuts them both'.

The lack of attention to the variety of and changes in Papuan worldviews since the 1960s is astonishing as newly emerging identities and related concerns and strategies lead to tensions in and between local communities and shape to a large extent the politics of the elite. In the virtual absence of a middle-class and very limited private investment in human development and the delivery of services, the powerful elites in Papua are to be found in the administrative sector and in religious institutions. Therefore, Papuan political power is in the hands of these new bureaucratic and religious elite.

Christian and Muslim leaders in Papua recognize that religion is an important source of inspiration for the people and that religious institutions, being the largest and most organized civil society organizations in Papua, should play an important role as mediators between the government and communities (Giay 2001). The varied ethnic and political landscape in Papua is accentuated by the timing and nature of contact with outside powers. In pre-colonial times, contact with regional others and internal and in-migration were perhaps the most significant factors in demographic, social and cultural change in Papua. More in general many coastal groups looked for centuries towards the west. In particular the coastal communities of the Kepala Burung and the Cenderawasih Bay maintained trade and marriage relationship with Maluku and Islam spread along certain coastal stretches.[11] In contrast, people in the highland regions lived relatively isolated in mountain valleys with little direct but extensive indirect trade networks extending to the coast (Ploeg 2001).

Cultural differences between the mountains and the north and the west coast changed markedly with the advent of Christian missionization and Dutch administration during the twentieth century. Mission activity, followed hesitantly by the government, affected the Cenderawasih Bay, the Kepala Burung, the north coast and coastal stretches such as Mimika and

10 Oosterhout 2000; Rutherford 2003; Stasch 2001, 2003; Timmer 2000a, 2000b, 2003. One of the reasons for this lack of attention to the cultural and social realities of Papuans is that since its incorporation in Indonesia access to the region for researchers has been severely restricted.

11 Chauvel 2005; Ellen 2003; Huizinga 1998; Kamma 1947-49; Swadling 1996; Timmer 2000b; Visser 1989.

Merauke along the southwest coast, while most groups in the highlands and communities in the southern plains remained 'untouched' until the 1960s. Encounters between highland people and the state and church intensified after the Indonesian government took over the territory from 1963 (Ploeg 2001; Hays 1993).

Shortly before and after the Second World War economic development was limited, while at later stages, new political developments took place. Especially the rapid expansion of administration and education had a major impact on the coastal people in Biak, Manokwari, Yapen en Sentani, and to a lesser extent in the Kepala Burung and Fak-fak. Papuans from these regions absorbed Dutch teachings at high schools in Netherlands New Guinea and were exposed to European life styles. Some were given the opportunity to enjoy education in Europe and the Pacific. The figures remained modest since in the early 1960s, only about 10,000 Papuans (of a total population estimated at around one million) were in government service while a smaller number was employed in the private sector (Timmer forthcoming).

Later generations grew up in the context of the Indonesian nation-state, undertook studies at Indonesian institutions and made careers in the Indonesian civil service, equipping them with the skills and language of modern Indonesia. Whereas many members of the old Papuan elite that were created by the Dutch were marginalized, the new generations of educated Papuans (still largely from coastal regions) found their way into the civil service. Participation of Papuans in the administration and commercial ventures was however still restricted. The Indonesian government was afraid that Papuans would gain too much of a voice in the administrative sector while banking facilities are few and tend to privilege Javanese, Buginese, Maluku and foreign investors. Moreover, the commercial infrastructure is poorly developed and bureaucratic approvals for trade are painfully slow, in particular for Papuans.

It was only in the late 1990s that sincere efforts were made to Papuanize the formal sector. Today, around 35% of the labour force in the government is Papuan which is a poor reflection of the demographic reality in which approximately 60% of the population is Papuan.[12] Nevertheless, over the last few years more Papuans have become legislators both at the district and provincial levels. Amid many people from elsewhere in Indonesia, the provincial bureaucracy is chiefly dominated by coastal Papuans from the Cenderawasih Bay islands of Biak and Yapen, Sentani, and, more recently from the Sorong and Ayamaru regions of the Kepala Burung. Muridan Widjojo (1998:3) signalled in this respect that the biggest problem facing Irian Jaya was social and cultural polarization and domination of the formal sec-

12 Don Flassy, personal communication, 23-4-2005.

tor by ethnic Biak, Ayamaru, Serui and Sentani. In contrast to the provincial bureaucracy, in the district governments in the highlands and south coastal regions the local population is more strongly represented notwithstanding the presence of a significant number of decision-makers from Biak and Yapen in the Cenderawasih Bay, the Sorong region of the Kepala Burung, and a few people from Java and Maluku.

Particularly among the recently ascending Sorong and Ayamaru elites, there is a remarkable acquaintance with Indonesian ways of doing politics. The acquired skills and knowledge of the present-day bureaucratic elite enables a number of influential people to establish links with Jakarta which primarily serves their own benefit. Highlanders and people from the south-coastal regions (Mimika, Merauke) are often consumed with envy about the power enjoyed by people from the Kepala Burung and the Cenderawasih Bay. Underlying this foremost regional cleavage in Papua is the serious lag in development of most regions of the highlands (Timmer forthcoming). Moreover, because of isolation and due to ongoing often poorly orchestrated TNI action, the highland region is currently the chief nursery of Papuan resistance to the Indonesian government. This Papuan resistance also translates into regional tensions as highlanders regularly challenge both the provincial government and coastal Papuans from Biak, Sorong and Sentani where they at times accuse of collaboration with 'Indonesia'. This tension highlights one of the main divisions within the Papuan nationalist movement which is illustrated by Rutherford (2003:xviii) recounting a joke in which a highlander tells another that when Papua gains independence all Biaks will become foreigners (*amberi*) while highlanders will become Biaks.

As mentioned, during the massive gatherings during the Papuan Spring Papuan leaders managed to balance representations from the highlands and the coast and Papuans felt united in their *memoria passionis*. With the advent of *pemekaran*, the tensions between elites from Biak, Yapen, Ayamaru and Sorong as well as between 'the coast' and 'the highlands' intensified. A recent Indonesia briefing by the International Crisis Group (ICG 2003d:1) outlines that the new *pemekaran* policy alongside a certain level of support for Otsus 'has generated intense acrimony within the governing elite in Papua between those who stand to gain from the division [...] and those who benefit more from the status quo'. Chauvel (2005:xi) notes that 'the jockeying for position that this policy unleashed suggests that regional and tribal interests remain politically salient'.

The protagonists

As indicated above, the *pemekaran* option was supported if not stimulated by a number of Papuan delegates who met with President Megawati, the Ministry of Home Affairs and BIN throughout 2002. In particular, malcontent Papuan political elements were mobilized by the above mentioned Ijie, and the Marine Brigadier General (retired) Abraham Atururi, who had lost against the current Governor, Jaap Solossa, during the election campaign for governorship in 1999 (ICG 2003d:8-9). Atururi enjoyed Dutch boarding school at primary level in Serui, Yapen during the heyday of Dutch efforts to develop Netherlands New Guinea. After the Dutch left New Guinea, Atururi attended the Navy National Academy after he finished Senior High School in Biak. Next he made a career in the Navy and became a Lieutenant Colonel and member of intelligence agency (BAKIN, Badan Koordinasi Intelijen Negara, currently BIN). He also served in the Paspanpres or the 'Security Guard for the President'. While still a Lieutenant Colonel, he was assigned as head of the Sorong District in 1992. After one five-year term in Sorong, he went to Jayapura to become one of the three Deputy Governors under Freddy Numberi. His term as Deputy Governor allowed him to rise in the military ranks and he earned his first star. During the Reformasi period and marking the end of the military's New Order *dwifungsi* ('dual function' of the military conflating national defence with nation-building), General Wiranto, the then Chief of the Armed Forces, demanded all active military personnel who were occupying civilian positions to choose whether they wanted to continue in the army or pursue a career as legislators. Atururi chose the latter as he aspired to become Governor of Irian Jaya but, as indicated, in 1999 he lost to Jaap Solossa.

Like Atururi, Solossa enjoyed Dutch education at primary and secondary level in Teminabuan and Manokwari respectively, and then Junior High School in Sorong. After the transfer of West New Guinea to Indonesia, he continued his education at Senior High School-level in Manokwari before studying Civil Administration at Universitas Cenderawasih in Jayapura for his undergraduate degree. Later, when he served as a member of the National Parliament, he used his spare time to pursue a Master Degree in Development Economics at Universitas Gajah Mada. He continued this specialization at postgraduate level at Universitas Padjadjaran in Bandung with a research on Special Autonomy for Papua. In May 2005, he received his doctorate. Dr Solossa has a large circle of acquaintances especially from the Ayamaru and Sorong elites who became unhappy with Atururi during his term as district head in Sorong. In a similar vein, Atururi is currently supported by elements of the Kepala Burung elite that are not happy with the current district head, John Piet Wanane, who is from the Ayamaru region.

Despite growing controversy over the status of the province, the Minister of Home Affairs, Hari Sabarno, inaugurated Atururi as the Governor of West Irian Jaya in November 2003, leading to a barrage of regional criticism. The

Speaker of the Papua provincial legislature and supporter of Solossa, John Ibo, said that the inauguration contradicted a recommendation issued by the People's Consultative Assembly during its latest annual session and urged Jakarta to revise the law on the division of Papua.

Atururi arrived in Manokwari in February 2003 to start work on the establishment of the new provincial headquarters. On his way from Jakarta he stopped in Jayapura to present to Speaker Ibo an official BIN statement signed by its head, Lieutenant General (retired) Hendropriyono, saying that Atururi had the authority to establish West Irian Jaya (Timmer 2004a:411). Exactly a year later, the Constitutional Court ruled against a lawsuit from a Special Autonomy Defence Team that sought to undo the division of Papua. Supported by Governor Solossa and elements of the Papuan elite in Jayapura, the Defence Team had argued that the establishment of the new province served the interests of the Megawati Sukarnoputri-led Indonesian Partai Demokrasi Indonesia Perjuangan, (PDI-P, Democratic Party of Struggle) which intended to weaken the dominant Golkar Party in the region through the *pemekaran* plan. The Team suggested that the PDI-P had economic interests in the Bintuni Bay where British Petroleum is establishing the Tangguh liquefied natural gas plant (ICG 2003d:9). The Team added that both the TNI and BIN had also a lot to gain with the province as the two institutions have economic interests in maintaining a high level of TNI presence in the region.

The Constitutional Court concluded that the establishment of West Irian Jaya remained valid although Law no. 45/1999 was no longer effective. Eight of the nine judges argued that the Otsus Law took effect after the new province and regencies were designed and that the law had annulled no state institution. The court ruling was seen as a victory for Atururi and left many in Jayapura, Sorong and elsewhere in Papua confused. While the media reported the decision as a win-win solution for all conflicting parties in Papua and Jakarta, John Ibo noted that it will lead to increasing disorder and growing loss of confidence in Jakarta's commitment to the problems in Papua (Timmer 2005:454-5).

One of the effects of the above-mentioned differences between the Sorong-Ayamaru elite which is often suspected of conspiring to control Papua as 'SOS' (Semua Orang Sorong, 'all-Sorong') and 'disadvantaged' highland tribes and 'backward' south coastal plains peoples was the significant local support for the establishment of a separate province of Central Irian Jaya in the Timika area. This new province was advocated by the head of the district of Timika, Clemens Tinal and the head of the Timika legislative council, Andreas Anggaibak. As Anggaibak said himself, he was encouraged by BIN to go ahead with the establishment of the new province (Chauvel and Bhakti 2004:41). In the region he enjoyed support from a group called 'Group of Seven Tribes'. When Anggaibak announced the official establishment of the province in late August 2003 riots broke out during which five people were killed and dozens were injured. Anggaibak's alliance met with opposition from a youth group of the Amungme people led by Thomas Uamang, Yopie Kilangin and Yohanes Deikme, with the support of the Amungme and other ethnic groups around Timika. This regional conflict about *pemekaran* is an extension of older disputes between the communities close to PT Freeport Indonesia copper and gold mining operations that relate to the misuse of company funds and collaboration of community leaders with the TNI in the region.[13] Exposing tensions between highland and north coastal people and in an attempt to gain a share of the riches of the Freeport mining venture, elements of the elite in Biak argued that Biak would be a better location for the new province's capital in April and May 2004. They proposed that Admiral Henk Wabiser should be appointed as acting Governor (Chauvel 2005:77).

Tensions at the regional level also played a role in the establishment of West Irian Jaya. New districts in West Irian Jaya like Fak-fak and Raja Ampat (which is rich in forest and nickel resources) felt uncomfortable with what they feared as domination by those from the Sorong and Ayamaru regions and opted to remain within the Province of Papua. Furthermore, during Atururi's lobbying for the establishment of West Irian Jaya, customary leaders in the region had an interest in the division plans, as it would lead to the establishment of 28 new regencies, including Teluk Bintuni, which would offer them an opportunity to occupy new administrative positions. The importance attached to the creation of the Teluk Bintuni regency is related to the above-mentioned operations of the Tangguh plant in the Bintuni Bay. The new regency, and the new province of West Irian Jaya of which it is part, will be abundantly rich in natural resources.

The *pemekaran* decree amplified cleavages within the Papuan elite of which one favours Otsus as a means for the development of Papua as a whole and is led by Governor Solossa who is supported by a number of civil society organizations and prominent Papuan intellectuals. Others were keen to establish their own provinces and districts to claim their own power positions and secure access to natural resources. Ethnic tensions along regional fault lines intensified as the pro-*pemekaran* players in Papua demanded a share of the fiscal transfers from the central government and wanted to increase control over the territory's riches. The resulting disunity among influential people in the Papuan bureaucratic elite weakened the support for Otsus and eased the implementation of the *pemekaran* law (McGibbon 2004:61).

13 Leith 2003; Ballard 2002; Muridan Widjojo 2003. Anggaibak, who is a former police man tried to control the so-called One Percent Fund that was set up 1996 by the Freeport mining company to support social development programs which met with opposition from other political players in the region.

Autonomy and its opportunities

Within the plans for the establishment of new districts and new provinces, almost no provision has been made to ensure that new government policies are adjusted to local circumstances and meet the aspirations of the people. The majority of government officials are accustomed to working with top-down programmes and accountability procedures that rarely involve the communities who figure as subjects in the plans and reports. The New Order government with its ambition to impose a layer of Indonesianness all over the archipelago propagated the idea that the lives of citizens in such remote and 'underdeveloped' regions as Papua had to be transformed according to fixed formats. The results are often unsettling in particular when long-standing community-based ways of doing things and local ways of resources management were disrupted. While development plans for Papua were designed to improve the living conditions of so-called 'isolated people' (*masyarakat terasing*) they often lead to estrangement. This in turn stimulated a tendency to reflect nostalgically on one's own unique non-state units such as the kinship group and the 'customary people' (*masyarakat adat*) whose rights should be restored.

Currently, decentralized governments at the district levels face the daunting task of finding ways to overcome deep-seated feelings of distrust towards the state, and to develop programs that acknowledge the complex varieties and recent changes in Papuan society. Newly recruited personnel are for the most part educated at schools for public administration with curricula are in accord with the New Order and its top-down philosophy. As such, they are ill-equipped to adjust themselves to new democratic and open-minded ways of governance.

Reflecting on the colonial context in the Australian-administered Territory of Papua and New Guinea in the 1960s, Peter Lawrence (1969) argues that the difficulty of establishing a Western type of legal system is that the groups concerned, that is, the Australians and the New Guineans, represent quite different, specialized social systems. Both systems had their own idiosyncratic process of social control that was not expected to function in a single legal framework. Today, the Papua New Guinea Government still faces the difficult challenge of binding a variety of distinct communities into an effective political and ideological organization (LiPuma 1995; Douglas 2000; May 2001, 2003). The present situation in Papua appears to suffer from a similar incompatibility between models of governance structured upon institutional principles of modern statehood and variety of everyday political and social realities. Otsus aims to counter this, but the formidable challenge facing decentralizing governments is beyond most administrators' imagination and not anticipated by the legislative or the executive bodies that enacted and implemented the *pemekaran* law.

Previously, the political and governmental situation in Papua was characterized as based on an 'outside' and 'Indonesian' government ruling a majority of Papuans through models of governance current in Java and not embracing or fully appreciating 'Papuan ways of doing things'. While there were a fair number of Papuans in the bureaucracy at all levels and a few Governors in the period from 1963 were ethnically Papuan, local communities saw the regional and provincial government as dominated by Javanese. Since more Papuans began to occupy seats in the formal sector the ideas about the government changed to a sense of domination of 'Indonesian politics' endorsed by Papuan elites.

Many criticize provincial leaders because they promise local communities development and access to resources while they actually profit from arrangements with elites in Jakarta, TNI and Javanese and foreign investors. This obviously leads to an unstable situation as political support at the local level will soon dwindle and break along regional or ethnic fault lines. Since administrative procedures lack transparency, the widespread feeling among Papuans that their own elite cannot be trusted will no doubt increase.

There is currently a growing tension between those who seek, find and use opportunities offered in the formal and commercial sectors and those who are denied such prospects. Papuan communities' responses to a corrupt administration and dishonest behaviour of their own elite are varied. In many of the locations where large-scale resource extraction takes place, such as Freeport mining in the Mimika region and the Tangguh project in the Bintuni Bay, as well as logging and fishery business, local communities organize themselves against neighbouring groups and their elites who also claim natural resources and compensation.

One effect of this development is the emergence of eccentric and charged revitalizations of customary structures and the establishment of customary organizations (*masyarakat adat*). The expectations of monetary flows that resource development projects might bring, and the related competing claims over land and resources, pose problems for local people who no longer know whom to trust and through whom to raise their voices with outside companies and the government. At the same, the government and the companies find it increasingly difficult to deal effectively with the dispersed forms of Papuan leadership.

On top of the resulting frustrations and tensions between groups and a growing gap between local communities and the formal sector, criminal and predatory business is increasingly entrenching itself in the instruments of the state. The ways in which this also affects local sentiments and longstanding discourses on identity, autonomy and independence, and leads to new regional and ethnic alliances, show parallels to situations in African countries as described by Jean-François Bayart, Stephen Ellis and Beatrice Hibou (1999), among others. Comparisons between problems with governance in Africa and the Pacific and Asian region may provide many analytical advantages.

For example, Mahmood Mamdani's (1996) emphasis on colonial legacies and what he calls a bifurcated state, characterized by friction between the creation of an urban civil society and a rural zone administrated by means of ethnic division and retribalized authority, puts central the super-ordinate structure of governance and state strategies. As shown in this chapter, an analysis of the legacies of the state and the emergence and politics of urban elites since the colonial epoch is crucial to understanding the social and political dynamics in present-day Papua.

However, as Jon Fraenkel (2004) points out, comparisons between Africa and Oceania and Asia ought to be done cautiously. A careful comparison between Papua and Africa is beyond the scope of this paper but let me make the point that the most obvious parallel between Papua and certain regions in Africa is, as said, the criminalization of the state in Papua. In the capacity of provincial legislator, district head, head of a department and so on, they not only gain influence over state resources but they also enjoy relative freedom to make profitable deals with resources extraction ventures. These businesses are largely unregulated exploitation of the minerals, oil, fish, and forest resources.

A striking example is rampant logging and the illegal trade of merbau *(kayu besi)* threatening the pristine forests of the region. (EIA/Telapak 2005; *Logging* 2002). Merbau (*kayu besi*) is a luxurious dark hardwood that is the main target of a billion-dollar trade route from Papua to the booming cities of China's Yangtze River delta. Another unsettling example is the involvement of the TNI and government officials in the gathering and trade of *gaharu* (eaglewood) that is sold for high prices to the Arab world.[14] One of the results is that wealth is taken away from the bottom up while opportunities for advancement are redistributed inside and outside Papua within limited elites by the provision of gifts, commercial opportunities, and so on. Politically and economically, Papua begins to show signs of the privatization of the state and the criminalization of the behaviour of power-holders.

14 SKP Merauke 2004. The rampant spread of the HIV/AIDS-virus is partly connected to the prostitution centres established and run by the TNI to service local and migrant workers. These prostitution centres are a principal source of the infection. Estimates suggest that the number of HIV-infected people in Papua stands at approximately 15,000 at present.

Conclusion

The post-Soeharto Reformasi period in Papua was marked by revivals of optimism about change and expectations of imminent far-reaching sovereignty. The prospect of justice, the acknowledgement of the 'true history of Papua', and increased respect for the Papuans, alternated with strong disappointment and mounting resentment towards 'Jakarta' due to renewed harsh and poorly controlled TNI operations. Amid a persistent undercurrent of distrust towards the national government many in Papua showed a remarkable ardour for entering into a bargaining process (albeit often with high opening bids, alarming policy-makers in Jakarta). Hopes that justice can be done for the Papuans were again visible during the recent national elections in which the people of Papua went to the polls in high numbers (Timmer 2005:448-50). Also the Otsus and *pemekaran* lobbies indicate that many in Papua want to participate actively in a political economy of dependence on and engagement with Jakarta.

Dependence is constructed and maintained as much by Papuans who support a dialogue with 'Jakarta' and are eager to cast votes during democratic elections, as by political actors who try to convince Jakarta of the importance of recognizing the grievances of the people of Papua, or merely seek to profit financially from this relationship. On the other hand, both the 'indigenous Papuans' and those generally labelled as 'immigrants' – the divisions between the two can never be clear, let alone desirable – have for a number of reasons quite a strong urge to live their lives largely autonomously. This is due to their *memoria passionis* and disappointment with the central government's policies towards Papua. When the need to distance oneself from unreliable elites and a decentralization that goes astray, people begin to revitalize traditions of relative freedom allegedly enjoyed in the past.

At the level of local communities, throughout history, people have been subject to forms of destabilization as the result of interactions with others and they continuously developed new strategies with locally specific inventiveness. Papuan people's potent histories of relative autonomy and their recent experiences with the church, the colonial government and Indonesian institutions are diverse. Generally, local institutions have been internally negotiated in response to the administration and the church. At the same time, from the district level up to the provincial bureaucracy and the national parliament, Papuan leaders and politicians increasingly usurp the powers of the civil service. Less promising is that in particular the district and provincial levels of the administration have become intertwined in personal patronage systems.

The voices for more autonomy in Papua are generally not about Papuan nationalism but are cast in opposition to the dominance of the state. The state has not brought what Papuans expected and is thus challenged by social, ethnic, religious and regional identities. Most Papuans treat the state with a high degree of suspicion. Only when the promise of commitment to and respect for their demands and aspirations is in the air, they want to engage with the state. Currently, there are two points of contention among the vast majority of people in Papua. One is the unpredictability of 'Jakarta' as the model of the state that the central government is propagating to Papua is unclear, and the other is frustration over the wealth and influence of Papuan elites whose agendas are often too detached from the circumstances they suggest to address.

To remain critical of what is going on in Papua, policy-makers (as well as Papua watchers) should be careful not to fall into the classical mistake of seeing that there is a united Papuan cause that is frustrated by 'Indonesia'. In fact, there has never been an en masse Papuan effort to struggle for secession from Indonesia or a 'compact, self-conscious, and organized community', as Chauvel (2005:3), among others, observes. There have always been strong divisions within Papua even when people organize in civil society organizations, government bodies, or alongside activist circles abroad. What most Papuans have in common though is a *memoria passionis* and the experiences of development programs and democratization efforts dogged by unfulfilled promises and failures. During the Papuan Spring this shared history was expressed Papua-wide in terms of a demand for the straightening of Papuan history and enhanced respect for the Papuans. But the attempts of organizing people into a united front were undermined by military operations and the *pemekaran* decree that was supported by elements of the Papuan elite. What remained was Otsus but this promising reform policy was frustrated by Papuan and Jakarta politics surrounding the *pemekaran* decree which brought to the surface a spate of old and enduring regional, political and personal tensions in the region. The *pemekaran* plan provided opportunities for disenchanted Papuan leaders and subsequently unleashed regional and ethnic sentiments as well as mutual distrust among Papuan leaders.

Finally, with respect to the increasing prominence of the informal economy in Papua, it is important to realize that already since the New Order period major parts of domestic Papua operated more as an unofficial or 'unconventional' economy than an economy of wage earners, formal institutions, and legal contracts. While it is true that a formidable number of people earn government wages, most rural people trade and exchange goods in and between communities in order to survive. Erring decentralization and the limited presence of meaningful development programs trigger fractionalization when people begin to compete for political and economic resources. Self-interest in this context is the result of a realistic view that relates to current and past development promises. People know that outsiders come and make promises about financial rewards, roads, bridges, sago factories, logging activities, fish factories and so on. Then things – people in Papua know from experience – are unlikely to be sustainable and will favour some over others. In these circumstances, elites and local people have a realistic view to get what they can while they can.

Hence what is often seen as greediness, is a response to the ongoing deferral of development alongside failing policies that aim at enhancing services to the people of Papua. In a region which is abundantly rich in natural resources, whose people do not share equally in the profits of resource development projects, and of which many people's dignities have been denied in violent ways for a long period of time, this kind of response is understandable. In other words, 'disorder' in Papua is not merely a condition created by 'Jakarta' or as a state of dereliction; it is a condition that offers opportunities for people in Papua who know how to play the system.

Glossary

Glossary

adat	custom
Afdeeling	administrative unit under Dutch colonial rule
agama	religion
Ajeg Bali	a discourse about the position of Balinese culture in present-day Indonesia
ajeg	strong, upright
aji krama	prices of tradition, for example bride-prices
arat sabulungan	indigenous religion of the Mentawai
aspirasi masyarakat	aspirations of the people
bangun	to construct
banjar	Balinese village unit with social, religious and political functions
beamtenstaat	a state as an apolitical administrative polity that was staffed by Dutch and 'native' officials – but with the Dutch firmly in control – for whom sound and centralized administration mattered most. It was a state that emphasized modern, efficient developmental governance
beras miskin	rice for the poor
berpolitik	politicking (is for instance also used to describe peoples' sneaky strategies to push through their own interests)
bupati	district head
camat	sub-district head
cukong	financier (usually from Chinese origin)
dakwah	Islamic missionary activity
dangdut	Malay-Indonesian pop music genre
datu maling	lord of thieves
desa adat	customary village
desa dinas	administrative village
desa pakraman	traditional Balinese village
desa	village
desentralisasi	decentralization
dewan	council
Dinas Sosial	Social Services

dinas	service
diproyekkan	making something into a project in order to get access to (part of the) project funding
dwifungsi	dual function of the military conflating national defence with nation-building
ekspedisi	expedition (an excursion undertaken for a specific purpose, but also a business that does cargo forwarding, such as sending parcels by ship)
Gereformeerde Zendingsbond	Dutch Reformed Mission
Gereja Toraja	Toraja church
Grooter Toradja	Greater Toraja
haj	pilgrimage to Mecca
haji	pilgrim to Mecca
haram	prohibited by Islam
harga diri	self respect, dignity
Hulubalang	Acehnese aristocrats
Idul Fitri	Islamic feast at the end of the month Ramadan
ikut manipulasi	join the manipulation
instruksi presiden (inpres)	presidential instruction
jatah	portion (bribe)
jawara	individual or group of persons who have a source of physical power (and supernatural knowledge), who dare to oppose injustice, and who protect weaker individuals or community groups; also known as *pendekar*
jihad	a holy struggle waged on behalf of Islam as a religious duty
kabihu	clan
kabupaten	district
kasus adat	customary law dispute
kawasan khusus	special region
kawin maling	marriage by theft
kayu besi	*merbau*, dark hard wood
kayu tangkapan	confiscated timber
kayu temuan	legal timber
kebal	invulnerability
kebudayaan	culture
kecamatan	sub-district
kejayaan Luwu	the greatness of Luwu as a kingdom
kelompok kritis	critical group
keluwuan	Luwu and Luwu-ness
kemajuan	progress
kepala desa	village head
kepala dinas	head of district agency
kerajaan	kingdom
kesenian	art
ketemuq	spirit loss

kiai langgar	Islamic religious teachers who are paid to give sermons or public lectures at privately owned small mosques
kiai pesantren	charismatic Islamic teachers who run residential schools
kiai	Islamic religious teacher
kolom	unit of 15 to 25 households of (GMIM) church members
kopi bangka	'Bangka coffee', the term used for tin sand by the Bangka tin sand mafia in Singapore
kota otonom	autonomous city
kota	city
kotamadya	municipality
krama	customary practice
kuno	old fashioned
landschap	territory under Dutch colonial rule
laskar	partisan militia
laskar jihad	militant Islamic group, also a particular group founded in Java early 2000
lurah	village head appointed by the government
madrasah	non-residential Islamic school
maju	developed, modern
maramba	Sumbanese aristrocrat
marapu	ancestral spirits (Sumbawa)
masyarakat adat	customary people, traditional/indigenous community
masyarakat terasing	isolated community
masyarakat	community, society
memoria passionis	*ingatan penderitaan* – the living memory of distress; refers in human rights activist circles in Papua to the memory general social and economic marginalization, frequent denial of dignity, and sometimes outright terror
mentobat	repent in the mosque
merdeka	freedom, independence
nagari	West Sumatran village
orang asli	original people
orang	people, person
pahlawan	hero
pahlawan nasional	national hero
pam swakarsa	local security groups
pamong praja	local aristocracy within the post independence administrative apparatus
Pancasila	five pillars, the Indonesian state principles
Panghulu	head of a matrilineage (Sumatra)
pecalang	traditional village police in Bali
pedanda	Brahman priest
pegawai negeri sipil	civil servant
pembangunan	development

pemekaran	(literally 'blossoming') administrative fragmentation
pemekaran daerah	administrative fragmentation of a region
pemetik	picker
penadah	middleman
pendapatan asli daerah	*see* PAD, locally raised revenues (districts taxes)
pendekar	(literally: sword master) individual or group of persons who have a source of physical power (and supernatural knowledge), who dare to oppose injustice, and who protect weaker individuals or community groups
pengajian	public Islamic lecture
perkeliruan	mistaken, confused, erroneous
pesantren	Islamic boarding school
petrus	penembakan misterius – mysterious shootings
prasasti	stone inscription
preman	thug, hoodlum
pribumi	son of the soil, native
proyekkan, diproyekkan	to make a project of ('the making of a government service program into a personally profitable business')
pusaka	ancestors' ritual weaponry
pusako	inherited property
putra asli daerah	autochthonous sons of the region
putra asli setempat	people originating from a certain place
putra daerah	child of the region, native son
raja kecil	little king
reformasi	reform(ation)
rompi	a multi-pocketed sleeveless vest
sasareu	someone from afar, outsider
serumpun	trans-national Malay solidarity
sharia, syariah	Islamic law
suku	ethnic group
surau	Islamic prayer centre
syarak	law
syuriah	council of religious scholars
tanah ulayat	village land (West Sumatra)
tauke	foreman, boss (usually from Chinese origin)
tebusan	ransom payment
terbelakang	backwards
transmigrasi	transmigration
Tuan Guru	Lombok's Islamic cleric
Tudang Sipulung	sit and discuss together (Buginese)
tukang protes	protest expert
Ulama, Ulema	Muslim religious teacher or leader
ulayat, tanah ulayat	village land (West Sumatra)
wakil bupati	deputy district head
warga	commoner groups (Bali)
warung	food stall
wilayah pemilu	electoral area
zelfbesturend landschap	self-governing territory

Abbreviations and acronyms

ABK Fraksi	Fraksi Amanat Bintang Keadilan – Mandate Star Justice Faction
ABRI	Angkatan Bersenjata Republik Indonesia – Indonesian Armed Forces
ABSSBK	Adat Basandi Syarak, Syarak Basandi Kitabullah – Adat is founded on the *syarak*, the *syarak* is founded on the holy Koran
AISS	Aku ingin sehat sejahtera – I would like to be healthy and prosperous
AMAN	Aliansi Masyarakat Adat Nusantara – Nusanatara Indigenous Peoples Alliance
APBD	Anggaran Pendapatan dan Belanja Daerah – the Regional Budget
APBN	Anggaran Pendapatan Belanja Negara – the State Budget
APDN	Akademi Pemerintahan Dalam Negeri – Domestic Government Academy
BAKIN	Badan Koordinasi Intelijen Negara (currently BIN) – State Coordinating Intelligence Service
BAKOR-P3PL	Badan Koordinasi Perjuangan Pembentukan Provinsi Luwu Coordinating Body for the Formation of Luwu Province
Bappeda	Badan Perencanaan dan Pembangunan Daerah – Regional Planning Board
BIDA	Batam Industrial Development Authority
BIN	Badan Intelijen Negara – National Intelligence Board
BKO	Bawah Kendali Operasi – Under Operational Control
BKPM	Badan Koordinasi Penanaman Modal – Investment Coordination Agency
BKPPLR	Badan Koordinasi Pembentukan Propinsi Luwu-Raya – Coordinating Body for the Formation of Luwu Raya Province
BKSAUA	Badan Kerjasama Antar Umat Beragama – Organization for Inter-Faith Cooperation
BOSOWA	Bone-Soppeng-Wajo – The regionally powerful political and economic Bugis areas in South Sulawesi
BP3ST	Badan Perjuangan Pemekaran Propinsi Sulawesi Timur – Body for the Struggle for Pemekaran of East Sulawesi Province
BPH	Badan Pemerintah Harian – Governing Council
brimob	brigade mobil – mobile police brigade
CSO	Civil Society Organization
DAD	Dewan Adat Dayak – Dayak Customary Council
DAK	Dana Alokasi Khusus – Special Allocation Fund

dandem	komandan distrik militer – head of regional military command
danrem	komandan resort militer – head of military command
DAU	Dana Alokasi Umum – General Allocation Fund
DCSB	Daftar Calon Sementara Baru – Provisional List of New Candidates
DDII	Dewan Dakwah Islamiyah Indonesia – the Indonesian Council for Islamic Appeals
denpom	detasemen polisi militer – military police detachment
dispenda	dinas pendapatan daerah – local government revenue collection agency
DOM	Daerah Operasi Militer – Area of (special) Military Operation
DPD	Dewan Pemerintah Daerah – Council of Local Government (in the 1950s)
DPD	Dewan Perwakilan Daerah – Regional Representative Council (after Reformasi)
DPR	Dewan Perwakilan Rakyat – People's Representative Assembly (Parliament)
DPRD (I and II)	Dewan Perwakilan Rakyat Daerah – Regional parliament on provincial (*propinsi*) level (DPRD Tingkat I) and on district (*kabupaten*) level (DPRD Tingkat II). In this volume DPRD is used for both levels with different translations depending on the context. Used translations are: Provincial assembly, Provincial parliament, District parliament, Regional parliament, Local parliament, Regional House of Representatives, Regional Legislative Council
FPPDP-LR	Front Penuntut Pemekaran Kabupaten dan Provinsi Luwu Raya – Front for the Demand of District Autonomy and Formation of Luwu Raya Province
FPPPL	Front Perjuangan Pembentukan Provinsi Luwu – Front for the Struggle for Formation of Luwu Province
GAM	Gerakan Aceh Merdeka – Free Aceh Movement
GMIM	Gereja Masehi Injili di Minahasa – Masehi Injili Church in Minahasa (Protestant)
GMKI	Gerakan Mahasiswa Kristen Indonesia – Indonesian Christian Student Movement
HAM	Hak Asasi Manusia – Human Rights
HMI	Himpunan Mahasiswa Islam – Islamic Students Union
HPH	Hak Pengusahaan Hutan – Timber Concession Permit
HPHH	Hak Pemungutan Hasil Hutan – Forest Product Harvest Concessions
ICMI	Ikatan Cendekiawan Muslim Indonesia – Association of Indonesian Muslim Intellectuals
ID	Institut Dayakologi – Institute for Dayakology
IDRD	Institute of Dayakology Research and Development
IJCC	Irian Jaya Crisis Centre
IKAS	Ikatan Keluarga Asal Sumba di Kupang – Union of Sumbanese Residing in Kupang
IPKI	Ikatan Pendukung Kemerdekaan Indonesia – League of Supporters of Indonesian Independence
IPMIL	Ikatan Pelajar Mahasiswa Indonesia Luwu – Indonesian Association

	of Luwu Students
IPPMEN	Ikatan Pemuda Pelajar Mentawai – Association for Young Mentawaian Students and Scholars
Kadin	Kamar Dagang Indonesia – Indonesian Chamber of Commerce and Industry
KAN	Kerapatan Adat Nagari – Village Adat Council
kanwil	kantor wilayah – regional office
kapolda	kepala kepolisian daerah – head of the provincial police
kapolres	kepala kepolisian resort – head of the county police
KBP	Kepala Bagian Perlengkapan – Head of the Provision Section
Kepri	Kepulauan Riau – Riau Archipelago
KKL	Kerukunan Keluarga Luwu – Association of Luwu People
KKN	Korupsi, Kolusi, Nepotisme – the Indonesian triad of corruption, collusion, and nepotism
KMI	Komite Indonesia Merdeka – Indonesia Freedom Committee
KN	Kerapatan Nagari – Village Council
kodam	komando daerah militer – military area commands
kodim	komando distrik militer – district military commands
kopassus	komando pasukan khusus – the army special forces
koramil	komando rayon militer – military precinct commands
korem	komando resort militer – military resort command
korpri	korps pegawai republik Indonesia – Indonesian civil service corps
koter	komando teritorial – territorial commands
KP (Keppres)	Keputusan Presiden – Presidential Decree
KPPPL	Komite Pusat Pembentukan Provinsi Luwu – Central Committee for the Formation of Luwu Province
KPPB	Komite Pembentukan Propinsi Banten – Committee for the Establishment of the Province of Banten
KPPSI	Komite Persiapan Penegakan Syariat Islam – Preparatory Committee for the Upholding of Islamic Law
KPU	Komite Pemilihan Umum – General Election Committee
KPUD	Kantor Pemilihan Umum Daerah – Regional General Election Committee
krismon	krisis moneter – monetary crisis
KTP	Kartu Tanda Penduduk – identity card
KUT	Kredit Usaha Tani – Farmer's Credit Program
LAN	Lembaga Adat Nagari – Village Adat Law Institution (West Sumatra)
LIPI	Lembaga Ilmu Pengetahuan Indonesia – Indonesian Institute of Sciences
LKAAM	Lembaga Kerapatan Adat Alam Minangkabau – Minangkabau-wide Association of Village Adat Councils
MABM	Majelis Adat Budaya Melayu – Malay Cultural and Customary Council
MAD	Majelis Adat Dayak – Dayak Customary Council
MPR	Majelis Rakyat Papua – Papuan People's Assembly
MPR	Majelis Permusyawaratan Rakyat – National Assembly
MUBES	Musyawarah Besar – Grand Meeting for Discussion
MUI	Majelis Ulama Indonesia – Council of Indonesian Islamic Scholars

muspida	musyawarah pimpinan daerah – meeting of local leaders
NICA	Netherlands-Indies Civil Administration
NU	Nahdlatul Ulama
NTT	Nusa Tenggara Timur
OPM	Organisasi Papua Merdeka – Free Papua Organization
Otsus	Otonomi Khusus – Special Autonomy
PAD	Pendapatan Asli Daerah – Locally Raised Revenues (district taxes)
PAN	Partai Amanat Nasional – Party of the National Message
Parkindo	Partai Kristen Indonesia – Indonesian Christian Party
Partindo	Partai Indonesia – Indonesia Party
PBB	Partai Bulan Bintang – Crescent and Star Party
PD	(Partai) Persatuan Dayak – Dayak Unity (Party)
PDI	Partai Demokrasi Indonesia – Indonesian Democratic Party
PDI-P	Partai Demokrasi Indonesia Perjuangan – Indonesian Democratic Party of Struggle
PDKB	Partai Demokrasi Kasih Bangsa – Love the Nation Democratic Party
PDR	Partai Daulat Rakyat – Islamic People's Sovereignty Party
Pepera	Penentuan Pendapat Rakyat – Act of Free Choice
Perda	Peraturan Daerah – District Regulation
PIKI	Persatuan Intelektual Kristen Indonesia – Indonesian Intellectual Christian Union
PKB	Partai Kebangkitan Bangsa – Party of the Awakening of the Nation
PKI	Partai Komunis Indonesia – Indonesian Communist Party
PKI	Partai Kemerdekaan Indonesia – Indonesian Freedom Party
PKK	Program Kesejahteraan Keluarga – Family Welfare Program
PKS	Partai Keadilan Sejahtera – Prosperous Justice Party
PLG	Pembangunan Lahan Gambut – Peat Land Development
Polri	Kepolisian Republik Indonesia – Indonesian National Police
PP	Peraturan Pemerintah – Government Regulation
PPDKB	Partai Pembela Demokrasi Kasih Bangsa – Defenders of Love the Nation Democratic Party
PPIM	Pusat Pengkajian Islam dan Minangkabau – Centre for Studies of Islam and Minangkabau
PPKTU	Panitia Pembentukan Kabupaten Toraja Utara – Committee for Establishment of North Toraja District
PPP	Partai Persatuan Pembangunan – Unity and Development Party
PPPSBBI	Persatuan Pendekar Persilatan dan Seni Budaya Banten Indonesia – Indonesian Association of Champions of Banten Martial Arts
PPPTTRB	Perhimpunan Pengelola dan Pekerja Tambang Timah Rakyat Bangka – The Association of Bangka Small-Scale Tin Miners and Operators
PPSDAK	Pembinaan Pengelolaan Sumber Daya Alam Kemasyarakatan – Strengthening Community Natural Resource Management
PRRI	Pemerintah Revolusioner Republik Indonesia – Revolutionary Government of the Indonesian Republic
PSDH	Provisi Sumber Daya Hutan – Forest Resource Royalty
PUIL	Persatuan Ummat Islam Lombok – Lombok Association for Muslims
RAPBD	Rancangan Anggaran Pendapatan dan Belanja Daerah

RFN	Rainforest Foundation Norway
RMI	Lembaga Ma'arif and Rabithah Ma'ahid Islamiyah
RMS	Republik Maluku Selatan – Republic of the South Moluccas
SARA	Suku Agama Ras Antargolongan – Ethnic, Religious, Race and Inter-class
sekda	sekretaris daerah – district secretary
sembako	sembilan bahan pokok – nine basic commodities (for example rice, sugar, cooking oil and so on)
SIJORI Growth Triangle	link of the economies of Singapore, Johore and the Riau Archipelago
SIPAD	Surat Izin Perdagangan Antar Daerah – Inter-Region Trading Licenses
STPDN	Sekolah Tinggi Pemerintahan Dalam Negeri – Civil Service College
TKI	Tenaga Kerja Indonesia – Indonesian migrant labourer
TKW	Tenaga Kerja Wanita – Female migrant labourer
TNI	Tentara Nasional Indonesia – Indonesian National Military
Trikora	Tri Komando Rakyat – People's Threefold Command
UD	Utusan Daerah – Regional Representative
UU	Undang Undang – Law
WALHI	Wahana Lingkungan Hidup Indonesia – Indonesian Forum for Environment
YCM	Yayasan Citra Mandiri – 'Vision for Autonomy' Foundation

About the authors

Lorraine V. Aragon is a cultural anthropologist who teaches at the University of North Carolina, Chapel Hill, NC, USA. She has conducted fieldwork in Central Sulawesi since 1984, and done comparative research in other areas of Indonesia and Southeast Asia. Her primary interests are religion, minorities and the state, language categories, migration, ownership concepts, forest subsistence, visual and performance arts, mass media, and intellectual property rights. She is the author of the monograph *Fields of the Lord; Animism, Christian minorities, and state development in Indonesia* (2000), and has published a number of articles on the Poso conflict.
aragon2@email.unc.edu

Franz von Benda-Beckmann is co-head of the project group 'Legal Pluralism' at the Max Planck Institute for Social Anthropology in Halle, Germany, and honorary professor at the Universities of Leipzig and Halle. He obtained his PhD with a thesis on 'Legal pluralism in Malawi' at the University of Kiel (1970), and his Habilitation in anthropology at the University of Zürich in 1979 with his book *Property in social continuity* (1979), based on field research in West Sumatra. He has co-edited several books and published numerous articles and book chapters on issues of property rights, social (in)security and legal pluralism in developing countries, and on legal anthropological theory. Most recently he co-edited (with K. von Benda-Beckmann and A. Griffiths) *Mobile people, mobile law; Expanding legal relations in a contracting world* (2005).
fbenda@eth.mpg.de

Keebet von Benda-Beckmann is co-head of the project group 'Legal Pluralism' at the Max Planck Institute for Social Anthropology at Halle, Germany, professor in anthropology of law at Erasmus University Rotterdam, the Netherlands, and honorary professor at the University of Leipzig and the Martin Luther University at Halle-Wittenberg. She wrote her dissertation on 'The broken stairways to consensus; Village justice and state courts in Minangkabau' (1984) and co-authored *De emancipatie van Molukse vrouwen in Nederland* [The emancipation of Maluku Women in the Netherlands] (1992).

She has carried out extensive comparative research in West Sumatra, on Ambon and in the Netherlands on dispute management, local forms of social security, and management of natural resources and decentralization. Two recent books she co-edited are *Coping with insecurity; An 'underall' perspective on social security in the Third World* (2000), and *Mobile people, mobile law; Expanding legal relations in a contracting world* (2005).
kbenda@eth.mpg.de

Myrna Eindhoven graduated in cultural anthropology and sociology of non-western societies at Leiden University. In 2000 she began writing her PhD dissertation on identity politics among the Mentawai indigenous peoples at the Amsterdam School for Social Science Research. This research is part of the WOTRO (Wetenschappelijk Onderzoek van de Tropen en Ontwikkelingslanden, Netherlands Foundation for the Advancement of Tropical Research) project 'Trans-national Society, Media and Citizenship; The Capacity of the State to Control Information and Communication; The Gulf Area and Indonesia'. She currently works at the Institute of Environmental Sciences at Leiden University on establishing a regional network for indigenous peoples in Southeast Asia.
eindhoven@cml.leidenuniv.nl

Erwiza Erman obtained her PhD at the University of Amsterdam in 1999 with a dissertation entitled 'Miners, managers and the state; A socio-political history of the Ombilin coal-mines, West Sumatra, 1892-1996'. She is a researcher at Lembaga Ilmu Pengetahuan Indonesia (LIPI, the Indonesian Institute of Sciences) in Jakarta. She has written extensively about the history of mining in Indonesia, including a book on the history of labour relations in the tin mines of Belitung, *Kesenjangan buruh majikan; Pengusaha, koeli dan penguasa; Industri timah Belitung, 1852-1940* [The employer-employee gap; Capitalists, coolies and colonial power in the Belitung tin industry, 1852-1940] (1995) and the chapter 'Labouring communities; Women's roles in the Ombilin coal mines of Sumatra', in: *Labour in Southeast Asia; Local processes in a globalised world* (2004).
erwizae@yahoo.com

Andi Faisal Bakti was awarded his PhD by the University of Quebec at Montreal in 1998, and conducted post-doctoral research in communications at McGill University in 2000. He is senior lecturer at the Faculty of Dakwah and Communication, State Islamic University Syarif Hidayatullah Jakarta. He has held research fellowships at the International Institute for Asian Studies (IIAS) and Koninklijk Instituut voor Taal-, Land- en Volkenkunde (KITLV, Royal Netherlands Institute of Southeast Asian and Caribbean Studies), both

in Leiden, and at the Oxford Centre for Islamic Studies, UK. His research interests include religious/cultural communication, civil society, good governance, regional autonomy, and human rights. Among his recent publications are: 'Good governance in Islam', in: *Islam, negara dan civil society* [Islam, state and civil society] (2005), 'Paramadina and its approach to culture and communication; An engagement in civil society', in: *Archipel* (2004), and 'Collective memories of the Qahhar movement', in: *Beginning to remember* (2005).
abakti@hotmail.com

Carole Faucher teaches Southeast Asian studies at Mahidol International University College in Thailand. She has recently conducted research at Tokyo University of Foreign Studies, KITLV in Leiden, and City University of Hong Kong. She obtained her undergraduate and MA degrees in anthropology from the Université de Montréal and her PhD in sociology from the National University of Singapore, where she then lectured between 1999 and 2003. She has been researching Singapore and the Riau Archipelago in Indonesia since 1995, focusing on the anthropology of emotion, ethnicity, collective memory, political anthropology and popular culture. She is co-editor (with Maribeth Erb and Priyambudi Sulistiyanto) of *Regionalism in post-Suharto Indonesia* (2005).
faucher.carole@hotmail.com

David Henley is a geographer who obtained his PhD from the Australian National University in 1992. He has been a researcher at the KITLV since 1993, initially as a member of the EDEN (Ecology, Demography and Economy in Nusantara) project on the environmental history of Indonesia. For this project he produced two monographs: *Fertility, food and fever; Population, economy and environment in North and Central Sulawesi, 1600-1930* (2005) and a forthcoming history of malaria and malaria control in Indonesia. His other books include *Jealousy and justice; The indigenous roots of colonial rule in northern Sulawesi* (2002) and *Nationalism and regionalism in a colonial context; Minahasa in the Dutch East Indies* (1996). Currently he coordinates the KITLV's project CREDIT (Credit, Risk and the Economy of Debt; Indonesian Trajectories) on credit and debt relations in Southeast Asian history. His other research interests include the institutional dynamics of colonial expansion, and the comparative history of Southeast Asia and tropical Africa.
henley@kitlv.nl

Syarif Hidayat has been a researcher at the Puslitbang Ekonomi dan Pembangunan (PEP, Centre for Economic and Development Studies) within the Indonesian Institute of Sciences (LIPI) in Jakarta since 1990. In 1999 he

obtained his PhD at Flinders University, Adelaide, South Australia, with a dissertation entitled 'Decentralised politics in a centralised political system; A study of local-state power in West Java and West Sumatra in New Order Indonesia'. He lectures part-time in the post-graduate programmes of Trisakti University (in economics) and National University (social and political sciences), both in Jakarta. Among his many recent publications on problems of regional autonomy are *Kegamangan Otonomi Daerah?* [Uncertain Regional Autonomy?] (2004), 'Decentralisation and regional autonomy in Indonesia', in: *Decentralisation, democratic governance, and civil society in comparative perspective* (2004), and 'Hidden autonomy; Understanding the nature of Indonesian decentralisation on a day-to-day basis', in: *Regionalism in post-Suharto Indonesia* (2005).
hidayat_syarif@hotmail.com

M. Isa Sulaiman graduated in history from Syiah Kuala University in Banda Aceh in 1977, and lectured there all his life. He obtained his PhD in 1985 at the Ecoles des Hautes Etudes en Sciences Sociales, Paris, with a dissertation (in French) on the struggle between aristocrats and religious leaders in Aceh during the years of occupation and revolution 1942-1951. This work, updated and expanded, was published in Indonesia as *Sejarah Aceh; Sebuah gugatan terhadap tradisi* (1997). After Reformasi he published a book on the Free Aceh Movement, *Aceh merdeka; Ideologi, kepemimpinan, dan gerakan* (2000). He combined wide research interests with social engagement. M. Isa Sulaiman died in the tsunami that swept Banda Aceh on 26 December 2004, shortly after completing his contribution to the present volume (see obituary in this book).

Gerry van Klinken is a research fellow with the KITLV research programme that led to the present book. His book on post-New Order ethnic conflict outside Java, *Communal violence and democratisation in Indonesia; Small town wars*, is forthcoming. After gaining a MSc in geophysics (Macquarie University, Sydney, 1978), he taught physics in universities in Malaysia and Indonesia (1979-1991). In 1996 he moved into Asian Studies with a PhD dissertation at Griffith University, Brisbane, which was published as *Minorities, modernity and the emerging nation; Christians in Indonesia, a biographical approach* (2003). Since then he has taught and researched at universities in Australia, Indonesia and the Netherlands. He edited the Australian quarterly magazine *Inside Indonesia* from 1996 to 2002 and frequently comments on Indonesia in the mass media. His recent research has been on human rights, ethnicity, post-authoritarian transition, and historical memory.
klinken@kitlv.nl

John M. MacDougall has a doctorate in anthropology from Princeton University. For the past ten years he has been researching religious movements and militias in Bali, Lombok and Jakarta. While his earlier research on Bali and Lombok focused primarily on rural minorities' conversion to formalized state religion, since Soeharto's fall in 1998 his interests have shifted to the way that organized crime and radicalized religion have decentralized identity and security among Indonesia's urban poor. John has worked for several different NGOs in Indonesia and East Timor. Most recently he studied organized crime and regional militias for the International Crisis Group in Jakarta (2002-2004). He is currently researching the political economy of trafficking networks for the International Organization for Migration in Jakarta.
msukarsa@yahoo.com

John F. McCarthy studied environmental science, sociology and anthropology in the Universities of Melbourne and Monash. He is the author of *The fourth circle; A political ecology of Sumatra's rainforest frontier* (2006). He has carried out various assignments with non-governmental organizations in Australia and Indonesia. He has participated in two Centre for International Forestry Research (CIFOR) projects on decentralization and forest policy in Indonesia. At this time and under a fellowship with the Van Vollenhoven Institute at Leiden University during 2001-2003, he carried out extended fieldwork in Central Kalimantan. John McCarthy teaches at the Asia Pacific School of Economics and Governance at the Australian National University in Canberra, and was previously a research fellow at the Asia Research Centre, Murdoch University, Australia.
mccarthy_johnf@yahoo.com.au

Dik Roth is a social anthropologist at the Law and Governance Group of Wageningen University in the Netherlands. He teaches, among others, on the socio-legal dimensions of development and natural resources management. He holds a PhD from Wageningen University. He has advised on land reform and farmer resettlement in Luwu, South Sulawesi, and has done extensive research in the same region on migration and transmigration, land reform, irrigation development, and local irrigation management. His most recent work on Indonesia focuses on decentralization and provincial politics in South Sulawesi. He is also researching river flood protection policies in the Netherlands. His most recent publication (co-edited with Rutgerd Boelens and Margreet Zwarteveen) is *Liquid relations; Contested water rights and legal complexity* (2005).
dik.roth@wur.nl

Arianto Sangaji is the director of Yayasan Tanah Merdeka, a NGO in Palu engaged in advocacy over land rights in Central Sulawesi. He is a frequent commentator in the Indonesian mass media about social issues in Central Sulawesi. Among his publications are *Masyarakat dan Taman Nasional Lore Lindu* [Society and the Lore Lindu National Park] (2004), and *Buruk INCO, rakyat digusur; Ekonomi politik pertambangan Indonesia* [Bad International Nickel Company, the people evicted; The political economy of mining in Indonesia] (2002).
antosangadji@yahoo.com

Jim Schiller lectures at Flinders University in Adelaide, South Australia. He completed his PhD in 1986 at Monash University with a dissertation that was published as *Developing Jepara in New Order Indonesia* (1996). His mainly Indonesia-focused research and consulting interests include local politics, democratic deepening, local governance, participation and accountability, decentralization, civil society and the state, the political party and election system, local resource politics, Islam and civil society, and Jepara studies. Recent publications include: *Jalan terjalnya reformasi politik lokal* [The steep road to local political reform] (2003); 'What is in an election? A local perspective on Indonesia's 2004 representative elections' (Biennial Conference Asian Studies Association of Australia (ASAA), July 2004); 'Looking for civil society; The 1999 election in Jepara', in: *RENAI, Jurnal Politik Lokal* (2002) and 'Indonesia; Living with uncertainty', in: *Policy, society and organisation* (1999).
Jim.Schiller@flinders.edu.au

Maria J.C. Schouten obtained a PhD in social-cultural sciences at the Free University in Amsterdam and is presently an associate professor at the Department of Sociology of the Universidade da Beira Interior in Covilhã (Portugal). She has been researching Minahasa, North Sulawesi, intermittently for the past 25 years, focusing on social change at the local level. Her current research is mainly about gender and health issues, as well as about religious minorities, in European and Southeast Asian contexts. Her publications include *Leadership and social mobility in a Southeast Asian society; Minahasa, 1677-1983* (1998); the introduction to *A Ásia do Sudeste; História, cultura e desenvolvimento* [Southeast Asia; History, culture and development] (1998), of which she was also the editor, and 'Antropologia e colonialismo em Timor português' [Anthropology and colonialism in Portuguese Timor], in: *Lusotopie; Timor, Les défis de l'indépendance* [Lusotopie; Timor, the challenge of independence] (2001).
schouten@sapo.pt

Henk Schulte Nordholt heads the research department of KITLV, and coordinated the KITLV research programme that led to the present book. He obtained his PhD in social sciences from the Free University in Amsterdam with a dissertation that was published as *The spell of power; A history of Balinese politics: 1650-1940* (1996). He taught anthropology and Asian history at the University of Amsterdam from 1985 to 2004. Schulte Nordholt's main fields of research include Balinese history, political violence, the anthropology of colonialism, and contemporary politics in Indonesia. From 2001 to 2004 he coordinated the KNAW-sponsored Indonesian-Dutch research programme 'Indonesia in Transition'. He has published 70 articles (many available through www.creamofscience.org) and 15 books and is a regular guest on Dutch television and radio programmes about the Indonesian political situation. Among his books are *Kriminalitas, identitas dan modernitas dalam sejarah Indonesia* [Criminality, identity and modernity in Indonesian history] (2002), and the edited volumes *Outward appearances; Dressing state and society in Indonesia* (1997), and *Time matters; Global and local time in Asian histories* (with Willem van Schendel, 2001).
schultenordholt@kitlv.nl

Taufiq Tanasaldy is a PhD candidate in the Department of Political and Social Change, RSPAS, Australian National University. He is also a research officer at the School of Humanities and Social Sciences, University of New South Wales at Australian Defence Force Academy. He formerly taught in the Department of International Relations at the University of Indonesia. Taufiq graduated from the University of Indonesia in Jakarta in 1995 and the Graduate School of International Studies, Korea University in Seoul in 1997. He obtained language proficiency certificates from Beijing Language and Cultural University and Korea University. In 2004, Taufiq conducted nine months of fieldwork in West Kalimantan for his PhD thesis to be entitled 'Ethnic politics in Indonesia; The case of Dayak politics in West Kalimantan'. Taufiq's recent articles appear in the *Korea Journal of International Studies* and *Global; Journal of International Studies*.
taufiq.tanasaldy@anu.edu.au

Jaap Timmer is a research fellow in the Centre for Pacific and Asian Studies at Radboud University Nijmegen, Netherlands. Until recently, he was a research fellow in the State, Society and Governance in Melanesia Project at the Research School of Pacific and Asian Studies, Australian National University. He has broad regional interests in Southeast Asia and the Southwest Pacific, with particular emphasis on Papua, Maluku and the Solomon Islands. He has undertaken consultancies for international NGOs and government agencies on programs for conflict resolution, special autonomy, and development.

Jaap Timmer is the author of *Living with intricate futures; Order and confusion in Imyan worlds, Irian Jaya, Indonesia* (2000).
jaap.timmer@chello.nl

Alex John Ulaen is an anthropologist and historian who specializes in North Sulawesi. Born in Talaud, he lives in Manado where he teaches at the Sam Ratulangi University. He has studied in France, Germany and Japan. His publications include *Nusa Utara; Dari lintasan niaga ke daerah perbatasan* [The Islands in the North; From trade route to border zone] (2003), a study of the history and peoples of the Sangir and Talaud Islands between Sulawesi and the Philippines.
aj_ulaen@yahoo.com

Jacqueline A.C. Vel works at the Van Volenhoven Institute in Leiden, and was formerly assistant professor in Asian Studies at the University of Amsterdam in the Department of Sociology and Cultural Anthropology. She is affiliated research fellow of the International Institute for Asian Studies (Leiden/Amsterdam). She worked as development worker and researcher on the island of Sumba in eastern Indonesia from 1984 until 1990. She obtained her PhD at Wageningen University in 1994 with a dissertation entitled 'The Uma-economy; Indigenous economics and development work in Lawonda, Sumba (Eastern Indonesia)'. Her current research, entitled 'Uma politics; Democracy and local political culture on Sumba (Indonesia)', is about Sumbanese who live outside Sumba. It concerns the creation of political identity, the national in the local, and performance in an illiberal democracy. Her most recent publication is 'Pilkada in East Sumba; An old rivalry in a new democratic setting', *Indonesia* (2005).
j.a.c.vel@law.leidenuniv.nl

Bibliography

A.B.G. Satria Naradha *see* Satria Naradha, A.B.G.

Abasa, Mona

2004 'Markets of faith; Jakartan Da'wa and Islamic gentrification', *Archipel* 67:173-202.

Abdul Aziz Saleh *see* Saleh, Abdul Aziz

Abdullah, Taufik

1995 'Bukan "mambangkik Batang Tarandam"', *Genta Budaya* 1:3-10.

1966 'Adat and Islam; An examination of conflict in Minangkabau', *Indonesia* 2:1-24.

Abdulsalam, Tammar

1997 'Aku bertutur tentang diriku; Sebuah autobiografi'. Pontianak: n.p.

Acciaioli, Greg

1985 'Culture as art; From practice to spectacle in Indonesia', *Canberra Anthropology* 8:148-74.

2001 'Memberdayakan kembali "kesenian Totua"; Revitalisasi adat masyarakat To Lindu di Sulawesi Tengah', *Antropologi Indonesia* 25-65:60-83.

2004 'From economic actor to moral agent; Knowledge, fate and hierarchy among the Bugis of Sulawesi', *Indonesia* 78:147-79.

Ade Chandra *see* Chandra, Ade

Adhuri, D. and L. Rachmawati

2004 'Ethnicity, inequality and conflict in Riau'. [Manuscript.]

Aditjondro, George Junus

1995 *Bali, Jakarta's colony; Social and ecological impacts of Jakarta-based conglomerates in Bali's tourist industry.* Perth: Asia Research Centre, Murdoch University. [Working Paper 58.]

2001 'Guns, pamphlets and handy-talkies; How the military exploited local ethno-religious tensions in Maluku to preserve their political and economic privileges', in: Ingrid Wessel and Georgia Wimhöfer (eds), *Violence in Indonesia,* pp. 100-28. Hamburg: Abera.

2003 'Prolog', in: Rinaldy Damanik, *Tragedi kemanusiaan Poso; Menggapai surya pagi melalui kegelapan malam,* pp. xvi-l. Jakarta: PBHI.

2004a 'Kerusuhan Poso dan Morowali; Akar permasalahan dan jalan keluarnya'. Paper, Propatria Symposium, Jakarta, 7 January.

2004b 'Kayu hitam, bisnis pos penjagaan, perdagangan senjata, dan proteksi modal besar; Ekonomi politik bisnis militer di Sulawesi Timur', *Jurnal Wacana* 17-3:137-77.

Adriani, N. and Alb.C. Kruyt

1950 *De Bare'e-sprekende Toradja's van Midden-Celebes*. Second edition. Amsterdam: Noord-Hollandsche Uitgevers Maatschappij. Three vols. [First edition 1912.]

Agrawal, Arun and Jesse C. Ribot

1999 'Accountability in decentralization; A framework with South Asian and African Cases', *Journal of Developing Areas* 33:473-502.

Agus A. Alua *see* Alua, Agus A.

Agung Alit *see* Alit, Agung

Agus Indiyanto *see* Indiyanto, Agus

Agus Sumule *see* Sumule, Agus

Agus Sutisna *see* Sutisna, Agus

Alfan Miko *see* Miko, Alfan

Alit, Agung

2004 'Praying contests', *Latitudes* 42:10-1.

Alua, Agus A.

2002a *MUBES Papua 2002, 23-26 Februari; 'Jalan sejarah, jalan kebenaran'*. Jayapura: Sekretariat Presidium Dewan Papua and Biro Penelitian STFT Fajar Timur. [Seri Pendidikan Politik Papua 3.]

2002b *Kongres Papua 2002, 21 Mei - 04 Juni; 'Marilah kita meluruskan sejarah Papua Barat'*. Jayapura: Sekretariat Presidium Dewan Papua and Biro Penelitian STFT Fajar Timur. [Seri Pendidikan Politik Papua 4.]

Amal, Ichlasul

1992 *Regional and central government in Indonesian politics; West Sumatra and South Sulawesi, 1949-1979*. Yogyakarta: Gadjah Mada University Press.

Amir, M.S.

1999 *Adat Minangkabau; Pola dan tujuan hidup orang Minang*. Jakarta: Mutiara Sumber Widya.

2005 *Tanya-jawab adat Minangkabau*. Jakarta: Karya Dunia Fikir.

Amnesty International

2002 'Indonesia; Grave human rights violations in Wasior, Papua'. www.amnesty.org/library/index/engasa210322002. [Accessed 2-3-2005.]

Andaya, Barbara Watson

1997 'Recreating a vision', *Bijdragen tot de Taal-, Land- en Volkenkunde* 153:483-508.

Andaya, Leonard Y.

1995 'The Bugis-Makassar diasporas', *Journal of the Malaysian Branch of the Royal Asiatic Society* 68(June):119-38.

Anderson, Benedict R.O'G.

1983 'Old state, new society; Indonesia's New Order in comparative historical perspective', *Journal of Asian Studies* 42:477-96.

1988 'Cacique democracy and the Philippines; Origins and dreams', *New Left Review* 169(May/June):3-33.

1990 'The idea of power in Javanese culture', in: Benedict R.O'G. Anderson (ed.), *Language and power; Exploring political cultures in Indonesia*, pp. 1-69. Ithaca, NY: Cornell University Press.

2001 (ed.) *Violence and the state in Suharto's Indonesia*. Ithaca, NY: Cornell University Press. [Studies on Southeast Asia 30.]

Andi Faisal Bakti *see* Bakti, Andi Faisal

Antlöv, Hans

2003 'Not enough politics? Regional autonomy and the democratic polity', in: Edward Aspinall and Greg Fealy (eds), *Local power and politics in Indonesia; Decentralisation and democratisation*, pp. 72-86. Singapore: ISEAS.

Antlöv, Hans and Sven Cederroth

2004 *Elections in Indonesia; The New Order and beyond*. London: Routledge-Curzon.

Aragon, Lorraine V.

2000 *Fields of the Lord; Animism, Christian minorities, and state development in Indonesia*. Honolulu: University of Hawai'i Press.

2001 'Communal violence in Poso, Central Sulawesi; Where people eat fish and fish eat people', *Indonesia* 72:45-79.

2002 'Migrasi, komoditi export dan sejarah hak pemakaian tanah di Sulawesi Tengah', in: Anu Lounela and R. Yando Zakaria (eds), *Berebut tanah; Beberapa kajian berspektif kampus dan kampong*. Yogyakarta: Insist.

2004 'Profiting from displacement', *Inside Indonesia* 77:14-5.

2005 'Mass media fragmentation and narratives of violent action in Sulawesi's Poso conflict', *Indonesia* 79:1-55.

Arianto Sangaji *see* Sangaji, Arianto

Ariel Heryanto *see* Heryanto, Ariel

Asia Foundation

2002 *Indonesia rapid decentralization appraisal; Second report*. Jakarta: Asia Foundation.

Asian Development Bank

2001 'Technical assistance to the Republic of Indonesia for support for decentralized education management'. Technical assistance report. [TAR-INO 34120.]

Asia Research Centre

2001 *Decentralization and development cooperation; Issues for donors*. Perth: Asia Research Centre. [Murdoch University for the Australian Agency for International Development (AUSAID) of the Department of Foreign Affairs and Trade.]

Aspinall, Edward Thomas

2000 *Political opposition and the transition from authoritarian rule; The case of Indonesia*. PhD thesis, Australian National University, Canberra.

2002 'Sovereignty, the successor state, and universal human rights; History and the international structuring of Acehnese nationalism', *Indonesia* 73:1-24.

Aspinall, Edward and Greg Fealy (eds)

2003 *Local power and politics in Indonesia; Decentralisation and democratisation*. Singapore: ISEAS.

Aspinall, Edward and Harold Crouch

2003 *The Aceh peace process; Why it failed*. Washington DC: East-West Center. [Policy Studies 1.]

Atkinson, Jane Monnig

1989 *The art and politics of Wana shamanship*. Berkeley, CA: University of California Press.

Avonius, Leena

2004 *Reforming Wetu Tel; Islam, adat and the promises of regionalism and post-New Order Lombok*. PhD thesis, Leiden University.

Awaloedin Djamin *see* Djamin, Awaloedin

Azrial, Yulfian

1994 *Budaya alam Minangkabau; Kurikulum muatan lokal Sumatera Barat 1994 untuk sekolah dasar untuk kelas 3, 4, 5, 6*. Padang: Angkasa Raya.

Baal, Jan van

1960 'Erring acculturation', *American Anthropologist* 62-1:108-21.

Badan Koordinasi Pembentukan Propinsi Luwu (BKPPL)

2000 *Pembentukan Propinsi Luwu Raya*. Jakarta: Badan Koordinasi Pembentukan Propinsi Luwu.

Badan Perencanaan Daerah Propinsi Banten

2002 *Banten dalam angka 2002*. Banten: Badan Perencanaan Daerah Propinsi Banten. [In cooperation with Badan Pusat Statistik Propinsi Banten.]

2003 *Banten dalam angka 2003*. Banten: Badan Perencanaan Daerah Propinsi Banten. [In cooperation with Badan Pusat Statistik Propinsi Banten.]

Badan Pusat Statistik (BPS)

1998 *Jumlah penduduk dan perkiraan jumlah tenaga kerja dan angkatan kerja propinsi Nusa Tenggara Barat menurut kabupaten 1998*. Jakarta: BPS.

Badan Pusat Statistik Kabupaten Wajo

2002 *Produk domestik regional bruto Kabupaten Wajo*. Wajo: BPS.

Badan Pusat Statistik Propinsi Kalimantan Barat

2001 *Karakteristik penduduk Kalimantan Barat hasil sensus penduduk 2000*. Pontianak: Badan Pusat Statistik Propinsi Kalimantan Barat. [Seri L2.2.1.1.]

Badan Pusat Statistik Kabupaten Sumba Barat

2001 *Sumba Barat dalam angka 2000*. Waikabubak: Badan Pusat Statistik Kabupaten Sumba Barat.

2003 *Sumba Barat dalam angka 2002*. Waikabubak: Badan Pusat Statistik/ Kabupaten Sumba Barat.

Badri, Muhammad Nasihuddin

2001 *Meniti tapak sejarah 66 tahun pondok pesantren Darunnahdlatain Nahdlatul Wathan Panco*. Pancor: Yayasan Pendidikan Hamzanwadi.

Bagus, I Gede Ngurah

2004 'The Parisada Hindu Dharma Indonesia in a society in transformation; The emergence of conflicts amidst differences and demands', in: Martin Ramstedt (ed.), *Hinduism in modern Indonesia; A minority religion between local, national, and global interests*, pp. 84-92. London/New York: RoutledgeCurzon.

Bahar, S. and Mohammed Zulfan Tadjoeddin

2004 *Masih ada harapan; Posisi sebuah etnik minoritas dalam hidup berbangsa dan bernegara*. Jakarta: Yayasan Sepuluh Agustus.

Bailey, Frederick G.
1983 *The tactical uses of passion; An essay on power, reason and reality*. Ithaca, NY: Cornell University Press.

Bakker, Frederik Lambertus
1993 *The struggle of the Hindu Balinese intellectuals; Developments in modern Hindu thinking in independent Indonesia*. Amsterdam: VU University Press.

Bakker, Heleen E. and Nico G. Schulte Nordholt (eds)
1996 *Corruption and legitimacy*. Amsterdam: SISWO.

Bakti, Andi Faisal
2004 *Communication and family planning in Indonesia; South Sulawesi Muslim perceptions of a global development program*. Leiden: INIS.

Baldwin, William L.
1983 *The world tin market*. Durham, NC: Duke University Press.

Bali membangun
2003 *Bali membangun 2002*. Denpasar: Bappeda.

Ballard, Chris
2002 'The signature of terror; Violence, memory, and landscape at Freeport', in: Bruno David and Meredith Wilson (eds), *Inscribed landscapes; Marking and making place*, pp. 13-26. Honolulu: University of Hawai'i Press.

Bamba, John
2000 'Land, rivers and forests; Dayak solidarity and ecological resilience', in: Janis B. Alcorn and Antoinette G. Royo (eds), *Indigenous social movement and ecological resilience; Lessons from the Dayak of Indonesia*, pp. 35-61. Washington: Biodiversity Support Program.
2002 'Freedom to violate; Reformasi and local responses in West Kalimantan'. Paper, International Conference of the Indonesian Transition to Democracy, Jakarta, 17-19 January.

Barnard, Timothy P.
1997 'Local heroes and national consciousness', *Bijdragen tot de Taal-, Land- en Volkenkunde* 153:509-26.

Barr, Christopher M.
1998 'Bob Hasan, the rise of Apkindo, and the shifting dynamics of control in Indonesia's timber sector', *Indonesia* 65:1-36.
2002 'Timber concession reform; Questioning the "sustainable logging" paradigm ', in: Carol J. Pierce Colfer and Ida Aju Pradnja Resosudarmo (eds), *Which way forward? People, forests and policymaking in Indonesia*, pp. 191-220. Washington DC: Resources for the Future. www.cifor.cgiar.org/acm/download/pub/pol-ch9.zip. [Last accessed 16-2-2006.]

Barr, John
2002 'The future could be genocide; Reflections on Papua'. Paper, Uniting Church in Australia National Assembly, Sydney, 10 June. www.westpapua.net/news/02/06/150602-terrorism.htm. [Last accessed 20-2-2006.]

Basry, Hassan
1961 *Kisah gerila Kalimantan; Dalam revolusi Indonesia 1945-1949*. Bandjarmasin: Jajasan Lektur Lambung Mangkurat.

Bayart, Jean-François, Stephen Ellis and Beátrice Hibou
1999 *The criminalization of the state in Africa*. Oxford: The International African Institute.

Bayly, C.A.
2004 *The birth of the modern world 1780-1914*. Oxford: Blackwell.

Benda, Harry J.
1966 'The pattern of administrative reforms in the closing years of Dutch rule in Indonesia', *Journal of Asian Studies* 25:589-605.

Benda-Beckmann, Franz von
1979 *Property in social continuity; Continuity and change in the maintenance of property relationships through time in Minangkabau, West Sumatra*. The Hague: Nijhoff. [KITLV, Verhandelingen 86.]

Benda-Beckmann, Franz von and Keebet von Benda-Beckmann
1978 'Residence in a Minangkabau nagari', *Indonesia Circle* 15:6-17.
1988 'Adat and religion in Minangkabau and Ambon', in: H. Claessen and D.S. Moyer (eds), *Time past, time present, time future; Essays in honour of professor P.E. de Josselin de Jong*, pp. 195-212. Dordrecht: Foris. [KITLV, Verhandelingen 131.]
2001 *Recreating the nagari; Decentralization in West Sumatra*. Halle/Saale: Max Planck Institute for Social Anthropology. [Working Paper 31.]
2004 *Struggles over communal property rights and law in Minangkabau, West Sumatra*. Halle/Saale: Max Planck Institute for Social Anthropology. [Working Paper 64.]
2005 'Democracy in flux; Time, mobility and sedentarization of law in Minangkabau, Indonesia', in: Franz von Benda-Beckmann, Keebet von Benda-Beckmann and Anne Griffiths (eds), *Mobile law, mobile people*, pp. 111-30. Dartmore: Ashgate.

Berry, Sara
1989 'Social institutions and access to resources', *Africa* 59-1:41-55.

Bertrand, Jacques
2004 *Nationalism and ethnic conflict in Indonesia*. Cambridge: Cambridge University Press.

Betke, Friedhelm and Hamonangan Ritonga
2004 'Rural East Indonesia; Who are the poor in East Sumba?', in: Hans Gsänger and Myriam Fernando (eds), *Poverty monitoring in Asia*, pp. 117-46. Colombo: Centre for Poverty Analysis.

Biezeveld, Renske Laura
2002 *Between individualism and mutual help; Social security and natural resources in a Minangkabau village*. Delft: Eburon.

Bigalke, Terence W.
2005 *Tana Toraja; A social history of an Indonesian people*. Singapore: Singapore University Press; Leiden: KITLV Press.

Bingling Yuan
2000 *Chinese democracies; A study of kongsis of West Borneo (1776-1884)*. PhD thesis, Leiden University, Leiden.

Bob Sugeng Hadiwinata *see* Hadiwinata, Bob Sugeng

Boroma, Suhendro
2002 'Awal gagasan dan pencanangan', in: Suhendro Boroma (ed.), *Kasih mengubah dunia*, pp. 3-11. Manado: Penerbit Jaringan Kerja Kasih (JAJAK) Sulut.

Bourchier, David
1990 'Crime, law and state authority in Indonesia', in: Arief Budiman (ed.), *State and civil society in Indonesia*, pp. 177-212. Clayton, Victoria: Centre of Southeast Asian Studies, Monash University.

Bowen, John R.
1986 'On the political construction of tradition; Gotong Royong in Indonesia', *Journal of Asian Studies* 45:545-61.

Broek, Theo van den and Alexandra Szalay
2001 'Raising the Morning Star; Six months in the developing independence movement in West Papua', *Journal of Pacific History* 36:77-92.

Brown, David
1994 *The state and ethnic politics in South-East Asia*. London: Routledge.

Brown, Ian
1997 *Economic change in South-East Asia c. 1830-1980*. Kuala Lumpur: Oxford University Press.

Bruinessen, Martin van
2002 'The violent fringes of Indonesia's radical Islam', *ISIM Newsletter* 11:7.
2004 'Post-Soeharto Muslim engagements with civil society and democratization', in: Hanneman Samuel and Henk Schulte Nordholt (eds), *Indonesia in transition; Rethinking 'civil society', 'region', and 'crisis'*, pp. 37-66. Yogyakarta: Pustaka Pelajar.

Budiardjo, Carmel and Liem Sioe Long
1983 *West Papua; The obliteration of a people*. London: Tapol.

Budiman, Arief, Barbara Hatley and Damien Kingsbury (eds)
1999 *Reformasi; Crisis and change in Indonesia*. Clayton, Victoria: Monash Asia Institute. [Monash Papers on Southeast Asia 50.]

Burns, Peter
2004 *The Leiden legacy; Concepts of law in Indonesia*. Leiden: KITLV Press. [Verhandelingen 191.]

Carmel Budiardjo *see* Budiardjo, Carmel

Carneiro, Robert L.
1970 'A theory of the origin of the state', *Science* 169:733-8.

Cederroth, Sven
1981 *The spell of the ancestors and the power of Mekkah; A Sasak community on Lombok*. Göteborg, Sweden: Acta Universitatis Gothoburgensis.

Chandra, Ade, A.R. Rizal, Erizal and Ronidin
2000 *Minangkabau dalam perubahan*. Padang: Yasmin Akbar.

Chatterjee, Partha
1993 *Nationalist thought and the colonial world; A derivative discourse*. Minneapolis: University of Minnesota Press.

Chauvel, Richard
2005 *Constructing Papuan nationalism; History, ethnicity, and adaptation.* Washington DC: East-West Center. [Policy Studies 14.]

Chauvel, Richard and Ikrar Nusa Bhakti
2004 *The Papua conflict; Jakarta's perceptions and policies.* Washington DC: East-West Center. [Policy Studies 5.]

Cohen, Margot
2003 'Going it alone', *Far Eastern Economic Review* (29-5-2003):48-51.

Collins, Elizabeth
2003 'The struggle for political reform in South Sumatra', in: Damien Kingsbury and Harry Aveling (eds), *Autonomy and disintegration in Indonesia,* pp. 157-76. London: RoutledgeCurzon.

Colombijn, Freek
2003 'When there is nothing to imagine; Nationalism in Riau', in: Peter J.M. Nas, Gerard A. Persoon and Rivke Jaffe (eds), *Framing Indonesian realities; Essays in symbolic anthropology in honour of Reimar Schefold,* pp. 333-65. Leiden: KITLV Press. [Verhandelingen 209.]
2005 'A cultural practice of violence in Indonesia; Lessons from history', in: Dewi Fortuna Anwar et al. (eds), *Violent internal conflicts in Asia Pacific; Histories, political economies and policies,* pp. 245-68. Jakarta: Yayasan Obor Indonesia.

Colombijn, Freek and J. Thomas Lindblad (eds)
2002 *Roots of violence in Indonesia; Contemporary violence in historical perspective.* Leiden: KITLV Press. [Verhandelingen 194.]

Conboy, Ken
2004 *Intel; Inside Indonesia's intelligence service.* Jakarta, Singapore: Equinox.

Connor, Linda and Adrian Vickers
2003 'Crisis, citizenship, and cosmopolitanism; Living in a local and global risk society in Bali', *Indonesia* 75:153-80.

Cornelis Lay *see* Lay, Cornelis

Coronese, Stefano
1986 *Kebudayaan suku Mentawai.* Jakarta: Grafidian Jaya.

Couteau, Jean
2002 'Bali; Crise en paradis', *Archipel* 64:231-54.

Cribb, Robert
1990 (ed.) *The Indonesian killings; Studies from Java and Bali.* Clayton, Victoria: Centre of Southeast Asian Studies, Monash University. [Monash Papers on Southeast Asia 21.]
2000 'From petrus to ninja; Death squads in Indonesia' in: Bruce B. Campbell and Arthur D. Brenner (eds), *Death squads in global perspective; Murder with deniability,* pp. 181-202. New York: St. Martin's Press.

Crouch, Harold A.
1978 *The army and politics in Indonesia.* Ithaca, NY: Cornell University.
1979 'Patrimonialism and military rule in Indonesia', *World Politics* 31:571-87.

Damanik, Rinaldy
2003 *Tragedi kemanusiaan Poso.* Palu, Indonesia: PBHI and LPS-HAM Sulteng.

Damciwar Dt. Bagindo Sampono *see* Sampono, Damciwar Dt. Bagindo

Darma Putra, I Nyoman

2003 'Bali pasca-bom; Konflik, kekerasan dan rekonstruksi identitas budaya menuju "Ajeg Bali"'. Paper, Kongres Kebudayaan, Bukittinggi, 19-23 October.

Davidson, Jamie S.

2002 *Violence and politics in West Kalimantan, Indonesia.* PhD thesis, University of Washington, Seattle.

2003 'The politics of violence on an Indonesian periphery', *South East Asia Research* 11-1:59-89.

Davidson, Jamie S. and Douglas Kammen

2002 'Indonesia's unknown war and the lineages of violence in West Kalimantan', *Indonesia* 73:53-87.

Dawood, Dayan and Sjafrizal

1989 'Aceh; The LNG boom and enclave development', in: Hal Hill (ed.), *Unity and diversity; Regional economic development in Indonesia since 1970*, pp. 107-23. Singapore: Oxford University Press.

Dayan Dawood *see* Dawood, Dayan

Degung Santikarma *see* Santikarma, Degung

Departemen Pertahanan RI

2003 *Indonesia; Mempertahankan tanah air memasuki abad 21.* Jakarta: Departemen Pertahanan RI. [White Paper of the Ministry of Defence.]

Dias Pradadimara *see* Pradadimara, Dias

Dick, Howard

2005 'Southeast Asia as an open system; Geopolitics and economic geography', in: Paul H. Kratoska, Remco Raben and Henk Schulte Nordholt (eds), *Locating Southeast Asia; Geographies of knowledge and the politics of space*, pp. 250-74. Singapore: National University of Singapore Press.

Djamin, Awaloedin

2002 'Pamswakarsa, siskamling dan satpam'. Paper, 22nd anniversary of SATPAM, Mataram, December.

Djoeroemana Siliwoloe *see* Siliwoloe, Djoeroemana

Djopari, J.R.G.

1993 *Pemberontakan organisasi Papua Merdeka.* Jakarta: Grasindo.

Djuweng, Stepanus (ed.)

1996 *Manusia Dayak; Orang kecil yang terperangkap modernisasi.* Pontianak: Institute of Dayakology Research and Development (IDRD).

Dobbin, Christine

1983 *Islamic revivalism in a changing peasant economy; Central Sumatra, 1784-1847.* London: Curzon.

Dormeirer-Frère, Alexandre and Jean-Luc Maurer

2002 'Le dilemme de la decentralization en Indonesie', *Archipel* 64:255-87.

Douglas, Bronwen

2000 *Weak states and other nationalisms? Emerging Melanesian paradigms.* Canberra: State, Society and Governance in Melanesia Project, Research School for Pacific and Asian Studies, The Australian National University. [State, Society and Governance in Melanesia Discussion Paper 2000/3.]

Drake, Richard Allen
1982 *The material provisioning of Mualang society in hinterland Kalimantan Barat, Indonesia*. PhD thesis, Michigan State University, East Lansing.

Drooglever, P.J.
2005 *Een daad van vrije keuze; De Papoea's van westelijk Nieuw-Guinea en de grenzen van het zelfbeschikkingsrecht*. Amsterdam: Boom.

Dwikora Putra *see* Putra, Dwikora

Dijk, Kees van
1981 *Rebellion under the banner of Islam; The Darul Islam in Indonesia*. The Hague: Nijhoff. [KITLV, Verhandelingen 94.]
2001 *A country in despair; Indonesia between 1997 and 2000*. Leiden: KITLV Press. [Verhandelingen 186.]
2002 'The good, the bad and the ugly; Explaining the unexplainable; Amuk massa in Indonesia', in: Freek Colombijn and Thomas J. Lindblad (eds), *Roots of violence in Indonesia; Contemporary violence in historical perspective*, pp. 277-97. Leiden: KITLV Press. [Verhandelingen 194.]

Ecip, S. Sinansari, Darwis Waru, Alip Yog Kunandar
2002 *Rusuh Poso, rujuk Malino*. Jakarta: Cahaya Timur.

Edy Utama *see* Utama, Edy

Eddy Hermanto *see* Hermanto, Eddy

EIA/Telapak
2005 'The last frontier; Illegal logging in Papua and China's massive timber theft'. London, Bogor: The Environmental Investigation Agency and Telapak. www.eia-international.org. [Last accessed, 5-5-2005.]

Eindhoven, Myrna
2002 'Translation and authenticity in Mentawaian activism', *Indonesia and the Malay World* 30:357-67.

Eisenstadt, S.N.
1973 *Traditional patrimonialism and modern neo-patrimonialism*. Beverly Hills, CA: Sage.

Eko Pasetyo *see* Prasetyo, Eko

Eldersveld, S.J., Samuel L., Lars Strömberg and Johan Wim Derksen
1995 *Local elites in Western democracies; A comparative analysis of urban political leaders in U.S., Sweden, and the Netherlands*. Oxford: Westview.

Ellen, Roy
2003 *On the edge of the Banda zone; Past and present in the social organization of a Moluccan trading network*. Honolulu: University of Hawai'i Press.

Emmerson, Donald K.
1983 'Understanding the New Order; Bureaucratic pluralism in Indonesia', *Asian Survey* 23:1220-41.
1999 (ed.) *Indonesia beyond Suharto; Polity, economy, society, transition*. Armonk, NY: Sharpe.

Erb, Maribeth, Carole Faucher and Priyambudi Sulistiyanto (eds)
2005 *Regionalism in post-Suharto Indonesia*. London: RoutledgeCurzon.

Eriksen, Thomas Hylland
1993 *Ethnicity and nationalism; Anthropological perspectives*. London: Pluto.

Erizal
2000a 'Adat basandi syarak, syarak basandi kitabullah', in: Ade Chandra, A.R. Rizal, Erizal, and Ronidin (eds), *Minangkabau dalam perubahan*, pp. 106-11. Padang: Yasmin Akbar.
2000b 'Adat Minang dan globalisasi saling tantang-menantang', in: Ade Chandra, A.R. Rizal, Erizal, and Ronidin (eds), *Minangkabau dalam perubahan*, pp. 122-8. Padang: Yasmin Akbar.

Erman, Erwiza
1994 'Dutch and Japanese policies in the mining sector'. Paper, Workshop Japanese Heritage, Amsterdam, October 1994.
1995 *Kesenjangan buruh-majikan; Pengusaha, koelie dan penguasa; Industri timah Belitung, 1852-1940*. Jakarta: Sinar Harapan.
2003 'Between pepper and tin; Experience of crisis in Bangka'. Paper, Workshop Social History of Crisis; Local and Comparative Studies, Leiden, 4-5 December.
2004 'Illegal mining in West Sumatra, Indonesia; Actors and access in the post-Suharto era'. Paper, Graduate School of International Development (GSID), Nagoya, February.
forthcoming 'Grounds of conflict between mining company and local community in West Sumatra', in: *Anthropology of mining*. Victoria: Monash University Press.

Erwiza Erman *see* Erman, Erwiza

Evans, Peter
1995 *Embedded autonomy; States and industrial transformation*. Princeton, NJ: Princeton University Press.

Fanany, Ismet
2003 'The first year of local autonomy; The case of West Sumatra', in: Damien Kingsbury and Harry Aveling (eds), *Autonomy and disintegration in Indonesia*, pp. 177-88. London: RoutledgeCurzon.

Fathurahman Zakaria *see* Zakaria, Fathurahman

Faucher, Carole
2005 'Regional autonomy, Malayness and power hierarchy in the Riau Archipelago', in: Maribeth Erb, Priyambudi Sulistiyanto and Carole Faucher (eds), *Regionalism in post-Suharto Indonesia*, pp. 125-40. London: RoutledgeCurzon.

Foley, Michael W. and Bob Edwards
1996 'The paradox of civil society', *Journal of Democracy* 7-3:38-52.

Ford, Michele
2003 'Who are the Orang Riau? Negotiating identity across geographic and ethnic divides', in: Edward Aspinall and Greg Fealy (eds), *Local power and politics in Indonesia; Decentralization and democracy*, pp. 132-47. Singapore: ISEAS.

Forth, Gregory L.
1981 *Rindi; An ethnographic study of a traditional domain in eastern Sumba*. The Hague: Nijhoff. [KITLV, Verhandelingen 93.]

1994 '"Post" modernism; Issues of meaning, cultural objectification and national-local distinctions in an eastern Indonesian community', in: Greg Acciaioli and Jennifer Nourse (eds), *Official rhetoric, popular response; Dialogue and resistance in Indonesia and the Philippines*, pp. 144-56. Adelaide, SA: University of Adelaide. [Special issue of *Social Analysis* 35.]

Fraenkel, Jon
2004 'The coming anarchy in Oceania? A critique of the "Africanisation" of the South Pacific thesis', *Commonwealth and Comparative Politics* 42-1:1-34.

Frans Maniagasi *see* Maniagasi, Frans

Frerks, Georg and Jan Michiel Otto
1996 *Decentralization and development; A review of development administrative literature*. Leiden: Van Vollenhoven Institute for Law and Administration in Non-Western Countries. [Research Report 96/2.]

Geertz, Clifford
1963 'The integrative revolution; Primordial sentiments and civil politics in the new states', in: Clifford Geertz (ed.), *Old societies and new states*, pp. 105-57. New York: Free Press.
1972 'Afterword; The politics of meaning', in: Claire Holt, Benedict R.O'G. Anderson and James Siegel (eds), *Culture and politics in Indonesia*, pp. 319-33. Ithaca, NY: Cornell University Press.
1979 *The religion of Java; The guest for modernity in Asia and Africa*. Chicago: University of Chicago Press. [First published 1960.]

George Junus Aditjondro *see* Aditjondro, George Junus

Gerth, H.H. and C. Wright Mills (eds)
1946 *From Max Weber; Essays in sociology*. New York: Oxford University Press.

Giay, Benny
2001 'Towards a New Papua; When they hear the sacred texts of the church, Papuans see a better future', *Inside Indonesia* 67:8-9.

Goh, Taro
1991 *Sumba bibliography*. Canberra: Australian National University.

Golden, Brigham
2003 'Political millenarianism and the economy of conflict; Reflections on Papua by an activist anthropologist'. Asia Society's Asian Social Issues Program (ASIP). www.asiasource.org/asip/papua_golden.cfm [Last accessed 16-2-2006].

Grimes, Charles E., Tom Therik, Barbara Dix Grimes and Max Jacob
1997 *A guide to the people and languages of Nusa Tenggara*. Kupang: Artha Wacana Press.

Grootenhuis, G.W.
1961 *Papoea-elite en politieke partijen*. Part 1. Hollandia: Gouvernement van Nederlands-Nieuw-Guinea. [Kantoor voor Bevolkingszaken, no. 299/61.]

GTZ (Deutsche Gesellschaft für Technische Zusammenarbeit)
2001a *Decentralization News* 6. Jakarta: GTZ. [March.]

2001b *Donor activities related to decentralization and local governance capacity building in Indonesia.* Jakarta: GTZ.

Gupta, Agil
1995 'Blurred boundaries; The discourse of corruption, the culture of politics, and the imagined state, *American Ethnologist* 22-2:375-402.

H.Ch.N.Dt. Bandaro *see* Latief, H.Ch.N.Dt. Bandaro

H. Mas'oed Abidin *see* Mas'oed Abidin, H.

H. Salmadanis *see* Salmandanis, H.

Habermas, Jürgen
1992 *The structural transformation of the public sphere.* Cambridge: Polity Press. [First published as *Strukturwandel der öffentlichkeit.* Darmstadt, RFA: Herman Luchterhand Verlag, 1962.]

Hadiwinata, Bob Sugeng
2003 *The politics of NGOs in Indonesia; Developing democracy and managing a movement.* London: RoutledgeCurzon.

Hadiz, Vedi R.
2003a 'Power and politics in North Sumatra; The uncompleted Reformasi', in: Edward Aspinall and Greg Fealy (eds), *Local power and politics in Indonesia; Decentralisation and democratisation,* pp. 119-31. Singapore: ISEAS.

2003b *Decentralisation and democracy in Indonesia; A critique of neo-institutionalist perspectives.* Hong Kong: City University of Hong Kong. [Southeast Asia Research Centre, Working Paper Series 47.]

2003c 'Reorganizing political power in Indonesia; A reconsideration of so-called "democratic transitions"', *The Pacific Review* 16:591-611.

Hadiz, Vedi R. and Richard Robison
2003 *Neo-liberal reforms and illiberal consolidations; The Indonesian paradox.* Hong Kong: City University of Hong Kong. [Southeast Asia Research Centre, Working Paper Series 53.]

Hamdan, Iwan Kusuma et al.
2004 'Mengawal aspirasi masyarakat Banten menuju Banten iman dan taqwa; Memori pengabdian DPRD Banten masa bakti 2001-2004'. Banten: Sekretariat DPRD Banten. [Manuscript.]

Harley
2004 'Keuntungan di balik tragedi kemanusian Poso'. [Manuscript.]

Harris-White, Barbara
2003 *India working; Essays on society and economy.* Cambridge: Cambridge University Press. [Series Contemporary South Asia 8.]

Harvey, Barbara Sillars
1974 *Tradition, Islam and rebellion; South Sulawesi 1905-1965.* PhD thesis, Cornell University, Ithaca, NY.

1977 *Permesta; Half a rebellion.* Ithaca, NY: Cornell University Press.

Hasbi, Mohammad, Mochtar Naim and Damciwar Dt. Bagindo Sampono (eds)
1990 *Nagari, desa dan pembangunan pedesaan di Sumatera Barat.* Padang: Yayasan Genta Budaya.

Hasrifendi and Lindo Karsyah
2003 *Utopia nagari Minangkabau.* Padang: IAIN-IB.

Hassan Basry *see* Basry, Hassan
Hays, Terence E.
1993 '"The New Guinea Highlands"; Region, culture area or fuzzy set?', *Current Anthropology* 34:141-64.
Hefner, Robert W.
1993 'Islam, state, and civil society; ICMI and the struggle for the Muslim middle class', *Indonesia* 56:1-37.
2000 *Civil Islam; Muslims and democratization in Indonesia*. Princeton, NJ: Princeton University Press.
Heidhues, Mary Somers
2003 *Gold diggers, farmers, and traders in the 'Chinese districts' of West Kalimantan, Indonesia*. Ithaca, NY: Cornell Southeast Asia Program Publications. [Studies on Southeast Asia 34.]
Henley, David
1996 *Nationalism and regionalism in a colonial context; Minahasa in the Dutch East Indies*. Leiden: KITLV Press. [Verhandelingen 168.]
2004 'Conflict, justice, and the stranger-king; Indigenous roots of colonial rule in Indonesia and elsewhere', *Modern Asian Studies* 38:85-144.
Hermanto, Kompol Eddy
2004 '"Illegal logging" di Kalimantan Tengah; Penanganannya dari kacamata profesionalisme berdasarkan paradigma baru Polri'. Manuscript.
Hernawan, J. Budi and Theo van den Broek
1999 'Dialog nasional Papua, sebuah kisah "Memoria Passionis"; Kisah ingatan penderitaan sebangsa', *Tifa Irian* 8 (March).
Heryanto, Ariel
1988 'The development of "development"', *Indonesia* 46:1-24.
Heyman, Josiah McC. and Alan Smart
1999 'States and illegal practices; An overview', in: Josiah McC. Heyman (ed.), *States and illegal practices*, pp.1-24. Oxford: Berg.
Hidayat, Syarif
2002 'Hidden autonomy; Understanding the nature of Indonesian decentralization on a day to day basis'. Paper, Workshop on Regional Autonomy in Indonesia, National University of Singapore, 13 May.
2003 'Desentralisasi dalam perspektif state-society relation; Rekonstruksi konsep dan pendekatan kebijakan', in: Syamsuddin Harris (ed.), *Desentralisasi dan otonomi daerah; Naskah akademik dan RUU usulan LIPI*, pp. 43-53. Jakarta: Pusat Penelitian Politik-LIPI dan PGRI.
Hill, Hal
1996 *The Indonesian economy since 1966; Southeast Asia's emerging giant*. Cambridge: Cambridge University Press.
Hofman, Bert and Kai Kaiser
2002 'The making of the Big Bang and its aftermath; A political economy perspective'. Paper, Conference 'Can Decentralization Help Rebuild Indonesia?', George State University, Atlanta, 1-3 May. http://isp-aysps.gsu.edu/fprc/ino/hofmankaiserAtlanta.pdf. [Last accessed 16-2-2006.]

Holtzappel, Coen, Martin Sanders and Milan Titus (eds)
2002 *Riding a tiger; Dilemmas of integration and decentralization in Indonesia.* Amsterdam: Rozenberg.

Hoskins, Janet
1993 *The play of time; Kodi perspectives on calendars, history and exchange.* Berkeley, CA: University of California Press.

Howe, Leo
2001 *Hinduism and hierarchy in Bali.* Oxford: James Curry; Santa Fe: School of American Research Press.

Huizinga, Fre
1998 'Relations between Tidore and the north coast of New Guinea in the nineteenth century', in: Jelle Miedema, Cecilia Odé and Rien A.C. Dam (eds), *Perspectives on the Bird's Head of Irian Jaya, Indonesia; Proceedings of the conference, Leiden, 13-17 October 1997,* pp. 385-419. Amsterdam: Rodopi.

Human Rights Watch
1997 'West Kalimantan; Communal violence in West Kalimantan'. www.hrw.org/reports/1997/wkali/. [Last accessed 16-2-2006.]
2002 'Breakdown; Four years of communal violence in Central Sulawesi'. *Human Rights Watch Report 14*: part 9(C). www.hrw.org/reports/2002/indonesia/. [Last accessed 16-2-2006.]

Huntington, Samuel P.
1996 *The clash of civilizations and the remaking of world order.* New York: Simon and Schuster.

Hurgronje, C. Snouck
1893-95 *De Atjehers.* Batavia: Landsdrukkerij.

Huydecoper van Nigtevecht, J.L.R.
1990 *Nieuw-Guinea; Het einde van een koloniaal beleid.* The Hague: SDU.

I Gde Pitana *see* Pitana, I Gde

I Gede Ngurah Bagus *see* Bagus, I Gede Ngurah

I Nyoman Darma Putra *see* Darma Putra, I Nyoman

ICG (International Crisis Group)
2001a *Indonesia; Violence and radical Muslims.* Jakarta, Brussels: ICG. [Indonesia Briefing, 10 October, www.crisisgroup.org/home/index.cfm?id=3007&l=1.]
2001b *Communal violence in Indonesia; Lessons from Kalimantan.* Jakarta/Brussels: ICG. [Asia Report 19, www.crisisgroup.org/home/index.cfm?id=1455&l=1.]
2001c *National police reform.* Jakarta, Brussels: ICG. [Asia Report 13, www.crisisgroup.org/home/index.cfm?id=1459&l=1.]
2002a *Al Qaeda in Southeast Asia; The case of the 'Ngruki network' in Indonesia.* Jakarta, Brussels; ICG. [Indonesia Briefing, 8 August, www.crisisgroup.org/home/index.cfm?id=3009&l=1.]
2002b *Indonesia; Resources and conflict in Papua.* Jakarta, Brussels: ICG. [Asia Report 39, www.crisisgroup.org/home/index.cfm?id=1449&l=1.]
2003a *Jemaah Islamiyah in Southeast Asia; Damaged but still dangerous.* Jakarta, Brussels: ICG. [Asia report 63, www.crisisgroup.org/home/index.cfm?id=1935&l=1.]

2003b *Aceh; Why the military option still won't work.* Jakarta, Brussels: ICG. [Asia Briefing, 9 May, www.crisisgroup.org/home/index.cfm?id=1777&l=1.]

2003c *The perils of private security; Guards and militias on Bali and Lombok.* Jakarta, Brussels: ICG. [Asia Report 67, www.crisisgroup.org/home/index.cfm?id=2353&l=1.]

2003d *Dividing Papua; How not to do it.* Jakarta, Brussels: ICG. [Asia Briefing 24, www.crisisgroup.org/home/index.cfm?id=1764&l=1.]

2004 *Jihad in Central Sulawesi.* Jakarta, Brussels: ICG. [Asia Report 74, www.crisisgroup.org/home/index.cfm?id=3006&l=1.]

2005 *Decentralisation and conflict in Indonesia; The Mamasa case.* Jakarta, Brussels: ICG. [Asia Briefing 37, www.crisisgroup.org/home/index.cfm?id=3406&l=1.]

Ichlasul Amal *see* Amal, Ichlasul

Ida Aju Pradnja Resosudarmo *see* Resosudarmo, Ida Aju Pradnja

Idrus Hakimy Dt. Rajo Panghulu *see* Rajo Panghulu, Idrus Hakimy Dt.

Illner, Michal

2000 'Issues of the decentralization reforms in former communist countries', *Informationen zur Raumentwicklung* 7:391-401.

Indiyanto, Agus

2005 'Coping with "crisis"; A field report from Koto Gadang, West Sumatra', in: Hanneman Samuel and Henk Schulte Nordholt (eds), *Indonesia in transition; Rethinking 'civil society', 'region' and 'crisis'*, pp. 221-34. Yogyakarta: Pustaka Pelajar.

Indria Samego *see* Samego, Indria

Ismail, T. Rivolsa

2004 'Acheh hanya Terima secuil', *Serambi Indonesia* (May 2004).

Ismet Fanany *see* Fanany, Ismet

Iwan Kusuma Hamdan *see* Hamdan, Iwan Kusuma

J. Budi Hernawan *see* Hernawan, J. Budi

James, Deborah and Albert Schrauwers

2003 'An apartheid of souls; Dutch and Afrikaner colonialism and its aftermath in Indonesia and South Africa; An introduction', *Itinerario; European Journal of Overseas History* 27-3/4:49-80.

Jaya, Wihana Kirana

2002 'Fiscal decentralisation and its impact on local government revenge in Indonesia', in: Minako Sakai (ed.), *Beyond Jakarta; Regional autonomy and local societies in Indonesia*, pp. 38-55. Adelaide: Crawford House.

Jaya, Wihana Kirana and Howard Dick

2001 'The latest crisis of regional autonomy in historical perspective', in: Grayson Lloyd and Shannon Smith (eds), *Indonesia today; Challenges of history*, pp. 216-28. Singapore: ISEAS.

Jenkins, Rob and Anne Marie Goetz

1999 'Accounts and accountability; Theoretical implications of the right-to-information movement in India', *Third World Quarterly* 20:603-22.

Jones, Gavin W.
1977 *The population of North Sulawesi*. Yogyakarta: Gadjah Mada University Press. [Department of Demography, Australian National University, Indonesian Population Monograph Series 1.]

Jouvenel, Bertrand de
1962 *On power*. Boston: Beacon.

Julipin, Vinsentius and Sekundus Pius
1987 *Dayak, krisis sosio-kultural; Materi diskusi panel dalam rangka temu wicara tokoh Dayak se-Kalimantan*. Pontianak: Institute of Dayakology Research and Development (IDRD).

Kadir, L.H.
1993 'Latar belakang keberadaan budaya kantuk dan catatan perjuangan politik suku Dayak di Kalimantan Barat; Sebuah catatan anak petani untuk generasinya'. Pontianak: n.p.

Kahn, Joel S.
1993 *Constituting the Minangkabau; Peasants, culture, and modernity in colonial Indonesia*. Providence: Berg.
1998 'Southeast Asian identities; Introduction', in: Joel S. Kahn (ed.), *Southeast Asian identities*, pp. 1-27. Singapore: ISEAS.

Kamma, F.C.
1947-49 'De verhouding tussen Tidore en de Papoesche eilanden in legende en historie', *Indonesië* 1:361-70, 536-59; 2:177-88, 256-75.

Kammen, Douglas and Siddharth Chandra
1999 *A tour of duty; Changing patterns of military politics in Indonesia in the 1990s*. Ithaca NY: Cornell University Press. [Cornell Modern Indonesia Project Publications 75.]
2003 'Security disorders; Sending troops is not going to solve regional conflicts', *Inside Indonesia* 73:6-7.

Kapita, Oemboe Hina
1976 *Sumba di dalam jangkauan jaman*. Waingapu: Gereja Kristen Sumba.

Kartodirdjo, Sartono
1966 *The peasants' revolt of Banten in 1888; Its conditions, course and sequel; A case study of social movements in Indonesia*. The Hague: Nijhoff. [KITLV, Verhandelingen 50.]

Khatib Mansur *see* Mansur, Khatib

Kato, Tsuyoshi
1982 *Matriliny and migration; Evolving Minangkabau traditions in Indonesia*. Ithaca, NY: Cornell University Press.

Kaudern, Walter
1925 *Structures and settlements in Central Celebes; Ethnographical studies in Celebes*. Vol.1. Göteborg: Elanders Bokytryckeri Aktiebolag.

Keane, Webb
1997 *Signs of recognition; Power and hazards of representation in an Indonesian society*. Berkeley: University of California Press.

Kell, Tim
1995 *The roots of Acehnese rebellion, 1989-1992*. Ithaca, NY: Cornell Modern Indonesia Project, Cornell University.

Kepulauan Riau
1999 *Kepulauan Riau pada masa dollar*. Jakarta: Departmen Pendidikan dan Kebudayaan.

Khatib Mansur *see* Mansur, Khatib

Khilnani, Sunil
2001 'The development of civil society', in: Sudipta Kaviraj and Sunil Khilnani (eds), *Civil society; History and possibilities*, pp. 11-32. Cambridge: Cambridge University Press.

King, Dwight Y.
1982 'Indonesia's New Order as a bureaucratic polity, a neopatrimonial regime or bureaucratic authoritarian regime; What difference does it make?' in: Benedict R. O'G. Anderson and Audrey Kahin (eds), *Interpreting Indonesian politics; Thirteen contributions to the debate*, pp. 104-16. Ithaca, NY: Cornell University Press. [Cornell Modern Indonesia Project Publications 62.]

King, Peter
2004 *West Papua and Indonesia since Suharto; Independence, autonomy or chaos?* Sydney: University of New South Wales Press.

King, Victor T.
1985 *The Maloh of West Kalimantan; An ethnographic study of social inequality and social change among an Indonesian Borneo People*. Dordrecht: Foris. [KITLV Verhandelingen 108.]

Kingsbury, Damien
2003 *Power politics and the Indonesian military*. London, New York: Routledge-Curzon

Kingsbury, Damien and Arief Budiman (eds)
2001 *Indonesia; The uncertain transition*. Adelaide: Crawford.

Kingsbury, Damien and Harry Aveling (eds)
2003 *Autonomy and disintegration in Indonesia*. London: RoutledgeCurzon.

Kingston, Jeffrey B.
1991 'Manipulating tradition; The state, adat, popular protest, and class conflict in colonial Lampung', *Indonesia* 51:21-45.

Kipp, Rita Smith
1993 *Dissociated identities; Ethnicity, religion, and class in an Indonesian society*. Ann Arbor: University of Michigan Press.

Kivlan Zen *see* Zen, Kivlan

Klinken, Gerry van
2002 'Indonesia's new ethnic elites', in: Henk Schulte Nordholt and Irwan Abdullah (eds), *Indonesia; In search of transition*, pp. 67-105. Yogyakarta: Pustaka Pelajar.
2003a 'Decentralisation, violence, and democracy; The colonial roots of ethnic conflict in Indonesia', in: Stanley Adi Prasetyo, A.E. Priyono, and Olle Törnquist (eds), *Indonesia's post-Soeharto democracy movement*, pp. 81-96. Jakarta: Demos.
2003b 'Ethnicity in Indonesia', in: Colin Mackerras (ed.), *Ethnicity in Asia*, pp. 64-87. London: RoutledgeCurzon.

2004 'Dayak ethnogenesis and conservative politics in Indonesia's outer Islands' in: Samuel Hanneman and Henk Schulte Nordholt (eds), *Indonesia in transition; Rethinking 'civil society', 'region' and 'crisis'*, pp. 107-28. Yogyakarta: Pustaka Pelajar.

2005 'New actors, new identities; Post-Suharto ethnic violence in Indonesia', in: Dewi Fortuna Anwar et al. (eds), *Violent internal conflicts in Asia Pacific; Histories, political economies and policies*, pp. 79-100. Jakarta: Yayasan Obor.

2006 'Colonizing Borneo; The creation of a Dayak province in Kalimantan', *Indonesia* 81(April):23-50.

forthcoming-a *Communal violence and democratisation in Indonesia; Small town wars.*

forthcoming-b 'Return of the sultans; The communitarian turn in local politics', in: James Davidson and David Henley (eds), *The revival of tradition in Indonesian politics*. London: Routledge.

Kruyt, Alb.C.

1930 'De To Wana op Oost-Celebes', *Tijdschrift voor Indische Taal-, Land- en Volkenkunde* 70:398-625.

1938 *De west-Toradja's op Midden-Celebes*. Five vols. Amsterdam: Noord-Hollandsche Uitgevers-Maatschappij. [Verhandelingen der Koninklijke Nederlandse Akademie van Wetenschappen, Afd. Letterkunde, nieuwe reeks 40.]

Kuipers, Joel C.

1990 *Power in performance; The creation of textual authority in Weyewa ritual speech*. Philadelphia: University of Pennsylvania Press.

1998 *Language, identity and marginality in Indonesia; The changing nature of ritual speech on the island of Sumba*. Cambridge: Cambridge University Press.

Laksono, Paschalis Maria

2002 *The common ground in the Kei Islands*. Yogyakarta: Galang.

Langen, K.F.H. van

1888 'De inrichting van het Atjehsche staatsbestuur onder het Sultanaat', *Bijdragen tot de Taal-, Land- en Volkenkunde* 37:381-471.

Lasahido, Tahmidy

2003 *Suara dari Poso; Kerusuhan, konflik, dan resolusi*. Jakarta Timur: Yappika.

Latief, H.Ch.N.Dt. Bandaro

2002 *Etnis dan adat Minangkabau*. Bandung: Angkasa.

Latief, H.Ch.N.Dt. Bandaro et al. (eds)

2004 *Minangkabau yang gelisah; Mencari strategi sosialisasi pewarisan adat dan budaya Minangkabau untuk generasi muda*. Bandung: Lubuk Agung.

Lawrence, Peter

1969 'The state versus stateless societies in Papua and New Guinea', in: B.J. Brown (ed.), *Fashion of law in New Guinea; Being an account of the past, present and developing system of laws in Papua and New Guinea*, pp. 15-37. Sydney: Butterworths.

Lay, Cornelis
2002 *Eksekutif dan legislatif di daerah; Penelitian tentang potensi konflik antara DPRD dan birokrasi di daerah.* Jakarta: Kementerian Riset dan Teknologi/LIPI.

Legge, John D.
1961 *Central authority and regional autonomy in Indonesia; A study in local administration, 1950-1960.* Ithaca, NY: Cornell University Press.

Leigh, Barbara
1991 'Making the Indonesian State; The role of school texts', *Review of Indonesian and Malaysian Affairs* 25-1:17-43.
1999 'Learning and knowing boundaries; Schooling in New Order Indonesia', *Sojourn* 14:34-56.

L.H. Kadir *see* Kadir, L.H.

Leirissa, R.Z.
1991 *PRRI-Permesta; Strategi membangun Indonesia tanpa komunis.* Jakarta: Pustaka Utama Grafiti.

Leith, Denise
2003 *The politics of power; Freeport in Suharto's Indonesia.* Honolulu, HI: University of Hawai'i Press.

Lev, Daniel
1985 'Colonial law and the genesis of the Indonesian State', *Indonesia* 4:57-74.

Liddle, R. William
1970 *Ethnicity, party, and national integration.* New Haven, London: Yale University Press.
2001 (ed.) *Crafting Indonesian democracy.* Bandung: Mizan.

Liem Soei Liong
2002 'It's the military, stupid!', in: Freek Colombijn and J. Thomas Lindblad (eds), *Roots of violence in Indonesia; Contemporary violence in historical perspective*, pp. 197-225. Leiden: KITLV Press. [Verhandelingen 194.]

LiPuma, Edward
1995 'The formation of nation-states and national cultures in Oceania', in: Robert J. Foster (ed.), *Nation making; Emergent identities in postcolonial Melanesia*, pp. 33-68. Ann Arbor: University of Michigan Press.

LKAAM (Lembaga Kerapatan Adat Alam Minangkabau)
2002 *Adat basandi syarak, syarak basandi kitabullah; Pedoman hidup banagari.* Padang: Sako Batuah.

Locke, John
1961 *A letter concerning toleration.* The Hague: Nijhoff. [First published 1689.]

Logging
2002 'The logging of West Papua', *Down to Earth Newsletter* 55. http//dte.gn.apc.org. [Last accessed 5-5-2005.]

Lombard, Denys
1967 *Le Sultanat d' Atjeh au temps d' Iskandar Muda 1607-1636.* Paris: École Française d'Extrême-Orient.

Lowry, Robert
1996 *The armed forces of Indonesia*. St. Leonards: Allen and Unwin.
Lubis, Sairul S.
1962 '10 Tahun PKI di NTB', *Gelora*. [Issue number unknown.]
Lutfi, Muchtar et al.
1977 *Sejarah Riau*. Pekanbaru: Universitas Riau Pekanbaru.
Lumenta, Dave
2001 'Reconstructing Iban identities over a glass of tuak; Notes from a fieldtrip to the Batang Kanyau Iban in West Kalimantan', *Antropologi Indonesia* 66:110-3.
Lumholtz, Carl
1920 *Through Central Borneo; An account of two years' travel in the land of the head-hunters between the years 1913 and 1917*. Vol. 1. New York: Scribners.
Lynch, Jake
2003 'Making peace newsworthy; Indonesian journalists attend a peace journalism training workshop in Manado', *Inside Indonesia* 74:29-30.
Lijphart, Arend
1966 *The trauma of decolonization; The Dutch and West New Guinea*. London, New Haven: Yale University Press. [Yale Studies in Political Science 17.]
1968 *The politics of accommodation; Pluralism and democracy in the Netherlands*. Berkeley, CA: University of California Press.
1977 *Democracy in plural societies; A contemporary exploration*. London, New Haven: Yale University Press.
M. Isa Sulaiman *see* Sulaiman, M. Isa
McAdam, Douglas, Sidney Tarrow and Charles Tilly
2001 *Dynamics of contention*. Cambridge/New York: Cambridge University Press.
McCarthy, John F.
2000 'The changing regime; Forest property and Reformasi in Indonesia', *Development and Change* 31-1:91-129.
2001a *Decentralization and forest management in Kapuas District*. Bogor, Indonesia: Centre for International Forestry Research (CIFOR). [Case Studies on Decentralisation and Forests in Indonesia 2.]
2001b *Decentralization, local communities and forest management in Barito Selatan*. Bogor, Indonesia: Centre for International Forestry Research (CIFOR). [Case Studies on Decentralisation and Forests in Indonesia 1.]
2004 'Changing to gray; Decentralization and the emergence of volatile socio-legal configurations in Central Kalimantan, Indonesia', *World Development* 32:1199-223.
forthcoming *The fourth circle; A political ecology of Sumatra's rainforest frontier*. Palo Alto, CA: Stanford University Press.
McCoy, Alfred W. (ed.)
1993 *An anarchy of families; State and family in the Philippines*. Madison, WI: University of Wisconsin, Center for Southeast Asian Studies.

McCulloch, Lesley
2000 'Trifungsi; The role of the Indonesian military in business'. Paper, Conference 'The Military as an Economic Player', Jakarta, 16-19 November.

McGibbon, Rodd
2004 *Secessionist challenges in Aceh and Papua; Is special autonomy the solution?* Washington DC: East-West Center. [Policy Studies 10.]

MacRae, Graeme S.
1997 *Economy, ritual and history in a Balinese tourist town.* PhD thesis, University of Auckland.

McVey, Ruth
1982 'The beamtenstaat in Indonesia', in: Benedict Anderson and Audrey Kahin (eds), *Interpreting Indonesian politics; Thirteen contributions to the debate,* pp. 84-91. Ithaca, NY: Cornell University Press. [Cornell Modern Indonesia Project publications 62.]
2000 (ed.) *Money and power in provincial Thailand.* Copenhagen: Nordic Institute of Asian Studies (NIAS).
2003 'Nation versus state in Indonesia', in: Damien Kingsbury and Harry Aveling (eds), *Autonomy and disintegration in Indonesia,* pp. 11-27. London: RoutledgeCurzon.

McWilliam, Andrew
2001 'Haumeni, not many; Renewed plunder and mismanagement in the Timorese sandalwood industry'. Working Paper 29, Research School of Pacific and Asian Studies, Australian National University, Canberra. http://rspas.anu.edu.au/rmap/workingpapers.php. [Last accessed 16-2-2006.]

MacIntyre, Andrew
1991 *Business and politics in Indonesia.* St. Leonards, NSW: Asian Studies Association of Australia. [Southeast Asia Publications Series 21.]
1994 (ed.) *Business and government in industrializing Asia.* St. Leonards, NSW: Allen and Unwin.

Mackie, Jamie and Andrew MacIntyre
1994 'Politics', in: Hal Hill (ed.), *Indonesia's New Order; The dynamics of socio-economic transformation,* pp. 1-53. St. Leonards: Allen and Unwin.

Maclean, Neil
1994 'Freedom or autonomy; A modern Melanesian dilemma', *Man* 29:667-88.

Magenda, Burhan Djabier
1989 *The surviving aristocracy in Indonesia; Politics in three provinces of the outer islands.* PhD thesis, Cornell University, Ithaca, NY.
1991 *East Kalimantan; The decline of a commercial aristocracy.* Ithaca, NY: Cornell University Press. [Cornell Modern Indonesia Project Publications 70.]

Majcherkiewicz, Tatiana
2000 'Great expectations; The regional administrative reform in Eastern Central Europe in anticipation of the EU'. Paper, The Ionian Conference 2000; Facing the challenges of the new millennium - Governance and citizenship in the European Union - the influence of culture, Corfu (Greece), 20-22 May.

Malley, Michael S.
1999 'Regions, centralization and resistance', in: Donald K. Emmerson (ed.), *Indonesia beyond Suharto; Polity, economy, society, transition*, pp. 71-105. Armonk, NY: Sharpe.
2003 'New rules, old structures and the limits of democratic decentralisation', in: Edward Aspinall and Greg Fealy (eds), *Local power and politics in Indonesia; Decentralisation and democratisation*, pp. 102-18. Singapore: ISEAS.
2004 'The origins of Indonesian decentralization'. Paper, KITLV/LIPI conference 'Renegotiating Boundaries; Local Politics in Post-Suharto Indonesia', Jakarta, 20-22 December.

Malo, Manasse
1995 'Social sector decentralization; The case of Indonesia'. Online Paper, International Development Research Centre, Ottawa, Canada. www.idrc.ca/socdev/pub/indones/Indones.html. [No longer online, try http://web.archive.org.]

Mamar, Sulaiman
2001 'Kesimpulan dan rekomendasi', in: Suriadi Mappangara (ed.), *Respon militer terhadap konflik sosial di Poso*, pp. 120-26. Palu: Yayasan Bina Warga Sulawesi Tengah.

Mamdani, Mahmood
1996 *Citizen and subject; Contemporary Africa and the legacy of late colonialism*. Princeton, NJ: Princeton University Press.
2001a *When victims become killers; Colonialism, nativism, and the genocide in Rwanda*. Princeton, NJ: Princeton University Press.
2001b 'Beyond settler and native as political identities; Overcoming the political legacy of colonialism', *Comparative Studies in Society and History* 43:651-64.

Manan, Imran
1984 *A traditional elite in continuity and change; The chiefs of the matrilineal lineages of the Minangkabau of West Sumatra, Indonesia*. PhD thesis, University of Illinois.

Maniagasi, Frans
2001 *Masa depan Papua; Merdeka, otonomi khusus dan dialog*. Jakarta: Millennium.

Mann, Michael
2005 *The dark side of democracy; Explaining ethnic cleansing*. Cambridge: Cambridge University Press.

Manning, Chris and Peter van Diermen (eds)
2000 *Indonesia in transition; Social aspects of Reformasi and crisis*. Singapore: ISEAS.

Mansur, Khatib
2001 *Perjuangan rakyat Banten menuju propinsi.* Jakarta: Antara Pustaka Utama.

Mappangara, Suriadi (ed.)
2001 *Respon militer terhadap konflik sosial di Poso.* Palu: Yayasan Bina Warga Sulawesi Tengah.

Mari Pangestu *see* Pangestu, Mari

Martinkus, John
2002 'Paradise betrayed; West Papua's struggle for independence', *Quarterly Essay* 7:1-83.

Mas'oed Abidin, H.
1997 *Islam dalam pelukan muhtadin Mentawai; 30 Tahun perjalanan Da'wah Ila'llah Mentawai menggapai cahaya iman 1967-1997.* Jakarta: Dewan Dakwah Islamiyah Indonesia.

Massewa, Muslim
2002 *Andi Djemma - Datu Luwu; Tahta bagi Republik.* Jakarta: Yayasan Bina Profesi dan Wirausaha (BENUA).

Mattulada, A.
1974 *Bugis Makassar; Manusia dan kebudayaannya.* Makassar: Universitas Hasanuddin. [Terbitan Khusus Berita Antropologi 15.]

May, Ron
2001 *State and society in Papua New Guinea; The first twenty-five years.* Canberra: ANU Press.
2003 'Turbulence and reform in Papua New Guinea', *Journal of Democracy* 14-1:154-65.

Meijering, M. et al.
1927 *Tot dankbaarheid genoopt; Gedenkboek ter gelegenheid van den 25-jarigen zendingsarbeid op Soemba vanwege de Gereformeerde kerken in Groningen, Drenthe en Overijssel.* Kampen: Kok.

Mietzner, Marcus
2003 'Business as usual? The Indonesian armed forces and local politics in the post-Soeharto era', in: Edward Aspinall and Greg Fealy (eds), *Local power and politics in Indonesia; Decentralisation and democratisation,* pp. 245-58. Singapore: ISEAS.

Migdal, Joel S.
2001 *State in society; Studying how states and societies transform and constitute one another.* Cambridge, New York: Cambridge University Press. [Cambridge Studies in Comparative Politics.]

Miko, Alfan et al.
2005 *Kembali ke nagari; Pengumpulan data-data dasar tentang perubahan dalam pemerintahan lokal di Minangkabau.* Halle: Max Planck Institute for Social Anthropology/Padang: SCDev. [Project Group Legal Pluralism.]

Miles, Douglas
1976 *Cutlass and crescent moon; A case study of social and political change in outer Indonesia.* Sydney: Centre for Asian Studies, University of Sydney.

Millar, S.
1989 *Bugis weddings; Rituals of social location in modern Indonesia*. Berkeley, CA: Centre for South East Asian Studies, University of California. [Monograph Series 29.]

Mochtar Nim *see* Naim, Mochtar

Mohammad Hasbi *see* Hasbi, Mohammad

Mona Abasa *see* Albasa, Mona

Morrell, Elizabeth
2002 'How many degrees of separation? Observations from South Sulawesi', *Antropologi Indonesia* 26:33-43.
2005 'Re-drawing Sulawesi's map; New provincial borders don't solve old problems', *Inside Indonesia* 82:18-9.

M.S. Amir *see* Amir, M.S.

Muhammad Nasihuddin Badri *see* Badri, Muhammad Nasihuddin

Muridan S. Widjojo *see* Widjojo, Muridan S.

Muslim Massewa *see* Massewa, Muslim

Naim, Mochtar
1990 'Nagari versus desa; Sebuah kerancuan structural', in: Mohammad Hasbi, Mochtar Naim and Damciwar Dt. Bagindo Sampono (eds), *Nagari, desa, dan pembangunan pedesaan di Sumatera Barat*, pp. 47-60. Padang: Yayasan Genta Budaya.

Nathan, M.
2003 'Decentralisation and conflict; A case study of Luwu, South Sulawesi'. Paper, Percik Seminar, Salatiga, Indonesia.

Navis, A.A.
1995 Discussion comment, in: Edy Utama (ed.), 'Intelektual Minangkabau mandek?', *Jurnal Kebudayaan Genta Budaya* 1:19. [Special issue.]

Needham, Rodney
1987 *Mamboru; History and structure in a domain of North-western Sumba*. Oxford: Clarendon.

Noorduyn, J.
1991 *A critical survey of studies on the languages of Sulawesi*. Leiden: KITLV Press. [Bibliographical Series 18.]

Nyoman Sukartha *see* Sukartha, Nyoman

Nyoman Widnyani *see* Widnyani, Nyoman

Obidzinski, Krystof
2003 *Logging in East Kalimantan, Indonesia; The historical expedience of illegality*. PhD thesis, University of Amsterdam.

Ockey, James S.
1992 *Business leaders, gangsters, and the middle class; Societal groups and civilian rule in Thailand*. PhD thesis, Cornell University, Ithaca, NY.

Oemboe Hina Kapita *see* Kapita, Oemboe Hina

Oki, Akira
1977 *Social change in the West Sumatran village; 1908-1945*. PhD thesis, Australian National University, Canberra.

Oosterhout, Dianne van
2000 'Tying the time string together; An end-of-time experience in Irian Jaya, Indonesia', *Ethnohistory* 47-1:67-99.
O'Rourke, Kevin
2002 *Reformasi; The struggle for power in post-Soeharto Indonesia*. Crows Nest, NSW: Allen and Unwin.
Osborne, Robin
1985 *Indonesia's secret war; The guerilla struggle in Irian Jaya*. Sydney: Allen and Unwin.
Ostrom, Elinor
1992 *Crafting institutions for self-governing irrigation systems*. San Francisco: ICS Press. [Institute for Contemporary Studies.]
Pangestu, Mari
1996 *Economic reform, deregulation and privatization; The Indonesian experience*. Jakarta: Centre for Strategic and International Studies (CSIS).
Parimartha, I Gde
2003 'Memahami desa adat, desa dinas dan desa pakraman; Suatu tinjauan historis, kritis'. Denpasar: Universitas Udayana. [Inaugural lecture.]
Parker, Lyn
2002 'The subjectification of citizenship; Student interpretations of school teachings in Bali', *Asian Studies Review* 26-1:3-37.
Paschalis Maria Laksono *see* Laksono, Paschalis Maria
Pelras, Christian
1976 'Pelapisan dan kekuasaan tradisional di Tanah Wajo'. Unpublished translation by Ida Husain. [Originally published as *Hiérarchie et pouvoir traditionnels en pays Wadjo*. Two vols. Paris: s.n., 1971.]
1996 *The Bugis*. Cambridge, MA: Blackwell.
2000 'Patron-client ties among Bugis and Makassarese of South Sulawesi', *Bijdragen tot de Taal-, Land-, en Volkenkunde* 156:15-54.
Peluso, Nancy Lee and Emily Harwell
2001 'Territory, custom, and the cultural politics of ethnic war in West Kalimantan Indonesia', in: Nancy Lee Peluso and Michael John Watts, *Violent environments*, pp. 83-116. Ithaca, NY: Cornell University Press.
Pemberton, John
1986 'Notes on the 1982 general election in Solo', *Indonesia* 41:1-22.
1994 *On the subject of 'Java'*. Ithaca, NY: Cornell University Press.
Pemilu Indonesia
2000 *Pemilu Indonesia dalam angka dan fakta tahun 1955-1999*. Jakarta: Biro Humas Komisi Pemilihan Umum.
Penders, C.L.M.
2002 *The West New Guinea debacle; Dutch decolonisation and Indonesia, 1945-1962*. Honolulu: University of Hawai'i Press, Leiden: KITLV Press.
Penduduk Indonesia
2001 *Hasil sensus penduduk tahun 2000*. Jakarta: BPS. [Seri L.2.2.]
Pepera
1972 *Penentuan pendapat rakjat (Pepera) di Irian Barat 1969*. Djajapura: Pemerintah Daerah Propinsi Irian Barat.

Perry, Martin

1998 'The Singapore Growth Triangle in the global and local economy', in: Victor R. Savage, Lily Kong and Warwick Neville (eds), *The Naga awakens; Growth and change in Southeast Asia*, pp. 87-112. Singapore: Times Academic Press.

Persoon, Gerardus Antonius

1994 *Vluchten of veranderen; Processen van verandering en ontwikkeling bij tribale groepen in Indonesië*. PhD thesis, Leiden University.

1998 'Isolated groups or indigenous peoples; Indonesia and the international discourse', *Bijdragen tot de Taal-, Land- en Volkenkunde* 154:281-304.

Persoon, Gerard and Reimar Schefold (eds)

1985 *Pulau Siberut; Pembangunan sosio-ekonomi, kebudayaan tradisional dan lingkungan hidup*. Jakarta: Bhratara.

Phongpaichit, Pasuk, Sungsidh Piriyarangsan and Nualnoi Treerat

1998 *Guns, girls, gambling, ganja; Thailand's illegal economy and public policy*. Chiang Mai: Silkworm Books.

Picard, Michel

1996 *Bali; Cultural tourism and touristic culture*. Singapore: Archipelago.

1997 'Cultural tourism, nation-building, and regional culture; The making of a Balinese identity' in: Michel Picard and Robert E. Wood (eds), *Tourism, ethnicity, and the state in Asian and Pacific societies*, pp. 181-214. Honolulu: University of Hawaii Press.

1999 'The discourse of kebalian; Transcultural constructions of Balinese identity', in: Raechelle Rubinstein and Linda H. Connor (eds), *Staying local in the global village; Bali in the twentieth century*, pp. 15-49. Honolulu: University of Hawaii Press.

2003 'Touristification and Balinization in a time of Reformasi', *Indonesia and the Malay World* 31:108-18.

2005 'Otonomi daerah in Bali; The call for special autonomy status in the name of kebalian', in: Maribeth Erb, Priyambudi Sulistiyanto and Carole Faucher (eds), *Regionalism in post-Suharto Indonesia*. London: RoutledgeCurzon.

Pitana, I Gde

1999 'Status struggles and the priesthood in contemporary Bali', in: Raechelle Rubinstein and Linda H. Connor (eds), *Staying local in the global village; Bali in the twentieth century*, pp. 181-201. Honolulu: University of Hawaii Press.

2001 'Sociology of the temple; Issues related to rivalry in status and power', in: Urs Ramseyer and I Gusti Raka Panji Tisna (eds), *Bali; Living in two worlds; A critical selfportrait*, pp. 117-27. Basel: Schwabe, Museum der Kulturen.

Ploeg, Anton

2001 'The other Western Highlands', *Social Anthropology* 9-1:25-43.

Ponsen, Madelon

2003 'Stille strijd; Democratie, identiteit en "veranderende continuïteiten" in het district Minahasa van een decentraliserend Indonesië'. MA thesis, University of Amsterdam.

Pouwer, Jan
1999 'The colonisation, decolonisation and recolonisation of West New Guinea', *Journal of Pacific History* 34-2:157-79.
PPIM (Pusat Pengkajian Islam dan Minangkabau)
2003 *Sumatera Barat 2003; Reaktualisasi adat basandi syarak, syaraka basandi kitabullah.* Padang: PPIM.
Pradadimara, Dias and Burhaman Junedding
2002 'Who is calling for Islamic law?', *Inside Indonesia* 72:12-3. www.insideindonesia.org/edit72/Politics Dias.htm. [Last accessed 20-2-2006.]
Prasetyo, Eko
2002 *Membela agama tuhan; Potret gerakan Islam dalam pusaran konflik global.* Yogyakarta: Insist.
Pratikno
2005 'Exercising freedom; Local autonomy and democracy in Indonesia, 1999-2001', in: Maribeth Erb, Priyambudi Sulistiyanto and Carole Faucher (eds), *Regionalism in post-Suharto Indonesia,* pp. 21-35. London: RoutledgeCurzon.
Pringle, Robert
2004 *A short history of Bali.* Crows Nest, NSW: Allen and Unwin.
Puskur (Pusat Kurikulum)
2002 *Kurikulum berbasis kompetensi.* Jakarta: Puskur [Pengelolaan Kurikulum Berbasis Kelas, Departemen Pendidikan Nasional.]
Putnam, Robert D.
1993 *Making democracy work.* Princeton, NJ: Princeton University Press.
2000 *Bowling alone; The collapse and revival of American community.* New York: Simon and Schuster.
Putra Dwikora and Wayan Supartha (eds)
2000 *K. Nadha; Sang perintis.* Denpasar: Pustaka Bali Post.
Putu Suasta *see* Suasta, Putu
Quinn, George
2003 'Coming apart and staying together at the center; Debates over provincial status in Java and Madura', in: Edward Aspinall and Greg Fealy (eds), *Local power and politics in Indonesia; Decentralisation and democratisation,* pp. 164-78. Singapore: ISEAS.
R.Z. Leirissa *see* Leirissa, R.Z.
Raffles, Thomas Stamford
1965 *The history of Java.* Kuala Lumpur: Oxford University Press. [First published 1817. London: Black, Parbury and Allen.]
Rajo Panghoeloe, Rasjid Manggis Dt.
1971 *Minangkabau; Sedjarah ringkas dan adatnja.* Padang: Sridharma.
Rajo Panghulu, Idrus Hakimy Dt.
2001 *Rangkaian mustika adat basandi syarak di Minangkabau.* Fifth edition. Bandung: PT Remaja Rosdakarya.
Ramstedt, Martin
2002 'Hinduism in modern Indonesia', in: Satish Chandra and Baladas Ghoshal (eds), *Indonesia; A new beginning?,* pp. 140-68. New Delhi:

Sterling.
2004 'Negotiating identities; Indonesian 'Hindus' between local, national, and global interests' in: Martin Ramstedt (ed.), *Hinduism in modern Indonesia; A minority religion between local, national, and global interests*, pp. 1-34. London, New York: RoutledgeCurzon.

Rasjid Manggis Dt. Rajo Panghoeloe *see* Rajo Panghoeloe, Rasjid Manggis Dt.

Ravault, Rene-Jean
1985 'Resisting media imperialism by coerseduction', *InterMedia* 13-3:32-7.
1986 'Défense de l'identité culturelle par les réseaux traditionnels de coerséduction', *International Political Science Review* 7-3:251-80.

Ray, David and Gary Goodpaster
2003 'Indonesian decentralization', in: Damien Kingsbury and Harry Aveling (eds), *Autonomy and disintegration in Indonesia*, pp. 75-95. London: RoutledgeCurzon.

Reenen, Joke van
1996 *Central pillars of the house; Sisters, wives, and mothers in a rural community in Minangkabau, West Sumatra*. PhD thesis, Research School CNWS, Leiden University.

Reid, Anthony
1979 *The blood of the people; Revolution and the end of traditional rule in northern Sumatra*. Kuala Lumpur: Oxford University Press.
1998 'Merdeka; The concept of freedom in Indonesia', in: David Kelly and Anthony Reid (eds), *Asian freedoms; The idea of freedom in East and Southeast Asia*, pp. 141-60. Cambridge: Cambridge University Press.
2003 *War, peace and the burden of history in Aceh*, Singapore: Asia Research Institute. [Working Paper Series 1.]

Reno, William
1995 *Corruption and state politics in Sierra Leone*. Cambridge/New York: Cambridge University Press.

Resosudarmo, Ida Aju Pradnja
2003 'Shifting power to the periphery; The impact of decentralization on forests and forest people', in: Edward Aspinall and Greg Fealy (eds), *Local power and politics in Indonesia; Decentralization and democracy*, pp. 230-44. Singapore: ISEAS.

Ribot, Jesse C.
1998 'Theorizing access; Forest profits along Senegals charcoal commodity chain', *Development and Change* 29:307-41.

Ribot, Jesse C. and Nancy Lee Peluso
2002 'A theory of access', *Rural Sociology* 62:153-81.

Rifai, Amzulian
2002 'Regional autonomy; The implications for the legal system', in: Minako Sakai (ed.), *Beyond Jakarta; Regional autonomy and local societies in Indonesia*, pp. 29-37. Adelaide: Crawford House.

Rinaldy Damanik, *see* Damanik, Rinaldy

T. Rivolsa Ismail *see* Ismail, T. Rivolsa

Riwut, Tjilik
1979 *Kalimantan membangun*. Jakarta: Sayakarta Agung.

1993 *Kalimantan membangun; Alam dan kebudayaan*. Edited by Nila Riwut and Agus Fahri Husein. Yogyakarta: PT Tiara Wacana Yogya.

Robertson-Snape, Fiona
1999 'Corruption, collusion and nepotism in Indonesia', *Third World Quarterly* 20:589-602.

Robinson, Geoffrey
1998 'Rawan is as rawan does; The origins of disorder in New Order Aceh', *Indonesia* 66:127-56.
2001 'People's war; Militias in East Timor and Indonesia', *South East Asia Research* 9:271-318.

Robinson, Kathryn May
1986 *Stepchildren of progress; The political economy of development in an Indonesian mining town*. Albany, NY: State University of New York Press.
1999 'Revisiting INCO', *Inside Indonesia* 60:24.
2000 'Gender, Islam and nationality; Indonesian domestic servants in the Middle East', in: Kathleen M. Adams and Sara Dickey (eds), *Home and hegemony; Domestic service and identity in South and Southeast Asia*, pp. 249-82. Ann Arbor: University of Michigan Press.
2002 'Inter-ethnic violence; The Bugis and the problem of explanation', in: Minako Sakai (ed.), *Beyond Jakarta; Regional autonomy and local societies in Indonesia*, pp. 145-72. Adelaide: Crawford House.

Robison, Richard
1986 *Indonesia; The rise of capital*. Sydney: Allen and Unwin.
1988 'Authoritarian states, capital-owning classes, and the politics of newly industrializing countries; The case of Indonesia', *World Politics* 61:52-74.
2002 'Indonesia; Crisis, oligarchy, and reform', in: Garry Rodan, Kevin Hewison and Richard Robison (eds), *The political economy of South-East Asia; Conflict, crises and change*, pp. 104-31. Second edition. Oxford: Oxford University Press.

Robison, Richard and Andrew Rosser
1998 'Contesting reform; Indonesia's New Order and the IMF', *World Development* 26:1593-609.

Robison, Richard and Vedi Hadiz
2004 *Reorganizing power in Indonesia; The polititics of oligarchy in an age of markets*. London: RoutledgeCurzon.

Roekaarts, C.
1985 *Dayak first draft*. Pontianak: Keuskupan Agung Pontianak, Biro PSE.

Rohdewohld, Rainer
2003 'Decentralisation and the Indonesian bureaucracy', in: Edward Aspinall and Greg Fealy (eds), *Local power and politics in Indonesia; Decentralisation and democratisation*, pp. 259-74. Singapore: ISEAS.

Rotberg, Robert I. (ed.)
2003 *State failure and state weakness in a time of terror*. Cambridge, MA: World Peace Foundation, Washington DC: Brookings Institution Press.

Roth, Dik

2002 'A national crisis in regional perspective; Some observations on Luwu District, South Sulawesi, Indonesia', in: Coen Holtzappel, Martin Sanders and Milan Titus (eds), *Riding a tiger; Dilemmas of integration and decentralization in Indonesia*, pp. 181-210. Amsterdam: Rozenberg.

2003 *Ambition, regulation and reality; Complex use of land and water resources in Luwu, South Sulawesi, Indonesia*. PhD thesis, Wageningen University, Wageningen.

2004 'From "Grooter Toradja" to "Toraja Raya"; Emergent ethnic identity, expansionism and political struggle in Tana Toraja and Luwu, South Sulawesi, Indonesia', in: Martin Ramstedt (ed.), *Hinduism in modern Indonesia*, pp. 160-83. London: RoutledgeCurzon.

Roth, Guenther

1968 'Personal rulership, patrimonialism and empire building in the New States', *World Politics* 20:194-206.

Rumate, Vekie A.

1999 *Kondisi ekonomi Sulawesi Utara di tengah krisis ekonomi*. Jakarta: Centre for Policy and Implementation Studies. [CPIS Monitoring dan Analisis 52/1999.]

Rutherford, Danilyn

1999 'Waiting for the end in Biak; Violence, order and a flag raising', *Indonesia* 67:39-59.

2003 *Raiding the land of the foreigners; The limits of the nation on an Indonesian frontier*. Princeton, NJ: Princeton University Press.

2005 'Nationalism and millenarianism in West Papua; Institutional power, interpretive practice, and the pursuit of Christian truth', in: June Nash (ed.), *Social movements; An anthropological reader*, pp. 146-67. Malden, MA: Blackwell.

Ryaas Rashid, M.

2003 'Regional autonomy and local politics in Indonesia', in: Edward Aspinall and Greg Fealy (eds), *Local power and politics in Indonesia; Decentralisation and democratisation*, pp. 63-71. Singapore: ISEAS.

Sakai, Minako

2002 (ed.) *Beyond Jakarta; Regional autonomy and local societies in Indonesia*. Adelaide: Crawford House.

2003a 'Resisting the mainland', in: Damien Kingsbury and Harry Aveling (eds), *Autonomy and disintegration in Indonesia*, pp. 189-200. London: RoutledgeCurzon.

2003b 'The privatisation of Padang cement; Regional identity and economic hegemony in the new era of decentralization', in: Edward Aspinall and Greg Fealy (eds), *Local power and politics in Indonesia: Decentralization and democratisation*, pp. 148-63. Singapore: ISEAS.

Saleh, Abdul Aziz

1990 'Reaksi terhadap Damciwar', in: Mohammad Hasbi, Mochtar Naim and Damciwar Dt. Bagindo Sampono (eds), *Nagari, desa dan pembangunan pedesaan di Sumatera Barat*, pp. 85-8. Padang: Yayasan Genta Budaya.

Saleh, Abdul Aziz and D. Flud van Giffen (eds)
1990 *Socio-cultural impacts of development; Some theoretical issues*. Padang: Andalas University, Research Centre. [Proceedings, Seminar on Socio-Cultural Impacts of Development.]

Salmadanis, H. and H. Duski Samad
2003 *Adat basandi syarak; Nilai dan aplikasinya menuju kembali ke nagari dan surau*. Jakarta: Kartika Insan Lestari Press.

Saltford, John
2000 'United Nations involvement with the act of self-determination in West-Irian (Indonesian West New Guinea) 1968 to 1969', *Indonesia* 69:71-92.

Samego, Indria
1998 *Bila ABRI berbisnis*. Bandung: Mizan.

Sampono, Damciwar Dt. Bagindo
1990 'Dampak perubahan nagari terhadap pembangunan pedesaan di Sumatera Barat', in: Mohammad Hasbi, Mochtar Naim and Damciwar Dt. Bagindo Sampono (eds), *Nagari, desa dan pembangunan pedesaan di Sumatera Barat*, pp. 73-82. Padang: Yayasan Genta Budaya.

Sangaji, Arianto
2003 'Rumput kering di balik anyir darah; Tragedi kemanusiaan Poso'. Manuscript, Palu, 15 September.
2002 *Buruk Inco rakyat digusur; Ekonomi politik pertambangan Indonesia*. Jakarta: Sinar Harapan.
2004 'Bara api dan bola panas; Politik identitas dan politik pemekaran di Sulawesi Timur'. Paper, KITLV Modern Indonesia Occasional Seminar Series, Leiden, 4 August.

Santikarma, Degung
2001a 'The power of Balinese culture', in: Urs Ramseyer and I Gusti Raka Panji Tisna (eds), *Bali; Living in two worlds; A critical self-portrait*, pp. 27-45. Basel: Schwabe, Museum der Kulturen.
2001b 'The burden of being exotic', *Latitudes* 1:22-26.

Sartono Kartodirdjo *see* Kartodirdjo, Sartono

Satria Naradha, A.B.G. (ed.)
2004 *Ajeg Bali; Sebuah cita-cita*. Denpasar: Bali Post.

Satu abad kota Selong
1998 *Satu abad kota Selong*. Selong, West Nusa Tenggara: East Lombok Regional Government.

Savirani, Amalinda
2004 'Local strongmen in new regional politics in Indonesia'. MA thesis, International School for Social Sciences and the Humanities, University of Amsterdam.

Saya Shiraishi *see* Shiraishi, Saya

Schefold, Reimar
1998 'The domestication of culture; Nation-building and ethnic diversity in Indonesia', *Bijdragen tot de Taal-, Land- en Volkenkunde* 154:259-80.

Schiller, Jim
1996 *Developing Jepara in New Order Indonesia*. Clayton, Victoria: Monash Asia Institute. [Monash Papers on Southeast Asia 40.]

2001 'Looking for civil society; The 1999 election in Jepara', *RENAI, Jurnal Politik Lokal and Sosial-Humaniora* 2-1:5-18.

Schrauwers, Albert

2000 *Colonial 'reformation' in the highlands of Central Sulawesi, Indonesia, 1892-1995*. Toronto: Toronto University Press.

Schulte Nordholt, Henk

1994 'The making of traditional Bali; Colonial ethnography and bureaucratic reproduction', *History and Anthropology* 8:89-127.

1996 *The spell of power; A history of Balinese politics 1650-1940*. Leiden: KITLV Press. [Verhandelingen 170.]

1999 'The making of traditional Bali; Colonial ethnography and bureaucratic reproduction', in: Peter Pels and Oscar Salemink (eds), *Colonial subjects; Essays on the practical history of anthropology*, pp. 241-81. Ann Arbor: University of Michigan Press.

2000 'Localizing modernity in colonial Bali during the 1930s', *Journal of Southeast Asian Studies* 31:101-14.

2001 'Plotting time in Bali; Articulating plurality', in: Willem van Schendel and Henk Schulte Nordholt (eds), *Time matters; Global and local time in Asian societies*, pp. 57-76. Amsterdam: VU University Press.

2002 'A genealogy of violence', in: Freek Colombijn and J. Thomas Lindblad (eds), *Roots of violence in Indonesia; Contemporary violence in historical perspective*, pp. 33-61. Leiden: KITLV Press. [Verhandelingen 194.]

2003 'Renegotiating boundaries; Access, agency and identity in post-Soeharto Indonesia', *Bijdragen tot de Taal-, Land- en Volkenkunde* 159:550-89.

Schulte-Nordholt, Henk and Gusti Asnan (eds)

2003 *Indonesia in transition; Work in progress*. Yogyakarta: Pustaka Pelajar.

Schulte Nordholt, Nico G.

1996 'Corruption and legitimacy in Indonesia; An exploration', in: Heleen E. Bakker, and Nico G. Schulte Nordholt (eds), *Corruption and legitimacy*, pp. 65-93. Amsterdam: SISWO.

Schulze, Kirsten E.

2002 'Laskar Jihad and the conflict in Ambon', *The Brown Journal of World Affairs* 9-1:57-96.

2004 *The Free Aceh Movement (GAM); Anatomy of a separatist organization*. Washington DC: East-West Center. [Policy Studies 2.]

Scott, James C.

1972 *Comparative political corruption*. Englewood Cliffs, NJ: Prentice-Hall.

1985 *Weapons of the weak; Everyday forms of peasant resistance*. New Haven, London: Yale University Press.

Sharp, Nonie (in association with Markus Wonggor Kaisiëpo)

1994 *The Morning Star in Papua Barat*. North Carlton: Arena.

Shiraishi, Saya

1997 *Young heroes; The Indonesian family in politics*. Ithaca, NY: Cornell University Press.

Sidel, John T.

1998 'Macet total; Logistics of circulation and accumulation in the demise of Indonesia's New Order', *Indonesia* 66:159-94.

1999 *Capital, coercion, and crime; Bossism in the Philippines.* Stanford: Stanford University Press.

Sihombing, Herman
1979 *Mentawai.* Jakarta: Pradnya Paramita.

Siliwoloe, Djoeroemana and Muana Nanga
2003 'Catatan kritis atas draft laporan hasil penelitian Tim Undana tentang pemekaran kabupaten Sumba Barat', *Suara Sumba* 3-6:6-7.

S. Sinansari Ecip *see* Ecip, S. Sinansari

Singh, Bilveer
2001 *The Indonesian military business complex; Origins, course and future.* Canberra: Strategic and Defence Studies Centre (SDSC), Australian National University. [Working Paper 354.]

Sjahmunir, A.M.
1996 *Kedudukan dan peranan Peraturan Daerah no. 13 tahun 1983 dalam proses pengambilan keputusan pada pemerintahan desa di Sumatera Barat.* PhD thesis. Universitas Gadjah Mada, Yogyakarta.

Skinner, George William and Edward M. Bruner
1959 *Local, ethnic, and national loyalties in village Indonesia; A symposium.* New York: Institute of Pacific Relations. [Yale University, Southeast Asia Studies, Cultural Report Series 8.]

SKP Merauke (Sekretariat Keadilan dan Perdamaian, Merauke)
2004 *Bisnis gaharu dan dampaknya terhadap kehidupan orang Awyu dan Wiyagar di Distrik Assue, Kabupaten Mappi Papua Selatan.* Merauke: Sekretariat Keadilan dan Perdamaian (SKP), Keuskupan Agung Merauke. [Laporan Kegiatan, Seri Sosial Ekonomi 01, www.hampapua.org/skp/skp06/var-05i.pdf, last accessed 16-2-2006.]

Slaats, Herman
1999 'Land titling and customary rights; Comparing land registration projects in Thailand and Indonesia', in: Toon van Meijl and Franz von Benda-Beckmann (eds), *Property rights and economic development; Land and natural resources in Southeast Asia and Oceania*, pp. 88-109. London: Kegan Paul.

Soekarno
2000 *Bebaskan Irian Barat;Kumpulan pidato Presiden Soekarno tentang pembebasan Irian Barat 17 Agustus 1961-17 Agustus 1962.* Yogyakarta: Ragam Media. [First published 1962.]

Somers Heidhues, Mary F.
1991 'The company island; A note on the history of Belitung', *Indonesia* 51:1-20.
1992 *Bangka tin and mentok pepper; Chinese settlement on an Indonesian island.* Singapore: ISEAS.

Stasch, Rupert
2001 'Giving up homicide; Korowai experience of witches and police (West Papua)', *Oceania* 72:33-52.
2003 'The forest, the city, and the subdistrict seat; Rural-urban articulations in the politics of sovereignty in West Papua'. Paper, Annual American Anthropological Association Meeting, Chicago.

Statistik Indonesia
2002 *Statistik Indonesia 2001*. Jakarta: Badan Pusat Statistik.

Stoler, Ann Laura
1995 *Race and the education of desire; Foucault's history of sexuality and the colonial order of things*. Durham and London: Duke University Press.

Stone Sweet, Alec
2002 'Judicialization and the construction of governance', in: Martin Shapiro and Alec Stone Sweet (eds), *On law, politics, and judicialization*, pp. 55-89. Oxford: Oxford University Press.

Suasta, Putu
2001 'Between holy waters and highways', in: Urs Ramseyer and I Gusti Raka Panji Tisna (eds), *Bali; Living in two worlds; A critical self-portrait*, pp. 37-44. Basel: Schwabe, Museum der Kulturen.

Suasta, Putu and Linda H. Connor
1999 'Democratic mobilization and political authoritarianism; Tourism developments on Bali', in: Raechelle Rubinstein and Linda H. Connor (eds), *Staying local in the global village; Bali in the twentieth century*, pp. 91-122. Honolulu: University of Hawaii Press.

Suhendro Boroma *see* Boroma, Suhendro

Sukartha, Nyoman, Ida Bagus Mayun and I Wayan Rupa
1993 *Peranan mabebasan dalam menyebarluaskan nilai-nilai budaya masyarakat Bali*. Jakarta: Departemen Pendidikan dan Kebudayaan.

Sulaiman, M. Isa
1997 *Sejarah Aceh; Sebuah gugatan terhadap tradisi*. Jakarta: Pustaka Sinar Harapan.
2000 *Aceh merdeka; Ideologi, kepemimpinan dan gerakan*. Jakarta: Pustaka Al-Kautsar.

Sulaiman Mamar *see* Mamar, Sulaiman

Sulawesi Utara
1991-2003 *Sulawesi Utara dalam angka [1990-2002]*. Manado: Badan Pusat Statistik Propinsi Sulawesi Utara. [Annual publication.]

Sullivan, Laurence
2003 *Challenges to special autonomy in the province of Papua, Republic of Indonesia*. Canberra: State, Society and Governance in Melanesia Project, Research School of Pacific and Asian Studies, The Australian National University. [State, Society and Governance in Melanesia Discussion Paper 2003/6.]

Sumule, Agus
2003a 'Swimming against the current; The drafting of the special autonomy bill for the Province of Papua and its passage through the National Parliament of Indonesia', *Journal of Pacific History* 38:353-69.
2003b (ed.) *Mencari jalan tengah; Otonomi khusus Provinsi Papua*. Jakarta: Gramedia.

Sundhaussen, Ulf
1988 *Politik militer Indonesia 1945-1967; Menuju dwifungsi ABRI*. Jakarta: LP3ES.

Suriadi Mappangara *see* Mappangara, Suriadi

Sutherland, Heather

1979 *The making of a bureaucratic elite; The colonial transformation of the Javanese priyayi*. Singapore: Heinemann.

Sutisna, Agus

2001 *Banten paska provinsi; Mengawal transisi, membangun demokrasi*. Banten: LSPB, Jakarta: Partnership for Governance Reform in Indonesia.

Swadling, Pamela

1996 *Plumes from paradise; Trade cycles in outer Southeast Asia and their impact on New Guinea and nearby islands until 1920*. Boroko: Papua New Guinea National Museum.

Syaikhu Usman *see* Usman, Syaikhu

Syarif Hidayat *see* Hidayat, Syarif

Tahmidy Lasahido *see* Lasahido, Tahmidy

Tambang Timah

1986 *Tin industry in Indonesia*. Jakarta: Desanti Grafika.

Tammar Absulsalam *see* Abdulsalam, Tammar

Taro Goh *see* Goh, Taro

Taufik Abdullah *see* Abdullah, Taufik

Tilly, Charles

2003 *The politics of collective violence*. Cambridge: Cambridge University Press.

Timmer, Jaap

1998 'Lost power, concealed knowledge, and the return of the Kingdom among the Imyan of the Bird's Head of Irian Jaya', in: Jelle Miedema, Cecilia Odé and Rien A.C. Dam (eds), *Perspectives on the Bird's Head of Irian Jaya, Indonesia; Proceedings of the Conference, Leiden, 13-17 October 1997*, pp. 79-116. Amsterdam: Rodopi.

2000a 'The return of the Kingdom; Agama and the Millennium among the Imyan of Irian Jaya, Indonesia', *Ethnohistory* 47:27-63.

2000b *Living with intricate futures; Order and confusion in Imyan Worlds, Irian Jaya, Indonesia*. PhD thesis, University of Nijmegen. Nijmegen: Centre for Pacific and Asian Studies, University of Nijmegen.

2003 *Narratives of government and church among the Imyan of Papua/Irian Jaya, Indonesia*. Canberra: State, Society and Governance in Melanesia Project, Research School of Pacific and Asian Studies, The Australian National University. [State, Society and Governance in Melanesia Discussion Paper 2003/5.]

2004a 'Melanesia in review; Issues and events, 2003 – West Papua', *The Contemporary Pacific* 17:409-19.

2004b 'Government, church, and millenarian critique in the Imyan tradition of the religious (Papua/Irian Jaya, Indonesia)', in: Holger Jebens (ed.), *Cargo, cult and culture critique*, pp. 117-36. Honolulu: University of Hawai'i Press.

2005 'Melanesia in review; Issues and events, 2004 – Papua', *The Contemporary Pacific* 16:448-56.

forthcoming 'A brief social and political history of Papua (1962-2004)', in: Andrew J. Marshall and Bruce M. Beehler (eds), *The ecology of Papua*. Hongkong: Periplus. [The Ecology of Indonesia Series, Volume IX.]

Tjilik Riwut *see* Riwut, Tjilik

Tocqueville de, Alexis

1961 *De la démocratie en Amérique*. Paris: Gallimard.

1969 *Democracy in America*. Garden City, NY: Anchor.

Törnquist, Olle

1990 'Rent capitalism, state, and democracy', in: Arief Budiman, (ed.), *State and civil society in Indonesia*, pp. 29-49. Clayton, Victoria: Monash Asia Institute. [Monash Papers on Southeast Asia 22.]

2000 (ed.) *Political violence; Indonesia and India in comparative perspective*. Oslo: Center for Development and the Environment (SUM), University of Oslo.

Tremewan, Christopher

1994 *The political economy of social control in Singapore*. Oxford: St. Martin's Press.

Tsing, Anna Lowenhaupt

2003 'The news in the provinces', in: Renato Rosaldo (ed.), *Cultural citizenship in island Southeast Asia; Nation and belonging in the hinterlands*, pp. 192-222. Berkeley, CA: University of California Press.

Turner, Mark and Owen Podger with Maria Sumarjono and Wayan K. Tirthayasa

2003 *Decentralization in Indonesia; Redesigning the state*. Canberra: Asia Pacific Press. [The Australian National University.]

Ukur, Fridolin

1971 *Tantang-djawab suku Dajak*. Jakarta: BPK Gunung Mulia.

UNDP (United Nations Development Program)

2001 *Good governance for the people involving the people; Partnership for governance reform*. Jakarta: Partnership for Governance Reform Secretariat.

Usman, Syaikhu

2002 'Regional autonomy in Indonesia; Field experiences and emerging challenges'. Working Paper, SMERU Research Institute, Jakarta, June.

Utama, Edy

1995 (ed.) 'Intelektual Minangkabau mandek?', *Jurnal Kebudayaan Genta Budaya* 1. [Special issue.]

1996a (ed.) 'Budaya lokal versus global', *Jurnal Kebudayaan Genta Budaya* 2. [Special issue.]

1996b (ed.) 'Nagari, demokrasi dan perubahan', *Jurnal Kebudayaan Genta Budaya* 3. [Special issue.]

Utomo, Yogi W.

2000 'Welcome, Bangka-Belitung and Gorontalo!', *Sabili* 8(14):76.

Vakiotis, Michael

1994 *Indonesian politics under Suharto; Order, development and pressure for change*. London: Routledge.

Veen, Roel van der

2004 *What went wrong with Africa? A contemporary history*. Amsterdam: KIT.

Vekie A. Rumate *see* Rumate, Vekie A.

Vel, Jacqueline

1994a *The Uma economy; Indigenous economics and development work in Lawonda, Sumba (Eastern Indonesia).* PhD thesis, Wageningen University, Wageningen.

1994b 'Manu Wolu and the birds' nests; The consequences of a deviant way to cope with insecurity', *Focaal* 22/23:35-46.

2001 'Tribal battle in remote island; Crisis and violence in Sumba (Eastern Indonesia)', *Indonesia* 72:141-58.

forthcoming *Uma politics; Democracy and contemporary political culture in Sumba.*

Velthoen, Esther

1997 'Wanderers, robbers and bad folk; The politics of violence, protection and trade in eastern Indonesia 1750-1850', in: Anthony Reid (ed.), *The last stand of Asian autonomies; Responses to modernity in the diverse states of Southeast Asia and Korea, 1750-1900*, pp. 367-88. New York: St. Martin's Press.

2004 'Hutan and kota; Contested visions of the nation-state in southern Sulawesi in the 1950s', in: Hanneman Samuel and Henk Schulte Nordholt (eds), *Indonesia in transition; Rethinking 'civil society', 'region', and 'crisis'*, pp. 147-74. Yogyakarta: Pustaka Pelajar.

Velthoen, Esther and Gregory L. Acciaioli

1993 'Fluctuating states, mobile populations; Shifting relations of Bajo to local rulers and Bugis traders in colonial eastern Sulawesi'. Paper, LIPI International Seminar on Bajau Communities, Jakarta, 22-25 November.

Vickers, Adrian

2001 'The New Order; Keeping up appearances', in: Grayson Lloyd and Shannon Smith (eds), *Indonesia today; Challenges of history*, pp. 72-84. Singapore: ISEAS.

2002 'Bali Merdeka? Internal migration, tourism and Hindu revivalism', in: Minako Sakai (ed), *Beyond Jakarta; Regional autonomy and local society in Indonesia*, pp. 80-100. Adelaide: Crawford House.

Vinsentus Julipin *see* Julipin, Vinsentius

Visser, Leontine

1989 'The Kamrau Bay area; Between Mimika and Maluku, a report of a short visit', *Irian, Bulletin of Irian Jaya* 17:65-76.

Vlasblom, Dirk

2004 *Papoea; Een geschiedenis.* Amsterdam: Mets and Schilt.

Volkman, Toby Alice

1985 *Feasts of honor; Ritual and change in the Toraja highlands.* Urbana: University of Illinois Press.

Volkstelling

1936 *Volkstelling 1930 – Census of 1930 in Netherlands India.* Vol. 5. Batavia: Landsdrukkerij. [Departement van Economische Zaken, Nederlands Indië.]

Vos, Reinout

1993 *Gentle Janus, merchant prince; The VOC and the tin trade diplomacy in the Malay World, 1740-1800.* Leiden: KITLV Press. [Verhandelingen 157.]

Vosmaer, J. Nicholas
1839 'Korte beschrijving van het zuid-oostelijk schiereiland van Celebes', *Verhandelingen van het Bataviaasch Genootschap van Kunsten en Wetenschappen* (VBG) 17:63-184.
Walsh, Pat and Betty Rouch
1999 'Updates on West Papua; In the shadow of East Timor, Australia has turned a blind eye to another history of genocide', *Arena Magazine* 43:6-9.
Warren, Carol
1994 *Centre and periphery in Indonesia; Environment, politics and human rights in the regional press (Bali).* Perth: Asia Research Centre, Murdoch University. [Working Paper 42.]
2004 'Adat-Balinese discourse and practice; Locating citizenship and the commonweal'. [Manuscript]
Warren, James F.
2003 *A tale of two centuries; The globalisation of maritime raiding and piracy in Southeast Asia at the end of the eighteenth and twentieth centuries.* Singapore: Asia Research Institute (ARI), National University of Singapore. [Working Paper Series 2.]
Wee, Vivienne
2002 *Ethno-nationalism in process; Atavism, ethnicity and indigenism in Riau.* Hong Kong: City University of Hong Kong. [Southeast Asia Research Centre Working Paper Series 22.]
Wessel, Ingrid and Georgia Wimhöfer (eds)
2001 *Violence in Indonesia.* Hamburg: Abera.
Westenenk, L.C.
1918 *De Minangkabausche nagari.* Weltevreden: Visser. [Mededelingen van het Bureau voor de Bestuurszaken der Buitenbezittingen, bewerkt door het Encyclopedisch Bureau.]
Wezeman, Pieter D.
2003 *Conflicts and small arms.* Solna: SIPRI.
White, Nicholas J.
2004 'The beginnings of crony capitalism; Business, politics and economic development in Malaysia, c. 1955-70', *Modern Asian Studies* 38:389-417.
Widjojo, Muridan S.
1998 'Pemberdayaan masyarakat adat; Infrastruktur kebangkitan Irian Jaya masa depan'. Paper, seminar Aspirasi Masyarakat Irian Jaya dan Pembangunan Nasional dalam Era Reformasi, Forum Rekonsiliasi Irian Jaya (FORERI), Jayapura, 19-20 November.
2003 'Govt needs to change to end Papua violence', *Jakarta Post* 30-8-2003.
Widnyani, Nyoman and I Ketut Widia
2002 *Pecalang desa pakraman Bali.* Denpasar: SIC.
Wielenga, D.K.
1949 *De zending op Soemba.* 's Gravenhage: Hoenderloo.
Wihana Kirana Jaya *see* Jaya, Wihana Kirana

Williams, Michael C.
1990 *Communism, religion, and revolt in Banten*. Athens, OH: Ohio University Center for International Studies. [Southeast Asia Series 86.]
Williams, Robert
1999 'New concepts for old?' *Third World Quarterly* 20:503-13.
Winters, Jeffrey A.
1988 'Indonesia; The rise of capital; A review essay', *Indonesia* 45:109-28.
1996 *Power in motion; Capital mobility and the Indonesian state*. Ithaca, NY: Cornell University Press.
World Bank
2003 'Decentralizing Indonesia; A regional public expenditure review'. East Asia Poverty Reduction and Economic Management Unit. [Report no. 26191-IND.]
Yinger, J. Milton
1985 'Ethnicity', *Annual Review of Sociology* 11:151-80.
Yogi W. Utomo *see* Utomo, Yogi W.
Yoshihara Kunio
1988 *The rise of ersatz capitalism in South-East Asia*. Kuala Lumpur: Oxford University Press.
Yulfian Azrial *see* Azrial, Yulfian
Zakaria, Fathurahman
2001 *Gerakan 30 September 1965; Rakyat NTB melawan bahaya merah*. Mataram: Sumurmas.
Zen, Kivlan
2004 *Konflik dan integrasi TNI-AD*. Jakarta: Institute for Policy Studies.
Zerner, Charles
2000 'Towards a broader vision of justice and nature conservation', in: Charles Zerner (ed.), *People, plants and justice*, pp. 2-20. New York: Columbia University Press.

Index

www.ingramcontent.com/pod-product-compliance
Lightning Source LLC
Chambersburg PA
CBHW071407230926
51846CB00001B/27
9789067182836